# NORTHERN CHEYENNE TONGUE RIVER, MONTANA 1904 - 1932 CENSUS
## 1927-1932
## VOLUME III
## INCLUDING BIRTHS & DEATHS
## 1925-1932
### WITH ILLUSTRATIONS

TRANSCRIBED BY
**JEFF BOWEN**

NATIVE STUDY
Gallipolis, Ohio
USA

Copyright © 2022
by Jeff Bowen

ALL RIGHTS RESERVED
No part of this publication can be reproduced
in any form or manner whatsoever
without previous written permission from the
Copyright holder or Publisher.

Native Study LLC
Gallipolis, OH
*www.nativestudy.com*

Library of Congress Control Number: 2021922089

ISBN: 978-1-64968-165-2

Book cover: "The Valley Of The Rosebud" ca 1905, Photographer: Edward S. Curtis (1868-1952). Photo shows a Cheyenne Indian, wearing a war bonnet headdress, on horseback at a pool of water.
- Title devised by Library staff. - Curtis no. 1407-5. Forms part of: Edward S. Curtis Collection (Library of Congress).
**Rights Advisory**
No known restrictions on publication. No renewal in Copyright Office.
Photos are complements of the McCracken Research Library, Buffalo Bill Center of the West, National Archives and the Library of Congress.

Made in the United States of America.

# Other Books and Series by Jeff Bowen

*Compilation of History of the Cherokee Indians and Early History of the Cherokees by Emmet Starr with Combined Full Name Index*
(Hardbound & Softbound)

*1901-1907 Native American Census Seneca, Eastern Shawnee, Miami, Modoc, Ottawa, Peoria, Quapaw, and Wyandotte Indians (Under Seneca School, Indian Territory)*

*1932 Census of The Standing Rock Sioux Reservation with Births And Deaths 1924-1932*

*Kiowa, Comanche, Apache, Fort Sill Apache, Wichita, Caddo and Delaware Indians Birth and Death Rolls 1924-1932*

*Census of The Blackfeet, Montana, 1897- 1901 Expanded Edition*

*Eastern Cherokee by Blood, 1906-1910, Volumes I thru XIII*

*Choctaw of Mississippi Indian Census 1929-1932 with Births and Deaths 1924-1931  Volume I*
*Choctaw of Mississippi Indian Census 1933, 1934 & 1937, Supplemental Rolls to 1934 & 1935 with Births and Deaths 1932-1938, and Marriages 1936-1938 Volume II*

*Eastern Cherokee Census Cherokee, North Carolina 1930-1939 Census 1930-1931 with Births And Deaths 1924-1931 Taken By Agent L. W. Page Volume I*
*Eastern Cherokee Census Cherokee, North Carolina 1930-1939 Census 1932-1933 with Births And Deaths 1930-1932 Taken By Agent R. L. Spalsbury   Volume II*
*Eastern Cherokee Census Cherokee, North Carolina 1930-1939 Census 1934-1937 with Births and Deaths 1925-1938 and Marriages 1936 & 1938 Taken by Agents R. L. Spalsbury And Harold W. Foght Volume III*

*Seminole of Florida Indian Census, 1930-1940 with Birth and Death Records, 1930-1938*

*Texas Cherokees 1820-1839 A Document For Litigation 1921*

*Starr Roll 1894  (Cherokee Payment Rolls) Districts: Canadian, Cooweescoowee, and Delaware Volume One*
*Starr Roll 1894 (Cherokee Payment Rolls) Districts: Flint, Going Snake, and Illinois   Volume Two*
*Starr Roll 1894 (Cherokee Payment Rolls) Districts: Saline, Sequoyah, and Tahlequah; Including Orphan Roll   Volume Three*

*Cherokee Intruder Cases  Dockets of Hearings 1901-1909  Volumes I & II*

# Other Books and Series by Jeff Bowen

*Indian Wills, 1911-1921 Records of the Bureau of Indian Affairs*
*Books One* thru *Seven*
*Native American Wills & Probate Records 1911-1921*

*Turtle Mountain Reservation Chippewa Indians 1932 Census with Births & Deaths, 1924-1932*

*Chickasaw By Blood Enrollment Cards 1898-1914 Volume I* thru *V*

*Cherokee Descendants East An Index to the Guion Miller Applications Volume I*
*Cherokee Descendants West An Index to the Guion Miller Applications Volume II (A-M)*
*Cherokee Descendants West An Index to the Guion Miller Applications Volume III (N-Z)*

*Applications for Enrollment of Seminole Newborn Freedmen, Act of 1905*

*Eastern Cherokee Census, Cherokee, North Carolina, 1915-1922, Taken by Agent James E. Henderson*    *Volume I (1915-1916)*
    *Volume II (1917-1918)*
    *Volume III (1919-1920)*
    *Volume IV (1921-1922)*

*Complete Delaware Roll of 1898*

*Eastern Cherokee Census, Cherokee, North Carolina, 1923-1929, Taken by Agent James E. Henderson*    *Volume I (1923-1924)*
    *Volume II (1925-1926)*
    *Volume III (1927-1929)*

*Applications for Enrollment of Seminole Newborn Act of 1905 Volumes I & II*

*North Carolina Eastern Cherokee Indian Census 1898-1899, 1904, 1906, 1909-1912, 1914 Revised and Expanded Edition*

*1932 Hopi and Navajo Native American Census with Birth & Death Rolls (1925-1931) Volume 1 - Hopi*
*1932 Hopi and Navajo Native American Census with Birth & Death Rolls (1930-1932) Volume 2 - Navajo*

*Western Navajo Reservation Navajo, Hopi and Paiute 1933 Census with Birth & Death Rolls 1925-1933*

*Cherokee Citizenship Commission Dockets 1880-1884 and 1887-1889 Volumes I* thru *V*

*Applications for Enrollment of Chickasaw Newborn Act of 1905 Volumes I* thru *VII*

# Other Books and Series by Jeff Bowen

*Cherokee Intermarried White 1906 Volume I thru X*

*Applications for Enrollment of Creek Newborn Act of 1905 Volumes I thru XIV*

*Applications for Enrollment of Choctaw Newborn Act of 1905 Volumes I thru XX*

*Choctaw By Blood Enrollment Cards 1898-1914 Volumes I thru XX*

*Oglala Sioux Indians Pine Ridge Reservation 1932 Census Book I*
*Oglala Sioux Indians Pine Ridge Reservation Birth and Death Rolls 1924-1932 Book II*

*Census of the Sioux and Cheyenne Indians of Pine Ridge Agency 1896 - 1897 Book I*
*Census of the Sioux and Cheyenne Indians of Pine Ridge Agency 1898 - 1899 Book II*

*Northern Cheyenne Tongue River, Montana 1904 - 1932 Census 1904-1916 Volume I*
*Northern Cheyenne Tongue River, Montana 1904 - 1932 Census 1917-1926 Volume II*

*Sac & Fox - Shawnee Estates 1885-1910 (Under Sac & Fox Agency) Volumes I-VIII*
*Sac & Fox - Shawnee Estates 1920-1924 (Under The Sac & Fox Agency, Oklahoma) & Wills 1889-1924 Volume IX*
*Sac & Fox - Shawnee Deaths, Cemetery, Births, & Marriage Cards (Under The Sac & Fox Agency, Oklahoma) 1853-1933 Volume X*
*Sac & Fox - Shawnee Marriages, Divorces, Estates Log Books Volumes 1 & 2, Log Book Births & Deaths (Under Sac & Fox Agency, Oklahoma)1846-1924 Volume XI*
*Sac & Fox - Shawnee Guardianships Part 1 (Under Sac & Fox Agency, Oklahoma) 1892-1909 Volume XII*
*Sac & Fox - Shawnee Guardianships, Part 2 (Under The Sac & Fox Agency, Oklahoma) 1902-1910 Volume XIII*
*Sac & Fox - Shawnee Guardianships, Part 3 (Under The Sac & Fox Agency, Oklahoma) 1906-1914 Volume XIV*

*Census of the Pima, Tohono O'odham (Papago), and Maricopa Indians of the Gila River, Ak Chin & Gila Bend Reservations 1932 with Birth and Death Rolls 1924-1932*

*Identified Mississippi Choctaw Enrollment Cards 1902-1909 Volumes I, II, III & IV*

Visit our website at **www.nativestudy.com** to learn more about these and other books and series by Jeff Bowen

This series isn't just dedicated to a gentleman named Bill Buckner, but it is also a tribute to a resourceful and caring individual.

# Table of Contents

| | |
|---|---|
| List of Illustrations | vi |
| Introduction | vii |
| Census Instructions | xix |
| Instructions To Enumerators | xx |
| Dull Knife Speech | lxxvii |

| | |
|---|---|
| Census of Northern Cheyenne | |
| 1927 | 1 |
| 1928 | 55 |
| 1929 | 111 |
| 1930 | 167 |
| 1931 | 217 |
|     Births, Deaths, Additions | 271 |
| 1932 | 279 |
| | |
| Birth Roll | 355 |
| Death Roll | 371 |
| | |
| Books and Resources | 391 |
| Index | 393 |

## LIST OF ILLUSTRATIONS

1. Big Crow and girl wearing headdresses — lxvi
2. Buffalo Calf Woman sitting in chair — lxvii
3. Cheyenne Indian and Son on horse — lxviii
4. George Long Roach holding hat — lxix
5. Richard and Sophie Wooden Leg — lxx
6. Holy Standing Woman & Mrs Martin Two Bulls — lxxi
7. Iron Hand and family — lxxii
8. Jean Poitra and daughter — lxxiii
9. Jessie Roman Nose holding baby — lxxiv
10. Lame Deer schoolchildren — lxxv

## INTRODUCTION

Most works of art come from some artist's dream or vision, but the inspiration within these pages, as much as we should celebrate the bravery and endurance of a people, there's another reason behind this series.

It comes from an author, Craig Johnson, the creator of the *Longmire* books and television series. Along with the cast and crew of the show, the storyteller Johnson plies his craft in telling about a broken sheriff. After losing his wife to cancer, Longmire tries finding his way through justice and serving others. He's known by his rigid character and unbending honesty thinking every human being deserves a chance in life. Longmire's best friend Henry Standingbear, portrayed by Lou Diamond Phillips, is a Cheyenne living on the reservation which is in close proximity to the Crow Reservation but in the story is near fictitious Absaroka County, Wyoming. In reality the Northern Cheyenne Reservation is in Lame Deer, Montana, and the Crow Reservation in Crow Agency, Montana (from 1884 to present-day). Johnson painstakingly points out through his storyline the characters' daily struggles, the Cheyenne people, who still endure to this day but with the same pride and will to live past the prejudice and the raw hate their ancestors dealt with in times past. These people have had to fight each day of their lives.

Longmire takes place in modern times, but he recognizes the Cheyenne struggle with life now. He sees them still managing that fight and doing it with the same will to survive as their predecessors did at Sand Creek or on the Washita.

So the inspiration to create a family record of censuses, along with images, in some instances matching the census records came from Longmire's creator and the fine people that worked so hard to entertain us yet let us understand it wasn't just TV but a real people that exist now and have a history we should all know about and understand.

This census book series has been extremely difficult when it comes to date of birth or age. It has been obvious while transcribing these Cheyenne censuses that they, the Cheyenne people, just wanted to live their lives peacefully and be left alone. They may have observed their age generally but were more concerned with living and caring for their families and their people.

Not every series challenged by this author has had the opportunity to have so many years in a working volume because of the smaller number of tribal members involved here. By having this smaller volume of people the tracking of each individual's age or year of birth or even miscues of correct names has greatly exposed the census takers' inconsistencies because of either, their education, abilities or concern or possibly the tribal member's knowledge of their own age or what year could have been pressed upon them by the individual taking the census at the time. Every effort has been taken to follow every year while checking and re-checking many times over every single individual's entry recorded within these pages so as to notate as closely as possible a correct day or year of each individual's age and name.

Keep in mind even years after the struggles you are about to read, the adjustments were slow because of distrust and the battle to save a culture and a people. Many times, first names will be changed or spelled differently as well as dates which you will observe.

The mold the Cheyenne were being forced into and the toil that prevailed upon so many wasn't taken lightly. The Cheyenne today are a strong people. Their ancestors were brave, proud and had strength down to their very souls. They lived a strict culture many couldn't understand or follow. They taught their children to respect the family and their elders no matter what. They not only showed them how to live but they also showed them how to die. They taught them the love and understanding of their very surroundings.

The more that was read about the Northern Cheyenne the more interesting it became. They fought because they were being pursued by a people that wanted their land and their lives, literally. The military had a policy of annihilation not assimilation as they at times falsely claimed; the actual documentation from historical records is clear about that very point. There were some within the ranks that did want mercy and compassion for the Cheyenne but that kind of thinking consumed few involved especially among the higher ranked officers and beyond.

George Bird Grinnell circa: 1915, in his, *The Fighting Cheyennes,* stated it better than anyone this author has read in years of research. Plainly stating the trouble between the Plains tribes and the white man or other Native American peoples for that matter. Grinnell simply says, "The hostility that was thus growing up between Indians and white men was racial. To the white man an Indian was an Indian, and the white man who had been robbed or threatened by an Indian felt himself justified in taking vengeance on the next Indian that he saw, without regard to whether he had been injured by that man or by men of that tribe. In the same way if an Indian had been killed by a white man the members of his tribe were ready to revenge the injury on the next white man that came along. Thus it came about that persons innocent of any fault were constantly punished for the harm done by one of their race. The guilty never suffered. As a result of this feeling neither Indians nor white men felt that they could trust one of the opposite race, and each held the other always in suspicion."[1]

---

[1] *The Fighting Cheyennes*; Pg. 96 Para 2.

Saying that the Northern Cheyenne were a courageous people is a huge understatement. They were ravaged by a people that couldn't hold a candle to a Cheyenne's soul or very depth of humanity held within. "Those under Little Wolf surrendered in southeastern Montana on March 27, 1879. Five years later, an executive order signed by President Chester A. Arthur created the Tongue River reservation in Montana, designated specifically for the Northern Cheyennes."[2]

The real trouble outside of normal tribal rivalries started when one of the collisions with the U.S. military took place. "The Cheyennes and Arapahoes had traditionally been friendly to the white man, and it wasn't until 1856 that an incident occurred between troops at Fort Laramie and a band of Northern Cheyennes, creating the first outbreak of hostilities by the tribes."[3] The history of the Plains tribes in general was a thing of beauty until the emigration of those seeking gold and land that wasn't theirs. The Cheyennes moved where the land's natural resources were abundant, buffalo for food, clothing, shelter, and fuel for heat that came from the land and clean water essential for life. But this time the landlords or owners were going to be driven from their homes. The military went to extremes to change life forever on the Plains. Men like G. A. Custer, John M. Chivington, and others set their sights on the destruction of innocent families. The first notice of trouble was circa 1856 then there was a steady stream that came from then on.

A few incidents can be mentioned but the frame of mind and what the Cheyennes were facing can be understood from a few quotes. From Major Scott J. Anthony while considering the winter of 1863 and the need to provide for the Cheyenne even though the Treaty of Fort Wise had been provided papers to sign previously in February of 1861. "Major Anthony was less compassionate about the welfare of the tribes. He wrote, "The Indians are all very destitute this season, and the government will be compelled to subsist them to a great extent, or allow them to starve to death, which would probably be much the easier way of disposing of them."[4] Colonel Chivington through a dispatch on May 31, 1864 states, "The Cheyennes will have to be soundly whipped before they will be quiet. If any of them are caught in your vicinity kill them, as that is the only way."[5] Major General Phil Sheridan to Custer receiving final orders before the fight at Washita in 1868, "Kill or hang every warrior. Bring back all women and children. Take good care of yourself, were the senior commander's parting orders."[6] This from Sheridan, and Custer in his final report said the loss of women and children couldn't be helped. After assuring the Cheyenne that there wouldn't be trouble Custer surrounded the village and attacked.

---

[2] *The Northern Cheyenne Exodus*; Pg. 13 Para 1.
[3] *The Sand Creek Massacre*; Pg. 5 Para 2.
[4] *The Sand Creek Massacre*; Pg. 35 Para 3.
[5] *The Sand Creek Massacre*; Pg. 83 Para 2.
[6] *Custer, Black Kettle, and the Fight On The Washita*: Pg. 142 Para 3.

On November 29, 1864 Chivington at Sand Creek made the first attempt to be rid of the friendly Cheyenne Chief Black Kettle, "When the attack first began, Black Kettle had quickly remembered the advice given him by the whites on several occasions. In 1860, Greenwood had given him a large American garrison-type flag, and he now tied the flag to the end of a long lodge pole, added a white flag beneath it, and hoisted it above his tent."[7] Chivington couldn't be reasoned with while a trader and friend of the Cheyenne William Bent tried to dissuade him from attacking. "Chivington stated that he was not authorized to make peace with the Indians and that he himself was then "on the warpath."[8]

From Grinnell's *Fighting Cheyennes* it can be seen the Cheyennes were promised peace before the slaughter, "Of what Major Wynkoop did after he returned with the chiefs from Denver to Fort Lyon or what he promised them I find no official record, but there is evidence in the testimony given before the Joint Special Committee of Congress in 1865. From this testimony it seems clear that Wynkoop did promise the chiefs protection and that relying on this promise, and on the circular to the friendlies sent out by Governor Evans, they moved in to Sand Creek, believing that peace had been made or soon would be made."[9] The Cheyennes thought they were safe. Black Kettle had made every effort to do the right thing. The most fatal mistake he made was to trust those in charge, the military authorities from the highest level. Chivington had taken the word of his superiors that attack was the way. He left with hundreds of men behind him just as dark was setting in, "John Smith says that the attack occurred between dawn and daylight, nearer sunrise than daybreak. The Indians discovered a large body of troops approaching. Some of the women at first thought they were buffalo, but others recognized them as troops and ran to Smith's lodge and called him out, asking him to go and see what the troops were and what they wanted. At the council of 1860 Black Kettle had been given a large American flag, and now he ran it up on a long lodge-pole before his lodge, with a small white flag under it as a sign that the camp was friendly."[10] It may be redundant by mentioning three times in three quotes about Black Kettle's American flag, but it bares necessity, to impress the evil and destruction of an innocent people.

George Bent was also present during the morning of the attack and gave testimony as to what he saw, "He sprang out of bed and ran out of the lodge. It was not yet day, but through the dim gray of the winter twilight he saw two bodies of horsemen, one on each side of the creek, charging down toward the camp. When I looked toward the chief's lodge [he says] I saw that Black Kettle had a large American

---

[7] *The Sand Creek Massacre*; Pg. 150 Para 2.
[8] *The Sand Creek Massacre*; Pg. 79 Para 2.
[9] *The Fighting Cheyennes*; 1915; Pg. 159 Para 1.
[10] *The Fighting Cheyennes*; 1915; Pg. 164 Para 2.

flag up on a long lodge-pole as a signal to the troop that the camp was friendly. Part of the warriors were running out toward the pony herds and the rest of the people were rushing about the camp in great fear. All the time Black Kettle kept calling out not to be frightened; that the camp was under protection and there was no danger. Then suddenly the troops opened fire on this mass of, men, women and children, and all began to scatter and run."[11] Also Bent stated that at the start Black Kettle and his wife along with White Antelope stood in front of his lodge after all the others had left only to realize they had to run. White Antelope stayed and died. During the flight Black Kettle's wife was shot, when he returned she had been shot nine times but was still alive. He managed to get her up and put her on a horse and got her to another camp. Troops later sent out to identify those who had been killed made mistakes on identities because of the needless mutilation by the soldiers. They thought Black Kettle was one of them and was reported dead. He wasn't a bodily victim this time but his heart was likely wounded to the very core. Seeing his people lying there, wondering, who is it that really needs to be called savage? "John Smith accompanied Lieutenant Colonel Bowen over the field to identify the dead, and he mistook a badly cut up body for that of Black Kettle."[12]

Chivington wasn't the only one that wanted to end the Cheyenne. At Washita on November 27, 1868, Black Kettle though Southern Cheyenne would soon come to realize his fears were real again. Approximately four years previously in almost the same manner at Sand Creek his village would be not just attacked this time it would be annihilated along with himself, only this time by George Armstrong Custer. "Custer blazed a crimson trail from one end of the Plains to the other. He was merciless to man and beast he was ruthless in treatment of his foes. An Indian was an Indian to him; and it is a matter of record that he killed more Indian women and children than warriors. That he never was successful in capturing an Indian warrior in battle can be substantiated. His sole prisoners of war were decrepit old men, squaws and papooses. Not once, during his ten years' crusade, did he ever defeat in battle the red knights who opposed him."[13]

It seems that the only way Custer could defeat the Cheyenne was to deceive them and then surround them. He sent scouts and they reported that the Cheyenne fighting strength was much weaker than that of Custer's, he knew he could over run them. "Custer was not long determining his plan of attack. This time there would be no opportunity for his intended victims to escape by flight. Before morning he could surround the village. At a given signal the encircling battle line would converge on

---

[11] *The Fighting Cheyennes* 1915; Pg. 170-171 Para 4-5.
[12] *The Sand Creek Massacre*; Pg. 153 Para 3.
[13] *Custer, Black Kettle, and the fight on the Washita*; Pg. 13-14 Para 3.

the unsuspecting Indians, who then would be completely at his mercy. It would be a wipe-out."[14]

What's interesting is during 1867 a Congressional investigation was initiated between Sand Creek (1864) and the Battle of Washita (1868). "The peace commission appointed by Congress in July, 1867, made its report January 7, 1868. An interesting conclusion which it reached was that in all cases investigated by the commission of difficulties which existed with Indians at the date of the commission's creation, and for some years previous, the cause of the difficulty was traced to the acts of white men—either civilians or soldiers."[15]

White civilians or soldiers not Indians, not Cheyennes, but land grabbers from every phase of European background. No matter how long they were in the United States five years or for twenty years, they were here to take what didn't belong to them. The Cheyenne tribe was small in consideration to other tribes so the consideration and promises made to them were all lies. They were promised much for their tribal holdings (land). Very little was coming. The powers that be cut back their promises in food, money and peace of mind. The thought was be rid of them and we can move on from there. The politicians who were going to ratify a treaty agreement stole out clauses cheating the Cheyenne then never mentioned that they took it upon themselves to change what was agreed upon. They never had to pay the personal price of their deception or lose out being they were a thousand miles away. It didn't affect them so why worry.

Custer would eventually meet his end at Little Big Horn by thinking he couldn't be defeated, but his arrogance became fatal. After the 7$^{th}$ Calvary's defeat the Cheyenne people would again pay a price for having the will to live and refusing those that pretended they knew what was good for the Cheyenne people. The tribes, Cheyenne, Sioux, Arapahoe, among others, tried to trust those that acted like their motives were the best but knew their promises were evil and empty. The whites never held up their end of the bargain, they never intended to. They just wanted what they wanted no matter the cost, likely filling their own pockets. There were other fights in between. They combed the land capturing many different tribal camps, one of them being Dull Knife's along with Little Wolf and other Cheyennes. Custer's last breath of brutality would come June 26, 1876. Come late November, Dull Knife and his people felt a life change coming. It was a matter of survival now. Another fight and more lost. He had lost family at Little Bighorn, a son and friends from his village. But every fight there were less and less of his people. This time there was less food, less ponies, and now hundreds of troopers again with endless resources, burning their

---

[14] *Custer, Black Kettle, and the fight on the Washita*: Pg. 148 Para 3.
[15] *The Fighting Cheyennes* 1915; Pg. 287 Para 1.

homes, along with more Cheyenne blood being poured upon their own land. They would seek out Crazy Horse's camp near the Tongue River. There being another fight with the blue coats in January, 1877. Crazy Horse was again plunged into hard times, barely able to feed his own or protect them from the harsh winter and devastation the military was creating. He took in the Cheyennes for a while but it wouldn't be long before hard feelings would unintentionally come between friends. A courageous people were being driven to surrender bodily but not in spirit. They'd try to work with those that twisted truth but knew if their promises failed they'd have to do something about it.

During the spring they were told they needed to go to the reservation in Oklahoma, the Darlington Agency. They wanted to stay home in the north; they were told by General Crook and a Colonel Ranald Mackenzie that after a year if they didn't like it in Oklahoma they could return home. But for now they could live with their Southern Cheyenne relatives where the climate was good, and there was plenty of food and supplies. They arrived and the welcome wasn't the best. Their relatives were already short of food, clothing and medicine, if any, and now there would be much less. The climate wasn't what they were used to and their original distrust was quickly turning from what was a feeling to factual reality through disease, a lack of support and sadly the burials of both young and old. "In his interviews with Little Wolf and others, ethnologist George B. Grinnell calculated that about 41 of Little Wolf's band lost their lives to disease during the winter of 1877-78, more than had been killed in battle during the Great Sioux War. Wild Hog claimed before a U.S. Senate Select Committee that over 50 Northern Cheyenne children died during the first winter at Darlington Agency, while Cheyenne historian Peter John Powell estimated 58 deaths of children from among the various camps."[16] They had to place their own destiny in their hands again even to the death. It was better to die fighting to be free rather than trapped while an invisible enemy, disease, choked the very breath from them. Denied their request to leave as promised, it was time to go home.

The notion to leave Darlington had been simmering in the hearts of the Cheyenne for a while but it was like an invitation had just been delivered when, "On September 9, 1878, mixed-blood Edmond Guerrier, interpreter for the army with the Cheyennes since the 1860s, rode into Little Wolf's camp and informed the Sweet Medicine chief that agent Miles wished to see him again. Little Wolf took with him Wild Hog and Old Crow (Crow). According to George Bent, Dull Knife was also present. "What do you want with me," Little Wolf demanded upon entering Miles office, "why did you send for me?" "Three of your young men have run off," Miles replied, "and now I want you to give me ten of your young men, to hold here as

---

[16] *Tell Them We Are Going Home*; Pg. 37 Para 3.

prisoners until I get back the three that have gone off. The soldiers will go after these three, and when they have brought them back, I will give the ten men their liberty."[17]

Little Wolf refused and tried to show his will to keep peace. As usual a white man's first thought was if bullied they'll cave. Clearly as always and in this situation Miles like most in positions of authority insisted on taking kindness for weakness. Miles insistence obviously helped the Cheyenne chiefs make a difficult decision. Not all would attempt to leave that had moved south around a year previous but, "At about 10 o'clock on the night of Sunday, September 9, 1878, long before the first streaks of dawn lightened the eastern skies, Dull Knife and Little Wolf led a procession of diversely aged men, woman, and children, with their ponies and dogs, setting out for their home in the north. As indicated, not all of the Northern Cheyennes who had arrived in August 1877 undertook the journey. Some had perished from starvation and disease during their detention, while others had melded—easily or uneasily—with kin among the communities at Darlington. Only 353 of the people who had arrived the previous year from Camp Robinson (a little more than a third of the original body—a fragment of the whole) slipped away in the shadows that night, optimistic about going home but heartsick at having to leave relatives behind."[18] As so many times before the people left their fires burning high as they emptied their skin covered homes and carrying all they could while moving like ghosts in the night. Even with the army's eyes upon them like birds of prey realizing hours later they had been duped by a people they failed to learn about or understand because of their own stupidity.

For approximately seven hundred miles or more the Cheyenne continued to evade some of the greatest military strategist of the time; only to be fooled by a few warriors that dwindled during each fight with their women, and children. Bone weary on their feet, starving while wearing rags, and leading exhausted ponies they showed themselves to be brilliant, cunning and disciplined while standing at death's door while daring it to come for them. Standing to fight when they had to they fought with limited ammunition and resources. They possessed strength that seemed to come out of nowhere. The Cheyennes' dangerous trek could likely be classified as one of the longest running fights in history. Many times the soldiers paid a price for chasing what they thought were a helpless people, as they stood their ground digging rifle pits they shielded their families behind them so they could live, and then in time only to slip off again in the dark leaving the blue jackets dumbfounded once more while having to lick their wounds and scratching their heads. The Cheyennes had a vision in their hearts of home again.

---

[17] *Tell Them We Are Going Home*; Pg. 41 Para 2.
[18] *January Moon*; Pg. 18 Para 1.

The Cheyenne between September 9, 1878 to January 9, 1879 understood what the meaning of sacrifice really meant. Whether warrior, woman or child they stood their ground no matter the cost, to go home. First a running fight with practically nothing for hundreds of miles then only to be pursued by even larger numbers they knew they had reached their home ground but felt it best to divide the two bands, Little Wolf went one way and Dull Knife hoping they could live among their Sioux brothers, headed towards the Red Cloud Agency only to find out that during their absence it had been moved approximately 60 miles away into the Dakota Territory. Then knowing his people couldn't stand much more; torn, tired and not only hungry but exposed to the harsh elements without supplies or warm clothing he, Dull Knife, did what he had to do to save lives, surrender, only to be delivered to Fort Robinson (Red Cloud Agency 1873 to 1877). Fort Robinson like the bad omen it was, a negative abusive future for the Cheyenne people. The soldiers left there with the Cheyenne to take them to Oklahoma. Crazy Horse died there, now they were being delivered back there once more as if to break them physiologically and as usual the politicians and the military completely failed to understand the spirit of the Cheyenne as they had proven time after time that their intestinal fortitude and intelligence was more than the so-called authorities could handle.

All of Dull Knife's people were placed in one building, ten yards wide and thirty yards long, with one woodstove in the center of the room. Previously a cavalry barrack there was no furniture and the new captives only had what blankets and clothing they brought with them. Searched for weapons during their surrender they preserved what little form of protection they could by disassembling rifles and pistols and having the woman and children slip the parts under their clothing or wear them as a form of hidden jewelry. Once in the room and alone the floor boards were torn up so they could keep the weapons or ammunition hidden in case of any future searches. There was peace for a while. There was freedom within limits and medical care received. Some were still sick from living down south but things weren't getting better for many. The temperatures were falling below zero and the ragged clothing wasn't enough. They were fed decently as the troops for a while. But Dull Knife knew they'd try to send them south once more and kept telling the commander and others of the base about the poor conditions there. Hoping they would listen again those far away in the east were quite willing to make a decision that wouldn't affect them. General Sheridan wanted more soldiers there likely feeling there would be a fight when the truth was revealed as to what their fate would be. But what would happen next reveals the seriousness of or consequences to come by reading this conversation between a clerk and a young girl, "Reflecting the people's feelings about returning south, a daughter of Chief Wild Hog coveted some calico that she saw in the post trader's store during the Indians' early weeks at Fort Robinson. When a clerk suggested that she might wait and purchase it at Sidney Barracks while en route back to the Indian Territory, the girl echoed the Cheyennes' doughty stance, responding that she was not going there. When the clerk asked where she would go if not to Sidney, She allegedly replied, "To Heaven."[19] The level of commitment even as openly stated as at this time couldn't be comprehended even by those who a little more than a decade and a half ago had seen bodies stacked like cord wood before their very eyes during the Civil War.

Four months to the day in below zero conditions late at night thinking the camp had settled in Dull Knife and his people would make their escape with their shadows full against the snow as the moon cast its bright light against each footstep. They had no choice during a time when their words fell on deaf ears. After refusing to agree to go back south, the new commanding officer Captain Henry Wessells decided that until the Cheyennes broke he would refuse them food or fuel to warm themselves. Even though some had requested clothing for them knowing the forced move south again was close, the snow was piling up and the Indian Commissioner said the request hadn't even been received till the end of December. They were again in rags and dressed for warmer weather now being starved and sick and frozen. Yet they made their break. Many died; some made it under unbelievable conditions not even mentioning the damage to those that did. Dull Knife near seventy years of age again made it with what family he had left walking to Dakota Territory.

"The earliest written reference to the people that became known as the Cheyenne was in a letter from the French explorer La Salle in 1680. He wrote that some Cheyenne visited him after traveling from their homeland on the headwaters of the Mississippi River in what is now Minnesota to the Illinois River in southwest Illinois. Like many tribes of that day, the Tsethasetas, as the Cheyenne called themselves, once lived in bark tepees and grew corn, beans and squash. However, they left their agricultural life by the close of the 17th century and began moving west to the Plains to seek the buffalo. Early traditions of the Algonquian-speaking Cheyenne say they were driven out of the north by a powerful enemy and settled after crossing a large body of water."[20]

"The Northern Cheyenne Indian Reservation (Cheyenne: *Tsėhéstáno*; formerly named the Tongue River) is home of the federally recognized Northern Cheyenne tribe. Located in southeastern Montana, the reservation is approximately 690 square miles (1,800 km$^2$) in size and home to approximately 5,000 Cheyenne people. The tribal and government headquarters are located in Lame Deer, also the home of the annual Northern Cheyenne pow wow.

The reservation is bounded on the east by the Tongue River and on the west by the Crow Reservation. There are small parcels of non-contiguous off-reservation

---

[19] *January Moon*; Pg. 49-50 Para 4.
[20] *Indian Nations of North America*-Cheyenne Intro; Pg. 164 Para 1.

trust lands in Meade County, South Dakota, northeast of the city of Sturgis. Its timbered ridges that extend into northwestern South Dakota are part of Custer National Forest and it is approximately 40 miles (64 km) east of the site of the 1876 Battle of the Little Bighorn.

According to tribal enrollment figures as of March 2013, there were approximately 10,050 enrolled tribal members, of which about 4,939 were residing on the reservation, with approximately 91% of the population Native American (full or part blood quantum) and 72.8% identifying as Cheyenne. Slightly more than a quarter of the population five years or older spoke a language other than English. Members of the Crow Nation also live on the reservation.

Lame Deer, Montana, with about 4,000 residents, of which 92% are American Indian, is the capital of the Northern Cheyenne nation. Chief Dull Knife College is located there. To the west is Muddy, Montana with about 600 residents, 94% American Indian, and further west Busby, Montana with about 700 residents, 90% American Indian. Busby was the site of the Tongue River Boarding School, opened in 1904.

The St. Labre Catholic boarding school is also on the reserve and educates children in pre-K-12. It serves nearly 450 students and embraces the North American culture while also celebrating catholic faith and educating children. They integrate North American culture within the school curriculum allowing for formal education to take place in addition to cultural education. Along with the school, this facility also runns[sic] a Shiloh Youth Group Home, Childcare Center, Community Outreach Services, Elderly Outreach Services, and a Work Incentive Program. These programs along with the school aim to educate the community members ad[sic] provide them with skills in order to become independent in any way they need. There is also a St. Labre museum which houses important Cheyenne artifacts and aims to display history of the culture and language in hopes people with[sic] learn from it."[21]

During the transcription of this series it was found that the National Archives according to their film catalog and within the film record itself goes from 1920 to 1922, leaving out 1921. This Northern Cheyenne book series itself contains twenty eight census years and comes from the National Archives Record Group M-595, film rolls 576-578. It contains, in most cases, the previous census number, present census number, Indian name, if given, but in rare cases, English name, relationship to head of household, date of birth or year, and sex. In many cases you will find brackets "[]" with explanatory notes.

The Northern Cheyennes' story along with their fellow tribes the Southern Cheyenne, the Northern and Southern Arapahoe as well as the numerous Sioux tribes

---

[21] Northern Cheyenne Indian Reservation; Wikipedia.

is a story of decimation. This is a story of fraud, a story of a larceny, pilfering, robbery, or whatever the worst description can be given. It's about murder and mutilation on a people. Northern Cheyenne wives, their sons and daughters, their infants, their beloved land suffered. An Indian people's source of life, the American Bison was wiped out for one reason, to destroy a peoples' way of life. The destruction was so great that those in power were willing to go to any extreme to exterminate a people that just wanted to be left alone. In the later part of these volumes you will find a complete list of every reference read during this study. It's important to read the history of such a courageous people and follow their example. Please forgive any mistakes in advance but an honest effort was made and hopefully as honest as possible because the old ones and those at present deserve the very best.

I want to thank every author listed and reference participant otherwise it wouldn't be possible to forward great resources to the folks looking for their ancestors.

\* This third volume (1927-1932) of the Northern Cheyenne Series after 24 years' worth of recorded censuses starting with the year 1928 changes format giving even greater detailed information concerning not only the Last Census Number, the Present Census Number (starting in 1930 just the Present Census Number), English Name, Relationship, Month and Year of Birth, Sex, and finally for the first time in this series Blood Quantum, which will indicate many individual's degree of blood in the previous two volumes. Central to these vital records you will also find Live Births 1925-1932; Deaths 1925-1932 with the Cause of Death in most cases along with some Additions. Also included are several illustrations. This volume is a great addition to the series being more detailed than ever due to the advanced nature and education of the personnel working to establish Northern Cheyenne records.

Also I would like to thank Samantha from the McCracken Research Library at the Buffalo Bill Center of the West for educating me on how to reference their photographs, as well helping me to learn which photos could be used in this Northern Cheyenne series. A great respect is personally felt for these wonderful people.

Jeff Bowen
Gallipolis, OH
*NativeStudy.com*

# Census Instructions

## INSTRUCTIONS

(A) A separate roll is to be made of each reservation; also, of each *rancheria* or reserve, and a separate roll of Indians allotted on the public domain or homesteading. The roll is to be based on enrollment and not on residence.

(B) Persons are to be listed by families alphabetically; that is, not only by the first letter of the surname, but also by the second and subsequent letters, when the first letter or letters are the same. For example: Abalon, Abbott, Abeon, Abend, Abict; Ball, Bell, Bill, Boll, Bull; Carley, Carmen, Carton, etc. Families having the same surname are also to be listed in this way, e. g.: Brown, Anson; Brown, Bill; Brown, Charles; Brown, David. In the case of English translations of Indian names, such as John *Flying-Elk*, Flying-Elk is the surname and is to be listed under F. In such cases the first word of the translated Indian name determines the alphabetical position. The best way to accomplish this will be to write the names of each family group on a separate card; then, arrange the cards alphabetically and type the names therefrom onto the census roll.

Members of a family are to be listed in the following order: Head, first; wife second; then children, whether sons or daughters, *in the order of their ages*; and lastly, all other relatives and persons living with the family who do not constitute another family group.

Annuity and per capita payment rolls are also to be prepared in the same manner.

(C) A family is composed of the following members:
1. Both parents and their unmarried children, if any, living with them; all other relatives and persons living with the family who do not constitute another family group.
2. Either parent and the unmarried children, if the other parent is dead; all other relatives and persons living with the family who do not constitute another family group.
3. A single person over 21 years of age, not living with a relative.

(D) For each person the following information is to be furnished:
1. NUMBER.—A number is to be assigned in serial order. Thus, the first person listed is to be numbered as "1," the second, as "2," and so on until the census is completed.
2. NAME.—If there are both an Indian and an English name, the allotment or annuity roll name is to be given. First, the last or surname; then, the given name in full. Ditto marks are to be used under the surname of the head for the surnames of the other members of one family.
3. SEX.—"M," for male; "F," for female.
4. AGE AT LAST BIRTHDAY.—Age in completed years at last birthday is to be shown. For infants under 1 year, age in completed months, expressed as twelfths of a year. Thus, 3 months as $\tfrac{3}{12}$ yr.
5. TRIBE.—Care is to be taken that tribe, not band or local name, is given. Thus, Ute tribe, not Pahvant, which is a band of Ute. Likewise, Hupa tribe, not Bear River, which is a local name for the members of the Hupa tribe living near Bear River.
6. DEGREE OF BLOOD.—"F," for full blood; "¼+," for one-fourth or more Indian blood; "–¼," for less than one-fourth Indian blood.
7. MARITAL STATUS.—"S," for a single or unmarried person; "M," for a married person; and "Wd," for widowed of either sex.
8. RELATIONSHIP TO HEAD OF FAMILY.—The head, whether husband or father, widow or unmarried person of either sex, is to be designated as such. For the other members, the appropriate term which designates the particular relationship the person bears to the head is to be used.
9. RESIDENCE.—
    (a) At *jurisdiction* where enrolled: Yes or no. The term jurisdiction includes all reservations and public domain allotments under the agency.
    (b) Or at another jurisdiction. The name of the jurisdiction is to be given.
    (c) Or elsewhere:
        1. Post office: Both the proper name of the post office and the class by which it is known (city, town, village, etc.) are to be given. Thus, Lewiston, city.
        2. County.
        3. State.
10. WARD.—Yes or no. Wardship depends primarily upon the ownership of individual property held in trust or upon membership in a tribe living on a Federal reservation. See Circular 2145.
11. ALLOTMENT, ANNUITY, AND IDENTIFICATION NUMBERS.—"Al," for allotment; "An," for annuity; and "Id," for identification, before the appropriate number or numbers. All numbers are to be shown.

(E) Rolls not prepared in strict conformity with the above instructions will be returned for correction.

[7-994.]

# Eleventh Census of the United States.
## JUNE 1, 1890.

# INSTRUCTIONS TO ENUMERATORS.

Under the Provisions of the Act of Congress
approved March 1, 1889.

DEPARTMENT OF THE INTERIOR,

CENSUS OFFICE.

**WASHINGTON:**
**GOVERNMENT PRINTING OFFICE.**
**1890.**

# GENERAL INSTRUCTIONS.

DEPARTMENT OF THE INTERIOR,
CENSUS OFFICE,
*Washington, D. C., May* 1, 1890.

Under the provisions of the act entitled "An Act to provide for taking the Eleventh and subsequent censuses," approved March 1, 1889, a census of the population, wealth, and industry of the United States is to be taken as of June 1, 1890. By the provisions of section 19 of said act the enumeration must be completed on or before the first day of July, and in any city having over ten thousand inhabitants under the census of 1880 the enumeration must be taken within two weeks from the first Monday of June.

One hundred and seventy-five supervisors of census, one or more to each state and territory and the District of Columbia, have been appointed by the President, by and with the advice and consent of the Senate.

## APPOINTMENT OF ENUMERATORS.

Upon the approval by the Superintendent of Census of the persons designated for appointment as enumerators in each district the supervisor will issue to each person so named a commission, signed by said supervisor and approved by the Superintendent of Census, authorizing and empowering him to execute and fulfill the duties of an enumerator in accordance with law, and setting forth the boundaries of the subdivision within which such duties are to be performed by him. Accompanying the commission will be a blank form of oath or affirmation [7–062], as required by section 8 of the act of March 1, 1889.

As soon as the commission and printed form of oath are received by the enumerator the receipt of the commission should be acknowledged to the supervisor on form 7–792, and the oath duly subscribed, in accordance with the instructions printed thereon, and transmitted to the supervisor before the first Monday of June, the date fixed by law for the commencement of the enumeration. These requirements must be strictly complied with, as no enumerator is qualified by law to enter upon his

(3)

4    INSTRUCTIONS TO ENUMERATORS.

duties until he has received his commission and filed his oath with the supervisor for his district. It is also provided by law that the enumerator, by accepting his commission and qualifying thereunder, binds himself to carry the work on to completion, unless incapacitated by sickness from so doing. For neglect or refusal to perform the duties required of him under the law he will be deemed guilty of a misdemeanor, and be liable upon conviction to a fine not exceeding five hundred dollars. An enumerator can not throw up the work, therefore, simply because of dissatisfaction or indolence.

### DUTIES OF ENUMERATORS.

It is the duty of each enumerator, after being duly qualified as above, to visit personally each dwelling in his subdivision, and each family therein, and each individual living out of a family in any place of abode, and by inquiry made of the head of such family, or of the member thereof deemed most credible and worthy of trust, and of such individual living out of a family, to obtain each and every item of information and all the particulars required by the act of March 1, 1889. All of this data is to be obtained as of date June 1, 1890.

In case no person shall be found at the usual place of abode of such family, or individual living out of a family, competent to answer the inquiries made in compliance with the requirements of the act, then it shall be lawful for the enumerator to obtain the required information, as nearly as may be practicable, from the family or families, or person or persons, living nearest to such place of abode. The term "individual living out of a family" is explained in the special instructions concerning Schedule No. 1 (page 20).

It is the prime object of the enumeration to obtain the name and the requisite particulars as to personal description of every person in the United States, except Indians not taxed.

### COURTESY ON THE PART OF ENUMERATORS.

It is the duty of an enumerator, in the exercise of his authority to visit houses and interrogate members of families resident therein, to exercise courtesy and consideration. A rude, peremptory, or overbearing demeanor would be an injustice to the families visited, and would render the members of those families less dis-

INSTRUCTIONS TO ENUMERATORS.  5

posed to give information with fullness and exactness, and would seriously retard the census work. On the other hand, it is not necessary that the enumerator should enter into prolix explanations or give time to anything beyond the strictly necessary work of interrogation. The enumerator should be *prompt, rapid, and decisive* in announcing his object and his authority and in making his inquiries, but in so doing he should not arouse any antagonism or give any offense.

### THE OBLIGATION TO GIVE INFORMATION.

It is not within the choice of any inhabitant of the United States whether he will or will not communicate the information required by the census law. By the fifteenth section of the act approved March 1, 1889, it is provided:

That each and every person more than twenty years of age, belonging to any family residing in any enumeration district or subdivision, and in case of the absence of the heads and other members of any such family, then any representative of such family, shall be, and each of them hereby is, required, if thereto requested by the Superintendent, supervisor, or enumerator, to render a true account to the best of his or her knowledge of every person belonging to such family in the various particulars required by law, and whoever shall willfully fail or refuse shall be guilty of a misdemeanor, and upon conviction thereof shall be fined in a sum not exceeding one hundred dollars.

Enumerators are cautioned, however, not to obtrude unnecessarily the compulsory feature of the enumeration. It will be found very generally that the persons called upon to give information will do so without objection or delay. It is only where information required by law is refused that the penalties for noncompliance need be referred to. The enumerator will then quietly but firmly point out the consequences of persistency in refusal.

### FALSE STATEMENTS.

It is further to be noted that the enumerator is not required to accept answers which he knows or has reason to believe are false. He has a right to a true statement on every matter respecting which he is bound to inquire. Should any person persist in making statements which are obviously erroneous, the enumerator should enter upon the schedule the facts as nearly as he can ascertain them by his own observation or by inquiry of credible persons.

6        INSTRUCTIONS TO ENUMERATORS.

This matter becomes of special importance with reference to the statements made concerning members of families who are mentally or physically defective. The law requires a return in the case of each insane, feeble-minded, idiotic, blind, or deaf person, or such as may be crippled, maimed, or deformed. It not infrequently happens that the persons interrogated are disposed to conceal, or even to deny, the existence of such infirmities on the part of members of their household, especially as regards children. In such cases, if the fact is personally known to the enumerator, or if ascertained by inquiry from neighbors, it should be entered on the schedules the same as if obtained from the head or some member of the family.

In the same way the enumerator is not bound by any statement concerning the values produced in agricultural or other occupations which he knows or has reason to believe to be false; also, regarding homes and farms which are reported as having no incumbrances resting upon them, no statement should be accepted which he believes to be false. His duty is to report the actual facts as nearly as he can ascertain them.

### PENALTY FOR DISCLOSING INFORMATION.

By the thirteenth section of the act of March 1, 1889, it is provided that "any supervisor or enumerator who shall, without the authority of the Superintendent, communicate to any person not authorized to receive the same any information gained by him in the performance of his duties, shall be deemed guilty of a misdemeanor, and upon conviction shall be fined not exceeding five hundred dollars."

The intent of this provision is to make the answers to all the inquiries confidential, and to prevent disclosures of information which would operate to the personal detriment or disadvantage of the person supplying the same. It is not within the discretion of the supervisor or enumerator to make public or give out for his private use or that of any other person any part of the information obtained by him. All requests, whether from newspapers, local officials, or individuals, for the total population of his subdivision, or other matters pertaining to the enumeration, should be referred to the Census Office for reply. The returns will be tabulated in this office without delay, and the correct

## INSTRUCTIONS TO ENUMERATORS.

official figures supplied as soon as ascertained. Furthermore, it should be the duty of the enumerator to state, in all cases where objection is raised, that the names and residences will not be used in the printed reports, nor will any statement be made concerning the business or operations of individual establishments.

### FALSE OR FICTITIOUS RETURNS.

The law (section 13) further provides:

If he (supervisor or enumerator) shall willfully or knowingly swear or affirm falsely, he shall be deemed guilty of perjury, and, on conviction thereof, shall be imprisoned not exceeding three years, and be fined not exceeding eight hundred dollars; or, if he shall willfully and knowingly make false certificates or fictitious returns, he shall be deemed guilty of a misdemeanor, and, upon conviction of either of the last-named offenses, he shall be fined not exceeding five thousand dollars and be imprisoned not exceeding two years.

By this provision the enumerator is placed under severe penalties to do the work required of him honestly and conscientiously. The boundaries of the subdivision allotted to each enumerator are clearly defined in his commission, and it is his duty to make a thorough and systematic canvass of the territory assigned to him, visiting each house and establishment in order and obtaining complete and truthful returns concerning each individual living or doing business therein, as required by the law and his oath of office.

### THE SCHEDULES OF INQUIRIES.

The schedules to be used by the census enumerators are as follows:

Schedule No. 1, relating to population.

Schedule No. 2, relating to agriculture.

Schedule No. 3, relating to general manufactures, and special schedules relating to particular industries.

Schedule No. 5, relating to persons who have died during the census year.

Supplemental Schedules Nos. 1 to 8, relating to persons mentally or physically defective, crippled, maimed, or deformed, or temporarily disabled by sickness or disease; also to homeless children, prisoners, and paupers.

Special Schedule, relating to surviving soldiers, sailors, and marines in the war of the rebellion, and widows of soldiers, sailors, and marines of that war.

8   INSTRUCTIONS TO ENUMERATORS.

In the exercise of the authority conferred on the Superintendent of Census by section 18 of the act of March 1, 1889, Schedule No. 4, relating to social statistics, has been withdrawn from the enumerators.

By the same section it is also provided that, in the discretion of the Superintendent, the mortality schedules and the general and special schedules for manufactures may be withheld from the enumerators, as explained in the special instructions relating to these schedules.

The schedules, in number deemed sufficient for the enumeration, will be sent by the supervisors of census to the enumerators by registered mail. A portfolio is provided for carrying the schedules needed for each day's work. The extra supply of schedules should be left at home in some safe place, and at the completion of each day's work a new supply sufficient to answer the wants of the next day should be placed in the portfolio, and the completed work carefully retained at home in the same order in which the enumeration is made from day to day.

It is expected that the enumerators will prosecute their work at all times with diligence and dispatch. The limitations as to the time in which the enumeration shall be completed make it the imperative duty of enumerators to so arrange their work as to finish within the time allowed by law. An ordinary day's work should cover at least ten hours, and it will often be the case that the enumerators will find it profitable to do considerable work during the early part of the evening. When the work can be prosecuted to advantage there is no objection to such an arrangement on the part of the enumerators.

## THE PLAN OF ENUMERATION IN INSTITUTIONS.

The statistics of population and other special data concerning persons residing in institutions will be taken by institution enumerators; that is, some official or other trustworthy person connected with the institution, who will be appointed specially for the purpose.

This plan of enumeration will not be extended to all institutions, but the appointment of special institution enumerators will be determined partly by the size of the institution and partly by its nature.

INSTRUCTIONS TO ENUMERATORS. 9

For those institutions where this plan of enumeration is to be carried out the enumerators for the districts in which such institutions are located will have no responsibility. Each enumerator will receive in advance of the enumeration due notification from the supervisor for his district as to the institutions which are not to be taken by him. It should be the duty of the enumerator, however, if there is any institution in his district, whatever may be its size or character, to satisfy himself by personal inquiry of the officer in charge whether a special institution enumerator has been appointed, and if not, to proceed to enumerate the population as in the case of all other houses visited by him. On the other hand, if a special institution enumerator has been appointed for it, then it has been withdrawn from his district, and he will leave it to be enumerated by the special institution enumerator.

### SOLDIERS AND SAILORS.

All soldiers of the United States army, civilian employés, and other residents at posts or on military reservations, will be enumerated in the same manner as has been provided for institutions, by the appointment of a special resident enumerator; and in all such cases where the district enumerator has been so notified such posts or military reservations should not be included as a part of his district. For posts not garrisoned, and any other posts not so withdrawn, the district enumerator will make the necessary inquiries, and if no special enumerator has been appointed he will include the residents of such posts as a part of his district equally with other elements of the population.

In a similar way all sailors and marines stationed on vessels and at the United States navy yards, as well as resident officers, with their families, will be specially enumerated and need not be taken by the district enumerator if, upon inquiry or by notification, he knows that such special provision has been made.

### SPECIAL ENUMERATION OF INDIANS.

The law provides that the Superintendent of Census may employ special agents or other means to make an enumeration of all Indians living within the jurisdiction of the United States, with such information as to their condition as may be obtainable, classifying them as to Indians taxed and Indians not taxed.

By the phrase "Indians not taxed" is meant Indians living on reservations under the care of government agents or roaming individually or in bands over unsettled tracts of country.

Indians not in tribal relations, whether full-bloods or half-breeds, who are found mingled with the white population, residing in white families, engaged as servants or laborers, or living in huts or wigwams on the outskirts of towns or settlements, are to be regarded as a part of the ordinary population of the country, and are to be embraced in the enumeration.

The enumeration of Indians living on reservations will be made by special agents appointed directly from this office, and supervisors and enumerators will have no responsibility in this connection.

Many Indians, however, have voluntarily abandoned their tribal relations or have quit their reservations and now sustain themselves. When enumerators find Indians off of or living away from reservations, and in no wise dependent upon the agency or government, such Indians, in addition to their enumeration on the population and supplemental schedules, in the same manner as for the population generally, should be noted on a special schedule [7-917] by name, tribe, sex, age, occupation, and whether taxed or not taxed.

The object of this is to obtain an accurate census of all Indians living within the jurisdiction of the United States and to prevent double enumeration of certain Indians.

Where Indians are temporarily absent from their reservations the census enumerators need not note them, as the special enumerator for the Indian reservation will get their names.

### ENUMERATORS' DAILY REPORT CARDS.

Two postal cards for each working-day of the period allowed for enumeration will be furnished to each enumerator, one [7-761] adressed to the supervisor of his district, and the other [7-762] addressed to the Superintendent of Census at Washington.

The cards addressed to supervisors are printed on gray paper, and those addressed to the Superintendent of Census on buff paper.

On the back of these cards is a printed form for a statement by the enumerator of the number of persons, farms, etc., enumerated by him during the day to which the report relates, and also a statement of the time actually and necessarily occupied in this service.

INSTRUCTIONS TO ENUMERATORS. 11

The enumerator will, at the close of each day, fill up and sign this report. If he is in the immediate neighborhood of a post-office on the following day he will deposit these cards in the mail; if not, he will hold them until such time as he has an opportunity, without undue trouble, to deposit them; but he will not on any account fail to make out and sign the reports of daily work at the time required.

As these reports will be used in determining the compensation of enumerators, it will be desirable for them to exercise great pains in this particular.

In those districts where the enumeration must be made in the first two weeks of June the working days actually allowed by law number twelve, and end with June 14. In a few districts it may happen that the time required to complete the enumeration will exceed this limit, and to cover such emergencies daily report cards are supplied for June 16, 17, and 18. The enumeration must be completed, however, within two weeks in all districts, wherever possible, and the necessity for using these additional cards must be avoided, except for unusual causes only.

Accompanying the daily report cards are two forms of certificate of completion of enumeration, which read as follows:

I certify that on the ―― day of ――――, 1890, I completed the enumeration of the district assigned me, and that the returns have been duly and truthfully made in accordance with law and my oath of office.

―――― ――――,
*Enumerator for District No. ――.*

As soon as the work in each district is finished the enumerator should date, sign, and mail both of these cards, one of which [7-763] is to be sent to the supervisor and the other [7-764] to the Superintendent of Census.

Blanks are also provided for the use of enumerators in making consolidated statements of the time actually and necessarily occupied each day in the prosecution of their work. Upon this form [7-794] should be entered the number of hours and minutes worked each day as recorded on the daily report cards at the close of each day's service, including the time occupied by enumerators in securing from physicians the corrections of the statements of the causes of deaths on Schedule No. 5, in hunting up delinquents and absentees, and in securing information omitted upon their first rounds.

INSTRUCTIONS TO ENUMERATORS.

## RETURN OF SCHEDULES TO SUPERVISORS.

When the work in an enumeration district is finished all the schedules not used, together with the portfolio, should be neatly packed and returned in the same package with the completed schedules. The schedules and portfolio should be placed between the two pieces of mill-board provided for their protection and securely tied, and then wrapped in heavy manilla paper in the same manner as when received by the enumerator. The wrapping paper on the package, as originally sent, if preserved and turned (when necessary) will form a suitable cover for the return of the completed work.

The label [7–696] bearing the printed address of the supervisor is to be used by enumerators for the return of the schedules, and should be pasted on the outside of the package and over the old label bearing the name and address of the enumerator (if the wrapping paper is not turned). This label has the word "registered" stamped thereon, and by attaching the same to the package of schedules it can be sent to the supervisor to whom addressed by registered mail. In signing registry receipts the enumerators are cautioned in all cases to add their official title to their names.

## COMPENSATION.

By the eleventh section of the act of March 1, 1889, the Superintendent of Census, with the approval of the Secretary of the Interior, is authorized to fix the rates of compensation to be allowed the enumerators in advance of the enumeration.

Uniform rates will be allowed for the enumeration of deaths occurring during the census year and for names on the supplemental schedules and veterans' special schedule as follows:

Cents.
For each death reported (Schedule No. 5).......................... 2
For each person mentally or physically defective, and for each
  prisoner, pauper, or homeless child enumerated (Supplemental Schedules Nos. 1 to 8) ............................................ 5
For each surviving person or widow of person, who had served
  in the army, navy, or marine corps of the United States in the
  war of the rebellion, enumerated (Veterans' Special Schedule) ............................................................................ 5

## INSTRUCTIONS TO ENUMERATORS. 13

For the return of living persons (Schedule No. 1), of farms (Schedule No. 2), and of establishments of productive industry (Schedule No. 3 and Special Schedules) the rates allowed will be determined according to the varying ease or difficulty of enumeration.

The minimum allowance for each living inhabitant will be 2 cents, for each farm reported 15 cents, and for each manufacturing establishment 20 cents. The minimum rate for living inhabitants will be paid generally in cities and in incorporated towns and villages having a population sufficient to form a separate enumeration district. In certain rural districts higher per capita rates will be allowed, according to the relative sparseness of population, difficulties of travel, and other considerations affecting the matter. In regions where, through sparseness of settlement or other difficulties, it would be impossible for an enumerator to earn fair pay at the maximum per capita rates a per diem allowance has been authorized. The rates of pay of the enumerators of the Tenth Census, and the amounts earned daily by them, have been carefully studied for the various sections of the country, and the inequalities which existed at that census have been eliminated as far as possible.

Each enumerator, before the commencement of the enumeration, will receive from his supervisor a circular announcing the rates of compensation to be paid for his work. At the completion of the enumeration, and after the schedules returned by him have been examined by the supervisor, as required by section 5 of the act of March 1, 1889, a certification of the amount due to each enumerator, in accordance with his returns and the rates authorized for his district, will be made by the supervisor to the Superintendent of Census, and the schedules for such district returned at the same time to the Census Office.

As soon as the schedules are received at the Census Office the statements of the supervisor as to the persons, farms, etc., enumerated will be verified, and vouchers in duplicate sent direct from this office to each enumerator, to be by him receipted in duplicate and returned to the Census Office. Upon the receipt of these vouchers, properly signed, the compensation due to each enumerator will be transmitted by mail in the form of a draft, payable to the order of the enumerator named therein.

# SPECIAL INSTRUCTIONS

RELATIVE TO THE ENTRIES TO BE MADE ON THE GENERAL AND SPECIAL SCHEDULES.

In making the entries, whether of names or figures, upon the schedules enumerators must be careful to write clearly and neatly, without interlineations, erasures, or blots, as the original schedules must be returned to the Census Office at Washington for examination and compilation, and are to be finally bound in book form as a permanent record.

Use *black ink* in filling the schedules, and be careful to follow instructions as to the marks and symbols to be used in certain cases. Great care should also be exercised in making the entries upon the proper line and in the proper column. A little heedlessness in this respect may produce the most serious confusion. The schedules have been arranged to help the enumerator to find the proper line and column through the use of dotted, plain, and heavy lines, so that the eye can be guided to find easily the correct place of entry.

The enumerator should also realize the necessity of having every question answered exactly as required by the instructions. In the work of compilation in the Census Office each inquiry is treated as if it were the only one on the schedule, and no reference is made to preceding or following answers. The plainest illustration of this point is the necessity of entering every person who is single as "single," even if it is an infant but a few days old. In counting single persons no reference is made to the age, as shown by a preceding inquiry.

Each schedule is provided with a space for the signature of the enumerator, and each schedule, as soon as filled, must be signed by the enumerator as his certification that the entries contained therein have been wholly made by him. The enumerator is prohibited by law from delegating to any other person his authority to enter dwellings and to interrogate their inhabitants. The work of enumeration must be done by him in person, and can not be performed by proxy. The only exception to this which can arise would be in case the services of an interpreter were necessary, and then only when specially authorized from the Census Office.

(15)

## SCHEDULE NO. 1.—POPULATION.

The schedule adopted for the enumeration of the population is what is known as the family schedule; that is, a separate schedule for each family, without regard to the number of persons in the family. Three forms of this schedule are provided for the use of enumerators, according as the families to be enumerated are made up of a large or small number of persons.

The single-sheet schedules [7–556a] are provided for use in enumerating families containing from 1 to 10 persons, the double-sheet schedules [7–556b] for use in enumerating families containing more than 10 but not over 20 persons, and the additional sheets [7–556c] for use in enumerating families containing more than 20 persons. In the case of large-families, boarding-houses, lodging-houses, hotels, institutions, schools, etc., containing more than 20 persons use the double sheet for 1 to 20 persons, and such number of the additional sheets as may be necessary. Whenever the additional sheets are used, be careful to write on each sheet, in the spaces provided therefor, the number of the supervisor's district, enumeration district, dwelling-house, and family, and also the name of the institution, school, etc., as the case may be. Also, at the heads of the columns in which the information concerning the several persons enumerated is entered, fill in the "tens" figures on the dotted lines preceding the printed unit figures, and continue to number the columns consecutively, as 21, 22, etc., until all the persons in the family have been enumerated.

Upon one or the other of these forms of the population schedule, according to the size of the family to be enumerated, is to be entered the name of every man, woman, and child who *on the 1st day of June*, 1890, shall have his or her usual place of abode within the enumerator's district. No child born between the 1st day of June, 1890, and the day of the enumerator's visit (say June 5, June 15, etc., as the case may be) is to be entered upon the schedule. On the other hand, every person who was a resident of the district upon the 1st day of June, 1890, but between that date and the day of the enumerator's visit shall have died, should be entered on the schedule precisely as if still living. The object of the schedule is to obtain a list of the inhabitants *on the 1st of June*, 1890, and all changes after that date, whether in the nature of gain or of loss, are to be disregarded in the enumeration.

INSTRUCTIONS TO ENUMERATORS. 17

In answering the several inquiries on the population and other schedules the space provided for each answer should be filled by a definite statement or a symbol used to denote either that the inquiry is not applicable to the person for whom the answers are being made or that the information can not be obtained. In all cases where the inquiry is not applicable use the following symbol: X. If for any reason it is not possible to obtain answers to inquiries which are applicable to the person enumerated, use the following symbol to denote this fact: ═══. The enumerator must bear in mind, however, that where he has every reason to suppose that he can supply the answer himself it is better than the symbol; and in any case the symbol should not be used until he has made every effort to ascertain the proper answer from the persons in the family or in the neighborhood, as required by law.

Illustrative examples of the manner of filling the population schedules and the use of these symbols are contained in printed sheets [7-975] which are supplied to enumerators.

## Supervisors' and Enumeration Districts.

The first thing to be entered at the head of each schedule is the number of the supervisor's district and of the enumeration district in which the work is performed. These numbers must be repeated for each family enumerated, and where additional sheets are used these numbers are to be carried to those sheets, as already stated.

## Civil Divisions.

Be careful to enter accurately the name of the city, town, township, precinct, etc., and distinguish carefully between the population of villages within townships and the remainder of such townships. The correct enumeration of the population of these minor civil divisions is especially important, and is of interest in the presentation in the printed reports of details concerning these small bodies of population. So far as possible, also, the population of small unincorporated villages and hamlets should be separately reported. Also enter at the head of each schedule, in the spaces provided therefor, the name of the county and state or territory in which the minor subdivision is located. In cities the street, street-number, and ward should be entered in the proper spaces, and in those cities where special sanitary districts have been established

2

## 18   INSTRUCTIONS TO ENUMERATORS.

for the purposes of the census enumeration the letters used to designate them should be added in some convenient space at the head of each schedule and encircled thus: (A), (B), (C), etc., according to the special letters used to distinguish these sanitary districts.

### Institutions.

Wherever an institution is to be enumerated, as a hospital, asylum, almshouse, jail, or penitentiary, the full name and title of the institution should be entered, and all persons having their usual place of abode in such institution, whether officers, attendants, inmates, or persons in confinement, should then be entered consecutively on the schedules as one family. If, as sometimes may be the case, a sheriff, warden, or other prison official may live in one end of the prison building, but separated by a partition wall from the prison proper, his family (including himself as its head) should be returned on a separate schedule, and should not be returned on the schedule upon which the prisoners are entered. Where the officers or attendants, or any of them, do not reside in the institution buildings, but live with their families in detached dwellings, no matter whether the houses are owned by the institution or located in the same grounds, they should be reported on separate schedules, but should be included as a part of the work of the special institution enumerator, where one is appointed, and should not be left to be taken by the district enumerator. It may happen also that some of the officers or attendants may reside wholly outside of the institution precincts, either in rented houses or houses owned by the institution, or by themselves, and in such cases they should be enumerated by the district enumerator and not by the special institution enumerator. The tour of duty of the special institution enumerator should not extend beyond the boundaries of the institution grounds, but should include all those persons and inmates whose usual places of abode are clearly within the territory controlled by the institution.

### Persons, Families, and Dwellings.

**A.—Number of dwelling-house in the order of visitation.**

In the space against the inquiry marked A is to be entered the number of the dwelling-house in the order of visitation. The

INSTRUCTIONS TO ENUMERATORS. 19

object of this inquiry is to ascertain the total number of dwelling-houses. A dwelling-house for the purposes of the census means any building or place of abode, of whatever character, material, or structure, in which any person is living at the time of taking the census. It may be a room above a warehouse or factory, a loft above a stable, a wigwam on the outskirts of a settlement, or a dwelling-house in the ordinary sense of that term. A tenement house, whether it contains two, three, or forty families, should be considered for the purposes of the census as one house. A building under one roof suited for two or more families, but with a dividing partition wall and a separate front door for each part of the building, should be counted as two or more houses. A block of houses under one roof, but with separate front doors, should be considered as so many houses, without regard to the number of families in each separate house in the block. Wholly uninhabited dwellings are not to be counted.

B.—Number of families in this dwelling-house.

The inquiry marked B calls for the number of families, whether one or more, in each dwelling-house. *Where there is more than one family in a dwelling-house, this inquiry should be answered only on the schedule for the first family enumerated and omitted on the schedules for the second and subsequent families enumerated in the same house,* to avoid duplication of results; the space on the schedules for the second and subsequent families should be filled, however, by an X, as not being applicable. An example of this character is given on the printed sheets illustrative of the manner of filling schedules.

C.—Number of persons in this dwelling-house.

The inquiry marked C calls for the number of persons in each dwelling-house, and where there is more than one family in the house the answer should represent the total number of persons included in the several families occupying the same house. Where there is but a single family to a house, the answer to this inquiry should be the same as for inquiry E. *Where there is more than one family in a dwelling-house this inquiry, as in the case of inquiry B, should be answered only on the schedule for the first family enumerated.*

D.—Number of family in the order of visitation.

In answer to the inquiry marked D enter the number, in the order of visitation, of each family residing in the district. The

## INSTRUCTIONS TO ENUMERATORS.

fact that more than one family is often found in a house makes the family number exceed, necessarily, the house number, as called for by inquiry A.

The word family, for the purposes of the census, includes persons living alone, as well as families in the ordinary sense of that term, and also all larger aggregations of people having only the tie of a common roof and table. A hotel, with all its inmates, constitutes but one family within the meaning of this term. A hospital, a prison, an asylum is equally a family for the purposes of the census. On the other hand, the solitary inmate of a cabin, a loft, or a room finished off above a store, and indeed all individuals living out of families, constitute a family in the meaning of the census act.

By "individuals living out of families" is meant all persons occupying lofts in public buildings, above stores, warehouses, factories, and stables, having no other usual place of abode; persons living solitary in cabins, huts, or tents; persons sleeping on river boats, canal boats, barges, etc., having no other usual place of abode, and persons in police stations having no homes. Of the classes just mentioned the most important, numerically, is the first, viz: those persons, chiefly in cities, who occupy rooms in public buildings, or above stores, warehouses, factories, and stables. In order to reach such persons the enumerator will need not only to keep his eyes open to all indications of such casual residence in his enumeration district, but to make inquiry both of the parties occupying the business portion of such buildings and also of the police. In the case, however, of tenement houses and of the so-called "flats" of the great cities as many families are to be recorded as there are separate tables.

A person's home is where he sleeps. There are many people who lodge in one place and board in another; all such persons should be returned as members of that family with which they lodge.

**E.—Number of persons in this family.**

The answer to this inquiry should correspond to the number of columns filled on each schedule, and care should be taken to have all the members of the family included in this statement and a column filled for each person in the family, including servants, boarders, lodgers, etc. Be sure that the person answering the inquiries thoroughly understands the question, and does not omit any person who should be counted as a member of the family.

## Names, Relationship to Head of Family, and whether Survivors of the War of the Rebellion.

**1. Christian name in full, initial of middle name, and surname.**

Opposite to the inquiry numbered 1 on the schedule are to be entered the names of all persons whose usual place of abode on the 1st day of June, 1890, was in the family enumerated. The census law furnishes no definition of the phrase "usual place of abode;" and it is difficult, under the American system of a protracted enumeration, to afford administrative directions which will wholly obviate the danger that some persons will be reported in two places and others not reported at all. Much must be left to the judgment of the enumerator, who can, if he will take the pains, in the great majority of instances satisfy himself as to the propriety of including or not including doubtful cases in his enumeration of any given family. In the cases of boarders at hotels or students at schools or colleges the enumerator can by one or two well-directed inquiries ascertain whether the person concerning whom the question may arise has at the time any other place of abode within another district at which he is likely to be reported. Seafaring men are to be reported at their land homes, no matter how long they may have been absent, if they are supposed to be still alive. Hence, sailors temporarily at a sailors' boarding or lodging house, if they *acknowledge any other home within the United States*, are not to be included in the family of the lodging or boarding house. Persons engaged in internal transportation, canal men, expressmen, railroad men, etc., if they habitually return to their homes in the intervals of their occupations, will be reported *as of their families*, and not where they may be temporarily staying on the 1st of June, 1890.

In entering the members of a family the name of the father, mother, or other ostensible head of the family (in the case of hotels, jails, etc., the landlord, jailer, etc.) is to be entered in the first column. It is desirable that the wife should be enumerated in the second column, and the children of the family proper should follow in the order of their ages, as will naturally be the case. The names of all other persons in the family, whether relatives, boarders, lodgers, or servants, should be entered successively in subsequent columns.

INSTRUCTIONS TO ENUMERATORS.

The christian name in full and initial of middle name of each person should be first entered and the surname immediately thereunder, as shown in the illustrative example.

**2. Whether a soldier, sailor, or marine during the civil war (U. S. or Conf.), or widow of such person.**

Write "Sol" for soldier, "Sail" for sailor, and "Ma" for marine. If the person served in the United States forces add "U. S." in parenthesis, and if in the Confederate forces add "Conf." in parenthesis, thus: Sol (U. S.); Sail (U. S.); Sol (Conf.), etc. In the case of a widow of a deceased soldier, sailor, or marine, use the letter "W" in addition to the above designations, as W. Sol (U. S.), W. Sol (Conf.), and so on.

The enumeration of the survivors of the late war, including their names, organizations, length of service, and the widows of such as have died, is to be taken on a special schedule prepared for the purpose, as provided for by the act of March 1, 1889, *and relates only to those persons, or widows of persons, who served in the army, navy, or marine corps of the United States in the late war.* The inquiry concerning the survivors of both the United States and Confederate forces is made on the population schedule so as to ascertain the *number* now living and the *number* who have died and have left widows.

**3. Relationship to head of family.**

Designate the head of a family, whether a husband or father, widow or unmarried person of either sex, by the word *"Head;"* other members of a family by *wife, mother, father, son, daughter, grandson, daughter-in-law, aunt, uncle, nephew, niece, servant,* or other properly distinctive term, according to the particular relationship which the person bears to the head of the family. Distinguish between *boarders,* who sleep and board in one place, and *lodgers,* who room in one place and board in another. If an inmate of an institution or school, write *inmate, pupil, patient, prisoner,* or some equivalent term which will clearly distinguish inmates from the officers and employés and their families. But all officers and employés of an institution who reside in the institution building are to be accounted, for census purposes, as one family, the head of which is the superintendent, matron, or other officer in charge. If more than one family resides in the institution building, group the members together and distinguish

INSTRUCTIONS TO ENUMERATORS. 23

them in some intelligible way. In addition to defining their natural relationship to the head of the institution or of their own immediate family, their official position in the institution, if any, should be also noted, thus: *Superintendent, clerk, teacher, watchman, nurse,* etc.

### Color, Sex, and Age.

**4. Whether white, black, mulatto, quadroon, octoroon, Chinese, Japanese, or Indian.**

Write *white, black, mulatto, quadroon, octoroon, Chinese, Japanese,* or *Indian,* according to the color or race of the person enumerated. Be particularly careful to distinguish between blacks, mulattoes, quadroons, and octoroons. The word "black" should be used to describe those persons who have three-fourths or more black blood; "mulatto," those persons who have from three-eighths to five-eighths black blood; "quadroon," those persons who have one-fourth black blood; and "octoroon," those persons who have one-eighth or any trace of black blood.

**5. Sex.**

Write *male* or *female,* as the case may be.

**6. Age at nearest birthday. If under one year, give age in months.**

Write the age in figures at nearest birthday in whole years, omitting months and days, for each person of one year of age or over. For children who on the 1st of June, 1890, were less than one year of age, give the age in months, or twelfths of a year, thus: $\frac{2}{12}$, $\frac{7}{12}$, $\frac{11}{12}$. For a child less than one month old, state the age as follows: $\frac{0}{12}$. The *exact* years of age for all persons one year old or over should be given whenever it can be obtained. In any event, do not accept the answer "don't know," but ascertain as nearly as possible the approximate age of each person. The general tendency of persons in giving their ages is to use the round numbers, as 20, 25, 30, 35, 40, etc. If the age is given as "about 25," determine, if possible, whether the age should be entered as 24, 25, or 26. Particular attention should be paid to this, otherwise it will be found when the results are aggregated in this office that a much more than normal number of persons have been reported as 20, 25, 30, 35, 40, etc., years of age, and a much less than normal at 19, 21, 24, 26, 29, 31, etc.

## Conjugal Condition and Children and Children Living.

**7. Whether single, married, widowed, or divorced.**

Write *single, married, widowed,* or *divorced,* according to the conjugal condition of the person enumerated. No matter how young the person may be, the conjugal condition, if "single," should be always stated.

**8. Whether married during the census year (June 1, 1889, to May 31, 1890).**

Write *yes* or *no,* as the case may be.

**9. Mother of how many children, and number of these children living.**

This inquiry is to be made concerning all women who are or have been married, including those widowed or divorced. The answers should be given in figures, as follows: 6—5; that is, mother of six (6) children, of which five (5) are living. If a woman who is or has been married has had no children, or if none are living, state the fact thus: 0—0 or 3—0, as the case may be.

## Place of Birth and Parent Nativity.

**10. Place of birth.**

Give the place of birth of the *person* whose name appears at the head of the column opposite inquiry 1, and for whom the entries are being made.

**11. Place of birth of Father.**

Give the place of birth of the *father* of the person for whom the entries are being made.

**12. Place of birth of Mother.**

Give the place of birth of the *mother* of the person for whom the entries are being made.

If the person (Inquiry 10), or father (Inquiry 11), or mother (Inquiry 12) were born in the United States, name the state or territory, or if of foreign birth name the country. The names of *countries,* and not of cities, are wanted. In naming the country of foreign birth, however, do not write, for instance, "Great Britain," but give the particular country, as *England, Scotland,* or *Wales.*

INSTRUCTIONS TO ENUMERATORS. 25

If the person, or father, or mother were born in a foreign country of American parents, write the name of the country and also the words *American Citizen*. If born at sea, write the words *At Sea;* if in the case of the father or mother the words "At Sea" be used, add the nationality of the father's father or mother's father.

If born in Canada or Newfoundland, write the word "English" or "French" after the particular place of birth, so as to distinguish between persons born in any part of British America of French and English extraction respectively. *This is a most important requirement, and must be closely observed in each case and the distinction carefully made.*

## Naturalization.

Inquiries 13, 14, and 15 should be made concerning only those adult *males* of foreign birth who are 21 years of age or over.

**13. Number of years in the United States.**

Give the answer in figures, as 1, 2, 3, 6, 10, etc., according to the number of years such person (as stated above) may have resided in the United States.

**14. Whether naturalized.**

Write *yes* or *no*, as the case may be.

**15. Whether naturalization papers have been taken out.**

If naturalized (Inquiry 14), use the symbol **X**; if not naturalized, (Inquiry 14), write *yes* or *no*, as the case may be, in answer to this inquiry (15).

## Profession, Trade, or Occupation, and Months Unemployed.

**16. Profession, trade, or occupation.**

This is a most important inquiry. Study these instructions closely, and in reporting occupations avoid the use of unmeaning terms. A person's occupation is the profession, trade, or branch of work upon which he chiefly depends for support, and in which he would ordinarily be engaged during the larger part of the year. General or indefinite terms which do not indicate the kind of work done by each person must not be used. You are under no obligation to give a person's occupation just as he expresses

xliii

it. If he can not tell intelligibly what he *is*, find out what he *does*, and describe his occupation accordingly. The name of the place worked in or article made or worked upon should not be used as the sole basis of the statement of a person's occupation. Endeavor to ascertain always *the character of the service rendered or kind of work done*, and so state it.

The illustrations given under each of the general classes of occupation show the nature of the answers which should be made to this inquiry. They are not intended to cover all occupations, but are indicative of the character of the answers desired in order to secure, for each person enumerated, properly descriptive designations of service rendered or work done by way of occupation and as the means of gaining a livelihood.

**Agricultural Pursuits.**—Be careful to distinguish between the *farm laborer*, the *farmer*, and *farm overseer*; also between the *plantation laborer*, the *planter*, and *plantation overseer*. These three classes must be kept distinct, and each occupation separately returned.

Do not confuse the *agricultural laborer*, who works on the farm or plantation, with the general or day laborer, who works on the road or at odd jobs in the village or town. Distinguish also between *woodchoppers* at work regularly in the woods or forests and the laborer, who takes a job occasionally at chopping wood.

Make a separate return for *farmers* and *planters* who own, hire, or carry on a farm or plantation, and for *gardeners, fruit growers, nurserymen, florists, vine-growers*, etc., who are engaged in raising vegetables for market or in the cultivation of fruit, flowers, seeds, nursery products, etc. In the latter case, if a man combines two or more of these occupations, be careful to so state it, as *florist, nurseryman and seed-grower*.

Avoid the confusion of the *garden laborer, nursery laborer*, etc., who hires out his services, with the proprietor gardener, florist, nurseryman, etc., who carries on the business himself or employs others to assist him.

Return as *dairymen* or *dairywomen* those persons whose occupation in connection with the farm has to do chiefly with the dairy. Do not confuse them with employés of butter and cheese or condensed milk factories, who should be separately returned by some distinctive term.

INSTRUCTIONS TO ENUMERATORS. 27

Return *stock-herders* and *stock-drovers* separately from *stock-raisers*.

Do not include *lumbermen, raftsmen, log-drivers*, etc., engaged in hauling or transporting lumber (generally by water) from the forest to the mill, with the employes of lumber yards or lumber mills.

**Fishing.**—For *fishermen* and *oystermen* describe the occupation as accurately as possible. Be careful to avoid the return of fishermen on vessels as sailors. If they gain their living by fishing, they should be returned as "fishermen," and not as sailors.

**Mining and Quarrying.**—Make a careful distinction between the *coal miners* and *miners of ores;* also between miners generally and *quarrymen*. State the *kind* of ore mined or stone quarried.

Do not return *proprietors* or *officials* of mining or quarrying companies as miners or quarrymen, but state their business or official position accurately.

**Professional Pursuits.**—This class includes *actors, artists* and *teachers of art, clergymen, dentists, designers, draughtsmen, engravers, civil engineers* and *surveyors, mechanical* and *mining engineers, government clerks* and *officials, journalists, lawyers, musicians* and *teachers of music, physicians, surgeons, professors* (in colleges and universities), *teachers* (in schools), and other pursuits of a professional nature. Specify each profession in detail, according to the fact. These are cited simply as illustrations of these classes of pursuits.

Distinguish between *actors, theatrical managers*, and *showmen*.

Make a separate return for *government clerks* occupying positions under the national, state, county, city, or town governments from clerks in offices, stores, manufacturing establishments, etc.; also distinguish *government officials*.

Return *veterinary surgeons* separately from other surgeons.

Distinguish *journalists, editors*, and *reporters* from *authors* and other *literary persons* who do not follow journalism as a distinct profession.

Return separately *chemists, assayers, metallurgists*, and other scientific persons.

**Domestic and Personal Service.**—Among this class of occupations are comprised *hotel keepers, boarding-house keepers, restaurant*

xlv

*keepers, saloon keepers*, and *bartenders*; *housekeepers, cooks*, and *servants* (in hotels, boarding-houses, hospitals, institutions, private families, etc.); *barbers* and *hairdressers; city, town*, and *general day laborers; janitors, sextons*, and *undertakers; nurses* and *midwives; watchmen, policemen*, and *detectives*. Specify each occupation or kind of service rendered in detail, according to the fact. The above are given only as examples of the occupations which would naturally be included under this general class of work.

Distinguish carefully between *housekeepers*, or women who receive a stated wage or salary for their services, and *housewives*, or women who keep house for their own families or for themselves, without any gainful occupation. The occupation of grown daughters who assist in the household duties without fixed remuneration should be returned as *"Housework—without pay."*

As stated under agricultural pursuits, do not confuse *day laborers*, at work for the city, town, or at odd jobs, with the agricultural laborer, at work on the farm or plantation or in the employ of gardeners, nurserymen, etc. State specifically the *kind* of work done in every instance.

*Clerks* in hotels, restaurants, and saloons should be so described and carefully distinguished from *bartenders*. In many instances bartenders will state their occupation as "clerk" in wine store, etc., but the character of the service rendered by such persons will readily determine whether they should be classed as "bartenders" or not.

*Stationary engineers* and *firemen* should be carefully distinguished from *engineers* and *firemen* employed on locomotives, steamboats, etc.

*Soldiers, sailors*, and *marines* enlisted in the service of the United States should be so returned. Distinguish between officers and enlisted men, and for civilian employes return the kind of service performed by them.

**Pursuits of Trade and Transportation.**—Distinguish carefully between *real estate agents, insurance agents, claim agents, commission agents*, etc. If a person is a real estate agent and also an auctioneer, as is often the case, return his occupation as *real estate agent and auctioneer.*

Return accountants, bookkeepers, clerks, cashiers, etc., separately, and state the kind of service rendered, as *accountant—*

## INSTRUCTIONS TO ENUMERATORS. 29

*insurance; bookkeeper—wholesale dry goods; clerk—gas company; cashier—music store.*

Do not confound a clerk with a salesman, as is often done, especially in dry goods stores, grocery stores, and provision stores. Generally speaking, the persons so employed are to be considered as salesmen, unless the bulk of their service is in the office on the books and accounts; otherwise they should be returned as *salesman—dry goods; salesman—groceries*, etc.

*Stenographers* and *typewriters* should be reported separately, and should not be described simply as "clerks."

Distinguish carefully between *bank clerks, cashiers in banks*, and *bank officials*, describing the particular position filled in each case. In no case should a *bank cashier* be confounded with cashiers in stores, etc.

Distinguish between foremen and overseers, packers and shippers, porters and helpers, and errand, office, and messenger boys in stores, etc., and state in each case the character of the duties performed by them, as *foreman—wholesale wool house; packer—crockery; porter—rubber goods; errand boy—dry goods; messenger boy—telegraph.*

State the kind of merchants and dealers, as *dry goods merchant, wood and coal dealer*, etc. Whenever a single word will express the business carried on, as *grocer*, it should be so stated.

In the case of hucksters and peddlers also state the kind of goods sold, as *peddler—tinware.*

Distinguish *traveling salesmen* from **salesmen** in stores, and state the kind of goods sold by them.

Return *boarding* and *livery-stable keepers* separately from *hostlers* and other stable employés.

Distinguish also between *expressmen, teamsters, draymen*, and *carriage and hack drivers.*

Steam railroad employés should be reported separately, according to the nature of their work, as *baggagemen, brakemen, conductors, laborers on railroad, locomotive engineers, locomotive firemen, switchmen, yardmen*, etc.

*Officials of railroad, telegraph, express*, and *other companies* should be separately returned and carefully distinguished from the employés of such companies.

*Boatmen, canalmen, pilots, longshoremen, stevedores,* and *sailors* (on steam or sailing vessels) should be separately returned.

xlvii

*Telegraph operators, telephone operators, telegraph linemen, telephone linemen, electric-light men,* etc., should be kept distinct, and a separate return made for each class.

**Manufacturing and Mechanical Pursuits.**—In reporting occupations pertaining to manufactures there are many difficulties in the way of showing the kind of work done rather than the article made or the place worked in. The nature of certain occupations is such that it is well nigh impossible to find properly descriptive terms without the use of some expression relating to the article made or place in which the work is carried on.

Do not accept " maker " of an article or " works in " mill, shop, or factory, but strive always to find out the particular work done.

Distinguish between persons who tend machines and the unskilled workman or laborer in mills, factories, and workshops.

Describe the proprietor of the establishment as a "manufacturer," and specify the branch of manufacture, as *cotton manufacturer,* etc. In no case should a manufacturer be returned as a " maker " of an article.

In the case of apprentices, state the trade to which apprenticed, as *Apprentice—carpenter,* etc.

Distinguish between *butchers,* whose business is to slaughter cattle, swine, etc., and *provision dealers,* who sell meats only.

Distinguish also between a *glover, hatter,* or *furrier* who actually make or make up in their own establishments all or part of the gloves, hats, or furs which they sell, and the person who simply deals in but does not make these articles.

Do not use the words "factory operative," but specify in every instance the kind of work done, as *cotton mill—spinner; silk mill—weaver,* etc.

Do not describe a person in a printing office as a "printer" where a more expressive term can be used, as *compositor, pressman, press feeder,* etc.

Make the proper distinction between a *clock* or *watch* " *maker* " and a *clock* or *watch* " *repairer.*" Do not apply the word "jeweler" to those who make watches, watch chains, or jewelry in large establishments.

Avoid in all cases the use of the word "mechanic," and state whether a *carpenter, mason, house painter, machinist, plumber,* etc.

Do not say "finisher," "molder," "polisher," etc., but state

INSTRUCTIONS TO ENUMERATORS. 31

the article finished, molded, or polished, as *brass finisher, iron molder, steel polisher*, etc.

Distinguish between *cloak makers, dressmakers, seamstresses, tailoresses*, etc. In the case of *sewing-machine operators*, specify the work done.

**Other Occupations.**—When a lawyer, merchant, manufacturer, etc., has retired from practice or business, say *retired lawyer, retired merchant*, etc.

The distinction to be made between *housewives, housekeepers*, and those assisting in *housework* has already been stated under "DOMESTIC AND PERSONAL SERVICE." For the large body of persons, particularly young women, who live at home and do nothing, make the return as " No occupation." With respect to infants and children too young to take any part in production or to be engaged in any stated occupation, distinguish between those at home and those attending school. For those too young to go to school, or who for some reason did not attend school during the census year, write the words *At home*, and for those who attended school during some part of the school year write the words, *At school—public*, or *At school—private*, according to the kind of school. If taught by a governess or tutor, it should be so stated. The *student* at college or engaged in special studies should be reported separately from *scholars in public or private schools*.

The doing of domestic errands or family chores out of school hours, where a child regularly attends school, should not be considered an occupation. But if a boy or girl, whatever the age, is earning money regularly by labor, contributing to the family support, or appreciably assisting in mechanical or agricultural industry, the kind of work performed should be stated.

**17. Months unemployed during the census year (June 1, 1889, to May 31, 1890).**

If a person having a gainful occupation was unemployed during any part of the census year it should be so stated in months and parts of months. If, as may often happen, a person was unemployed at his usual occupation for some time during the census year and yet found other temporary employment for some part or the whole of the time, this fact should be clearly stated. For instance, a person's occupation may be that of "Farm laborer," at which he may have had no employment for three months during the census year. During two of these three months, however, he may have worked in a shoe shop, so that, so far as actual idleness is concerned, he was only out of work one month. In all such cases, where the non-employment returned in answer to Inquiry 17 does not represent actual idleness as regards the person's usual occupation given in answer to Inquiry 16, indicate the number of months unemployed at occupation by inserting the figures, in parenthesis, after the name of the occupation itself. In the case just cited, and as shown in the "illustrative example," the answer to Inquiry 16 would appear as "Farm laborer (3)" and the answer to Inquiry 17 as "1." For all persons not engaged in gainful occupations the symbol "X" should be used.

### School Attendance, Illiteracy, and Language Spoken.

**18. Attendance at school (in months) during the census year (June 1, 1889, to May 31, 1890).**

For all persons between the ages of five and seventeen, inclusive, the attendance at school during the census year should be in all cases stated in months and parts of months. Where a person within the above ages did not attend school at all during the census year write "0," and for all other persons to whom the inquiry is not applicable use the symbol "X."

*Inquiries numbered 19 and 20 relate to illiteracy, and are to be made only of or concerning persons ten years of age or over.*

**19. Able to read.**

Write *yes* or *no*, as the case may be.

**20. Able to write.**

Write *yes* or *no*, as the case may be.

A person may not be able to read or write the English language and yet may be able to read or write (or both) their native language, as French, Spanish, Italian, etc. If in such cases a person can read or write (or both) some language, the answer to Inquiry 19 and Inquiry 20 should be "yes," according to the fact. If not able to so read or write the answer should be "no." For all persons *under ten* years of age use the symbol "X."

INSTRUCTIONS TO ENUMERATORS. 33

**21. Able to speak English. If not, the language or dialect spoken.**

*This inquiry should also be made of or concerning every person ten years of age or over.* If the person is able to speak English so as to be understood in ordinary conversation, write *English;* otherwise, write the name of the language or dialect in which he usually expresses himself, as *German, Portuguese, Canadian French, Pennsylvania Dutch,* etc. For all persons *under* ten years of age use the symbol "X."

### Mental and Physical Defects, etc.

**22. Whether suffering from acute or chronic disease, with name of disease and length of time afflicted.**

If a person is suffering from acute or chronic disease so as to be unable to attend to ordinary business or duties, give the name of the disease and the length of time that it has lasted.

**23. Whether defective in mind, sight, hearing, or speech, or whether crippled, maimed, or deformed, with name of defect.**

If a person is mentally or physically defective, state the nature of the defect.

**24. Whether a prisoner, convict, homeless child, or pauper.**

If the person is a prisoner, convict, homeless child, or pauper, be careful to so state, as *"prisoner," "pauper,"* etc.

**25. Supplemental schedule and page.**

If answers are required to Inquiries 22, 23, or 24, indicate in this space the number of the Supplemental Schedule and page of schedule on which the special inquiries relating to such person have been answered. (See instructions concerning Supplemental Schedules.)

### Ownership of Homes and Farms.

**26. Is the home you live in hired, or is it owned by the head or by a member of the family?**

If hired, say *Hired;* if owned, say *Owned,* and indicate whether owned by *head, wife, son, daughter,* or other member of family, as *Owned—head; Owned—wife; Owned—son,* etc. If there is more than one son or daughter in the family, and the home is owned by one of them, indicate which one by using the figure at the head of

3

the column in which the name, etc., of the person is entered, as *Owned—son* (4).

**27. If owned by head or member of family, is the home free from mortgage incumbrance?**

If free from incumbrance, say *Free;* if mortgaged, say *Mortgaged.*

**28. If the head of family is a farmer, is the farm which he cultivates hired, or is it owned by him or by a member of his family?**

To be answered in the same manner as for Inquiry 26.

**29. If owned by head or member of family, is the farm free from mortgage incumbrance?**

To be answered in the same manner as for Inquiry 27.

**30. If the home or farm is owned by head or member of family, and mortgaged, give the post-office address of owner.**

In answer to this inquiry the post-office address of the owner of a *mortgaged* home or farm must be correctly stated; that is, the post-office at which the owner (whether head of family, wife, son, daughter, etc.) usually receives his or her mail.

*In all cases where it can not be definitely ascertained whether the home or farm is mortgaged or not return the post-office address of the owner, so that this office can communicate with such persons.*

In connection with the definition of mortgage incumbrance it should be stated that judgment notes or confessions of judgment, as in Pennsylvania and Virginia, the deeds of trust of many states, deeds with vendor's lien clause, bonds or contracts for title that are virtually mortgages, crop liens or mortgages upon crops, and all other legal instruments that partake of the nature of mortgages upon real estate, are to be regarded as such; but mechanics' liens are not to be regarded as mortgage incumbrances upon homes or farms.

The enumerator should be careful to use the local name for the mortgage incumbrance when making the inquiries, and should not confine himself to the word "mortgage" when it will be misunderstood.

Some of the difficulties which will arise in connection with the prosecution of the inquiries concerning homes and farms, and how they are to be treated, may be mentioned, as follows:

1. A house is not necessarily to be considered as identical with

INSTRUCTIONS TO ENUMERATORS. 35

a home and to be counted only once as a home. If it is occupied as a home by one or more tenants, or by owner and one or more tenants, it is to be regarded as a home to each family.

2. If a person owns and cultivates what has been two or more farms and lives on one, they are not to be taken as more than one farm.

3. If a person owns and cultivates what has been two or more farms and all are not mortgaged, the several farms are to be counted as one farm and as mortgaged.

4. If a person hires both the farm he cultivates and the home he lives in, or owns both, the home is to be considered as a part of the farm.

5. If a person owns the home he lives in and hires the farm he cultivates, or owns the farm he cultivates and hires the home he lives in, both farm and home are to be entered upon the schedule, and separately.

6. If the tenant of a farm and its owner live upon it, either in the same house or in different houses, the owner is to be regarded as owning the home he lives in and the tenant as hiring the farm he cultivates. If the owner simply boards with the tenant no account is to be made of the owner.

7. If the same person owns and cultivates one farm and hires and cultivates another farm, he is to be entered upon the schedule as owning the farm he cultivates.

8. The head of a family may own and cultivate a farm and his wife may own another farm which is let to tenant, perhaps to her husband. In such case only the farm which is owned by the head of the family is to be considered, but the rented farm is to be taken account of when its tenant's family is visited.

9. A person who cultivates a farm is not to be regarded as hiring it if he works for a definite and fixed compensation in money or fixed quantity of produce, but he is to be regarded as hiring it if he pays a rental for it or is to receive a share of the produce, even though he may be subject to some direction and control by the owner.

SCHEDULE NO. 2.—AGRICULTURE.

"Farms" for the purposes of the agricultural schedule include, besides what are commonly known as farms, all considerable

INSTRUCTIONS TO ENUMERATORS.

nurseries, orchards, and market gardens owned by separate parties, which are cultivated for pecuniary profit, and employ as much as the labor of one able-bodied workman during the year. Mere cabbage and potato patches, family vegetable gardens, and ornamental lawns, not constituting a portion of a farm for general agricultural purposes, will be excluded. No farm will be reported of less than three acres unless five hundred dollars' worth of produce has been actually sold from it during the year. The latter proviso will allow the inclusion of many market gardens in the neighborhood of large cities, where, although the area is small, a high state of cultivation is maintained and considerable values are produced.

A farm is what is owned or leased by one man and cultivated under his care. A distant wood-lot or sheep-pasture, even if in another subdivision or district, is to be treated as a part of the farm; but wherever there is a resident overseer or a manager there a separate farm is to be reported.

The amounts of the various crops may be estimated according to the best judgment of the proprietor or manager where no exact account is kept.

Special instructions as to certain inquiries are contained on the schedule. Those instructions and the following additional explanations should receive the careful attention of all enumerators.

*Improved* or *unimproved land* should be carefully noted. All land once plowed is *improved* unless afterward abandoned for cultivation, like the "old fields" of the South. Western enumerators will pay special attention to this instruction, and not be guided by local customs. Rocky, hill, and mountain pastures are *not improved*, but fields used for pasture as a part of a rotation of crops *are* improved.

Weeks of hired labor should be obtained by adding together the number of weeks *each* individual of the help employed was at work, thus: one man hired by the year should be counted as 52 weeks; another man for twenty-six weeks as 26 weeks; two men in hay and in harvest each six weeks as 12 weeks, and one woman in the dairy for a year as 52 weeks; making a total for that farm of 142 weeks of hired labor.

Farmers should be encouraged to give as full and complete answers to the various questions as possible, and the fact should be impressed upon them that they, above all others, are interested

INSTRUCTIONS TO ENUMERATORS. 37

in having the returns of the census as near the truth as it is possible to get them.

SCHEDULE NO. 3 AND SPECIAL SCHEDULES.—MANUFACTURES.

The following schedules are provided for the collection of the statistics of manufactures:

GENERAL SCHEDULE NO. 3 [7–560].

To be used to report establishments whose operations do not come within the scope of either of the special schedules.

SPECIAL SCHEDULES.

No. 1. Agricultural Implements.
No. 2. Paper Mills.
No. 3. Boots and Shoes. (Not including custom work and repairing, which should be returned on General Schedule No. 3.)
No. 4. Leather, Tanned and Curried.
No. 5. Lumber Mills and Saw Mills. (Including their remanufactures. Planing mills and sash, door, and blind factories separately conducted should be returned on General Schedule No. 3.) Timber products not produced by lumber mills and saw mills must be separately returned on Special Schedule No. 5 a.
No. 6. Brick Yards.
No. 7. Flour and Grist Mills.
No. 8. Cheese, Butter, and Condensed Milk Factories. (Not including farm products, which should be returned by enumerators on Schedule No. 2—Agriculture.)
No. 9. Slaughtering and Meat Packing. (Not including retail butchering establishments.)
No. 10. Chemical Manufactures.
No. 11. Clay and Pottery Products.
No. 12. Coke. (Not to be taken by enumerators.)
No. 13. Cotton Manufactures.
No. 14. Dyeing and Finishing of Textiles.
No. 15. Electrical Industry. (Not to be taken by enumerators.)
No. 16. Glass. (Not to be taken by enumerators.)
No. 17. Manufactured Gas. (Not to be taken by enumerators.)
No 18. Iron and Steel. (Not to be taken by enumerators.)
No. 19. Printing, Publishing, and the Periodical Press.

## INSTRUCTIONS TO ENUMERATORS.

No. 20. Shipbuilding.
No. 21. Silk and Silk Goods.
No. 22. Wool Manufactures.
No. 23. Hosiery and Knit Goods.
No. 24. Carriages and Wagons.
No. 25. Salt Works. (Not to be taken by enumerators.)
No. 26. Leather, Patent, Enameled, and Morocco.

Of the foregoing special schedules the following will be mailed direct from the Census Office to the manufacturers before the time for beginning the enumeration, with the request that the schedules be properly filled out ready for the enumerator when he calls:

No. 2. Paper Mills.
No. 10. Chemical Manufactures.
No. 11. Clay and Pottery Products.
No. 13. Cotton Manufactures.
No. 14. Dyeing and Finishing of Textiles.
No. 20. Shipbuilding.
No. 21. Silk and Silk Goods.
No. 22. Wool Manufactures.
No. 23. Hosiery and Knit Goods.
No. 26. Leather, Patent, Enameled, and Morocco.

In the event that it shall be found by the enumerator that an establishment of the character noted above has not received a schedule upon which to make its return, the enumerator must at once report the fact to the supervisor of his district, in order that the schedule may be forwarded to be filled and taken up by the enumerator before the completion of his work.

The statistics of iron and steel, of coke, of glass, of the electrical industry, of manufactured gas, and of salt will be collected by expert special agents without regard to locality. Enumerators will not visit establishments of these classes.

In cities and towns of importance as manufacturing centers without regard to population the collection of the general statistics of manufactures has been entirely withdrawn from the enumerators and the duty assigned to special agents appointed for each city or town of this class.

A list of the cities and towns in which the collection of these statistics has been withdrawn from the enumerators in each supervisor's district will be furnished the supervisor in order that enumerators may be properly instructed in this respect. To guard against possible failure to collect the statistics of these establishments in localities for which special agents are not to be appointed, enumerators, in the absence of specific instructions from the supervisors, should ascertain beyond the possibility of a doubt whether or not they are to enumerate the establishments of productive industry in their respective districts.

In the rural districts, and in cities and towns for which no special agents are to be appointed, as set forth in the preceding paragraph, the statistics of manufactures will be collected by the enumerators appointed to collect the statistics of population and agriculture and during the progress of the work of enumerating the inhabitants.

It is for the information and guidance of enumerators with respect to this duty that these special instructions are provided.

Enumerators shall personally visit each establishment of productive industry, except those above noted, within their respective districts, and obtain upon the proper schedule a return of the operations of such establishment during the census year, June 1, 1889, to May 31, 1890; in the case, however, of establishments whose books of accounts are balanced at a different date, the return may be for the fiscal year of the establishment most nearly conforming to the census year.

The term "Establishment of Productive Industry" must be understood in its broadest sense to embrace not only mills and factories, but also the operations of all small establishments and the mechanical trades, as *blacksmithing, coopering, masonry and bricklaying, mechanical dentistry, wheelwrighting*, etc.

Restaurants, saloons, and barber shops, the compounding of individual prescriptions by druggists and apothecaries, the operations of retail mercantile establishments, transportation corporations and lines, and professional services (except mechanical dentistry, as above noted) are not considered as coming within the meaning of the law in this connection. In case it shall be claimed by any person engaged in the lines of business herein exempt from enumeration that the operations of his establishment are in the nature of productive industry, the facts, together with proper explanatory notes, shall be reported at once to this office through the supervisor of census.

Great care must be taken by enumerators to guard against the

INSTRUCTIONS TO ENUMERATORS.

omission from their returns of any establishment that comes properly within the scope of their investigation. They should have their eyes open to every indication of the presence of productive industry, and should supplement personal observation by frequent and persistent inquiry.

In the event of an establishment located in one enumeration district having an office located in another enumeration district at which the desired information is to be obtained, the enumerator in whose district the establishment is located shall report the facts at once to this office through the supervisor, with such explanation as may be necessary to insure the procurement of a return of the operations of such establishment.

In filling page 1 and question 1, page 3, of the general and special schedules enumerators should be careful to insert correctly the name and address of the corporation, firm, or individual carrying on the business, and with sufficient fullness to enable the Census Office to conduct such subsequent correspondence as may be necessary.

In question 3, general schedule, the kind of business and character of product should be described as specifically as possible, as, for example, "fishing hooks," "hoisting apparatus," "skirt supporters," "speaking tubes," "building hardware," "toys," "fireworks," etc. General terms should be avoided where specific and technical terms will more clearly express the character of the product. Attention is called to the explanatory notes printed on the general and special schedules for manufactures.

It is not necessary to explain at length the use of the word "materials" in respect to manufactures. It will be enough to say that what is the product of one establishment often becomes the material of another, as the product of the foundry may become the material of the machine shop, or the product of the furnace may become the material of the forge and mill, or the product of the woolen mill may become the material of the clothing manufacturer.

The cost of materials and values of products must be reported for all establishments returned upon the general or special schedules. Care must be taken to report clearly and fully (question 7) the kinds, quantities, and cost of the more important materials used by each establishment, and to report in like manner (question 8) the kinds, quantities, and values of the

INSTRUCTIONS TO ENUMERATORS. 41

principal products. The kinds and quantities of materials and products noted in the questions on the special schedules must be reported in detail for all establishments returned upon either of such special schedules.

Care should be taken to assure manufacturers that the details of their business will not be made public or communicated to any but authorized employes of the Census Office. The returns of manufacturing establishments will be used only for the purposes of tabulation, and no publication will be made in the census reports that will disclose the operations of individual establishments. This assurance is set forth on each schedule over the signature of the Superintendent of Census.

### SCHEDULE NO. 5.—MORTALITY.

Special instructions for filling this schedule [7–417] are printed on the schedule itself, and need not be repeated here.

In certain cities and localities Schedule No. 5 has been withdrawn from the enumerators, as authorized by section 18 of the act of March 1, 1889, and the supervisors have been instructed to so inform the enumerators. All other enumerators not so informed will make the inquiries, as provided for on Schedule No. 5.

In the following states there is a more or less complete local registration of deaths which gives, in almost all cases, the name, age, and sex of those who have died, but does not give certain other items which are called for in the mortality schedule:

Alabama, Connecticut, Massachusetts, Minnesota, New Hampshire, New Jersey, New York, Rhode Island, and Vermont.

In these states the enumerators from whom the schedules are not withdrawn are advised and instructed to consult these local records for the purpose of making their lists of deaths complete as to number; and if they can arrange to copy the names, sex, and age from the local records before starting on their rounds they will then find it easy to fill out the data called for on the mortality schedules.

In all the states many towns and cities from 5,000 to 15,000 inhabitants have a local registration of deaths which is more or less complete, and in all places where such local registration exists the enumerators should consult the records and, if possible, obtain lists of names, with age and sex, to aid them in their work of obtaining a complete record of deaths.

42        INSTRUCTIONS TO ENUMERATORS.

In the following cities special sanitary districts have been created and the enumerators' districts arranged with reference to keeping the population of each of these sanitary districts distinct: Allegheny City, Baltimore, Boston, Brooklyn, Buffalo, Charleston, Chicago, Cincinnati, Cleveland, District of Columbia, Kansas City, Minneapolis, Nashville, New Orleans, New York City, Philadelphia, Pittsburgh, Saint Louis, Saint Paul, San Francisco, and Yonkers.

The letter used to designate each sanitary district should be entered on the population, mortality, and supplemental schedules in every instance.

### SUPPLEMENTAL SCHEDULES.

In addition to the general schedules for population, agriculture, and manufactures, already described, there are eight supplemental schedules which call for special information concerning the insane, feeble-minded and idiotic, deaf, blind, those diseased and physically defective (not otherwise enumerated), children in benevolent institutions, prisoners, and paupers, as follows:

No. 1.—Statistics of Insanity.
No. 2.—Statistics of Feeble-mindedness and Idiocy.
No. 3.—Statistics of the Deaf.
No. 4.—Statistics of the Blind.
No. 5.—Statistics of Persons Diseased and Physically Defective.
No. 6.—Statistics of Benevolence.
No. 7.—Statistics of Crime.
No. 8.—Statistics of Pauperism.

Each person belonging to the several classes indicated above is to be entered first upon the regular population schedule, with all the particulars required in the case of any inhabitant. This information is to be transferred to the supplemental schedule of his class, as explained on the schedules themselves, and in addition make the special inquiries called for on each supplemental schedule. For each person thus entered on the supplemental schedule the enumerator will receive additional compensation and at higher rates (5 cents for each name) than for entries upon the regular population schedule.

In transferring to the supplemental schedule the answers to certain inquiries on the population schedule it will be necessary to use abbreviations, owing to the width of the columns, as follows:

3. Write *Hd*, for head of family; *Wfe*, for wife; *Son; Dau*, for

daughter; *Gd-son*, for grandson; *Gd-dau*, for granddaughter; *Dau-in-law*, for daughter-in-law; *Aunt*; *Unc*, for uncle; *Neph*, for nephew; *Niece*; *Svt*, for servant; *Bdr*, for boarder; *Ldgr*, for lodger. Write *Inm*, for inmate; *Pu*, for pupil; *Pat*, for patient; *Pr*, for prisoner.

4. Write *W*, for white; *B*, for black; *Mu*, for mulatto; *Qd*. for quadroon; *Oc*, for octoroon; *Ch*, for Chinese; *Jp*, for Japanese; *In*, for Indian.

5. Write *M*, for male; *F*, for female.

7. Write *Sg*, for single; *Mr*, for married; *Wd*, for widow; *Dv*, for divorced.

Under "Physical defects" write *yes* in the column or columns indicating the particular defect or defects reported, except in "defective speech," which is to be answered as indicated in the inquiry itself.

In all other respects the answers as made on the population schedule can be transferred without abbreviation to the spaces provided on the supplemental schedules.

The nature of the information called for by these supplemental schedules is fully explained upon the schedules themselves.

Enumerators will take notice that the persons enumerated on the supplemental schedules, whether in or out of institutions, may belong to more than one of the special classes. For example, the pauper insane in hospitals and asylums for the insane are to be enumerated both as insane and as paupers, and all the questions contained on both of these schedules are to be filled, in order that they may be in proper shape for the work to be done upon them in the Census Office when received. The same remark applies to insane prisoners, to deaf or blind children in orphan schools or in homes for the friendless, and in many similar cases. A full description is to be made of each person belonging to more than one of the special classes on each of the schedules for each of the classes to which he belongs. For this double work double pay will be allowed.

Some of the questions contained on the supplemental schedules can not be answered by means of a personal interview with each person so enumerated, but can be answered by examination of the institution records, if in an institution. In all such cases it will be expected and required that the enumerator shall examine the records and reply to each special question as fully as may be possible.

INSTRUCTIONS TO ENUMERATORS.

Wherever there is a city or town lock-up in which prisoners are retained usually for but a single night or a night and a day the enumerator will be expected to visit it on the first Monday of June, to ascertain whether there are any prisoners then in confinement in it, and not to delay such visit until a later date.

Enumerators should understand that the object of the inquiry relating to paupers is to ascertain the number of persons who were on the first day of June wholly or partly, but permanently, supported at the expense of the poor fund belonging to any state, county, city, or town. From this class should be excluded all persons not inmates of almshouses who receive only temporary aid at their homes. But all inmates of almshouses should be reported on the pauper schedule, also those not in almshouses who are boarded out at public expense or kept on any private farm or in any private house at public expense. In every enumeration district an effort should be made, in advance of entering upon the work of enumeration, to find out, if the enumerator does not already know, whether any county or town paupers are kept for pay by any of the inhabitants of the district, and all such should be reported, subject to the caution given above.

Care must be exercised in the case of every almshouse, lock-up, police station, jail, prison, hospital, asylum, school, or other institution to write the name of the institution in full at the top of each page of the general and supplemental schedules.

SPECIAL SCHEDULE.—SURVIVING SOLDIERS, ETC.

The provision of the act of March 1, 1889, under which the special enumeration of survivors of the war of the rebellion is made, reads as follows:

That said Superintendent shall, under the authority of the Secretary of the Interior, cause to be taken on a special schedule of inquiry, according to such form as he may prescribe, the names, organizations, and length of service of those who had served in the Army, Navy, or Marine Corps of the United States in the war of the rebellion, and who are survivors at the time of said inquiry, and the widows of soldiers, sailors, or marines.

The entries concerning each survivor or widow should be carefully and accurately made, so that the printed reports may contain only thoroughly trustworthy information.

Spaces are provided on the special schedule for the entry of fifty names, or, more properly, terms of service. The spaces are numbered consecutively from 1 to 50, and cover the four pages comprised

INSTRUCTIONS TO ENUMERATORS.   45

in each schedule. The inquiries made concerning each survivor or widow call for the repetition of the number of the house and family as returned on the general Population Schedule (No. 1), the name, rank, company, regiment, or vessel, date of enlistment, date of discharge, and length of service (in years, months, and days) on the upper half of each page, and the post-office address, disability incurred, and general remarks on the lower half of each page.

The column headed "Remarks" is intended to be used to cover any points not included in the foregoing inquiries and which are necessary to a complete statement of a person's term of service.

In the case of persons having served in more than one organization, use as many spaces as may be necessary to cover their various terms of service.

In the case of widows of deceased soldiers, sailors, or marines, make the entry of her name on the dotted line, as follows: Lucretia A., widow of ---------------------- Ashton, John R. filling out the record of his service during the war, and giving under "Post-office address" the present address of the widow.

Where a person enlisted under an assumed name, and was so borne on the muster-rolls, but who has since resumed his lawful name, and under which he would be enumerated on the population schedule, make the entry on the special schedule for survivors as follows: John H. Brown, alias ---------------------- Galbreath, James H.

In this case the man's real name is John H. Brown, but the name under which he served was James H. Galbreath.

The attention of enumerators is called specially to the fact that from a number of the states there were *two*, and in some instances *three*, and even *four* regiments mustered into the service of the United States at different dates during the war whose designations were the same or so nearly similar as to be easily confounded with each other. For example: In Massachusetts the Sixth Regiment of Infantry was organized in August and September, 1862, to serve nine months, and was mustered out June 3, 1863; the Sixth Regiment of Militia Infantry was organized April 22, 1861, to serve three months, and was mustered out in July, 1861, and the Sixth Regiment of Militia Infantry was organized in July, 1864, to serve one hundred days, and was mustered out October 27, 1864. So also there were two organizations from that state—among several similar duplications—called the Second Unattached Company Militia Infantry: one organized May 3, 1864, to serve ninety days, and mustered out August 6, 1864, and the other organized August 7, 1864, to serve one hundred days, and mustered out November 15, 1864. In Ohio the Sixtieth Infantry (one year's service) was organized in February, 1862, and mustered out November 10, 1862 and the Sixtieth Infantry (three years' service) was organized in the months of February, March, April, and May, 1864, and mustered out July 28, 1865. The Eighty-eighth Infantry (three months' service) was organized in June, 1862, and mustered out September 26, 1862, and the Eighty-eighth Infantry (three years' service) was organized from September 24, 1862, to August 3, 1863, and was mustered out July 3, 1865. In Missouri the First Regiment Infantry was organized in April and May, 1861, to serve three months; two companies were mustered out in July and August, 1861, and the remaining companies reorganized for three years' service, and the designation changed to the First Missouri Light Artillery September 1, 1861; the First Regiment U. S. Reserve Corps, Missouri, was organized May 7, 1861, to serve three months, and mustered out August 20, 1861; the First Regiment U. S. Reserve Corps, Missouri, was organized September 3-14, 1861, to serve during the war in Missouri, and mustered out in September and October, 1862; and the First Regiment (state militia) was organized from December, 1861, to May, 1862, to serve during the war in Missouri, and mustered out by companies from December, 1864, to May, 1865. In Pennsylvania the Twentieth Regiment Volunteer Infantry was organized April 30, 1861, to serve three months, and was mustered out August 6, 1861; and the Twentieth Regiment Militia Infantry was organized June 17, 1863, to serve during the emergency, and mustered out August 10, 1863.

Enumerators should also be careful to distinguish between the *arms* of the service, and in giving the record of the service of a soldier state whether he belonged, for example, to the Cavalry, Artillery (heavy or light), Engineers, or Infantry.

All men *who were mustered into the military service of the United States during the late war* should be enumerated.

Robert P. Porter,
*Superintendent of Census.*

# MISCELLANEOUS PHOTOGRAPHS

## NORTHERN CHEYENNE INDIAN RESERVATION
## LAME DEER, MONTANA

The following illustration names are within this set or are a party with a family name or relation of the same; or the photograph itself was taken at or near Lame Deer.

Photographer: Thomas Bailey Marquis, 1869-1935  (1922-1935)

Big Crow and girl wearing eagle feather headdresses and bead necklaces in front of log building. Big Crow fought at the Battle of Little Bighorn.

PN.165.3.72
McCracken Research Library, Buffalo Bill Center of the West

Photographer: Thomas Bailey Marquis, 1869-1935 (1922-1935)

Buffalo Calf Woman sitting in wooden chair wearing blanket in front of log building. She is the wife of Sun Road.

PN.165.1.84
McCracken Research Library, Buffalo Bill Center of the West

Photographer: Arthur Rothstein, 11915-1985 (June 1939)

Cheyenne Indian and Son on horse, Tongue River Reservation, Montana.

Library of Congress

Photographer: Thomas Bailey Marquis, 1869-1935 (1922-1935)

George Long Roach, with braided hair and wearing earrings, holding hat standing behind Model T Ford automobile. Man walking next to wooden building in background.

PN.165.2.36
McCracken Research Library, Buffalo Bill Center of the West

Photographer: Thomas Bailey Marquis, 1869-1935 (1922-1925[sic])

Richard Wooden Leg, with hand drum, kneeling next to wife Sophie, holding beaded horsehide bag, in front of log house. Hills in background right. John Wooden Leg is the grandson of Richard. Richard Wooden Leg fought at the Battle of Little Bighorn and was a Native American Judge.

PN.165.1.4
McCracken Research Library, Buffalo Bill Center of the West

Photographer: Thomas Bailey Marquis, 1869-1935 (1922-1935)

Holy Standing Woman holding reins and standing next to Mrs. Martin Two Bulls, wrapped in wool blanket, holding puppy, and wearing a stocking cap in wagon. Son, Joseph Two Bulls in wagon. Man, Oliver Sponge or possibly Martin Two Bulls in wagon. Unknown boy with stocking cap hanging over side. Snow, hills, and trees in background.

PN.165.1.117
McCracken Research Library, Buffalo Bill Center of the West

Photographer: Thomas Bailey Marquis, 1869-1935 (1922-1935)

Iron Hand with family in front of wooden house near doorway. Back row, left to right: Charlie White Wolf, Henry Iron Hand, August Scalpcane. Middle row: Mrs. James Atwood, Mrs. Iron Hand, Waldo Atwood, Iron Hand. Front row: Mary Atwood, Henry Scalpcane. Willis Iron Hand. Dog [lying] in front left of group. Charlie White Wolf was a Southern Cheyenne.

PN.165.1.109
McCracken Research Library, Buffalo Bill Center of the West

Photographer: Thomas Bailey Marquis, 1869-1935 (1922-1935)

Jean Poitra's daughter sitting on dog with mother holding onto her in front of Log house in Busby, Montana

PN.165.1.9
McCracken Research Library, Buffalo Bill Center of the West

Photographer: Thomas Bailey Marquis, 1869-1935 (1922-1935)

Jessie Roman Nose with blanket and shawl on head holding baby in front of wooden building

PN.165.2.87
McCracken Research Library, Buffalo Bill Center of the West

Photographer: Thomas Bailey Marquis, 1869-1935 (1926)

Lame Deer, Montana, schoolchildren standing for class picture outside their classroom. Front row, left to right: John Stands in Timber, Jr., Max High Walking, unknown, Ira Issues, Henry Scalpcane, Grace Rowland, Harriet King, Rose King. Back row left to right: George Texas, James King (wearing ball cap), Sam Dives Backwards, Ramona Brady, Rose Red Cherries, Fannie Walks Along, Elsie Tall Whiteman. Emma King (lady) is standing behind the children.

PN.165.2.130
McCracken Research Library, Buffalo Bill Center of the West

"You people have lied to us. Here your streams run slow and sluggish; the water is not good; our children sicken and die. My young warriors have been out for nearly two moons, and find no buffaloes; you said there were plenty; they find only the skeletons; the white hunters have killed them for their hides. Take us back to the land of our fathers. I am done."

Dull Knife (Morning Star)
*The Border and The Buffalo* 1967 John R. Cook

# CENSUS OF NORTHERN CHEYENNE

-of-

TONGUE RIVER RESERVATION, MONT.

June 30, 1927,

TONGUE RIVER AGENCY,

C. B. Lohmiller, Superintendent.

TONGUE RIVER.
124
1927

RECAPITULATION[sic].

Census of the **Northern Cheyenne** Indians of **Tongue River** Agency, _____ on June 30, **1927**, taken by **C.B. Lohmiller**, Superintendent.

Total last census . . . . . . . . . . . . . . . . . . . . . . . . . . . . . . . . . . . . . . . . . . 1440

    Added by enrollment or picked up on account of omission from
    previous census rolls . . . . . . . . . . . . . . . . . . . . . . . . . . . . . . . . . 29

    Added by births - unreported previous years . . . . . . . . . . . ____
                    current year . . . . . . . . . . . . . . . . . . . . . . 48     48

    Total . . . . . . . . . . . . . . . . . . . . . . . . . . . . . . . . . . . . . . . . . . . . . 1517

Dropped from rolls on account of enrollment elsewhere,
    elsewhere, duplication, etc. . . . . . . . . . . . . . . . . . . . . . . . . ____

Dropped on account of deaths unreported
    previous years . . . . . . . . . . . . . . . . . . . . . . . . . ____

Dropped on account of deaths during
    current year . . . . . . . . . . . . . . . . . . . . . . . . . 68     ____

    Total dropped . . . . . . . . . . . . . . . . . . . . . . . . . . . . . . . . . . . . . . 68

Total this census roll (should agree with last number on roll).     1449

    Total males . . . . . . . . . . . . . . . . . . . . . . . . . . . 722

    Total females . . . . . . . . . . . . . . . . . . . . . . . . . 727     1449

    Total adults - males . . . . . . . . . . 410
                  females . . . . . . . . 394     804

    Total minors - males . . . . . . . . . 312
                  females . . . . . . . 333     645

    Total minors of school age - male . . . . . . . . 184
                             female . . . . . . 212     396

    Total minors under school age - male . . . . . 120
                              female . . . 129     249

    Total number of families . . . . . . . . . . . . . . 310

Census of the **Northern Cheyenne** Indians of **Tongue River** Agency, **Mont.** on **June 30, 1927** taken by **C.B. Lohmiller**, Superintendent.

**Key:** Last Number; Present Number; Indian Name; English Name; Relationship; Month, Year, of Birth; Sex;

| | | |
|---|---|---|
| 1182; | 1; | Americanhorse, Austin; hsbd.; Oct. 1878; M. (Texas) |
| 1183; | 2; | Americanhorse, Maude; wife; Apr. 1883; F. |
| 1184; | 3; | Americanhorse, Lucy; dau.; Nov. 1910; F. |
| 1185; | 4; | Americanhorse, (Peter) George; son; Sept. 1914; M. |

8;  5;  Americanhorse, Bessie; sgle.; Nov. 1905[?]; F. [First shows as 1 yr. 1908.]

1;  6;  Americanhorse, Flora; mthr.; -- 1861; F.

3;  7;  Americanhorse, George; hsbd.; Oct. 1881; M.
4;  8;  Americanhorse, Minnie; wife; Dec. 1884[?]; F. [1907-26 birth yr., 1885-1886.]
5;  9;  Americanhorse, James; son; Nov. 1911; M.
6;  10; Americanhorse, Marie; dau.; Jun. 1914; F.
7;  11; Americanhorse, Lucy; dau.; Aug. 1918; F.

9;  12; Americanhorse, Rueben[sic]; son; Nov. 1917[?]; M. [Shows 1918, birth 1918.]
    13; Americanhorse, Albert; son; Jul. 1912; M. (Mike Badhorse)
Children of Geo. Deafy Americanhorse Dec'd.

10; 14; Americanhorse, Willis; fthr.; Oct. 1892; M.
11; 15; Americanhorse, Ernest; son; Nov. 1911; M.
12; 16; Americanhorse, Laura Martha; dau.; Jun. 1914; F.
13; 17; Americanhorse, Madge; dau.; Dec. 1916; F.
14; 18; Americanhorse, Grace; dau.; Apr. 1918; F.

2;  19; Americanhorse, Walter; hsbd.; Oct. 1890; M.

18; 20; Ant, James; hsbd.; Feb. 1903; M.
19; 21; Ant, Hannah; wife; May 1900; F. [Highwalking]
    22; Ant; Bertha; dau.; Jan. 1925; F.

15; 23; Ant, Walter; hsbd.; Jan. 1880; M.
16; 24; Ant, Helen; wife; May 1882; F.
17; 25; Ant, June; dau.; Jan. 1920; F.
    26; Ant, Paul; son; Mar. 1927; M.

20; 27; Arapahoechief, Maude; wdw.; Dec. 1846[?]; F. [1904-23, birth year 1844.]

1194; 28; Atwood, James; hsbd.; Mar. 1891; M. (Twentystands)
1195; 29; Atwood, Cecelia; wife; Jan. 1898; F.
1196; 30; Atwood, Mary Lucy; dau.; May 1914; F.

Census of the **Northern Cheyenne** Indians of **Tongue River** Agency, **Mont.** on **June 30, 1927** taken by **C.B. Lohmiller**, Superintendent.

Key: Last Number; Present Number; Indian Name; English Name; Relationship; Month, Year, of Birth; Sex;

1197; 31; Atwood, Herbert; son; Aug. 1922; M.

21; 32; Baldeagle, Hugh; hsbd.; May 1858; M.
22; 33; Baldeagle, Minnie; wife; Sept. 1859; F.

1109; 34; Bearchum, Alex; son; Mar. 1901; M. s-son Frank Stumphorn

23; 35; Bearchum, Benjamin Jr.; son; Mar. 1919; M. [Junior] s-son Ed. Womanleggins

24; 36; Bearcomesout, Charles; hsbd.; Oct. 1880; M.
26; 37; Bearcomesout, Harold; son; Mar. 1908; M.
27; 38; Bearcomesout, Pius; son; Sept. 1915; M.

28; 39; Bearquiver, Edward; hsbd.; Sept. 1881; M.
29; 40; Bearquiver, Maggie; wife; May 1881; F.
30; 41; Bearquiver, Edna; dau.; Dec. 1912; F.
31; 42; Bearquiver, Claude; son; Nov. 1916; M.
32; 43; Bearquiver, James; son; Jun. 1920; M.
33; 44; Bearquiver, Martin; son; Aug, 1922; M.
     45; Bearquiver, Grace; dau.; May 1927; F.

34; 46; Beartusk, Jerome; hsdb.; Aug. 1885; M.
35; 47; Beartusk, Lucy; wife; Jan. 1893; F.
37; 48; Beartusk, Edith; dau.; Apr. 1916; F.
38; 49; Beartusk, Alice; dau.; Apr. 1917; F.
39; 50; Beartusk, Gladys; dau.; Jan. 1919; F. [Nellie]
40; 51; Beartusk, Kenneth; son; Dec. 1920; M.
42; 52; Beartusk, Bertha Elizabeth; dau.; Mar. 1923; F.
43; 53; Beartusk, Jerome Jr.; son; Dec. 1925; M.

44; 54; Beaverheart, Thomas; hsdb.; May 1863[?]; M. [1904-15, birth year 1857; 1916-24, birth year 1859; 1925-27 birth year 1863.]
45; 55; Beaverheart, Nellie; wife; Mar. 1857; F.
46; 56; Beaverheart, David; son; Apr. 1890; M. [Name Davis in 1926.]

47; 57; Bigback, Charles; hsbd.; Mar. 1863[?]; M. [Birth year 1865.]
48; 58; Bigback, Clara; wife; Jul. 1869; F.

49; 59; Bigback, John; Sgle.; Feb. 1904; M. [Henry in 1919.]

50; 60; Bigback, James; hsbd.; Aug. 1894; M.
51; 61; Bigback, Jennie; wife; May 1898; F.
52; 62; Bigback, Gladys; dau; Jul. 1920; F.
53; 63; Bigback, Robert; son; Dec. 1923; M.

Census of the **Northern Cheyenne** Indians of **Tongue River** Agency, **Mont.** on **June 30, 1927** taken by **C.B. Lohmiller**, Superintendent.

**Key:** Last Number; Present Number; Indian Name; English Name; Relationship; Month, Year, of Birth; Sex;

54;   64;   Bigback, Stephen; wdr.; Apr. 1892; M.

55;   65;   Bigbeaver, August; hsbd.; Mar. 1861; M.
       66;   Bigbeaver, Annie Marie; dau.; Jun. 1911; F.

57;   67;   Bigcrow, Andrew; hsbd.; Mar. 1854; M.
58;   68;   Bigcrow, Jennie; wife; Nov. 1888; F.
59;   69;   Bigcrow, Sarah Angela; dau.; Aug. 1912; F.

60;   70;   Bigfoot, John; hsbd.; -- 1881; M.

61;   71;   Bigfoot, White; hsbd.; Oct. 1875; M.
62;   72;   Bigfoot, Louisa; wife; Sept. 1885; F.
63;   73;   Bigfoot, Louis; son; Jun. 1911; M.

65;   74;   Bigfoot, Davis; hsbd.; May 1898; M.
66;   75;   Bigfoot, Lucy; wife; Oct. 1900; F.
68;   76;   Bigfoot, Alice; dau.; Jan. 1921; F.   [1926 Census birth 1923, name Martha same #. Shows up in 1925 birth year as 1923, also as Martha.]
       77;   Bigfoot, Mary; dau. Apr. 1924; F.

69;   78;   Bighead, Kate; wdw.; Jul. 1847; F.

70;   79;   Bigheadman, Benjamin; hsbd.; Jul. 1889; M.
71;   80;   Bigheadman, Julia; wife; Jul. 1894; F.
72;   81;   Bigheadman, Gladys; dau.; Sept. 1918; F. [1926 Census name Lucille same #.]
      82;   Bigheadman, Lucy; dau. Oct. 1924; F.

74;   83;   Bigheadman, Blair; hsbd.; Jun. 1892; M.
75;   84;   Bigheadman, Clara; wife; Apr. 1901; F.
76;[sic] 85;   Bigheadman, Grover; son; Jul. 1919; M.
[sic];   86;   Bigheadman, August; son; Aug. 1922; M.
      87;   Bigheadman, Julia; dau.; Dec. 1924; F.
      88;   Bigheadman, Mary; dau. June 1926; F.
85;   89;   Bigheadman, Betty Nora; dau; Jan. 1915; F. g-dau. John Twomoons
86;   90;   Bigheadman, Frank (Biddle); son; Aug. 1917; M. g-son John Twomoons [1918 year Lucy g dt.] (Children of Ben. Bigheadman)

77;   91;   Bigheadman, John; hsbd.; Jun. 1849[sic]; M. [1904-25, birth year 1853.]
78;   92;   Bigheadman, Nellie; wife; Oct. 1853; F.

80;   93;   Bigheadman, William; hsbd.; Dec. 1886; M.
81;   94;   Bigheadman, Nellie; wife; Jun. 1891; F.

Census of the **Northern Cheyenne** Indians of **Tongue River** Agency, **Mont.** on **June 30, 1927** taken by **C.B. Lohmiller**, Superintendent.

**Key:** Last Number; Present Number; Indian Name; English Name; Relationship; Month, Year, of Birth; Sex;

84; 95; Bigheadman, Richard; son; Apr. 1909; M. (Richard Rowland)
82; 96; Bigheadman, Grace; dau.; May 1918; F.
83; 97; Bigheadman, Kathleen; dau.; Mar. 1925; F.
98; Bigheadman, Doris; dau.; Jun. 1926; F.

87; 99; Biglefthand, Peter; hsbd.; Nov. 1867; M.
88; 100; Biglefthand, Patty; wife; Dec. 1875; F. [1904-16 Birth year 1875; 1917-26 birth year 1885.]
89; 101; Biglefthand, Raphael; son; Sept. 1912; M. [1915-#72 was Daisy, female.]

90; 102; Bigleg, Hinton; hsbd.; May 1887[?]; M. [Shows up in 1911, birth year 1911-26, 1883.]
91; 103; Bigleg, Anne; wife; Jan. 1879; F.

92; 104; Bignose, George; sgle.; Aug. 1897; M.

93; 105; Bignose, Samuel; sgle.; May 1891; M.

94; 106; Bignose, James; hsbd.; Oct. 1863; M.
95; 107; Bignose, Rachael[sic]; wife; Jul. 1855[?]; F.

96; 108; Bites, Sally; wdw.; Oct. 1866; F.

97; 109; Bites, James; hsbd.; Sept. 1900; M.
98; 110; Bites, Sally; wife; Jan 1905; F. [Crazymule]
111; Bites, Florence; dau.; Jul. 1926; F.

99; 112; Bixby, Benjamin; hsbd.; Oct. 1887[?]; M. [1904-1918 birth year is 1886. 1919-26, 1866.]
100; 113; Bixby, Gertrude; wife; May 1893[sic]; F. [Whitepowder 1904-07; Tallwhiteman 1908; Bixby 1909-1927; 1904-08 Birth year 1887; 1909-13 birth year 1888; 1914-26 1883; 1927 1893.]
101; 114; Bixby, Anne; dau.; Sept. 1913; F.
102; 115; Bixby, James; son; Dec. 1915; M. [Jessie Daughter 1916-19.]

104; 116; Bixby, Edward; hsbd.; Mar. 1891; M. [1904-18 birth year 1890; 1919-26 birth year 1898; 1927 1891.]
117; Bixby, Eva Kelsey; wife; ---; F. (Married white woman)
105; 118; Bixby, Edward George; son; Jul. 1922; M. [1924 Clara, dau; F. 1925-26 Jack.]
106; 119; Bixby, Elsie Virginia; dau.; Dec. 1923; F. [Vianne 1925-26.]
120; Bixby, William Lawrence; son; Mar. 1925; M.

103; 121; Bixby, Jessie; wdw.; May 1853; F.

Census of the **Northern Cheyenne** Indians of **Tongue River** Agency, **Mont.** on **June 30, 1927** taken by **C.B. Lohmiller**, Superintendent.

Key: Last Number; Present Number; Indian Name; English Name; Relationship; Month, Year, of Birth; Sex;

107;  122;  Blackbird, Isaac; hsbd.; June 1864; M.
108;  123;  Blackbird, Sallie; wife; Mar. 1872; F.

109;  124;  Blackcrane, Charles; hsbd.; Jun. 1865; M.
110;  125;  Blackcrane, Clara; wife; Dec. 1866[?]; F. [1920 Clara Blackeagle, wdw, #102, birth year 1845. Charles wife in 1920, Edith birth year 1866.]

111;  126;  Blackeagle, William; fthr.; Jun. 1888[?]; M.
[#126, William-Censuses 1904-1915 Birth year 1886. 1916-1918 Birth year 1896; 1919 Birth year 1906 [sic]; 1920-26 Census birth year again 1896.]
112;  127;  Blackeagle, Carl; son; Sept. 1911; M.

113;  128;  Blackhorse, Rueben[sic]; hsbd.; July 1853[?]; M.
114;  129;  Blackhorse, Lena; wife; Dec. 1876[sic]; F. [1904-26 birth year 1862-3.]
115;  130;  Blackhorse, Anna; dau.; July 1913; F. [Anna 1927.?]
[#115, Son, Arthur in 1913-14 Censuses. Name Ada 1915-19. Name Ida 1920-26.]

116;  131;  Blackhorse, Alex; hsbd.; Oct. 1897; M.
117;  132;  Blackhorse, Mary; wife; Jun. 1903; F.
118;  133;  Blackhorse, Francis; son; July 1922; M. [1923-26 name Merton.]
      134;  Blackhorse, Alice; dau; Sept. 1924; F.

      135;  Blackree, Alice; mthr.; Mar. 1909; F.
      136;  Blackree, Anna; dau.; Aug. 1923; F.

 56;  137;  Blackree, Emma; wdw.; Jun. 1851; F. [1924 last name Bigbeaver.]

119;  138;  Blackree, Paul; hsbd.; Oct. 1878; M.
120;  139;  Blackree, Jennie; wife; May 1881; F.

122;  140;  Blackstone, Charles; hsbd.; Dec. 1860[?]; M.
123;  141;  Blackstone, Lena; s-dau[?]; Jul. 1878; F.
[#141, Previous & 1923 Census dau, 1924 wife.]

124;  142;  Blackstone, Arthur; hsbd.; Dec. 1892; M.
125;  143;  Blackstone, Nellie[sic]; wife; Aug. 1900[sic]; F. [1906-26 birth year 1905. #143, Name Sallie, Mother Nellie. Nee Littlehead]

129;  144;  Blackwhetstone, Nellie; wdw.; Mar. 1864; F.

130;  145;  Blackwolf, Bennie; hsbd.; Jun. 1897; M. [1904-1923 name Alex.]
131;  146;  Blackwolf, Ella; wife; Dec. 1900; F.
132;  147;  Blackwolf, Henry; son; Oct. 1920; M. [1925 Census Thomas.]
133;  148;  Blackwolf, James; son; Aug. 1923; M. [1925 Census Alfred.]
      149;  Blackwolf, Ruth; dau.; Jan. 1927; F.

Census of the **Northern Cheyenne** Indians of **Tongue River** Agency, **Mont.** on **June 30, 1927** taken by **C.B. Lohmiller**, Superintendent.

**Key:** Last Number; Present Number; Indian Name; English Name; Relationship; Month, Year, of Birth; Sex;

134; 150; Blackwolf, John; hsbd.; Aug. 1870; M.
135; 151; Blackwolf, Nellie; wife; Jul. 1874; F.
136; 152; Blackwolf, Alex; son; May 1906; M.
[#152, Name Busby, a brother Alex born 1897 in 1916 census, married in 1917.]
137; 153; Blackwolf, Gladys; dau.; Jan. 1914; F. [Prev. Census Mary.]

138; 154; Blindman, Arthur; wdr.; Nov. 1868; M.

139; 155; Bluehawk, Louis; wdr.; Jun. 1850[sic]; M. [1904-19 Born 1861.]

140; 156; Bobtailhorse, Thomas; hsbd.; Jul. 1850; M.
141; 157; Bobtailhorse, Gertrude; wife; Dec. 1851; F.

142; 158; Bolson, Gail; dau.; Jul.1915; F. [1925 s-son, M,] (dau. Rena LeFever)
143; 159; Bolson, Frank; son; Aug. 1917; M. (son Rena LeFever)
144; 160; Bolson, Roy Guy; son; Dec. 1919; M. (son Rena LeFever)

145; 161; Boxelder, Laura; wdw.; Jan. 1872; F.

146; 162; Brady, Arthur; hsbd.; Dec. 1840; M.
147; 163; Brady, Ellen; wife; Dec. 1853; F.

148; 164; Brady, Alex; hsbd.; Dec. 1898; M. [1904-15 birth year 1898; 1916-26 1893.]
149; 165; Brady, Josie; wife; Dec. 1902; F. [Pine]
150; 166; Brady, Charles; son; Nov. 1923; M.

152; 167; Brady, James R.; son; Dec. 1909; M. (Son of Jennie Brady Wolfvoice)

153; 168; Brady, George; hsbd.; July 1881; M.
154; 169; Brady, Flossie; wife; Feb. 1897; F.
155; 170; Brady, Elmore; son; Mar. 1907; M.
156; 171; Brady, James Henry; son; Apr. 1913; M.
157; 172; Brady, Howard; son; Nov. 1915[sic]; M.
158  173; Brady, Romona Lucy; dau.; Dec.1917[?]; F.
159; 174; Brady, Wilson; son; Oct. 1918; M.
160; 175; Brady, Martha; dau.; Feb. 1921; F.
161; 176; Brady, Roy; son; Jan. 1925; M.

162; 177; Braidedlocks, William; hsbd.; Oct. 1851; M.
163; 178; Braidedlocks, Gertie; wife; May 1852; F.

164; 179; Brownbird, Joseph; hsbd.; Sept. 1865; M.
165; 180; Brownbird, Anna; wife; Oct. 1865; F.

Census of the __Northern Cheyenne__ Indians of __Tongue River__ Agency, __Mont.__ on __June 30, 1927__ taken by __C.B. Lohmiller__, Superintendent.

**Key:** Last Number; Present Number; Indian Name; English Name; Relationship; Month, Year, of Birth; Sex;

166; 181; Buffalohorn, John; hsbd.; Apr.1862[sic]; M. [1904-25 birth year 1869.]
167; 182; Buffalohorn, Lena; wife; May 1870; F. [Birth year 1848[sic], 1920-22.]

168; 183; Buffalohump, Samuel; hsbd.; July 1845; M.
169; 184; Buffalohump, Nora; wife; Aug. 1848; F.

171; 185; Burns, George; hsbd.; Mar. 1895; M.
Burns, Belle; wife; ---; --. (Not enrolled)

172; 186; Burns, Robert J.; hsbd.; Sept. 1897; M.
Burns, Hattie; wife; ---; --. (Not enrolled)
173; 187; Burns, Phyllis Roberta; dau.; Mar. 1926; F.

174; 188; Burns, Gertrude; wdw.; July 1846; F.

175; 189; Burns, Julia; wife; Feb. 1872; F.
Burns, James; hsbd.; ---; --. (White not enrolled)
176; 190; Burns, James C., Jr.; son; July 1908; M.
177; 191; Burns, Margaret; dau.; Sept. 1911; F.
178; 192; Burns, Anna Grace; dau.; Aug. 1913; F.

179; 193; BeMent, Emma Burns; wife; June 1901; F.
180; 194; BeMent, Jacqueline (Maxine); dau.; Oct. 1922; F.
181; 195; BeMent, Clarence Jr.; son.; Nov.1924; M. [Max in 1925. Mickie in 1926.]
182; 196; BeMent, Jesse; son; Mar. 1924; M. [Joseph in 1925.]

183; 197; Beirdneau, Adeline; wife; Feb. 1899; F.
184; 198; Beirdneau, Betty Belle, dau.; Apr. 1923; F.
185; 199; Beirdneau, Barbara Marie; dau.; Apr. 1926; F.

186; 200; Burns, Lizzie; wife; Jan. 1873; F.
Burns, Patrick; hsbd.; ---;---. (White not enrolled)
187; 201; Burns, Josephine; s-dau.; July 1918; F. (Small) [Had a Kitty Small in 1925. Adopt-dau., in 1925-26.]

188; 202; Callsfirst, Andrew; hsbd.; June 1888; M.
189; 203; Callsfirst, Jennie; wife; July 1872; F.
190; 204; Callsfirst, Mary; dau.; Sept. 1911; --. [1924 Annie.]

191; 205; Chasingbear, Flora; mthr.; Mar. 1882; F.
192; 206; Chasingbear, Laura; dau.; May 1916; F.
207; Chasingbear, Robert; son; July 1924; M.

Census of the **Northern Cheyenne** Indians of **Tongue River** Agency, **Mont.** on **June 30, 1927** taken by **C.B. Lohmiller**, Superintendent.

**Key:** Last Number; Present Number; Indian Name; English Name; Relationship; Month, Year, of Birth; Sex;

193; 208; Chasingbear, Willis; hsbd.; Mar. 1895; M.
194; 209; Chasingbear, Madge; wife; Apr. 1898[sic]; F. [Powderface]

195; 210; Chubby, John; hsbd.; Nov. 1875; M.
196; 211; Chubby, Anne; wife; Dec. 1885; F.
198; 212; Chubby, Rhoda; dau.; Jan. 1920; F.

199; 213; Clubfoot, Floyd; hsbd.; Mar. 1888; M. [In 1904, 15 yrs., old.]
200; 214; Clubfoot, Stella; wife; Apr. 1896[?]; F. [Weaselbear]
[#214, No record 1904-07; 1908 birth 1890; 1909-23 birth 1893.]
201; 215; Clubfoot, Norman; Son; Nov. 1916; M.
[1917 shows Norman died in 1916. In 1918-23 Census as born 1916 and alive?]
202; 216; Clubfoot, Verle; Son; Mar. 1923; M.
203; 217; Clubfoot, Flossie; dau.; Dec. 1925; F.

204; 218; Clubfoot, Frank; hsbd.; Mar. 1891; M. [1904-23 birth year 1891.]
205; 219; Clubfoot, Lucy Alice; wife; Feb. 1893[?]; F.
[#219, 1915-18 birth year is 1898; 1920 its 1896; 1923 its 1886; 1924-6 its 1893.]
206; 220; Clubfoot, James; son; Oct. 1922; M.

207; 221; Clubfoot, John; hsbd.; Dec. 1860[?]; M. [1904-13 shows birth year 1863. 1814-26 birth year 1854.]
208; 222; Clubfoot, Minnie; wife; July 1870; F.

209; 223; Clubfoot, Willis; sgle.; Mar. 1891; M.

210; 224; Clubfoot, Joseph; sgle.; July 1900; M.

211; 225; Colhoff, Emma; wife; Sept. 1894; F.
         Colhoff, William; hsbd.; ---; --. (Not enrolled)
212; 226; Colhoff, Maxine; dau.; May 1916; F.
213; 227; Colhoff, Edward; son.; May 1918; M.
214; 228; Colhoff, Annie Gladys; dau.; Apr. 1922; F.
215; 229; Colhoff, William Rowland; son; Apr. 1924; M.
     230; Colhoff, George; son; Jan. 1927; M.

216; 231; Comestogether, Ida; wdw.; 1860[sic]; F. [1904-19 birth year 1841. 1920-26 birth year 1854. 1927 birth year 1860.]

217; 232; Cooley, Julia; wife; Nov. 1891; F.
         Cooley, Al; hsbd.; ---; --. (Not enrolled)
218; 233; Cooley, Violet; dau.; Mar. 1914; F.
219; 234; Cooley, Junior; son; May 1916; M.
220; 235; Cooley, Francis; son; Oct. 1922; M.
221; 236; Cooley, Vera; dau.; Jan. 1925; F.

Census of the **Northern Cheyenne** Indians of **Tongue River** Agency, **Mont.** on **June 30, 1927** taken by **C.B. Lohmiller**, Superintendent.

**Key:** Last Number; Present Number; Indian Name; English Name; Relationship; Month, Year, of Birth; Sex;

222; 237; Crawling, Charles; fthr.; Aug. 1884; M.
223; 238; Crawling, Martha; dau.; Jan. 1917; F.

225; 239; Crazymule, John[sic]; hsbd.; Mar. 1870; M.
[#239; In 1919 name Joseph, previous #220, birth year 1881. Mixed with another family not in 1920 census.] [Between 1920-22 Census takers mixed up #218 John and #220 Joseph's names and wifes and names.]
226; 240; Crazymule, Jennie; wife; Feb. 1857; F. [Issues]

228; 241; Crazymule, James Paul; son; Nov. 1910; M. Children of Lizzie Crazymule Yellownose and Joseph Crazymule
229; 242; Crazymule, Charles; son; Nov. 1919; M. [Raymond in 1926.]
243; Crazymule, Xavier; son; Nov. 1921; M.

230; 244; Crazymule, Joseph; hsbd.; Mar. 1881; M.
231; 245; Crazymule, Sarah; wife; July 1873; F.
232; 246; Crazymule, Eva; dau.; May 1909; F. [Wyoming in 1926.]

233; 247; Crook, George; hsbd.; Jan. 1864[?]; M. [1904-25 Birth year 1871.]
234; 248; Crook, Theresa; wife; Nov. 1866; F.
235; 249; Crook, Alice; dau.; Jan. 1908; F.

236; 250; Crook, Rosa; wdw.; Aug. 1865; F.

237; 251; Crook, Albert; sgle.; Apr. 1901; M.

238; 252; Crookednose, Nicholas; hsbd.; June 1867; M.
239; 253; Crookednose, Susie; wife; Sept. 1872; F.

240; 254; Curley, Hattie; wdw.; Aug. 1856; F.

241; 255; Curley, Thomas; hsbd.; Nov. 1889; M.
242; 256; Curley, Esther; wife; Dec. 1895; F.
243; 257; Curley, Ella; dau.; Apr. 1925; F.
258; Curley, Baby; son; Feb. 1927; M.

244; 259; Deafy, David; hsbd.; May 1898; M. [Americanhorse]
245; 260; Deafy, Anna; wife; Dec. 1895[?]; F. [Horseroads; 1904-25 Birth year 1897.]
246; 261; Deafy, Willis; son; Nov. 1917; M.
247; 262; Deafy, Elsie; dau.; July 1925; F.

248; 263; Deafy, James; hsbd.; Aug. 1870[?]; M. [1904-25 Birth year 1873.]

Census of the **Northern Cheyenne** Indians of **Tongue River** Agency, **Mont.** on **June 30, 1927** taken by **C.B. Lohmiller**, Superintendent.

**Key:** Last Number; Present Number; Indian Name; English Name; Relationship; Month, Year, of Birth; Sex;

249; 264; Deafy, Mary; wife; May 1874; F. [1904-11 birth year 1874. 1912-26 birth year 1880. Name Walkingwoman 1904-06. 1907 no first name. 1908- Walkingwoman-Maria. 1908-10 name Maria. 1911-26 name Mary.]
250; 265; Deafy, Carrie; dau.; June 1910; F. [Jessie in 1926.]

251; 266; Divesbackwards, John; hsbd.; Jan. 1870; M.

252; 267; Divesbackwards, Rufus; hsbd.; Feb. 1890; M.
253; 268; Divesbackwards, Nancy; wife; Mar. 1882; F.
254; 269; Divesbackwards, Sam; son; Apr. 1918; M. [1926 name Irving.]
255; 270; Divesbackwards, Strane; son; May 1920; M.
271; Divesbackwards, Grace; dau.; Feb. 1925; F.

257; 272; Divesbackwards, Louisa; sgle.; Aug. 1917; F. g-dau, Mary Shavedhead

258; 273; Dog, Louis; hsbd.; May 1855; M.
259; 274; Dog, Maude; wife; Mar. 1866; F.

260; 275; Dullknife, Bessie; sgle.; Mar. 1870; F.

261; 276; Duster, Albert; hsbd.; Apr. 1889; M.
262; 277; Duster, Vinnie; wife; Sept. 1896; F.
569;[sic]278; Duster, Mabel; dau.; July 1913; F. (mother Amelia Limpy) [1926 name May Limpy Prev. #516.]
263; 279; Duster, Annie; dau.; Dec. 1920; F.
264; 280; Duster, Bessie; dau.; July 1924; F.

270; 281; Eaglefeathers, Oliver; hsbd.; Sept. 1895; M.
271; 282; Eaglefeathers, Julia; wife; June 1895; F.
272; 283; Eaglefeathers, Simon; son; Mar. 1922; M.
273; 284; Eaglefeathers, Rosie; dau.; July 1925; F.

267; 285; Eaglefeathers, Jacob; hsbd.; Sept. 1874; M.
269; 286; Eaglefeathers, Bernice; dau.; Oct. 1917[sic]; F. [First shows in 1923 census with birth year as 1920. Nothing in 1917-22.]
268; 287; Eaglefeathers, Mildred; dau.; May 1920[sic]; F. [1917 shows birth year as 1916. 1918-26 as 1915.]

276; 288; Eastman, Mary G.; wife; Dec. 1876; F.
Eastman, Mike; hsbd.; ---; --. (Not enrolled)
274; 289; Eastman, Margaret; dau.; May 1903; F.
277; 290; Eastman, Pearl; dau.; June 1907; F.
278; 291; Eastman, Robert; son; Mar. 1911; M.
279; 292; Eastman, Letha; dau.; Apr. 1913; F. [Son, Carl in 1916 Census.]
280; 293; Eastman, Rose; dau.; Sept. 1915; F.

Census of the **Northern Cheyenne** Indians of **Tongue River** Agency, **Mont.** on **June 30, 1927** taken by **C.B. Lohmiller**, Superintendent.

**Key:** Last Number; Present Number; Indian Name; English Name; Relationship; Month, Year, of Birth; Sex;

281; 294; Eastman, Louisa; dau.; Mar. 1918; F.
41; 295; Beartusk, Myrtle; g-dau.; Aug. 1913; F. [Julia 1926.] (mother Lucy Beartusk)

283; 296; Eastman, Charles; sgle.; Feb. 1901; M.

284; 297; Eastman, Perry; hsbd.; Nov. 1895; M.
285; 298; Eastman, Mary; wife; Feb. 1893; F.

286; 299; Elkshoulder, Henry; hsbd.; 1894[sic]; M. [1904-26 birth year 1884.]
287; 300; Elkshoulder, Bessie; wife; Aug. 1893; F.
288; 301; Elkshoulder, Curtis; son; Feb. 1908; M.
289; 302; Elkshoulder, Lucy; dau.; Mar. 1917; F.
290; 303; Elkshoulder, Sylvia; dau.; July 1922; F.
291; 304; Elkshoulder, George; son; Dec. 1925; M. [Adolph in 1926.]

403; 305; Elliot, Elizabeth Harris; wife; Apr. 1906; F.
Elliot, ---; hsbd.; ---; --. (Not enrolled)

292; 306; Eyesyellow, Wilbur; hsbd.; July 1868; M.
293; 307; Eyesyellow, Daisy; wife; Sept. 1856; F.

294; 308; Farr, Jessie; wdw.; Jan. 1899[sic]; F. [1908-26 birth year 1890.]
295; 309; Farr, Alice; dau.; Feb. 1910; F. [Jessie in 1920.]
296; 310; Farr, Frank; son; July 1917; M.
297; 311; Farr, Eyelyn[sic]; dau.; Dec. 1914; F.

298; 312; Fasthorse, Clara; sgle.; May 1913; F.
[1913-1917 Census #312- name Raymond M.; S. Son; Male.]

299; 313; Fightingbear, Edgar; hsbd.; Oct.1874; M.
300; 314; Fightingbear, Alice; Wife; Jun. 1893; F.
301; 315; Fightingbear, Julia; dau.; July 1911; F.
302; 316; Fightingbear, Dora; dau.; Mar. 1915; F. [1926 name Fannie.]
303; 317; Fightingbear, Elmer; son; Apr. 1921; M.
304; 318; Fightingbear, Herbert; son; Sept. 1923, M.
305; 319; Fightingbear, Emma; dau.; May 1926; F.

306; 320; Fightingbear, Willis; sgle.; June 1899; M.

307; 321; Fingers, Otis; wdr.; Oct. 1868[?]; M. [1904-25 Birth year 1867.]
308; 322; Fingers, Joseph; son; Aug. 1914; M. [1917 Census Daughter. Josie 1915-20.]

309; 323; Firecrow, Peter; hsbd.; Apr. 1887; M.
310; 324; Firecrow, Joseph; son; Oct. 1923; M. [Josephine; dau; F., in 1926]

Census of the **Northern Cheyenne** Indians of **Tongue River** Agency, **Mont.** on **June 30, 1927** taken by **C.B. Lohmiller**, Superintendent.

**Key:** Last Number; Present Number; Indian Name; English Name; Relationship; Month, Year, of Birth; Sex;

311; 325; Firewolf, John; hsbd.; Apr. 1877; M.
312; 326; Firewolf, Josephine; wife; Jan. 1875; F.

313; 327; Fisher, Eugene; hsbd.; July 1878; M.
314; 328; Fisher, Kitty; wife; Apr. 1890; F.
315; 329; Fisher, Eugene, Jr.; son; Dec. 1912; M.
316; 330; Fisher, Langburn; son; July 1915; M.
317; 331; Fisher, J. Allen; son; Mar. 1917; M. [1917 Census name Ira.]
318; 332; Fisher, Alliwitchie; dau.; May 1919; F. [1919 Census name Pearl.]
319; 333; Fisher, Calleaus; son; May 1919; M. [1919 Census name Earl.]
320; 334; Fisher, Russell; son; Nov. 1921; M.
321; 335; Fisher, Phyllis Helen; dau.; Mar. 1924; F.
336; Fisher; Bernidine; son; Dec. 1926; M.

322; 337; Fisher, Lena; mthr.; May 1876; F.
323; 338; Fisher, Alice; dau.; Aug. 1898; F.
326; 339; Fisher, John; son; July 1901; M.
327; 340; Fisher, Henry; son; Aug. 1905; M.
328; 341; Fisher, Isabelle; dau.; June 1908; F.
324; 342; Fisher, Richard; son; Nov. 1912; M.
325; 343; Fisher, Harold; son; Jan. 1920; M.

329; 344; Fliesabout, William; hsbd.; Feb. 1879; M.
330; 345; Fliesabout, Minnie; wife; Dec. 1882; F.
332; 346; Fliesabout, June; dau.; Jun. 1923; F. [Martin; son; F[sic], in 1926.]

333; 347; Flying, Debs; wdr.; Feb. 1886; M.
334; 348; Flying, Frank; son; Oct. 1915; M.
335; 349; Flying, Parker; son; Apr. 1918; M.

336; 350; Flying, Myra; mthr.; June 1867; F.
337; 351; Flying, Ruth; dau.; Dec. 1916; F.

338; 352; Flying, Thomas; hsbd.; Mar. 1869; M.
339; 353; Flying, Margaret; wife; Mar. 1866; F. [Highbear]

340; 354; Flying, Pauline; dau.; June 1916; F. [Male, Paul in 1920.]

341; 355; Foot, Jennie; wife; June 1890; F.
Foot, Albert; hsbd.; ---;--. (Not enrolled)
342; 356; Foot, Thelma; dau.; June 1913; F. [1917 Census name Daisy.]
343; 357; Foot, Bertha; dau.; Dec. 1919; F.
344; 358; Foot, Edward; son.; Apr. 1918; M.
345; 359; Foot, Eva; dau.; May 1923; F.

Census of the **Northern Cheyenne** Indians of **Tongue River** Agency, **Mont.** on **June 30, 1927** taken by **C.B. Lohmiller**, Superintendent.

**Key:** Last Number; Present Number; Indian Name; English Name; Relationship; Month, Year, of Birth; Sex;

811; 360;     Fox, Jessie; dau.; Aug.1918; F. dau. Mary Redbird [Margaret in 1926.]
812; 361;     Fox, Marie; dau.; Oct. 1922; F. dau. Mary Redbird [Max, M., 1922-25.]

346; 362;     Ghostbull, Arthur; hsbd.; Feb. 1870[sic]; M. [1904-26 birth year 1874.]
347; 363;     Ghostbull, Sarah; wife; Sept. 1867[?]; F. 1905-08 birth year 1868, 1909-11 birth year 1861, 1912-13 birth year 1866, 1914 birth year 1851, 1915-26 birth year 1861.]
348; 364;     Ghostbull, Eva (Mary); dau.; Mar. 1908; F.

349; 365;     Grasshopper, Isaac; wdr.; June 1850; M.

350; 366;     Grasshopper, Frank; sgle.; Sept. 1906; M. son of Mrs. Stanley Lamewoman. [Arthur in 1926.]

351; 367;     Grasshopper, Susie; s-dau.; Apr. 1909; F. s-dau. Stanley Lamewoman
352; 368;     Grasshopper, Mary; s-dau.; Aug. 1914; F. s-dau. Stanley Lamewoman

353; 369;     Gray, Edward; hsbd.; Apr. 1873; M.
354; 370;     Gray, Nellie; wife; Sept. 1874; F.
355; 371;     Gray, Teddy; son; Aug. 1915; M.

356; 372;     Gray, John; hsbd.; Aug. 1902[?]; M. [1904 shows up as 1 yr. old.]
1356; 373;     Gray, Kate Wolfname; wife; Mar. 1900; F. [Ida in 1926.]

357; 374;     Gray, Bessie; div-wife; July 1904; F. [1920 #917, name Sandcrane.]
358; 375;     Gray, Rose Marie; dau.; Nov.1923; F.

359; 376;     Greasydog, Fannie; sgle.; June 1897; F.

361; 377;     Hairlessbear, Hilda; dau.; Mar. 1912[?]; F. [States in 1913 census, Born 3/8/1913.] dau. Mrs. John Chubby

362; 378;     Hairyhand, Henry; wdr.; Oct. 1855; M.

363; 379;     Hankeringwolf, Peter; hsbd.; Sept. 1834; M.

365; 380;     Hardground, Ernest; hsbd.; July 1896; M.
366; 381;     Hardground, Mary; wife; Aug. 1895[?]; F.
367; 382;     Hardground, Ethel; dau.; Feb. 1921; F.
368; 383;     Hardground, Katie; dau.; Sept. 1923; F.
369; 384;     Hardground, Elda; dau.; Apr. 1926; F.

370; 385;     Hardground, Jane; dau.; Mar. 1915; F. s-dau. Lee Spottedblackbird.

371; 386;     Hardground, Robert; hsbd.; Nov. 1876; M.
373; 387;     Hardground, Roland; son; July 1909; M. [Rowland in 1926.]

Census of the **Northern Cheyenne** Indians of **Tongue River** Agency, **Mont.** on **June 30, 1927** taken by **C.B. Lohmiller**, Superintendent.

**Key:** Last Number; Present Number; Indian Name; English Name; Relationship; Month, Year, of Birth; Sex;

374;  388;  Hardground, Lucy; dau.; Sept. 1911; F. [Rena in 1926.]
375;  389;  Hardground, Lyla; dau.; Feb. 1914; F.

363;  390;  Hardground, Albert; hsbd.; June 1899; M.
1080; 391;  Hardground, Ruth; wife; May 1908; F. [Standingelk]

377;  392;  Hardground, George; sgle.; Apr. 1901[sic]; M.
[George's birth year, Censuses 1904-08 is 1898. 1909-13 is 1897. 1914-18 is 1895.]

378;  393;  Hardground, Thomas; sgle; Aug. 1903; M.

379;  394;  Hardrobe, Colonel; fthr.; Feb. 1856[sic]; M.

380;  395;  Hardrobe, Albert; sgle.; July 1896; M.

381;  396;  Hardrobe, Fannie; dau.; Oct. 1880; F.

      397;  Hardrobe, Mollie; g-dau.; Oct. 1919; F. dau. Mrs. Louis Magpie

382;  398;  Hardrobe, Margaret; dau.; Apr. 1918; F. [name Lucy and birth year 1911 in 1926. s-dau Willis Medicinebull.] dau. Ruth Yellownose

384;  399;  Harris, Edward; hsbd.; Jan. 1887; M.
385;  400;  Harris, Bessie; wife; May 1891[?]; F. [1911-26 birth year 1888-89.]
386;  401;  Harris, May; dau.; May 1911; F.
387;  402;  Harris, Nellie; dau.; May 1914; F.
388;  403;  Harris, Dorothy; dau.; May 1919; F.
389;  404;  Harris, Hubert George; son; Jan. 1922; M. [Lawrence Edw. In 1926.]

390;  405;  Harris, Sallie; wdw.; Sept. 1850; F.

391;  406;  Harris, Bryan; wdr.; Apr. 1898; M.
392;  407;  Harris, Carl; son; Oct. 1921; M.

395;  408;  Harris, William; hsbd.; Jan. 1877; M.
396;  409;  Harris, Margaret; wife; May 1884; F.
397;  410;  Harris, George; son; Sept. 1907; M.
394;  411;  Harris, Lucy; dau.; Jan. 1908; F.
398;  412;  Harris, Julia; dau.; Dec. 1910; F.
399;  413;  Harris, Agnes; dau.; Sept. 1912[?]; F. [Shows up in 1914 census as being born in 1913. 1914-16 birth year as 1913, 1917-26 birth year as 1915.]
400;  414;  Harris, Raymond; son; Apr. 1915; M.
401;  415;  Harris, Mary; dau.; Apr. 1919; F. [1920 name Leota.]
402;  416;  Harris, Florence; dau.; Spet.[sic] 1923; F. [1925 son Joseph, M.]

409;  417;  Hart, Frank; hsbd.; July 1898; M.

18

Census of the __Northern Cheyenne__ Indians of __Tongue River__
Agency,_**Mont.**_ on __June 30, 1927__ taken by__ **C.B. Lohmiller**__,
Superintendent.

**Key:** Last Number; Present Number; Indian Name; English Name; Relationship; Month, Year, of Birth; Sex;

410; 418; Hart, Rose Alice; wife; May 1907; F. [Hairlessbear]

404; 419; Hart, Charles; hsbd.; May 1880; M.
405; 420; Hart, Louisa; wife; Sept. 1885; F.
406; 421; Hart, Mattie Lizzie; dau.; July 1911; F. [Censuses 1912-18 name is Katie.]
407; 422; Hart, Eva; dau.; Dec. 1913[sic]; F. [Census 1916-20 birth year 1915.]
408; 423; Hart, Jessie Dianna; dau.; Apr. 1917; F.

411; 424; Headswift, Charles; fthr.; Mar. 1867; M.
412; 425; Headswift, Frank; son; Jun. 1911; M.

413; 426; Highbear, William; hsbd.; Mary[sic]1888[?]; M.
414; 427; Highbear, Minnie; wife; May 1897[?]; F.
[Most censuses show birth year 1896.]

415; 428; Highwalking, Nellie; wdw.; Apr. 1859[sic]; F. [Born 1850 from 1904-16.]

416; 429; Highwalking, Floyd; hsbd.; Apr. 1888; M.
417; 430; Highwalking, Belle; wife; Jun. 1893; F.
418; 431; Highwalking, Max; son; Jan. 1917; M.
419; 432; Highwalking, George; son; Mar. 1913; M. [David in 1926.]

408; 433; Hisbadhorse[sic], Richard; hsbd.; Aug. 1848; M.
[Hisbadhorses 1904-26.]
421; 434; Hisbadhorse, Rhoda; wife; Jun. 1856[sic]; F.
[1904-26 birth year 1840.]

424; 435; Hisbadhorses, Willis; hsbd.; Aug. 1898; M.
428; 436; Hisbadhorses, Ernest; son; May 1917; M. [1924 s-son. Eugene in 1926.]
429; 437; Hisbadhorses, Medaris; son; Aug. 1921; M. [Bird; son; 1917; in 1926.]
427; 438; Hisbadhorses, Fannie; dau.; Oct. 1922; F. [Josephine in 1926.]

431; 439; Hollowbreast, Hubert; hsbd.; May 1875; M.
427;[sic]440; Hollowbreast, Mary; wife; Apr. 1896; F. [Previous censuses name Hattie Hisbadhorses. 1926 Hisbadhorses, wdw. #426.]
432; 441; Hollowbreast, Donald; son; Mary[sic]1917; M. [James in 1926.]
430; 442; Hollowbreast, Richard; son; Oct. 1925; M. [1926 Richard Hisbadhorses.]

Census of the **Northern Cheyenne** Indians of **Tongue River** Agency, **Mont.** on **June 30, 1927** taken by **C.B. Lohmiller**, Superintendent.

**Key:** Last Number; Present Number; Indian Name; English Name; Relationship; Month, Year, of Birth; Sex;

433; 443; Hollowbreast, William; hsbd.; Mar. 1900[?]; M. [1925 birth year 1893. Birth year 1866 in 1926. Birth year 1900 in 1920. 1904-15 there is a Willie Hollowbreast that has a birth year of 1900. Father same as William in 1920.]
Hollowbreast, Edith; wife; ---; --. (Not enrolled)

434; 444; Hollowwood, Richard; hsbd.; July 1856[sic]; M. [1904-26 birth year 1866.]
435; 445; Hollowwood, Minnie; wife; Aug. 1856; F.

436; 446; Horn, Annie Wolfname; wife; May 1900; F. [Name Alice 1904-20.]
Horn, Miles; hsbd.; ---; --. (Not enrolled)
438; 447; Horn, Rose; dau.; June 1921; F.
439; 448; Horn, Wilena; dau.; Mar. 1923; F.
449; Horn, Margaret; dau.; July 1926; F.

440; 450; Horseroads, Thomas; hsbd.; Sept. 1878; M.
441; 451; Horseroads, Lucy; wife; Aug. 1887; F.
442; 452; Horseroads, Sallie; dau.; Nov. 1921; F.
443; 453; Horseroads, Ida; dau.; Jan. 1924; F.
454; Horseroads, Cora; dau.; Nov. 1926; F.

444; 455; Howlingantelope, Albert; hsbd.; Apr. 1874; M.
445; 456; Howlingantelope, Eva; wife; May 1880; F.

275; 457; Ironhand, William; hsbd.; Nov. 1882; M.
446; 458; Ironhand, Sally; wife; July 1884; F.
447; 459; Ironhand, Henry; son; June 1910; M.
448; 460; Ironhand, Willis; son; Jan. 1915; M.
461; Ironhand, Jane; dau.; Feb. 1927; F.

449; 462; Ironshirt, Jennie; mthr.; July 1858; F.

450; 463; Ironshirt, Fred; hsbd.; July 1831; M.
451; 464; Ironshirt, Nora; wife; Aug. 1850; F.

452; 465; Ironshirt, Robert; wdr.; July 1902; M.

454; 466; Irontooth, Susan; wdw.; -- 1834; F.

459; 467; Issues, John; hsbd.; -- 1863; M.
460; 468; Issues, Clara; wife; Mar. 1870; F. [Blackmedicine; 1904-17, Birth year 1868; she becomes Issues 1915, 1918-25 birth year changed to 1863, 1926 to 1878. 1927 to 1870.]

455; 469; Issues, Francis; wdr.; Mar. 1897; M.

20

Census of the **Northern Cheyenne** Indians of **Tongue River** Agency, **Mont.** on **June 30, 1927** taken by **C.B. Lohmiller**, Superintendent.

**Key:** Last Number; Present Number; Indian Name; English Name; Relationship; Month, Year, of Birth; Sex;

457; 470; Issues, Ira; son; Feb. 1920[?]; M. [1919 name Ira, 1920-23, George.]
458; 471; Issues, Irene; dau.; May 1921; F.

461; 472; Killsback, James; hsbd.; July 1863; M. [Census #461, name Joseph Killsacross in 1926.]
462; 473; Killsback, Amelia; wife; Dec. 1878; F.

463; 474; Killsnight, Charles; hsbd.; June 1890; M. [Div. Husb. of Minnie Killsnight noted as such in 1926.]
464; 475; Killsnight, Rosa; wife; Feb. 1899[?]; F. [Birth year 1903 in 1926.]
465; 476; Killsnight, Anna; Dau.; Mar. 1911; F. [Florence in 1926.]
466; 477; Killsnight, Robert; son; Jan. 1913; M.
467; 478; Killsnight, Rosa; dau.; Apr. 1915; F.
468; 479; Killsnight, Susan; dau.; May 1917; F.
469; 480; Killsnight, Hubert; son; Feb. 1919; M. [Brighton in 1926.]
470; 481; Killsnight, Bessie; dau.; Feb. 1920; F. [Margaret in 1926. Birth year 1923.]
471; 482; Killsnight, Margaret; dau.; Feb. 1924; F.
483; Killsnight, Dorothy; dau.; Feb. 1927; F.

472; 484; Killsnight, Rose; mthr.; Apr. 1881[sic]; F. [1904-24 Birth 1884.]
473; 485; Killsnight, Carrie; dau.; May 1911; F.

474; 486; Killsnight, William Jr.; sgle.; Oct. 1904; M.

475; 487; Killsnight, Hugh; hsbd.; Aug. 1866; M.
476; 488; Killsnight, Clara; wife; Sept. 1872; F.

477; 489; Killsnight, Cole; sgle.; Feb. 1905; M.

478; 490; Killsnight, William Sr.; hsbd.; Apr. 1856; M.
479; 491; Killsnight, Cora; wife; June 1860; F.
480; 492; Killsnight, Martin; son; Jan. 1907; M.

481; 493; Killsnight, Willis; hsbd.; Mar. 1895; M. [Rutherford in 1926.]
482; 494; Killsnight, Carrie; wife; May 1890; F. [Whitemoon]
484; 495; Killsnight, Flossie; dau.; Feb. 1924; F. [Sage in 1926.]
485; 496; Killsnight, James; son; Apr. 1926; M.

486; 497; Killsnightwoman, ---; mthr.; Apr. 1858; F.

487; 498; Killsontop, John; hsbd.; Aug. 1906; M. Separated
499; Killsontop, June; dau.; Apr. 1927; F. (Mary Strangeowl is mother of child.)

Census of the **Northern Cheyenne** Indians of **Tongue River** Agency, **Mont.** on **June 30, 1927** taken by **C.B. Lohmiller**, Superintendent.

Key: Last Number; Present Number; Indian Name; English Name; Relationship; Month, Year, of Birth; Sex;

488; 500; Killsontop, Mamie; wife; Mar. 1897; F. Separated
489; 501; Killsontop, Ida; dau.; Oct. 1924; F.

490; 502; Kingfisher, Herman; hsbd.; Apr. 1867; M.
491; 503; Kingfisher, Carrie; wife; Aug. 1876; F.

429;[sic]504; Kingfisher, Willis; hsbd.; Sept. 1896; M.
493; 505; Kingfisher, Minnie; wife; July 1896; F.
495; 506; Kingfisher, Isabelle; dau.; Sept. 1918; F.
     507; Kingfisher, Charles; son; June 1921; M.
     508; Kingfisher, Louise; dau.; Oct. 1922; F.
     509; Kingfisher, Ellen; dau.; June 1926; F.

496; 510; Kinzel, Alice; wife; Mar. 1893; F.
         Kinzel, Jerry; hsbd.; ---; --. (Not enrolled)
497; 511; Kinzel, Emma Loua[sic]; dau.; June 1917; F.
498; 512; Kinzel, Helan[sic] Louise; dau.; Mar. 1920; F.
499; 513; Kinzel, Cecelia Leah; dau.; July 1924; F.

     514; Knows-His-Gun, Frances; wife; Oct.1904; F.
         Knows-His-Gun, Hector; hsb.; ---; --. (Not enrolled)
     515; Knows-His-Gun, Sylvester; son; Sept. 1926; M.

500; 516; LaFever, Rena (Eastman); wife; Aug. 1896[?]; F. (Married white man)
     517; LaFever, Kenneth; son; Dec. 1925; M. [#501; Herman; son; birth year 1925 in 1926.]

502; 518; Lamebear, Benjamin; hsbd.; July 1894; M.
503; 519; Lamebear, Clara; wife; May 1894; F.
504; 520; Lamebear, Eva; dau.; Nov. 1910[sic]; F. [Birth year 1916 first shows in 1917.]
505; 521; Lamebear, Cora; dau.; Apr. 1919; F.
506; 522; Lamebear, Charles; son; Oct. 1921; M.
507; 523; Lamebear, Will; son; Jan. 1926; M.

508; 524; Lamewoman, Nellie; sgle.; July 1854; F.

     525; Lamewoman, Sam; son; Oct. 1912; M. (Sam Littlebear)
511; 526; Lamewoman, Mary; dau.; Aug. 1917; F. (s-dau. Ed Womanleggins) [Same previous number name Minnie birth year 1916. Has a sister named Mary #510 birth year 1914.]

512; 527; Lamewoman, Stanley; hsbd.; Aug. 1889; M.
513; 528; Lamewoman, Augusta; wife; July 1885; F.
514; 529; Lamewoman, Virgil; son; Feb. 1922; M.

Census of the **Northern Cheyenne** Indians of **Tongue River** Agency, **Mont.** on **June 30, 1927** taken by **C.B. Lohmiller**, Superintendent.

**Key:** Last Number; Present Number; Indian Name; English Name; Relationship; Month, Year, of Birth; Sex;

510; 530; Lamewoman, Jessie; dau.; June 1914; F. [In 1926 #510; Mary; s-dau; 1914; F. (s-dau Edward Womanleggins).]

516; 531; Lastbull, Fred; hsbd.; Jan. 1888; M.
               Lastbull, Maywoman; wife; ---; --. (Enrolled in Okla.)

517; 532; Lennon, Mary (Burns); wife; June 1906; F.
               Lennon, Thomas; hsbd.; ---; M. (Not enrolled white)
       533; Lennon, Arthur George; son; Nov. 1926; M.

518; 534; Lightning, Frank; wdr.; Aug. 1871; M.

525; 535; Limberhand, Richard; sgle.; Aug. 1905; M.

526; 536; Limberhand, James; sgle.; Oct. 1902[?]; M.

519; 537; Limberhand, Nathan; hsbd.; Mar. 1876; M.
520; 538; Limberhand, Artie; wife; Sept. 1883; F.
521; 539; Limberhand, Elmore; son; Jan. 1909; M.
522; 540; Limberhand, Bennie; son; Jan. 1912[?]; M.
523; 541; Limberhand, Jennie; dau.; Nov. 1915; F.
524; 542; Limberhand, Doris; Dau.; May 1922; F.

527; 543; Limpy, Benjamin; hsbd.; Oct. 1892; M.
528; 544; Limpy, Hattie[sic]; wife; June 1894; F.
[#544; Hallie Killsacross #271, 1914 census. 1915-16 Hallie Limpy.]
529; 545; Limpy, Anna; dau.; Jan. 1915; F. [Son, Jack 1916- 19; Jean in 1926.]
530; 546; Limpy, Rosa; Dau.; Aug. 1919; F. [#530 Elnora; birth year1921 in 1926.]
       547; Limpy, Jessie; dau.; Nov. 1922; F.

531; 548; Limpy, Charles; hsbd.; Oct. 1857; M.
532; 549; Limpy, Nellie; wife; July 1854; F.

534; 550; Limpy, Fred; hsbd.; Apr. 1884; M.
535; 551; Limpy, Amelia; wife; May 1885; F. [Womanleggins]
536;[sic]552; Limpy, Mamie; dau.; Dec. 1907; F.
537; 553; Limpy, Frank; son; May 1911; M.
538; 554; Limpy, Mary; dau.; May 1913; F. [#506, Limpy, Mary; D.; 6 Mo; in 1909. #538 May Limpy birth year 1913 in 1926.]
539; 555; Limpy, Henry; son; Aug. 1919; M. [1920 Census Fred Jr.]
540; 556; Limpy, Cora; dau.; Nov. 1925; F.

541; 557; Littlebear, Paul; hsbd.; July 1887; M.
542; 558; Littlebear, Rosa; wife; Aug. 1887; F.
545; 559; Littlebear, May; dau.; May 1908; F. [Anne in 1926.]

Census of the **Northern Cheyenne** Indians of **Tongue River** Agency, **Mont.** on **June 30, 1927** taken by **C.B. Lohmiller**, Superintendent.

Key: Last Number; Present Number; Indian Name; English Name; Relationship; Month, Year, of Birth; Sex;

543; 560; Littlebear, Flossie; dau.; Apr. 1912; F. [Mary in 1926.]
544; 561; Littlebear, Clara; dau.; Apr. 1916; F.
562; Littlebear, Two-birds; son; Dec. 1923; M.
563; Littlebear, Lucille; dau.; July 1926; F.

546; 564; Littlebird, Peter; hsbd.; May 1870; M.
547; 565; Littlebird, Jennie; wife; July 1892; F.
548; 566; Littlebird, Joseph; son; Sept. 1912; M.
549; 567; Littlebird, Julia; dau.; June 1922; F.
550; 568; Littlebird, James Wm.; son; June 1925; M.

552; 569; Littlebird, Harry; s-son; Aug. 1918; M. s-son Leo Whitecrane
1274; 570; Littlebird, James; s-son; July 1919; M. s-son Leo Whitecrane
[Previous #1274; Littlebird, Elsie; s-dau; birth year 1920; F in 1926.]

553; 571; Littlechief, Victor; hsbd.; Jan. 1877; M.
554; 572; Littlechief, Louisa; wife; Mar. 1875; F.
555; 573; Littlechief, Lucille; dau.; Feb. 1911; F. [Lizzie in 1926.]

556; 574; Littlecoyote, Henry; fthr.; Sept. 1875; M.
557; 575; Littlecoyote, Daniel; son; Oct. 1910; M.

558; 576; Littleeagle, Charles; hsbd.; May 1867; M.
559; 577; Littleeagle, Mary; wife; June 1878; F.
560; 578; Littleeagle, Clara; dau.; Aug. 1905; F.

561; 579; Littleeyes, Eva; sgle.; July 1893; F. Lives with Zac Rowland

562; 580; Littlehawk, Dora; wdw.; Jan. 1869; F.

563; 581; Littlehead, Charles; hsbd.; June 1869; M.
564; 582; Littlehead, Nellie; wife; Dec. 1882; F.
565; 583; Littlehead, Frank; son; Nov. 1909; M.
566; 584; Littlehead, George; son; May 1920; M. [1920 name John.]

567; 585; Littlehead, Rena; s-dau.; Nov. 1919; F. s-dau. Oliver Eaglefeathers. [Mildred in 1926.]

568; 586; Littlehead, John; hsbd.; -- 1894; M.

569; 587; Littleoldman, Fern; s-dau.; Aug. 1917; F. s.-dau. Chas. Sharpnose [#569; Littleman, Julia; s-dau; 1915; F. (s-dau Fred Limpy) in 1926.]

570; 588; Littlemouth, Clara; wdw.; July 1859; F.

Census of the **Northern Cheyenne** Indians of **Tongue River** Agency, **Mont.** on **June 30, 1927** taken by **C.B. Lohmiller**, Superintendent.

**Key:** Last Number; Present Number; Indian Name; English Name; Relationship; Month, Year, of Birth; Sex;

571; 589; Littlemouth, John; hsbd.; Oct. 1894[?]; M. [Keeps changing year of birth.]
572; 590; Littlemouth, Jennie; wife; Sept. 1898; F.
573; 591; Littlemouth, Evelyn; dau; May 1921; F.
574; 592; Littlemouth, James; son; June 1922; M.
575; 593; Littlemouth, Mary; dau.; Apr. 1924; F.

576; 594; Littleoldman, Thomas; son; Dec. 1913; M.

578; 595; Littlesun, Jack; son; Aug. 1920; M.
579; 596; Littlesun, Horace; son; Sept. 1922; M.
Children of Bessie Littlesun Wolfchum.

580; 597; Littlesun, Frank; hsbd.; Oct. 1884; M.
581; 598; Littlesun, Anna; wife; June 1892; F.
582; 599; Littlesun, Alfred; son; Dec. 1912; M.

583; 600; Littlesun, Samuel; hsbd.; July 1858; M.
584; 601; Littlesun, Cora; wife; Sept. 1864; F.

585; 602; Littlewhirlwind, George; hsbd.; Jan. 1901; M.
1229; 603; Littlewhirlwind, Martha; wife; Oct. 1909; F. [Fannie Walksalong in 1926.]

586; 604; Littlewhiteman, Aaron; hsbd.; Dec. 1862; M.
587; 605; Littlewhiteman, Sadie; wife; Apr. 1866; F.
588; 606; Littlewhiteman, Wesley; sgle.; Aug. 1897; M.

589; 607; Littlewhiteman, Frank; hsbd.; 1901; M.
590; 608; Littlewhiteman, Emma; wife; Oct. 1900; F. [#964 in 1919 shows as Lightning, Emma; g dt; 1901; F. Grandparents Shortsioux in census as birth year 1901 starting in 1912 or 11 years old.]
591; 609; Littlewhiteman, Leon; son; Aug. 1920; M. [John in 1926.]
592; 610; Littlewhiteman, Margaret; dau.; July 1922; F.
       611; Littlewhiteman, John; son; Oct. 1925; M.

593; 612; Littlewhiteman, David; hsbd.; Feb. 1869; M.
594; 613; Littlewhiteman, Agnes; wife; July 1872; F.
595; 614; Littlewhiteman, Peter; son; Apr. 1906; M.

596; 615; Littlewhiteman, James; hsbd.; June 1895; M.
597; 616; Littlewhiteman, Gusta; wife; Sept. 1897; F. [Littlesun]
599; 617; Littlewhiteman, Kitty; dau.; Sept. 1923; F.
       618; Littlewhiteman, Charles; son; Sept. 1925; M. [In 1926 #600; as Charles (Albert); son; 1925; M.]

Census of the **Northern Cheyenne** Indians of **Tongue River** Agency, **Mont.** on **June 30, 1927** taken by **C.B. Lohmiller**, Superintendent.

Key: Last Number; Present Number; Indian Name; English Name; Relationship; Month, Year, of Birth; Sex;

607; 619; Littlewhiteman, Milton; hsbd.; Sept. 1884[?]; M. [Most previous cenuses 1886.]

608; 620; Littlewhiteman, Rosa; wife; Sept. 1882; F.

601; 621; Littlewhiteman, Henry; hsbd.; Jan. 1891; M.
602; 622; Littlewhiteman, Josie; wife; Feb. 1897; F. [Weaselbear; Prev. Marriage Woodenlegs.]
603; 623; Littlewhiteman, Edith; dau.; Dec. 1912[sic]; F. [Birth 1915.]
604; 624; Littlewhiteman, Rosa; Dau.; Sept. 1915[sic]; F. [Birth 1920.]
605; 625; Littlewhiteman, Agnes; dau.; Oct. 1921; F.
626; Littlewhiteman, Bessie; dau.; May 1926; F.

606; 627; Littlewhiteman, Charles; son; Feb.1915; M. s-son Dan Seminole

609; 628; Littlewhiteman, Florence; dau; Feb. 1915; F. s-dau Chas. Spottedwolf

610; 629; Littlewhiteman, Stanley; hsbd.; July 1888; M.
611; 630; Littlewhiteman, Grace; wife; -- 1894; F. [1920- #1300, name Walkingbear.]
612; 631; Littlewhiteman, Milton; son; Dec. 1914; M.
613; 632; Littlewhiteman, Aaron; son; Dec. 1921; M.
614; 633; Littlewhiteman, Adrain; son; Dec. 1923; M. [Name Hillman; birth 1924 in 1926.]
634; Littlewhiteman, Sadie; dau.; Jan. 1927; F.

615; 635; Littlewolf, Frank; hsbd.; Feb. 1877; M.
616; 636; Littlewolf, Kate; wife; Mar. 1883; F.
617; 637; Littlewolf, May; dau.; Mar. 1911; F.
618; 638; Littlewolf, Susan; dau.; June 1914; F.
619; 639; Littlewolf, Mary; dau.; Feb. 1922; F.

621; 640; Littlewolf, Laura; wdw.; Nov. 1852; F.

622; 641; Littlewolf, Lena; dau.; Dec. 1878[sic]; F.
[Lena #641; Censuses 1904-09 birth year is 1880; 1910 birth year is 1890; 1911-13 birth year is 1876; 1914-17 birth year is 1881; 1918 birth year is 1851; 1919-26 birth year is 1878.]

623; 642; Littlewolf, Robert; hsbd.; June 1882[?]; M. [1904-1913 birth year 1882. 1914-26 birth year 1877.]
624; 643; Littlewolf, May; wife; June 1894; F. [Prev. #373 name Harris; 1920.]
625; 644; Littlewolf, Charles (Homer); son; July 1908[sic]; M.[Birth year 1918 in 1919.]
626; 645; Littlewolf, Geraldine; dau.; Dec. 1921; F.
646; Littlewolf, Eva; dau.; Apr. 1925; F.

Census of the **Northern Cheyenne** Indians of **Tongue River** Agency, **Mont.** on **June 30, 1927** taken by **C.B. Lohmiller**, Superintendent.

**Key:** Last Number; Present Number; Indian Name; English Name; Relationship; Month, Year, of Birth; Sex;

627; 647; Littlewolf, Mary; sgle.; Nov. 1903; F.

628; 648; Littlewolf, William; hsbd.; Aug. 1883; M.
629; 649; Littlewolf, May; wife; Dec. 1890; F.
630; 650; Littlewolf, Mamie; dau.; July 1912[?]; F.
631; 651; Littlewolf, William Jr; son; Oct. 1914[?]; M.
632; 652; Littlewolf, Claude; son; Dec. 1916[?]; M.

633; 653; Littleyellowman, Hugh; sgle.; -- 1885; M.

634; 654; Littleyellowman, Jake; hsbd.; Oct. 1861; M.
635; 655; Littleyellowman, Gertrude; wife; Aprl 1875; F.

636; 656; Littleyellowman, Eddie; hsbd.; -- 1892; M. [birth year 1890 in 1926.]
Littleyellowman, ---; wife; ---; --. (Not enrolled here)

638;[sic]657; Littleyellowman, Richard; son; Jul. 1890; M. [#638 in 1926 is Eddie Littleyellowman; sgle; birth year 1890. In 1926 #636 is Richard; husb; birth year 1892.]

639; 658; Lonebull, Louis; sgle.; Aug. 1858; M.

640; 659; Loneelk, Wilson; sgle.; Mar. 1911; M. (Lives with Nellie Redeagle)

641; 660; Lonetravelingwolf, Mabel; dau.; June 1910; F. dau. Jane Walkingbird

642; 661; Lonewolf, Charles; hsbd.; June 1883; M.
643; 662; Lonewolf, Rosa; wife; Dec. 1890; F. [1917 Census name was Mary.]
644; 663; Lonewolf, James; son; July 1915; M. [Lloyd in 1926.]
645; 664; Lonewolf, Ella; dau.; May 1925; F.

647; 665; Longjaw, Frank; hsbd.; Apr. 1900; M.
985; 666; Longjaw, Cora Sharpnose; wife; May 1901; F.
667; Longjaw, Robert; son; Mar. 1927; M.

648; 668; Longjaw, Charles; hsbd.; Mar. 1846[?]; M. [1904-08 birth year 1843. 1909-13 birth year 1856-7. 1914-26 birth year 1857.]
650; 669; Longjaw, Clara; wife; Apr. 1862; F.
651; 670; Longjaw, Charles Jr.; g-son; Jul. 1915; M.

658; 671; Longjaw, James; hsbd.; May 1881; M.
659; 672; Longjaw, Nellie; wife; Jan. 1896; F.

652; 673; Longjaw, Elmer; hsbd.; Dec. 1883[?]; M.

Census of the __**Northern Cheyenne**__ Indians of __**Tongue River**__ Agency, __**Mont.**__ on __**June 30, 1927**__ taken by __**C.B. Lohmiller**__, Superintendent.

**Key:** Last Number; Present Number; Indian Name; English Name; Relationship; Month, Year, of Birth; Sex;

653; 674; Longjaw, Lena; wife; Aug. 1886; F. [From 1814 to 1817 Censuses have birth year as 1866.]
654; 675; Longjaw, Albert; son; June 1912; M.
655; 676; Longjaw, Henry; son; Jan. 1916; M.
656; 677; Longjaw, Clara; dau.; Jan. 1919; F.
      678; Longjaw, James; son; Dec. 1923; M.

661; 679; Longroach, George; hsbd.; Apr. 1882; M.
662; 680; Longroach, Nellie; wife; June 1888; F.
663; 681; Longroach, Harry; son; Jan. 1911; M.
664; 682; Longroach, James; son; Nov. 1914; M.
665; 683; Longroach, Mary; dau.; Mar. 1917; F. [Name Vita 1917-26.]
666; 684; Longroach, Frank; son; Feb. 1920; M.
667; 685; Longroach, Regina; dau.; Sept. 1923; F. [Veria in 1923.]
      686; Longroach, May; dau.; Aug. 1926; F.

668; 687; Looksatbareground, Jas.; hsbd.; May 1878; M.
669; 688; Looksatbareground, Julia; wife; May 1852; F. [1924 wd., Elkshoulders.]

670; 689; Looksbehind, James; hsbd.; -- 1885; M. (James Nightwalking)
            Looksbehind, ---; wife; ---; --. (Not enrolled)
      690; Looksbehind, James Jr.; son; May 1927; M.

671; 691; Looksbehind, Charles; hsbd.; Oct. 1860; M.
            Looksbehind, ---; wife; ---; --. (Not enrolled)
672; 692; Looksbehind, Thomas; son; July 1907[sic]; M. [1904-24 birth year 1903, 1 year old in 1904 census. 1925-26 birth year 1923.]

673; 693; Looksbehind, Sallie; div.; Oct. 1859; F.
674; 694; Looksbehind, Pius; g-son; Mar. 1912; M. (Redneck)

675; 695; Lostleg, Gertrude; wdw.; Nov. 1859; F.

676; 696; Lostleg, Nelson; hsbd.; July 1891; M.
677; 697; Lostleg, James; son; Dec. 1915; M. [Ernest George in 1926.]
678; 698; Lostleg, Theodorea (Virginia); dau.; Feb. 1919; F. [Son Theodore in 1920.]

679; 699; Magpie, Albert; fthr.; Apr. 1886; M. [Prev. censuses from 1904-15 name is Youngmagpie with same birth year, none in 1913, Magpie in 1916. As early as 1907 a first wife Julia born 1887. Anne is a second wife starting in 1919. Anne is not in 1925.]
680; 700; Magpie, Anna Mary; dau.; Dec. 1919; F. [Minnie in 1926.]
681; 701; Magpie, Gilbert; son; Aug. 1922; M. [#681 in 1926 was Magpie, Eva; dau; 1919; F.]

Census of the **Northern Cheyenne** Indians of **Tongue River** Agency, **Mont.** on **June 30, 1927** taken by **C.B. Lohmiller**, Superintendent.

**Key:** Last Number; Present Number; Indian Name; English Name; Relationship; Month, Year, of Birth; Sex;

682; 702; Magpie, Rose; dau.; Sept. 1925; M. [#682 in 1926 was Magpie, Edward; son; 1923; M.]

683; 703; Magpie, Louis; hsbd.; Oct. 1885; M.
684; 704; Magpie, Mira[sic]; wife; July 1894; F.
685; 705; Magpie, Eddie; son; Apr. 1910[sic]; M. [Shows in 1906, #705; Eddy; M; S; 2mo.]

687; 706; Manbear, Lena; mthr.; Aug. 1867; F.
688; 707; Manbear, Lizzie; dau.; Aprl. 1902; F.
689; 708; Manbear, Walters Coolidge; g-son; Feb. 1926; M.

690; 709; Marrowbone, Jessie; mthr.; -- 1888; F. Children enrolled at Pine Ridge.

694; 710; Medicine, Sampson; hsbd.; Sept. 1876; M.
695; 711; Medicine, Anna; wife; Feb. 1879; F.

696; 712; Medicine, Jennie; sgle.; Mar. 1902; F.

697; 713; Medicinebear, Maggie; wdw.; June 1847; F.

698; 714; Medicinebird, Nelson; hsbd.; Aug. 1875; M.
699; 715; Medicinebird, Ella; wife; Feb. 1883; F.
700; 716; Medicinebird, Homer; son; Mar. 1914; M.

701; 717; Medicinebull, Robert; hsbd.; Aug. 1860; M.
702; 718; Medicinebull, Maggie; wife; July 1862; F.

703; 719; Medicinebull, Willis; hsbd.; Apr. 1887; M.
704; 720; Medicinebull, Anne; wife; May 1902[?]; F. [Swallow] [Birth year 1905 in 1926.]
708; 721; Medicinebull, Fred; son; Oct. 1925; M.

706; 722; Medicinebull, James; son; Aug. 1910; M.
707; 723; Medicinebull, Ruth; dau.; June 1913; F. [Birth year 1911 in 1926.]

705; 724; Medicinebull, Donald; son; May 1922; M. Mother, Ruth Yellownose

709; 725; Medicineelk, Basil; hsbd.; Jan. 1894; M.
710; 726; Medicineelk, Jennie; wife; Sept. 1904; F. [Eaglefeathers]
711; 727; Medicineelk, Spencer; son; July 1917; M.

713; 728; Medicineelk, Harold; hsbd.; July 1865; M.
714; 729; Medicineelk, John; g-son; Oct. 1908; M. [Sandwoman]

29

Census of the **Northern Cheyenne** Indians of **Tongue River** Agency, **Mont.** on **June 30, 1927** taken by **C.B. Lohmiller**, Superintendent.

**Key:** Last Number; Present Number; Indian Name; English Name; Relationship; Month, Year, of Birth; Sex;

715; 730; Medicineelk, James Edw.; sgle.; son; Apr. 1902; M.
716; 731; Medicineelk, Thomas; hsbd.; July 1906[?]; M. [Birth year 1904 in 1926.]
1178; 732; Medicineelk, Nellie Teeth; wife; Oct. 1912; F.

717; 733; Medicineelk, Andrew; hsbd.; May 1898[sic]; M.
718; 734; Medicineelk, Maggie; wife; Jan. 1903; F. [Bearquiver]
719; 735; Medicineelk, Peter; son; Mar. 1926; M.

720; 736; Medicineflying, John; hsbd.; Sept. 1882; M.
721; 737; Medicineflying, Bertha; wife; Feb. 1885; F.
722; 738; Medicineflying, Jennie; dau.; Feb. 1910; F. [Bernice from 1910-23.]
723; 739; Medicineflying, Helen; dau.; Aug. 1916; F.
724; 740; Medicineflying, Agnes; dau.; May 1920; F.
726; 741; Medicineflying, Phyllis; dau.; July 1924; F. [Birth year 1925 in 1926.]

727; 742; Medicinetop, James; wdr[?]; May 1861; M.

728; 743; Medicinetop, John; hsbd.; Jan. 1885; M.
729; 744; Medicinetop, Ida; wife; May 1890; F.
730; 745; Medicinetop, Clarence; son; Oct. 1910; M.
731; 746; Medicinetop, Marjorie; dau.; Apr. 1914[sic]; F. [Birth year 1917.]
732; 747; Medicinetop, Phyllis; dau.; Sept. 1922; F.
733; 748; Medicinetop, Roy; son; Aug. 1924; M. [Birth year 1925 in 1926.]

735; 749; Merritt, Wesley; hsbd.; Oct. 1876; M.
736; 750; Merritt, Josie; wife; May 1863; F.

739; 751; Mexicancheyenne, Ernest; hsbd.; Dec. 1889[sic]; M.
740; 752; Mexicancheyenne, Mary; wife; July 1899; F.
741; 753; Mexicancheyenne, Hilda; dau.; June 1919; F.
742; 754; Mexicancheyenne. Mary Victoria; dau.; Aug. 1921; F.
743; 755; Mexicancheyenne. Rudolph; son; Feb. 1925; M. [Anabelle; dau; 1925.]

744; 756; Mexicancheyenne, Marion; hsbd.; July 1887; M.
745; 757; Mexicancheyenne, Emma; wife; June 1893; F.
746; 758; Mexicancheyenne, James; son; July 1914; M.
747; 759; Mexicancheyenne, Rosa; dau.; Nov. 1918; F.
748; 760; Mexicancheyenne, Margaret; dau.; Dec. 1920; F. [Ethel in 1926.]
749; 761; Mexicancheyenne, Mary; dau.; Jan. 1925; F.

738; 762; Mexicancheyenne, Dorothy; dau.; July 1908; F.

751; 763; Oldbull, Daniel; fthr.; Oct. 1870; M.
752; 764; Oldbull, Thomas; son; Nov. 1910; M.

Census of the **Northern Cheyenne** Indians of **Tongue River** Agency, **Mont.** on **June 30, 1927** taken by **C.B. Lohmiller**, Superintendent.

**Key:** Last Number; Present Number; Indian Name; English Name; Relationship; Month, Year, of Birth; Sex;

754; 765; Onebear, James; hsbd.; July1900; M.
755; 766; Onebear, Maggie; wife; Mar. 1903; F. [Seminole]
756; 767; Onebear, Robert; son; Dec. 1925; M.

757; 768; Parker, Alvin O.; hsbd.; June 1879; M.
Parker, Mildred; wife; ---; --. (Not enrolled)
758; 769; Parker, Clyde Spencer; son; Nov. 1922; M.
759; 770; Parker, Verda Faye; dau.; Sept. 1924; F.
771; Parker, Shirley Rose; dau.; Jan. 1927; F.

760; 772; Parker, Charles A. Jr.; hsbd.; July 1885; M.
Parker, Marie; wife; ---; --. (Not enrolled)
761; 773; Parker, Theresa; dau.; Mar. 1912; F.
774; Parker, Gabriel; son; Oct. 1926; M.

762; 775; Parker, Edwin H.; sgle.; Apr. 1895; M.

649; 776; Parker, Guy; hsbd.; Sept. 1891; M. [Prev. # out of order.]
Parker, Gertrude; wife; ---; --. (Not enrolled)
763; 777; Parker, Winfred; son; April 1914; M.
764; 778; Parker, Alice; dau.; Feb. 1917; F.
765; 779; Parker, Stella; dau.; Apr.1919; F.
766; 780; Parker, Vincent Albert; son; June 1925; M.

282; 781; Pease, Ida (Eastman); wife; Feb. 1906; F.
Pease, George; hsbd.; ---; --. (Not enrolled)

767; 782; Pine, Frank; wdr.; July 1863; M.

768; 783; Pine, Rutherford; hsbd.; June 1886; M.
769; 784; Pine, Julia; wife; Aug. 1896[sic]; F. [In 1916 marries Julia Blackcrane nee Kingfisher; in 1912 she is 18 years old, birth year is 1894 from 1904-16. Gave birth year as 1884 from 1917-26.]
770; 785; Pine, Cecelia; dau.; Jan. 1916; F.
771; 786; Pine, Daniel; son; Sept. 1923; M.

772; 787; Pine, Wilson; hsbd.; Mar. 1886; M.
773; 788; Pine, Nora; wife; July 1888; F.
774; 789; Pine, Alexander; son; Nov. 1917; M.
775; 790; Pine, John; son; Apr. 1922; M.
776; 791; Pine, Sarah; dau.; Aug. 1924; F.

777; 792; Playingbear, Henry; hsbd.; Jan. 1877; M.
778; 793; Playingbear, Mildred; Wife; April 1880[?]; F. [1904-17 birth year 1881-82, 1918-26 birth year 1888.]

Census of the **Northern Cheyenne** Indians of **Tongue River** Agency, **Mont.** on **June 30, 1927** taken by **C.B. Lohmiller**, Superintendent.

**Key:** Last Number; Present Number; Indian Name; English Name; Relationship; Month, Year, of Birth; Sex;

779; 794; Playingbear, Mary; dau.; Feb. 1911; F.
780; 795; Playingbear, John; son; May 1915; M.

781; 796; Plentycamps, Clara; wdw.; Aug. 1845; F.

782; 797; Porcupine, Albert; hsbd.; July 1848; M.
783; 798; Porcupine, Julia; wife; Apr. 1866; F.

786; 799; Powderface, John; hsbd.; May 1866; M.

784; 800; Powderface, Julia; s-dau.; Aug. 1913; F. (s-dau. Wilson Pine)
785; 801; Powderface, Fern; s-dau.; July 1918; F. (s-dau. Wilson Pine)

788; 802; Powell, Mary; wife; Nov. 1881; F.
Powell, Edward; hsbd.; ---;--. (Not enrolled)
789; 803; Powell, Deyo; son; June 1907[sic]; M. [Birth year 1909, 6 mo's old.]
790; 804; Powell, Howard; son; Feb. 1912; M.

791; 805; Powell, Clay; hsbd.; Nov. 1904; M.
Powell, Ollie; ---; --. (Not enrolled)

792; 806; Prairiebear, Arthur; hsbd.; Mar. 1882; M.
793; 807; Prairiebear, Sally; wife; Oct. 1885; F.

794; 808; Redbeads, John; hsbd.; Nov. 1871; M.
795; 809; Redbeads, Nancy; wife; Apr. 1876; F
796; 810; Redbeads, Susie; dau.; May 1913; F.
797; 811; Redbeads, Clara; dau.; June 1915; F.
798; 812; Redbeads, Georgia; dau.; July 1917; F. [Name Gloria 1917-20.]

799; 813; Redbird, Joseph; hsbd.; Oct. 1899; M. [Middle name Francis in 1910.]
814; Redbird, William; son; June 1922; M.
801; 815; Redbird, Allen; son; May 1925, M. [First shows in 1925 with birth in 1924. Same Prev. #, Helena; dau; 1925, F. in 1926. ]

802; 816; Redbird, William; hsbd.; July 1876; M.
803; 817; Redbird, Florence; wife; June 1877; F.
804; 818; Redbird, Lena; dau.; Nov. 1920; F. [Susie in 1926.]

810; 819; Redbird, Mary; mthr.; Aug. 1897; F.

814; 820; Redbreath, Charles; hsbd.; Apr. 1879; M.
815; 821; Redbreath, Betty; wife; Jan. 1908; F. [Yellownose]
817; 822; Redbreath, Elina Jane; dau.; June 1925; F. [Elina June in 1926.]

32

Census of the **Northern Cheyenne** Indians of **Tongue River** Agency, **Mont.** on **June 30, 1927** taken by **C.B. Lohmiller**, Superintendent.

**Key:** Last Number; Present Number; Indian Name; English Name; Relationship; Month, Year, of Birth; Sex;

818; 823; Redcherries, Teddy; wdr[?]; -- 1888; M.
820; 824; Redcherries, William; hsbd.; June 1890; M.
821; 825; Redcherries, Bessie; wife; Feb. 1894; F.
256; 826; Redcherries, Anna; dau.; May 1910; F. [Woodenthigh-Killsontop; #256, Divesbackward, May; s-dau; 1910; F., in 1926.]
822; 827; Redcherries, Alice; dau.; Aug. 1912; F.
823; 828; Redcherries, Rose; dau.; Apr. 1916; F.
824; 829; Redcherries, Frank; son; May 1919; M.
830; Redcherries, Margaret; dau.; Sept. 1923; F.

825; 831; Redeagle, Jennie; wdw.; Sept. 1841[?]; F.
[Jennie #831, Census 1904-14 birth year 1851; 1915-18 birth year 1852. 1919-26 birth year 1832.]

826; 832; Redeagle, Nellie; wdw.; Aug. 1872; F.

827; 833; Redeagle, Willis; sgle.; Dec. 1901; M.

828; 834; Redfox, James; hsbd.; Apr. 1865; M.
829; 835; Redfox, Cora; wife; July 1867; F.

830; 836; Redfox, Jennie; wdw.; Dec. 1873; F.

831; 837; Redfox, Robert; hsbd.; Mar. 1900; M.
832; 838; Redfox, Cecelia; wife; June 1894; F.
839; Redfox, Edna; dau.; Mar. 1927; M[sic].

834; 840; Redneck, Curtis; hsbd.; Jan. 1888; M.
835; 841; Redneck, Josie; wife; Dec. 1896; F.

836; 842; Redneck, David; fthr.; Sept. 1891; M.
843; Redneck, Minnie; dau.; Aug. 1919; F.

837; 844; Redneck, Clyde; son; Aug. 1912; M. son Maude Shields Whitewolf

840; 845; Redneck, Henry; hsbd.; Aug. 1882; M.
841; 846; Redneck, Fannie; wife; July 1884[?]; F. [Birth year 1887 in 1926.]
842; 847; Redneck, Grace; dau.; Mar. 1910; F.
839; 848; Redneck, Dora; dau.; Oct. 1914[?]; F. [Birth year 1908 in 1926.]
843; 849; Redneck, Homer; son; July 1917; M.
844; 850; Redneck, Florence; dau.; Apr. 1921; F.
845; 851; Redneck, John; son; May 1925; M.

846; 852; Rednose, Paul; hsbd.; June 1876; M.
847; 853; Rednose, Lucy; wife; May 1870; F.

Census of the __Northern Cheyenne__ Indians of __Tongue River__ Agency, __Mont.__ on __June 30, 1927__ taken by __C.B. Lohmiller__, Superintendent.

**Key:** Last Number; Present Number; Indian Name; English Name; Relationship; Month, Year, of Birth; Sex;

848; 854; Rednose, Sarah (Mae); dau.; Nov. 1914; F.

849; 855; Redowl, Mabel; wdw.; July 1846[?]; F.[Birth year 1840 in 1926.]

850; 856; Redrobe, Fred; hsbd.; Oct. 1867; M.
851; 857; Redrobe, Nora; wife; Apr. 1869; F.
852; 858; Redrobe, Louis; son; Nov. 1892; M.

853; 859; Redrobe, Jasper; sgle.; July 1900; M.

854; 860; Redrobe, William; hsbd.; Aug. 1897; M.
855; 861; Redrobe, Alice; wife; May 1884[?]; F. [1907-19, birth year 1884-5. 1904 nee-Killsnight; 1905-6 Risingsun, 1907-19 Shell, 1920-27 Redrobe.]

856; 862; Redwater, Thaddeus; hsbd.; Mar. 1875; M.
Redwater, Martha; wife; ---; --. (Not enrolled)

857; 863; Redwater, Cecelia; Div.; Feb. 1872; F.

858; 864; Redwoman, Frank; hsbd.; Feb. 1889; M.
865; Redwoman, Ella; wife; Mar. 1900; F.
859; 866; Redwoman, Flossie Alice; dau.; Sept. 1911; F.
860; 867; Redwoman, Eugene; son; Feb. 1923; M.
868; Redwoman, Joe; son; May 1924; M.

861; 869; Redwoman, Manuel; hsbd.; July 1881; M.
862; 870; Redwoman, Olive; wife; Aug. 1891; F.
871; Redwoman, Edna; dau.; July 1926; F.

750; 872; Redwoman, Julia; dau.; July 1909; F. Mother, Mrs. Jno. Chubby [Same prev., # in 1926 Nicetalker, Clarice; s-dau; 1909; F. (s-dau John Chubby).]

863; 873; Ridgebear, Charles; fthr.; -- 1882; M.

864; 874; Ridgebear, Willis; hsbd.; July 1887; M.
865; 875; Ridgebear, Rilla; wife; Mar. 1898; F.
866; 876; Ridgebear, Bessie Agnes; dau.; Nov. 1918; F.
867; 877; Ridgebear, Carrie; dau.; Apr. 1921; F. [Katie in 1926.]
878; Ridgebear, Anna; dau.; Jan. 1927; F.

868; 879; Ridgewalker, Robert; hsbd.; June 1860[sic]; M.
869; 880; Ridgewalker, Ethel; wife; June 1870; F.
870; 881; Ridgewalker, Frank; son; Apr. 1908; M.

871; 882; Risingfire, Bessie; wdw.; Nov. 1856[?]; F.

Census of the **Northern Cheyenne** Indians of **Tongue River** Agency, **Mont.** on **June 30, 1927** taken by **C.B. Lohmiller**, Superintendent.

**Key:** Last Number; Present Number; Indian Name; English Name; Relationship; Month, Year, of Birth; Sex;

| | | |
|---|---|---|
| 872; | 883; | Risingsun, Oliver; hsbd.; May 1900; M. |
| 873; | 884; | Risingsun, Martha (Elizabeth); wife; Aug. 1907; F. [Flying] |
| | 885; | Risingsun, Teddy; son; Oct. 1926; M. |

| | | |
|---|---|---|
| 874; | 886; | Risingsun, Peter; hsbd.; Aug. 1887; M. |
| 875; | 887; | Risingsun, Bessie; wife; Nov. 1892; F. |
| 876; | 888; | Risingsun, Maude; dau.; Jun. 1913; F. [Jessie in 1926.] |
| ----; | 889; | Risingsun, Harry; son; Apr. 1921[?]; M. [Birth year 1918 #877 in 1926.] |
| 878; | 890; | Risingsun, Lyman; son; July 1923; M. |
| 879; | 891; | Risingsun, James; son; Dec. 1925; M. |

| | | |
|---|---|---|
| 880; | 892; | Risingsun, Philip; hsbd.; Aug. 1862; M. |
| 881; | 893; | Risingsun, Nora; wife; Jan. 1868; F. |
| 882; | 894; | Risingsun, John; son; June 1895; M. |
| 883; | 895; | Risingsun, William; son; June 1904[?]; M. [Birth year 1910 in 1926.] |
| 884; | 896; | Risingsun, Alice; dau.; Dec. 1909; F. |

| | | |
|---|---|---|
| 885; | 897; | Robinson, Nellie; wife; Oct. 1897; F. |
| | | Robinson, Major; hsbd.; ---;--. (Not enrolled) |
| 886; | 898; | Robinson, David; son; Aug. 1918; M. |
| 887; | 899; | Robinson, Cornelius Clay; son; June 1920; M. |
| ----; | 900; | Robinson, Eloise Elaine; dau.; Mar. 1922; F. [Previous #888, In 1926.] |

890; 901; Rockroads, Nora; wdw.; Dec. 1870[?]; F. [1904-18 birth year 1868. 1919-26 birth year 1983.]

| | | |
|---|---|---|
| 891; | 902; | Rockroads, Mack; hsbd.; Mar. 1893; M. |
| 892; | 903; | Rockroads, Nellie; wife; Nov. 1893; F. |
| 894; | 904; | Rockroads, Thomas; son; Apr. 1917; M. |

[1918 Census #902; Name is Lettie, female.]

896; 905; Rockroads, Mary; dau.; Feb. 1926; F.

897; 906; Romannose, Louis; hsbd.; Sept. 1882; M.
[Louis's Birth year 1882, 1904-13; 1862, 1914-20. 1882 in 1922-27.]

| | | |
|---|---|---|
| 898; | 907; | Romannose, Mary; wife; May 1890; F. |
| 899; | 908; | Romannose, George; son; July 1910; M. |
| 900; | 909; | Romannose, Blanche; dau.; Sept. 1914; F. [Helen in 1926.] |
| 901; | 910; | Romannose, Julia; dau.; Apr. 1916[?]; F. [Name May and birth year 1919 in 1926.] |
| 902; | 911; | Romannose, Willeatte; dau.; Oct. 1921; F. |
| 903; | 912; | Romannose, Montana; dau.; Nov. 1923; F. |

| | | |
|---|---|---|
| 905; | 913; | Rondeau, Antoine; hsbd.; Apr. 1887; M. |
| 906; | 914; | Rondeau, Louisa; wife; June 1889; F. [Birth year 1886 in 1926.] |

Census of the **Northern Cheyenne** Indians of **Tongue River** Agency, **Mont.** on **June 30, 1927** taken by **C.B. Lohmiller**, Superintendent.

**Key:** Last Number; Present Number; Indian Name; English Name; Relationship; Month, Year, of Birth; Sex;

| | | |
|---|---|---|
| 907; | 915; | Rondeau, Clara; dau.; Dec. 1912; F. |
| 809;[sic]916; | | Rondeau, Charles; son; May 1920; M. [Dau, Marie in 1920.] [#909 in 1926.] |

| | | |
|---|---|---|
| 910; | 917; | Rondeau, William; hsbd.; Mar. 1866[?]; M. [Birth year 1887 in 1926.] |
| 911; | 918; | Rondeau, Henry; son; Mar. 1911; M. |
| 912; | 919; | Rondeau, John R.; son; Mar. 1912[?]; M. [Born 1913] |

| | | |
|---|---|---|
| 913; | 920; | Roundstone, Flora; wife; Apr. 1888; F. [Twobulls] |
| | | Roundstone, Fred; hsbd.; ---;--. (Not enrolled) |
| 914; | 921; | Roundstone, Martin; son; Nov. 1911; M. |
| 915; | 922; | Roundstone, Sarah; dau.; May 1920; F. |
| | 923; | Roundstone, Paul; son; Apr. 1922; M. |
| | 924; | Roundstone, Ruth; dau.; July 1926; F. |

| | | |
|---|---|---|
| 916; | 925; | Rowland, Sally; wdw.; Sept. 1854; F. [Previously Annie-Anna.] |

| | | |
|---|---|---|
| 917; | 926; | Rowland, Clay; hsbd.; Feb. 1880; M. |
| | | Rowland, Jennie; wife; ---; --. (Note[sic] enrolled) |

| | | |
|---|---|---|
| 918; | 927; | Rowland, Thomas.; hsbd.; Dec. 1892; M. |
| 919; | 928; | Rowland, Daisy; wife; Mar. 1900; F. [Fightingbear, Ellen in 1924.] |
| 920; | 929; | Rowland, Lizzie; dau.; Nov. 1913; F. |
| 921; | 930; | Rowland, Lillian; dau.; Nov. 1916; F. |
| 922; | 931; | Rowland, Blanche; dau.; Aug. 1925; F. |

| | | |
|---|---|---|
| 923; | 932; | Rowland, Willis; hsbd.; Apr. 1862; M. |
| 924; | 933; | Rowland, Helen; wife; May 1868; F. [Sarah 1908-1919.] |
| 925; | 934; | Rowland, Grace; s-dau; Nov. 1914[?]; F. (Cora Littlewhiteman) |

[Shows adopted and birth year 1916 in 1926.]

| | | |
|---|---|---|
| 826; | 935; | Rowland, William; hsbd.; Sept. 1896; M. |
| | | Rowland, Elizabeth; wife; ---; --. (not enrolled) |
| 927; | 936; | Rowland, Chester Clay; son; June 1920; M. |
| 928; | 937; | Rowland, Wilma; dau.; Oct. 1924; F. |
| 929; | 938; | Rowland, Allen Edsel; son; Feb. 1926; M. |

| | | |
|---|---|---|
| 930; | 939; | Rowland, George; hsbd.; Jan. 1898; M. |
| 931; | 940; | Rowland, Frank; son; May 1924; M. |
| | 941; | Rowland, Carrie; dau.; Nov. 1926; F. |

| | | |
|---|---|---|
| [sic]; | 942; | Rowland, Jesse; sgle.; Feb. 1884; M. [Name Frank and previous #932 in 1926.] |

Census of the **Northern Cheyenne** Indians of **Tongue River** Agency, **Mont.** on **June 30, 1927** taken by **C.B. Lohmiller**, Superintendent.

**Key:** Last Number; Present Number; Indian Name; English Name; Relationship; Month, Year, of Birth; Sex;

| | | |
|---|---|---|
| 935; | 943; | Rowland, Joe; hsbd.; Dec. 1902[?]; M. [In 1926 #935; Jose; son; birth year 1900.] |
| 933; | 944; | Rowland, Zac; hsbd.; Dec. 1868; M. |
| 934; | 945; | Rowland, Edna; wife; Oct. 1876; F. |
| 936; | 946; | Rowland, Claude; sgle.; Apr. 1904; M. s-son Hinton Bigleg |
| 937; | 947; | Rowland, Benjamin; sgle.; July 1908; M. s-son Hinton Bigleg |
| 938; | 948; | Rowland, Benton; hsbd; Dec. 1898; M. |
| | | Rowland, Annie; wife; ---; --; (not enrolled) |
| | 949; | Rowland, Marie; dau.; May 1926; F. |
| 1220; | 950; | Rowland, Emma Bites; mthr.; July 1895[sic]; F. [Twomoons in 1926, Born 1893] |
| 939; | 951; | Rowland, Alice; dau.; July 1910[?]; F. [Birth year 1912 in 1926.] |
| 942; | 952; | Russell, John; fthr.; Sept. 1893; M. |
| 943; | 953; | Russell, Stella Mildred; dau.; Feb. 1916; F. |
| 944; | 954; | Russell, May; dau.; May 1924; F. |
| | 955; | Russell, Joseph Melvin; son; Dec. 1925; M. |
| | 956; | Russell, Inez Irma; dau.; Mar. 1927; F. |
| 945; | 957; | Russell, William; hsbd.; May 1873; M. |
| 946; | 958; | Russell, Sadie; wife; Apr. 1886; F. |
| 947; | 959; | Russell, Fred; son; July 1908; M. |
| 948; | 960; | Russell, Earl; son; Aug. 1915; M. |
| 949; | 961; | Russell, Mary; dau.; Sept. 1918; F. [Mildred in 1926.] |
| 950; | 962; | Russell, Clara; dau.; May 1922; F. |
| 951; | 963; | Russell, Herman; son May 1925; M. |
| 952; | 964; | Russell, Frank; hsbd.; Dec. 1898[?]; M. (Separated) |
| 953; | 965; | Russell, Jessie; wife; Oct. 1905[sic]; F. [Rockroads (Rhoda) all numbers past and present coincide, shows up in 1915, birth year 1913.] |
| | 966; | Russell, Ford; son; Mar. 1925; M. |
| 954; | 967; | Sansaver[sic], Lillian; dau.; July 1906; F. [Sansover mother was a Miles in 1915. Sansover in 1917 #741] [dau-Rhoda Seminole.] |
| 955; | 968; | Sanchez, Pauline; dau.; Mar. 1915; F. Children Cecelia Redfox. |
| 956; | 969; | Sanchez, Cecelia; dau.; Apr. 1922; F. |
| 957; | 970; | Sandcrane, Henry; husb.; Oct. 1889; M. |
| 958; | 971; | Sandcrane, Anne; wife; July 1895; F. |

37

Census of the **Northern Cheyenne** Indians of **Tongue River** Agency, **Mont.** on **June 30, 1927** taken by **C.B. Lohmiller**, Superintendent.

**Key:** Last Number; Present Number; Indian Name; English Name; Relationship; Month, Year, of Birth; Sex;

959; 972; Sandcrane, Emily May; dau.; Oct. 1920; F.
973; Sandcrane, Harry; son; June 1926; M.
960; 974; Sandcrane, John; hsbd.; Jan. 1873; M.
961; 975; Sandcrane, Ruth; wife; Dec. 1878; F.
962; 976; Sandcrane, Isabelle; dau.; May 1914; F.

963; 977; Scalpcane, August Paul; sgle.; Feb. 1906[sic]; M.
964; 978; Scalpcane, Otto; bro.; Nov. 1914[sic]; M.
965; 979; Scalpcane, Henry; bro.; Nov. 1919; M. [Rudolph in 1926.]

970; 980; Seminole, John; hsbd.; Feb. 1879[?]; M. [Birth year 1881 in 1926.]
971; 981; Seminole, Fred; son; Jun. 1915; M.

966; 982; Seminole, Dan; hsbd.; Aug. 1894; M.
967; 983; Seminole, Jennie; wife; July 1896; F.
984; Seminole, Anna; dau.; June 1920; F.
968; 985; Seminole, Margaret; dau.; Jan. 1922; F.
969; 986; Seminole, Alfred; son; Mar. 1924; M.

974; 987; Seminole, Josephine; mthr.; Apr. 1891; F.
975; 988; Seminole, Lawrence (Smoky); son; Dec. 1911; M. [g-son in 1926.]

976; 989; Seminole, Louis; fthr.; June 1884; M.
977; 990; Seminole, Delbert; son; June 1911; M.
978; 991; Seminole, Hannah; dau.; Nov. 1912[?]; F. [1917 Census Son Theodore. Birth year 1915 in 1926.]

813; 992; Seminole, Max; son; Nov. 1924; M. (son of Mary Redbird) [1926 #813 entry; Redbird, Maxine; g-g-son; 1924; M.] (g-g-son Joseph Tangledhornelk)

979; 993; Seminole Miles; hsbd.; 1869[?]; M. [Birth year 1875 in 1926.]
980; 994; Seminole, Rhoda; wife; Mar. 1892[?]; F. [Birth year in 1926 is 1879]
981; 995; Seminole, Lorraine; dau.; June 1916; F.
982; 996; Seminole, David; son; Apr. 1919; M.

983; 997; Sharpnose, Bessie; wdw.; July 1846; F.

984; 998; Sharpnose, Edward Chas.; hsbd.; May 1896[sic]; M.
422; 999; Sharpnose, Josephine; wife; Jun. 1902; F. [Hisbadhorses]

986; 1000; Shavedhead, Jean; wife; June 1901; F. [Swallow]
Shavedhead, Jeffrey; hsbd.; ---; --. (not enrolled)
987; 1001; Shavedhead, Charles; son; June 1924; M. [Same Previous #, Jeffrey, Jr. and birth year 1925 in 1926.]

Census of the **Northern Cheyenne** Indians of **Tongue River** Agency, **Mont.** on **June 30, 1927** taken by **C.B. Lohmiller**, Superintendent.

**Key:** Last Number; Present Number; Indian Name; English Name; Relationship; Month, Year, of Birth; Sex;

    1002;        Shavedhead, Anna Marjorie; dau.; Oct. 1926; F.

988; 1003;       Shavedhead, Mary; wdw.; June 1865; F.

989; 1004;       Shavedhead, James; hsbd.; Nov. 1899; M.
990; 1005;       Shavedhead, Alice; wife; Feb. 1907[?]; F. [Medicineflying]
991; 1006;       Shavedhead, Anna; dau; Sept. 1925; F. [Hyacinth in 1926.]

992; 1007;       Shell, Joseph; hsbd.; Feb. 1881; M.
993; 1008;       Shell, Julia; wife; Sept. 1901[?]; F. [Previous #530 in 1906, censuses 1906-19, wife Alice [Risingsun] Shell, birth year 1885.] [Julia starts census 1920.]

995; 1009;       Shell, Minnie; Wdw.; June 1882[?]; F. [Killsnight] [Birth year 1892 in 1926.]
996; 1010;       Shell, Elsie; dau; Jan. 1926; F.

997; 1011;       Shepherd, Mollie; wife; Apr. 1895; F.
                   Shepherd, Clarence; hsbd.; ---; --. (Not enrolled)

998; 1012;       Shortsioux, Mary; orp.; June 1914; F. [dau Maggie Longears.]

1029; 1013;     Sherman, Ethel Parker; wife; May 1883; F.
                   Sherman, George; hsbd.; ---; --. (Not enrolled)
1135; 1014;     Sherman, Frances; dau.; Dec. 1908; F.
1130; 1015;     Sherman, George Jr.; son; Oct. 1911; M.
1131; 1016;     Sherman, Otto; son; June 1913; M.
1132; 1017;     Sherman, Wretha; dau.; Aug. 1915; F.
1133; 1018;     Sherman, Carl; son; Dec. 1918; M.
1134; 1019;     Sherman, Clarence Oliver; son; July 1922; M.

999; 1020;       Shoulderblade, Benedict; hsbd.; Sept. 1874; M.

1005; 1021;     Shoulderblade, Fred; hsbd.; Oct. 1861; M.
1007; 1022;     Shoulderblade, Richard; son; Aug. 1911; M.

1008; 1023;     Shoulderblade, Pius; hsbd.; May 1889; M.
1009; 1024;     Shoulderblade, Ethel; wife; Aug. 1893; F.
1010; 1025;     Shoulderblade, Thomas; son; Oct. 1915; M.
1011; 1026;     Shoulderblade, Francis; son; Mar. 1917; M. [1917 Census William]
1012; 1027;     Shoulderblade, Wendel; son; Aug. 1920; M.
1013; 1028;     Shoulderblade, Everett John; son; Jun. 1923; M.

1015; 1029;     Silloway, Veta (Burns); wife; Apr. 1904; F.
                   Silloway, Lloyd; hsbd.; ---; --. (Not enrolled)

Census of the **Northern Cheyenne** Indians of **Tongue River** Agency, **Mont.** on **June 30, 1927** taken by **C.B. Lohmiller**, Superintendent.

**Key:** Last Number; Present Number; Indian Name; English Name; Relationship; Month, Year, of Birth; Sex;

1016; 1030; Sioux, Thomas; hsbd.; Nov. 1870; M.
1018; 1031; Sioux, Henry; s-son; June 1911; M. [Divesbackwards; Name Jacob; and listed as g-son; in 1926.]

1019; 1032; Sittingman, Charles; hsbd.; Oct. 1866[sic]; M. [1904-18 birth 1868.]
1020; 1033; Sittingman, Lucy; wife; May 1866[sic]; F. [Born 1868.]

1021; 1034; Sittingman, Edward; sgle.; June 1900; M. [Edwin in 1926.]

1022; 1035; Small, Josephine; wife; Feb. 1892; F.
            Small, Thomas; hsbd.; ---; --. (Not enrolled)
1023; 1036; Small, Victor; son; Aug. 1912; M.
1024; 1037; Small, Edward; son; Nov. 1913; M.
1025; 1038; Small, Max Joe; son; Apr. 1915; M.
       1039; Small, Ivan; son; Apr. 1920; M.
       1040; Small, Thomas; son; Dec. 1921; M.
1026; 1041; Small, Horace; son; July 1923; M.
1027; 1042; Small, Melvin; son; Feb. 1924; M.
       1043; Small, Worth; son; Feb. 1927; M.

1028; 1044; Smith, John; hsbd.; June 1875; M. [Birth year 1878 in 1926.]
1029; 1045; Smith, Blanche; wife; Mar. 1880; F. [Birth year 1883 in 1926.]

1030; 1046; Soldierwolf, John; hsbd.; Apr. 1883; M.
1031; 1047; Soldierwolf, Mary; wife; Apr. 1888; F.
1032; 1048; Soldierwolf, Thos. Chas.; son; June 1910; M.
1033; 1049; Soldierwolf, Aurora; dau.; Jan. 1915; F.
1034; 1050; Soldierwolf, Lucy; dau.; Oct. 1917; F.
1035; 1051; Soldierwolf, Kenneth; son; July 1920; M.
1036; 1052; Soldierwolf, Katherine; dau.; May 1922; F.

1038; 1053; Spang, Alfonso; hsbd.; Jan. 1887; M.
            Spang, Margie; wife; ---; --. (Not enrolled)

1044; 1054; Spang, Alban; sgle.; Sept. 1892; M.

1051; 1055; Spang, Deyo; hsbd.; Dec. 1888; M.
            Spang, Lucille; wife; ---; --. (Not enrolled)
1052; 1056; Spang, Bruce Spencer; son; June 1924; M.
       1057; Spang, Dale Cooper; son; July 1926; M.

1050; 1058; Spang, James; div.; July 1899; M.

1039; 1059; Spang, Lucy; wife; May 1869; F.
            Spang, A.D.; hsb.; ---; --. (Not enrolled)

Census of the **Northern Cheyenne** Indians of **Tongue River** Agency, **Mont.** on **June 30, 1927** taken by **C.B. Lohmiller**, Superintendent.

**Key:** Last Number; Present Number; Indian Name; English Name; Relationship; Month, Year, of Birth; Sex;

| | |
|---|---|
| 1042; 1060; | Spang, Sarah; dau.; Aug. 1904; F. |
| 1043; 1061; | Spang, Harriet; sgle.; Oct. 1905; F. [Birth 1906.] |
| 1040; 1062; | Spang, Edith; dau.; Dec. 1909; F. |
| 1041; 1063; | Spang, Cash; son; Oct. 1911; M. |

| | |
|---|---|
| 1046; 1064; | Spang, Roy; husb; Sept. 1895; M. |
| 1047; 1065; | Spang, Jessie; wife; May 1907; F. |
| 1048; 1066; | Spang, Regina Susanna; dau.; June 1922; F. [Regina Rosetta in 1926.] |
| 1049; 1067; | Spang, Lyman; son; Aug. 1923; M. |

| | |
|---|---|
| 1045; 1068; | Spang, Wilfred; hsbd.; May 1901; M. |
| 1416; 1069; | Spang, Alice Yellowhorse; wife; June 1908; F. |

| | |
|---|---|
| 1053; 1070; | Sponge, Alfred; hsbd.; July 1996[sic]; M. |
| 1054; 1071; | Sponge, Josie; wife; Sept. 1901; F. [Shoulderblade] [1922 was #958, Scott.] |

| | |
|---|---|
| 1055; 1072; | Sponge, Oliver; hsbd.; Mar. 1898; M. |
| 1056; 1073; | Sponge, Clara; wife; May 1905; F. [Tangleyellowhair] |

1058; 1074; Spottedblackbird, Lee; hsbd.; June 1859; M. [Birth year 1854 in 1926.]
[#1074, Didn't pickup a first name until 1915 name, Lee; or Leo.]
1059; 1075; Spottedblackbird, Clara; wife; Oct. 1874; F. [Birth year 1854 in 1926.]

| | |
|---|---|
| 1060; 1076; | Spottedelk, Charles; fthr.; Mar. 1863[?]; M. |
| 1061; 1077; | Spottedelk, August; son; July 1897; M. |

1062; 1078; Spottedelk, Alex; wdr.; Nov. 1900; M.

| | |
|---|---|
| 1065; 1079; | Spottedhawk, Hugh; hsbd.; Apr. 1867; M. |
| 1066; 1080; | Spottedhawk, Ruth; niece; Dec. 1907; F. [Medicinebird] |

| | |
|---|---|
| 1067; 1081; | Spottedwolf, Charles; hsbd.; Oct. 1892; M. |
| 1068; 1082; | Spottedwolf, Lena; wife; Sept. 1892; F. |
| 1069; 1083; | Spottedwolf, Julia Eva; dau; Apr. 1913; F. |
| 1070; 1084; | Spottedwolf, Piney; dau.; Sept. 1921; F. |
| 1085; | Spottedwolf, John; Oct. 1923; M. |
| 1086; | Spottedwolf, Earl; July 1926; M. |

| | |
|---|---|
| 1071; 1087; | Spottedwolf, Patrick; hsbd.; Nov. 1887; M. |
| 1072; 1088; | Spottedwolf, Jean; wife; Oct. 1901; F. |
| 1073; 1089; | Spottedwolf, Ruby; dau.; Sept. 1920; F. |
| 1074; 1090; | Spottedwolf, Phyllis; dau.; Oct. 1923; F. |
| 1075; 1091; | Spottedwolf, Eugene; son; Aug. 1925; M. |

Census of the **Northern Cheyenne** Indians of **Tongue River** Agency, **Mont.** on **June 30, 1927** taken by **C.B. Lohmiller**, Superintendent.

**Key:** Last Number; Present Number; Indian Name; English Name; Relationship; Month, Year, of Birth; Sex;

1077; 1092;    Standingelk, Nina; sgle.; June 1907; F.
1078; 1093;    Standingelk, Frank; hsbd.; June 1874; M.
1079; 1094;    Standingelk, Fannie; wife; Apr. 1878; F.
1081; 1095;    Standingelk, George; son; Apr. 1910[sic]; M.
1082; 1096;    Standingelk, Flora; dau.; Apr. 1921; F.

1083; 1097;    Standingelk, Francis; hsbd.; Apr. 1901; M.
      1098;    Standingelk, Annie; wife; May 1907; F.
      1099;    Standingelk, Roy; son; Aug. 1926; M.

1084; 1100;    Standingelk, Henry; wdr.; June 1891; M.

1085; 1101;    Standingelk, Lockwood; wdr.; June 1890; M.

1086; 1102;    Standingelk, Robert B.; hsbd.; Oct. 1870; M.
1087; 1103;    Standingelk, Sally; wife; Sept. 1895; F.
1088; 1104;    Standingelk, Ella; dau.; Dec. 1918; F.
      1105;    Standingelk, (Clara) Jennie; dau.; May 5, 1927; F.

1090; 1106;    Standingelk, Alex; hsbd.; Mar. 1896; M.
1091; 1107;    Standingelk, Nora; wife; July 1903; F.
1092; 1108;    Standingelk, Geneva; dau.; Mar. 1922; F.
1093; 1109;    Standingelk, Margaret; dau.; Nov. 1924; F.

1094; 1110;    Standsintimber, John; hsbd.; Mar. 1886; M.
1095; 1111;    Standsintimber, Josie; wife; Mar. 1898; F.
1096; 1112;    Standsintimber, Josephine; dau.; June 1920; F.
1097; 1113;    Standsintimber, John Jr.; son; Oct.1921; M.

121; 1114;    Star, May Blackree; sgle.; Dec.1904; F. [Minnie in 1926.]

1099; 1115;    Standsout, Sallie; wdw.; Aug. 1847; F.

1100; 1116;    Starvingbear, James; fthr; Apr. 1876; M.
1102; 1117;    Starvingbear, Mary; dau.; Mar. 1907; F. [Lottie in 1926.]
1101; 1118;    Starvingbear, Jack; son; Feb. 1914; M. [Rosco in 1926.]

1103; 1119;    Strangeowl, John; hsbd.; Sept. 1872[?]; M. [Birth year 1876 in 1926.]
1104; 1120;    Strangeowl, Gertie; wife; Nov. 1868; F.
1105; 1121;    Strangeowl, Mary; Dau.; Feb. 1909; F.

1106; 1122;    Strangeowl, James; sgle; June 1904; M.

1107; 1123;    Stumphorn, Frank; hsbd.; Oct. 1843; M.
1108; 1124;    Stumphorn, Annie; wife; July 1855; F. [Shortsioux, Wdw.]

Census of the **Northern Cheyenne** Indians of **Tongue River** Agency, **Mont.** on **June 30, 1927** taken by **C.B. Lohmiller**, Superintendent.

**Key:** Last Number; Present Number; Indian Name; English Name; Relationship; Month, Year, of Birth; Sex;

1110; 1125; Stumphorn, Anna.; wdw.; Sept. 1851[sic]; F. [Birth year 1842.]

1111; 1126; Sunbear, John; wdr.; July 1843[sic]; M. [1904-15 Birth year 1856. 1916-27 Birth year 1843.]

1112; 1127; Sunbear, Michael; hsbd.; -- 1891; M.
　　　　　　Sunbear, ---; wife; --; --. (not enrolled)
1128;　　　Sunbear, Herman; son; Aug. 1923; M.
1113; 1129; Sunbear, Deyo; son; -- 1924; M.

1114; 1130; Sunroads, David; hsbd.; Sept. 1881; M.
1115; 1131; Sunroads, Lizzie; wife; Mar. 1883; F.

1116; 1132; Sunroads, John; hsbd.; July 1843; M.
1117; 1133; Sunroads, Lena; wife; Mar. 1845; F.

1118; 1134; Swallow, William; hsbd.; Feb. 1874; M. [Birth year 1873-4.] [William #1134; 1904-15 born 1873, 1916-17 born 1897, 1918-26 born 1863.]
1119; 1135; Swallow, Gertrude; wife; Mar. 1896; F. [Redbreath]
1120; 1136; Swallow, Mary; dau.; May 1907; F. [Previously name Anne.]
　816; 1137; Percy Redbreath (Walter); son; Nov. 1919[?]; M.
[Birth year 1922 in 1926.]

1121; 1138; Swallow, Edward; sgle.; Mar. 1902; M.

　　1139; Swallow, Oliver; sgle.; Apr. 1899; M.

1122; 1140; Sweetmedicine, David; hsbd.; Mar. 1863[sic]; M. [Birth year 1868]
1123; 1141; Sweetmedicine, Clara; wife; Dec. 1870; F.
1124; 1142; Sweetmedicine, Jacob; son; Apr. 1894; M.

1125; 1143; Sweetmedicine, Joseph; sgle.; Dec. 1898; M.

1027; 1144; Sweetmedicine, Ellen; wife; July 1897; F. former wife of Wm. Sweetmedicine.

1126; 1145; Sweetmedicine, William; hsbd.; -- 1889; M.

1128; 1146; Sweetmedicine, Alta; dau.; -- 1913[sic]; F. [1915-Son, Thomas; M.]

1142; 1147; Tallbull, Albert; sgle.; Apr. 1906; M. [Birth year 1902 in 1926.]

1136; 1148; Tallbull, Charles; hsbd.; Oct. 1887; M.
1137; 1149; Tallbull, Mary; wife; May 1893; F.
1138; 1150; Tallbull, Joseph; son; June 1915; M.

43

Census of the __Northern Cheyenne__ Indians of __Tongue River__ Agency, __Mont.__ on __June 30, 1927__ taken by __C.B. Lohmiller__, Superintendent.

**Key:** Last Number; Present Number; Indian Name; English Name; Relationship; Month, Year, of Birth; Sex;

1139; 1151;   Tallbull, Henry; son; Dec. 1917; M.
1140; 1152;   Tallbull, William; son; Jan. 1921; M.
1141; 1153;   Tallbull, Nelson; son; Oct. 1923; M.
      1154;   Tallbull, Cecil Russell; son; Jan. 1927; M.

1143; 1155;   Tallbull, Nora; wdw.; June 1858[sic]; F.

1144; 1156;   Tallwhiteman, Jasper; fthr.; July 1893[?]; M. [Birth year 1891 in 1926.]
1145; 1157;   Tallwhiteman, John E.; son; Oct. 1914; M.
1146; 1158;   Tallwhiteman, Agnes; dau.; May 1924; F. [1925 census Dan son, M., same #. Name Rilla in 1926.]

1148; 1159;   Tallwhiteman, John; hsbd.; Apr. 1886; M.
1149; 1160;   Tallwhiteman, Eleanor; wife; Mar. 1898; F.
1150; 1161;   Tallwhiteman, Clarence; son; July 1912; M.
1151; 1162;   Tallwhiteman, Florence; dau.; May 1914; F.
1152; 1163;   Tallwhiteman, Jasper; son; July 1916; M.
1153; 1164;   Tallwhiteman, Alice; dau.; May 1920; F.
1154; 1165;   Tallwhiteman, Tug; son.; June 1922; M.
1155; 1166;   Tallwhiteman, Agnes; dau.; July 1925; F.

1156; 1167;   Tallwhiteman, Joseph; sgle.; June 1847; M.

1157; 1168;   Tallwhiteman, Patrick; hsbd.; June 1888; M.
1158; 1169;   Tallwhiteman, Florence; wife; July 1900; F.
1159; 1170;   Tallwhiteman, Alice; dau.; Jan. 1916; F.
1160; 1171;   Tallwhiteman, Laura; dau.; June 1923; F.

1162; 1172;   Tangledhornelk, Nellie; wdw.; -- 1853; F. [1904-18 no "d" in last name.]

1163; 1173;   Tangledyellowhair, Chas.; hsbd.; Feb. 1892; M. [1904-18 no "d" in last name.]
1164; 1174;   Tangledyellowhair, Georgia Marion; wife; Sept. 1891; F. [Talks]
1165; 1175;   Tangledyellowhair, Roberta; dau.; Sept.1924; F.
      1176;   Tangledyellowhair, Bert; son; Oct. 1926; M.

1167; 1177;   Tangledyellowhair, David; fthr.; June 1898[?]; M. [1904-18 no "d" in last name. Birth year 1894 in 1926.]
1168; 1178;   Tangledyellowhair, Clara; dau.; Oct. 1919; F.
1169; 1179;   Tangledyellowhair, Winona; dau.; Jan. 1922; F.

1170; 1180;   Tangledyellowhair, James; hsbd.; Jan. 1869; M. [1904-18 no "d" in last name.]

Census of the **Northern Cheyenne** Indians of **Tongue River** Agency, **Mont.** on **June 30, 1927** taken by **C.B. Lohmiller**, Superintendent.

**Key:** Last Number; Present Number; Indian Name; English Name; Relationship; Month, Year, of Birth; Sex;

1171; 1181;   Tangledyellowhair, Minnie; wife; Dec. 1870[?]; F. [Birth year 1873 in 1926.]

1172; 1182;   Tangledyellowhair, Josie; wdw.; Mar. 1848[?]; M. [1904-18 no "d" in last name. Birth year 1846 in 1926.]

1174;[sic]1183;   Teeth, Charles; hsbd.; Mar. 1863[?]; M. [Birth year 1865 in 1926.]
1174; 1184;   Teeth, Sallie; wife; Apr. 1873; F.

1175; 1185;   Teeth, John; hsbd.; May 1889; M.
1176; 1186;   Teeth, Edith; wife; Oct. 1902; F.
1177; 1187;   Teeth, Franklin; son; Oct. 1909; M.
1179; 1188;   Teeth, Earl; son; Jun. 1916; M.
1180; 1189;   Teeth, Montana; dau.; Apr. 1922; F.
1181; 1190;   Teeth, Elsie; dau.; Sept. 1925; F.

1186; 1191;   Threefingers, John; hsbd.; Mar. 1862[?]; M. [Birth year 1878[?] in 1926. #1191-Various ages starting 1904, in 1913-1920 birth year 1868 changes again in 1922.]
1187; 1192;   Threefingers, Pansy; wife; July 1876[?]; F. [Birth year 1878 in 1926.]

1188; 1193;   Threefingers, William; hsbd.; Sept. 1901; M.
1189; 1194;   Threefingers, Ruth Maude; wife; Oct. 1907; F. [Medicinebird]

1190; 1195;   Turkeylegs, John; hsbd.; July 1859; M.
1191; 1196;   Turkeylegs, Lydia; wife; Aug. 1874; F.
1192; 1197;   Turkeylegs, Lawence; son; July 1906; M. [Name James in 1926.]

1198; 1198;   Twin, Louis James; hsbd.; Dec. 1887[?]; M. [Birth year 1889 in 1926.]
1199; 1199;   Twin, Bessie; wife; Mar. 1886; F.
1200; 1200;   Twin, Margaret; dau.; Apr. 1918; F.
1201; 1201;   Twin, Edna; Dau.; July 1924; F.

1202; 1202;   Twobirds, Peter; hsbd.; May 1878; M.
1203; 1203;   Twobirds, Leonora[sic]; wife; July 1872; F.
1206; 1204;   Twobirds, Jacob; son; Jan. 1901; M.
1205; 1205;   Twobirds, Walter; son; Aug. 1908[?]; M.

1207; 1206;   Twobulls, Martin; hsbd.; July 1891; M.
1208; 1207;   Twobulls, Eleanor; wife; May 1900; F.
1209; 1208;   Twobulls, William; son; Sept. 1920; M.

1210; 1209;   Twobulls, Kate; wdw.; Aug. 1865; F.

1211; 1210;   Twofeathers, John; hsbd.; Apr. 1857; M. [1904-22 Twofeathers.]

Census of the **Northern Cheyenne** Indians of **Tongue River** Agency, **Mont.** on **June 30, 1927** taken by **C.B. Lohmiller**, Superintendent.

**Key:** Last Number; Present Number; Indian Name; English Name; Relationship; Month, Year, of Birth; Sex;

| | | |
|---|---|---|
| 1212; 1211; | Twofeathers, Clara; wife; May 1870; F. | |
| 1213; 1212; | Twofeathers, Ethel; dau.; Sept. 1908; F. | |
| | | |
| 1214; 1213; | Twomoons, Bert; fthr.; Nov.1887; M. | |
| 1215; 1214; | Twomoons, Margaret; wife; Aug. 1892; F. [Americanhorse] | |
| 1216; 1215; | Twomoons, George; son; Jan. 1920; M. | |
| 1216; | Twomoons, Austin; son; Feb. 1927; M. | |
| | | |
| 1217; 1217; | Twomoons, John; wdr.; Apr. 1855; M. | |
| | | |
| 1219; 1218; | Twommons[sic], William; hsbd.; May 1884; M. | |
| | | |
| 1221; 1219; | Walkingbear, Charles; hsbd.; May 1876; M. | |
| 1222; 1220; | Walkingbear, Jennie; wife; Spet[sic]. 1872; F. | |
| | | |
| 1223; 1221; | Walkingbear, David; hsbd.; June 1897; M. (Separated) | |
| | | |
| 1224; 1222; | Walkingbear, Mannie; wife; Aug. 1897; F. (Separated) | |
| | | |
| 1225; 1223; | Walkingbird, Jane; mthr.; Mar. 1867; F. | |
| | | |
| 1226; 1224; | Walkinghorse, John; hsbd.; Aug. 1857; M. | |
| 1227; 1225; | Walkinghorse, Olive; wife; Sept. 1866; F. | |
| | | |
| 1228; 1226; | Walksalong, Hugh; fthr.; Apr. 1885[sic]; M. | |
| 1230; 1227; | Walksalong, Flora; dau.; May 1915; F. [Previous census 1916-19, Fred son.] | |
| 1231; 1228; | Walksalong, Eugenia; dau.; June 1920; F. | |
| | | |
| 1232; 1229; | Walkseasy, Nora; wdw.; Mar. 1864; F. | |
| | | |
| 1233; 1230; | Walkslast, Richard; hsbd.; Mar. 1856; M. | |
| 1234; 1231; | Walkslast, Anne; wife; July 1862[?]; F. [Birth year 1859, 1904-22.] | |
| 1235; 1232; | Walkslast, Frank; g-son; Mar. 1908; M. | |
| | | |
| 1242; 1233; | Walkslast, James; sgle.; Sept. 1905; M. [Clement in 1926.] | |
| | | |
| 1236; 1234; | Walksnice, Adolph; hsbd.; Apr. 1878; M. | |
| 1237; 1235; | Walksnice, Flora; wife; Oct. 1884; F. | |
| 1238; 1236; | Walksnice, Dick; son; May 1911; M. | |
| | | |
| 1239; 1237; | Walksnice, John; hsbd.; Sept. 1905; M. | |
| 1240; 1238; | Walksnice, Mary; wife; Jan. 1903; F. [Crookednose] | |
| 1239; | Walksnice, Agnes; dau.; Aug. 1926; F. | |

Census of the **Northern Cheyenne** Indians of **Tongue River** Agency, **Mont.** on **June 30, 1927** taken by **C.B. Lohmiller**, Superintendent.

**Key:** Last Number; Present Number; Indian Name; English Name; Relationship; Month, Year, of Birth; Sex;

265; 1240;   Wallowing, Rufus; hsbd.; Nov. 1887[?]; M. (Dustybuffalo) [Rollingbull] Name changed to "Wallowing" see 57750-26. [First name Rutherford misspelled starting in 1918.]
266; 1241;   Wallowing, Stella; wife; July 1885; F.

1241; 1242;   Walters, George; hsb.; Sept. 1897; M.
             Walters, Lillian Cook; wife; ---; --. (not enrolled)

1243; 1243;   Wanderingmedicine, Wm.; sgle.; Apr. 1869[?]; M. [Birth year 1856 in 1926.]

1201; 1244;   Waters[sic], Frank; husb.; 1875; M. [1904-20, name is Water. Birth year 1877 in 1926.]
             Waters, Sarah; wife; --; --. (Not enrolled)
1377; 1245;   Waters, Joseph; a-son[sic]; July 1922; M. [1346; 1377; Woodenlegs, Martin; son; 1922; in 1926.]

1245; 1246;   Weaselbear, Frank; hsbd.; Sept. 1861; M.
1246; 1247;   Weaselbear, Mary; wife; Feb. 1870; F.
1247; 1248;   Weaselbear, Sarah; dau.; June 1913; F.

1248; 1249;   Weaselbear, Hugh; fthr.; -- 1889; M.
1249; 1250;   Weaselbear, Andrew; son; Apr. 1915; M.
1250; 1251;   Weaselbear, Busby; son; July 1922; M.

1251; 1252;   Weaselbear, Cordelia; dau.; May 1917; F. Mrs. Henry Littlewhiteman, Mother [Clarice in 1926.]

1252; 1253;   Whirlwind, Thomas; div.; Oct. 1876; M. (Divorced)

1253; 1254;   Whirlwind, Rose; div.; Dec. 1892; F. (Divorced)

1254; 1255;   Whistlingelk, Charles; hsbd.; Jan. 1876; M.
1255; 1256;   Whistlingelk, Josie; wife; June 1884; F. [1904-20, birth year 1884. Birth year 1874 in 1926.]
1256; 1257;   Whistlingelk, Blanche Alice ; dau.; July 1909; F.
1257; 1258;   Whistlingelk, Harriet Julia; dau.; June 1913; F. [1913-22 son, Henry, M.]
1258; 1259;   Whistlingelk, Alfred; son; Jan. 1917; M.
1258;[sic]1260;   Whistlingelk, Lois; dau.; Dec. 1926; F.

1259; 1261;   Whistlingelk, John; hsbd.; Apr. 1904; M.
1260; 1262;   Whistlingelk, Flora; wife; May 1906; F. [Redrobe]
       1263;   Whistlingelk, May; dau.; Mar. 1926; F.

1261; 1264;   White, Stamper; hsbd.; Apr. 1898; M.

Census of the **Northern Cheyenne** Indians of **Tongue River** Agency, **Mont.** on **June 30, 1927** taken by **C.B. Lohmiller**, Superintendent.

Key: Last Number; Present Number; Indian Name; English Name; Relationship; Month, Year, of Birth; Sex;

1262; 1265;  White, Lottie; wife; Mar. 1903; F. [Rowland]
1263; 1266;  White, Pearl; dau.; Aug. 1923; F.
1267;  White, Ben; son; Dec. 1926; M.

1265; 1268;  Whitebear, Joseph; hsbd.; -- 1896; M.

1268; 1269;  Whitebird, Frank; sgle.; Feb. 1902; M.

1269; 1270;  Whitebird, Lena; wdw.; Oct. 1855; F. [1904-13, birth year 1855; 1914-23 has birth year as 1885. Corrected in 1924 to 1855. Husband George was born approximately 1852.]

1270; 1271;  Whitebuffalo, John; hsbd.; Mar. 1871; M.
1271; 1272;  Whitebuffalo, Ella; wife; Aug. 1867; F.

1272; 1273;  Whitecrane, Leo; hsbd.; June 1895; M.
1273; 1274;  Whitecrane, Ella; wife; July 1901; F. [Littlebird]
1275; 1275;  Whitecrane, Victor; son; June 1924; M.
1276;  Whitecrane, Elmer; son; Dec. 1926; M.

1276; 1277;  Whitecrane, Charles; wdr.; Apr. 1876; M.

1277; 1278;  Whitedirt, Arthur; hsbd.; Apr. 1875; M.
1278; 1279;  Whitedirt, Maggie; wife; June 1875[sic]; F. [1905-1919 birth year 1872.]
1279; 1280;  Whitedirt, Charlie; son; June 1905; M.
1280; 1281;  Whitedirt, Jennie; dau.; Feb. 1911; F.

1281; 1282;  Whitefrog, Nellie; wdw.; May 1861; F.

1283; 1283;  Whitehawk, Emma; wdw.; Sept. 1883; F.
1284; 1284;  Whitehawk, Verlie; dau.; Mar. 1918; F.

1285; 1285;  Whitehawk, Mary; wdw.; July 1858[sic]; F. [1904-18 birth year 1838.]

1286; 1286;  Whitehawk, Charles Jno.; hsbd.; Apr. 1899[?]; M. [1905-09 Name is Chase. Years 1905-13 birth year 1898. 1914-16 birth year 1889.]
1287; 1287;  Whitehawk, Ida; wife; June 1898; F.
1288; 1288;  Whitehawk, Mary; dau.; Sept. 1919; F.
1289; 1289;  Whitehawk, Marguerite; dau.; Nov. 1920; F. [Same #1251 John, 1922-25, son, M.; Same prev., #1289 Emma; dau; 1922 in 1926.]

1290; 1290;  Whitehorse, George; wdr.; Feb. 1850; M.

1291; 1291;  Whitemoon, George; sgle.; Nov.1854; M. [Birth year 1851 in 1926.]

48

Census of the **Northern Cheyenne** Indians of **Tongue River** Agency, **Mont.** on **June 30, 1927** taken by **C.B. Lohmiller**, Superintendent.

Key: Last Number; Present Number; Indian Name; English Name; Relationship; Month, Year, of Birth; Sex;

| | |
|---|---|
| 1292; 1292; | Whitemoon, Hugh; div.; Apr. 1881; M. |
| 1293; 1293; | Whiteshirt, Jean; mthr.; July 1899; F. |
| 1294; 1294; | Whiteshirt, Caroline; dau.; Nov. 1921; F. [Name Alice in 1926.] |
| 1296; 1295; | Whiteshirt, Dottie; dau.; Apr. 1925; F. |
| 1297; 1296; | Whitewolf, Frank; hsbd.; Mar. 1847; M. |
| 1298; 1297; | Whitewolf, Julia; wife; July 1854; F. |
| 1299; 1298; | Whitewolf, Anne Lucy; dau.; Apr. 1904; F. |
| 1300; 1299; | Whitewolf, Charles Isadore; hsbd.; Aug. 1890; M. [Birth year 1887 in 1926.] |
| 1301; 1300; | Whitewolf, Belle; wife; May 1902; F. |
| 1302; 1301; | Whitewolf, Joseph; son; Mar. 1921; M. |
| 1302; | Whitewolf, George; son; June 1923; M. |
| 1304; 1303; | Whitewolf, Maude Shields; wife; Oct. 1891; F. |
| | Whitewolf, Grover; hsbd.; --; --. (Not enrolled) |
| 1305; 1304; | Whitewolf, Everett; son; Mar. 1914; M. |
| 1306; 1305; | Whitewolf, Carrie; dau.; June1916; F. [Philip son, M., 1920 census.] |
| 1307; 1306; | Whitewolf, Wilson; son; May 1919[?]; M. [1919-20 birth year 1918.] |
| 1308; 1307; | Whitewolf, Thomas; son; Nov. 1921; M. |
| 1309; 1308; | Whitewolf, Martin Owen; son; Feb. 1923; M. |
| 1310; 1309; | Whitewolf, Calvin Mexican; son; Jan. 1925; M. [Clara dau, F., 1925 census, same #.] |
| 1311; 1310; | Wildhog, Bird; hsbd.; June 1869; M. |
| 1312; 1311; | Wildhog, Lydia; wife; Oct. 1872; F. |
| 1317; 1312; | Wildhog, Alice Viola; dau.; Jan. 1907[?]; F. [Birth year 1901 in 1926.] |
| 1313; 1313; | Wildhog, Willie; son; July 1910; M. |
| 1314; 1314; | Wildhog, Julia; dau.; June 1913; F. [Susie in 1926.] |
| 1315; 1315; | Wildhog, Anne; dau.; Sept. 1895; F. |
| 1316; 1316; | Wildhog, John; son; Oct. 1898; M. |
| 1318; 1317; | Wildhog, Vida[sic]; sgle.; Mar. 1905[?]; F. [Note: Viola in 1906-25. Shows as 2 months old in 1906 yet majority of census years show the year of birth as 1907.] |
| 1319; 1318; | Wildhog, Mary Anne; mthr.; Dec. 1903; F. [Birth date 1905 in 1926.] |
| 1320; 1319; | Wildhog, Opal; dau.; Jan. 1925; F. |
| 1321; 1320; | Wilson, Martha; wife; May 1894; F. |
| | Wilson, James; hsbd.; --; --. (Not enrolled) |
| 1323; 1321; | Wilson, Arthur; son; Sept. 1918; M. [1919 name James Jr.] |

Census of the **Northern Cheyenne** Indians of **Tongue River** Agency, **Mont.** on **June 30, 1927** taken by **C.B. Lohmiller**, Superintendent.

**Key:** Last Number; Present Number; Indian Name; English Name; Relationship; Month, Year, of Birth; Sex;

1322; 1322; Wilson, Esther Martha; dau.; Aug. 1920; F.
1324;[sic]1323; Wilson, Alice; dau.; July 1921; F. [#1324 in 1926 was Josephine.]
1324; Wilson, Florence; dau.; Sept. 1922; F.
[sic]; 1325; Wilson, Josephine; dau.; Nov. 1924; F.
1326; Wilson, James Jr.; son; Dec. 1926; M.

1325; 1327; Wolf, William; hsbd.; Apr. 1872; M.
1326; 1328; Wolf, Rosa; wife; May 1877; F. [nee Crow / Bigbeaver.]
1329; 1329; Wolf, Fannie Lucy; dau.; Mar. 1916; F.

1330; 1330; Wolfblack, Dallas; hsbd.; Apr. 1882[?]; M. [1904-14 birth year 1885; 1915-23, 1872; 1924-27, 1882.]
1332; 1231; Wolfblack, Rose; wife; June 1890; F. [Whitemoon]
1334; 1332; Wolfblack, Gladys; dau.; Dec. 1915; F.
1335; 1333; Wolfblack, Oran; son; Apr. 1924; M.
1336; 1334; Wolfblack, Harry; son; Jan. 1926; M.

1337; 1335; Wolfchief, Harshey; hsbd.; Aug. 1852; M.
1338; 1336; Wolfchief, Anna; wife; July 1861[sic]; F. [Whiteelk]

1339; 1337; Wolfchief, Josie; wdw.; July 1843; F.

1340; 1338; Wolfchief, Richard; hsbd.; Apr. 1892; M.
1341; 1339; Wolfchief, Flora; wife; Sept. 1891; F.
1342; 1340; Wolfchief, Alice; dau.; Nov. 1912; F.
1341; Wolfchief, Ann; dau.; May 1927; F.

1345; 1342; Wolfchum, Paul; hsbd.; Oct. 1893; M. [Birth year 1890 in 1926.]
577; 1343; Wolfchum, Bessie Littlesun; wife; June 1890; F.
1344; Wolfchum, Walker; son; Dec. 1926; M.

1346; 1345; Wolfchum, Lily; dau.; May 1916; F. With Adolph Walksnice. [1917 Census name Betty.]

1347; 1346; Wolfear, Willis; hsbd.; Jan. 1884; M.
1348; 1347; Wolfear, Sophia; wife; May 1872; F.

1349; 1348; Wolfname, Paul; hsbd.; Dec. 1886; M.
1350; 1349; Wolfname, Annie; wife; Feb. 1892; F.
1351; 1350; Wolfname, Martha Grace; dau.; June 1910; F.
1352; 1351; Wolfname, Henry; son; Sept. 1912; M.
1353; 1352; Wolfname, Wilbur Paul; son; Oct. 1921; M.

1354; 1353; Wolfname, William; hsbd.; Jan. 1854; M.
1355; 1354; Wolfname, Bessie; wife; May 1854; F.

Census of the **Northern Cheyenne** Indians of **Tongue River** Agency, **Mont.** on **June 30, 1927** taken by **C.B. Lohmiller**, Superintendent.

**Key:** Last Number; Present Number; Indian Name; English Name; Relationship; Month, Year, of Birth; Sex;

1355;  Wolfname, Grace; dau.; June 1916; F. s-dau. Miles Horn

1357; 1356;  Wolfroads[sic], Mack; hsbd.; July 1878; M.
1358; 1357;  Wolfroads, Jennie; wife; Aug. 1877; F.
1359; 1358;  Wolfroads, Maude; dau.; July 1910; F.
1360; 1359;  Wolfroads, Rosa Charlotte; dau.; Jan. 1914; F. [Norman, son, M., same # 1922-23. Birth year 1920 in 1926.]

1361; 1360;  Wolftooth, Young; hsbd.; Nov. 1881; M.
1362; 1361;  Wolftooth, Mary; dau.; May 1918; F.
1363; 1362;  Wolftooth, Norman; son; July 1920; M.
1365; 1363;  Wolftooth, Doris; dau.; Nov. 1925; F.

1366; 1364;  Wolfvoice, Grover; hsbd.; Apr. 1890; M.
151; 1365;  Wolfvoice, Jennie Brady; wife; May 1882[sic]; F. [1904-1922 birth year 1888.]
1367; 1366;  Wolfvoice, Anne; dau.; Feb. 1918; F.
1367;  Wolfvoice, Dewey; son; Mar. 1927; M.

1368; 1368;  Womanleggins, Edward; hsbd.; Apr. 1888; M.
1369; 1369;  Womanleggins, Mannie[sic]; wife; Nov. 1891; F. [Lamewoman]
1370; 1370;  Womanleggins, Mabel; dau.; Aug. 1915; F. (Mabel Badhorses) [1917-20 son, Junior, M.; Name is June in 1926.]

1371; 1371;  Woodenlegs[sic], Richard; hsbd.; Aug. 1859; M.
1372; 1372;  Woodenlegs, Sophia; wife; May 1859[sic]; F.

1373; 1373;  Woodenlegs[sic], Tom; hsbd.; July 1887; M. (Tom Seminole)
1374; 1374;  Woodenlegs, Jessie; wife; Nov. 1905[sic]; F. [Spottedelk; shows 6mo., 1908 census.]
1375; 1375;  Woodenlegs, John; son; Nov. 1909; M.
1376;  Woodenlegs, Mabel; dau; Mar. 1927; F.

1378; 1377;  Woodenthigh, Arthur; hsbd.; Nov. 1883; M.
1379; 1378;  Woodenthigh, Eva; wife; Dec. 1887; F.
1380; 1379;  Woodenthigh, Esther; dau.; Apr. 1910; F.
1381; 1380;  Woodenthigh, Alice; dau.; Feb. 1914; F.
1382; 1381;  Woodenthigh, Peter; a-son; May 1918; M. [Birth year 1916 in 1926.]

1383; 1382;  Woodenthigh, Chester; hsbd.; Sept. 1884; M.
1384; 1383;  Woodenthigh, Lena; wife; Sept. 1890; F.
1385; 1384;  Woodenthigh, Philip; son; May 1915; M.
1386; 1385;  Woodenthigh, John; son; June 1916; M.
1386;  Woodenthigh, Melvin; son; Nov. 1923; M.

Census of the **Northern Cheyenne** Indians of **Tongue River** Agency, **Mont.** on **June 30, 1927** taken by **C.B. Lohmiller**, Superintendent.

**Key:** Last Number; Present Number; Indian Name; English Name; Relationship; Month, Year, of Birth; Sex;

| | |
|---|---|
| 1387; 1387; | Woodpecker, James; hsbd.; Mar. 1901; M. |
| 1388; 1388; | Woodpecker, Mary; wife; May 1904; F. [Littlewhiteman] |
| 1390; 1389; | Woodpecker, Ralph; sgle.; Dec. 1907; M. |
| 1389; 1390; | Woodpecker, Donald; sgle.; July 1909; M. |
| | |
| 1391; 1391; | Woundedeye, Davis; hsbd.; June 1885; M. |
| 1392; 1392; | Woundedeye, Susie May; wife; Aug. 1903; F. |
| 1393; 1393; | Woundedeye, Milton; son; Apr. 1920; M. |
| 1394; 1394; | Woundedeye, Charles; son; Nov. 1922; M. [Ross] |
| 1395; | Woundedeye, Veta; dau.; Jan. 1927; F. |
| | |
| 1395; 1396; | Woundedeye, Paul; son; June 1911; M. |
| | |
| 1396; 1397; | Woundedeye, Ford; hsbd.; Apr. 1882; M. |
| 1397; 1398; | Woundedeye, Florence; wife; May 1890; F. |
| 1398; 1399; | Woundedeye, Winfield; son; Apr. 1908; M. |
| 1399; 1400; | Woundedeye, Laura; dau.; Nov. 1909; F. |
| 1400; 1401; | Woundedeye, Victoria; dau.; Jan. 1922; F. |
| 1401; 1402; | Woundedeye, Fordson; son; Jan. 1919; M. |
| 1403; | Woundedeye, Ruth; dau.; Apr. 1927; F. |
| | |
| 1402; 1404; | Yellowfox, William; hsbd.; May 1900; M. |
| 1403; 1405; | Yellowfox, Margaret; wife; Mar. 1905; F. [Yellownose] |
| | |
| 1405; 1406; | Yelloweagle, Kate; wdw.; Apr. 1852; F. |
| | |
| 1406; 1407; | Yelloweyes, Abram; hsbd.; July 1874; M. |
| 1407; 1408; | Yelloweyes, Nora; wife; Feb. 1877; F. |
| | |
| 1408; 1409; | Yelloweyes, Oliver; hsbd.; July 1901; M. |
| 1409; 1410; | Yelloweyes, Gertrude; wife; May 1905[?]; F. [Brownbird] |
| 1410; 1411; | Yelloweyes, Mary; dau.; Nov. 1924; F. |
| | |
| 1411; 1412; | Yellowfox, Robert; hsbd.; July 1875; M. |
| 1412; 1413; | Yellowfox, Carrie; wife; Nov. 1882; F. |
| 1413; 1414; | Yellowfox, Frank; son; July 1901; M. |
| 1414; 1415; | Yellowfox, Charles; son; Oct. 1908; M. |
| 1415; 1416; | Yellowfox, William; son; Aug. 1922; M. |
| | |
| 1417; 1417; | Yellowhorse, Julia; s-dau.; May 1913; F. s-dau Milton Littlewhiteman. |
| | |
| 1418; 1418; | Yellownose, Robert; hsbd.; Sept. 1859[?]; M. [Birth year 1865 in 1926.] |
| 1419; 1419; | Yellownose, Anne; wife; Mar. 1867; F. |
| | |
| 1420; 1420; | Yellownose, George; hsbd.; Nov. 1896; M. [Birth year 1895. 1904-17.] |

Census of the **Northern Cheyenne** Indians of **Tongue River** Agency, **Mont.** on **June 30, 1927** taken by **C.B. Lohmiller**, Superintendent.

**Key:** Last Number; Present Number; Indian Name; English Name; Relationship; Month, Year, of Birth; Sex;

| | | |
|---|---|---|
| 227; 1421; | Yellownose, Lizzie; wife; Apr. 1891; F. [Crazymule] | |
| 1422; | Yellownose, Ruth; div.; Sept. 1898; F. | |
| 1421; 1423; | Yellowrobe, Charles; hsbd.; June 1892; M. | |
| 1422; 1424; | Yellowrobe, Alice; wife; May 1898; F. | |
| 1423; 1425; | Yellowrobe, Ruth; dau.; Mar. 1917; F. [Name Ruana in 1926.] | |
| 1424; 1426; | Yellowrobe, Martha; dau.; Jan. 1926; F. | |
| 1425; 1427; | Yellowrobe, Jasper; sgle.; Dec. 1894; M. | |
| 1426; 1428; | Yellowrobe, Adolph; sgle.; Nov. 1900; M. | |
| 1427; 1429; | Yellowrobe, William; hsbd.; Oct. 1865; M. | |
| 1428; 1430; | Yellowrobe, Minnie; wife; Jan. 1857; F. [Birth year 1859 in 1926.] | |
| 1429; 1431; | Youngbear, George; hsbd.; Aug. 1882; M. | |
| 1430; 1432; | Youngbear, Cora; wife; July 1888[?]; F. [Birth year 1890. 1904-1919.] | |
| 1431; 1433; | Youngbear, Arthur; son; Aug. 1913; M. | |
| 1432; 1434; | Youngbear, Ralph; son; Oct. 1921[sic]; M. [Shows up in 1920. Born 1919.] | |
| 1433; 1435; | Youngbird, James; hsbd.; Sept. 1857; M. | |
| 1434; 1436; | Youngbird, Clara; wife; May 1863; F. | |
| 1435; 1437; | Youngbird, John; hsbd.; Sept. 1884; M. | |
| 1436; 1438; | Youngbird, Anne; wife; Feb. 1885; F. [Looksbehind] | |
| 1331; 1439; | Youngbird, Carl; son; Apr. 1912; M. [Birth year 1923 in 1926.] | |
| 1440; | Gillispie, Parker, May; Wife; May 1888; F. | |
| 1441; | Littleyellowman, May; dau.; -- 1916; F. | |
| 1442; | Littleyellowman, Rose; dau.; Mar. 1923; F. | |
| 1443; | Littleyellowman, Susie; dau.; Feb. 1921; F. | |
| 1444; | Looksbehind, Roy; son; -- 1921; M. (Nightwalking) James Looksbehind- Fthr. | |
| 1445; | Looksbehind, Camilla; dau.; Aug. 1923; F. | |
| 1446; | Redcherries, Miller; son; Nov. 1920; M. Teddy Redcherries- Fthr. | |
| 1447; | Whitecrow, Alfred; son; Dec. 1910; M. Teddy Redcherries- Fthr. | |
| 1448; | Wheeler, Dewitt, Carlton; hsbd.; Dec. 1892; M. | |
| 1449; | Wheeler, Dewitt, Philip; son; Nov. 1916; M. | |

Census of the **Northern Cheyenne** Indians of **Tongue River** Agency, **Mont.** on **June 30, 1927** taken by **C.B. Lohmiller**, Superintendent.

Key: Last Number; Present Number; Indian Name; English Name; Relationship; Month, Year, of Birth; Sex;

R E C A P I T U L A T I O N  O F  C E N S U S

```
Total Males.........................722
Total Females......................727  1449
Males over 21.....................410
Females over 18..................394
Males under 21...................410
Females under 18................333
                                1,449
```

Last Year's census showed a total of 1440
This "      "    shows   "   "   1449

Total increase............................   9

54

# CENSUS OF NORTHERN CHEYENNE

-of-

## TONGUE RIVER RESERVATION, MONT.

June 30, 1928,

TONGUE RIVER AGENCY,

C. B. Lohmiller, Superintendent.

TONGUE RIVER.
124

1928

Census of the **Northern Cheyenne** Indians of **Tongue River** Agency, **Mont.** on **June 30, 1928** taken by **C.B. Lohmiller**, Superintendent.

**Key:** Last Number; Present Number; Indian Name; English Name; Relationship; Month, Year, of Birth; Sex; Blood Quantum

1; 1; Americanhorse, Austin; hsbd.; Oct. 1878; M; F
2; 2; Americanhorse, Maude; wife; Apr. 1883; F; F
3; 3; Americanhorse, Lucy; dau.; Nov. 1910; F; F
4; 4; Americanhorse, (Peter) George; son; Sept. 1914; M; F [Texas]

5; 5; Americanhorse, Bessie; sgle.; Nov. 1905[?]; F; F [First shows as 1 yr. 1908.]

6; 6; Americanhorse, Flora; mthr; -- 1861; F. F

7; 7; Americanhorse, George; hsbd.; Oct. 1881; M. F
8; 8; Americanhorse, Minnie; wife; Dec. 1884[?]; F. F [1907-26 birth yr., 1885-1886.]
9; 9; Americanhorse, James; son; Nov. 1911; M. F
10; 10; Americanhorse, Marie; dau.; June 1914; F. F
11; 11; Americanhorse, Lucy; dau.; Aug. 1918; F. F

12; 12; Americanhorse, Rueben[sic]; son; Nov. 1917[?]; M. F [Shows 1918, birth 1918.]
13; 13; Americanhorse, Albert; son; July 1912; M. F (Mike Badhorse)

14; 14; Americanhorse, Willis; fthr; Oct. 1892; M. F
15; 15; Americanhorse, Ernest; son; Nov. 1911; M. F
16; 16; Americanhorse, Laura Martha; dau; June 1914; F. F
17; 17; Americanhorse, Madge; dau; Dec. 1916; F. F
18; 18; Americanhorse, Grace; dau; Apr. 1918; F. F

19; 19; Americanhorse, Walter; hsb; Oct. 1890; M. F

20; 20; Ant, James; hsbd.; Feb. 1903; M. F
21; 21; Ant, Hannah; wife; May 1900; F. F [Highwalking]
22; 22; Ant, Bertha; dau; Jan. 1925; F. F

23; 23; Ant, Walter; hsbd; Jan. 1880; M. F
24; 24; Ant, Helen; wife; May 1882; F. F
25; 25; Ant, June; dau.; Jan. 1920; F. F
26; 26; Ant, Paul; son; Mar. 1927; M. F

27; ---; Arapahoechief, Maude; wdw; Dec. 1846[?]; F. F Died April 15, 1928 [1904-23, birth year 1844.]

28; 27; Atwood, James; hsbd.; Mar. 1891; M. F (Twentystands)
29; 28; Atwood, Cecelia; wife; Jan. 1898; F. F
30; 29; Atwood, Mary Lucy; dau.; May 1914; F. F

Census of the **Northern Cheyenne** Indians of **Tongue River** Agency, **Mont.** on **June 30, 1928** taken by **C.B. Lohmiller**, Superintendent.

**Key:** Last Number; Present Number; Indian Name; English Name; Relationship; Month, Year, of Birth; Sex; Blood Quantum

31; 30; Atwood, Herbert; son; Aug. 1922; M. F
---; ---; Atwood, Walter; son; Jan. 1928; M. F Died Feb. 16, 1928
---; ---; Atwood, Baby ; son; Jan. 1928; M. F Died Jan. 26, 1928

32; 31; Baldeagle, Hugh; hsbd; May 1858; M. F
33; 32; Baldeagle, Minnie; wife; Sept. 1859; F. F

34; 33; Bearchum, Frank; son; Mar. 1901; M. 3/4 S-son Frank Stumphorn [Name Alex in 1926.]

35; 34; Bearchum, Benjamin Jr.; son; Mar. 1919; M. 5/8 [Junior] s-son Ed. Womanleggins

36; 35; Bearcomesout, Charles; hsbd; Oct. 1880; M. F
37; 36; Bearcomesout, Harold; son; Mar. 1908; M. F
38; 37; Bearcomesout, Pius; son; Sept. 1915; M. F

39; 38; Bearquiver, Edward; hsbd.; Sept. 1881; M. F
40; ---; Bearquiver, Maggie; wife; May 1881; F. F Died April 1, 1928
41; 39; Bearquiver, Edna; dau.; Dec. 1912; F. F
42; 40; Bearquiver, Claude; son; Nov. 1916; M. F
43; 41; Bearquiver, James; son; June 1920; M. F
44; 42; Bearquiver, Martin; son; Aug. 1922; M. F
45; 43; Bearquiver, Grace; dau.; May 1927; F. F

46; 44; Beartusk, Jerome; hsdb; Aug. 1885; M. F
47; 45; Beartusk, Lucy; wife; Jan. 1893; F. 1/8
48; 46; Beartusk, Edith; dau.; Apr. 1916; F. 1/2
49; 47; Beartusk, Alice; dau.; Apr. 1917; F. 1/2
50; 48; Beartusk, Gladys; dau.; Jan. 1919; F. 1/2 [Nellie]
51; 49; Beartusk, Kenneth; son; Dec. 1920; M. 1/2
52; 50; Beartusk, Bertha Elizabeth; dau.; Mar. 1923; F. 1/2
53; 51; Beartusk, Jerome Jr.; son; Dec. 1925; M. ½

54; 52; Beaverheart, Thomas; hsdb.; May 1863[?]; M. F [1904-15, birth year 1857; 1916-24, birth year 1859; 1925-28 birth year 1863.]
55; 53; Beaverheart, Nellie; wife; Mary[sic] 1857; F. F
56; 54; Beaverheart, David; son; Apr. 1890; M. F [Name Davis in 1926.]

197; 55; Beirdneau, Adeline; wife; Feb. 1899; F. 1/8
       ; Beirdneau, Al; hsbd; -- ---; --. (White)
198; 56; Beirdneau, Betty Belle, dau.; Apr. 1923; F. 1/16
199; 57; Beirdneau, Barbara Marie; dau.; Apr. 1926; F. 1/16
     58; Beirdneau, Albert Lee; son; Feb. 16, 1928; M. 1/16

Census of the **Northern Cheyenne** Indians of **Tongue River** Agency, **Mont.** on **June 30, 1928** taken by **C.B. Lohmiller**, Superintendent.

**Key:** Last Number; Present Number; Indian Name; English Name; Relationship; Month, Year, of Birth; Sex; Blood Quantum

193; 59; BeMent, Emma Burns; Wife; June 1901; F. 1/8
194; 60; BeMent, Jacqueline; dau.; Oct. 1922; F. 1/16
195; 61; BeMent, Clarence Jr.; son.; Nov.1923; M. 1/16 [Max in 1925. Mickie in 1926.]
196; 62; BeMent, Jesse; son; Mar. 1924; M. 1/16 [Joseph in 1925.]
63; BeMent, Geraldine; dau.; Feb. 1, '27; F. 1/16 Unreported last census
64; BeMent, Celia Camille; dau.; Jan. 19/28; F. 1/16

57; 65; Bigback, Charles; hsbd.; Mar. 1863[?]; M. F [Birth year 1865.]
58; 66; Bigback, Clara; wife; July 1869; F. F

59; 67; Bigback, John; Sgle; Feb. 1904; M. F [Henry in 1919.]

60; 68; Bigback, James; hsbd; Aug. 1894; M. F
61; 69; Bigback, Jennie; Wife; May 1898; F. F
62; 70; Bigback, Gladys; dau.; July 1920; F. F
63; 71; Bigback, Robert; son; Dec. 1923; M. F

64; 72; Bigback, Stephen; wdr.; Apr. 1892; M. F

65; 73; Bigbeaver, August; hsbd.; Mar. 1861; M. F
66; 74; Bigbeaver, Annie Marie; dau.; June 1911; F. F

67; 75; Bigcrow, Andrew; hsbd.; Mar. 1854; M. F
68; 76; Bigcrow, Jennie; Wife; Nov. 1888; F. F
69; 77; Bigcrow, Sarah Angela; dau.; Aug. 1912; F. F

70; 78; Bigfoot, John; hsbd; -- 1881; M. F

71; 79; Bigfoot, White; hsbd.; Oct. 1875; F.[sic] F
72; 80; Bigfoot, Louisa; wife; Sept. 1885; F. F
73; 81; Bigfoot, Louis; son; June 1911; M. F

74; 82; Bigfoot, Davis; hsbd; May 1898; M. F
75; 83; Bigfoot, Lucy; wife; Oct. 1900; F. F
76; 84; Bigfoot, Alice; dau.; Jan. 1921; F. F [1926 Census birth 1923, name Martha same #. Shows up in 1925 birth year as 1923, also as Martha.]
77; 85; Bigfoot, Mary; dau.; Apr. 1924; F. F
86; Bigfoot, James; son; Dec. 15/27; M. F

78; 87; Bighead, Kate.; wdw.; July 1847; F. F

79; 88; Bigheadman, Benjamin; hsbd.; July 1889; M. F
80; 89; Bigheadman, Julia; wife; July 1894; F. F

Census of the **Northern Cheyenne** Indians of **Tongue River** Agency, **Mont.** on **June 30, 1928** taken by **C.B. Lohmiller**, Superintendent.

**Key:** Last Number; Present Number; Indian Name; English Name; Relationship; Month, Year, of Birth; Sex; Blood Quantum

81; 90; Bigheadman, Gladys; dau.; Sept. 1918; F. F [1926 Census name Lucille same #.]
82; ---; Bigheadman, Lucy; dau.; Oct. 1924; F. F Died April 17, 1928
91; Bigheadman, Laura; dau.; July 1927; F. F

83; 92; Bigheadman, Blair; hsbd.; June 1892; M. F
84; 93; Bigheadman, Clara; wife; Apr. 1901; F. F
85; 94; Bigheadman, Grover; son; July 1919; M. F
86; 95; Bigheadman, August; son; Aug. 1922; M. F
87; 96; Bigheadman, Julia; dau.; Dec. 1924; F. F
88; ---; Bigheadman, Mary; dau.; June 1926; F. F Died March 4, 1928

89; 97; Bigheadman, Betty Nora; dau.; Jan. 1915; F. F g-dau. John Twomoons
90; 98; Bigheadman, Frank (Biddle); son; Aug. 1917; M. F g-son. John Twomoons [1918 year Lucy g dt.] (Children of Ben. Bigheadman)

91; 99; Bigheadman, John; hsbd.; June 1849[sic]; M. F [1904-25, birth year 1853.]
92; 100; Bigheadman, Nellie; wife; Oct. 1853; F. F

93; 101; Bigheadman, William; hsbd; Dec. 1886; M. F
94; 102; Bigheadman, Nellie; wife; June 1891; F. F
95; 103; Bigheadman, Richard; son; Apr. 1909; M. F (Richard Rowland)
96; 104; Bigheadman, Grace; dau.; May 1918; F. F
97; 105; Bigheadman, Kathleen; dau.; Mar. 1925; F. F
98; 106; Bigheadman, Dorla; dau.; June 1926; F. F

99; ---; Biglefthand, Peter; hsbd.; Nov. 1867; M. F Died February 18, 1928

100; 107; Biglefthand, Patty; wife; Dec. 1875; F. F [1904-16 Birth year 1875; 1917-26 birth year 1885.]
101; 108; Biglefthand, Raphael; son; Sept. 1912; M. F [1915-#72 was Daisy, female.]

102; 109; Bigleg, Hinton; hsbd.; May 1887[?]; M. F [Shows up in 1911, birth year 1911-26, 1883.]
103; 110; Bigleg, Anne; wife; Jan. 1879; F. 1/4

104; 111; Bignose, George; sgle; Aug. 1897; M. F

105; 112; Bignose, Samuel; sgle.; May 1891; M. F

106; 113; Bignose, James; hsbd.; Oct. 1863; M. F

Census of the **Northern Cheyenne** Indians of **Tongue River** Agency, **Mont.** on **June 30, 1928** taken by **C.B. Lohmiller**, Superintendent.

**Key:** Last Number; Present Number; Indian Name; English Name; Relationship; Month, Year, of Birth; Sex; Blood Quantum

107; 114; Bignose, Rachel; wife; July 1855[?]; F. F

108; 115; Bites, Sally; wdw.; Oct. 1866; F. F

109; 116; Bites, James; hsbd.; Sept. 1900; M. F
110; 117; Bites, Sally; wife; Jan. 1905; F. F [Crazymule]
111; 118; Bites, Florence; dau.; July 1926; F. F

112; 119; Bixby, Benjamin; hsbd.; Oct. 1887[?]; M. 1/4 [1904-1918 birth year is 1886. 1919-26, 1866.]
113; 120; Bixby, Gertrude; wife; May 1893[sic]; F. 3/4 [Whitepowder 1904-07; Tallwhiteman 1908; Bixby 1909-1927; 1904-08 Birth year 1887; 1909-13 birth year 1888; 1914-26 1883; 1927 1893.]
114; 121; Bixby, Annie; dau.; Sept. 1913; F. 1/2
115; 122; Bixby, James; son; Dec. 1915; M. 1/2 [Jessie Daughter 1916-19.]

116; 123; Bixby, Edward; hsbd.; Mar. 1891; M. 1/4 [1904-18 birth year 1890; 1919-26 birth year 1898; 1927 1891.]
118; 124; Bixby, Edward George; son; July 1922; M. 1/8 [1924 Clara, dau; F. 1925-26 Jack.]
119; 125; Bixby, Elsie Virginia; dau; Dec. 1923; F. 1/8 [Vianne 1925-26.]
120; 126; Bixby, William Lawrence; son; Mar. 1925; M. 1/8

121; 127; Bixby, Jessie; wdw; May 1853; F. 1/2

122; 128; Blackbird, Isaac; hsbd; June 1863; M. F [Birth year 1864 in 1927.]
123; 129; Blackbird, Sallie; wife; Mar. 1872; F. F

124; ---; Blackcrane, Charles; hsbd.; June 1864; M. F  Died March 18, 1928
125; 130; Blackcrane, Clara; wife; Dec. 1866[?]; F. F [1920 Clara Blackeagle, wdw, #102, birth year 1845. Charles wife in 1920, Edith birth year 1866.]

126; 131; Blackeagle, William; hsbd; June 1888[?]; M. F
[#131, William-Censuses 1904-1915 Birth year 1886. 1916-1918 Birth year 1896; 1919 Birth year 1906 [sic]; 1920-26 Census birth year again 1896.]
127; 132; Blackeagle, Carl; son; Sept. 1911; M. F

128; 133; Blackhorse, Rueben[sic]; hsbd; July 1853[?]; M. F
129; 134; Blackhorse, Lena; wife; Dec. 1876[sic]; F. F [1904-26 birth year 1862-3.]
130; 135; Blackhorse, Anna; dau; July 1913; F. F [Anna 1927.?]
[#135, Son, Arthur in 1913-14 Censuses. Name Ada 1915-19. Name Ida 1920-26.]

131; 136; Blackhorse, Alex; hsbd.; Oct. 1897; M. F
132; 137; Blackhorse, Mary; wife; June 1903; F. F

Census of the **Northern Cheyenne** Indians of **Tongue River** Agency, **Mont.** on **June 30, 1928** taken by **C.B. Lohmiller**, Superintendent.

**Key:** Last Number; Present Number; Indian Name; English Name; Relationship; Month, Year, of Birth; Sex; Blood Quantum

133; 138; Blackhorse, Francis; son; July 1922; M. F [1923-26 name Merton.]
134; 139; Blackhorse, Alice; dau; Sept. 1924; F. F

135; 140; Blackree, Alice; mthr; Mar. 1909; F. F
136; 141; Blackree, Anna; dau; Aug. 1923; F. F

137; ---; Blackree, Emma; wdw; June 1851; F. F Died Nov. 24, 1927 [1924 last name Bigbeaver.]

138; 142; Blackree, Paul; hsbd; Oct. 1878; M. F
139; 143; Blackree, Jennie; wife; May 1881; F. F

140; 144; Blackstone, Charles; hsbd.; Dec. 1860[?]; M. F
144; ---; Blackstone, Nellie; wife; Mar. 1864; F. F Died May 23, 1928 [Blackwhetstone]

141; 145; Blackstone, Lena; s-dau[?]; Jul. 1878; F. 7/8
[#145, Previous & 1923 Census dau, 1924 wife.]

142; 146; Blackstone, Arthur; hsbd; Dec. 1892; M. F
143; 147; Blackstone, Nellie[sic]; wife; Aug. 1900[sic]; F. F [1906-26 birth year 1905. #147, Name Sallie, Mother Nellie. Nee Littlehead]
        148; Blackstone, Louis; son; Oct. 21/27; M. F

145; 149; Blackwolf, Bennie; hsbd; June 1897; M. F [1904-1923 name Alex.]
146; 150; Blackwolf, Ella; wife; Dec. 1900; F. F
147; 151; Blackwolf, Henry; son; Oct. 1919; M. F [1925 Census Thomas.]
148; 152; Blackwolf, James; son; Aug. 1923; M. F [1925 Census Alfred.]
149; 153; Blackwolf, Ruth; dau; Jan. 1927; F. F

150; 154; Blackwolf, John; hsbd; Aug. 1870; M. F
151; 155; Blackwolf, Nellie; wife; July 1874; F. F
152; 156; Blackwolf, Alex; son; May 1906; M. F
[#156, Name Busby, a brother Alex born 1897 in 1916 census, married in 1917.]
153; 157; Blackwolf, Mary; dau; Jan. 1914; F. F

154; 158; Blindman, Arthur; wdr; Nov. 1868; M. F

155; 159; Bluehawk, Louis; wdr; June 1850[sic]; M. 1/2 [1904-19 Born 1861.]

156; 160; Bobtailhorse, Thomas; hsbd; July 1850; M. F
157; 161; Bobtailhorse, Gertrude; wife; Dec. 1851; F. F

Census of the **Northern Cheyenne** Indians of **Tongue River** Agency, **Mont.** on **June 30, 1928** taken by **C.B. Lohmiller**, Superintendent.

**Key:** Last Number; Present Number; Indian Name; English Name; Relationship; Month, Year, of Birth; Sex; Blood Quantum

158; 162; Bolson, Gail; dau; July1915; F. 1/8 [1925 s-son, M,] (Children of Rena LeFever)
159; 163; Bolson, Frank; son; Aug. 1917; M. 1/8
160; 164; Bolson, Roy Guy; son; Dec. 1919; M. 1/8

161; 165; Boxelder, Laura; wdw; Jan. 1872; F. F

162; 166; Brady, Arthur; hsbd; Dec. 1840; M. F
163; 167; Brady, Ellen; wife; Dec. 1853; F. F

164; 168; Brady, Alex; hsbd.; Dec. 1898; M. F [1904-15 birth year 1898; 1916-26 1893.]
165; 169; Brady, Josie; wife; Dec. 1902; F. F [Pine]
166; 170; Brady, Charles; son; Nov. 1923; M. F

167; ---; Brady, James R.; son; Dec. 1909; M. F Died December 4, 1927

168; 171; Brady, George; hsbd; July 1881; M. F
169; 172; Brady, Flossie; wife; Feb. 1897; F. 3/4
170; 173; Brady, Elmore; son; Mar. 1907; M. F
171; 174; Brady, James Henry; son; Apr. 1913; M. F
172; 175; Brady, Howard; son; Nov. 1915[sic]; M. F
173  176; Brady, Romona Lucy; dau; Dec.1917[?]; F. F
174; 177; Brady, Wilson; son; Oct. 1918; M. F
175; 178; Brady, Martha; dau; Feb. 1921; F. 7/8
176; 179; Brady, Roy; son; Jan. 1925; M. 7/8

177; 180; Braidedlocks, William; hsbd; Oct. 1851; M. F
178; 181; Braidedlocks, Gertie; wife; May 1852; F. F

179; 182; Brownbird, Joseph; hsbd; Sept. 1865; M. F
180; 183; Brownbird, Anna; wife; Oct. 1865; F. F

181; 184; Buffalohorn, John; hsbd; Apr.1862[sic]; M. F [1904-25 birth year 1869.]
182; 185; Buffalohorn, Lena; wife; May 1870; F. F [Birth year 1848[sic], 1920-22.]

183; 186; Buffalohump, Samuel; hsbd; July 1845; M. F
184; 187; Buffalohump, Nora; wife; Aug. 1848; F. F

185; 188; Burns, George; hsbd; Mar. 1895; M. 1/8
Burns, Belle; wife; ---; --. (Not enrolled)

Census of the **Northern Cheyenne** Indians of **Tongue River** Agency, **Mont.** on **June 30, 1928** taken by **C.B. Lohmiller**, Superintendent.

**Key:** Last Number; Present Number; Indian Name; English Name; Relationship; Month, Year, of Birth; Sex; Blood Quantum

186; 189;     Burns, Robert J.; hsbd; Sept 1897; M. 1/8
                Burns, Hattie Walker; wife; ---; --. (White)
187; 190;     Burns, Phyllis Roberta; dau.; Mar. 1926; F. 1/16
                Burns, Robert J. Jr.; son; Feb. 15/28; M. 1/16 Died February 15, 1928

188; 191;     Burns, Gertrude; wdw; July 1846; F. F

189; 192;     Burns, Julia; wife; Feb. 1872; F. 1/4
190; 193;     Burns, James C., Jr.; son; July 1908; M. 1/8
191; 194;     Burns, Margaret; dau.; Sept. 1911; F. 1/8
192; 195;     Burns, Anna Grace; dau.; Aug. 1913; F. 1/8

200; 196;     Burns, Lizzie; wife; Jan. 1873; F. 1/4
                Burns, Patrick; hsbd.; ---;--. (White)
201; 197;     Burns, Josephine; s-dau.; July 1918; F. 1/4 (Small) [Had a Kitty Small in 1925. Adopt-dau., in 1925-26.]

202; 198;     Callsfirst, Andrew; hsbd; June 1888; M. F
203; 199;     Callsfirst, Jennie; wife; July 1872; F. 3/4
204; 200;     Callsfirst, Mary; dau.; Sept 1911; F. 7/8 [1924 Annie.]

205; 201;     Chasingbear, Flora; mthr; Mar. 1882; F. F
206; 202;     Chasingbear, Laura; dau; May 1916; F. F
207; 203;     Chasingbear, Robert; son; July 1924; M. F

208; 204;     Chasingbear, Willis; hsbd; Mar. 1895; M. F
209; 205;     Chasingbear, Madge; wife; Apr. 1898[sic]; F. F [Powderface]

210; 206;     Chubby, John; hsbd.; Nov. 1875; M. F
211; 207;     Chubby, Anne; wife; Dec. 1885; F. F
212; 208;     Chubby, Rhoda; dau.; Jan. 1920; F. F

213; 209;     Clubfoot, Floyd; hsbd; Mar. 1888; M. F [In 1904, 15 yrs., old.]
214; 210;     Clubfoot, Stella; wife; Apr 1896[?]; F. F [Weaselbear]
[#210, No record 1904-07; 1908 birth 1890; 1909-23 birth 1893.]
215; 211;     Clubfoot, Norman; son; Nov. 1916; M. F
[1917 shows Norman died in 1916. In 1918-23 Census as born 1916 and alive?]
216; 212;     Clubfoot, Verle; Son; Mar. 1923; M. F
217; 213;     Clubfoot, Flossie; dau; Dec. 1925; F. F

218; 214;     Clubfoot, Frank; hsbd; Mar. 1891; M. F [1904-23 birth year 1891.]
219; 215;     Clubfoot, Lucy Alice; wife; Feb. 1893[?]; F. F
[#215, 1915-18 birth year is 1898; 1920 its 1896; 1923 its 1886; 1924-6 its 1893.]
220; 216;     Clubfoot, James; son; Oct. 1922; M. F

Census of the **Northern Cheyenne** Indians of **Tongue River** Agency, **Mont.** on **June 30, 1928** taken by **C.B. Lohmiller**, Superintendent.

**Key:** Last Number; Present Number; Indian Name; English Name; Relationship; Month, Year, of Birth; Sex; Blood Quantum

221; 217; Clubfoot, John; hsbd; Dec. 1860[?]; M. F [1904-13 shows birth year 1863. 1814-26 birth year 1854. 1927-28 birth year 1860.]
222; 218; Clubfoot, Minnie; wife; July 1870; F. F

223; 219; Clubfoot, Willis; sgle; Mar. 1891; M. F

224; 220; Clubfoot, Joseph; sgle; July 1900; M. F

225; 221; Colhoff, Emma; wife; Sept. 1894; F. 3/4
Colhoff, William; hsbd.; ---; --. (Not enrolled)
226; 222; Colhoff, Maxine; dau; May 1916; F. 3/4
227; 223; Colhoff, Edward; son.; May 1918; M. 3/4
228; 224; Colhoff, Annie Gladys; dau; Mar.[?] 1921; F. 3/4 [Birth month Apr., year 1922 in 1927.]
229; 225; Colhoff, William Rowland; son; Apr. 1924; M. 3/4
230; 226; Colhoff, George; son; Jan. 1927; M. 3/4

231; ---; Comestogether, Ida; wdw; 1860[sic]; F. F Died June 19, 1928 [1904-19 birth year 1841. 1920-26 birth year 1854. 1927-28 birth year 1860.]

232; 227; Cooley, Julia; wife; Nov. 1891; F. 1/8
Cooley, Al; hsbd.; ---; --. (White)
233; 228; Cooley, Violet; dau; Mar. 1914; F. 1/16
234; 229; Cooley, Junior; son; May 1916; M. 1/16
235; 230; Cooley, Francis; son; Oct. 1922; M. 1/16
236; 231; Cooley, Vera; dau.; Jan. 1925; F. 1/16

237; 232; Crawling, Charles; fthr; Aug. 1884; M. F
238; 233; Crawling, Martha; dau.; Jan. 1917; F. F

239; 234; Crazymule, John[sic]; hsbd.; Mar. 1870; M. F
[#234; In 1919 name Joseph, previous #220, birth year 1881. Mixed with another family not in 1920 census.] [Between 1920-22 Census takers mixed up #218 John and #220 Joseph's names and wifes and names.]
240; 235; Crazymule, Jennie; wife; Feb. 1857; F. F [Issues]

241; 236; Crazymule, James Paul; son; Nov. 1910; M. F Children of Lizzie Yellownose and Joseph Crazymule.
242; 237; Crazymule, Charles; son; Nov. 1919; M. F [Raymond in 1926.]
243; 238; Crazymule, Xavier; son; Nov. 1921; M. F

244; 239; Crazymule, Joseph; hsbd.; Mar. 1881; M. F
245; 240; Crazymule, Sarah; wife; July 1873; F. F
246; 241; Crazymule, Eva; dau; May 1909; F. F [Wyoming in 1926.]

Census of the **Northern Cheyenne** Indians of **Tongue River** Agency, **Mont.** on **June 30, 1928** taken by **C.B. Lohmiller**, Superintendent.

**Key:** Last Number; Present Number; Indian Name; English Name; Relationship; Month, Year, of Birth; Sex; Blood Quantum

247; 242; Crook, George; hsbd.; Jan. 1864[?]; M. F [1904-25 Birth year 1871.]
248; 243; Crook, Theresa; wife; Nov. 1866; F. F
249; 244; Crook, Alice; dau; Jan. 1908; F. F

250; 245; Crook, Rosa; wdw.; Aug. 1965[sic]; F. F

251; 246; Crook, Albert; sgle; Apr. 1901; M. F

252; 247; Crookednose, Nicholas; hsbd.; June 1867; M. F
253; 248; Crookednose, Susie; wife; Sept. 1872; F. F

254; 249; Curley, Hattie; wdw; Aug. 1856; F. F

255; 250; Curley, Thomas; hsbd; Nov. 1889; M. F
256; 251; Curley, Esther; wife; Dec. 1895; F. F
257; 252; Curley, Ella; dau; Apr. 1925; F. F
258; 253; Curley, Logan; Son; Feb. 1927; M. F

259; 254; Deafy, David; hsbd; May 1898; M. F [Americanhorse]
260; 255; Deafy, Anna; wife; Dec. 1895[?]; F. F [Horseroads; 1904-25 Birth year 1897.]
261; 256; Deafy, Willis; son; Nov. 1917; M. F
262; 257; Deafy, Elsie; dau; July 1925; F. F

263; 258; Deafy, James; hsbd; Aug. 1870[?]; M. F [1904-25 Birth year 1873.]
264; 259; Deafy, Mary; wife; May 1874; F. F [1904-11 birth year 1874. 1912-26 birth year 1880. Name Walkingwoman 1904-06. 1907 no first name. 1908-Walkingwoman-Maria. 1908-10 name Maria. 1911-28 name Mary.]
265; 260; Deafy, Carrie; dau.; June 1910; F. F [Jessie in 1926.]

266; 261; Divesbackwards, John; hsbd.; Jan. 1870; M. F [Depending the on census taker they spell Divesbackwards at the end with or without an "s".]

267; 262; Divesbackwards, Rufus; hsbd.; Feb. 1890; M. F
268; 263; Divesbackwards, Nancy; wife; Mar. 1882; F. F
269; 264; Divesbackwards, Sam; son; Apr. 1918; M. F [1926 name Irving.]
270; 265; Divesbackwards, Strane; son; May 1920; M. F
271; 266; Divesbackwards, Grace; dau; Feb. 1925; F. F

272; 267; Divesbackwards, Louisa; g-dau.; Aug. 1917; F. 7/8 g-dau, Mary Shavedhead

273; 268; Dog, Louis; hsbd; May 1855; M. F
274; 269; Dog, Maude; wife; Mar 1866; F. F

Census of the __Northern Cheyenne__ Indians of __Tongue River__ Agency, __Mont.__ on __June 30, 1928__ taken by __C.B. Lohmiller__, Superintendent.

**Key:** Last Number; Present Number; Indian Name; English Name; Relationship; Month, Year, of Birth; Sex; Blood Quantum

275; 270; Dullknife, Bessie; sgle; Mar. 1870; F. F

276; 271; Duster, Albert; hsbd; Apr. 1889; M. F
277; 272; Duster, Vinnie; wife; Sept 1896; F. F
278; 273; Duster, Mabel; dau; July 1913; F. F (Amelia Limpy, mother) [1926 name May Limpy Prev. #516.]
279; 274; Duster, Annie; dau; Dec. 1920; F. F
280; 275; Duster, Bessie; dau; July 1924; F. F

281; 276; Eaglefeathers, Oliver; hsbd.; Sept 1895; M. F
282; 277; Eaglefeathers, Julia; wife; June 1895; F. 3/4
283; 278; Eaglefeathers, Simon; son; Mar. 1922; M. 7/8
284; 279; Eaglefeathers, Rosie; dau; July 1925; F. 7/8

285; 280; Eaglefeathers, Jacob; hsbd; Sept 1874; M. F
286; ---; Eaglefeathers, Bernice; dau; Oct. 1917[sic]; F. F Died December 26, 1927 [First shows in 1923 census with birth year as 1920. Nothing in 1917-22.]
287; 281; Eaglefeathers, Mildred; dau; May 1920[sic]; F. F [1917 shows birth year as 1916. 1918-26 as 1915.]

288; 282; Eastman, Mary G.; wife; Dec. 1876; F. 1/4
Eastman, Mike; hsbd.; ---; --. (White)
289; 283; Eastman, Margaret; dau; May 1903; F. 1/8
291; 284; Eastman, Robert; son; Mar 1911; M. 1/8
293; 285; Eastman, Rose; dau; Sept 1915; F. 1/8
294; 286; Eastman, Louisa; dau; Mar. 1918; F. 1/8
295; 287; Eastman, Myrtle; g-dau; Aug. 1913; F. 1/16 [Julia 1926.] (Lucy Beartusk, mother)

296; 288; Eastman, Charles; wdr.; Feb 1901; M. 1/8

297; 289; Eastman, Perry; hsbd; Nov. 1895; M. 1/8
298; 290; Eastman, Mary; wife; Feb. 1893; F. F

299; 291; Elkshoulder, Henry; hsbd; July 1894[sic]; M. F [1904-26 birth year 1884.]
300; 292; Elkshoulder, Bessie; wife; Aug 1893; F. F
301; 293; Elkshoulder, Curtis; son; Feb. 1908; M. F
302; 294; Elkshoulder, Lucy; dau.; Mar. 1917; F. F
303; 295; Elkshoulder, Sylvia; dau.; July 1922; F. F
304; 296; Elkshoulder, George; son; Dec. 1925; M. F [Adolph in 1926.]

305; 297; Elliot, Elizabeth H.; wife; Apr. 1906; F. 3/8
Elliot, Lafe; hsbd.; ---; --. (White)

67

Census of the **Northern Cheyenne** Indians of **Tongue River** Agency, **Mont.** on **June 30, 1928** taken by **C.B. Lohmiller**, Superintendent.

**Key:** Last Number; Present Number; Indian Name; English Name; Relationship; Month, Year, of Birth; Sex; Blood Quantum

        298;       Elliot, Edwin, Francis; son; Jan 8/28; M. 5/8

306; 299;      Eyesyellow, Wilbur; hsbd.; July 1868; M. F
307; 300;      Eyesyellow, Daisy; wife; Sept 1856; F. F

308; 301;      Farr, Jessie; wdw; Jan. 1899[sic]; F. 1/4 [1908-26 birth year 1890.]
310; 302;      Farr, Frank; son; July 1917; M. 1/8
311; 303;      Farr, Evelyn; dau.; Dec. 1914; F. 1/8

312; 304;      Fasthorse, Clara; sgle; May 1913; F. F
[1913-1917 Census #312- name Raymond M.; S. Son; Male.]

313; 305;      Fightingbear, Edgar; hsbd; Oct.1874; M. F
314; 306;      Fightingbear, Alice; Wife; June 1893; F. F
315; 307;      Fightingbear, Julia; dau.; July 1911; F. F
316; 308;      Fightingbear, Dora; dau.; Mar. 1915; F. F [1926 name Fannie.]
317; 309;      Fightingbear, Elmer; son; Apr. 1921; M. F

318; 310;      Fightingbear, Herbert; son; Sept 1923, M. F
319; 311;      Fightingbear, Emma; dau; May 1926; F. F

320; 312;      Fightingbear, Willis; sgle; June 1899; M. F

321; 313;      Fingers, Otis; wdr.; Oct. 1868[?]; M. F [1904-25 Birth year 1867.]
322; 314;      Fingers, Joseph; son; Aug. 1914; M. F [1917 Census Daughter, Josie 1915-20.]

323; 315;      Firecrow, Peter; hsbd; Apr. 1887; M. F
324; 316;      Firecrow, Joseph; son; Oct. 1923; M. F [Josephine; dau; F., in 1926]

325; 317;      Firewolf, John; hsbd.; Apr. 1877; M. F
326; 318;      Firewolf, Josephine; wife; Jan. 1875; F. F

327; 319;      Fisher, Eugene; hsbd; July 1878; M. 1/2
328; 320;      Fisher, Kitty; wife; Apr. 1890; F. 1/8
329; 321;      Fisher, Eugene, Jr.; son; Dec. 1912; M. 1/4
330; 322;      Fisher, Langburn; son; July 1915; M. 1/4
331; 323;      Fisher, J. Allen; son; Mar. 1917; M. 1/4 [1917 Census name Ira.]
332; 324;      Fisher, Alliwitchie; dau; May 1919; F. 1/4 [1919 Census name Pearl.]
333; 325;      Fisher, Calleaus; son; May 1919; M. 1/4 [1919 Census name Earl.]
334; 326;      Fisher, Russell; son; Nov. 1921; M. 1/4
335; 327;      Fisher, Phyllis Helen; dau.; Mar. 1924; F. 1/4
336; 328;      Fisher; Bernidine; son; Dec. 1926; M. 1/4

Census of the **Northern Cheyenne** Indians of **Tongue River** Agency, **Mont.** on **June 30, 1928** taken by **C.B. Lohmiller**, Superintendent.

**Key:** Last Number; Present Number; Indian Name; English Name; Relationship; Month, Year, of Birth; Sex; Blood Quantum

337; 329; Fisher, Lena; mthr; May 1876; F. F
338; 330; Fisher, Alice; dau; Aug 1898; F. F
339; 331; Fisher, John; son; July 1901; M. F
340; 332; Fisher, Henry; son; Aug 1905; M. F
341; 333; Fisher, Isabelle; dau.; June 1908; F. F
342; 334; Fisher, Richard; son; Nov. 1912; M. F
343; 335; Fisher, Harold; son; Jan 1920; M. F

344; 336; Fliesabout, William; hsbd; Feb 1879; M. F
345; 337; Fliesabout, Minnie; wife; Dec 1882; F. F
346; 338; Fliesabout, June; dau; June 1923; F. F [Martin; son; F[sic], in 1926.]

347; 339; Flying, Debs; wdr; Feb 1886; M. F
348; 340; Flying, Frank; son; Oct. 1915; M. F
349; 341; Flying, Parker; son; Apr 1918; M. F

350; 342; Flying, Myra; mthr; June 1867; F. F
351; 343; Flying, Ruth; dau; Dec. 1916; F. F

352; 344; Flying, Thomas; hsbd; Mar. 1869; M. F
353; 345; Flying, Margaret; wife; Mar. 1866; F. F [Highbear]

354; 346; Flying, Pauline; dau.; June 1916; F. 7/8 (Mrs. Geo. Brady, Mother) [Male, Paul in 1920 #150 under Brady.]

355; Foot, Jennie; wife; June 1890; F. 3/4 Died Sept. 27, 1927
356; 347; Foot, Thelma; dau.; June 1913; F. 5/8 [1917 Census name Daisy.]
357; 348; Foot, Bertha; dau.; Dec. 1919; F. 5/8
358; 349; Foot, Edward; son.; Apr. 1918; M. 5/8
359; 350; Foot, Eva; dau; May 1923; F. 5/8

1422; 351; Foot, Ruth Yellownose; wife; Sept. 1898; F. F
Foot, Albert; hsbd.; ---; --; (Not enrolled)

360; 352; Fox, Margaret; dau.; Aug.1918; F. F [Jessie in 1927.]
361; 353; Fox, Marie; dau.; Oct. 1922; F. F [Max, M., 1922-25.]

362; 354; Ghostbull, Arthur; hsbd; Feb. 1870[sic]; F.[sic] F [1904-26 birth year 1874.]
363; 355; Ghostbull, Sarah; wife; Sept. 1867[?]; F. F 1905-08 birth year 1868, 1909-11 birth year 1861, 1912-13 birth year 1866, 1914 birth year 1851, 1915-26 birth year 1861.]
364; 356; Ghostbull, Eva Mary; dau; Mar. 1908; F. F

1440; 357; Gillispie, May Parker; wife; May 1888; F. ¼

Census of the **Northern Cheyenne** Indians of **Tongue River** Agency, **Mont.** on **June 30, 1928** taken by **C.B. Lohmiller**, Superintendent.

**Key:** Last Number; Present Number; Indian Name; English Name; Relationship; Month, Year, of Birth; Sex; Blood Quantum

365; 358; Grasshopper, Isaac; wdr.; June 1850; M. F
366; 359; Grasshopper, Frank; sgle; Sept. 1906; M. F son of Mrs. Stanley Lamewoman. [Arthur in 1926.]

367; 360; Grasshopper, Susie; s-dau; Apr. 1909; F. F Dau. of Mrs. Stanley Lamewoman.
368; 361; Grasshopper, Mary; s-dau; Aug. 1914; F. F Dau. of Mrs. Stanley Lamewoman.

369; 362; Gray, Edward; hsbd; Apr. 1873; M. F
370; 363; Gray, Nellie; wife; Sept. 1874; F. F
371; 364; Gray, Teddy; son; Aug. 1915; M. F

372; 365; Gray, John; hsbd; Aug. 1902[?]; M. F [1904 shows up as 1 yr. old.]
373; 366; Gray, Kate Wolfname; wife; Mar. 1900; F. F [Ida in 1926.]
Gray, Baby; son; Dec. 11/27; M. F

374; 367; Gray, Bessie; Div.; July 1904; F. F [1920 #917, name Sandcrane.]
375; 368; Gray, Rose Marie; dau; Nov.1923; F. F

376; 369; Greasydog, Fannie; sgle; June 1897; F. F

377; 370; Hairlessbear, Hilda; dau.; Mar. 1912[?]; F. F (Mrs. John Chubby, mother) [States in 1913 census, Born 3/8/1913.]

378; 371; Hairyhand, Henry; wdr.; Oct. 1855; M. F

379; 372; Hankeringwolf, Peter; wdr.; Sept. 1834; M. F

380; 373; Hardground, Ernest; hsbd; July 1896; M. F
381; 374; Hardground, Mary; wife; Aug. 1895[?]; F. F
382; 375; Hardground, Ethel; dau.; Feb. 1921; F. F
383; 376; Hardground, Katie; dau.; Sept. 1923; F. F
384; Hardground, Elda; dau; Apr. 1926; F. F Died January 31, 1928

385; 377; Hardground, Jane; dau.; Mar. 1915; F. F s-dau. Lee Spottedblackbird.

386; 378; Hardground, Robert; hsbd.; Nov. 1876; M. F
387; 379; Hardground, Roland; son; July 1909; M. F [Rowland in 1926.]
388; 380; Hardground, Lucy; dau.; Sept 1911; F. F [Rena in 1926.]
389; 381; Hardground, Lyla; dau.; Feb. 1914; F. F

390; 382; Hardground, Albert; hsbd; June 1899; M. F
391; 383; Hardground, Ruth; wife; May 1908; F. F [Standingelk]

Census of the __Northern Cheyenne__ Indians of __Tongue River__
Agency, __Mont.__ on __June 30, 1928__ taken by __C.B. Lohmiller__,
Superintendent.

**Key:** Last Number; Present Number; Indian Name; English Name; Relationship; Month, Year, of Birth; Sex; Blood Quantum

392; 384; Hardground, George; sgle.; Apr. 1901[sic]; M. F [George's birth year, Censuses 1904-08 is 1898. 1909-13 is 1897. 1914-18 is 1895.]

393; 385; Hardground, Thomas; sgle.; Aug. 1903; M. F

394; 386; Hardrobe, Colonel; wdr.; Feb. 1856[sic]; M. F

395; 387; Hardrobe, Albert; sgle; July 1896; M. F

396; 388; Hardrobe, Fannie; dau.; Oct. 1880; F. F

397; 389; Hardrobe, Mollie; g-dau; Oct. 1919; F. F dau. Mrs. Louis Magpie

398; 390; Hardrobe, Margaret; dau.; Apr. 1918; F. F [name Lucy and birth year 1911 in 1926. s-dau Willis Medicinebull.] dau. Ruth Yellownose Foot.

406; 391; Harris, Bryan; wdr.; Apr. 1898; M. 1/4
407; 392; Harris, Carl; son; Oct. 1921; M. 5/8

599;[sic]393; Harris, Edward; hsbd; Jan. 1887; M. 1/4
400; 394; Harris, Bessie; wife; May 1889; F. F [1911-26 birth year 1888-89.]
401; 395; Harris, May; dau.; May 1911; F. 5/8
402; 396; Harris, Nellie; dau.; May 1914; F. 5/8
403; 397; Harris, Dorothy; dau.; May 1919; F. 5/8
404; 398; Harris, Hubert Geo.; son; Jan. 1922; M. 5/8 [Lawrence Edw. In 1926.]
       399; Harris, Inez Romona; dau.; Dec. 9. 1927; F. 5/8

405; 400; Harris, Allie; wdr.[sic]; Sept. 1850; F. 1/2 [Sallie]

408; 401; Harris, William; hsbd; Jan. 1877; M. 1/4
409; 402; Harris, Margaret; wife; May 1884; F. 1/2
410; 403; Harris, George; son; Sept. 1907; M. 3/8
411; 404; Harris, Lucy; dau.; Jan. 1908; F. 3/8
412; 405; Harris, Julia; dau.; Dec. 1910; F. 3/8
413; 406; Harris, Agnes; dau.; Sept. 1912[?]; F. 3/8 [Shows up in 1914 census as being born in 1913. 1914-16 birth year as 1913, 1917-26 birth year as 1915.]
414; 407; Harris, Raymond; son; Apr. 1915; M. 3/8
415; 408; Harris, Mary; dau.; Apr. 1919; F. 3/8 [1920 name Leota.]
416; 409; Harris, Florence; dau.; Sept. 1923; F. 3/8 [1925 son Joseph, M.]

419; 410; Hart, Charles; hsbd; May 1880; M. F
420; 411; Hart, Louisa; wife; Sept. 1885; F. 1/4
421; 412; Hart, Mattie Lizzie; dau.; July 1911; F. 5/8 [Censuses 1912-18 name is Katie.]

Census of the **Northern Cheyenne** Indians of **Tongue River** Agency, **Mont.** on **June 30, 1928** taken by **C.B. Lohmiller**, Superintendent.

**Key:** Last Number; Present Number; Indian Name; English Name; Relationship; Month, Year, of Birth; Sex; Blood Quantum

422; 413; Hart, Eva; dau; Dec. 1913[sic]; F. 5/8 [Census 1916-20 birth year 1915.]
423; 414; Hart, Jessie Diana; dau; Apr 1917; F. 5/8

417; 415; Hart, Frank; hsbd; July 1898; M. 7/8
418; 416; Hart, Rose Alice; wife; May 1907; F. F [Hairlessbear]

424; 417; Headswift, Charles; fthr; Mar. 1867; M. F
425; 418; Headswift, Frank; son; June 1911; M. F

426; 419; Highbear, William; hsbd; Mar. 1888[?]; M. F
427; 420; Highbear, Minnie; wife; May 1897[?]; F. F [Most censuses show birth year 1896.]

428; 421; Highwalking, Nellie; wdw; Apr. 1859[sic]; F. F [Born 1850 from 1904-16.]

429; 422; Highwalking, Floyd; hsbd; Apr. 1888; M. F
430; 423; Highwalking, Belle; wife; June 1893; F. F
431; 424; Highwalking, Max; son; Jan. 1917; M. F
432; 425; Highwalking, George; son; Mar. 1913; M. F [David in 1926.]

433; Hisbadhorse[sic], Richard; hsbd.; Aug. 1848; M. F Died Sept. 6, 1927 [Hisbadhorses 1904-26.]
434; 426; Hisbadhorse, Rhoda; wife; June 1856[sic]; F. F [1904-26 birth year 1840.]

435; 427; Hisbadhorses, Willis; hsbd; Aug. 1898; M. F
436; 428; Hisbadhorses, Ernest; son; May 1917; M. F [1924 s-son. Eugene in 1926.]
437; 429; Hisbadhorses, Medaris; son; Aug. 1921; M. F [Bird; son; 1917; in 1926.]
438; 430; Hisbadhorses, Fannie; dau; Oct. 1922; F. F [Josephine in 1926.]

439; 431; Hollowbreast, Hubert; hsbd.; May 1875; M. F
440; 432; Hollowbreast, Mary; wife; Apr. 1896; F. F [Previous censuses name Hattie Hisbadhorses. 1926 Hisbadhorses, wdw. #426.]
441; 433; Hollowbreast, Donald; son; May1917; M. F [James in 1926.]
442; Hollowbreast, Richard; son; Oct. 1925; M. F Died April 15, 1928 [1926 Richard Hisbadhorses.]

443; 434; Hollowbreast, William; hsbd.; Mar. 1900[?]; M. F [1925 birth year 1893. Birth year 1866 in 1926. Birth year 1900 in 1920. 1904-15 there is a Willie Hollowbreast that has a birth year of 1900. Father same as William in 1920.]

72

Census of the **Northern Cheyenne** Indians of **Tongue River** Agency, **Mont.** on **June 30, 1928** taken by **C.B. Lohmiller**, Superintendent.

**Key:** Last Number; Present Number; Indian Name; English Name; Relationship; Month, Year, of Birth; Sex; Blood Quantum

                     Hollowbreast, Edith; wife; ---; --. (White)

444; 435;    Hollowwood, Richard; hsbd; July 1856[sic]; M. F [1904-26 birth year 1866.]
445; 436;    Hollowwood, Minnie; wife; Aug. 1856; F. F

446; 437;    Horn, Annie Wolfname; wife; May 1900; F. F [Name Alice 1904-20.]
                     Horn, Miles; hsbd; ---; --. (not enrolled)
447; 438;    Horn, Rose; dau; June 1921; F. F
448; 439;    Horn, Wilena; dau; Mar. 1923; F. F
449; 440;    Horn, Margaret; dau; July 1926; F. F
       441;    Horn, Celia; dau; May 7/28; F. F

450; 442;    Horseroads, Thomas; hsbd; Sept. 1878; M. F
451; 443;    Horseroads, Lucy; wife; Aug. 1887; F. F
452;         Horseroads, Sallie; dau.; Nov. 1921; F. F Died February 29, 1928
453; 444;    Horseroads, Ida; dau.; Jan. 1924; F. F
454; 445;    Horseroads, Cora; dau.; Nov. 1926; F. F

455; 446;    Howlingantelope, Albert; hsbd; Apr. 1874; M. F
456; 447;    Howlingantelope, Eva; wife; May 1880; F. F

290; 448;    Huff, Pearl Eastman; wife; June 1907; F. 1/8
                     Huff, Patrick; hsbd; ---; M. F (Not enrolled)
       449;    Huff, Elsie Margaret; dau; Dec. 23/27; F. ¼

457; 450;    Ironhand, William; hsbd; Nov. 1882; M. F
458; 451;    Ironhand, Sally; wife; July 1884; F. F
459; 452;    Ironhand, Henry; son; June 1910; M. F
460; 453;    Ironhand, Willis; son; Jan. 1915; M. F
461; 454;    Ironhand, Jane; dau; Feb. 1927; F. F

462; 455;    Ironshirt, Jennie; mthr; July 1858; F. F

463; 456;    Ironshirt, Fred; hsbd; July 1831; M. F
464; 457;    Ironshirt, Nora; wife; Aug. 1850; F. F

465; 458;    Ironshirt, Robert; wdr; July 1902; M. F

466; 459;    Irontooth, Susan; wdr[sic]; -- 1834; F. F

467; 460;    Issues, John; hsbd; -- 1863; M. F

Census of the **Northern Cheyenne** Indians of **Tongue River** Agency, **Mont.** on **June 30, 1928** taken by **C.B. Lohmiller**, Superintendent.

**Key:** Last Number; Present Number; Indian Name; English Name; Relationship; Month, Year, of Birth; Sex; Blood Quantum

468; 461; Issues, Clara; wife; Mar. 1870; F. F [Blackmedicine; 1904-17, Birth year 1868; she becomes Issues 1915, 1918-25 birth year changed to 1863, 1926 to 1878. 1927 to 1870.]

469; 462; Issues, Francis; wdr; Mar. 1897; M. F
470; 463; Issues, Ira; son; Feb. 1920[?]; M. F [1919 name Ira, 1920-23, George.]
471; 464; Issues, Irene; dau.; May 1921; F. F

472; 465; Killsback, James; hsbd.; July 1863; M. F [Census #461, name Joseph Killsacross in 1926.]
473; 466; Killsback, Amelia; wife; Dec. 1878; F. F

474; 467; Killsnight, Charles; hsbd.; June 1890; M. F
475; 468; Killsnight, Rosa; wife; Feb. 1899[?]; F. F [Birth year 1903 in 1926.]
476; 469; Killsnight, Anna; dau.; Mar. 1911; F. F [Florence in 1926.]
477; 470; Killsnight, Robert; son; Jan. 1913; M. F
478; 471; Killsnight, Rosa; dau.; Apr. 1915; F. F
479; 472; Killsnight, Susan; dau; May 1917; F. F
480; 473; Killsnight, Hubert; son; Feb. 1919; M. F [Brighton in 1926.]
481; 474; Killsnight, Bessie; dau.; Feb. 1920; F. F [Margaret in 1926. Birth year 1923.]
482; 475; Killsnight, Margaret; dau; Feb. 1924; F. F
483; 476; Killsnight, Dorothy; dau; Feb. 1927; F.

484; Killsnight, Rose; wdw; Apr. 1881[sic]; F. F Died June 25, 1928. [1904-24 Birth 1884.]
485; 477; Killsnight, Carrie; dau; May 1911; F. F

486; 478; Killsnight, William Jr.; sgle; Oct. 1904; M. F

487; 479; Killsnight, Hugh; hsbd; Aug. 1866; M. F
488; 480; Killsnight, Clara; wife; Sept. 1872; F. F

489; 481; Killsnight, Cole; sgle; Feb. 1903; M. F [Birth year 1905 in 1927.]

490; 482; Killsnight, William Sr.; hsbd; Apr. 1856; M. F
491; 483; Killsnight, Cora; wife; June 1860; F. F

492; 484; Killsnight, Martin; hsbd; Jan. 1907; M. F
309; 485; Killsnight, Alice Farr; wife; Feb. 1910; F. 1/8 [Jessie in 1920.]

493; 486; Killsnight, Willis; hsbd.; Mar. 1895; M. F [Rutherford in 1926.]
494; 487; Killsnight, Carrie; wife; May 1890; F. F [Whitemoon]
495; 488; Killsnight, Flossie; dau; Feb. 1923; M.[sic] F [Sage in 1926.]

Census of the **Northern Cheyenne** Indians of **Tongue River** Agency, **Mont.** on **June 30, 1928** taken by **C.B. Lohmiller**, Superintendent.

**Key:** Last Number; Present Number; Indian Name; English Name; Relationship; Month, Year, of Birth; Sex; Blood Quantum

| | | |
|---|---|---|
| 496; | 489; | Killsnight, James; son; Apr. 1926; M. F |
| | 490; | Killsnight, Ralph; son; Apr. 7/28; M. F |

497; 491; Killsnightwoman, ---; wdw; Apr. 1858; F. F

| | | |
|---|---|---|
| 498; | 492; | Killsontop, John; hsbd; Aug. 1906; M. F |
| 1121; | 493; | Killsontop, Mary Strangeowl; wife; Feb. 1909; F. F |
| 499; | 494; | Killsontop, June; dau.; Apr. 1927; F. F |

| | | |
|---|---|---|
| 500; | 495; | Killsontop, Mamie; div.; Mar. 1897; F. F |
| 501; | 496; | Killsontop, Ida; dau; Oct. 1924; F. F |

| | | |
|---|---|---|
| 502; | 497; | Kingfisher, Herman; hsbd; Apr. 1867; M. F |
| 503; | 498; | Kingfisher, Carrie; wife; Aug. 1876; F. F |

| | | |
|---|---|---|
| 504; | 499; | Kingfisher, Willis; hsbd; Sept. 1896; M. F |
| 505; | 500; | Kingfisher, Minnie; wife; July 1896; F. F |
| 506; | 501; | Kingfisher, Isabelle; dau.; Sept. 1918; F. F |
| 507; | 502; | Kingfisher, Charles; son; June 1921; M. F |
| 508; | 503; | Kingfisher, Louise; dau.; Oct. 1922; F. F |
| 509; | 504; | Kingfisher, Ellen; dau.; June 1926; F. F |
| | 505; | Kingfisher, Angela; dau.; May 23/28; F. F |

| | | |
|---|---|---|
| 510; | 506; | Kinzel, Alice; wife; Mar. 1893; F. 1/4 |
| 511; | 507; | Kinzel, Emma Loua[sic]; dau.; June 1917; F. 1/8 |
| 512; | 508; | Kinzel, Helen Louise; dau.; Mar. 1920; F. 1/8 |
| 513; | 509; | Kinzel, Cecelia Leah; dau.; July 1924; F. 1/8 |
| | 510; | Kinzel, Virgil Bruce; son; Oct. 9/27; M. 1/8 |

| | | |
|---|---|---|
| 514; | 511; | Knows-His-Gun, Frances; wife; Oct.1904; F. F |
| | | Knows-His-Gun, Hector; hsbd; ---; --. (Not enrolled) |
| 515; | 512; | Knows-His-Gun, Sylvester; son; Sept 1926; M. F |

| | | |
|---|---|---|
| 516; | 513; | LaFever, Rena Eastman; wife; Aug. 1896[?]; F. 1/8 |
| | | LaFever, I.B.; hsbd; ---; --; (White) |
| 517; | 514; | LaFever, Kenneth; son; Dec. 1925; M. 1/16 [#501; Herman; son; birth year 1925 in 1926.] |

| | | |
|---|---|---|
| 518; | 515; | Lamebear, Benjamin; hsbd; July 1894; M. F |
| 519; | 516; | Lamebear, Clara; wife; May 1894; F. F |
| 520; | 517; | Lamebear, Eva; dau; Nov. 1910[sic]; F. F [Birth year 1916 first shows in 1917.] |
| 521; | 518; | Lamebear, Cora; dau.; Apr. 1919; F. F |
| 522; | 519; | Lamebear, Charles; son; Oct. 1921; M. F |

Census of the **Northern Cheyenne** Indians of **Tongue River** Agency, **Mont.** on **June 30, 1928** taken by **C.B. Lohmiller**, Superintendent.

**Key:** Last Number; Present Number; Indian Name; English Name; Relationship; Month, Year, of Birth; Sex; Blood Quantum

523;                Lamebear, Will; son; Jan. 1926; M. F Died June 10, 1928

524;   520;   Lamewoman, Nellie; sgle; July 1854; F. F

525;   521;   Lamewoman, Sam; son; Oct. 1912; M. F (Sam Littlebear)
526;   522;   Lamewoman, Mary; dau.; Aug. 1917; F. F s-dau. Ed Womanleggins [Same previous number name Minnie birth year 1916. Has a sister named Mary #510 birth year 1914.]

527;   523;   Lamewoman, Stanley; hsbd.; Aug. 1889; M. F
528;   524;   Lamewoman, Augusta; wife; July 1885; F. F
529;   525;   Lamewoman, Virgil; son; Feb. 1822[sic]; M. F
530;   526;   Lamewoman, Jessie; dau.; June 1914; F. F

531;   527;   Lastbull, Fred; hsbd; Jan. 1888; M. F
              Lastbull, Maywoman; wife; ---; --. (No enrolled)

532;   528;   Lennon, Mary Burns; wife; June 1906; F. 1/8
              Lennon, Thomas; hsbd; ---; --. (White)
533;   529;   Lennon, Arthur George; son; Nov. 1926; M. 1/16

534;   530;   Lightning, Frank; wdr; Aug. 1871; M. F

535;   531;   Limberhand, Richard; sgle.; Aug. 1905; M. F

536;   532;   Limberhand, James; sgle; Oct. 1902[?]; M. F

537;   533;   Limberhand, Nathan; hsbd.; Mar. 1876; M. F
538;   534;   Limberhand, Artie; wife; Sept. 1883; F. F
539;   535;   Limberhand, Elmore; son; Jan. 1909; M. F
540;   536;   Limberhand, Bennie; son; Jan. 1912[?]; M. F
541;   537;   Limberhand, Jennie; dau.; Nov. 1915; F. F
542;   538;   Limberhand, Doris; dau.; May 1922; F. F

543;   539;   Limpy, Benjamin; hsbd.; Oct. 1892; M. F
544;   540;   Limpy, Hattie[sic]; wife; June 1894; F. F
[#540; Hallie Killsacross #271, 1914 census. 1915-16 Hallie Limpy.]
545;   541;   Limpy, Anna; dau.; Jan. 1915; F. F [Son, Jack 1916- 19; Jean in 1926.]
546;   542;   Limpy, Rosa; dau.; Aug. 1919; F. F [#530 Elnora; birth year1921 in 1926.]
547;   543;   Limpy, Jessie; dau.; Nov. 1922; F. F

548;   544;   Limpy, Charles; hsbd; Oct. 1857; M. F

Census of the **Northern Cheyenne** Indians of **Tongue River** Agency, **Mont.** on **June 30, 1928** taken by **C.B. Lohmiller**, Superintendent.

**Key:** Last Number; Present Number; Indian Name; English Name; Relationship; Month, Year, of Birth; Sex; Blood Quantum

549; 545; Limpy, Nellie; wife; July 1854; F. F

550; 546; Limpy, Fred; hsbd; Apr. 1884; M. 1/2
551; 547; Limpy, Amelia; wife; May 1885; F. F [Womanleggins]
552; 548; Limpy, Mamie; dau.; Dec. 1907; F. 3/4
553; 549; Limpy, Frank; son; May 1911; M. 3/4
554; 550; Limpy, Mary; dau; May 1913; F. 3/4 [#506, Limpy, Mary; D.; 6 Mo; in 1909. #538 May Limpy birth year 1913 in 1926.]
555; 551; Limpy, Henry; son; Aug. 1919; M. 3/4 Lives with g-fthr. Nathan Limberhand. [1920 Census Fred Jr.]
556; 552; Limpy, Cora; dau; Nov 1925; F. 3/4
Limpy, Elnora; dau.; June 1927; F. 3/4 Unreported last year Died Sept. 9, 1927

557; 553; Littlebear, Paul; hsbd.; July 1887; M. F
558; 554; Littlebear, Rosa; wife; Aug. 1887; F. F
559; 555; Littlebear, May; dau; May 1908; F. F [Anne in 1926.]
560; 556; Littlebear, Flossie; dau; Apr. 1912; F. F [Mary in 1926.]
561; 557; Littlebear, Clara; dau.; Apr. 1916; F. F
562; 558; Littlebear, Two Birds; son; Dec. 1923; M. F
563; 559; Littlebear, Lucille; dau.; July 1926; F. F

564; 560; Littlebird, Peter; hsbd.; May 1870; M. F
565; 561; Littlebird, Jennie; wife; July 1892; F. F
566; 562; Littlebird, Joseph; son; Sept. 1912; M. F
567; 563; Littlebird, Julia; dau.; June 1922; F. F
568; 564; Littlebird, James Wm.; son; June 1925; M. F
569; 565; Littlebird, Harry; s-son; Aug. 1918; M. F s-son Leo Whitecrane
570; 566; Littlebird, James; s-son; July 1919; M. F s-son Leo Whitecrane
[#570, Previous #1274; Littlebird, Elsie; s-dau; birth year 1920; F in 1926.]

571; 567; Littlechief, Victor; hsbd; Jan. 1877; M. F
572; 568; Littlechief, Louisa; wife; Mar. 1875; F. F
573; 569; Littlechief, Lucille; dau.; Feb. 1911; F. F

574; 570; Littlecoyote, Henry; fthr; Sept. 1875; M. F
575; 571; Littlecoyote, Daniel; son; Oct. 1910; M. F

576; 572; Littleeagle, Charles; hsbd; May 1867; M. F
577; 573; Littleeagle, Mary; wife; June 1878; F. F
578; 574; Littleeagle, Clara; dau.; Aug. 1905; F. F

579; 575; Littleeyes, Eva; sgle; July 1893; F. F Lives with Zac Rowland

Census of the **Northern Cheyenne** Indians of **Tongue River** Agency, **Mont.** on **June 30, 1928** taken by **C.B. Lohmiller**, Superintendent.

**Key:** Last Number; Present Number; Indian Name; English Name; Relationship; Month, Year, of Birth; Sex; Blood Quantum

580; 576; Littlehawk, Dora; wdw; Jan. 1869; F. F

581; 577; Littlehead, Charles; hsbd.; June 1869; M. F
582; 578; Littlehead, Nellie; wife; Dec. 1882; F. F
583; 579; Littlehead, Frank; son; Nov. 1909; M. F
584; 580; Littlehead, George; son; May 1920; M. F [1920 name John.]

585; 581; Littlehead, Rena; s-dau.; Nov. 1919; F. F s-dau. Oliver Eaglefeathers. [Mildred in 1926.]

586; 582; Littlehead, John; hsbd; -- 1894; M. F

587; 583; Littleoldman, Fern; s-dau; Aug. 1917; F. F s.-dau. Chas. Sharpnose [#569; Littleman, Julia; s-dau; 1915; F. (s-dau Fred Limpy) in 1926.]

588; 584; Littlemouth, Clara; wdw; July 1859; F. F

589; 585; Littlemouth, John; hsbd.; Oct. 1894[?]; M. F [Keeps changing year of birth.]
590; 586; Littlemouth, Jennie; wife; Sept 1898; F. F
591; 587; Littlemouth, Evelyn; dau; May 1921; F. F
592; 588; Littlemouth, James; son; June 1922; M. F
593; 589; Littlemouth, Mary; dau; Apr 1924; F. F
Littlemouth, Baby; son; Mar. 20/28; M. F Died March 29, 1928

594; 590; Littleoldman, Thomas; son; Dec. 1913; M. F

595; 591; Littlesun, Jack; son; Aug. 1920; M. F
596; 592; Littlesun, Horace; son; Sept. 1922; M. F
Children of Bessie Littlesun Wolfchum.

597; 593; Littlesun, Frank; hsbd; Oct. 1884; M. F
598; 594; Littlesun, Anna; wife; June 1892; F. F
599; 595; Littlesun, Alfred; son; Dec. 1912; M. F

600; 596; Littlesun, Samuel; hsbd; July 1858; M. F
601; 597; Littlesun, Cora; wife; Sept. 1864; F. F

602; 598; Littlewhirlwind, George; hsbd; Jan. 1901; M. F
603; 599; Littlewhirlwind, Martha; wife; Oct. 1909; F. F [Fannie Walksalong in 1926.]
Littlewhirlwind, Ellen; dau; July 1927; F. F Died Sept. 17, 1927

604; 600; Littlewhiteman, Aaron; hsbd; Dec. 1862; M. 1/2

Census of the __**Northern Cheyenne**__ Indians of **Tongue River** Agency, **Mont.** on **June 30, 1928** taken by **C.B. Lohmiller**, Superintendent.

**Key:** Last Number; Present Number; Indian Name; English Name; Relationship; Month, Year, of Birth; Sex; Blood Quantum

605; 601; Littlewhiteman, Sadie; wife; Apr. 1866; F. F
606; 602; Littlewhiteman, Wesley; sgle; Aug. 1897; M. 3/4

607; 603; Littlewhiteman, Frank; hsbd; Nov. 1901; M. 3/4
608; 604; Littlewhiteman, Emma; wife; Oct. 1900; F. F [#964 in 1919 shows as Lightning, Emma; g dt; 1901; F. Grandparents Shortsioux in census as birth year 1901 starting in 1912 or 11 years old.]
609; 605; Littlewhiteman, Leon; son; Aug. 1920; M. 7/8 [John in 1926.]
610; 606; Littlewhiteman, Margaret; dau; July 1922; F. 7/8
611; Littlewhiteman, John; son; Oct. 1925; M. 7/8 Died October 27, 1927

612; 607; Littlewhiteman, David; hsbd; Feb. 1869; M. 1/2
613; 608; Littlewhiteman, Agnes; wife; July 1872; F. F
614; 609; Littlewhiteman, Peter; son; Apr. 1906; M. 3/4

615; 610; Littlewhiteman, James; hsbd; June 1895; M. 3/4
616; 611; Littlewhiteman, Gusta; wife; Sept 1897; F. F [Littlesun]
617; 612; Littlewhiteman, Kitty; dau; Sept 1923; F. 7/8
618; 613; Littlewhiteman, Charles; son; Sept 1925; M. 7/8 [In 1926 #600; as Charles (Albert); son; 1925; M.]

619; 614; Littlewhiteman, Milton; hsbd; Sept 1884[?]; M. [Most previous cenuses 1886.]
620; 615; Littlewhiteman, Rosa; wife; Sept 1882; F. F

621; 616; Littlewhiteman, Henry; hsbd; Jan. 1891; M. 3/4
622; 617; Littlewhiteman, Josie; wife; Feb. 1897; F. F [Weaselbear; Prev. Marriage Woodenlegs.]
623; 618; Littlewhiteman, Edith; dau.; Dec. 1912[sic]; F. 7/8 [Birth 1915.]
624; 619; Littlewhiteman, Rosa; dau.; Sept. 1915[sic]; F. 7/8 [Birth 1920.]
625; 620; Littlewhiteman, Agnes; dau.; Oct. 1921; F. 7/8
626; 621; Littlewhiteman, Bessie; dau.; May 1926; F. 7/8

627; 622; Littlewhiteman, Charles; son; Feb.1915; M. 7/8 s-son Dan Seminole

628; 623; Littlewhiteman, Florence; dau.; Feb. 1915; F. 7/8 s-dau. Chas. Spottedwolf

629; 624; Littlewhiteman, Stanley; hsbd; July 1888; M. 3/4
630; 625; Littlewhiteman, Grace; wife; -- 1894; F. F [1920- #1300, name Walkingbear.]
631; 626; Littlewhiteman, Milton; son; Dec. 1914; M. 7/8
632; 627; Littlewhiteman, Aaron; son; Dec. 1921; M. 7/8
633; 628; Littlewhiteman, Adrain; son; Dec. 1923; M. 7/8 [Name Hillman; birth 1924 in 1926.]

Census of the **Northern Cheyenne** Indians of **Tongue River** Agency, **Mont.** on **June 30, 1928** taken by **C.B. Lohmiller**, Superintendent.

**Key:** Last Number; Present Number; Indian Name; English Name; Relationship; Month, Year, of Birth; Sex; Blood Quantum

634; 629; Littlewhiteman, Sadie; dau; Jan. 1927; F. 7/8

635; 630; Littlewolf, Frank; hsbd; Feb. 1877; M. F
636; 631; Littlewolf, Kate; wife; Mar. 1883; F. F
637; 632; Littlewolf, May; dau; Mar. 1911; F. F
638; 633; Littlewolf, Susan; dau.; June 1914; F. F
639; 634; Littlewolf, Mary; dau.; Feb. 1922; F. F

640; 635; Littlewolf, Laura; wdw; Nov. 1852; F. F

641; 636; Littlewolf, Lena; sgle; Dec. 1878[sic]; F. F
[Lena #636; Censuses 1904-09 birth year is 1880; 1910 birth year is 1890; 1911-13 birth year is 1876; 1914-17 birth year 1881; 1918 birth year is 1851; 1919-28 birth year is 1878.]

642; 637; Littlewolf, Robert; hsbd; June 1882[?]; M. F [1904-1913 birth year 1882. 1914-26 birth year 1877.]
643; 638; Littlewolf, May; wife; June 1894; F. F [Prev. #373 name Harris; 1920.]
644; 639; Littlewolf, Charles Homer; son; July 1908[sic]; M. F [Birth year 1918 in 1919.]
645; 640; Littlewolf, Geraldine; dau.; Dec. 1921; F. F
646; 641; Littlewolf, Eva; dau.; Apr. 1925; F. F
642; Littlewolf, Laban; son; June 4/28; M. F

647; 643; Littlewolf, Mary; sgle; Nov. 1903; F. F

648; 644; Littlewolf, William; hsbd; Aug. 1883; M. F
649; 645; Littlewolf, May; wife; Dec. 1890; F. F
650; 646; Littlewolf, Mamie; dau; July 1912[?]; F. F
651; 647; Littlewolf, William Jr; son; Oct. 1914[?]; M. F
652; 648; Littlewolf, Claude; son; Dec. 1916[?]; M. F

656; 649; Littleyellowman, Eddie; hsbd; -- 1892; M. F [birth year 1890 in 1926.]

653; 650; Littleyellowman, Hugh; sgle; -- 1885; M. F

654; 651; Littleyellowman, Jake; hsbd; Oct. 1861; M. F
655; 652; Littleyellowman, Gertrude; wife; Apr. 1875; F. F

1441; 653; Littleyellowman, May; dau; -- 1916; F. F
1442; 654; Littleyellowman, Rose; dau; Mar. 1923; F. F
1443; 655; Littleyellowman, Susie; dau.; Feb. 1921; F. F

Census of the **Northern Cheyenne** Indians of **Tongue River** Agency, **Mont.** on **June 30, 1928** taken by **C.B. Lohmiller**, Superintendent.

**Key:** Last Number; Present Number; Indian Name; English Name; Relationship; Month, Year, of Birth; Sex; Blood Quantum

657; 656; Littleyellowman, Richard; son; July 1890; M. F

658; 657; Lonebull, Louis; sgle; Aug. 1858; M. F

659; 658; Loneelk, Wilson; sgle; Mar. 1911; M. F (Lives with Nellie Redeagle)

660; 659; Lonetravelingwolf, Mabel; dau.; June 1910; F. F dau. Jane Walkingbird

661; 660; Lonewolf, Charles; hsbd; June 1883; M. F
662; 661; Lonewolf, Rose; wife; Dec. 1890; F. [1917 Census name was Mary. 1927 name is Rosa.]
663; 662; Lonewolf, James; son; July 1915; M. F [Lloyd in 1926.]
664; 663; Lonewolf, Ella; dau; May 1925; F. F

665; 664; Longjaw, Frank; hsbd; Apr. 1900; M. F
666; 665; Longjaw, Cora Sharpnose; wife; May 1901; F. F
667; 666; Longjaw, Robert; son; Mar. 1927; M. F

668; 667; Longjaw, Charles; hsbd; Mar. 1846[?]; M. F [1904-08 birth year 1843. 1909-13 birth year 1856-7. 1914-26 birth year 1857.]
669; 668; Longjaw, Clara; wife; Apr. 1862; F. F
670; 669; Longjaw, Charles Jr.; g-son; July 1915; M. F

671; 670; Longjaw, James; hsbd; May 1881; M. F
672; 671; Longjaw, Nellie; wife; Jan. 1896; F. F
672; Longjaw, Donald; son; Nov. 27/27; M. F

673; 673; Longjaw, Elmer; hsbd; Dec. 1883[?]; M. F
674; 674; Longjaw, Lena; wife; Aug. 1886; F. F
[From 1814 to 1817 Censuses have birth year as 1866.]
675; 675; Longjaw, Albert; son; June 1912; M. F
676; 676; Longjaw, Henry; son; Jan. 1916; M. F
677; 677; Longjaw, Clara; dau; Jan. 1919; F. F
678; Longjaw, James; son; Dec. 1923; M. F Died Dec. 3, 1927

679; 678; Longroach, George; hsbd; Apr. 1882; M. F
680; 679; Longroach, Nellie; wife; June 1888; F. F
681; 680; Longroach, Harry; son; Jan 1911; M. F
682; 681; Longroach, James; son; Nov. 1914; M. F
683; 682; Longroach, Mary; dau; Mar. 1917; F. F [Name Vita 1917-26.]
684; 683; Longroach, Frank; son; Feb. 1920; M. F
685; 684; Longroach, Regina; dau; Sept. 1923; F. F [Veria in 1923.]
686; Longroach, May; dau; Aug. 1926; F. F Died March 3, 1928

Census of the **Northern Cheyenne** Indians of **Tongue River** Agency, **Mont.** on **June 30, 1928** taken by **C.B. Lohmiller**, Superintendent.

**Key:** Last Number; Present Number; Indian Name; English Name; Relationship; Month, Year, of Birth; Sex; Blood Quantum

687; 685; Looksatbareground, Jas.; hsbd; May 1878; M. F
688; 686; Looksatbareground, Julia; wife; May 1852; F. F [1924 wd., Elkshoulders.]

689; 687; Looksbehind, James; hsbd; -- 1885; M. F (James Nightwalking)
1444; 688; Looksbehind, Roy; son; -- 1921; M. F
1445; 689; Looksbehind, Camilla; dau; Aug. 1923; F. F
690; 690; Looksbehind, James Jr.; son; May 1927; M. F

691; 691; Looksbehind, Charles; hsbd; Oct. 1860; M. F
692; 692; Looksbehind, Thomas; son; July 1907[sic]; M. F [1904-24 birth year 1903, 1 year old in 1904 census. 1925-26 birth year 1923.]

693; 693; Looksbehind, Sallie; div.; Oct. 1859; F. F
694; 694; Looksbehind, Pius; g-son; Mar. 1912; M. F (Redneck)

695; Lostleg, Gertrude; wdw; Nov. 1859; F. F Died. Aug. 12, 1927

696; 695; Lostleg, Nelson; hsbd; July 1891; M. F
697; 696; Lostleg, James; son; Dec. 1915; M. F [Ernest George in 1926.]
698; 697; Lostleg, Virginia Theodorea; dau; Feb. 1919; F. F [Son Theodore in 1920.]

699; 698; Magpie, Albert; fthr; Apr. 1886; M. F [Prev. censuses from 1904-15 name is Youngmagpie with same birth year, none in 1913, Magpie in 1916. As early as 1907 a first wife Julia born 1887. Anne is a second wife starting in 1919. Anne is not in 1925.]
700; 699; Magpie, Anna Mary; dau; Dec. 1919; F. F [Minnie in 1926.]
701; 700; Magpie, Gilbert; son; Aug. 1922; M. F [#681 in 1926 was Magpie, Eva; dau; 1919; F.]
702; Magpie, Rose; dau; Sept. 1925; M. F Died December 10, 1927 [#682 in 1926 was Magpie, Edward; son; 1923; M.]

703; 701; Magpie, Louis; hsbd; Oct. 1885; M. F
704; 702; Magpie, Mira[sic]; wife; July 1894; F. F
705; 703; Magpie, Eddie; son; Apr. 1910[sic]; M. F [Shows in 1906, #705; Eddy; M; S; 2mo.]

706; 704; Manbear, Lena; mthr; Aug. 1867; F. F
707; 705; Manbear, Lizzie; dau; Apr. 1902; F. F
708; 706; Manbear, Walters Coolidge; g-son; Feb. 1926; M. 3/4

709; 707; Marrowbone, Jessie; mthr; -- 1888; F. F Children enrolled at Pine Ridge.

Census of the **Northern Cheyenne** Indians of **Tongue River** Agency, **Mont.** on **June 30, 1928** taken by **C.B. Lohmiller**, Superintendent.

**Key:** Last Number; Present Number; Indian Name; English Name; Relationship; Month, Year, of Birth; Sex; Blood Quantum

710; 708; Medicine, Sampson; hsbd; Sept. 1876; M. F
711; 709; Medicine, Anna; wife; Feb. 1879; F. F

712; 710; Medicine, Jennie; sgle; Mar. 1902; F. F

713; 711; Medicinebear, Maggie; wdw; June 1847; F. F

714; 712; Medicinebird, Nelson; hsbd; Aug. 1875; M. F
715; 713; Medicinebird, Ella; wife; Feb. 1883; F. F
716; 714; Medicinebird, Homer; son; Mar. 1914; M. F

717; 715; Medicinebull, Robert; hsbd; Aug. 1860; M. F
718; 716; Medicinebull, Maggie; wife; July 1862; F. F

719; 717; Medicinebull, Willis; hsbd; Apr. 1887; M. F
720; 718; Medicinebull, Anne; wife; May 1902[?]; F. F [Swallow] [Birth year 1905 in 1926.]
721; 719; Medicinebull, Fred; son; Oct. 1925; M. F

722; 720; Medicinebull, James; son; Aug. 1910; M. F
723; 721; Medicinebull, Ruth; dau; June 1913; F. F [Birth year 1911 in 1926.]

724; Medicinebull, Donald; son; May 1922; M. F Died March 23, 1928 [Mother, Ruth Yellownose.]

725; 722; Medicineelk, Basil; hsbd; Jan. 1894; M. F
726; 723; Medicineelk, Jennie E.; wife; Sept. 1904; F. F [Eaglefeathers]
727; 724; Medicineelk, Spencer; son; July 1917; M. F
725; Medicineelk, Sarah Alice; dau.; Apr. 20/28; F. F

728; 726; Medicineelk, Harold; wdr; July 1865; M. F
729; 727; Medicineelk, John; g-son; Oct. 1908; M. F [Sandwoman]

730; 728; Medicineelk, James Edw; sgle; Apr. 1902; M. F

731; 729; Medicineelk, Thomas; hsbd; July 1906[?]; M. F [Birth year 1904 in 1926.]
732; 730; Medicineelk , Nellie T.; wife; Oct. 1912; F. F
731; Medicineelk , William; son; Mar. 5/28; M. F

733; 732; Medicineelk, Andrew; hsbd; May 1898[sic]; M. F
734; 733; Medicineelk, Maggie; wife; Jan. 1903; F. F [Bearquiver]
735; 734; Medicineelk, Peter; son; Mar. 1926; M. F
735; Medicineelk, Claude; son; Dec. 4/27; M. F

Census of the **Northern Cheyenne** Indians of **Tongue River** Agency, **Mont.** on **June 30, 1928** taken by **C.B. Lohmiller**, Superintendent.

**Key:** Last Number; Present Number; Indian Name; English Name; Relationship; Month, Year, of Birth; Sex; Blood Quantum

736; 736; Medicineflying, John; hsbd.; Sept. 1882; M. F
737; 737; Medicineflying, Bertha; wife; Feb. 1885; F. F
738; 738; Medicineflying, Jennie; dau.; Feb. 1910; F. F [Bernice from 1910-23.]
739; 739; Medicineflying, Helen; dau.; Aug. 1916; F. F
740; 740; Medicineflying, Agnes; dau; May 1920; F. F
741; 741; Medicineflying, Phyllis; dau; July 1924; F. F [Birth year 1925 in 1926.]

742; 742; Medicinetop, James; wdr; May 1861; M. F

743; 743; Medicinetop, John; hsbd.; Jan. 1885; M. F
744; 744; Medicinetop, Ida; wife; May 1890; F. F
745; 745; Medicinetop, Clarence; son; Oct. 1910; M. F
746; 746; Medicinetop, Marjorie; dau; Apr. 1914[sic]; F. F [Birth year 1917.]
747; 747; Medicinetop, Phyllis; dau; Sept 1922; F. F
748; 748; Medicinetop, Roy; son; Aug 1924; M. F [Birth year 1925 in 1926.]
749; Medicinetop, Lena; dau; Oct. 24/27; F. F

749; 750; Merritt, Wesley; hsbd; Oct. 1876; M. F
750; 751; Merritt, Josie; wife; May 1863; F. F

751; 752; Mexicancheyenne, Ernest; hsbd.; Dec. 1889[sic]; M. 1/2
752; 753; Mexicancheyenne, Mary; wife; July 1899; F. F
753; 754; Mexicancheyenne, Hilda; dau; June 1919; F. 3/4
754; 755; Mexicancheyenne. Mary Victoria; dau; Aug. 1921; F. 3/4
755; 756; Mexicancheyenne. Rudolph; son; Feb. 1925; M. 3/4 [Anabelle; dau; 1925.]

756; 757; Mexicancheyenne, Marion; hsbd; July 1887; M. 1/2
757; 758; Mexicancheyenne, Emma; wife; June 1893; F. F
758; 759; Mexicancheyenne, James; son; July 1914; M. 3/4
759; 760; Mexicancheyenne, Rosa; dau; Nov. 1918; F. 3/4
760; 761; Mexicancheyenne, Margaret; dau; Dec. 1920; F. 3/4 [Ethel in 1926.]
761; 762; Mexicancheyenne, Mary; dau; Jan. 1925; F. 3/4
763; Mexicancheyenne, Mabel Ann; dau; Feb. 2/28; F. 3/4

763; 764; Oldbull, Daniel; fthr; Oct. 1870; M. F
764; 765; Oldbull, Thomas; son; Nov. 1910; M. F

765; 766; Onebear, James; hsbd; July 1900; M. 3/4
766; 767; Onebear, Maggie; wife; Mar. 1903; F. 3/4 [Seminole]
767; 768; Onebear, Robert; son; Dec. 1925; M. 3/4

768; 769; Parker, Alvin O.; hsbd; June 1879; M. 1/4
Parker, Mildred; wife; ---; --. (White)

Census of the **Northern Cheyenne** Indians of **Tongue River** Agency, **Mont.** on **June 30, 1928** taken by **C.B. Lohmiller**, Superintendent.

**Key:** Last Number; Present Number; Indian Name; English Name; Relationship; Month, Year, of Birth; Sex; Blood Quantum

769; 770; Parker, Clyde Spencer; son; Nov. 1922; M. 1/8
770; 771; Parker, Verda Faye; dau; Sept 1924; F. 1/8
771; 772; Parker, Shirley Rose; dau; Jan. 1927; F. 1/8

772; 773; Parker, Charles A Jr.; hsbd; July 1885; M. 1/4
Parker, Marie; wife; ---; F. 1/4 (Not enrolled)
773; 774; Parker, Theresa; dau; Mar. 1912; F. 1/4
774; 775; Parker, Gabriel; son; Oct. 1926; M. 1/4

775; 776; Parker, Edwin H.; sgle; Apr. 1895; M. 1/4

776; 777; Parker, Guy; hsbd; Sept 1891; M. 1/4
Parker, Gertrude; wife; ---; --. (Not enrolled)
777; 778; Parker, Winfred; son; Apr. 1914; M. 1/4
778; 779; Parker, Alice; dau; Feb. 1917; F. 1/4
779; 780; Parker, Stella; dau; Apr.1919; F. 1/4
780; Parker, Vincent Albert; son; July 1925; M. 1/4 Died March 11, 1928 [birth month June in 1927.]

781; 781; Pease, Ida (Eastman); wife; Feb. 1906; F. 1/8
Pease, George; hsbd; ---; --. (Not enrolled)

782; 782; Pine, Frank; wdr; July 1863; M. F

783; 783; Pine, Rutherford; hsbd; June 1886; M. F
784; 784; Pine, Julia; wife; Aug. 1896[sic]; F. F [In 1916 marries Julia Blackcrane nee Kingfisher; in 1912 she is 18 years old, birth year is 1894 from 1904-16. Gave birth year as 1884 from 1917-26.]
785; 785; Pine, Cecelia; dau; Jan. 1916; F. F
786; 786; Pine, Daniel; son; Sept. 1923; M. F

787; 787; Pine, Wilson; hsbd; Mar. 1886; M. F
788; 788; Pine, Nora; wife; July 1888; F. F
789; 789; Pine, Alexander; son; Nov. 1917; M. F
790; 790; Pine, John; son; Apr. 1922; M. F
791; 791; Pine, Sarah; dau; Aug. 1924; F. F

792; 792; Playingbear, Henry; hsbd; Jan. 1877; M. F
793; 793; Playingbear, Mildred; wife; April 1880[?]; F. F [1904-17 birth year 1881-82, 1918-26 birth year 1888.]
794; 794; Playingbear, Mary; dau; Feb. 1911; F. F
795; 795; Playingbear, John; son; May 1915; M. F

796; 796; Plentycamps, Clara; wdw; Aug. 1845; F. F

Census of the **Northern Cheyenne** Indians of **Tongue River** Agency, **Mont.** on **June 30, 1928** taken by **C.B. Lohmiller**, Superintendent.

**Key:** Last Number; Present Number; Indian Name; English Name; Relationship; Month, Year, of Birth; Sex; Blood Quantum

797; 797; Porcupine, Albert; hsbd; July 1848; M. F
798; 798; Porcupine, Julia; wife; Apr. 1866; F. F

799; 799; Powderface, John; hsbd; May 1866; M. F

800; 800; Powderface, Julia; s-dau.; Aug. 1913; F. F s-dau. Wilson Pine
801; 801; Powderface, Fern; s-dau.; July 1918; F. F s-dau. Wilson Pine

802; 802; Powell, Mary; wife; Nov. 1881; F. 1/2
          Powell, Edward; hsbd.; ---;--. (White)
803; 803; Powell, Deyo; son; June 1907[sic]; M. 1/4 [Birth year 1909, 6 mo's old.]
804; 804; Powell, Howard; son; Feb. 1912; M. 1/4

805; 805; Powell, Clay; div.; Nov. 1904; M. 1/4

806; 806; Prairiebear, Arthur; hsbd.; Mar. 1882; M. F
807; 807; Prairiebear, Sally; wife; Oct. 1885; F. F

808; 808; Redbeads, John; hsbd; Nov. 1871; M. F
809; 809; Redbeads, Nancy; wife; Apr. 1878; F. F [Birth year 1876 in 1927.]
810; 810; Redbeads, Susie; dau; May 1913; F. F
811; 811; Redbeads, Clara; dau; June 1915; F. F
812; 812; Redbeads, Georgia; dau; July 1917; F. F [Name Gloria 1917-20.]

813; 813; Redbird, Joseph; hsbd; Oct. 1899; M. F [Middle name Francis in 1910.]
762; 814; Redbird, Dorothy M.C.; wife; July 1908; F. 3/4 [Mexicancheyenne]
814; 815; Redbird, William; son; June 1922; M. F
815; 816; Redbird, Allen; son; May 1925, M. F [First shows in 1925 with birth in 1924. Same Prev. #, Helena; dau; 1925, F. in 1926.]
      817; Redbird, David; son; May 22/28; M. 7/8

816; 818; Redbird, William; hsbd; July 1876; M. F
817; 819; Redbird, Florence; wife; June 1877; F. 3/4
818; 820; Redbird, Lena; dau.; Nov. 1920; F. 7/8 [Susie in 1926.]

820; 821; Redbreath, Charles; hsbd; Apr. 1879; M. F
821; 822; Redbreath, Betty; wife; Jan. 1908; F. F [Yellownose]
822; 823; Redbreath, Elina Jane; dau.; June 1925; F. F [Elina June in 1926.]
      824; Redbreath, George; son; July 1927; M. F

823; 825; Redcherries, Teddy; wdr[?]; -- 1888; M. F
1446; 826; Redcherries, Miller; son; Nov. 1920; M. F

Census of the **Northern Cheyenne** Indians of **Tongue River** Agency, **Mont.** on **June 30, 1928** taken by **C.B. Lohmiller**, Superintendent.

**Key:** Last Number; Present Number; Indian Name; English Name; Relationship; Month, Year, of Birth; Sex; Blood Quantum

824;  827;  Redcherries, William; hsbd; June 1890; M. F
825;  828;  Redcherries, Bessie; wife; Feb. 1894; F. F
826;  829;  Redcherries, Anna; dau; May 1910; F. F [Woodenthigh-Killsontop; #256, Divesbackward, May; s-dau; 1910; F., in 1926.]
827;  830;  Redcherries, Alice; dau; Aug. 1912; F. F
828;  831;  Redcherries, Rose; dau.; Apr. 1916; F. F
829;  832;  Redcherries, Frank; son; May 1919; M. F
830;  833;  Redcherries, Margaret; dau; Sept 1923; F. F
        834;  Redcherries, Katie; dau; Sept 3/27; F. F

831;  835;  Redeagle, Jennie; wdw; Sept 1841[?]; F. F
[Jennie #835, Census 1904-14 birth year 1851; 1915-18 birth year 1852. 1919-26 birth year 1832.]

832;  836;  Redeagle, Nellie; wdw; Aug. 1872; F. F

833;  837;  Redeagle, Willis; sgle; Dec. 1901; M. F

834;  838;  Redfox, James; hsbd; Apr. 1865; M. F
835;  839;  Redfox, Cora; wife; July 1867; F. F

836;  840;  Redfox, Jennie; Wdw; Dec. 1873; F. F

837;  841;  Redfox, Robert; hsbd.; Mar. 1900; M. F
838;  842;  Redfox, Cecelia; wife; June 1894; F. F
839;  843;  Redfox, Edna; dau; Mar. 1927; M[sic]. F

840;  844;  Redneck, Curtis; hsbd; Jan. 1888; M. 3/4
841;  845;  Redneck, Josie; wife; Dec. 1896; F. F

842;  846;  Redneck, David; fthr.; Sept. 1891; M. 3/4
843;  847;  Redneck, Minnie; dau.; Aug. 1919; F. 7/8

844;  848;  Redneck, Clyde; son; Aug. 1912; M. 7/8 son Maude Shields Whitewolf.

845;  849;  Redneck, Henry; hsbd; Aug. 1882; M. F
846;  850;  Redneck, Fannie; wife; July 1884[?]; F. F [Birth year 1887 in 1926.]
847;  851;  Redneck, Grace; dau; Mar. 1910; F. F
848;  852   Redneck, Dora; dau; Oct. 1914[?]; F. F [Birth year 1908 in 1926.]
849;  853;  Redneck, Homer; son; July 1917; M. F
850;  854;  Redneck, Florence; dau; Apr 1921; F. F
851;  855;  Redneck, John; son; May 1925; M. F

Census of the **Northern Cheyenne** Indians of **Tongue River** Agency, **Mont.** on **June 30, 1928** taken by **C.B. Lohmiller**, Superintendent.

**Key:** Last Number; Present Number; Indian Name; English Name; Relationship; Month, Year, of Birth; Sex; Blood Quantum

852; 856; Rednose, Paul; hsbd; June 1876; M. F
853; 857; Rednose, Lucy; wife; May 1870; F. 1/2
854; 858; Rednose, Sarah Mae; dau.; Nov. 1914; F. F

855; 859; Redowl, Mabel; wdw; July 1846[?]; F. F [Birth year 1840 in 1926.]

856; 860; Redrobe, Fred; hsbd; Oct. 1867; M. F
857; 861; Redrobe, Nora; wife; Apr. 1869; F. F
858; 862; Redrobe, Louis; son; Nov. 1892; M. F

859; 863; Redrobe, Jasper; sgle; July 1900; M. F

860; 864; Redrobe, William; hsbd; Aug. 1897; M. F
861; 865; Redrobe, Alice; wife; May 1884[?]; F. F [1907-19, birth year 1884-5. 1904 nee-Killsnight; 1905-6 Risingsun, 1907-19 Shell, 1920-28 Redrobe.]

862; 866; Redwater, Thaddeus; hsbd; Mar. 1875; M. F
Redwater, Martha; wife; ---; --. (Not enrolled)

863; 867; Redwater, Cecelia; div.; Feb. 1872; F. F

864; 868; Redwoman, Frank; hsbd; Feb. 1889; M. F
865; Redwoman, Ella; wife; Mary[sic] 1900; F. F Died April 21, 1928
866; 869; Redwoman, Flossie Alice; dau; Sept. 1911; F. F
867; 870; Redwoman, Eugene; son; Feb. 1923; M. F
868; 871; Redwoman, Joe; son; May 1924; M. F
872; Redwoman, George; son; Apr. 4/28; M. F

869; 873; Redwoman, Manuel; hsbd.; July 1881; M. F
870; 874; Redwoman, Olive; wife; Aug. 1891; F. F
871; 875; Redwoman, Edna; dau; July 1926; F. F
876; Redwoman, Paul; son; June 11/28; M. F
827;[sic]877; Redwoman, Julia; dau.; July 1909; F. F dau-Mrs. John Chubby [1926 Nicetalker, Clarice; s-dau; 1909; F. (s-dau John Chubby). Prev. #872.]

873; 878; Ridgebear, Charles; fthr; -- 1882; M. F

874; 879; Ridgebear, Willis; hsbd; July 1887; M. F
875; 880; Ridgebear, Rilla; wife; Mar. 1898; F. F
876; 881; Ridgebear, Bessie Agnes; dau; Nov. 1918; F. F
877; 882; Ridgebear, Carrie; dau; Apr 1921; F. F [Katie in 1926.]
878; 883; Ridgebear, Anna; dau; Jan. 1927; F. F

879; 884; Ridgewalker, Robert; hsbd; June 1860[sic]; M. F

Census of the **Northern Cheyenne** Indians of **Tongue River** Agency, **Mont.** on **June 30, 1928** taken by **C.B. Lohmiller**, Superintendent.

**Key:** Last Number; Present Number; Indian Name; English Name; Relationship; Month, Year, of Birth; Sex; Blood Quantum

880; 885; Ridgewalker, Ethel; wife; June 1870; F. 3/4
881; 886; Ridgewalker, Frank; son; Apr 1908; M. 7/8

882; 887; Risingfire, Bessie; wdw; Nov. 1856[?]; F. F

883; 888; Risingsun, Oliver; hsbd; May 1900; M. F
884; 889; Risingsun, Elizabeth Martha; wife; Aug. 1907; F. F [Flying]
885; 890; Risingsun, Teddy; son; Oct. 1926; M. F

886; 891; Risingsun, Peter; hsbd; Aug. 1887; M. F
887; 892; Risingsun, Bessie; wife; Nov. 1892; F. F
888; 893; Risingsun, Maude; dau.; June 1923[?]; F. F [Jessie in 1926. Birth year 1913 in 1927.]
889; 894; Risingsun, Harry; son; Apr 1921[?]; M. F [Birth year 1918 #877 in 1926.]
890; 895; Risingsun, Lyman; son; July 1923; M. F
891; 896; Risingsun, James; son; Dec. 1925; M. F

892; 897; Risingsun, Philip; hsbd.; Aug. 1862; M. F
893; 898; Risingsun, Nora; wife; Jan. 1868; F. F
894; 899; Risingsun, John; son; June 1895; M. F
895; 900; Risingsun, William; son; June 1904[?]; M. F [Birth year 1910 in 1926.]
896; 901; Risingsun, Alice; dau; Dec. 1909; F. F

897; 902; Robinson, Nellie; wife; Oct. 1897; F. 1/8
Robinson, Major; hsbd; ---;--. (not enrolled)
898; 903; Robinson, David; son; Aug. 1918; M. 1/8
899; 904; Robinson, Cornelius Clay; son; June 1920; M. 1/8
900; 905; Robinson, Eloise Elaine; dau; Mar. 1922; F. 1/8 [Previous #888, In 1926.]

901; 906; Rockroads, Nora; wdw; Dec. 1870[?]; F. F [1904-18 birth year 1868. 1919-26 birth year 1983.]
907; Rockroads, Mary; dau; Aug. 1913; F. F    Omitted last census

902; 908; Rockroads, Mack; hsbd; Mar. 1893; M. F
903; 909; Rockroads, Nellie; wife; Nov. 1893; F. F
904; 910; Rockroads, Thomas; son; Apr. 1917; M. F
[1918 Census #902; Name is Lettie, female.]
905; Rockroads, Mary; dau.; Feb. 1826[sic]; F. F Died Feb. 8, 1928

906; 911; Romannose, Louis; hsbd; Sept 1882; M. F
[Louis's Birth year 1882, 1904-13; 1862, 1914-20. 1882 in 1922-28.]

Census of the **Northern Cheyenne** Indians of **Tongue River** Agency, **Mont.** on **June 30, 1928** taken by **C.B. Lohmiller**, Superintendent.

**Key:** Last Number; Present Number; Indian Name; English Name; Relationship; Month, Year, of Birth; Sex; Blood Quantum

907; 912; Romannose, Mary; wife; May 1890; F. F
908; 913; Romannose, George; son; July 1910; M. F
909; 914; Romannose, Blanche; dau; Sept 1914; F. F [Helen in 1926.]
910; 915; Romannose, Julia; dau; Apr. 1916[?]; F. F [Name May and birth year 1919 in 1926.]
911; 916; Romannose, Willeatte; dau; Oct. 1921; F. F
912; 917; Romannose, Montana; dau; Nov. 1923; F. F

913; 918; Rondeau, Antoine; hsbd; Apr. 1887; M. 1/2
914; 919; Rondeau, Louisa; wife; June 1889; F. 1/4 [Birth year 1886 in 1926.]
915; 920; Rondeau, Clara; dau; Dec. 1912; F. 3/8
916; 921; Rondeau, Charles; son; May 1920; M. 3/8 [Dau, Marie in 1920.] [#909 in 1926.]

917; 922; Rondeau, William; hsbd; Mar. 1866[?]; M. 1/2 [Birth year 1887 in 1926.]
918; 923; Rondeau, Henry; son; Mar. 1911; M. 3/8
919; 924; Rondeau, John R.; son; Mar. 1912[?]; M. 3/8 [Born 1913]

920; 925; Roundstone, Flora; wife; Apr. 1888; F. F [Twobulls]
Roundstone, Fred; hsbd.; ---;--. (not enrolled)
921; 926; Roundstone, Martin; son; Nov. 1911; M. F
922; 927; Roundstone, Sarah; dau; May 1920; F. F
923; 928; Roundstone, Paul; son; Apr. 1922; M. F
924; 929; Roundstone, Ruth; dau.; July 1926; F. F

925; 930; Rowland, Sally; wdw; Sept. 1854; F. F [Previously Annie-Anna.]

926; 931; Rowland, Clay; hsbd; Feb. 1880; M. 3/4
Rowland, Jennie; wife; ---; --. (Not enrolled)

942; 932; Rowland, Jesse; sgle; Feb. 1884; M. 3/4 [Name Frank and previous #932 in 1926.]

943; 933; Rowland, Joe; hsbd.; Dec. 1902[?]; M. 3/4 [In 1926 #935; Jose; son; birth year 1900.]

927; 934; Rowland, Thomas.; hsbd; Dec. 1892; M. 3/4
928; 935; Rowland, Daisy; wife; Mar. 1900; F. F [Fightingbear, Ellen in 1924.]
929; 936; Rowland, Lizzie; dau; Nov. 1913; F. 7/8
930; 937; Rowland, Lillian; dau; Nov 1916; F. 7/8
931; 938; Rowland, Blanche; dau; Aug. 1925; F. 7/8
939; Rowland, Don; son; Jan. 22/28; M. 7/8

Census of the **Northern Cheyenne** Indians of **Tongue River** Agency, **Mont.** on **June 30, 1928** taken by **C.B. Lohmiller**, Superintendent.

**Key:** Last Number; Present Number; Indian Name; English Name; Relationship; Month, Year, of Birth; Sex; Blood Quantum

932; 940; Rowland, Willis; hsbd; Apr 1862; M. 1/2
933; 941; Rowland, Helen; wife; May 1868; F. F [Sarah 1908-1919.]
934; 942; Rowland, Grace; s-dau; Nov. 1914[?]; F. 7/8 (Cora Littlewhiteman) [Shows adopted and birth year 1916 in 1926.]

935; 943; Rowland, William; hsbd; Sept. 1896; M. 3/4
 Rowland, Elizabeth A.; wife; ---; --. (Not enrolled)
936; 944; Rowland, Chester Clay; son; June 1920; M. 1/2
937; Rowland, Wilma; dau.; Oct. 1924; F. Dropped See O.L. L-C 12899-28, 3258-27 FGT [NOTE FROM 1925 Census Entries, Roll #'s Prev- Pres., 883; 877; Rowland, William; husb; 1896; M.; Roll #'s Prev- Pres., 884; 878; Rowland, Chester Clay; s-son; 1920; M. (Wife and dau. not enrolled here). No blood quantum mentioned in 1928 Census for Wilma.]
938; 945; Rowland, Allen Edsel; son; Feb. 1926; M. 1/2
 946; Rowland, Ardith Faye; dau; Apr 30/28; F. 1/2

939; 947; Rowland, George; hsbd; Jan. 1898; M. 3/4
 Rowland, Frances; wife; ---; --; --; (Not enrolled)
940; 948; Rowland, Frank; son; May 1924; M. 7/8
941; 949; Rowland, Carrie; dau; Nov. 1926; F. 7/8

944; 950; Rowland, Zac; hsbd; Dec. 1868; M. 1/2
945; 951; Rowland, Edna; wife; Oct. 1876; F. F

946; 952; Rowland, Claude; sgle; Apr. 1904; M. 3/8 s-son Hinton Bigleg

947; 953; Rowland, Benjamin; sgle; July 1908; M. 3/8 s-son Hinton Bigleg

948; 954; Rowland, Benton; hsbd; Dec. 1898; M. 3/4
 Rowland, Annie; wife; ---; --; --; (not enrolled)
949; 955; Rowland, Marie; dau; May 1926; F. 7/8
 956; Rowland, Eugene A; son; Aug 13/27; M. 7/8 Unreported this year

950; 957; Rowland, Emma Bites; mthr; July 1895[sic]; F. F [Twomoons in 1926, Born 1893]
951; 958; Rowland, Alice; dau; July 1910[?]; F. 7/8 [Birth year 1912 in 1926.]

952; 959; Russell, John; hsbd; Sept. 1893; M. 3/4
 Russell, ---; wife --- ---; --. --
953; 960; Russell, Stella Mildred; dau; Feb. 1916; F. 7/8
954; 961; Russell, May; dau; May 1924; F. 7/8
955; Russell, Joseph Melvin; son; Dec. 1925; M. 7/8 Unreported this year Died August 29, 1927.
[956]; 962; Russell, Inez Irma; dau; Mar. 1927; F. 7/8

Census of the **Northern Cheyenne** Indians of **Tongue River** Agency, **Mont.** on **June 30, 1928** taken by **C.B. Lohmiller**, Superintendent.

**Key:** Last Number; Present Number; Indian Name; English Name; Relationship; Month, Year, of Birth; Sex; Blood Quantum

957; 963; Russell, William; hsbd; May 1873; M. F
958; Russell, Sallie; wife; Apr. 1886; F. F Died Sept. 28, 1927 [Name Sadie in 1927.]
959; 964; Russell, Fred; son; July 1908; M. F
960; 965; Russell, Earl; son; Aug. 1915; M. F
961; 966; Russell, Mary; dau; Sept. 1918; F. F [Mildred in 1926.]
962; 967; Russell, Clara; dau; May 1922; F. F
963; 968; Russell, Herman; son; May 1925; M. F

964; 969; Russell, Frank; hsbd; Dec. 1898[?]; M. 3/4 (Separated)
965; 970; Russell, Jessie; wife; Oct. 1905[sic]; F. F [Rockroads (Rhoda) all numbers past and present coincide, shows up in 1915, birth year 1913.]
966; 971; Russell, Ford; son; Mar. 1925; M. 7/8

967; 972; Sansaver[sic], Lillian; dau; July 1906; F. 1/2 dau-Rhoda Seminole [Sansover mother was a Miles in 1915. Sansover in 1917 #741]

968; 973; Sanchez, Pauline; dau; Mar. 1915; F. 1/2 Children of Cecleia[sic] Redfox.
969; 974; Sanchez, Cecelia; dau; Apr. 1922; F. 1/2

970; 975; Sandcrane, Henry; husb; Oct. 1889; M. F
971; Sandcrane, Anne; wife; July 1895; F. F Died Sept. 19, 1927
972; 976; Sandcrane, Emily May; dau; Oct. 1920; F. F
973; Sandcrane, Harry; son; June 1926; M. F Died Jan. 30, 1928

974; 977; Sandcrane, John; hsbd.; Jan. 1873; M. F
975; 978; Sandcrane, Ruth; wife; Dec. 1878; F. F
976; 979; Sandcrane, Isabelle; dau; May 1914; F. F

977; 980; Scalpcane, August Paul; sgle; Feb. 1906[sic]; M. F
978; 981; Scalpcane, Otto; bro.; Nov. 1914[sic]; M. F
979; 982; Scalpcane, Henry; bro; Nov. 1919; M. F [Rudolph in 1926.]

980; 983; Seminole, John; hsbd; Feb. 1879[?]; M. 3/4 [Birth year 1881 in 1926.]
981; 984; Seminole, Fred; son; Jun. 1915; M. 7/8
819; 985; Seminole, Mary Redbird; wife; Aug. 1897; F. F

982; 986; Seminole, Dan; hsbd.; Aug. 1894; M. 3/4
983; 987; Seminole, Jennie; wife; July 1896; F. F
984; 988; Seminole, Anna; dau; June 1920; F. 7/8
985; 989; Seminole, Margaret; dau; Jan. 1922; F. 7/8
986; 990; Seminole, Alfred; son; Mar. 1924; M. 7/8

Census of the **Northern Cheyenne** Indians of **Tongue River** Agency, **Mont.** on **June 30, 1928** taken by **C.B. Lohmiller**, Superintendent.

Key: Last Number; Present Number; Indian Name; English Name; Relationship; Month, Year, of Birth; Sex; Blood Quantum

987; 991; Seminole, Josephine; mthr; Apr. 1891; F. 3/4
988; 992; Seminole, Lawrence (Smoky); son; Dec. 1911; M. 7/8 [g-son in 1926.]
Seminole, Baby; dau; Nov. 24/27; F 7/8 Died December 1, 1927

989; 993; Seminole, Louis; fthr; June 1884; M. 3/4
990; 994; Seminole, Delbert; son; June 1911; M. 7/8
991; 995; Seminole, Hannah; dau; Nov. 1912[?]; F. 7/8 [1917 Census Son Theodore. Birth year 1915 in 1926.]

992; 996; Seminole, Max; son; Nov. 1924; M. 7/8 son-Mary Redbird [1926 #813 entry; Redbird, Maxine; g-g-son; 1924; M.] (g-g-son Joseph Tangledhornelk)

993; 997; Seminole Miles; Div.; 1869[?]; M. 3/4 [Birth year 1875 in 1926.]

994; 998; Seminole, Rhoda; Div.; Mar. 1892[?]; F. 1/4 [Birth year in 1926 is 1879.]
995; 999; Seminole, Lorraine; dau; June 1916; F. 1/2
996; 1000; Seminole, David; son; Apr. 1919; M. 1/2

997; Sharpnose, Bessie; wdw; July 1846; F. F Died Sept. 28, 1927

998; Sharpnose, Edward Chas.; hsbd; May 1896[sic]; M. F Died Aug. 23, 1927 [Birth year 1897-98.]
999; 1001; Sharpnose, Josephine; wife; June 1902; F. F [Hisbadhorses]
Sharpnose, Baby; son; May 1927; M. F Unreported last year Died Aug. 25, 1927

1000; 1002; Shavedhead, Jean; wife; June 1901; F. F [Swallow]
Shavedhead, Jeffrey; hsbd; ---; M. (not enrolled)
1001; 1003; Shavedhead, Charles; son; June 1924; M. F [Jeffrey, Jr. and birth year 1925 in 1926.]
1002; 1004; Shavedhead, Anna Marjorie; dau; Oct. 1926; F. F

1003; 1005; Shavedhead, Mary; wdw; June 1965[sic]; F. F

1004; 1006; Shavedhead, James; hsbd; Nov. 1899; M. F
1005; 1007; Shavedhead, Alice; wife; Feb. 1907[?]; F. F [Medicineflying; age 3 in 1910. Birth 1906-07.]
1006; 1008; Shavedhead, Anna; dau; Sept 1925; F. F [Hyacinth in 1926.]
1009; Shavedhead, Lucille; dau; Nov. 31/28; F. F

1007; 1010; Shell, Joseph; hsbd; Feb. 1881; M. F

Census of the **Northern Cheyenne** Indians of **Tongue River** Agency, **Mont.** on **June 30, 1928** taken by **C.B. Lohmiller**, Superintendent.

**Key:** Last Number; Present Number; Indian Name; English Name; Relationship; Month, Year, of Birth; Sex; Blood Quantum

1008; 1011; Shell, Julia; wife; Sept 1901[?]; F. F [Previous #530 in 1906, censuses 1906-19, wife Alice [Risingsun] Shell, birth year 1885.] [Julia starts census 1920.]

1009; 1012; Shell, Minnie; wdw; June 1882[?]; F. F [Killsnight] [Birth year 1892 in 1926.]
1010; Shell, Elsie; dau; Jan. 1926; F. F Died February 21, 1928

1011; 1013; Shepherd, Mollie; wife; Apr. 1895; F. 1/2
Shepherd, Clarence; hsbd; ---; M. F (Not enrolled)

1012; 1014; Shortsioux, Mary; dau; June 1914; F. 7/8 [dau Maggie Longears.]

1013; 1015; Sherman, Ethel Parker; wife; May 1883; F. 1/4
Sherman, George; hsbd; ---; --. (White)
1014; 1016; Sherman, Frances; dau; Dec. 1908; F. 1/8
1015; 1017; Sherman, George Jr.; son; Oct. 1911; M. 1/8
1016; 1018; Sherman, Otto; son; June 1913; M. 1/8
1017; 1019; Sherman, Wretha; dau; Aug. 1915; F. 1/8
1018; 1020; Sherman, Carl; son; Dec. 1918; M. 1/8
1019; 1021; Sherman, Clarence; son; July 1922; M. 1/8

1020; 1022; Shoulderblade, Benedict; hsbd; Sept. 1874; M. F

1021; 1023; Shoulderblade, Fred; hsbd; Oct. 1861; M. F
1022; 1024; Shoulderblade, Richard; son; Aug. 1911; M. F

1023; 1025; Shoulderblade, Pius; hsbd.; May 1889; M. F
1024; 1026; Shoulderblade, Ethel; wife; Aug. 1893; F. 3/4
1025; 1027; Shoulderblade, Thomas; son; Oct. 1915; M. 7/8
1026; 1028; Shoulderblade, Francis; son; Mar. 1917; M. 7/8 [1917 Census William]
1027; 1029; Shoulderblade, Wendel; son; Aug. 1920; M. 7/8
1028; 1030; Shoulderblade, Everett John; son; Jun. 1923; M. 7/8
1031; Shoulderblade, Fern; dau; 2/23/28; F. 7/8

1029; 1032; Silloway, Veta Burns; wife; Nov. 1904; F. 1/8 [Birth month Apr., in 1927.]
Silloway, Lloyd; hsbd.; ---; --. (not enrolled) white

1030; 1033; Sioux, Thomas; hsbd; Nov. 1870; M. F
1031; 1034; Sioux, Henry; s-son; June[?]. 1911; M. F [#1018, Divesbackwards; Name Jacob; and listed as g-son; in 1926. June birth month in 1927.]

1032; 1035; Sittingman, Charles; hsbd; Oct. 1866[sic]; M. F [1904-18 birth 1868.]

Census of the __Northern Cheyenne__ Indians of __Tongue River__
Agency, __Mont.__ on __June 30, 1928__ taken by __C.B. Lohmiller__,
Superintendent.

**Key:** Last Number; Present Number; Indian Name; English Name; Relationship; Month, Year, of Birth; Sex; Blood Quantum

1033; 1036;    Sittingman, Lucy; wife; May 1866[sic]; F. F [Born 1868.]

1034; 1037;    Sittingman, Edward; hsbd.; June 1900; M. F [Edward in 1927.]
1287; 1038;    Sittingman, Ida Whitehawk; wife; June 1898; F. F

1035; 1039;    Small, Josephine; wife; Feb. 1892; F. 1/2
              Small, Thomas; hsbd; ---; --. (White)
1036; 1040;    Small, Victor; son; Aug. 1912; M. 1/4
1037; 1041;    Small, Edward; son; Nov. 1913; M. 1/4
1038; 1042;    Small, Max Joe; son; Apr. 1915; M. 1/4
1039; 1043;    Small, Ivan; son; Apr. 1920; M. 1/4
1040; 1044;    Small, Thomas; son; Dec. 1921; M. 1/4
1041; 1045;    Small, Horace; son; July 1923; M. 1/4
1042; 1046;    Small, Melvin; son; Feb. 1924; M. 1/4
1043; 1047;    Small, Worth; son; Feb. 1927; M. 1/4

1044; 1048;    Smith, John; hsbd; June 1875; M. F [Birth year 1878 in 1926.]
1045; 1049;    Smith, Blanche; wife; Mar. 1880; F. F [Birth year 1883 in 1926.]

1046; 1050;    Soldierwolf, John; hsbd; Apr. 1883; M. F
1047; 1051;    Soldierwolf, Mary; wife; Apr. 1888; F. F
1048; 1052;    Soldierwolf, Thos. Chas.; son; June 1910; M. F
1049; 1053;    Soldierwolf, Aurora; dau; Jan. 1915; F. F
1050; 1054;    Soldierwolf, Lucy; dau; Oct. 1917; F. F
1051; 1055;    Soldierwolf, Kenneth Jas.; son; July 1920; M. F
1052; 1056;    Soldierwolf, Katherine; dau; May 1922; F. F

1053; 1057;    Spang, Alfonso; hsbd; Jan 1887; M. 1/8
              Spang, Margie; wife; ---; --. (White)

1054; 1058;    Spang, Alban; hsbd; Sept 1892; M. 1/8
              Spang, Ruth; wife; ---; --. (White)

1055; 1059;    Spang, Deyo; hsbd; Dec. 1888; M. 1/8
              Spang, Lucille; wife; ---; --. (White)
1056; 1060;    Spang, Bruce Spencer; son; June 1924; M. 1/16
1057; 1061;    Spang, Dale Cooper; son; July 1926; M. 1/16

1058; 1062;    Spang, James; hsbd; July 1899; M. 1/8
              Spang, Nina Dawson; wife; --- --; (White)
        1063;    Spang, James Russell; son; May 13/27; M. 1/16 Unreported last census
        1064;    Spang, Shirley Ann; dau; May 19/28; F. 1/16

Census of the **Northern Cheyenne** Indians of **Tongue River** Agency, **Mont.** on **June 30, 1928** taken by **C.B. Lohmiller**, Superintendent.

**Key:** Last Number; Present Number; Indian Name; English Name; Relationship; Month, Year, of Birth; Sex; Blood Quantum

1059; 1065;    Spang, Lucy; wife; May 1869; F. 1/4
               Spang, A.D.; hsbd; ---; --. (White)
1060; 1066;    Spang, Sarah; dau.; Aug. 1904; F. 1/8
1061; 1067;    Spang, Harriet; sgle; Oct. 1905; F. 1/8 [Birth 1906.]
1062; 1068;    Spang, Edith; dau.; Dec. 1909; F. 1/8
1063; 1069;    Spang, Cash; son; Oct. 1911; M. 1/8

1064; 1070;    Spang, Roy; husb; Sept. 1896; M. 1/8
1065; 1071;    Spang, Jessie; wife; May 1907; F. F
1066; 1072;    Spang, Regina Susanna; dau; June 1922; F. 1/4 [Regina Rosetta in 1926.]
1067; 1073;    Spang, Lyman; son; Aug. 1923; M. 1/4

1068; 1074;    Spang, Wilfred; hsbd; May 1901; M. 1/8
1069; 1075;    Spang, Alice Yellowhorse; wife; June 1908; F. F
      1076;    Spang; Norman; son; Sept 1927; M. 1/2

1070; 1077;    Sponge, Alfred; hsbd; July 1896; M. F
1071; 1078;    Sponge, Josie; wife; Sept 1901; F. F [Shoulderblade] [1922 was #958, Scott.]

1072; 1079;    Sponge, Oliver; hsbd; Mar. 1898; M. F
1073; 1080;    Sponge, Clara; wife; May 1905; F. F [Tangleyellowhair]
      1081;    Sponge, Paul; son; Dec. 10/27; M. F

1074; 1082;    Spottedblackbird, Lee; hsbd; June 1859; M. F [Birth year 1854 in 1926.]
[#1082, Didn't pickup a first name until 1915 name, Lee; or Leo.]
1075; 1083;    Spottedblackbird, Clara; wife; Oct. 1874; F. F [Birth year 1854 in 1926.]

1076; 1084;    Spottedelk, Charles; fthr; Mar. 1863[?]; M. F
1077; 1085;    Spottedelk, August; son; July 1897; M. F

1078; 1086;    Spottedelk, Alex; wdr.; Nov. 1900; M. F

1079; 1087;    Spottedhawk, Hugh; hsbd; Apr. 1867; M. F
1080; 1088;    Spottedhawk, Ruth; Neice[sic]; Dec. 1907; F. F [Medicinebird]

1081; 1089;    Spottedwolf, Charles; hsbd; Oct. 1892; M. F
1082; 1090;    Spottedwolf, Lena; wife; Sept. 1892; F. F
1083; 1091;    Spottedwolf, Julia Eva; dau.; Apr. 1913; F. F
1084; 1092;    Spottedwolf, Piney; dau; Sept. 1921; F. F
1085; 1093;    Spottedwolf, John; son; Oct. 1923; M. F
1086;          Spottedwolf, Earl; son; July 1926; M. F
      1094;    Spottedwolf, Baby; dau; Nov. 22/27; F. F

Census of the **Northern Cheyenne** Indians of **Tongue River** Agency, **Mont.** on **June 30, 1928** taken by **C.B. Lohmiller**, Superintendent.

**Key:** Last Number; Present Number; Indian Name; English Name; Relationship; Month, Year, of Birth; Sex; Blood Quantum

1087; 1095; Spottedwolf, Patrick; hsbd; Nov. 1887; M. F
1088; 1096; Spottedwolf, Jean; wife; Oct. 1901; F. 1/2
1089; 1097; Spottedwolf, Ruby; dau; Sept. 1920; F. 3/4
1090; 1098; Spottedwolf, Phyllis; dau; Oct. 1923; F. 3/4
1091; 1099; Spottedwolf, Eugene; son; Aug. 1925; M. 3/4
1100; Spottedwolf, Mollie; dau; Sept 28/27; F. 3/4

1092; 1101; Standingelk, Nina; sgle; June 1907; F. F

1093; 1102; Standingelk, Frank; hsbd; June 1874; M. F
1094; 1103; Standingelk, Fannie; wife; Apr. 1878; F. F
1095; 1104; Standingelk, George; son; Apr. 1910[sic]; M. F
1096; 1105; Standingelk, Flora; dau; Apr. 1921; F. F

1097; 1106; Standingelk, Francis; hsbd; Apr. 1901; M. F
1098; 1107; Standingelk, Annie; wife; May 1907; F. F
1099; 1108; Standingelk, Roy; son; Aug 1926; M. F

1100; 1109; Standingelk, Henry; wdr.; June 1891; M. F

1101; 1110; Standingelk, Lockwood; wdr.; June 1890; M. F

1102; 1111; Standingelk, Robert B.; hsbd.; Oct. 1870; M. F
1103; 1112; Standingelk, Sally; wife; Sept 1895; F. F
1104; 1113; Standingelk, Ella; dau; Dec. 1918; F. F
1105; 1114; Standingelk, (Clara) Jennie; dau; May 1927; F. F

1106; 1115; Standingelk, Alex; hsbd.; Mar. 1896; M. F.
1107; 1116; Standingelk, Nora; wife; July 1903; F. F
1108; 1117; Standingelk, Geneva; dau; Mar. 1922; F. F
1109; 1118; Standingelk, Margaret; dau; Nov. 1924; F. F
Standingelk, Mary; dau; Oct. 24/27; F. F Died January 15, 1928

1110; 1119; Standsintimber, John; hsbd; Mar. 1886; M. F
1111; 1120; Standsintimber, Josie; wife; Mar. 1898; F. 3/4
1112; 1121; Standsintimber, Josephine; dau; June 1920; F. 7/8
1113; 1122; Standsintimber, John Jr.; son; Oct.1921; M. 7/8
1123; Standsintimber, Elva; dau; Apr. 21/28; F. 7/8

1114; 1124; Star, May Blackree; sgle; Dec.1904; F. F [Minnie in 1926.]

1115; 1125; Standsout, Sallie; wdw; Aug. 1847; F. F

1116; 1126; Starvingbear, James; fthr; Apr. 1876; M. F

Census of the **Northern Cheyenne** Indians of **Tongue River** Agency, **Mont.** on **June 30, 1928** taken by **C.B. Lohmiller**, Superintendent.

Key: Last Number; Present Number; Indian Name; English Name; Relationship; Month, Year, of Birth; Sex; Blood Quantum

1117; 1127;   Starvingbear, Mary; dau.; Mar. 1907; F. F [Lottie in 1926.]
1118; 1128;   Starvingbear, Jack; son; Feb. 1914; M. F [Rosco in 1926.]

1119; 1129;   Strangeowl, John; hsbd; Sept. 1872[?]; M. F [Birth year 1876 in 1926.]
1120; 1130;   Strangeowl, Gertie; wife; Nov. 1868; F. F

1122; 1131;   Strangeowl, James; sgle; June 1904; M. F

1123; 1132;   Stumphorn, Frank; hsbd.; Oct. 1843; M. F
1124; 1133;   Stumphorn, Annie; wife; July 1855; F. F [Shortsioux, Wdw.]

1125; 1134;   Stumphorn, Anna.; wdw; Sept. 1851[sic]; F. F [Birth year 1842.]

1126; 1135;   Sunbear, John; wdr; July 1843[?]; M. F [1904-15 birth year 1856. 1916-28 birth year 1843.]

1127; 1136;   Sunbear, Michael; hsbd; -- 1891; M. F
              Sunbear, ---; wife; --; --. (Not enrolled)
1128; 1137;   Sunbear, Herman; son; Aug. 1923; M. F
1129; 1138;   Sunbear, Deyo; son; -- 1924; M. F

1130; 1139;   Sunroads, David; hsbd.; Sept. 1881; M. F
1131; 1140;   Sunroads, Lizzie; wife; Mar. 1883; F. F

1132; 1141;   Sunroads, John; hsbd; July 1843; M. F
1133; 1142;   Sunroads, Lena; wife; Mar. 1845; F. F

1134; 1143;   Swallow, William; hsbd; Feb. 1874; M. F [Birth year 1873-4.]
[William #1143; 1904-15 born 1873, 1916-17 born 1897, 1918-26 born 1863.]
1135; 1144;   Swallow, Gertrude; wife; Mar. 1896; F. F [Redbreath]
1136; 1145;   Swallow, Mary; dau; May 1907; F. F [Previously name Anne.]
1137; 1146;   Percy Redbreath; son; Nov. 1919[?]; M. F [Birth year 1922 in 1926.]

1138; 1147;   Swallow, Edward; sgle; Mar. 1902; M. F

1139; 1148;   Swallow, Oliver; sgle; Apr. 1899; M. F

1140; 1149;   Sweetmedicine, David; hsbd.; Mar. 1863[sic]; M. F [Birth year 1868]
1141; 1150;   Sweetmedicine, Clara; wife; Dec. 1870; F. F
1142; 1151;   Sweetmedicine, Jacob; son; Apr. 1894; M. F

1143; 1152;   Sweetmedicine, Joseph; sgle.; Dec. 1898; M. F

Census of the **Northern Cheyenne** Indians of **Tongue River**
Agency, **Mont.** on **June 30, 1928** taken by **C.B. Lohmiller**,
Superintendent.

**Key:** Last Number; Present Number; Indian Name; English Name; Relationship; Month, Year, of Birth; Sex; Blood Quantum

1044; 1153;      Sweetmedicine, Ellen; Div. wife; July 1897; F. F

1145; 1154;      Sweetmedicine, William; Div. hsbd.; -- 1889; M. F
1146; 1155;      Sweetmedicine, Alta; dau; -- 1913[sic]; F. F [1915-Son, Thomas; M.]

1147; 1156;      Tallbull, Albert; sgle; Apr. 1906; M. F [Birth year 1902 in 1926.]

1148; 1157;      Tallbull, Charles; hsbd; Oct. 1887; M. F
1149; 1158;      Tallbull, Mary; wife; May 1893; F. F
1150; 1159;      Tallbull, Joseph; son; June 1915; M. F
1151; 1160;      Tallbull, Henry; son; Dec. 1917; M. F
1152; 1161;      Tallbull, William; son; Jan. 1921; M. F
1153; 1162;      Tallbull, Nelson; son; Oct. 1923; M. F
1154; 1163;      Tallbull, Cecil Russell; son; Jan. 1927; M. F

1155; 1164;      Tallbull, Nora; wdw; June 1858[sic]; F. F

1156; 1165;      Tallwhiteman, Jasper; fthr; July 1893[?]; M. F [Birth year 1891 in 1926.]
1157;      Tallwhiteman, John; son; Oct. 1914; M. F Died Sept. 19, 1927
1158; 1166;      Tallwhiteman, Agnes; dau; May 1924; F. F [1925 census Dan son, M., same #. Name Rilla in 1926.]

1159; 1167;      Tallwhiteman, John; hsbd; Apr. 1886; M. F
1160; 1168;      Tallwhiteman, Eleanor; wife; Mar. 1898; F. F
1161; 1169;      Tallwhiteman, Clarence; son; July 1912; M. F
1162; 1170;      Tallwhiteman, Florence; dau; May 1914; F. F
1163; 1171;      Tallwhiteman, Jasper; son; July 1916; M. F
1164; 1172;      Tallwhiteman, Alice; dau; May 1920; F. F
1165; 1173;      Tallwhiteman, Tug; son; June 1922; M. F
1166; 1174;      Tallwhiteman, Agnes; dau; July 1925; F. F

1167;      Tallwhiteman, Joseph; sgle; June 1847; M. F Died February 16, 1928

1168; 1175;      Tallwhiteman, Patrick; hsbd; June 1888; M. F
1169; 1176;      Tallwhiteman, Florence; wife; July 1900; F. F
1170; 1177;      Tallwhiteman, Alice; dau; Jan. 1916; F. F
1171; 1178;      Tallwhiteman, Laura; dau; June 1923; F. F

1172; 1179;      Tangledhornelk, Nellie; wdw; -- 1853; F. F [1904-18 no "d" in last name.]

1173; 1180;      Tangledyellowhair, Chas.; hsbd; Feb. 1892; M. F [1904-18 no "d" in last name.]

Census of the **Northern Cheyenne** Indians of **Tongue River** Agency, **Mont.** on **June 30, 1928** taken by **C.B. Lohmiller**, Superintendent.

**Key:** Last Number; Present Number; Indian Name; English Name; Relationship; Month, Year, of Birth; Sex; Blood Quantum

1174; 1181;   Tangledyellowhair, Georgia Marion; wife; Sept. 1891; F. F [Talks]
1175; 1182;   Tangledyellowhair, Roberta; dau; Sept 1924; F. F
1176; 1183;   Tangledyellowhair, Bert; son; Oct. 1926; M. F

1177; 1184;   Tangledyellowhair, David; fthr; June 1898[?]; M. F [1904-18 no "d" in last name. Birth year 1894 in 1926.]
1178; 1185;   Tangledyellowhair, Clara; dau; Oct. 1919; F. F
1179; 1186;   Tangledyellowhair, Winona; dau; Jan. 1922; F. F
         1187;   Tangledyellowhair, Lariath; son; Apr. 14/28; M. F

1180; 1188;   Tangledyellowhair, James; hsbd; Jan. 1869; M. F [1904-18 no "d" in last name.]
1181; 1189;   Tangledyellowhair, Minnie; wife; Dec. 1870[?]; F. F [Birth year 1873 in 1926.]

1182; 1190;   Tangledyellowhair, Josie; wdw.; Mar. 1848[?]; M. F [1904-18 no "d" in last name. Birth year 1846 in 1926.]

1183; 1191;   Teeth, Charles; hsbd; Mar. 1863[?]; M. F [Birth year 1865 in 1926.]
1184;         Teeth, Sallie; wife; Apr. 1873; F. F Died April 17, 1928

1185; 1192;   Teeth, John; hsbd; May 1889; M. F
1186; 1193;   Teeth, Edith; wife; Oct. 1902; F. F
1187; 1194;   Teeth, Franklin; son; Oct. 1909; M. F
1188; 1195;   Teeth, Earl; son; June 1916; M. F
1189; 1196;   Teeth, Montana; dau; Apr. 1922; F. F
1190; 1197;   Teeth, Elsie; dau; Sept 1925; F. F

1191; 1198;   Threefingers, John; hsbd; Mar. 1862[?]; M. F [Birth year 1878[?] in 1926. #1198-Various ages starting 1904, in 1913-1920 birth year 1868 changes again in 1922.]
1192; 1199;   Threefingers, Pansy; wife; July 1876[?]; F. F [Birth year 1878 in 1926.]

1193; 1200;   Threefingers, William; hsbd; Sept. 1901; M. F
1194; 1201;   Threefingers, Ruth Maude; wife; Oct. 1907; F. F [Medicinebird]

1195; 1202;   Turkeylegs, John; hsbd; July 1859; M. F
1196; 1203;   Turkeylegs, Lydia; wife; Aug. 1874; F. F
1197; 1204;   Turkeylegs, Lawrence; son; July 1906; M. F [Name James in 1926.]

1198; 1205;   Twin, Louis James; hsbd; Dec. 1887[?]; M. F [Birth year 1889 in 1926.]
1199; 1206;   Twin, Bessie; wife; Mar. 1886; F. F
1200; 1207;   Twin, Margaret; dau; Apr. 1918; F. F

Census of the **Northern Cheyenne** Indians of **Tongue River** Agency, **Mont.** on **June 30, 1928** taken by **C.B. Lohmiller**, Superintendent.

**Key:** Last Number; Present Number; Indian Name; English Name; Relationship; Month, Year, of Birth; Sex; Blood Quantum

1201; 1208;      Twin, Edna; dau; July 1924; F. F

1202; 1209;      Twobirds, Peter; hsbd; May 1878; M. F
1203; 1210;      Twobirds, Lenora; wife; July 1872; F. F
1204; 1211;      Twobirds, Jacob; son; Jan. 1901; M. F
1205; 1212;      Twobirds, Walter; son; Aug. 1908[?]; M. F

1206; 1213;      Twobulls, Martin; hsbd; July 1891; M. F
1207; 1214;      Twobulls, Eleanor; wife; May 1900; F. F
1208; 1215;      Twobulls, William; son; Sept 1920; M. F
         1216;      Twobulls, Alice; dau; Aug. 1927; F. F

1209; 1217;      Twobulls, Kate; wdw; Aug. 1865; F. F

1210; 1218;      Twofeathers, John; hsbd; Apr. 1857; M. F [1904-22 Twofeathers.]
1211; 1219;      Twofeathers, Clara; wife; May 1870; F. F
1212; 1220;      Twofeathers, Ethel; dau; Sept 1908; F. F

1213; 1221;      Twomoons, Bert; hsbd; Nov.1887; M. F
1214; 1222;      Twomoons, Margaret; wife; Aug. 1892; F. F [Americanhorse]
1215; 1223;      Twomoons, George; son; Jan. 1920; M. F
1216; 1224;      Twomoons, Austin; son; Feb. 1927; M. F

1217; 1225;      Twomoons, John; wdr.; Apr. 1855; M. F

1218; 1226;      Twomoons, William; hsbd; May 1884; M. F

1219; 1227;      Walkingbear, Charles; hsbd.; May 1876; M. F
1220; 1228;      Walkingbear, Jennie; wife; Sept 1872; F. F

1221; 1229;      Walkingbear, David; hsbd; June 1897; M. F (Separated)

1222; 1230;      Walkingbear, Mamie; wife; Aug. 1897; F. F (Separated) [Mannie in 1927]

1223; 1231;      Walkingbird, Jane; mthr; Mar. 1867; F. F

1224; 1232;      Walkinghorse, John; hsbd.; Aug. 1857; M. F
1225; 1233;      Walkinghorse, Olive; wife; Sept 1866; F. F

1226; 1234;      Walksalong, Hugh; fthr; Apr. 1885[sic]; M. F
1227; 1235;      Walksalong, Flora; dau; May 1915; F. F [Previous census 1916-19, Fred son.]
1238; 1236;      Walksalong, (Mary) Eugenia; dau; June 1920; F. F

Census of the **Northern Cheyenne** Indians of **Tongue River** Agency, **Mont.** on **June 30, 1928** taken by **C.B. Lohmiller**, Superintendent.

**Key:** Last Number; Present Number; Indian Name; English Name; Relationship; Month, Year, of Birth; Sex; Blood Quantum

1237;      Walksalong, Carol; dau; Jan. 10/28; F. F

1229; 1238;      Walkseasy, Nora; wdw; Mar. 1864; F. F

1230; 1239;      Walkslast, Richard; hsbd; Mar. 1856; M. F
1231; 1240;      Walkslast, Anne; wife; July 1862[?]; F. F [Birth year 1859, 1904-22.]
1232; 1241;      Walkslast, Frank; g-son; Mar. 1908; M. F

1233; 1242;      Walkslast, James; sgle; Sept 1905; M. F [Clement in 1926.]

1234; 1243;      Walksnice, Adolph; hsbd; Apr. 1878; M. F
1235; 1244;      Walksnice, Flora; wife; Oct. 1884; F. F
1236; 1245;      Walksnice, Dick; son; May 1911; M. F

1237; 1246;      Walksnice, John; hsbd; Sept. 1905; M. F
1238; 1247;      Walksnice, Mary; wife; Jan. 1903; F. F [Crookednose]
1239; 1248;      Walksnice, Agnes; dau.; Aug. 1926; F. F

1240; 1249;      Wallowing, Rufus; hsbd; Nov. 1887[?]; M. F (Dustybuffalo) [Rollingbull] Name changed to "Wallowing" see 57750-26. [First name Rutherford misspelled starting in 1918.]
1241; 1250;      Wallowing, Stella; wife; July 1885; F. 1/4

1242; 1251;      Walters, George; hsbd; Sept. 1897; M. 1/2
                 Walters, Lillian Cook; wife; ---; --. (Not enrolled)

1243; 1252;      Wanderingmedicine, Wm.; sgle; Apr. 1869[?]; M. F [Birth year 1856 in 1926.]

1244; 1253;      Waters[sic], Frank; husb; 1875; M. [1904-20, name is Water. Birth year 1877 in 1926.]
                 Waters, Sarah; wife; --; --. (Not enrolled)
1245; 1254;      Waters, Joseph; s-son; July 1922; M. 7/8 [1346; 1377; Woodenlegs, Martin; son; 1922; in 1926.]

1246; 1255;      Weaselbear, Frank; hsbd; Sept 1861; M. F
1247; 1256;      Weaselbear, Mary; wife; Feb. 1870; F. F
1248; 1257;      Weaselbear, Sarah; dau.; June 1913; F. F

1249; 1258;      Weaselbear, Hugh; fthr; -- 1889; M. F
1250; 1259;      Weaselbear, Andrew; son; Apr. 1915; M. F
1251; 1260;      Weaselbear, Busby; son; July 1922; M. F

Census of the **Northern Cheyenne** Indians of **Tongue River** Agency, **Mont.** on **June 30, 1928** taken by **C.B. Lohmiller**, Superintendent.

**Key:** Last Number; Present Number; Indian Name; English Name; Relationship; Month, Year, of Birth; Sex; Blood Quantum

1252; 1261;   Weaselbear, Cordelia; dau; May 1917; F. F s-dau-Henry Littlewhiteman. [Clarice in 1926.]

1448; 1462;   Wheeler, Dewitt Carlton; hsbd; Dec. 1892; M. 1/2
1449; 1463;   Wheeler, Dewitt Philip; son; Nov. 1916; M. 1/2

1253; 1264;   Whirlwind, Thomas; div.; Oct. 1876; M. F

1254; 1265;   Whirlwind, Rose; div.; Dec. 1892; F. F

1255; 1266;   Whistlingelk, Charles; hsbd.; Jan. 1876; M. F
1256; 1267;   Whistlingelk, Josie; wife; June 1884[?]; F. F [1904-20, birth year 1884. Birth year 1874 in 1926.]
1258;[sic]1268;   Whistlingelk, Alice ; dau; June 1913[?]; F. F [Birth year 1909 in 1927.]
1259; 1269;   Whistlingelk, Alfred; son; Jan. 1917; M. F
1260; 1270;   Whistlingelk, Lois; dau; Dec. 1926; F. F

1261; 1271;   Whistlingelk, John; hsbd; Apr. 1904; M. F
1262; 1272;   Whistlingelk, Flora; wife; May 1906; F. F [Redrobe]
1263; 1273;   Whistlingelk, May; dau; Mar. 1926; F. F

1264; 1274;   White, Stamper; hsbd.; Apr. 1898; M. F
1265; 1275;   White, Lottie; wife; Mar. 1903; F. 3/4 [Rowland]
1266; 1276;   White, Pearl; dau; Aug. 1923; F. 7/8
1267; 1277;   White, Ben; son; Dec. 1926; M. 7/8

1268; 1278;   Whitebear, Joseph; hsbd; -- 1896; M. F

1269; 1279;   Whitebird, Frank; sgle; Feb. 1902; M. F

1270; 1280;   Whitebird, Lena; wdw; Oct. 1855; F. F [1904-13, birth year 1855; 1914-23 has birth year as 1885. Corrected in 1924 to 1855. Husband George was born approximately 1852.]

1271; 1281;   Whitebuffalo, John; hsbd; Mar. 1871; M. F
1272; 1282;   Whitebuffalo, Ella; wife; Aug. 1867; F. F

1273; 1283;   Whitecrane, Leo; hsbd; June 1895; M. F
1274; 1284;   Whitecrane, Ella; wife; July 1901; F. F [Littlebird]
1275; 1285;   Whitecrane, Victor; son; June 1924; M.
1276;         Whitecrane, Elmer; son; Dec. 1926; M. F Died February 23, 1928

1277; 1286;   Whitecrane, Charles; wdr.; Apr. 1876; M. F

Census of the **Northern Cheyenne** Indians of **Tongue River** Agency, **Mont.** on **June 30, 1928** taken by **C.B. Lohmiller**, Superintendent.

**Key:** Last Number; Present Number; Indian Name; English Name; Relationship; Month, Year, of Birth; Sex; Blood Quantum

1447; 1287; Whitecrow, Alfred; son; Dec. 1910; M. F [Teddy Redcherries- Fthr.]

1278; 1288; Whitedirt, Arthur; hsbd; Apr. 1875; M. F
1279; 1289; Whitedirt, Maggie; wife; June 1875[sic]; F. F [1905-1919 birth year 1872.]
1281; 1290; Whitedirt, Jennie; dau; Feb. 1911; F. F

1280; 1291; Whitedirt, Charlie; Son[sic]; June 1905; M. F
1259;[sic]1292; Whitedirt, Julia Whistlingelk; wife; July 1909[?]; F. F [1913-22 son, Henry, M.; #1259 is Alfred a brother in 1927. Birth month June, year 1913, in 1927.]

1282; 1293; Whitefrog, Nellie; wdw; May 1861; F. F

1283; 1294; Whitehawk, Emma; wdw; Sept 1883; F. F
1284; 1295; Whitehawk, Verlie; dau; Mar. 1918; F. F

1285; 1296; Whitehawk, Mary; wdw; July 1858[sic]; F. F [1904-18 birth year 1838.]

1286; 1297; Whitehawk, Charles Jno; hsbd; Apr. 1899[?]; M. F [1905-09 Name is Chase. Years 1905-13 birth year 1898. 1914-16 birth year 1889.]
1288; 1298; Whitehawk, Mary; dau; Sept. 1919; F. F
1289; 1299; Whitehawk, Marguerite; dau; Nov. 1920; F. F [Same #1251 John, 1922-25, son, M.; Same prev., #1289 Emma; dau; 1922 in 1926.]

1290; 1300; Whitehorse, George; wdr.; Feb. 1850; M. F

1291; 1301; Whitemoon, George; hsbd; Nov.1854; M. F [Birth year 1851 in 1926.]

1292; 1302; Whitemoon, Hugh; Div.; Apr. 1881; M. F

1293; 1303; Whiteshirt, Jean; mthr; July 1899; F. F
1294; 1304; Whiteshirt, Caroline; dau; Nov. 1921; F. F [Name Alice in 1926.]
1295; Whiteshirt, Dottie; dau; Apr. 1925; F. F Died March 29, 1928

1296; 1305; Whitewolf, Frank; hsbd; Mar. 1847; M. F
1297; 1306; Whitewolf, Julia; wife; July 1854; F. F
1298; 1307; Whitewolf, Anne Lucy; dau.; Apr. 1925[sic]; F. F [Birth year 1904 in 1927.]

1299; 1308; Whitewolf, Charles Isadore; hsbd.; Aug. 1890; M. F [Birth year 1887 in 1926.]
1300; 1309; Whitewolf, Belle; wife; May 1902; F. F
1301; 1310; Whitewolf, Joseph; son; Mar. 1921; M. F

Census of the **Northern Cheyenne** Indians of **Tongue River** Agency, **Mont.** on **June 30, 1928** taken by **C.B. Lohmiller**, Superintendent.

**Key:** Last Number; Present Number; Indian Name; English Name; Relationship; Month, Year, of Birth; Sex; Blood Quantum

| | |
|---|---|
| 1302; 1311; | Whitewolf, George; son; June 1923; M. F |
| 1312; | Whitewolf, Fred; son; Feb. 20/28; M. F |

| | |
|---|---|
| 1303; 1313; | Whitewolf, Maude Shields; W.; Oct. 1891; F. F |
| | Whitewolf, Grover; hsbd; --; --. (Not enrolled) |
| 1304; 1314; | Whitewolf, Everett; son; Mar. 1914; M. F |
| 1305; 1315; | Whitewolf, Carrie; dau.; June 1916; F. F [Philip son, M., 1920 census.] |
| 1306; 1316; | Whitewolf, Wilson; son; May 1919[?]; M. F [1919-20 birth year 1918.] |
| 1307; 1317; | Whitewolf, Thomas; son; Nov. 1921; M. F |
| 1308; 1318; | Whitewolf, Martin Owen; son; Feb. 1923; M. F |
| 1309; 1319; | Whitewolf, Calvin Mexican; son; Jan 1925; M. F [Clara dau, F., 1925 census, same #.] |

| | |
|---|---|
| 1310; 1320; | Wildhog, Bird; hsbd; June 1869; M. F |
| 1311; 1321; | Wildhog, Lydia; wife; Oct. 1872; F. F |
| 1312; 1322; | Wildhog, Alice Viola; dau; Jan. 1907[?]; F. F [Birth year 1901 in 1926.] |
| 1313; | Wildhog, Willie; son; July 1910; M. F Died May 12, 1928 |
| 1314; 1323; | Wildhog, Julia; dau; June 1913; F. F [Susie in 1926.] |
| 1315; 1324; | Wildhog, Anne; dau; Sept. 1895; F. F |
| 1316; 1325; | Wildhog, John; son; Oct. 1898; M. M[sic] |

1317; 1326; Wildhog, Vida[sic]; sgle; Mar. 1905[?]; F. F [Note: Viola in 1906-25. Shows as 2 months old in 1906 yet majority of census years show the year of birth as 1907.]

| | |
|---|---|
| 1318; 1327; | Wildhog, Mary Anne; mthr; Dec. 1903; F. F [Birth date 1905 in 1926.] |
| 1319; 1328; | Wildhog, Opal; dau; Jan. 1925; F. F |

| | |
|---|---|
| 1320; 1329; | Wilson, Martha; wife; May 1894; F. 1/2 |
| | Wilson, James; hsbd; --; --. (White) |
| 1321; 1330; | Wilson, Arthur; son; Sept 1918; M. 1/4 [1919 name James Jr.] |
| 1322; 1331; | Wilson, Esther Martha; dau.; Sept 1920; F. 1/4 [Birth month Aug., in 1927.] |
| 1323; 1332; | Wilson, Alice; dau; July 1921; F. 1/4 [#1324 in 1926 was Josephine.] |
| 1324; 1333; | Wilson, Florence; dau; Sept 1922; F. 1/4 |
| 1325; 1334; | Wilson, Josephine; dau; Nov. 1924; F. 1/4 |
| 1326; 1335; | Wilson, James Jr.; son; Dec. 1926; M. 1/4 |

| | |
|---|---|
| 1327; 1336; | Wolf, William; hsbd; Apr. 1872; M. F |
| 1328; 1337; | Wolf, Rosa; wife; May 1877; F. F [nee Crow / Bigbeaver.] |
| 1329; 1338; | Wolf, Fannie Lucy; dau.; Mar. 1916; F. F |

Census of the **Northern Cheyenne** Indians of **Tongue River** Agency, **Mont.** on **June 30, 1928** taken by **C.B. Lohmiller**, Superintendent.

**Key:** Last Number; Present Number; Indian Name; English Name; Relationship; Month, Year, of Birth; Sex; Blood Quantum

1330; 1339;   Wolfblack, Dallas; hsbd; Apr. 1882[?]; M. F [1904-14 birth year 1885; 1915-23, 1872; 1924-28, 1882.]
1331; 1340;   Wolfblack, Rose; wife; June 1890; F. F [Whitemoon]
1332; 1341;   Wolfblack, Gladys; dau; Dec. 1915; F. F
1333; 1342;   Wolfblack, Oran; son; Apr. 1924; M. F
1334;         Wolfblack, Harry; son; Jan. 1926; M. F Died April 26, 1928

1335; 1343;   Wolfchief, Harshey; hsbd; Aug. 1852; M. F
1336; 1344;   Wolfchief, Anna; wife; July 1861[sic]; F. F [Whiteelk]

1337; 1345;   Wolfchief, Josie; wdw; July 1843; F. F

1338; 1346;   Wolfchief, Richard; hsbd; Apr. 1892; M. F
1339; 1347;   Wolfchief, Flora; wife; Sept. 1891; F. F
1340; 1348;   Wolfchief, Alice; dau; Nov. 1912; F. F
1341; 1349;   Wolfchief, Ann; dau.; May 1927; F. F

1342; 1350;   Wolfchum, Paul; hsbd; Oct. 1893; M. F [Birth year 1890 in 1926.]
1343; 1351;   Wolfchum, Bessie Sun[sic]; wife; June 1890; F. f [Littlesun in 1927.]
1344; 1352;   Wolfchum, Walker; son; Dec. 1926; M. F

1345; 1353;   Wolfchum, Lily; dau; May 1916; F. F Lives with Adolph Walksnice. [1917 Census name Betty.]

1346; 1354;   Wolfear, Willis; hsbd.; Jan 1884; M. F
1347; 1355;   Wolfear, Sophia; wife; May 1872; F. F

1348; 1356;   Wolfname, Paul; hsbd; Dec. 1886; M. F
1349;         Wolfname, Anna; wife; Feb. 1892; F. F Died Aug. 21, 1927
1350; 1357;   Wolfname, Martha; dau; June 1910; F. F
1351; 1358;   Wolfname, Henry; son; Sept 1912; M. F
1352; 1359;   Wolfname, Wilbur Paul; son; Oct. 1921; M. F

1353; 1360;   Wolfname, William; hsbd; Jan. 1854; M. F
1354; 1361;   Wolfname, Bessie; wife; May 1854; F. F

1355; 1362;   Wolfname, Grace; dau; June 1916; F. F s-dau. Miles Horn

1356; 1363;   Wolfroads[sic], Mack; hsbd; July 1878; M. F
1357;         Wolfroads, Jennie; wife; Aug. 1877; F. F Died April 11, 1928
1358; 1364;   Wolfroads, Maude; dau; July 1910; F. F
1359; 1365;   Wolfroads, Rose Charlotte; dau.; Jan. 1914; F. F [Norman, son, M., same # 1922-23. Birth year 1920 in 1926. Name Rosa in 1927.]

Census of the **Northern Cheyenne** Indians of **Tongue River** Agency, **Mont.** on **June 30, 1928** taken by **C.B. Lohmiller**, Superintendent.

**Key:** Last Number; Present Number; Indian Name; English Name; Relationship; Month, Year, of Birth; Sex; Blood Quantum

1360; 1366;      Wolftooth, Young; hsbd; Nov. 1881; M. F
1361; 1367;      Wolftooth, Mary; dau; May 1918; F. 1/2
1362; 1368;      Wolftooth, Norman; son; July 1920; M. 3/4
1363; 1369;      Wolftooth, Doris; dau; Nov. 1925; F. 3/4

1364; 1370;      Wolfvoice, Grover; hsbd; Apr. 1890; M. F
1365; 1371;      Wolfvoice, Jennie Brady; wife; May 1882[sic]; F. F [1904-1922 birth year 1888.]
1366; 1372;      Wolfvoice, Anne; dau; Feb. 1918; F. F
1367; 1373;      Wolfvoice, Dewey; son; Mar. 1927; M. F

1368; 1374;      Womanleggins, Edward; hsbd.; Apr. 1888; M. F
1369; 1375;      Womanleggins, Mannie[sic]; wife; Nov. 1891; F. F [Lamewoman]
1370; 1376;      Womanleggins, Mabel; dau; Aug. 1915; F. F (Mabel Badhorses) [1917-20 son, Junior, M.; Name is June in 1926.]

1371; 1377;      Woodenlegs[sic], Richard; hsbd; Aug. 1859; M. F
1372; 1378;      Woodenlegs, Sophia; wife; May 1859[sic]; F. F

1373; 1379;      Woodenlegs[sic], Tom; hsbd; July 1887; M. 3/4 (Tom Seminole)
1374; 1380;      Woodenlegs, Jessie; wife; Nov. 1905[sic]; F. F [Spottedelk; shows 6mo., 1908 census.]
1375; 1381;      Woodenlegs, John; son; Nov. 1909; M. 7/8
1376; 1382;      Woodenlegs, Mabel; dau.; Mar. 1927; F. 7/8

1377; 1383;      Woodenthigh, Arthur; hsbd; Nov. 1883; M. F
1378; 1384;      Woodenthigh, Eva; wife; Dec. 1887; F. F
1379; 1385;      Woodenthigh, Esther; dau; Apr. 1910; F. F
1380; 1386;      Woodenthigh, Alice; dau; Feb. 1914; F. F
1381; 1387;      Woodenthigh, Peter; a-son; May 1918; M. 1/2 [Birth year 1916 in 1926.]

1382; 1388;      Woodenthigh, Chester; hsbd; Sept. 1884; M. F
1383; 1389;      Woodenthigh, Lena; wife; Sept 1890; F. F
1384; 1390;      Woodenthigh, Philip; son; May 1915; M. F
1385; 1391;      Woodenthigh, John; son; June 1916; M. F
1386; 1392;      Woodenthigh, Melvin; son; Nov. 1923; M. F

1382; 1393;      Woodpecker, James; hsbd; Mar. 1901; M. F
1388; 1394;      Woodpecker, Mary; wife; May 1904; F. 3/4 [Littlewhiteman]

1389;      Woodpecker, Ralph; sgle; Dec. 1907; M. F Died Sept 28, 1927

1390; 1395;      Woodpecker, Donald; sgle; July 1909; M. F

Census of the **Northern Cheyenne** Indians of **Tongue River** Agency, **Mont.** on **June 30, 1928** taken by **C.B. Lohmiller**, Superintendent.

**Key:** Last Number; Present Number; Indian Name; English Name; Relationship; Month, Year, of Birth; Sex; Blood Quantum

| | |
|---|---|
| 1391; 1396; | Woundedeye, Davis; hsbd; June 1885; M. F |
| 1392; 1397; | Woundedeye, Susie May; wife; Aug 1903; F. F |
| 1393; 1398; | Woundedeye, Milton; son; Apr 1920; M. F |
| 1394; 1928 | Woundedeye, Charles; son; Nov. 1922; M. F [Ross] Died June 27, |
| 1395; 1399; | Woundedeye, Veta; dau; Jan. 1927; F. F |
| | |
| 1397; 1400; | Woundedeye, Ford; hsbd; Apr 1882; M. F |
| 1398; 1401; | Woundedeye, Florence; wife; May 1890; F. F |
| 1399; 1402; | Woundedeye, Winfield; son; Apr. 1909; M. F [Birth year 1908 in 1927.] |
| 1401; 1403; | Woundedeye, Victoria; dau; Jan 1922; F. F |
| 1402; | Woundedeye, Fordson; son; Jan. 1919; M. F Died April 17, 1928 |
| 1403; 1404; | Woundedeye, Ruth; dau; Apr. 1927; F. F |
| | |
| 1400; 1405; | Woundedeye, Laura; mthr; Nov. 1909; F. F |
| 1406; | Woundedeye, Hayes; son; June 26/28; M. F |
| 1396; 1407; | Woundedeye, Paul; son; June 1911; M. F |
| | |
| 1404; 1408; | Yellowfox, William; hsbd; May 1900; M. F |
| 1405; 1409; | Yellowfox, Margaret; wife; Mar. 1905; F. F [Yellownose] |
| | Yellowfox, Arthur; son; Nov. 1/27; M. F Died Nov. 26, 1927 |
| | |
| 1406; 1410; | Yelloweagle, Kate; wdw; Apr. 1852; F. F |
| | |
| 1407; 1411; | Yelloweyes, Abram; hsbd; July 1874; M. F |
| 1408; 1412; | Yelloweyes, Nora; wife; Feb. 1877; F. F |
| | |
| 1409; 1413; | Yelloweyes, Oliver; hsbd; July 1901; M. F |
| 1410; 1414; | Yelloweyes, Gertrude; wife; May 1905[?]; F. F [Brownbird] |
| 1411; 1415; | Yelloweyes, Mary; dau; Nov. 1924; F. F |
| 1416; | Yelloweyes, Ruth; dau; Nov. 6/27; F. F |
| | |
| 1412; 1417; | Yellowfox, Robert; hsbd; July 1875; M. F |
| 1413; 1418; | Yellowfox, Carrie; wife; Nov. 1882; F. F |
| 1414; 1419; | Yellowfox, Frank; son; July 1901; M. F |
| 1415; 1420; | Yellowfox, Charles; son; Oct. 1908; M. F |
| 1416; | Yellowfox, William; son; Aug. 1922; M. F Died Nov. 11, 1927 |
| | |
| 1417; 1421; | Yellowhorse, Julia; s-dau; May 1913; F. F s-dau. Milton Littlewhiteman. |
| | |
| 1418; 1422; 1926.] | Yellownose, Robert; hsbd; Sept 1859[?]; M. F [Birth year 1865 in |
| 1419; 1423; | Yellownose, Anne; wife; Mar. 1867; F. F |

Census of the **Northern Cheyenne** Indians of **Tongue River** Agency, **Mont.** on **June 30, 1928** taken by **C.B. Lohmiller**, Superintendent.

**Key:** Last Number; Present Number; Indian Name; English Name; Relationship; Month, Year, of Birth; Sex; Blood Quantum

| | |
|---|---|
| 1420; 1424; | Yellownose, George; hsbd; Nov. 1896; M. F [Birth year 1895. 1904-17.] |
| 1227; [Crazymule] | Yellownose, Lizzie; wife; Apr. 1891; F. F Died July 10, 1927 |
| 1425; | Yellownose, Mary; dau; July 1927; F. F |
| | |
| 1423; 1426; | Yellowrobe, Charles; hsbd; June 1892; M. F |
| 1424; 1427; | Yellowrobe, Alice; wife; May 1898; F. F |
| 1425; 1428; | Yellowrobe, Ruth; dau; Mar. 1917; F. F [Name Ruana in 1926.] |
| 1426; 1429; | Yellowrobe, Martha; dau; Jan 1926; F. F |
| | |
| 1427; 1430; | Yellowrobe, Jasper; sgle; Dec. 1894; M. F |
| | |
| 1428; 1431; | Yellowrobe, Adolph; sgle; Nov. 1900; M. F |
| | |
| 1429; 1432; | Yellowrobe, William; hsbd; Oct. 1865; M. F |
| 1430; 1433; | Yellowrobe, Minnie; wife; Jan. 1857; F. F [Birth year 1859 in 1926.] |
| | |
| 1431; 1434; | Youngbear, George; hsbd; Aug. 1882; M. -- |
| 1432; 1435; 1919.] | Youngbear, Cora; wife; July 1888[?]; F. 3/4 [Birth year 1890. 1904-1919.] |
| 1433; 1436; | Youngbear, Arthur; son; Aug. 1913; M. 7/8 |
| 1434; 1437; 1919.] | Youngbear, Ralph; son; Oct. 1921[sic]; M. 7/8 [Shows up in 1920. Born 1919.] |
| 1438; | Youngbear, Mary; dau; Dec. 20/27; F. 7/8 |
| | |
| 1435; 1439; 1927.] | Youngbird, James; hsbd; Sept. 1867[?]; M. F [Birth year 1857 in 1927.] |
| 1436; 1440; | Youngbird, Clara; wife; May 1863; F. F |
| | |
| 1437; 1441; | Youngbird, John; hsbd; Sept 1884; M. F |
| 1438; 1442; | Youngbird, Anne; wife; Feb. 1885; F. F [Looksbehind] |
| 1439; 1443; | Youngbird, Carl; son; Apr. 1912; M. F [Birth year 1923 in 1926.] |
| | |
| 292; 1444; | Schaffer, Letha; wife; Apr. 1913; F. 1/8 [Son, Carl in 1916 Census. Eastman in 1927] |
| | Schaffer, George; hsbd.; -- ---; --. (Not enrolled) |

Census of the **Northern Cheyenne** Indians of **Tongue River** Agency, **Mont.** on **June 30, 1928** taken by **C.B. Lohmiller**, Superintendent.

**Key:** Last Number; Present Number; Indian Name; English Name; Relationship; Month, Year, of Birth; Sex; Blood Quantum

R E C A P I T U L A T I O N   O F   C E N S U S

```
Total males..........................720
Total females.......................734  1444
Males over 21.......................409
Females over 18....................374
Males under 21.....................411
Females under 18.................350
                                   1,444
```

Last year's census showed a total of 1449
This  "          "   shows  "   "   "  1444

Total decrease............................  5

# CENSUS OF NORTHERN CHEYENNE

-of-

## TONGUE RIVER RESERVATION, MONT.

June 30, 1929,

TONGUE RIVER AGENCY,

C. B. Lohmiller, Superintendent.

TONGUE RIVER.
124

1929

* 5-130

## UNITED STATES DEPARTMENT OF THE INTERIOR
### OFFICE OF INDIAN AFFAIRS

### I. CENSUS RECAPITULATION SHEET

Census of the __Northern Cheyenne__ Tribe of the __Tongue River__ Reservation of the __Tongue River__ Jurisdiction, as of __June__, __30__, __1929__
(Month) (Day) (Year)

taken by __C. B. Lohmiller__, Superintendent.

|  | Male | Female | Total |
|---|---|---|---|
| 1. Total last census | 720 | 724 | 1444 |
| 2. Additions | 33 | 27 | 60 |
|    a. Because of enrollment by Departmental authority | 0 | 0 | 0 |
|    b. *Male erroneously shown as female* | 1 | 0 | 1 |
|    c. Because of birth | 32 | 27 | 59 |
|       1. Unreported previous years | 3 | 1 | 4 |
|       2. Current year | 29 | 26 | 55 |
| 3. Total last census plus additions to roll | 753 | 751 | 1504 |
| 4. Subtractions | 23 | 20 | 43 |
|    a. Because of illegal or wrongful enrollment— |  |  |  |
|       *Male erroneously shown as female* | 0 | 1 | 1 |
|    b. Because of death | 23 | 19 | 42 |
|       1. Unreported previous years | 0 | 1 | 1 |
|       2. Current year | 23 | 18 | 41 |
| 5. Total this census (should agree with last number on current roll) | 730 | 731 | 1461 |

* (No. 778 this years census correctly shown as male; last year shown as female.)

5-130

## UNITED STATES DEPARTMENT OF THE INTERIOR
### OFFICE OF INDIAN AFFAIRS

## I. CENSUS RECAPITULATION SHEET

Census of the  Northern Cheyenne  Tribe of the  Tongue River  Reservation of the  Tongue River  Jurisdiction, as of  June , 30 , 19 29  taken by  C. B. Lohmiller , Superintendent.

|  | Male | Female | Total |
|---|---|---|---|
| 1. Total last census | 720 | 724 | 1444 |
| 2. Additions | 32 | 27 | 59 |
|     a. Because of enrollment by Departmental authority | 0 | 0 | 0 |
|     b. Because of omission from previous census rolls | 0 | 0 | 0 |
|     c. Because of birth | 32 | 27 | 59 |
|         1. Unreported previous years | 3 | 1 | 5 |
|         2. Current year | 29 | 26 | 55 |
| 3. Total last census plus additions to roll | 752 | 751 | 1503 |
| 4. Subtractions | 23 | 19 | 42 |
|     a. Because of illegal or wrongful enrollment— Departmental authority | 0 | 0 | 0 |
|     b. Because of death | 23 | 19 | 42 |
|         1. Unreported previous years | 0 | 1 | 1 |
|         2. Current year | 23 | 18 | 41 |
| 5. Total this census (should agree with last number on current roll) | *730 | 731 | 1461 |

\* (No. 778 this years census correctly shown as male; last year shown as female.)

## II. CENSUS RECAPITULATION SHEET

**UNITED STATES DEPARTMENT OF THE INTERIOR**
**OFFICE OF INDIAN AFFAIRS**

### II. CENSUS RECAPITULATION SHEET

| AGE GROUP | MIXED-BLOOD | | | DEGREE OF BLOOD FULL-BLOOD | | | TOTAL | | |
|---|---|---|---|---|---|---|---|---|---|
| | TOTAL | MALE | FEMALE | TOTAL | MALE | FEMALE | TOTAL | MALE | FEMALE |
| Under one year, | 17 | 8 | 9 | 38 | 21 | 17 | 55 | 29 | 26 |
| 1 to 3 years, | 33 | 22 | 11 | 58 | 22 | 36 | 91 | 44 | 47 |
| 4 to 9 " | 76 | 38 | 38 | 140 | 65 | 75 | 216 | 103 | 113 |
| 10 to 19 " | 100 | 44 | 56 | 219 | 96 | 123 | 319 | 140 | 179 |
| 20 to 29 " | 32 | 14 | 18 | 129 | 61 | 68 | 161 | 75 | 86 |
| 30 to 39 " | 40 | 25 | 15 | 149 | 77 | 72 | 189 | 102 | 87 |
| 40 to 49 " | 24 | 15 | 9 | 123 | 73 | 50 | 147 | 88 | 59 |
| 50 to 59 " | 12 | 4 | 8 | 102 | 58 | 44 | 114 | 62 | 52 |
| 60 to 69 " | 6 | 6 | 0 | 80 | 43 | 37 | 86 | 49 | 37 |
| 70 to 79 " | 3 | 1 | 2 | 61 | 29 | 32 | 64 | 30 | 34 |
| 80 to 89 " | 0 | 0 | 0 | 17 | 7 | 10 | 17 | 7 | 10 |
| 90 and over, | 0 | 0 | 0 | 2 | 1 | 1 | 2 | 1 | 1 |
| Unknown, | 0 | 0 | 0 | 0 | 0 | 0 | 0 | 0 | 0 |
| TOTAL, | 343 | 177 | 166 | 1118 | 553 | 565 | 1461 | 720 | 731 |

Census of the __Northern Cheyenne__ tribe of the __Tongue River Agency__ jurisdiction as of __June 30, 1929__ taken by __C.B. Lohmiller__, Superintendent.

**Key:** Present Number; Last Number; Indian Name; English Name; Sex; Month, Year, of Birth; Degree of Blood "F-Fullblood, M-Mixed Blood"; Marital Status; Relationship;

1; 1; Americanhorse, Austin; M; 10-1878; F; M; Head
2; 2; Americanhorse, Maude; F; 4-1883; F; M; Wife
3; 3; Americanhorse, Lucy; F; 11-1910; F; S; Dau
4; 4; Americanhorse, George; M; 9-1914; F; s; Son [Texas]

5; 5; Americanhorse, Bessie; F; 11-1905[?]; F; S; Head [First shows as 1 yr. 1908.]

6; 6; Americanhorse, Flora; F; -- 1861; F; Wd; Head

7; 7; Americanhorse, George; M; 10-1881; F; M; Head
8; 8; Americanhorse, Minnie; F; 12-1884[?]; F; M; Wife [1907-26 birth yr., 1885-1886.]
9; 9; Americanhorse, James; M; 11-1911; F; S; Son
10; 10; Americanhorse, Marie; F; 6-1914; F; S; Dau
11; 11; Americanhorse, Lucy; F; 8-1918; F; S; Dau

12; 12; Americanhorse, Reuben; M; 11-1917[?]; F; S; Orp. [Shows 1918, birth 1918.]
13; 13; Americanhorse, Albert; M; 7-1912; F; S; Orp. [Mike Badhorse]

14; 14; Americanhorse, Willis; M; 10-1892; F; M; Head
15; 15; Americanhorse, Ernest; M; 11-1911; F; S; Son
16; 16; Americanhorse, Laura Martha; F; 6-1914; F; S; Dau
17; 17; Americanhorse, Madge; F; 12-1916; F; S; Dau
18; 18; Americanhorse, Grace; F; 4-1918; F; S; Dau

19; 19; Americanhorse, Walter; M; 10-1890; F; H; Head

20; 20; Ant, James; M; 2-1903; F; H; Head
21; 21; Ant, Hannah; F; 5-1900; F; M; Wife [Highwalking]
22; 22; Ant, Bertha; F; 1-1925; F; S; Dau
23; Ant, Ralph; M; 10-18-1928; F; S; Son

24; 23; Ant, Walter; M; 1-1880; F; M; Head
25; 24; Ant, Helen; F; 5-1882; F; M; Wife
26; 25; Ant, June; F; 1-1920; F; S; Dau
27; 26; Ant, Paul; M; 3-1927; F; S; Son

28; 27; Atwood, James; M; 3-1891; F; M; Head [Twentystands]
29; 28; Atwood, Cecelia; F; 1-1898; F; M; Wife
30; 29; Atwood, Mary; F; 5-1914; F; S; Dau
31; 30; Atwood, Herbert; M; 8-1222[sic]; F; S; Son

32; 31; Baldeagle, Hugh; M; 5-1858; F; M; Head

Census of the **Northern Cheyenne** tribe of the **Tongue River Agency** jurisdiction as of **June 30, 1929** taken by **C.B. Lohmiller**, Superintendent.

**Key:** Present Number; Last Number; Indian Name; English Name; Sex; Month, Year, of Birth; Degree of Blood "F-Fullblood, M-Mixed Blood"; Marital Status; Relationship;

33; 32; Baldeagle, Minnie; F; 9-1859; F; M; Wife

34; 33; Bearchum, Frank; M; 3-1901; M; S; Head

35; 34; Bearchum, Benjamin Jr.; M; 3-1919; M; S; S-Son [Junior] S-son Ed. Womanleggins

36; 35; Bearcomesout, Charles; M; 10-1880; F; Wd; Head
37; 36; Bearcomesout, Harold; M; 3-1908; F; S; Son
38; 37; Bearcomesout, Pius; M; 9-1915; F; S; Son

39; 38; Bearquiver, Edward; M; 9-1881; F; Wd; Head
40; 39; Bearquiver, Edna; F; 12-1912; F; S; Dau
41; 40; Bearquiver, Claude; M; 11-1916; F; S; Son
42; 41; Bearquiver, James; M; 6-1920; F; S; Son
43; 42; Bearquiver, Martin; M; 8-1922; F; S; Son
44; 43; Bearquiver, Grace; F; 8-1927; F; S; Dau

45; 44; Beartusk, Jerome; M; 8-1885; F; Div; Head

46; 45; Beartusk, Lucy; F; 1-1893; M; Div; Head
47; 46; Beartusk, Edith; F; 4-1916; M; S; Dau
48; 47; Beartusk, Alice; F; 4-1917; M; S; Dau
49; 48; Beartusk, Gladys; F; 1-1919; M; S; Dau [Nellie]
50; 49; Beartusk, Kenneth; M; 12-1920; M; S; Son
51; 50; Beartusk, Bertha Eliz.; F; 3-1923; M; S; Dau
52; 51; Beartusk, Jerome Jr.; M; 12-1925; M; S; Son

53; 52; Beaverheart, Thomas; M; 5-1863[?]; F; M; Head [1904-15, birth year 1857; 1916-24, birth year 1859; 1925-28 birth year 1863.]
54; 53; Beaverheart, Nellie; F; 3-1857; F; M; Wife
55; 54; Beaverheart, David; M; 4-1890; F; S; Son [Name Davis in 1926.]

56; 55; Beirdneau, Adeline; F; 2-1899; M; Wd; Head
57; 56; Beirdneau, Betty Belle, F; 4-1923; M; S; Dau
58; 57; Beirdneau, Barbara Marie; F; 4-1926; M; S; Dau
59; 58; Beirdneau, Albert Lee; M; 2-16-1928; M; S; Son

60; 59; BeMent, Emma; F; 6-1901; M; M; Head [Burns]
61; 60; BeMent, Jacqueline; F; 10-1922; M; S; Dau
62; 61; BeMent, Clarence Jr.; M; 11-1923; M; S; Son [Max in 1925. Mickie in 1926.]
63; 62; BeMent, Jesse; M; 3-1925; M; S; Son [Joseph in 1925. Birth year 1924 in 1928.]
64; 63; BeMent, Geraldine; F; 2-1-27; M; S; Dau

Census of the __Northern Cheyenne__ tribe of the __Tongue River Agency__ jurisdiction as of __June 30, 1929__ taken by __C.B. Lohmiller__, Superintendent.

**Key:** Present Number; Last Number; Indian Name; English Name; Sex; Month, Year, of Birth; Degree of Blood "F-Fullblood, M-Mixed Blood"; Marital Status; Relationship;

65; 64; BeMent, Celia Camille; F; 1-19-28; M; S; Dau

66; 65; Bigback, Charles; M; 3-1863[?]; F; M; Head [Birth year 1865.]
67; 66; Bigback, Clara; F; 7-1869; F; M; Wife
68; 72; Bigback, Stephen; M; 4-1892; F; S; Son
69; 67; Bigback, John; M; 2-1904; F; S; Son [Henry in 1919.]

70; 68; Bigback, James; M; 8-1894; F; M; Head
71; 69; Bigback, Jennie; F; 5-1898; F; M; Wife
72; 70; Bigback, Gladys; F; 7-1920; F; S; Dau
73; 71; Bigback, Robert; M; 12-1923; F; S; Son

74; 73; Bigbeaver, August; M; 3-1861; F; M; Head
75; 74; Bigbeaver, Annie Marie; F; 6-1911; F; S; Dau

76; 75; Bigcrow, Andrew; 3-Mar. 1854; F; M; Head
77; 76; Bigcrow, Jennie; F; 11-1888; F; M; Wife
78; 77; Bigcrow, Sarah Angela; F; 8-1912; F; S; Dau

79; 78; Bigfoot, John; M; -- 1881; F; M; Head

80; 79; Bigfoot, White; M; 10-1875; F; M; Head
81; 80; Bigfoot, Louisa; F; 9-1885; F; M; Wife
82; 81; Bigfoot, Louis; M; 6-1911; F; S; Son

83; 82; Bigfoot, Davis; M; 5-1898; F; M; Head
84; 83; Bigfoot, Lucy; F; 10-1900; F; M; Wife
85; 84; Bigfoot, Alice; F; 1-1921; F; S; Dau [1926 Census birth 1923, name Martha same #. Shows up in 1925 birth year as 1923, also as Martha.]
86; 85; Bigfoot, Mary; F; 4-1924; F; S; Dau
86; Bigfoot, James; M; 12-15-27; F; S; Son Died 12-3-1928

87; Bighead, Kate; F; 7-1847; F; Wd; Head Died 2-23-1929

87; 88; Bigheadman, Benjamin; M; 7-1889; F; M; Head
88; 89; Bigheadman, Julia; F; 7-1894; F; M; Wife
89; 90; Bigheadman, Gladys; F; 9-1918; F; S; Dau [1926 Census name Lucille same #.]
90; 91; Bigheadman, Laura; F; 7-1927; F; S; Dau

91; 92; Bigheadman, Blair; M; 6-1892; F; M; Head
92; 93; Bigheadman, Clara; F; 4-1901; F; M; Wife
93; 94; Bigheadman, Grover; M; 7-1919; F; S; Son
94; 95; Bigheadman, August; M; 8-1922; F; S; Son
95; 96; Bigheadman, Julia; F; 12-1924; F; S; Dau

Census of the __Northern Cheyenne__ tribe of the __Tongue River Agency__ jurisdiction as of __June 30, 1929__ taken by __C.B. Lohmiller__, Superintendent.

**Key:** Present Number; Last Number; Indian Name; English Name; Sex; Month, Year, of Birth; Degree of Blood "F-Fullblood, M-Mixed Blood"; Marital Status; Relationship;

96; 97; Bigheadman, Betty Nora; F; 1-1915; F; S; G-Dau G.-dau. J. Twomoon[sic]
97; 98; Bigheadman, Frank Biddle; M; 8-1917; F; S; G-Son G-Son J. Twomoon[sic] [1918 year Lucy g dt. Children of Ben. Bigheadman.]

98; 99; Bigheadman, John; M; 6-1849[sic]; F; M; Head [1904-25, birth year 1853.]
99; 100; Bigheadman, Nellie; F; 10-1853; F; M; Wife

100; 101; Bigheadman, William; M; 12-1886; F; M; Head (Whitehorse)
101; 102; Bigheadman, Nellie; F; 6-1891; F; M; Wife
102; 103; Bigheadman, Richard; M; 4-1909; F; S; Son [Richard Rowland]
103; 104; Bigheadman, Grace; F; 5-1918; F; S; Dau
104; 105; Bigheadman, Kathleen; F; 3-1925; F; S; Dau
105; 106; Bigheadman, Dorla; F; 6-1926; F; S; Dau
106; Bigheadman, Elizabeth; F; 11-1928; F; S; Dau

107; 109; Bigleg, Hinton; M; 5-1887[?]; F; M; Head [Shows up in 1911, birth year 1911-26, 1883.]
108; 110; Bigleg, Annie; F; 1-1879; M; M; Wife
109; 952; Rowland, Claude; M; 4-1904; M; S; S-son
110; 953; Rowland, Benjamin; M; 7-1908; M; S; S-son

111; 111; Bignose, George; M; 8-1897; F; S; Head

112; 112; Bignose, Samuel; M; 5-1891; F; S; Head

113; 113; Bignose, James; M; 10-1863; F; M; Head
114; 114; Bignose, Rachel; F; 7-1855[?]; F; M; Wife
115; 484;[sic] Redneck, Clyde; M; 8-1912; F; S; Grson [7/8, son of Maude Shields Whitewolf. Last number in 1928 #848.]

116; 115; Bites, Sally; F; 10-1866; F; Wd; Head

117; 116; Bites, James; M; 9-1900; F; M; Head
118; 117; Bites, Sally; F; 1-1905; F; M; Wife [Crazymule]
119; 118; Bites, Florence; F; 7-1926; F; S; Dau
120; Bites, James Jr.; M; 5-5-1929; F; S; Son

121; 119; Bixby, Benjamin; M; 10-1887[?]; M; M; Head [1904-1918 birth year is 1886. 1919-26, 1866.]
122; 120; Bixby, Gertrude; F; 5-1893[sic]; M; M; Wife [Whitepowder 1904-07; Tallwhiteman 1908; Bixby 1909-1929; 1904-08 Birth year 1887; 1909-13 birth year 1888; 1914-26 1883; in 1927, 1893.]
123; 121; Bixby, Annie; F; 9-1913; M; S; Dau

Census of the **Northern Cheyenne** tribe of the **Tongue River Agency** jurisdiction as of **June 30, 1929** taken by **C.B. Lohmiller**, Superintendent.

**Key:** Present Number; Last Number; Indian Name; English Name; Sex; Month, Year, of Birth; Degree of Blood "F-Fullblood, M-Mixed Blood"; Marital Status; Relationship;

124; 122; Bixby, James; M; 12-1915; M; S; Son [Jessie Daughter 1916-19.]

125; 123; Bixby, Edward; M; 3-1891; M; M; Head [1904-18 birth year 1890; 1919-26 birth year 1898; in 1929, 1891.]
126; 124; Bixby, Edward George; M; 7-1922; M; S; Son [1924 Clara, dau; F. 1925-26 Jack.]
127; 125; Bixby, Elsie Virginia; F; 12-1923; M; S; Dau [Vianne 1925-26.]
128; 126; Bixby, Wm. Lawrence; M; 3-1925; M; S; Son
129; Bixby, Hattie Caroline; F; 7-24-1928; M; S; Dau

130; 127; Bixby, Jessie; F; 5-1853; M; Wd; Head

131; 128; Blackbird, Isaac; M; 6-1863; F; M; Head [Birth year 1864 in 1927.]
132; 129; Blackbird, Sallie; F; 3-1872; F; M; Wife

133; 130; Blackcrane, Clara; F; 12-1866[?]; F; Wd; Head [1920 Clara Blackeagle, wdw, #102, birth year 1845. Charles wife in 1920, Edith birth year 1866.]

134; 131; Blackeagle, William; M; 6-1888[?]; F; Wd[sic]; Head [#131, William-Censuses 1904-1915 Birth year 1886. 1916-1918 Birth year 1896; 1919 Birth year 1906 [sic]; 1920-26 Census birth year again 1896.]
135; 132; Blackeagle, Carl; M; 9-1911; F; S; Son

136; 133; Blackhorse, Rueben[sic]; M; 7-1853[?]; F; M; Head
137; 134; Blackhorse, Lena; F; 12-1876[sic]; F; M; Wife [1904-26 birth year 1862-3.]
138; 135; Blackhorse, Anna; F; 7-1913; F; S; Dau [Anna 1927.?] [#135, Son, Arthur in 1913-14 Censuses. Name Ada 1915-19. Name Ida 1920-26.]

139; 136; Blackhorse, Alex; M; 10-1897; F; M; Head
140; 137; Blackhorse, Mary; F; 6-1903; F; M; Wife
141; 138; Blackhorse, Francis; M; 7-1922; F; S; Son [1923-26 name Merton.]
142; 139; Blackhorse, Alice; F; 9-1924; F; S; Dau
Blackhorse, Charles; M; 2-1928; F; S; Son Died 8-4-1928

143; 140; Blackree, Alice; F; 3-1909; F; Div; Head
144; 141; Blackree, Anna; F; 8-1923; F; S; Dau

145; 142; Blackree, Paul; M; 10-1878; F; M; Head
146; 143; Blackree, Jennie; F; 5-1881; F; M; Wife

147; 144; Blackstone, Charles; M; 12-1860[?]; F; Wd[sic]; Head

148; 145; Blackstone, Lena; F; 7-1878; F; S; S-Dau[?] [7/8 blood in 1928.]

Census of the **Northern Cheyenne** tribe of the **Tongue River Agency** jurisdiction as of **June 30, 1929** taken by **C.B. Lohmiller**, Superintendent.

**Key:** Present Number; Last Number; Indian Name; English Name; Sex; Month, Year, of Birth; Degree of Blood "F-Fullblood, M-Mixed Blood"; Marital Status; Relationship;

[#145, Previous & 1923 Census dau, 1924 wife.]

149; 146; Blackstone, Arthur; M; 12-1892; F; M; Head
150; 147; Blackstone, Nellie[sic]; F; 8-1900[sic]; F; M; Wife [1906-26 birth year 1905. #147, Name Sallie, Mother Nellie. Nee Littlehead]
151; 148; Blackstone, Louis; M; 10-21-27; F; S; Son

152; 149; Blackwolf, Bennie; M; 6-1897; F; M; Head [1904-1923 name Alex.]
153; 150; Blackwolf, Ella; F; 12-1900; F; M; Wife
154; 151; Blackwolf, Henry; M; 10-1919; F; S; Son [1925 Census Thomas.]
155; 152; Blackwolf, James; M; 8-1923; F; S; Son [1925 Census Alfred.]
156; 153; Blackwolf, Ruth; F; 1-1927; F; S; Dau

157; 154; Blackwolf, John; M; 8-1870; F; M; Head
158; 155; Blackwolf, Nellie; F; 7-1874; F; M; Wife
159; 156; Blackwolf, Alex; M; 5-1906; F; S; Son [#156, Name Busby, a brother Alex born 1897 in 1916 census, married in 1917.]
160; 157; Blackwolf, Mary; F; 1-1914; F; S; Dau

161; 158; Blindman, Arthur; M; 11-1868; F; Wd[sic]; Head

162; 159; Bluehawk, Louis; M; 6-1850[sic]; M; Wd[sic]; Head [1904-19 Born 1861.]

163; 160; Bobtailhorse, Thomas; M; 7-1850; F; M; Head
164; 161; Bobtailhorse, Gertrude; F; 12-1851; F; M; Wife

165; 162; Bolson, Gail; F; 7-1915; M; S; Dau [1925 s-son, M,] (Children of Rena LeFever)
166; 163; Bolson, Frank; M; 8-1917; M; S; Son
167; 164; Bolson, Roy Guy; M; 12-1919; M; S; Son

168; 165; Boxelder, Laura; F; 1-1872; F; Wd; Head

169; 166; Brady, Arthur; M; 12-1840; F; M; Head
170; 167; Brady, Ellen; F; 12-1853; F; M; Wife

171; 168; Brady, Alex; M; 12-1898; F; M; Head [1904-15 birth year 1898; 1916-26 1893.]
172; 169; Brady, Josie; F; 12-1902; F; M; Wife [Pine]
173; 170; Brady, Charles; M; 11-1923; F; S; Son

174; 171; Brady, George; M; 7-1881; F; M; Head
175; 172; Brady, Flossie; F; 2-1897; M; M; Wife
176; 173; Brady, Elmore; M; 3-1907; F; S; Son

Census of the __Northern Cheyenne__ tribe of the __Tongue River Agency__
jurisdiction as of __June 30, 1929__ taken by __C.B. Lohmiller__, Superintendent.
**Key:** Present Number; Last Number; Indian Name; English Name; Sex; Month, Year, of Birth; Degree of Blood "F-Fullblood, M-Mixed Blood"; Marital Status; Relationship;

177;  174;  Brady, James Henry; M; 4-1913; F; S; Son
178;  175;  Brady, Howard; M; 11-1915[sic]; F; S; Son
179   176;  Brady, Romona Lucy; F; 12-1917[?]; F; S; Dau
180;  177;  Brady, Wilson; M; 10-1918; F; S; Son
181;  178;  Brady, Martha; F; 2-1921; M; S; Dau
182;  179;  Brady, Roy; M; 1-1925; M; S; Son
183;        Brady; Pearl; F; 7-14-1928; M; S; Dau
184;  346;  Flying, Pauline; F; 6-1916; M; S; S-Dau [Male, Paul in 1920 #150 under Brady.]

185;  180;  Braidedlocks, William; M; 10-1851; F; M; Head
186;  181;  Braidedlocks, Gertie; F; 5-1852; F; M; Wife

187;  182;  Brownbird, Joseph; M; 9-1865; F; M; Head
188;  183;  Brownbird, Anna; F; 10-1865; F; M; Wife

189;  184;  Buffalohorn, John; M; 4-1862[sic]; F; M; Head [1904-25 birth year 1869.]
190;  185;  Buffalohorn, Lena; F; 5-1870; F; M; Wife [Birth year 1848[sic], 1920-22.]

191;  186;  Buffalohump, Samuel; M; 7-1845; F; M; Head
192;  187;  Buffalohump, Nora; F; 8-1848; F; M; Wife

193;  188;  Burns, George; M; 3-1895; M; M; Head

194;  189;  Burns, Robert J.; M; 9-1897; M; M; Head
195;  190;  Burns, Phyllis Roberta; F; 3-1926; M; S; Dau

196;  191;  Burns, Gertrude; F; 7-1846; F; Wd; Head

197;  192;  Burns, Julia; F; 2-1872; M; Wd; Head
198;  193;  Burns, James C. Jr.; M; 7-1908; M; S; Son
199;  194;  Burns, Margaret; F; 9-1911; M; S; Dau
200;  195;  Burns, Anna Grace; F; 8-1913; M; S; Dau

201;  196;  Burns, Lizzie; F; 1-1873; M; M; Head
202;  197;  Burns, Josephine; F; 7-1918; M; S; A-Dau 1/4 (Small) [Had a Kitty Small in 1925. Adopt-dau., in 1925-26.]

203;  198;  Callsfirst, Andrew; M; 6-1888; F; M; Head
204;  199;  Callsfirst, Jennie; F; 7-1872; M; M; Wife

205;  201;  Chasingbear, Flora; F; 3-1882; F; Wd; Head
206;  202;  Chasingbear, Laura; F; 5-1916; F; S; Dau

123

Census of the __Northern Cheyenne__ tribe of the __Tongue River Agency__ jurisdiction as of __June 30, 1929__ taken by __C.B. Lohmiller__, Superintendent.

**Key:** Present Number; Last Number; Indian Name; English Name; Sex; Month, Year, of Birth; Degree of Blood "F-Fullblood, M-Mixed Blood"; Marital Status; Relationship;

207; 203; Chasingbear, Robert; M; 7-1924; F; S; Son

208; 204; Chasingbear, Willis; M; 3-1895; F; M; Head
209; 205; Chasingbear, Madge; F; 4-1898[sic]; F; M; Wife [Powderface]

210; 206; Chubby, John; M; 11-1875; F; M; Head
211; 207; Chubby, Anne; F; 12-1885; F; M; Wife
212; 208; Chubby, Rhoda; F; 1-1920; F; S; Dau
213; 370; Hairlessbear, Hilda; F; 3-1912[?]; F; S; S-Dau [States in 1913 census, Born 3/8/1913.]

214; 209; Clubfoot, Floyd; M; 3-1888; F; M; Head [In 1904, 15 yrs., old.]
215; 210; Clubfoot, Stella; F; 4-1896[?]; F; M; Wife [Weaselbear] [#210, No record 1904-07; 1908 birth 1890; 1909-23 birth 1893.]
216; 211; Clubfoot, Norman; M; 11-1916; F; S; Son [1917 shows Norman died in 1916. In 1918-23 Census as born 1916 and alive?]
212; Clubfoot, Verle; M; 3-1923; F; S; Son Died 10-27-28
217; 213; Clubfoot, Flossie; F; 12-1925; F; S; Dau

218; 214; Clubfoot, Frank; M; 3-1891; F; M; Head [1904-23 birth year 1891. 1926-birth year 1899.]
219; 215; Clubfoot, Lucy Alice; F; 2-1893[?]; F; M; Wife
[#215, 1915-18 birth year is 1898; 1920 its 1896; 1923 its 1886; 1924-29 its 1893.]
220; 216; Clubfoot, James; M; 10-1922; F; S; Son

221; 217; Clubfoot, John; M; 12-1860[?]; F; M; Head [1904-13 shows birth year 1863. 1814-26 birth year 1854. 1927-29 birth year 1860.]
222; 218; Clubfoot, Minnie; F; 7-1870; f; M; Wife
223; 219; Clubfoot, Willis; M; 3-1891; F; S; Son
224; 220; Clubfoot, Joseph; M; 7-1900; F; S; Son

225; 221; Colhoff, Emma; F; 9-1894; M; M; Head
226; 222; Colhoff, Maxine; F; 5-1916; M; S; Dau
227; 223; Colhoff, Edward; M; 5-1918; M; S; Son
228; 224; Colhoff, Annie Gladys; F; 3[?]-1921; M; S; Dau [Birth month Apr., year 1922 in 1927.]
229; 225; Colhoff, Wm. Rowland; M; 4-1924; M; S; Son 3/4
230; 226; Colhoff, George; M; 1-1927; M; S; Son

231; 227; Cooley, Julia; F; 11-1891; M; M; Head
232; 228; Cooley, Violet; F; 3-1914; M; S; Dau
233; 229; Cooley, Junior; M; 5-1916; M; S; Son
234; 230; Cooley, Francis; M; 10-1922; M; S; Son
235; 231; Cooley, Vera; F; 1-1925; M; S; Dau

Census of the __Northern Cheyenne__ tribe of the __Tongue River Agency__
jurisdiction as of __June 30, 1929__ taken by __C.B. Lohmiller__, Superintendent.

**Key:** Present Number; Last Number; Indian Name; English Name; Sex; Month, Year, of Birth; Degree of Blood "F-Fullblood, M-Mixed Blood"; Marital Status; Relationship;

236; 232;    Crawling, Charles; M; 8-1884; F; Wd; Head
237; 233;    Crawling, Martha; F; 1-1917; F; S; Dau

238; 234;    Crazymule, John[sic]; M; 3-1870; F; M; Head [#234; In 1919 name Joseph, previous #220, birth year 1881. Mixed with another family not in 1920 census.] [Between 1920-22 Census takers mixed up #218 John and #220 Joseph's names and wifes and names.]
239; 235;    Crazymule, Jennie; wife; 2-1857; F; M; Wife [Issues]
240; 236;    Crazymule, James Paul; M; 11-1910; F; S; Son [James, Charles, Xavier, Children of Lizzie Yellownose and Joseph Crazymule.]
241; 237;    Crazymule, Charles; M; 11-1919; F; S; Son [Raymond in 1926.]
242; 238;    Crazymule, Xavier; M; 11-1921; F; S; Son

243; 239;    Crazymule, Joseph; M; 3-1881; F; M; Head
244; 240;    Crazymule, Sarah; F; 7-1873; F; M; Wife
245; 241;    Crazymule, Eva; F; 5-1909; F; S; Dau [Wyoming in 1926.]

246; 242;    Crook, George; M; 1-1864[?]; F; M; Head [1904-25 Birth year 1871.]
247; 243;    Crook, Theresa; F; 11-1866; F; M; Wife
248; 244;    Crook, Alice; F; 1-1908; F; S; Dau

249; 245;    Crook, Rosa; F; 8-1965[sic]; F; Wd; Head
250; 246;    Crook, Albert; M; 4-1901; F; S; Son

251; 247;    Crookednose, Nicholas; M; 6-1867; F; M; Head
252; 248;    Crookednose, Susie; F; 9-1872; F; M; Wife

253; 249;    Curley, Hattie; F; 8-1856; F; Wd; Head

254; 250;    Curley, Thomas; M; 11-1889; F; M; Head
255; 251;    Curley, Esther; F; 12-1895; F; M; Wife
256; 252;    Curley, Ella; F; 4-1925; F; S; Dau
257; 253;    Curley, Logan; M; 2-1927; F; S; Son

258; 254;    Deafy, David; M; 5-1898; F; M; Head [Americanhorse]
259; 255;    Deafy, Anna; F; 12-1895[?]; F; M; Wife [Horseroads; 1904-25 Birth year 1897.]
260; 256;    Deafy, Willis; M; 11-1917; F; S; Son
261; 257;    Deafy, Elsie; F; 7-1925; F; S; Dau

262; 258;    Deafy, James; M; 8-1870[?]; F; Wd[sic] Head [1904-25 Birth year 1873.]
      259;    Deafy, Mary; F; 5-1874; F; M; Wife Died 12-30-28 [1904-11 birth year 1874. 1912-26 birth year 1880. Name Walkingwoman 1904-06. 1907 no first name. 1908-Walkingwoman-Maria. 1908-10 name Maria. 1911-28 name Mary.]

Census of the **Northern Cheyenne** tribe of the **Tongue River Agency** jurisdiction as of **June 30, 1929** taken by **C.B. Lohmiller**, Superintendent.

**Key:** Present Number; Last Number; Indian Name; English Name; Sex; Month, Year, of Birth; Degree of Blood "F-Fullblood, M-Mixed Blood"; Marital Status; Relationship;

263; 260; Deafy, Carrie; F; 6-1910; F; S; Dau [Jessie in 1926.]

264; 261; Divesbackward, John; M.; 1-1870; F; Wd[sic]; Head [Depending the on census taker they spell Divesbackwards at the end with or without an "s".]

265; 262; Divesbackward, Rufus; M; 2-1890; F; M; Head
266; 263; Divesbackward, Nancy; F; 3-1882; F; M; Wife
267; 264; Divesbackward, Sam; M; 4-1918; F; S; Son [1926 name Irving.]
268; 265; Divesbackward, Strane; M; 5-1920; F; S; Son
269; 266; Divesbackward, Grace; F; 2-1925; F; S; Dau

270; 268; Dog, Louis; M; 5-1855; F; M; Head
271; 269; Dog, Maude; F; 3-1866; F; M; Wife

272; 270; Dullknife, Bessie; F; 3-1870; F; Wd; Head

273; 271; Duster, Albert; M; 4-1889; F; M; Head
274; 272; Duster, Vinnie; F; 9-1896; F; M; Wife
275; 273; Duster, Mabel; F 7-1913; F; S; Dau [Amelia Limpy, mother, 1926 name May Limpy Prev. #516.]
276; 274; Duster, Annie; F; 12-1920; F; S; Dau
277; 275; Duster, Bessie; F; 7-1924; F; S; Dau

278; 276; Eaglefeathers, Oliver; M; 9-1895; F; M; Head
279; 277; Eaglefeathers, Julia; F; 6-1895; M; M; Wife

280; 278; Eaglefeathers, Simon; M; 3-1922; M; S; Son
281; 279; Eaglefeathers, Rosie; F; 7-1925; M; S; Dau
282; Eaglefeathers, Milton; M; 1-12-1929; M; S; Son
283; 581; Littlehead, Rena; F; 11-1919; M; S; S-Dau [Mildred in 1926.]

284; 280; Eaglefeathers, Jacob; M; 9-1874; F; Wd; Head
285; 281; Eaglefeathers, Mildred; F; 5-1920[sic]; F; S; Dau [1917 shows birth year as 1916. 1918-26 as 1915.]

286; 282; Eastman, Mary G.; F; 12-1876; M; M; Head
287; 283; Eastman, Margaret; F; 5-1903; M; S; Dau
288; 284; Eastman, Robert; M; 3-1911; M; S; Son
289; 285; Eastman, Rose; F; 9-1915; M; S; Dau
290; 286; Eastman, Louisa; F; 3-1918; M; S; Dau
291; 287; Eastman, Myrtle; F; 8-1913; M; S; G-Dau [Julia 1926. Lucy Beartusk, mother.]

292; 288; Eastman, Charles; M; 2-1901; M; Wd[sic]; Head

Census of the **Northern Cheyenne** tribe of the **Tongue River Agency** jurisdiction as of **June 30, 1929** taken by **C.B. Lohmiller**, Superintendent.

**Key:** Present Number; Last Number; Indian Name; English Name; Sex; Month, Year, of Birth; Degree of Blood "F-Fullblood, M-Mixed Blood"; Marital Status; Relationship;

293; 289;    Eastman, Perry; M; 11 1895; M; M; Head
294; 290;    Eastman, Mary; F; 2-1893; F; M; Wife

295; 291;    Elkshoulder, Henry; M; 7-1894[sic]; F; M; Head [1904-26 birth year 1884.]
296; 292;    Elkshoulder, Bessie; F; 8-1893; F; M Wife
297; 293;    Elkshoulder, Curtis; M; 2-1908; F; S; Son
298; 294;    Elkshoulder, Lucy; F; 3-1917; F; S; Dau
299; 295;    Elkshoulder, Sylvia; F; 7-1922; F; S; Dau
300; 296;    Elkshoulder, George; M; 12-1925; F; S; Son [Adolph in 1926.]
301;    Elkshoulder, Calvin; M; 8-5-1928; F; S; Son

302; 297;    Elliot, Elizabeth H.; F; 4-1906; M; M; Head
303; 398;[sic] Elliot, Edwin Francis; M; 1-8-1928; M; S; Son
304;    Elliot, Loretta May; F; 4-13-1929; M; S; Dau

305; 299;    Eyesyellow, Wilbur; M; 7-1868; F; M; Head
306; 300;    Eyesyellow, Daisy; F; 9-1856; F; M; Wife

307; 301;    Farr, Jessie; F; 1-1899[sic]; M; Wd; Head[1908-26 birth year 1890.]
308; 303;    Farr, Evelyn; F; 12-1914; M; S; Dau
309; 302;    Farr, Frank; M; 7-1917; M; S; Son

310; 305;    Fightingbear, Edgar; M; 10-1874; F; M; Head
311; 306;    Fightingbear, Alice; F; 6-1893; F; M; Wife
312; 307;    Fightingbear, Julia; F; 7-1911; F; S; Dau
313; 308;    Fightingbear, Dora; F; 3-1915; F; S; Dau [1926 name Fannie.]
314; 309;    Fightingbear, Elmer; M; 4-1921; F; S; Son
315; 310;    Fightingbear, Herbert; M; 9-1923, F; S; Son
316; 311;    Fightingbear, Emma; F; 5-1926; F; S; Dau
   Fightingbear, Baby; M; 6-11-1929; F; S; Son Died 6-15-1929

317; 312;    Fightingbear, Willis; M; 6-1899; F; S; Head

318; 313;    Fingers, Otis; M; 10-1868[?]; F; Wd[sic]; Head [1904-25 Birth year 1867.]
319; 314;    Fingers, Joseph; M; 8-1914; F; S; Son [1917 Census Daughter, Josie 1915-20.]

320; 315;    Firecrow, Peter; M; 4-1887; F; Wd[sic]; Head
321; 316;    Firecrow, Joseph; M; 10-1923; F; S; Son [Josephine; dau; F., in 1926]

322; 317;    Firewolf, John; M; 4-1877; F; M; Head
323; 318;    Firewolf, Josephine; F; 1-1875; F; M; Wife

Census of the __Northern Cheyenne__ tribe of the __Tongue River Agency__ jurisdiction as of __June 30, 1929__ taken by __C.B. Lohmiller__, Superintendent.

**Key:** Present Number; Last Number; Indian Name; English Name; Sex; Month, Year, of Birth; Degree of Blood "F-Fullblood, M-Mixed Blood"; Marital Status; Relationship;

324; 319; Fisher, Eugene; M; 7-1878; M; M; Head
325; 320; Fisher, Kitty; F; 4-1890; M; M; Wife
326; 321; Fisher, Eugene, Jr.; M; 12-1912; M; S; Son
327; 322; Fisher, Langburn; M; 7-1915; M; S; Son
328; 323; Fisher, J. Allen; M; 3-1917; M; S; Son [1917 Census name Ira.]
329; 324; Fisher, Alliwitchie; F; 5-1919; M; S; Dau [1919 Census name Pearl.]
330; 325; Fisher, Calleaus; M; 5-1919; M; S; Son [1919 Census name Earl.]
331; 326; Fisher, Russell; M; 11-1921; M; S; Son
332; 327; Fisher, Phyllis Helen; F; 3-1924; M; S; Dau
333; 328; Fisher; Bernidine; M; 12-1926; M; S; Son

334; 331; Fisher, John; M; 7-1901; F; M; Head
335; 794; Fisher, Mary P.; F; 2-1911; F; M; Wife [Playingbear]

336; 336; Fliesabout, William; M; 2-1879; F; M; Head
337; 337; Fliesabout, Minnie; F; 12-1882; F; M; Wife
338; 338; Fliesabout, June; F; 6-1923; F; S; Dau [Martin; son; F[sic], in 1926.]

339; 339; Flying, Debs; M; 2-1886; F; Wd[sic]; Head
340; 340; Flying, Frank; M; 10-1915; F; S; Son
341; 341; Flying, Parker; M; 4-1918; F; S; Son

342; 342; Flying, Myra; F; 6-1867; F; Wd; Head
343; 343; Flying, Ruth; F; 12-1916; F; S; Dau

344; 344; Flying, Thomas; M; 3-1869; F; Wd; Head
345; Flying, Margaret; F; 3-1866; F; M; Wife [Highbear] Died 9-21-1928

345; 1016; Fontenelle, Frances; F; 12-1908; M; M; Head [Sherman]

346; 351; Foot, Ruth Yellownose; F; 9-1898; F; M; Head
347; 347; Foot, Thelma; F; 6-1913; M; S; S-Dau [1917 Census name Daisy.]
348; 348; Foot, Bertha; F; 12-1919; M; S; S-Dau
349; 349; Foot, Edward; M; 4-1918; M; S; S-Son
350; 350; Foot, Eva; F; 5-1923; M; S; S-Dau
351; Foot, Sylvia; F; 11-19-1928; M; S; Dau

352; 354; Ghostbull, Arthur; M; 2-1870[sic]; F; M; Head [1904-26 birth year 1874.]
353; 355; Ghostbull, Sarah; F; 9-1867[?]; F; M; Wife 1905-08 birth year 1868, 1909-11 birth year 1861, 1912-13 birth year 1866, 1914 birth year 1851, 1915-26 birth year 1861.]
354; 356; Ghostbull, Eva Mary; F; 3-1908; F; S; Dau

355; 357; Gillispie, May Parker; F; 5-1888; M; M; Head

Census of the __Northern Cheyenne__ tribe of the __Tongue River Agency__ jurisdiction as of __June 30, 1929__ taken by __C.B. Lohmiller__, Superintendent.

**Key:** Present Number; Last Number; Indian Name; English Name; Sex; Month, Year, of Birth; Degree of Blood "F-Fullblood, M-Mixed Blood"; Marital Status; Relationship;

356; 358; Grasshopper, Isaac; M; 6-1850; F; Wd[sic]; Head

357; 359; Grasshopper, Frank; M; 9-1906; F; S; Head [Son of Mrs. Stanley Lamewoman.] [Arthur in 1926.]

358; 362; Gray, Edward; M; 4-1873; F; M; Head
359; 363; Gray, Nellie; F; 9-1874; F; M; Wife
360; 364; Gray, Teddy; M; 8-1915; F; S; Son

361; 365; Gray, John; M; 8-1902[?]; F; M; Head [1904 shows up as 1 yr. old.]
362; 366; Gray, Kate Wolfname; F; 3-1900; F; M; Wife [Ida in 1926.]

363; 367; Gray, Bessie; F; 7-1904; F; Div; Head [1920 #917, name Sandcrane.]
364; 368; Gray, Rose Marie; F; 11-1923; F; S; Dau
365; Gray, Peter; M; 11-29-1928; F; S; Son

366; 369; Greasydog, Fannie; F; 6-1897; F; S; Head

367; 371; Hairyhand, Henry; M; 10-1855; F; Wd[sic]; Head

368; 372; Hankeringwolf, Peter; M; 9-1834; F; Wd[sic]; Head

369; 373; Hardground, Ernest; M; 7-1896; F; M; Head
370; 374; Hardground, Mary; F; 8-1895[?]; F; M; Wife
371; 375; Hardground, Ethel; F; 2-1921; F; S; Dau
372; 376; Hardground, Katie; F; 9-1923; F; S; Dau

373; 378; Hardground, Robert; M; 11-1876; F; M; Head
374; 107; Biglefthand, Patty; F; 12-1875; F; M; Wife [1904-16 Birth year 1875; 1917-26 birth year 1885.]
375; 379; Hardground, Roland; M; 7-1909; F; S; Son [Rowland in 1926.]
376; 380; Hardground, Lucy; F; 9-1911; F; S; Dau [Rena in 1926.]
377; 381; Hardground, Lyla; F; 2-1914; F; S; Dau
378; 108; Biglefthand, Raphael; M; 9-1912; F; S; S-Son [1915-#72 was Daisy, female.]

379; 382; Hardground, Albert; M; 6-1899; F; M; Head
383; Hardground, Ruth; F; 5-1908; F; M; Wife [Standingelk] Died 6-12-1929
380; Hardground, Mary; F; 3-12-1929; F; S; Dau

381; 384; Hardground, George; M; 4-1901[sic]; f; S; Head
[George's birth year, Censuses 1904-08 is 1898. 1909-13 is 1897. 1914-18 is 1895.]

385; Hardground, Thomas; M; 8-1903; F; S; Head Died 12-3-1928

Census of the __Northern Cheyenne__ tribe of the __Tongue River Agency__
jurisdiction as of __June 30, 1929__ taken by __C.B. Lohmiller__, Superintendent.

**Key:** Present Number; Last Number; Indian Name; English Name; Sex; Month, Year, of Birth; Degree of Blood "F-Fullblood, M-Mixed Blood"; Marital Status; Relationship;

382; 386; Hardrobe, Colonel; M; 2-1856[sic]; F; Wd[sic]; Head
383; 388; Hardrobe, Fannie; F; 10-1880; F; S; Dau
384; 387; Hardrobe, Albert; M; 7-1896; F; S; Son
385; 390; Hardrobe, Margaret; F; 4-1918; F; S; G-Dau [name Lucy and birth year 1911 in 1926. s-dau Willis Medicinebull. dau. Ruth Yellownose Foot.]
386; 389; Hardrobe, Mollie; F; 10-1919; F; S; G-Dau. [Mrs. Louis Magpie]

387; 391; Harris, Bryan; M; 4-1898; M; M; Head
388; 1088; Spottedhawk, Ruth; F; 12-1907; F; M; Wife [Spottedhawk, Medicinebird]
389; 392; Harris, Carl; M; 10-1921; M; S; Son

390; 393; Harris, Edward; M; 1-1887; M; M; Head
391; 394; Harris, Bessie; F; 5-1889; F; M; Wife
392; 395; Harris, May; F; 5-1911; M; S; Dau
393; 396; Harris, Nellie; F; 5-1914; M; S; Dau
394; 397; Harris, Dorothy; F; 5-1919; M; S; Dau
395; 398; Harris, Hubert; M; 1-1922; M; S; Son [Lawrence Edw. In 1926.]
396; 399; Harris, Inez Romona; F; 12-9-1927; M; S; Dau

397; 400; Harris, Sallie; F; 9-1850; M; Wd; Head [Allie in 1928]

398; 401; Harris, William; M; 1-1877; M; M; Head
399; 402; Harris, Margaret; F; 5-1884; M; M; Wife
400; 403; Harris, George; M; 9-1907; M. S; Son
401; 404; Harris, Lucy; F; 1-1908; M; S; Dau
402; 405; Harris, Julia; F; 12-1910; M; S; Dau
403; 406; Harris, Agnes; F; 9-1912[?]; M; S; Dau [Shows up in 1914 census as being born in 1913. 1914-16 birth year as 1913, 1917-26 birth year as 1915.]
404; 407; Harris, Raymond; M; 4-1915; M; S; Son
405; 408; Harris, Mary; F; 4-1919; M; S; Dau [1920 name Leota.]
406; 409; Harris, Florence; F; 9-1923; M; S; Dau [1925 son Joseph, M.]

407; 410; Hart, Charles; M; 5-1880; F; M; Head
408; 411; Hart, Louisa; F; 9-1885; M; M; Wife
409; 412; Hart, Mattie Lizzie; F; 7-1911; M; S; Dau [Censuses 1912-18 name is Katie.]
410; 413; Hart, Eva; F; 12-1913[sic]; M; S; Dau [Census 1916-20 birth year 1915.]
411; 414; Hart, Jessie Diana; F; 4-1917; M; S; Dau

412; 415; Hart, Frank; M; 7-1898; M; M; Head
413; 416; Hart, Alice; F; 5-1907; F; M; Wife [Hairlessbear]
414; Hart, Edna; F; 11-16-1927; M; S; Dau

Census of the __Northern Cheyenne__ tribe of the __Tongue River Agency__ jurisdiction as of __June 30, 1929__ taken by __C.B. Lohmiller__, Superintendent.

**Key:** Present Number; Last Number; Indian Name; English Name; Sex; Month, Year, of Birth; Degree of Blood "F-Fullblood, M-Mixed Blood"; Marital Status; Relationship;

415; 417;     Headswift, Charles; M; 3-1867; F; Wd[sic]; Head
416; 418;     Headswift, Frank; M; 6-1911; F; S; Son

417; 419;     Highbear, William; M; 3-1888[?]; F; M; Head
418; 420;     Highbear, Minnie; F; 5-1897[?]; F; M; Wife [Most censuses show birth year 1896.]

419; 421;     Highwalking, Nellie; F; 4-1859[sic]; F; Wd; Head [Born 1850 from 1904-16.]

420; 422;     Highwalking, Floyd; M; 4-1888; F; M; Head
421; 423;     Highwalking, Belle; F; 6-1893; F; M; Wife
422; 424;     Highwalking, Max; M; 1-1917; F; S; Son
423; 425;     Highwalking, George; M; 3-1913; F; S; Son [David in 1926.]

424; 426;     Hisbadhorse, Rhoda; F; 6-1856[sic]; F; Wd; Head [1904-26 birth year 1840.]

425; 427;     Hisbadhorses, Willis; M; 8-1898; F; M; Head
426; 428;     Hisbadhorses, Ernest; M; 5-1917; F; S; Son [1924 s-son. Eugene in 1926.]
427; 429;     Hisbadhorses, Medaris; M; 8-1921; F; S; Son [Bird; son; 1917; in 1926.]
428; 430;     Hisbadhorses, Fannie; M[sic]; 10-1922; F; S; Son[sic] [Josephine in 1926.]

429; 431;     Hollowbreast, Hubert; M; 5-1875; F; M; Head
430; 432;     Hollowbreast, Mary; F; 4-1896; F; M; Wife [Previous censuses name Hattie Hisbadhorses. 1926 Hisbadhorses, wdw. #426.]
431; 433;     Hollowbreast, Donald; M; 5-1917; F; S; Son [James in 1926.]
432;     Hollowbreast, Edward; M; 4-7-1929; F; S; Son

433; 434;     Hollowbreast, William; M; 3-1900[?]; F; M; Head [1925 birth year 1893. Birth year 1866 in 1926. Birth year 1900 in 1920. 1904-15 there is a Willie Hollowbreast that has a birth year of 1900. Father same as William in 1920.]
434; 643;     Hollowbreast, Mary; F; 11-1903; F; M; Wife [Littlewolf]

435; [435;]     Hollowwood, Richard; M; 7-1856[sic]; F; M; Head [1904-26 birth year 1866.]
436;     Hollowwood, Minnie; wife; 8-1856; F; M; Wife Died 5-14-1929

436; 437;     Horn, Annie Wolfname; F; 5-1900; F; M; Head [Name Alice 1904-20.]
437; 438;     Horn, Rose; F; 6-1921; F; S; Dau
438; 439;     Horn, Wilena; F; 3-1923; F; S; Dau

Census of the __Northern Cheyenne__ tribe of the __Tongue River Agency__ jurisdiction as of __June 30, 1929__ taken by __C.B. Lohmiller__, Superintendent.

**Key:** Present Number; Last Number; Indian Name; English Name; Sex; Month, Year, of Birth; Degree of Blood "F-Fullblood, M-Mixed Blood"; Marital Status; Relationship;

439; 440;     Horn, Margaret; F; 7-1926; F; S; Dau
440; 441;     Horn, Celia; F; 5-7-1928; F; S; Dau

441; 442;     Horseroads, Thomas; M; 9-1878; F; M; Head
442; 443;     Horseroads, Lucy; F; 8-1887; F; M; Wife
443; 444;     Horseroads, Ida; F; 1-1924; F; S; Dau
444; 445;     Horseroads, Cora; F; 11-1926; F; S; Dau

445; 446;     Howlingantelope, Albert; M; 4-1874; F; M; Head
446; 447;     Howlingantelope, Eva; F; 5-1880; F; M; Wife
447; 304;     Fasthorse, Clara; F; 5-1913; F; S; G-Dau

448; 448;     Huff, Pearl; F; 6-1907; M; M; Head [Eastman]
449; 449;     Huff, Elsie Margaret; F; 12-23-1927; M; S; Dau

450; 450;     Ironhand, William; M; 11-1882; F; M; Head
451; 451;     Ironhand, Sally; F; 7-1884; F; M; Wife
452; 452;     Ironhand, Henry; M; 6-1910; F; S; Son
453; 453;     Ironhand, Willis; M; 1-1915; F; S; Son
454; 454;     Ironhand, Jane; F; 2-1927; F; S; Dau

455; 455;     Ironshirt, Jennie; F; 7-1858; F; Wd; Head

        456;     Ironshirt, Fred; M; 7-1831; F; M; Head Died 3-18-1929
456; 457;     Ironshirt, Nora; F; 8-1850; F; Wd; Wife

475; 458;     Ironshirt, Robert; M; 7-1902; F; Wd[sic]; Head

458; 459;     Irontooth, Susan; F; --1834; F; Wd; Head

459; 460;     Issues, John; M; -- 1863; F; M; Head
460; 461;     Issues, Clara; F; 3-1870; F; M; Wife [Blackmedicine; 1904-17, Birth year 1868; she becomes Issues 1915, 1918-25 birth year changed to 1863, 1926 to 1878. 1927 to 1870.]

461; 462;     Issues, Francis; M; 3-1897; F; M; Head
462; 548;     Issues, Mamie Limpy; F; 12-1907; M; M; Wife
463; 463;     Issues, Ira; M; 2-1920[?]; F; S; Son [1919 name Ira, 1920-23, George.]
464; 464;     Issues, Irene; F; 5-1921; F; S; Dau

465; 465;     Killsback, James; M; 7-1863; F; M; Head [Census #461, name Joseph Killsacross in 1926.]
466; 466;     Killsback, Amelia; F; 12-1878; F; M; Wife

467; 467;     Killsnight, Charles; M; 6-1890; F; M; Head

Census of the **Northern Cheyenne** tribe of the **Tongue River Agency**
jurisdiction as of **June 30, 1929** taken by **C.B. Lohmiller**, Superintendent.

**Key:** Present Number; Last Number; Indian Name; English Name; Sex; Month, Year, of Birth; Degree of
Blood "F-Fullblood, M-Mixed Blood"; Marital Status; Relationship;

| | | |
|---|---|---|
| 468; | 468; | Killsnight, Rosa; F; 2-1899[?]; F; M; Wife [Birth year 1903 in 1926.] |
| 469; | 469; | Killsnight, Anna; F; 3-1911; F; S; Dau [Florence in 1926.] |
| | 470; | Killsnight, Robert; M; 1-1913; F; S; Son Died 1-12-1929 |
| 470; | 471; | Killsnight, Rosa; F; 4-1915; F; S; Dau |
| 471; | 472; | Killsnight, Susan; F; 5-1917; F; S; Dau |
| 472; | 473; | Killsnight, Hubert; M; 2-1919; F; S; Son [Brighton in 1926.] |
| 473; | 474; | Killsnight, Bessie; F; 2-1920; F; S; Dau [Margaret in 1926. Birth year 1923.] |
| 474; | 475; | Killsnight, Margaret; F; 2-1924; F; S; Dau |
| 475; | 476; | Killsnight, Dorothy; F; 2-1927; F; S; Dau |
| 476; | | Killsnight, Jennie; F; 3-12-1929; F; S; Dau |
| | | |
| 477; | 478; | Killsnight, William Jr.; M; 10-1904; F; S; Head |
| 478; | 477; | Killsnight, Carrie; F; 5-1911; F; S; Sis |
| | | |
| 479; | 479; | Killsnight, Hugh; M; 8-1866; F; M; Head |
| 480; | 480; | Killsnight, Clara; F; 9-1872; F; M; Wife |
| | | |
| 481; | 482; | Killsnight, William Sr.; M; 4-1856; F; M; Head |
| 482; | 483; | Killsnight, Cora; F; 6-1860; F; M; Wife |
| 483; | 481; | Killsnight, Cole; M; 2-1905; F; S; Son [Birth year 1903 in 1928.] |
| | | |
| 484; | 484; | Killsnight, Martin; M; 1-1907; F; M; Head |
| | 485; | Killsnight, Alice Farr; F; 2-1910; M; M; Wife [Jessie in 1920. Died 6-6-1928] |
| 485; | | Killsnight, Kitty Belle; F; 11-9-1928; M; S; Dau |
| | | |
| 486; | 486; | Killsnight, Willis; M; 3-1895; F; M; Head [Rutherford in 1926.] |
| 487; | 487; | Killsnight, Carrie; F; 5-1890; F; M; Wife [Whitemoon] |
| 488; | 488; | Killsnight, Flossie; F; 2-1923; F; S; Dau [Sage in 1926.] |
| 489; | 489; | Killsnight, James; M; 4-1926; F; S; Son |
| 490; | 490; | Killsnight, Ralph; M; 4-7-1928; F; S; Son |
| | | |
| 491; | 491; | Killsnightwoman, ---; F; 4-1858; F; Wd; Head |
| | | |
| 492; | 492; | Killsontop, John; M; 8-1906; F; M; Head |
| 493; | 493; | Killsontop, Mary; F; 2-1909; F; M; Wife [Strangeowl] |
| 494; | 494; | Killsontop, June; F; 4-1927; F; S; Dau |
| 495; | | Killsontop, Levern; M; 1-1-1929; F; S; Son |
| | | |
| 496; | 495; | Killsontop, Mamie; F; 3-1897; F; Div; Head |
| 497; | 496; | Killsontop, Ida; F; 10-1924; F; S; Dau |
| | | |
| | 497; | Kingfisher, Herman; M; 4-1867; F; M; Head Died 12-2-1928 |
| 498; | 498; | Kingfisher, Carrie; F; 8-1876; F; Wd; Wife |

Census of the **Northern Cheyenne** tribe of the **Tongue River Agency** jurisdiction as of **June 30, 1929** taken by **C.B. Lohmiller**, Superintendent.

**Key:** Present Number; Last Number; Indian Name; English Name; Sex; Month, Year, of Birth; Degree of Blood "F-Fullblood, M-Mixed Blood"; Marital Status; Relationship;

| | | |
|---|---|---|
| 499; | 499; | Kingfisher, Willis; M; 9-1896; F; M; Head |
| 500; | 500; | Kingfisher, Minnie; F; 7-1896; F; M; Wife |
| 501; | 501; | Kingfisher, Isabelle; F; 9-1918; F; S; Dau |
| 502; | 502; | Kingfisher, Charles; M; 6-1921; F; S; Son |
| 503; | 503; | Kingfisher, Louise; F; 10-1922; F; S; Dau |
| 504; | 504; | Kingfisher, Ellen; F; 6-1926; F; S; Dau |
| 505; | 505; | Kingfisher, Angela; F; 5-23-1928; F; S; Dau |
| | | |
| 506; | 506; | Kinzel, Alice; F; 3-1893; M; M; Head |
| 507; | 507; | Kinzel, Emma Loua[sic]; F; 6-1917; M; S; Dau |
| 508; | 508; | Kinzel, Helen Louise; F; 3-1920; M; S; Dau |
| 509; | 509; | Kinzel, Cecelia Leah; F; 7-1924; M; S; Dau |
| 510; | 510; | Kinzel, Virgil Bruce; M; 10-9-1927; M; S; Son |
| | | |
| 511; | 511; | Knows-His-Gun, Frances; F; 10-1904; F; M; Head |
| 512; | 512; | Knows-His-Gun, Sylvester; M; 9-1926; F; S; Son |

513; 513; LaFever, Rena Eastman; F; 8-1896[?]; M; M; Head
514; 514; LaFever, Kenneth; M; 12-1925; M; S; Son [#501; Herman; son; birth year 1925 in 1926.]

515; 515; Lamebear, Benjamin; M; 7-1894; F; M; Head
516; 516; Lamebear, Clara; F; 5-1894; F; M; Wife
517; 517; Lamebear, Eva; F; 11-1910[sic]; F; S; Dau [Birth year 1916 first shows in 1917.]
518; 518; Lamebear, Cora; F; 4-1919; F; S; Dau
519; r19[sic]; Lamebear, Charles; M; 10-1921; F; S Son

520; 520; Lamewoman, Nellie; F; 7-1854; F; Wd; Head

521; 521; Lamewoman, Sam; M; 10-1912; F; M; Head [Sam Littlebear; 1928 Sam is a son.]
522; 958; Lamewoman, Alice R.; F; 7-1910; M; M; Wife [Rowland; 7/8 [Birth year 1912 in 1926.]

523; 523; Lamewoman, Stanley; M; 8-1889; F; M; Head
524; 524; Lamewoman, Augusta; F; 7-1885; F; M; Wife
525; 526; Lamewoman, Jessie; F; 6-1914; F; S; Dau
526; 525; Lamewoman, Virgil; M; 2-1822[sic]; F; S; Son
527; 361; Grasshopper, Mary; F; 8-1914; F; S; S-Dau.

528; 527; Lastbull, Fred; M; 1-1888; F; M; Head

529; 528; Lennon, Mary Burns; F; 6-1906; M; M; Head
530; 529; Lennon, Arthur George; M; 11-1926; M; S; Son

Census of the __Northern Cheyenne__ tribe of the __Tongue River Agency__ jurisdiction as of __June 30, 1929__ taken by __C.B. Lohmiller__, Superintendent.

**Key:** Present Number; Last Number; Indian Name; English Name; Sex; Month, Year, of Birth; Degree of Blood "F-Fullblood, M-Mixed Blood"; Marital Status; Relationship;

531; 530; Lightning, Frank; m; 8-1871; F; Wd[sic]; Head

532; 531; Limberhand, Richard; M; 8-1905; F; M; Head
533; 970; Limberhand, Jessie; F; 10-1905[sic]; F; M; Wife [Rockroads (Rhoda) all numbers past and present coincide, shows up in 1915, birth year 1913. 1926 last name Russell, wife, husband Frank, separated.]
534; Limberhand, Doris; F; 10-15-1928; F; S; Dau

535; 533; Limberhand, Nathan; M; 3-1876; F; M; Head
536; 534; Limberhand, Artie; F; 9-1883; F; M; Wife
537; 532; Limberhand, James; M; 10-1902[?]; F; S; Son
538; 535; Limberhand, Elmore; M; 1-1909; F; S; Son
539; 536; Limberhand, Bennie; M; 1-1912[?]; F; S; Son
540; 537; Limberhand, Jennie; F; 11-1915; F; S; Dau
541; 538; Limberhand, Doris; F; 5-1922; F; S; Dau

542; 539; Limpy, Benjamin; M; 10-1892; F; M; Head
543; 540; Limpy, Hattie[sic]; F; 6-1894; F; M; Wife
[#540; Hallie Killsacross #271, 1914 census. 1915-16 Hallie Limpy.]
544; 541; Limpy, Anna; F; 1-1915; F; S; Dau [Son, Jack 1916-19; Jean in 1926.]
545; 542; Limpy, Rosa; F; 8-1919; F; S; Dau [#530 Elnora; birth year1921 in 1926.]
546; 543; Limpy, Jessie; F; 11-1922; F; S; Dau

547; 544; Limpy, Charles; M; 10-1857; F; M; Head
548; 545; Limpy, Nellie; F; 7-1854; F; M; Wife

549; 546; Limpy, Fred; M; 4-1884; M; M; Head
550; 547; Limpy, Amelia; F; 5-1885; F; M; Wife [Womanleggins]
551; 549; Limpy, Frank; M; 5-1911; M; S; Son
552; 550; Limpy, Mary; F; 5-1913; M; S; Dau [#506, Limpy, Mary; D.; 6 Mo; in 1909. #538 May Limpy birth year 1913 in 1926.]
553; 551; Limpy, Henry; M; 8-1919; M; S; Son Lives with g-f N. Limberhand. [1920 Census Fred Jr.]
554; 552; Limpy, Cora; F; 11-1925; M; S; Dau
555; Limpy, Benjamin; M; 6-10-1929; M; S; Son

556; 553; Littlebear, Paul; M; 7-1887; F; M; Head
557; 554; Littlebear, Rosa; F; 8-1887; F; M; Wife
558; 555; Littlebear, May; F; May 1908; F; S; Dau [Anne in 1926.]
559; 556; Littlebear, Flossie; F; 4-1912; F; S; Dau [Mary in 1926.]
560; 557; Littlebear, Clara; F; 4-1916; F; S; Dau
561; 558; Littlebear, Two-Birds; M; 12-1923; F; S; Son
562; 559; Littlebear, Lucille; F; 7-1926; F; S; Dau
563; Littlebear, Carol; F; 12-2-1928; F; S; G-Dau Dau. of 658

Census of the __Northern Cheyenne__ tribe of the __Tongue River Agency__ jurisdiction as of __June 30, 1929__ taken by __C.B. Lohmiller__, Superintendent.

**Key:** Present Number; Last Number; Indian Name; English Name; Sex; Month, Year, of Birth; Degree of Blood "F-Fullblood, M-Mixed Blood"; Marital Status; Relationship;

564; 560; Littlebird, Peter; M; 5-1870; F; M; Head
565; 561; Littlebird, Jennie; F; 7-1892; F; M; Wife
566; 562; Littlebird, Joseph; M; 9-1912; F; S; Son
567; 563; Littlebird, Julia; F; 6-1922; F; S; Dau
568; 564; Littlebird, James Wm.; M; 6-1925; F; S; Son

569; 567; Littlechief; Victor; M; 1-1877; F; M; Head
570; 568; Littlechief; Louisa; F; 3-1875; F; M; Wife
571; 569; Littlechief; Lucille; F; 2-1911; F; S; Dau

572; 570; Littlecoyote, Henry; M; 9-1875; F; Wd[sic]; Head
573; 571; Littlecoyote, Daniel; M; 10-1910; F; S; Son

574; 572; Littleeagle, Charles; M; 5-1867; F; M; Head
575; 573; Littleeagle, Mary; F; 6-1878; F; M; Wife
576; 574; Littleeagle, Clara; F; 8-1905; F; S; Dau

577; 575; Littleeyes, Eva; F; 7-1893; F; S; Head [Lives with Zac Rowland]
Littleeyes, Baby; M; 1-19-1928; F; S; Son Died 10-19-1928

578; 576; Littlehawk, Dora; F; 1-1869; F; Wd; Head

579; 577; Littlehead, Charles; M; 6-1869; F; M; Head
580; 578; Littlehead, Nellie; F; 12-1882; F; M; Wife
581; 579; Littlehead, Frank; M; 11-1909; F; S; Son
582; 580; Littlehead, George; M; 5-1920; F; S; Son [1920 name John.]

583; 582; Littlehead, John; M; -- 1894; F; M; Head

584; 584; Littlemouth, Clara; F; 7-1859; F; Wd; Head

585; 585; Littlemouth, John; M; 10-1894[?]; F; M; Head [Keeps changing year of birth.]
586; 586; Littlemouth, Jennie; F; 9-1898; F; M; Wife
587; 587; Littlemouth, Evelyn; F; 5-1921; F; S; Dau
588; 588; Littlemouth, James; M; 6-1922; F; S; Son
589; 589; Littlemouth, Mary; F; 4-1924; F; S; Dau

590; 593; Littlesun, Frank; M; 10-1884; F; M; Head
591; 594; Littlesun, Anna; F; 6-1892; F; M; Wife
592; 595; Littlesun, Alfred; M; 12-1912; F; S; Son
Littlesun, Baby; M; 3-13-1929; F; S; Son Died 3-13-1929
Littlesun, Baby; M; 3-13-1929; F; S; Son Died 3-17-1929
593; 590; Littleoldman, Thomas; M; 12-1913; F; S; S-Son

Census of the __Northern Cheyenne__ tribe of the __Tongue River Agency__ jurisdiction as of __June 30, 1929__ taken by __C.B. Lohmiller__, Superintendent.

**Key:** Present Number; Last Number; Indian Name; English Name; Sex; Month, Year, of Birth; Degree of Blood "F-Fullblood, M-Mixed Blood"; Marital Status; Relationship;

594; 596;  Littlesun, Samuel; M; 7-1858; F; M; Head
595; 597;  Littlesun, Cora; F; 9-1864; F; M; Wife
596; 591;  Littlesun, Jack; M; 8-1920; F; S; G-Son
597; 592;  Littlesun, Horace; M; 9-1922; F; S; G-Son
[Children of Bessie Littlesun Wolfchum.]

598; 598;  Littlewhirlwind, George; M; 1-1901; F; M; Head
599; 599;  Littlewhirlwind, Martha; F; 10-1909; F; M; Wife [Fannie Walksalong in 1926.]
600;         Littlewhirlwind, Anna; F; 11-30-1928; F; S; Dau

601; 600;  Littlewhiteman, Aaron; M; 12-1862; M; M; Head
602; 601;  Littlewhiteman, Sadie; F; 4-1866; F; M; Wife
603; 602;  Littlewhiteman, Wesley; M; 8-1897; M; S; Son
604; 800;  Powderface, Julia; F; 8-1913; F; S; G-Dau [S-dau. Wilson Pine]

605; 603;  Littlewhiteman, Frank; M; 11-1901; M; M; Head
606; 604;  Littlewhiteman, Emma; F; 10-1900; F; M; Wife [#964 in 1919 shows as Lightning, Emma; g dt; 1901; F. Grandparents Shortsioux in census as birth year 1901 starting in 1912 or 11 years old.]
607; 605;  Littlewhiteman, Leon; M; 8-1920; M; S; Son [John in 1926.]
608; 606;  Littlewhiteman, Margaret; F; 7-1922; M; S; Dau

609; 607;  Littlewhiteman, David; M; 2-1869; M; M; Head
610; 608;  Littlewhiteman, Agnes; F; 7-1872; F; M; Wife
611; 609;  Littlewhiteman, Peter; M; 4-1906; M; S; Son

612; 610;  Littlewhiteman, James; M; 6-1895; M; M; Head
613; 611;  Littlewhiteman, Gusta; F; 9-1897; F. M; Wife [Littlesun]
614; 612;  Littlewhiteman, Kitty; F; 9-1923; M; S; Dau
615; 613;  Littlewhiteman, Charles; M; 9-1925; M; S; Son [In 1926 #600; as Charles (Albert); son; 1925; M.]

616; 614;  Littlewhiteman, Milton; M; 9-1884[?]; M; M; Head [Most previous cenuses 1886.]
617; 615;  Littlewhiteman, Rosa; F; 9-1882; F; M; Wife
618; 1421; Yellowhorse, Julia; F; 5-1913; F; S; S-Dau.

619; 616;  Littlewhiteman, Henry; M; 1-1891; M; M; Head
620; 617;  Littlewhiteman, Josie; F; 2-1897; F; M; wife [Weaselbear; Prev. Marriage Woodenlegs.]
621; 618;  Littlewhiteman, Edith; F; 12-1912[sic]; M; S; Dau [Birth 1915.]
622; 619;  Littlewhiteman, Rosa; F; 9-1915[sic]; M; S; Dau [Birth 1920.]
623; 620;  Littlewhiteman, Agnes; F; 10-1921; M; S; Dau
624; 621;  Littlewhiteman, Bessie; F; 5-1926; F; M; Dau

Census of the **Northern Cheyenne** tribe of the **Tongue River Agency** jurisdiction as of **June 30, 1929** taken by **C.B. Lohmiller**, Superintendent.

**Key:** Present Number; Last Number; Indian Name; English Name; Sex; Month, Year, of Birth; Degree of Blood "F-Fullblood, M-Mixed Blood"; Marital Status; Relationship;

625; 624; Littlewhiteman, Stanley; M; 7-1888; M; M; Head
626; 625; Littlewhiteman, Grace; F; -- 1894; F; M; Wife [1920- #1300, name Walkingbear.]
627; 626; Littlewhiteman, Milton; M; 12-1914; M; S; Son
628; 627; Littlewhiteman, Aaron; M; 12-1921; M; S; Son
629; 628; Littlewhiteman, Adrain; M; 12-1923; M; S; Son [Name Hillman; birth 1924 in 1926.]
630; 629; Littlewhiteman, Sadie; F; 1-1927; M; S; Dau
631; Littlewhiteman, Warren; M; 8-9-1928; M; S; Son

632; 630; Littlewolf, Frank; M; 2-1877; F; M; Head
633; 631; Littlewolf, Kate; F; 3-1883; F; M; Wife
634; 632; Littlewolf, May; F; 3-1911; F; S; Dau
635; 633; Littlewolf, Susan; F; 6-1914; F; S; Dau
636; 634; Littlewolf, Mary; F; 2-1922; F; S; Dau

637; 635; Littlewolf, Laura; F; 11-1852; F; Wd; Head
638; 636; Littlewolf, Lena; F; 12-1878[sic]; F; S; Dau
[Lena #636; Censuses 1904-09 birth year is 1880; 1910 birth year is 1890; 1911-13 birth year is 1876; 1914-17 birth year 1881; 1918 birth year is 1851; 1919-29 birth year is 1878.]

639; 637; Littlewolf, Robert; M; 6-1882[?]; F; M; Head [1904-1913 birth year 1882. 1914-26 birth year 1877.]
640; 638; Littlewolf, May; F; 6-1894; F; M; Wife [Prev. #373 name Harris; 1920.]
641; 639; Littlewolf, Charles Homer; M; 7-1908[sic]; S; Son [Birth year 1918 in 1919.]
642; 640; Littlewolf, Geraldine; F; 12-1921; F; S; Dau
643; 641; Littlewolf, Eva; F; 4-1925; F; S; Dau
644; 642; Littlewolf, Laban; M; 6-4-1928; F; S; Son

645; 644; Littlewolf, William; M; 8-1883; F; M; Head
646; 645; Littlewolf, May; F; 12-1890; F; M; Wife
647; 646; Littlewolf, Mamie; F; 7-1912[?]; F; S; Dau
648; 647; Littlewolf, William Jr; M; 10-1914[?]; F; S; Son
649; 648; Littlewolf, Claude; M; 12-1916[?]; F; S; Son

656; 649; Littleyellowman, Eddie; M; -- 1892; F; M; Head [birth year 1890 in 1926.]
651; 653; Littleyellowman, May; F; -- 1916; F; S; Dau
652; 655; Littleyellowman, Susie; F; 2-1921; F; S; Dau
653; 654; Littleyellowman, Rose; F; 3-1923; F; S; Dau
Littleyellowman, J. Ernest; M; 3-17-1929; F; S; Son

Census of the **Northern Cheyenne** tribe of the **Tongue River Agency** jurisdiction as of **June 30, 1929** taken by **C.B. Lohmiller**, Superintendent.

**Key:** Present Number; Last Number; Indian Name; English Name; Sex; Month, Year, of Birth; Degree of Blood "F-Fullblood, M-Mixed Blood"; Marital Status; Relationship;

654; 650; Littleyellowman, Hugh; M; -- 1885; F; M; Head

655; 651; Littleyellowman, Jake; M; 10-1861; F; M; Head
656; 329; Littleyellowman, Lena Fisher; F; 5-1876; F; M; Wife
657; 330; Fisher, Alice; F; 8-1898; F; S; S-Dau
658; 332; Fisher, Henry; M; 8-1905; F; S; S-Son
659; 333; Fisher, Isabelle; F; 6-1908; F; S; S-Dau
660; 334; Fisher, Richard; M; 11-1912; F; S; S-Son
661; 335; Fisher, Harold; M; 1-1920; F; S; S-Son

662; 656; Littleyellowman, Richard; M; 7-1890; F; S; Head

663; 657; Lonebull, Louis; M; 8-1858; F; Wd[sic]; Head

664; 660[sic]; Lonewolf, Charles; M; 6-1883; F; M; Head
665; 661; Lonewolf, Rose; F; 12-1890; F; M; Wife [1917 Census name was Mary. 1927 name is Rosa.]
666; 662; Lonewolf, James; M; 7-1915; F; S; Son [Lloyd in 1926.]
667; 663; Lonewolf, Ella; F; 5-1925; F; S; Dau

668; 660[sic]; Longjaw, Frank; M; 4-1900; F; M; Head
669; 738; Longjaw, Bernice; F; 2-1910; F; M; Wife [Medicineflying; Jennie in 1928.]
     665; Longjaw, Cora; F; 5-1901; F; M; Wife Died 9-1927 [Sharpnose]
670; 666; Longjaw, Robert; M; 3-1927; F; S; Son

671; 667; Longjaw, Charles; M; 3-1846[?]; F; M; Head [1904-08 birth year 1843. 1909-13 birth year 1856-7. 1914-26 birth year 1857.]
672; 668; Longjaw, Clara; F; 4-1862; F; M; Wife
673; 669; Longjaw, Charles Jr.; M; 7-1915; F; S; G-son

674; 670; Longjaw, James; M; 5-1881; F; M; Head
675; 671; Longjaw, Nellie; F; 1-1896; F; M; Wife
676; 672; Longjaw, Donald; M; 11-27-1927; F; S; Son

677; 673; Longjaw, Elmer; M; 12-1883[?]; F; M; Head
678; 674; Longjaw, Lena; F; 8-1886; F; M; Wife
[From 1814 to 1817 Censuses have birth year as 1866.]
679; 675; Longjaw, Albert; M; 12-1912; F; S; Son
680; 676; Longjaw, Henry; M; 1-1916; F; S; Son
681; 677; Longjaw, Clara; F; 1-1919; F; S; Dau

682; 678; Longroach, George; M; 4-1882; F; M; Head
683; 679; Longroach, Nellie; F; 6-1888; F; M; Wife
684; 680; Longroach, Harry; M; 1-1911; F; S; Son

Census of the **Northern Cheyenne** tribe of the **Tongue River Agency** jurisdiction as of **June 30, 1929** taken by **C.B. Lohmiller**, Superintendent.

**Key:** Present Number; Last Number; Indian Name; English Name; Sex; Month, Year, of Birth; Degree of Blood "F-Fullblood, M-Mixed Blood"; Marital Status; Relationship;

685; 681; Longroach, James; M; 11-1914; F; S; Son
686; 682; Longroach, Mary; F; 4-1917; F; S; Dau [Name Vita 1917-26. Birth month March in 1928.]
687; 683; Longroach, Frank; M; 2-1920; F; S; Son
688; 684; Longroach, Regina; F; 9-1923; F; S; Dau [Veria in 1923.]

689; 685; Looksatbareground, James; M; 5-1878; F; M; Head
690; 686; Looksatbareground, Julia; F; 5-1852; F; M; Wife [1924 wd., Elkshoulders.]

691; 691; Looksbehind, Charles; M; 10-1860; F; M; Head

692; 692; Looksbehind, Thomas; M; 7-1907[sic]; F; M; Head [1904-24 birth year 1903, 1 year old in 1904 census. 1925-26 birth year 1923.]
693; 1257; Looksbehind, Sarah W.B.; F; 6-1913; F; M; Wife [Weaselbear]

694; 687; Looksbehind, James; M; -- 1885; F; M; Head (James Nightwalking)
695; 688; Looksbehind, Roy; M; -- 1921; F; S; Son
696; 689; Looksbehind, Camilla; F; 8-1923; F; S; Dau
697; 690; Looksbehind, James Jr.; M; 5-1927; F; S; Son

698; 693; Looksbehind, Sallie; F; 10-1859; F; S; Head
699; 694; Redneck, Pius; M; 3-1912; F; S; G-son

700; 695; Lostleg, Nelson; M; 7-1891; F; Wd[sic]; Head
701; 696; Lostleg, James; M; 12-1915; F; S; Son [Ernest George in 1926.]
702; 697; Lostleg, Virginia; F; 2-1919; F; S; Dau [Son Theodore in 1920.]

703; 698; Magpie, Albert; M; 4-1886; F; Wd[sic]; Head [Prev. censuses from 1904-15 name is Youngmagpie with same birth year, none in 1913, Magpie in 1916. As early as 1907 a first wife Julia born 1887. Anne is a second wife starting in 1919. Anne is not in 1925.]
704; 699; Magpie, Anna Mary; F; 12-1919; F; S; Dau [Minnie in 1926.]
705; 700; Magpie, Gilbert; M; 8-1922; F; S; Son [#681 in 1926 was Magpie, Eva; dau; 1919; F.]

706; 701; Magpie, Louis; M; 10-1885; F; M; Head
707; 702; Magpie, Mira[sic]; F; 7-1894; F; M; Wife
708; 703; Magpie, Eddie; M; 4-1910[sic]; F; S; Son [Shows in 1906, #705; Eddy; M; S; 2mo.]

709; 704; Manbear, Lena; F; 8-1867; F; Wd; Head
710; 705; Manbear, Lizzie; F; 4-1902; F; S; Dau
711; 706; Manbear, Walters Collidge[sic]; M; 2-1926; M; S; G-Son

Census of the **Northern Cheyenne** tribe of the **Tongue River Agency** jurisdiction as of **June 30, 1929** taken by **C.B. Lohmiller**, Superintendent.

**Key:** Present Number; Last Number; Indian Name; English Name; Sex; Month, Year, of Birth; Degree of Blood "F-Fullblood, M-Mixed Blood"; Marital Status; Relationship;

712; 707; Marrowbone, Jessie; F; -- 1888; F; M; Head [Children enrolled at Pine Ridge.]

713; 708; Medicine, Sampson; M; 9-1876; F; M; Head
714; 709; Medicine, Anna; F; 2-1879; F; M; Wife
715; 710; Medicine, Jennie; F; 3-1902; F; S; Dau

711; Medicinebear, Maggie; F; 6-1847; F; Wd; Head Died 7-8-1928

716; 712; Medicinebird, Nelson; M; 8-1875; F; M; Head
717; 713; Medicinebird, Ella; F; 2-1883; F; M; Wife
718; 714; Medicinebird, Homer James; M; 3-1914; F; S; Son

719; 715; Medicinebull, Robert; M; 8-1860; F; M; Head
720; 716; Medicinebull, Maggie; F; 7-1862; F; M; Wife

721; 717; Medicinebull, Willis; M; 4-1887; F; M; Head
722; 718; Medicinebull, Anne; F; 5-1902[?]; F; M; Wife [Swallow] [Birth year 1905 in 1926.]
723; 719; Medicinebull, Fred; M; 10-1925; F; S; Son
724; 720; Medicinebull, James; M; 8-1910; F; S; Son
725; 721; Medicinebull, Ruth; F; 6-1913; F; S; Dau [Birth year 1911 in 1926.]

726; 722; Medicineelk, Basil; M; 1-1894; F; M; Head
727; 723; Medicineelk, Jennie; F; 9-1904; F; M; Wife [Eaglefeathers]
728; 724; Medicineelk, Spencer; M; 7-1917; F; S; Son
729; 725; Medicineelk, Sarah Alice; F; 4-20-1928; F; S; Son

730; 726; Medicineelk, Harold; M; 7-1865; F; Wd[sic]; Head
731; 727; Medicineelk, John; M; 10-1908; F; S; Son [Sandwoman; G-son in 1928]
732; 728; Medicineelk, James; M; 4-1902; F; S; Son

733; 729; Medicineelk, Thomas; M; 7-1906[?]; F; M; Head [Birth year 1904 in 1926.]
734; 730; Medicineelk , Nellie T.; F; 10-1912; F; M; Wife
735; 731; Medicineelk , William; M; 3-5-1928; F; S; Son

736; 732; Medicineelk, Andrew; M; 5-1898[sic]; F; M; Head
737; 733; Medicineelk, Maggie; F; 1-1903; F; M; Wife [Bearquiver]
738; 734; Medicineelk, Peter; M; 3-1926; F; S; Son
739; 735; Medicineelk, Claude; M; 12-4-1927; F; S; Son

740; 736; Medicineflying, John; M; 9-1882; F; M; Head
741; 737; Medicineflying, Bertha; F; 2-1885; F; M; Wife
742; 739; Medicineflying, Helen; F; 8-1916; F; S; Dau

Census of the **Northern Cheyenne** tribe of the **Tongue River Agency** jurisdiction as of **June 30, 1929** taken by **C.B. Lohmiller**, Superintendent.

**Key:** Present Number; Last Number; Indian Name; English Name; Sex; Month, Year, of Birth; Degree of Blood "F-Fullblood, M-Mixed Blood"; Marital Status; Relationship;

| | | |
|---|---|---|
| 743; | 740; | Medicineflying, Agnes; F; 5-1920; F; S; Dau |
| 744; | 741; | Medicineflying, Phyllis; F; 7-1924; F; S; Dau [Birth year 1925 in 1926.] |
| 745; | | Medicineflying, Clifford; M; 5-12-1929; F; S; Son |
| 746; | [742;] | Medicinetop, James; M; 5-1861; F; Wd[sic]; Head |
| 747; | 743; | Medicinetop, John; M; 1-1885; F; M; Head |
| 748; | 744; | Medicinetop, Ida; F; 5-1890; F; M; Wife |
| 749; | 745; | Medicinetop, Clarence; M; 10-1910; F; S; Son |
| 750; | 746; | Medicinetop, Marjorie; F; 4-1914[sic]; F; S; Dau [Birth year 1917.] |
| 751; | 747; | Medicinetop, Phyllis; F; 9-1922; F; S; Dau |
| 752; | 748; | Medicinetop, Roy; M; 8-1924; F; S; Son [Birth year 1925 in 1926.] |
| 753; | 749; | Medicinetop, Lena; F; 10-24-1927; F; S; Dau |
| 754; | | Medicinetop, Edward; 3-15-1929; F; S; Son |
| 755; | 750; | Merritt, Wesley; M; 10-1876; F; M; Head |
| 756; | 751; | Merritt, Josie; F; 5-1863; F; M; Wife |
| 757; | 752; | Mexicancheyenne, Ernest; M; 12-1889[sic]; M; M; Head |
| 758; | 753; | Mexicancheyenne, Mary; F; 7-1899; F; M; Wife |
| 759; | 754; | Mexicancheyenne, Harriet; F; 6-1919; M; S; Dau [Hilda in 1928.] |
| 760; | 755; | Mexicancheyenne. Mary Victoria; F; 8-1921; M; S; Dau |
| 761; | 756; | Mexicancheyenne. Rudolph; M; 2-1925; M; S; Son [Anabelle; dau; 1925.] |
| 762; | | Mexicancheyenne. Anna Joyce; F; 8-15-1928; M; S; Dau |
| 763; | 757; | Mexicancheyenne, Marion; M; 7-1887; M; M; Head |
| 764; | 758; | Mexicancheyenne, Emma; F; 6-1893; F; M; Wife |
| 765; | 759; | Mexicancheyenne, James; M; 7-1914; M; S; Son |
| 766; | 760; | Mexicancheyenne, Rosa; F; 11-1918; M; S; Dau |
| 767; | 761; | Mexicancheyenne, Margaret; F; 12-1920; M; S; Dau [Ethel in 1926.] |
| 768; | 762; | Mexicancheyenne, Mary; F; 1-1925; M; S; Dau |
| 769; | 763; | Mexicancheyenne, Mabel Ann; F; 2-2-1928; M; S; Dau |
| 770; | 764; | Oldbull, Daniel; M; 10-1870; F; Wd[sic]; Head |
| 771; | 765; | Oldbull, Thomas; M; 11-1910; F; S; Son |
| 772; | 766; | Onebear, James; M; 7-1900; M; M; Head |
| 773; | 767; | Onebear, Maggie; F; 3-1903; M; M; Wife [Seminole] |
| 774; | 768; | Onebear, Robert; M; 12-1925; M; S; Son |
| 775; | 769; | Parker, Alvin O.; M; 6-1879; M; M; Head |
| 776; | 770; | Parker, Clyde Spencer; M; 11-1922; M; S; Son |
| 777; | 771; | Parker, Verda Faye; F; 9-1924; M; S; Dau |
| 778; | 772; | Parker, Shirley Rose; M[sic]; 1-1927; M; S; Son[sic] |

Census of the **Northern Cheyenne** tribe of the **Tongue River Agency** jurisdiction as of **June 30, 1929** taken by **C.B. Lohmiller**, Superintendent.

**Key:** Present Number; Last Number; Indian Name; English Name; Sex; Month, Year, of Birth; Degree of Blood "F-Fullblood, M-Mixed Blood"; Marital Status; Relationship;

779;                Parker, Donald Edward; M; 8-25-1928; M; S; Son

780; 773;        Parker, Charles A Jr.; M; 7-1885; M; M; Head
781; 774;        Parker, Theresa; F; 3-1912; M; S; Dau
782; 775;        Parker, Gabriel; M; 10-1926; M; S; Son

783; 776;        Parker, Edwin H.; M; 4-1895; M; S; Head

784; 777;        Parker, Guy; M; 9-1891; M; M; Head
785; 778;        Parker, Winfred; M; 4-1914; M; S; Son
786; 779;        Parker, Alice; M; 2-1917; M; S; Dau
787; 780;        Parker, Stella; dau; 4-1919; M; S; Dau

788; 781;        Pease, Ida; F; 2-1906; M; M; Head [Eastman]

789; 782;        Pine, Frank; M; 7-1863; F; Wd[sic]; Head

790; 783;        Pine, Rutherford; M; 6-1886; F; M; Head
791; 784;        Pine, Julia; F; 8-1896[sic]; F; M; Wife [In 1916 marries Julia Blackcrane nee Kingfisher; in 1912 she is 18 years old, birth year is 1894 from 1904-16. Gave birth year as 1884 from 1917-26.]
792; 785;        Pine, Cecelia; F; 1-1916; F; S; Dau
793; 786;        Pine, Daniel; M; 9-1923; F; S; Son

794; 787;        Pine, Wilson; M; 3-1886; F; M; Head
795; 788;        Pine, Nora; F; 7-1888; F; M; Wife
796; 789;        Pine, Alexander; M; 11-1917; F; S; Son
797; 790;        Pine, John; M; 4-1922; F; S; Son
798; 791;        Pine, Sarah; F; 8-1924; F; S; Dau
799; 801;        Powderface, Fern; F; 7-1918; F; S; S-Dau

800; 792;        Playingbear, Henry; M; 1-1877; F; M; Head
801; 793;        Playingbear, Mildred; F; 4-1880[?]; F; M; Wife [1904-17 birth year 1881-82, 1918-26 birth year 1888.]
802; 795;        Playingbear, John; M; 5-1915; F; S; Son

803; 796;        Plentycamps, Clara; F; 8-1845; F; Wd; Head

          797;   Porcupine, Albert; M; 7-1848; F; M; Head Died 5-19-1929
804; 798;        Porcupine, Julia; F; 4-1866; F; M; Wife

805; 799;        Powderface, John; M; 5-1866; F; Wd[sic]; Head

806; 802;        Powell, Mary; F; 11-1881; M; M; Head

143

Census of the __Northern Cheyenne__ tribe of the __Tongue River Agency__ jurisdiction as of __June 30, 1929__ taken by __C.B. Lohmiller__, Superintendent.

**Key:** Present Number; Last Number; Indian Name; English Name; Sex; Month, Year, of Birth; Degree of Blood "F-Fullblood, M-Mixed Blood"; Marital Status; Relationship;

807; 803; Powell, Deyo; M; 6-1907[sic]; M; S; Son [Birth year 1909, 6 mo's old.]
808; 804; Powell, Howard; M; 2-1912; M; S; Son

809; 805; Powell, Clay; M; 11-1904; M; S; Head

810; 806; Prairiebear, Arthur; M; 3-1882; F; M; Head
811; 807; Prairiebear, Sally; F; 10-1885; F; M; Wife
812; Prairiebear, Louis; M; 11-2-1928; F; S; Son

813; 808; Redbeads, John; M; 11-1871; F; M; Head
814; 809; Redbeads, Nancy; F; 4-1878; F; M; Wife [Birth year 1876 in 1927.]
815; 810; Redbeads, Susie; F; 5-1913; F; S; Dau
816; 811; Redbeads, Clara; F; 6-1915; F; S; Dau
817; 812; Redbeads, Georgia; F; 7-1917; F; S; Dau [Name Gloria 1917-20.]

818; 813; Redbird, Joseph; M; 10-1899; F; M; Head [Middle name Francis in 1910.]
819; 814; Redbird, Dorothy M.C.; F; 7-1908; M; M; Wife [Mexicancheyenne]
820; 815; Redbird, William; M; 6-1922; F; S; Son
821; 816; Redbird, Allen; M; 5-1925; F; S; Son [First shows in 1925 with birth in 1924. Same Prev. #, Helena; dau; 1925, F. in 1926.]
822; 817; Redbird, David; M; 5-22-1928; M; S; Son

823; 818; Redbird, William; M; 7-1876; F; M; Head
824; 819; Redbird, Florence; F; 6-1877; M; M; Wife
825; 820; Redbird, Lena; F; 11-1920; M; S; Dau [Susie in 1926.]
826; Redbird, Samuel; M; 11-22-1928; M; S; Son

827; 821; Redbreath, Charles; M; 4-1879; F; M; Head
828; 822; Redbreath, Betty; F; 1-1908; F; M; Wife [Yellownose]
829; 823; Redbreath, Elina Jane; F; 6-1925; F; S; Dau [Elina June in 1926.]
830 824; Redbreath, George; M; 7-1927; F; S; Son

831; 825; Redcherries, Teddy; M; -- 1888; F; M; Head
832; 826; Redcherries, Miller; M; 11-1920; F; S; Son

833; 827; Redcherries, William; M; 6-1890; F; M; Head
834; 828; Redcherries, Bessie; F; 2-1894; F; M; Wife
835; 830; Redcherries, Alice; F; 8-1912; F; S; Dau
836; 831; Redcherries, Rose; F; 4-1916; F; S; Dau
837; 832; Redcherries, Frank; M; 5-1919; F; S; Son
838; 833; Redcherries, Margaret; F; 9-1923; F; S; Dau
839 834; Redcherries, Katie; M; 9-3-1927; F; S; Dau

Census of the **Northern Cheyenne** tribe of the **Tongue River Agency** jurisdiction as of **June 30, 1929** taken by **C.B. Lohmiller**, Superintendent.

**Key:** Present Number; Last Number; Indian Name; English Name; Sex; Month, Year, of Birth; Degree of Blood "F-Fullblood, M-Mixed Blood"; Marital Status; Relationship;

840; 828[sic]; Redcherries, Anna; F; 5-1910; F; S; Head [Woodenthigh-Killsontop; #256, Divesbackward, May; s-dau; 1910; F., in 1926.]
841; 829[sic]; Redcherries, Wallace; M; 2-4-1929; F; S; Son

842; 835; Redeagle, Jennie; F; 9-1841[?]; F; Wd; Head [Jennie #835, Census 1904-14 birth year 1851; 1915-18 birth year 1852. 1919-26 birth year 1832.]

843; 836; Redeagle, Nellie; F; 8-1872; F; Wd; Head
844; 837; Redeagle, Willis; M; 12-1901; F; S; Son
845; 658; Lonelek[sic], Wilson; M; 3-1911; F; S; Neph.

846; 838; Redfox, James; M; 4-1865; F; M; Head
847; 839; Redfox, Cora; F; 7-1867; F; M; Wife

848; 840; Redfox, Jennie; F; 12-1873; F; Wd; Head

849; 841; Redfox, Robert; M; 3-1900; F; M; Head
850; 842; Redfox, Cecelia; F; 6-1894; F; M; Wife
851; 843; Redfox, Edna; F; 3-1927; F; S; Dau
852; 973; Sanchez, Pauline; F; 3-1915; M; S; S-Dau
853; 974; Sanchez, Cecelia; F; 4-1922; M; S; S-Dau

854; 844; Redneck, Curtis; M; 1-1888; M; M; Head
855; 845; Redneck, Josie; F; 12-1896; M; M; Wife

856; 846; Redneck, David; M; 9-1891; M; M; Head
857; 847; Redneck, Minnie; F; 8-1919; M; S; Dau

858; 849; Redneck, Henry; M; 8-1882; F; M; Head
859; 850; Redneck, Fannie; F; 7-1884[?]; F; M; Wife [Birth year 1887 in 1926.]
860; 851; Redneck, Grace; F; 3-1910; F; S; Dau
861; 852 Redneck, Dora; F; 10-1914[?]; F; S; Dau [Birth year 1908 in 1926.]
862; 853; Redneck, Homer; M; 7-1917; F; S; Son
863; 854; Redneck, Florence; F; 4-1921; F; S; Dau
864; 855; Redneck, John; M; 5-1925; F; S; Son

865; 856; Rednose, Paul; M; 6-1876; F; M; Head
866; 857; Rednose, Lucy; F; 5-1870; F; M; Wife [1/2 in 1928.]
867; 858; Rednose, Sarah Mae; F; 11-1914; F; S; Dau

868; 859; Redowl, Mabel; F; 7-1946[?sic]; F; Wd; Head [Birth year 1840 in 1926.]

869; 860; Redrobe, Fred; M; 101867; F; M; Head
870; 861; Redrobe, Nora; F; 4-1869; F; M; Wife

145

Census of the __Northern Cheyenne__ tribe of the __Tongue River Agency__ jurisdiction as of __June 30, 1929__ taken by __C.B. Lohmiller__, Superintendent.

Key: Present Number; Last Number; Indian Name; English Name; Sex; Month, Year, of Birth; Degree of Blood "F-Fullblood, M-Mixed Blood"; Marital Status; Relationship;

871;  862;    Redrobe, Louis; M; 11-1892; F; S; Son

872;  863;    Redrobe, Jasper; M; 7-1900; F; S; Head

873;  864;    Redrobe, William; M; 8-1897; F; M; Head
874;  865;    Redrobe, Alice; F; 5-1884[?]; F; M; Wife [1907-19, birth year 1884-5. 1904 nee-Killsnight; 1905-6 Risingsun, 1907-19 Shell, 1920-28 Redrobe.]
875;  1261;   Weaselbear, Cordelia; F; 5-1917; F; S; Niece [s-dau-Henry Littlewhiteman. Clarice in 1926.]

876;  866;    Redwater, Thaddeus; M; 4[?]-1875; F; S; Head [Birth month March in 1928.]

877;  867;    Redwater, Cecelia; F; 2-1872; F; Div; Head

878;  868;    Redwoman, Frank; M; 2-1889; F; Wd; Head
879;  869;    Redwoman, Flossie Alice; F; 9-1911; F; S; Dau
880;  870;    Redwoman, Eugene; M; 2-1923; F; S; Son
881;  871;    Redwoman, Joe; M; 5-1924; F; S; Son
882;  872;    Redwoman, George; M; 4-4-1928; F; S; Son

883;  873;    Redwoman, Manuel; M; 7-1881; F; M; Head
884;  874;    Redwoman, Olive; F; 8-1891; F; M; Wife
885;  875;    Redwoman, Edna; F; 7-1926; F; S; Dau
886;  876;    Redwoman, Paul; M; 6-11-1927[?]; F; S; Son [Birth year 1928 in 1928.]
887;          Redwoman, Donald; M; 7-10-1928; F; S; Son

888;  878;    Ridgebear, Charles; M; -- 1882; F; M; Head

889;  879;    Ridgebear, Willis; M; 7-1887; F; M; Head
890;  880;    Ridgebear, Rilla; F; 3-1898; F; M; Wife
891;  881;    Ridgebear, Bessie Agnes; F; 11-1918; F; S; Dau
892;  882;    Ridgebear, Carrie; F; 4-1921; F; S; Dau [Katie in 1926.]
893;  883;    Ridgebear, Anna; F; 1-22-1927; F; S; Dau
894;          Ridgebear, James; M; 3-2-1929; F; S; Son

895;  884;    Ridgewalker, Robert; M; 6-1860[sic]; F; M; Head
896;  885;    Ridgewalker, Ethel; F; 6-1870; M; M; Wife
897;  886;    Ridgewalker, Frank; M; 4-1908; M; S; Son

898;  887;    Risingfire, Bessie; F; 11-1856[?]; F; Wd; Head

899;  888;    Risingsun, Oliver; M; 5-1900; F; M; Head
900;  889;    Risingsun, Elizabeth; F; 8-1907; F; M; Wife [Flying]
901;  890;    Risingsun, Teddy; M; 10-1926; F; S; Son

146

Census of the **Northern Cheyenne** tribe of the **Tongue River Agency** jurisdiction as of **June 30, 1929** taken by **C.B. Lohmiller**, Superintendent.

Key: Present Number; Last Number; Indian Name; English Name; Sex; Month, Year, of Birth; Degree of Blood "F-Fullblood, M-Mixed Blood"; Marital Status; Relationship;

902; 891; Risingsun, Peter; M; 8-1887; F; Wd[sic]; Head
892; Risingsun, Bessie; F; 11-1892; F; M; Wife Died 8-19-1928
903; 893; Risingsun, Maude; F; 6-1913; F; S; Dau
904; 894; Risingsun, Harry; M; 4-1921[?]; F; S; Son [Birth year 1918 #877 in 1926.]
905; 895; Risingsun, Lyman; M; 7-1923; F; S; Son
906; 896; Risingsun, James; M; 12-1925; F; S; Son
907; Risingsun, Ruby; F; 9-19-1928; F; S; Dau
908; Risingsun, Pearl; F; 9-19-1928; F; S; Dau

909; 897; Risingsun, Philip; M; 8-1862; F; M; Head
910; 898; Risingsun, Nora; F; 1-1868; F; M; Wife
911; 899; Risingsun, John; M; 6-1895; F; S; Son
912; 900; Risingsun, William; M; 6-1904[?]; F; S; Son [Birth year 1910 in 1926.]
913; 901; Risingsun, Alice; F; 12-1909; F; S; Dau

914; 902; Robinson, Nellie; F; 10-1897; M; M; Head
915; 903; Robinson, David; M; 8-1918; M; S; Son
916; 904; Robinson, Cornelius Clay; M; 6-1920; M; S; Son
917; 905; Robinson, Eloise Elaine; F; 3-1922; M; S; Dau [Previous #888, In 1926.]
918; Robinson, Buell; M; 7-30-1928; M; S; Son

919; 906; Rockroads, Nora; F; 12-1870[?]; F; Wd; Head [1904-18 birth year 1868. 1919-26 birth year 1983.]
920; 907; Rockroads, Mary; F; 8-1913; F; S; Dau

921; 908; Rockroads, Mack; M; 4[?]-1893; F; M; Head [March was birth month in 1928.]
922; 909; Rockroads, Nellie; F; 11-1893; F; M; Wife
923; 910; Rockroads, Thomas; M; 4-1917; F; S; Son [1918 Census #902; Name is Lettie, female.]

924; 911; Romannose, Louis; M; 9-1882; F; M; Head [Louis's Birth year 1882, 1904-13; 1862, 1914-20. 1882 in 1922-28.]
925; 912; Romannose, Mary; F; 5-1890; F; M; Wife
926; 913; Romannose, George; M; 7-1910; F; S; Son
927; 914; Romannose, Blanche; F; 9-1914; F; S; Dau [Helen in 1926.]
928; 915; Romannose, Julia; F; 4-1916[?]; F; S; Dau [Name May and birth year 1919 in 1926.]
929; 916; Romannose, Willeatte; F; 10-1921; F; S; Dau
930; 917; Romannose, Montana; F; 11-1923; F; S; Dau
931; Romannose, Eva Louise; 7-26-1928; F; S; Dau

932; 918; Rondeau, Antoine; M; 4-1887; M; M; Head

Census of the __Northern Cheyenne__ tribe of the __Tongue River Agency__
jurisdiction as of __June 30, 1929__ taken by __C.B. Lohmiller__, Superintendent.

**Key:** Present Number; Last Number; Indian Name; English Name; Sex; Month, Year, of Birth; Degree of Blood "F-Fullblood, M-Mixed Blood"; Marital Status; Relationship;

933; 919; Rondeau, Louisa; F; 6-1889; M; M; Wife [Birth year 1886 in 1926.]
934; 920; Rondeau, Clara; F; 12-1912; M; S; Dau
935; 921; Rondeau, Charles; M; 5-1920; M; S; Son [Dau, Marie in 1920.] [#909 in 1926.]

936; 922; Rondeau, William; M; 3-1866[?]; M; Wd[sic]; Head [Birth year 1887 in 1926.]
937; 923; Rondeau, Henry; M; 3-1911; M; S; Son
938; 924; Rondeau, John R.; M; 3-1912[?]; M; S; Son [Born 1913]

939; 925; Roundstone, Flora; F; 4-1888; F; M; Head [Twobulls]
940; 926; Roundstone, Martin; M; 11-1911; F; S; Son
941; 927; Roundstone, Sarah; F; 15[sic]-1920; F; S; Dau
942; 928; Roundstone, Paul; M; 4-1922; F; S; Son
943; 929; Roundstone, Ruth; F; 7-1926; F; S; Dau

944; 930; Rowland, Sally; F; 9-1854; F; Wd; Head [Previously Annie-Anna.]

945; 931; Rowland, Clay T.; M; 2-1880; M; M; Head

946; 933; Rowland, Joe; M; 12-1902[?]; M; M; Head [In 1926 #935; Jose; son; birth year 1900.]

947; 934; Rowland, Thomas.; M; 12-1892; M; M; Head
948; 935; Rowland, Daisy; F; 3-1900; F; M; Wife [Fightingbear, Ellen in 1924.]
949; 936; Rowland, Lizzie; F; 11-1913; M; S; Dau
950; 937; Rowland, Lillian; F; 11-1916; M; S; Dau
951; 938; Rowland, Blanche; F; 8-1925; M; S; Dau
952; 939; Rowland, Don; M; 1-22-1928; M; S; Son

953; 940; Rowland, Willis; M; 4-1862; M; M; Head
954; 941; Rowland, Helen; F; 5-1868; F; M; Wife [Sarah 1908-1919.]
955; 932; Rowland, Jesse; M; 2-1884; M; S; Neph. [Name Frank and previous #932 in 1926.]
956; 942; Rowland, Grace; F; 11-1914[?]; M; S; A-Dau (Cora Littlewhiteman) [Shows adopted and birth year 1916 in 1926.]
957; 948; Rowland, Frank; M; 5-1924; M; S;; G-Son

958; 943; Rowland, William; M; 9-14-1896; M; M; Head [Birth year 1896 in 1928.]
959; 944; Rowland, Chester Clay; M; 6-1920; M; S; Son
960; 945; Rowland, Allen Edsel; M; 2-1926; M; S; Son
961; 946; Rowland, Ardith Faye; F; -30-1928; M; S; Dau

947; Rowland, George; M; 1-1898; M; M; Head Died 1-29-1929

Census of the __Northern Cheyenne__ tribe of the __Tongue River Agency__ jurisdiction as of __June 30, 1929__ taken by __C.B. Lohmiller__, Superintendent.

**Key:** Present Number; Last Number; Indian Name; English Name; Sex; Month, Year, of Birth; Degree of Blood "F-Fullblood, M-Mixed Blood"; Marital Status; Relationship;

962; 949; Rowland, Carrie; F; 11-1926; M; S; Dau

963; 950; Rowland, Zac; M; 12-1868; M; M; Head
964; 951; Rowland, Edna; F; 10-1876; F; M; Wife

965; 954; Rowland, Benton; M; [12]-1898; M; M; Head
966; 955; Rowland, Marie; F; [5]-1926; M; S; Dau
967; 956; Rowland, Eugene A; M; 8-13-1927; M; S; Son

968; 959; Russell, John; M; 9-1893; M; M; Head
969; 960; Russell, Stella Mildred; F; 2-1916; M; S; Dau
970; 961; Russell, May; F; 5-1924; M; S; Dau
971; 962; Russell, Inez Irma; F; 3-1927; M; S; Dau
972; Russell, John Jr.; M; 3-31-1929; M; S; Son

973; 963; Russell, William; M; 5-1873; F; M; Head
974; 964; Russell, Fred; M; 7-1908; F; S; Son
975; 965; Russell, Earl; M; 8-1915; F; S; Son
976; 966; Russell, Mary; F; 9-1918; F; S; Dau [Mildred in 1926.]
977; 967; Russell, Clara; F; 5-1922; F; S; Dau
978; 968; Russell, Herman; M; 5-1925; F; S; Son

979; 969; Russell, Frank; M; 12-1898[?]; M; M; Head 3/4 (Separated)
980; 1153; Russell, Ellen; F; 7-1897; F; M; Wife [Sweetmedicine]
971; Russell, Ford; M; 3-1925; M; S; Son Died 8-8-1928

981; 972; Sansaver[sic], Lillian; F; 7-1906; M; S; Head [dau-Rhoda Seminole; Sansover mother was a Miles in 1915. Sansover in 1917 #741]

982; 975; Sandcrane, Henry; M; 10-1889; F; Wd[sic]; Head
983; 976; Sandcrane, Emily May; F; 10-1920; F; S; Dau

984; 977; Sandcrane, John; M; 1-1873; F; M; Head
985; 978; Sandcrane, Ruth; F; 12-1878; F; M; Wife
986; 979; Sandcrane, Isabelle; F; 5-1914; F; S; Dau
987; 583; Littleoldman, Fern; F; 8-1917; F; S; G-Dau [s.-dau. Chas. Sharpnose, #569; Littleman, Julia; s-dau; 1915; F. (s-dau Fred Limpy) in 1926.]

988; 980; Scalpcane, August; M; 2-1906[sic]; F; S; Head
989; 981; Scalpcane, Otto; M; 11-1914[sic]; F; S; Bro.
990; 982; Scalpcane, Henry; M; 11-1919; F; S; Bro. [Rudolph in 1926.]

991; 983; Seminole, John; M; 2-1879[?]; M; M; Head 3/4 [Birth year 1881 in 1926.]
992; 985; Seminole, Mary Redbird; F; 8-1897; F; M; Wife

149

Census of the **Northern Cheyenne** tribe of the **Tongue River Agency** jurisdiction as of **June 30, 1929** taken by **C.B. Lohmiller**, Superintendent.

**Key:** Present Number; Last Number; Indian Name; English Name; Sex; Month, Year, of Birth; Degree of Blood "F-Fullblood, M-Mixed Blood"; Marital Status; Relationship;

993; 984; Seminole, Fred; M; 6-1915; M; S; Son
994; 996; Seminole, Max; M; 11-1924; M; S; Son [son-Mary Redbird, 1926 #813 entry; Redbird, Maxine; g-g-son; 1924; M.; g-g-son Joseph Tangledhornelk]
Seminole, Helen May; F; 1-13-1929; M; S; Dau Died 1-19-1929
995; 352; Fox, Margaret; F; 8-1918; F; S; S-Dau [Jessie in 1927.]
996; 353; Fox, Marie; F; 11-1922; F; S; S-Dau [Max, M., 1922-25.]

997; 986; Seminole, Dan; M; 8-1894; M; M; Head
998; 987; Seminole, Jennie; F; 7-1896; F; M; Wife
999; 988; Seminole, Anna; F; 6-1920; M; S; Dau
1000; 989; Seminole, Margaret; F; 1-1922; M; S; Dau
1001; 990; Seminole, Alfred; M; 3-1924; M; S; Son
1002; Seminole, Beatrice; F; 8-27-1928; M; S; Dau
1003; 622; Littlewhiteman, Charles; M; 2-1915; M; S; S-Son

1004; 991; Seminole, Josephine; F; 4-1891; M; S; Head
1005; 992; Seminole, Lawrence; M; 12-1911; M; S; Son [g-son in 1926.]

1006; 993; Seminole, Louis; M; 6-1884; M; Wd[sic]; Head
1007; 994; Seminole, Delbert; M; 6-1911; M; S; Son
1008; 995; Seminole, Hannah; F; 11-1912[?]; M; S; Dau [1917 Census Son Theodore. Birth year 1915 in 1926.]

1009; 997; Seminole Miles; M; 1869[?]; M; Div; Head [Birth year 1875 in 1926.]

1010; 998; Seminole, Rhoda; F; 3-1882[?]; M; Div; Head [Birth year in 1926 is 1879; Birth year in 1928 is 1892.]
1011; 999; Seminole, Lorraine; F; 6-1916; M; S; Dau
1012; 1000; Seminole, David; F; 4-1919; M; S; Son

1013; 1001; Sharpnose, Josephine; F; 6-1902; F; Wd; Head [Hisbadhorses]

1014; 1002; Shavedhead, Jean; F; 6-1901; F; M; Head [Swallow]
1015; 1003; Shavedhead, Charles; M; 6-1924; F; S; Son [Jeffrey, Jr. and birth year 1925 in 1926.]
1016; 1004; Shavedhead, Anna Marjorie; F; 10-1926; F; S; Dau

1017; 1005; Shavedhead, Mary; F; 6-1965[sic]; F; Wd; Head
1018; 267; Divesbackwards, Louisa; F; 8-1917; F; S; G-Dau [States 7/8 blood in 1928.]

1019; 1006; Shavedhead, James; M; 11-1899; F; M; Head
1020; 1007; Shavedhead, Alice; F; 2-1907[?]; F; M; Wife [Medicineflying; age 3 in 1910. Birth 1906-07.]

Census of the __Northern Cheyenne__ tribe of the __Tongue River Agency__ jurisdiction as of __June 30, 1929__ taken by __C.B. Lohmiller__, Superintendent.

**Key:** Present Number; Last Number; Indian Name; English Name; Sex; Month, Year, of Birth; Degree of Blood "F-Fullblood, M-Mixed Blood"; Marital Status; Relationship;

1021; 1008;     Shavedhead, Anna; F; 9-1925; F; S; Dau [Hyacinth in 1926.]
1022; 1009;     Shavedhead, Lucille; F; 11-31-1928; F; S; Dau

1023; 1010;     Shell, Joseph; M; 2-1881; F; M; Head
1024; 1011;     Shell, Julia; F; 9-1901[?]; F; M; Wife [Previous #530 in 1906, censuses 1906-19, wife Alice [Risingsun] Shell, birth year 1885.] [Julia starts census 1920.]

1025; 1012;     Shell, Minnie; F; 6-1882[?]; F; Wd; Head [Killsnight] [Birth year 1892 in 1926.]

1026; 1013;     Shepherd, Mollie; F; 4-1895; M; M; Head

1027; 1014;     Shortsioux, Mary; F; 6-1914; M; S; Dau    Dau of Maggie Longears, Crow Agency, Mont.

1028; 1015;     Sherman, Ethel; F; 5-1883; M; M; Head
1029; 1016[sic];    Sherman, George Jr.; F; 11-1911; M; S; Son
1030; 1018;     Sherman, Otto; M; 6-1913; M; S; Son
1031; 1019;     Sherman, Wretha; F; 8-1915; M; S; Dau
1032; 1020;     Sherman, Carl; M; 12-1918; M; S; Son
1033; 1021;     Sherman, Clarence; M; 7-1922; M; S; Son

1034; 1022;     Shoulderblade, Benedict; M; 9-1874; F; M; Head

1035; 1023;     Shoulderblade, Fred; M; 10-1861; F; M; Head
1036; 1024;     Shoulderblade, Richard; M; 8-1911; F; S; Son

1037; 1025;     Shoulderblade, Pius; M; 5-1889; F; M; Head
1038; 1026;     Shoulderblade, Ethel; F; 8-1893; M; M; Wife
1039; 1027;     Shoulderblade, Thomas; M; 10-1915; M; S; Son
1040; 1028;     Shoulderblade, Francis; M; 3-1917; M; S; Son [1917 Census William]
1041; 1029;     Shoulderblade, Wendel; M; 8-1920; M; S; Son
1042; 1030;     Shoulderblade, Everett John; M; 6-1923; M; S; Son
1043; 1031;     Shoulderblade, Fern; F; 2-23-1928; M; S; Dau

1044; 1032;     Silloway, Veta; F; 11-1904; M; M; Head [Birth month Apr., in 1927.]

1045; 1033;     Sioux, Thomas; M; 11-1870; F; Wd; Head
1046; 1034;     Sioux, Henry; M; 6[?]-1911; F; S; A-Son [#1018, Divesbackwards; Name Jacob; and listed as g-son; in 1926. June birth month in 1927.]

1047; 1035;     Sittingman, Charles; M; 10-1866[sic]; F; M; Head [1904-18 birth 1868.]
1048; 1036;     Sittingman, Lucy; F; 5-1866[sic]; F; M; Wife [Born 1868.]

Census of the **Northern Cheyenne** tribe of the **Tongue River Agency** jurisdiction as of **June 30, 1929** taken by **C.B. Lohmiller**, Superintendent.

**Key:** Present Number; Last Number; Indian Name; English Name; Sex; Month, Year, of Birth; Degree of Blood "F-Fullblood, M-Mixed Blood"; Marital Status; Relationship;

| | |
|---|---|
| 1049; 1037; | Sittingman, Edward; M; 6-1900; F; M; Head [Edward in 1927. Was Edwin in 1926.] |
| 1050; 1038; | Sittingman, Ida Whitehawk; F; 6-1898; F; M; Wife |

| | |
|---|---|
| 1051; 1039; | Small, Josephine; F; 2-1892; M; M; Head |
| 1052; 1040; | Small, Victor; M; 8-1912; M; S; Son |
| 1053; 1041; | Small, Edward; M; 11-1913; M; S; Son |
| 1054; 1042; | Small, Max Joe; M; 4-1915; M; S; Son |
| 1055; 1043; | Small, Ivan; M; 4-1920; M; S; Son |
| 1056; 1044; | Small, Thomas; M; 12-1921; M; S; Son |
| 1057; 1045; | Small, Horace; M; 7-1923; M; S; Son |
| 1058; 1046; | Small, Melvin; M; 2-1924; M; S; Son |
| 1059; 1047; | Small, Worth; M; 2-1927; M; S; Son |
| | Small, Vera Sue; F; 12-20-1928; M; S; Dau Died 2-24-1929 |

| | |
|---|---|
| 1060; 1048; | Smith, John; M; 6-1875; F; M; Head [Birth year 1878 in 1926.] |
| 1061; 1049; | Smith, Blanche; F; 3-1880; F; M; Wife [Birth year 1883 in 1926.] |

| | |
|---|---|
| 1062; 1050; | Soldierwolf, John; M; 4-1883; F; M; Head |
| 1063; 1051; | Soldierwolf, Mary; F; 4-1888; F; M; Wife |
| 1064; 1052; | Soldierwolf, Thos. Chas.; M; 6-1910; F; S; Son |
| 1065; 1053; | Soldierwolf, Aurora; F; 1-1915; F; S; Dau |
| 1066; 1054; | Soldierwolf, Lucy; F; 10-1917; F; S; Dau |
| 1067; 1055; | Soldierwolf, James Kenneth; M; 7-1920; F; S; Son |
| 1068; 1056; | Soldierwolf, Katherine; F; 5-1922; F; S; Dau |

| | |
|---|---|
| 1069; 1057; | Spang, Alfonso; M; 1-1887; M; M; Head |
| 1070; 200; | Spang, Mary C.; F; 9-1911; M; M; Wife [1924 Annie. Callsfirst in 1928.] |

| | |
|---|---|
| 1073; 1059; | Spang, Deyo; M; 12-1888; M; M; Head |
| 1074; 1060; | Spang, Bruce Spencer; M; 6-1924; M; S; Son |
| 1075; 1061; | Spang, Dale Cooper; M; 7-1926; M; S; Son |

| | |
|---|---|
| 1076; 1062; | Spang, James; M; 7-1899; M; M; Head |
| 1077; 1063; | Spang, James Russell; M; 5-13-1927; M; S; Son |
| 1078; 1064; | Spang, Shirley Ann; F; 5-19-1928; M; S; Dau |

| | |
|---|---|
| 1079; 1065; | Spang, Lucy; F; 5-1869; M; M; Head |
| 1080; 1066; | Spang, Sarah; F; 8-1904; M; S; Dau |
| 1081; 1067; | Spang, Harriet; F; 10-1905; M; S; Dau [Birth 1906.] |
| 1082; 1068; | Spang, Edith; F; 12-1909; M; S; Dau |
| 1083; 1069; | Spang, Cash; M; 10-1911; M; S; Son |

| | |
|---|---|
| 1084; 1070; | Spang, Roy; M; 9-1896; M; M; Head |

Census of the __Northern Cheyenne__ tribe of the __Tongue River Agency__ jurisdiction as of __June 30, 1929__ taken by __C.B. Lohmiller__, Superintendent.

**Key:** Present Number; Last Number; Indian Name; English Name; Sex; Month, Year, of Birth; Degree of Blood "F-Fullblood, M-Mixed Blood"; Marital Status; Relationship;

1085; 1322;   Spang, Viola Alice; F; 1-1907[?]; F; M; Wife [Wildhog; Birth year 1901 in 1926.]
1086; 1072;   Spang, Regina Susanna; F; 6-1922; M; S; Dau [Regina Rosetta in 1926.]
1087; 1073;   Spang, Lyman; M; 8-1923; M; S; Son

1088; 1071;   Spang, Jessie; F; 5-1907; F; Div; Head

1089; 1074;   Spang, Wilfred; M; 5-1901; M; M; Head
1090; 1075;   Spang, Alice Y.H.; F; 6-1908; F; M; Wife [Yellowhorse]
1091; 1076;   Spang; Norman; M; 9-1927; M; S; Son

1092; 1077;   Sponge, Alfred; M; 7-1896; F; M; Head
1093; 1078;   Sponge, Josie; F; 9-1901; F; M; Wife [Shoulderblade] [1922 was #958, Scott.]

1094; 1079;   Sponge, Oliver; M; 3-1898; F; M; Head
1095; 1080;   Sponge, Clara; F; 5-1905; F; M; Wife [Tangleyellowhair]
1096; 1081;   Sponge, Paul; M; 12-10-1927; F; S; Son

1097; 1082;   Spottedblackbird, Lee; M; 6-1859; F; M; Head [Birth year 1854 in 1926. #1082. Didn't pickup a first name until 1915 name, Lee; or Leo.]
1098; 1083;   Spottedblackbird, Clara; F; 10-1874; F; M; Wife [Birth year 1854 in 1926.]
1099;  377;   Hardground, Jane; F; 3-1915; F; S; G-Dau [A s-dau in 1928.]

1100; 1084;   Spottedelk, Charles; M; 3-1863[?]; F; Wd; Head
1101; 1085;   Spottedelk, August; M; 7-1897; F; S; Son
1102; 1086;   Spottedelk, Alex; M; 11-1900; F; Wd[sic]; Son

1103; 1087;   Spottedhawk, Hugh; M; 4-1867; F; M; Head

1104; 1089;   Spottedwolf, Charles; M; 10-1892; F; M; Head
1105; 1090;   Spottedwolf, Lena; F; 9-1892; F; M; Wife
1106; 1091;   Spottedwolf, Julia Eva; F; 4-1913; F; S; Dau
1107; 1092;   Spottedwolf, Piney; F; 9-1921; F; S; Dau
1108; 1093;   Spottedwolf, John; M; 10-1923; F; S; Son
1109; 1094;   Spottedwolf, Lena; F; 11-22-1927; F; S; Dau
1110;  623;   Littlewhiteman, Florence; F; 2-1915; M; S; S-Dau

1111; 1095;   Spottedwolf, Patrick; M; 11-1887; F; M; Head
1112; 1096;   Spottedwolf, Jean; F; 10-1901; M; M; Wife
1113; 1097;   Spottedwolf, Ruby; F; 9-1920; M; S; Dau
1114; 1098;   Spottedwolf, Phyllis; F; 10-1923; M; S; Dau
1115; 1099;   Spottedwolf, Eugene; M; 8-1925; M; S; Son

Census of the __Northern Cheyenne__ tribe of the __Tongue River Agency__ jurisdiction as of __June 30, 1929__ taken by __C.B. Lohmiller__, Superintendent.

**Key:** Present Number; Last Number; Indian Name; English Name; Sex; Month, Year, of Birth; Degree of Blood "F-Fullblood, M-Mixed Blood"; Marital Status; Relationship;

1116; 1100;    Spottedwolf, Mollie; F; 9-28-1927; M; S; Dau

1117; 1267;    Squinteye, Josie; F; 6-1884[?]; F; M; Head [Whistlingelk; 1904-20, birth year 1884. Birth year 1874 in 1926.]
1118; 1268;    Whistlingelk, Alice; F; 6-1913[?]; F; S; Dau [Birth year 1909 in 1927.]
1119; 1269;    Whistlingelk, Alfred; M; 1-1917; F; S; Son
1120; 1270;    Whistlingelk, Lois; F; 12-1926; F; S; Dau

1121; 1101;    Standingelk, Nina; F; 6-1907; F; S; Head

1122; 1102;    Standingelk, Frank; M; 6-1874; F; M; Head
1123; 1103;    Standingelk, Fannie; F; 4-1878; F; M; Wife
        1104;    Standingelk, George; M; 4-1910[sic]; F; S; Son Died Aug. 7, 1928
1124; 1105;    Standingelk, Flora; F; 4-1921; F; S; Dau

1125; 1106;    Standingelk, Francis; F; 4-1901; F; M; Head
1126; 1107;    Standingelk, Annie; F; 5-1907; F; M; Wife
1127; 1108;    Standingelk, Roy; M; 8-1926; F; S; Son

1128; 1109;    Standingelk, Henry; M; 6-1891; F; Wd[sic]; Head

1129; 1110;    Standingelk, Lockwood; M; 6-1890; F; Wd[sic]; Head

1130; 1111;    Standingelk, Robert B.; M; 10-1870; F; M; Head
1131; 1112;    Standingelk, Sally; F; 9-1895; F; M; Wife
1132; 1113;    Standingelk, Ella; F; 12-1918; F; S; Dau
1133; 1114;    Standingelk, Jennie Clara; F; 5-1927; F; S; Dau

1134; 1115;    Standingelk, Alex; M; 3-1896; F; M; Head F.
1135; 1116;    Standingelk, Nora; F; 7-1903; F; M; Wife
1136; 1117;    Standingelk, Geneva; F; 3-1922; F; S; Dau
1137; 1118;    Standingelk, Margaret; F; 11-1924; F; S; Dau

1138; 1119;    Standsintimber, John; M; 3-1886; F; M; Head [Family Part Blood in 1928.]
1139; 1120;    Standsintimber, Josie; F; 3-1898; F[sic; 3/4]; M; Wife
1140; 1121;    Standsintimber, Josephine; F; 6-1920; F[sic; 7/8]; S; Dau
1141; 1122;    Standsintimber, John Jr.; M; 10-1921; F[sic; 7/8]; S; Son
1142; 1123;    Standsintimber, Elva; F; 4-21-1928; F[sic; 7/8]; S; Dau

1143; 1124;    Star, May Blackree; F; 12-1904; F; S; Head [Star, Blackree in 1928; Minnie in 1926.]

1144; 1125;    Standsout, Sallie; F; 8-1847; F; Wd; Head

Census of the __Northern Cheyenne__ tribe of the __Tongue River Agency__ jurisdiction as of __June 30, 1929__ taken by __C.B. Lohmiller__, Superintendent.

**Key:** Present Number; Last Number; Indian Name; English Name; Sex; Month, Year, of Birth; Degree of Blood "F-Fullblood, M-Mixed Blood"; Marital Status; Relationship;

| | |
|---|---|
| 1145; 1126; | Starvingbear, James; M; 4-1876; F; Wd[sic]; Head |
| 1146; 1127; | Starvingbear, Mary; F; 3-1907; F; S; Dau [Lottie in 1926.] |
| 1147; 1128; | Starvingbear, Jack; M; 2-1914; F; S; Dau[sic] [Rosco in 1926.] |
| 1148; | Bearcomesout, Herbert; M; 9-12-1928; F; S; G-son Son of 1146 |

| | |
|---|---|
| 1149; 1129; | Strangeowl, John; M; 9-1872[?]; F; M; Head [Birth year 1876 in 1926.] |
| 1150; 1130; | Strangeowl, Gertie; F; 11-1868; F; M; Wife |
| 1151; 1131; | Strangeowl, James; M; 6-1904; F; S; Son |

| | |
|---|---|
| 1152; 1132; | Stumphorn, Frank; M; 10-1843; F; M; Head |
| 1153; 1133; | Stumphorn, Annie; F; 7-1855; F; M; Wife [Shortsioux, Wdw.] |

| | |
|---|---|
| 1154; 1134; | Stumphorn, Anna.; F; 9-1851[sic]; F; Wd; Head [Birth year 1842.] |

1135; Sunbear, John; M; 7-1843[?]; F; Wd[sic]; Head Died 2-19-1929 [1904-15 birth year 1856. 1916-28 birth year 1843.]

| | |
|---|---|
| 1155; 1136; | Sunbear, Michael; M; -- 1891; F; M; Head |
| 1156; 1137; | Sunbear, Herman; M; 8-1923; F; S; Son |
| 1157; 1138; | Sunbear, Deyo; M; -- 1924; F; S; Son |

| | |
|---|---|
| 1158; 1139; | Sunroads, David; M; 9-1881; F; M; Head |
| 1159; 1140; | Sunroads, Lizzie; F; 3-1883; F; M; Wife |

| | |
|---|---|
| 1160; 1141; | Sunroads, John; M; 7-1843; F; M; Head |
| 1161; 1142; | Sunroads, Lena; F; 3-1845; F; M; Wife |

1162; 1143; Swallow, William; M; 2-1874; F; M; Head [Birth year 1873-4.] [William #1143; 1904-15 born 1873, 1916-17 born 1897, 1918-26 born 1863.]

| | |
|---|---|
| 1163; 1144; | Swallow, Gertrude; F; 3-1896; F; S[sic]; Wife [Redbreath] |
| 1164; 1145; | Swallow, Mary; F; 5-1907; F; S; Dau [Previously name Anne.] |
| 1165; 1146; | Percy Redbreath; M; 11-1919[?]; F; S; Son [Birth year 1922 in 1926.] |

| | |
|---|---|
| 1166; 1147; | Swallow, Edward; M; 3-1902; F; S; Head |

| | |
|---|---|
| 1167; 1148; | Swallow, Oliver; M; 4-1899; F; S; Head |

| | |
|---|---|
| 1168; 1149; | Sweetmedicine, David; M; 3-1863[sic]; F; M; Head [Birth year 1868] |
| 1169; 1150; | Sweetmedicine, Clara; F; 12-1870; F; M; Wife |
| 1170; 1151; | Sweetmedicine, Jacob; M; 4-1894; F; S; Son |
| 1171; 1152; | Sweetmedicine, Joseph; M; 12-1898; F; S; Son |

| | |
|---|---|
| 1172; 1154; | Sweetmedicine, William; M; -- 1889; F; M; Head |

Census of the **Northern Cheyenne** tribe of the **Tongue River Agency** jurisdiction as of **June 30, 1929** taken by **C.B. Lohmiller**, Superintendent.

**Key:** Present Number; Last Number; Indian Name; English Name; Sex; Month, Year, of Birth; Degree of Blood "F-Fullblood, M-Mixed Blood"; Marital Status; Relationship;

1173; 1155; Sweetmedicine, Alta; F; -- 1913[sic]; F; S; Dau [1915-Son, Thomas; M.]

1174; 1156; Tallbull, Albert; M; 4-1906; F; S; Head [Birth year 1902 in 1926.]

1175; 1157; Tallbull, Charles; M; 10-1887; F; M; Head
1176; 1158; Tallbull, Mary; F; 5-1893; F; M; Wife
1177; 1159; Tallbull, Joseph; M; 6-1915; F; S; Son
1178; 1160; Tallbull, Henry; M; 12-1917; F; S; Son
1179; 1161; Tallbull, William; M; 1-1921; F; S; Son
1180; 1163;[sic] Tallbull, Nelson; M; 10-1923; F; S; Son
1181; 1164;[sic] Tallbull, Cecil Russell; M; 1-1927; F; S; Son
1182; Tallbull, Nellie; F; 1-5-1929; F; S; Dau

1183; 1164; Tallbull, Nora; F; 6-1858[sic]; F; Wd; Head

1184; 1165; Tallwhiteman, Jasper; M; 7-1893[?]; F; Wd[sic]; Head [Birth year 1891 in 1926.]
1185; 1166; Tallwhiteman, Agnes; F; 5-1924; F; S; Dau [1925 census Dan son, M., same #. Name Rilla in 1926.]

1186; 1167; Tallwhiteman, John; M; 4-1886; F; M; Head
1187; 1168; Tallwhiteman, Eleanor; F; 3-1898; F; M; Wife
1188; 1169; Tallwhiteman, Clarence; M; 7-1912; F; S; Son
1189; 1170; Tallwhiteman, Florence; F; 5-1914; F; S; Dau
1190; 1171; Tallwhiteman, Jasper; M; 7-1916; F; S; Son
1191; 1172; Tallwhiteman, Alice; F; 5-1920; F; S; Dau
1192; 1173; Tallwhiteman, Tug; M; 6-1922; F; S; Son
1193; 1174; Tallwhiteman, Agnes; F; 7-1925; F; S; Dau

1175; Tallwhiteman, Patrick; M; 6-1888; F; Wd[sic]; Head

1194; 1179; Tangledhornelk, Nellie; F; -- 1853; F; Wd; Head [1904-18 no "d" in last name.]

1195; 1180; Tangledyellowhair, Chas.; M; 2-1892; F; M; Head [1904-18 no "d" in last name.]
1196; 1181; Tangledyellowhair, Georgia; F; 9-1891; F; M; Wife [Talks]
1197; 1182; Tangledyellowhair, Roberta; F; 9-1924; F; S; Dau
1198; 1183; Tangledyellowhair, Bert; M; 10-1926; F; S; Son
1199; Tangledyellowhair, Marie; F; 3-31-1929; F; S; Dau

1200; 1184; Tangledyellowhair, David; M; 6-1898[?]; F; M; Head [1904-18 no "d" in last name. Birth year 1894 in 1926.]
1201; 1176; Tangledyellowhair, Florence; F; 7-1900; F; M; Wife [Tallwhiteman]

156

Census of the __Northern Cheyenne__ tribe of the __Tongue River Agency__ jurisdiction as of __June 30, 1929__ taken by __C.B. Lohmiller__, Superintendent.

**Key:** Present Number; Last Number; Indian Name; English Name; Sex; Month, Year, of Birth; Degree of Blood "F-Fullblood, M-Mixed Blood"; Marital Status; Relationship;

1202; 1185;     Tangledyellowhair, Clara; F; 10-1919; F; S; Dau
1203; 1186;     Tangledyellowhair, Winona; F; 1-1922; F; S; Dau
1204; 1187;     Tangledyellowhair, Lariath; M; 4-14-1928; F; S; Son
1205; 1177;     Tallwhiteman, Alice; F; 1-1916; F; S; S-Dau
1206; 1178;     Tallwhiteman, Laura; F; 6-1923; F; S; S-Dau

1207; 1188;     Tangledyellowhair, James; M; 1-1869; F; M; Head [1904-18 no "d" in last name.]
1208; 1189;     Tangledyellowhair, Minnie; F; 12-1870[?]; F; M; Wife [Birth year 1873 in 1926.]

1209; 1190;     Tangledyellowhair, Josie; F; 3-1848[?]; F; Wd; Head [1904-18 no "d" in last name. Birth year 1846 in 1926.]

1210; 1191;     Teeth, Charles; M; 3-1863[?]; F; Wd[sic]; Head [Birth year 1865 in 1926.]

1211; 1192;     Teeth, John; M; 5-1889; F; M; Head
1212; 1193;     Teeth, Edith; F; 10-1902; F; M; Wife
1213; 1194;     Teeth, Franklin; M; 10-1909; F; S; Son
1214; 1195;     Teeth, Earl; M; 6-1916; F; S; Son
1215; 1196;     Teeth, Montana; F; 4-1922; F; S; Dau
1216; 1197;     Teeth, Elsie; F; 9-1925; F; S; Dau

1217; 1198;     Threefingers, John; M; 3-1862[?]; F; M; Head [Birth year 1878[?] in 1926. #1198-Various ages starting 1904, in 1913-1920 birth year 1868 changes again in 1922.]
1218; 1199;     Threefingers, Pansy; F; 7-1876[?]; F; M; Wife [Birth year 1878 in 1926.]

1219; 1200;     Threefingers, William; M; 9-1901; F; Wd[sic]; Head
       1201;     Threefingers, Ruth Maude; F; 10-1907; F; M; Wife Died 1-10-1929 [Medicinebird]

1220; 1202;     Turkeylegs, John; M; 7-1859; F; M; Head
1221; 1203;     Turkeylegs, Lydia; F; 8-1874; F; F[sic]; Wife
1222; 1204;     Turkeylegs, Lawrence; M; 7-1906; F; S; Son [Name James in 1926.]

1223; 1205;     Twin, Louis James; M; 12-1887[?]; F; M; Head [Birth year 1889 in 1926.]
1224; 1206;     Twin, Bessie; F; 3-1886; F; M; Wife
1225; 1207;     Twin, Margaret; F; 4-1918; F; S; Dau
       1208;     Twin, Edna; F; 7-1924; F; S; Dau Died 5-1-1929

1226; 1209;     Twobirds, Peter; M; 5-1878; F; M; Head

Census of the __Northern Cheyenne__ tribe of the __Tongue River Agency__ jurisdiction as of __June 30, 1929__ taken by __C.B. Lohmiller__, Superintendent.

**Key:** Present Number; Last Number; Indian Name; English Name; Sex; Month, Year, of Birth; Degree of Blood "F-Fullblood, M-Mixed Blood"; Marital Status; Relationship;

| | |
|---|---|
| 1227; 1210; | Twobirds, Lenora; F; 7-1872; F; M; Wife |
| 1228; 1211; | Twobirds, Jacob; M; 1-1901; F; S; Son |
| 1212; | Twobirds, Walter; M; 8-1908[?]; F; S; Son Died 6-15-1929 |
| | |
| 1229; 1213; | Twobulls, Martin; M; 7-1891; F; M; Head |
| 1230; 1214; | Twobulls, Eleanor; F; 5-1900; F; M; Wife |
| 1231; 1215; | Twobulls, William; M; 9-1920; F; S; Son |
| 1232; 1216; | Twobulls, Alice; F; 8-1927; F; S; Dau |
| | |
| 1233; 1217; | Twobulls, Kate; F; 8-1865; F; Wd; Head |
| | |
| 1234; 1218; | Twofeathers, John; M; 4-1857; F; M; Head |
| 1235; 1219; | Twofeathers, Clara; F; 5-1870; F; M; Wife |
| 1236; 1220; | Twofeathers, Ethel; F; 9-1908; F; S; Dau |
| | |
| 1237; 1221; | Twomoons, Bert; M; 11-1887; F; M; Head |
| 1238; 1222; | Twomoons, Margaret; F; 8-1892; F; M; Wife [Americanhorse] |
| 1239; 1223; | Twomoons, George; M; 1-1920; F; S; Son |
| 1240; 1224; | Twomoons, Austin; M; 2-1927; F; S; Son |
| | |
| 1241; 1225; | Twomoons, John; M; 4-1855; F; Wd; Head |
| | |
| 1242; 1226; | Twomoons, William; M; 5-1884; F; M; Head |
| 1243; 957; | Twomoons, Emma Bites; F; 7-1895[sic]; F; M; Wife [Rowland] |
| | |
| 1244; 1227; | Walkingbear, Charles; M; 5-1876; F; M; Head |
| 1245; 1228; | Walkingbear, Jennie; F; 9-1872; F; M; Wife |
| | |
| 1246; 1229; | Walkingbear, David; M; 6-1897; F; Div.; Head |
| | |
| 1247; 1230; | Walkingbear, Mannie; F; 8-1897; F; Div.; Head [Mamie in 1928.] |
| | |
| 1248; 1231; | Walkingbird, Jane; F; 3-1867; F; Wd; Head |
| 1249; 659; | Lonetravelingwolf, Mabel; F; 6-1910; F; S; G-Dau |
| | |
| 1250; 1232; | Walkinghorse, John; M; 8-1857; F; M; Head |
| 1251; 1233; | Walkinghorse, Olive; F; 9-1866; F; M; Wife |
| | |
| 1252; 1234; | Walksalong, Hugh; M; 4-1885[sic]; F; M; Head |
| 1253; 1235; | Walksalong, Flora; F; 5-1915; F; S; Dau [Previous census 1916-19, Fred son.] |
| 1254; 1236; | Walksalong, Mary Eugenia; F; 6-1920; F; S; Dau |
| 1255; 1237; | Walksalong, Carol; F; 1-10-1928; F; S; Dau |
| | |
| 1256; 1238; | Walkseasy, Nora; F; 3-1864; F; Wd; Head |

Census of the __Northern Cheyenne__ tribe of the __Tongue River Agency__ jurisdiction as of __June 30, 1929__ taken by __C.B. Lohmiller__, Superintendent.

**Key:** Present Number; Last Number; Indian Name; English Name; Sex; Month, Year, of Birth; Degree of Blood "F-Fullblood, M-Mixed Blood"; Marital Status; Relationship;

1257; 1239; walkslast[sic], Richard; M; 3-1856; F; M; Head
1258; 1240; Walkslast, Anne; F; 7-1862[?]; F; M; Wife [Birth year 1859, 1904-22.]
1259; 1241; Walkslast, Frank; M; 3-1908; F; S; G-Son

1260; 1242; Walkslast, James; M; 9-1905; F; S; Head [Clement in 1926.]

1261; 1243; Walksnice, Adolph; M; 4-1878; F; M; Head
1262; 1244; Walksnice, Flora; F; 10-1884; F; M; Wife
1263; 1245; Walksnice, Dick; M; 5-1911; F; S; Son
1264; 1353; Wolfchum, Lily; F; 5-1916; F; S; G-Dau [1917 Census name Betty.]

1265; 1246; Walksnice, John; M; 9-1905; F; M; Head
1266; 1247; Walksnice, Mary; F; 1-1903; F; M; Wife [Crookednose]
1267; 1248; Walksnice, Agnes; F; 8-1926; F; S; Dau

1268; 1249; Wallowing, Rufus; M; 11-1887[?]; F; M; Head [Dustybuffalo, Rollingbull] Name changed to "Wallowing" see 57750-26. [First name Rutherford misspelled starting in 1918.]
1269; 1250; Wallowing, Stella; F; 7-1885; M; M; Wife

1270; 1251; Walters, George; M; 9-1897; M; M; Head

1271; 1252; Wanderingmedicine, William; M; 4-1869[?]; F; M; Head [Birth year 1856 in 1926.]
1272; 652; Wanderingmedicine, Gertrude; F; 4-1875; F; M; Wife [Littleyellowman]

1273; 1253; Waters[sic], Frank; M; 1875; F; M; Head [1904-20, name is Water. Birth year 1877 in 1926.]
1274; 1254; Waters, Joseph; M; 7-1922; M; S; A-Son [1346; 1377; Woodenlegs, Martin; son; 1922; in 1926. S-son in 1928.]

1275; 1255; Weaselbear, Frank; M; 9-1861; F; M; Head
1276; 1256; Weaselbear, Mary; F; 2-1870; F; M; Wife

1277; 1258; Weaselbear, Hugh; M; -- 1889; F; M; Head
1278; 1259; Weaselbear, Andrew; M; 4-1915; F; S; Son
1279; 1260; Weaselbear, Busby; M; 7-1922; F; S; Son

1280; 1462; Wheeler, Dewitt Carlton; M; 12-1892; M; M; Head
1281; 1463; Wheeler, Dewitt Philip; M; 11-1916; M; S; Son

1282; 1264; Whirlwind, Thomas; M; 10-1876; F; Div.; Head

Census of the __Northern Cheyenne__ tribe of the __Tongue River Agency__ jurisdiction as of __June 30, 1929__ taken by __C.B. Lohmiller__, Superintendent.

**Key:** Present Number; Last Number; Indian Name; English Name; Sex; Month, Year, of Birth; Degree of Blood "F-Fullblood, M-Mixed Blood"; Marital Status; Relationship;

1283; 1265;   Whirlwind, Rose; F; 12-1892; F; Div.; Head

1284; 1266;   Whistlingelk, Charles; M; 1-1876; F; Div.; Head

1285; 1271;   Whistlingelk, John; M; 4-1904; F; M; Head
1286; 1272;   Whistlingelk, Flora; F; 5-1906; F; M; Wife [Redrobe]
1287; 1273;   Whistlingelk, May; F; 3-1926; F; S; Dau

1288; 1274;   White, Stamper; M; 4-1898; F; M; Head
1289; 1275;   White, Lottie; F; 3-1903; M; M; Wife [Rowland]
1290; 1276;   White, Pearl; F; 8-1923; M; S; Dau
1291; 1277;   White, Ben; M; 12-1926; M; S; Son

1292; 1278;   Whitebear, Joseph; M; -- 1896; F; Div.; Head

1293; 1279;   Whitebird, Frank; M; 2-1902; F; M; Head
1294; 877;   Whitebird, Julia Redwoman; F; 7-1909; F; M; Wife [1926 Nicetalker, Clarice; s-dau; 1909; F. Also s-dau John Chubby.]

1295; 1280;   Whitebird, Lena; F; 10-1855; F; Wd; Head [1904-13, birth year 1855; 1914-23 has birth year as 1885. Corrected in 1924 to 1855. Husband George was born approximately 1852.]

1296; 1281;   Whitebuffalo, John; M; 3-1871; F; M; Head
1297; 1282;   Whitebuffalo, Ella; F; 8-1867; F; M; Wife
1298; 1407;   Woundedeye, Paul; M; 6-1911; M[?]; S; G-Son [1928 listed as fullblood.]

1299; 1283;   Whitecrane, Leo; M; 6-1896; F; M; Head [Birth year 1895 in 1928.]
1300; 1284;   Whitecrane, Ella; F; 7-1901; F; M; Wife [Littlebird]
1301; 656;[sic]   Littlebird, Harry; M; 8-1918; F; S; S-son
1302; 566;   Littlebird, James; M; 7-1919; F; S; S-son [Previous #1274; Littlebird, Elsie; s-dau; birth year 1920; F in 1926.]
1303; 1285;   Whitecrane, Victor; son; June 1924; M.
1304;   Whitecrane, Eva; F; 12-5-1928; F; S; Dau

   1286;   Whitecrane, Charles; M;; 4-1876; F; Wd[sic]; Head Died 1-20-1928

1305; 1287;   Whitecrow, Alfred; M; 12-1910; F; S; Head [Teddy Redcherries-Fthr.]

1306; 1288;   Whitedirt, Arthur; M; 4-1875; F; M; Head
1307; 1289;   Whitedirt, Maggie; F; 6-1875[sic]; F; M; Wife [1905-1919 birth year 1872.]
1308; 1290;   Whitedirt, Jennie; F; 2-1911; F; S; Dau

Census of the __Northern Cheyenne__ tribe of the __Tongue River Agency__ jurisdiction as of __June 30, 1929__ taken by __C.B. Lohmiller__, Superintendent.
**Key:** Present Number; Last Number; Indian Name; English Name; Sex; Month, Year, of Birth; Degree of Blood "F-Fullblood, M-Mixed Blood"; Marital Status; Relationship;

1309; 1291; Whitedirt, Charlie; M; 6-1905; F; M; Head
1310; 1292; Whitedirt, Julia W.E.; F; 7-1909[?]; F; M; Wife [Whistlingelk]
1311; Whitedirt, Leona; F; 12-7-1928; F; S; Dau

1312; 1293; Whitefrog, Nellie; F; 5-1861; F; Wd; Head

1313; 1294; Whitehawk, Emma; F; 9-1883; F; Wd; Head
1314; 1295; Whitehawk, Verlie; F; 3-1918; F; S; Dau

1315; 1296; Whitehaw[sic], Mary; F; 7-1858[sic]; F; Wd; Head [1904-18 birth year 1838.]

1316; 1297; Whitehawk, Charles John; M; 4-1899[?]; F; M; Head [1905-09 Name is Chase. Years 1905-13 birth year 1898. 1914-16 birth year 1889.]
1317; 1298; Whitehawk, Mary; F; 9-1919; F; S; Dau
1318; 1299; Whitehawk, Marguerite; F; 11-1920; F; S; Dau [Same #1251 John, 1922-25, son, M.; Same prev., #1289 Emma; dau; 1922 in 1926.]

1319; 1300; Whitehorse, George; M; 2-1850; F; Wd[sic]; Head

1320; 1301; Whitemoon, George; M; 11-1854; F; M; Head [Birth year 1851 in 1926.]

1321; 1302; Whitemoon, Hugh; M; 4-1881; F; S; Head

1322; 1305; Whitewolf, Frank; M; 3-1847; F; M; Head
1323; 1306; Whitewolf, Julia; F; 7-1854; F; M; Wife
1307; Whitewolf, Anne Lucy; F; 4-1904; F; S; Dau Die Dec. 29-1928

1324; 1308; Whitewolf, Charles Isadore; M; 8-1890; F; M; Head [Birth year 1887 in 1926.]
1325; 1309; Whitewolf, Belle; F; 5-1902; F; M; Wife
1326; 1310; Whitewolf, Joseph; M; 3-1921; F; S; Son
1327; 1311; Whitewolf, George; M; 6-1923; F; S; Son
1328; 1312; Whitewolf, Fred; M; 2-20-1928; F; S; Son

1329; 360; Whitewolf, Susie G.H.; F; 4-1909; F; m; Head [Grasshopper; Dau. of Mrs. Stanley Lamewoman.]

1313; Whitewolf, Maude; F; 10-1891; F; M; Head Died 3-25-1929 [Shields]
1330; 1314; Whitewolf, Everett; M; 3-1914; F; S; Son
1331; 1315; Whitewolf, Carrie; F; 6-1916; F; S; Dau [Philip son, M., 1920 census.]
1332; 1316; Whitewolf, Wilson; M; 5-1919[?]; F; S; Son [1919-20 birth year 1918.]
1333; 1317; Whitewolf, Thomas; M; 11-1921; F; S; Son
1334; 1318; Whitewolf, Martin Owen; M; 2-1923; F; S; Son

Census of the __Northern Cheyenne__ tribe of the __Tongue River Agency__ jurisdiction as of __June 30, 1929__ taken by __C.B. Lohmiller__, Superintendent.

**Key:** Present Number; Last Number; Indian Name; English Name; Sex; Month, Year, of Birth; Degree of Blood "F-Fullblood, M-Mixed Blood"; Marital Status; Relationship;

1335; 1319;     Whitewolf, Calvin Mexican; M; 1-1925; F; S; Son [Clara dau, F., 1925 census, same #.]

1336; 1320;     Wildhog, Bird; M; 6-1869; F; M; Head
1337; 1321;     Wildhog, Lydia; F; 10-1872; f; M; Wife
1338; 1324;     Wildhog, Anne; F; 9-1895; F; S; Dau
1339; 1325;     Wildhog, John; M; 10-1898; F; S; Son
1340; 1326;     Wildhog, Vida[sic]; F; 3-1905[?]; F; S; Dau [Viola in 1906-25. Shows as 2 months old in 1906 yet majority of census years show the year of birth as 1907.]
1341; 1323;     Wildhog, Julia; F; 8-1913; F; S; Dau [Susie in 1926. Birth month June in 1928.]
1342; 1327;     Wildhog, Mary Anne; F; 12-1903; F; S; Dau [Birth date 1905 in 1926.]
1343; 1328;     Wildhog, Opal; F; 1-1925; F; S; G-Dau Dau of 1342

1344; 1329;     Wilson, Martha; F; 5-1894; M; M; Head
1345; 1330;     Wilson, Arthur; M; 9-1918; M; S; Son [1919 name James Jr.]
1346; 1331;     Wilson, Esther Martha; F; 8-1920; M; S; Dau [Birth month September in 1928.]
1347; 1332;     Wilson, Alice; F; 7-1921; M; S; Dau [#1324 in 1926 was Josephine.]
1348; 1333;     Wilson, Florence; F; 9-1922; M; S; Dau
1349; 1334;     Wilson, Josephine; F; 11-1924; M; S; Dau
1350; 1335;     Wilson, James Jr.; M; 12-1926; M; S; Son
1351;           Wilson, George; M; 4-24-1929; M; S; Son

1352; 1336;     Wolf, William; M; 4-1872; F; M; Head
1353; 1337;     Wolf, Rosa; F; 5-1877; F; M; Wife [nee Crow / Bigbeaver.]
1354; 1338;     Wolf, Fannie Lucy; F; 3-1916; F; S; Dau

1355; 1339;     Wolfblack, Dallas; M; 4-1882[?]; F; M; Head [1904-14 birth year 1885; 1915-23, 1872; 1924-28, 1882.]
1356; 1340;     Wolfblack, Rosa; F; 6-1890; F; M; Wife [Whitemoon; Rose in 1928.]
1357; 1341;     Wolfblack, Gladys; F; 12-1915; F; S; Dau
1358; 1342;     Wolfblack, Oran; M; 4-1924; F; S; Son
1359;           Wolfblack, Mary; F; 4-8-1929; F; S; Dau

1360; 1343;     Wolfchief, Harshey; M; 8-1852; F; M; Head
1361; 1344;     Wolfchief, Anna; F; 7-1861[sic]; F; M; Wife [Whiteelk]

1362; 1345;     Wolfchief, Josie; F; 7-1843; F; Wd; Head

1363; 1346;     Wolfchief, Richard; M; 4-1892; F; M; Head
1364; 1347;     Wolfchief, Flora; M; 9-1891; F; M; Wife
1365; 1348;     Wolfchief, Alice; F; 11-1912; F; S; Dau

Census of the __Northern Cheyenne__ tribe of the __Tongue River Agency__
jurisdiction as of __June 30, 1929__ taken by __C.B. Lohmiller__, Superintendent.

**Key:** Present Number; Last Number; Indian Name; English Name; Sex; Month, Year, of Birth; Degree of Blood "F-Fullblood, M-Mixed Blood"; Marital Status; Relationship;

| | |
|---|---|
| 1366; 1349; | Wolfchief, Ann; F; 5-1927; F; S; Dau |
| 1367; | Wolfchief, Norman; M; 3-7-1929; F; S; Son |

1368; 1350;  Wolfchum, Paul; M; 10-1893; F; M; Head [Birth year 1890 in 1926.]
1369; 1351;  Wolfchum, Bessie L. Sun[sic]; F; 6-1890; F; M; Wife [Littlesun in 1927.]
1370; 1352;  Wolfchum, Walker; M; 12-1926; F; S; Son
1371;        Wolfchum, John; M; 11-10-1928; F; S; Son

1372; 1354;  Wolfear, Willis; M; 1-1884; F; M; Head
1373; 1355;  Wolfear, Sophia; F; 5-1872; F; M; Wife

[?]   1356;  Wolfname, Paul; M; 12-1886; F; M; Head
1374; 1357;  Wolfname, Martha; F; 6-1910; F; S; Dau
1375; 1358;  Wolfname, Henry; M; 9-1912; F; S; Son
1376; 1359;  Wolfname, Wilbur Paul; M; 10-1921; F; S; Son

1377; 1360;  Wolfname, William; M; 1-1854; F; M; Head
1378; 1361;  Wolfname, Bessie; F; 5-1854; F; M; Wife
1379; 1362;  Wolfname, Grace; F; 6-1916; F; S; G-Dau Dau of 436.

1380; 1363;  Wolfroads[sic], Mack; M; 7-1878; F; M; Head
1381; 1364;  Wolfroads, Maude; F; 7-1910; F; S; Dau
1382; 1365;  Wolfroads, Rose Charlotte; F; 1-1914; F; S; Dau [Norman, son, M., same # 1922-23. Birth year 1920 in 1926. Name Rosa in 1927.]

1383; 1366;  Wolftooth, Young; M; 11-1881; F; M; Head
1384; 1367;  Wolftooth, Mary; F; 5-1918; M; S; Dau
1385; 1368;  Wolftooth, Norman; M; 7-1920; M; S; Son
1386; 1369;  Wolftooth, Doris; F; 11-1925; M; S; Dau
1387;        Wolftooth, Wayne; M; 5-30-1928; M; S; Son

1388; 1370;  Wolfvoice, Grover; M; 4-1890; F; M; Head
1389; 1371;  Wolfvoice, Jennie Brady; F; 5-1882[sic]; F; M; Wife [1904-1922 birth year 1888.]
1390; 1372;  Wolfvoice, Anne; F; 2-1918; F; S; Dau
1391; 1373;  Wolfvoice, Dewey; M; 3-1927; F; S; Son

1392; 1374;  Womanleggins, Edward; M; 4-1888; F; M; Head
1393; 1375;  Womanleggins, Mannie[sic]; F; 11-1891; F; M; Wife [Lamewoman]
1394; 1376;  Womanleggins, Mabel; F; 8-1915; F; S; S-Dau (Badhorses) [1917-20 son, Junior, M.; Name is June in 1926.]
1395;  522;  Lamewoman, Mary; F; 8-1917; F; S; S-dau. [Same previous number name Minnie birth year 1916. Has a sister named Mary #510 birth year 1914.]

1396; 1377;  Woodenlegs[sic], Richard; M; 8-1859; F; M; Head

Census of the __Northern Cheyenne__ tribe of the __Tongue River Agency__ jurisdiction as of __June 30, 1929__ taken by __C.B. Lohmiller__, Superintendent.

**Key:** Present Number; Last Number; Indian Name; English Name; Sex; Month, Year, of Birth; Degree of Blood "F-Fullblood, M-Mixed Blood"; Marital Status; Relationship;

1397; 1378;    Woodenlegs, Sophia; F; 5-1859[sic]; F; M; Wife

1398; 1379;    Woodenlegs[sic], Tom; M; 7-1887; M; M; Head (Seminole)
1399; 1380;    Woodenlegs, Jessie; F; 11-1905[sic]; F; M; Wife [Spottedelk; shows 6mo., 1908 census.]
1400; 1381;    Woodenlegs, John; M; 11-1909; M; S; Son
1401; 1382;    Woodenlegs, Mabel; F; 3-1927; M; S; Dau

1402; 1382;[sic]  Woodenthigh, Arthur; M; 11-1883; F; M; Head
1403; 1384;    Woodenthigh, Eva; F; 12-1887; F; M; Wife
1404; 1385;    Woodenthigh, Esther; F; 4-1910; F; S; Dau
1405; 1386;    Woodenthigh, Alice; F; 2-1914; F; S; Dau
1406; 1387;    Woodenthigh, Peter; M; 5-1918; F; S; A-Son [Birth year 1916 in 1926.]

1407; 1388;    Woodenthigh, Chester; M; 9-1884; M; M; Head [Fullblood in 1928.]

1408; 1389;    Woodenthigh, Lena; F; 9-1890; F; M; Head
1409; 1390;    Woodenthigh, Philip; M; 5-1915; F; S; Son
1410; 1391;    Woodenthigh, John; M; 6-1916; F; S; Son
1411; 1392;    Woodenthigh, Melvin; M; 11-1923; F; S; Son

1412; 1393;    Woodpecker, James; M; 3-1901; F; M; Head
1413; 1394;    Woodpecker, Mary; F; 5-1904; M; M; Wife [Littlewhiteman]

1414; 1395;    Woodpecker, Donald Charles; M; 7-1909; F; S; Head

1415; 1396;    Woundedeye, Davis; M; 6-1885; F; M; Head
1416; 1397;    Woundedeye, Susie May; F; 8-1903; F; M; Wife
1417; 1398;    Woundedeye, Milton; M; 4-1920; F; S; Son
1418; 1399;    Woundedeye, Veta; F; 1-1927; F; S; Dau

1419; 1400;    Woundedeye, Ford; M; 4-1882; F; M; Head
1420; 1401;    Woundedeye, Florence; F; May 1890; F; M; Wife
1421; 1402;    Woundedeye, Winfield; M; 4-1909; F; S; Son [Birth year 1908 in 1927.]
1422; 1403;    Woundedeye, Victoria; F; 1-1922; F; S; Dau
1423; 1404;    Woundedeye, Ruth; F; 4-1927; F; S; Dau

1424; 1405;    Woundedeye, Laura; F; 11-1909; F; S; Head
1425; 1406;    Woundedeye, Hayes; M; 6-26-1928; F; S; Son

1426; 1408;    Yellowfox, William; hsbd; May 1900; M. F
1427; 1409;    Yellowfox, Margaret; wife; Mar. 1905; F. F [Yellownose]
                Yellowfox, Baby; F; 9-8-1928; F; S; Dau Died 4-28- 1929

Census of the __Northern Cheyenne__ tribe of the __Tongue River Agency__
jurisdiction as of __June 30, 1929__ taken by __C.B. Lohmiller__, Superintendent.

**Key:** Present Number; Last Number; Indian Name; English Name; Sex; Month, Year, of Birth; Degree of Blood "F-Fullblood, M-Mixed Blood"; Marital Status; Relationship;

1428; 1410;  Yelloweagle, Kate; F; 4-1852; F; Wd; Head

1429; 1411;  Yelloweyes, Abram; M; 7-1874; F; M; Head
1430; 1412;  Yelloweyes, Nora; F; 2-1877; F; M; Wife

1431; 1413;  Yelloweyes, Oliver; M; 7-1901; F; M; Head
1432; 1414;  Yelloweyes, Gertrude; F; 5-1905[?]; F; M; Wife [Brownbird]
1433; 1415;  Yelloweyes, Mary; F; 11-1924; F; S; Dau
[1416];  Yelloweyes, Ruth; F; 11-6-1927; F; S; Dau

1434; 1417;  Yellowfox, Robert; M; 7-1875; F; M; Head
1435; 1418;  Yellowfox, Carrie; F; 11-1882; F; M; Wife
1436; 1419;  Yellowfox, Frank; M; 7-1901; F; S; Son
1437; 1420;  Yellowfox, Charles; M; 10-1908; F; S; Son

1438; 1422;  Yellownose, Robert; M; 9-1857[?]; F; M; Head [Birth year 1865 in 1926. Birth year 1859 in 1928.]
1423;  Yellownose, Anne; F; 5[?]-1863[?]; F; M; Wife Died 3-10-1929 [Birth year 1867; Birth month March in 1928.]

1439; 1424;  Yellownose, George; M; 11-1896; F; M; Head [Birth year 1895. 1904-17.]
1440; 1425;  Yellownose, Mary; F; 7-1927; F; S; Dau

1441; 1426;  Yellowrobe, Charles; M; 6-1892; F; M; Head
1442; 1427;  Yellowrobe, Alice; F; 5-1898; F; M; Wife
1443; 1428;  Yellowrobe, Ruth; F; 3-1917; F; S; Dau [Name Ruana in 1926.]
1444; 1429;  Yellowrobe, Martha; F; 1-1926; F; S; Dau
Yellowrobe, Alfred; M; 5-12-1929; F; S; Son Died 5-14-1929

1445; 1430;  Yellowrobe, Jasper; M; 12-1894; F; M; Head
1446; 1303;  Yellowrobe, Jean W.S.; F; 7-1899; F; M; Wife [Whiteshirt]
1447; 1304;  Yellowrobe, Caroline W.S.; F; 11-1921; F; S; S-Dau [Name Alice in 1926.]
1448;  Yellowrobe, Moses; M; 2-7-1929; F; S; Son

1449; 1432;  Yellowrobe, William; M; 10-1865; F; M; Head
1450; 1433;  Yellowrobe, Minnie; F; 1-1857; F; M; Wife [Birth year 1859 in 1926.]
1431;  Yellowrobe, Adolph; M; 11-1900; F; S; Son Died 10-24-1928

1451; 1434;  Youngbear, George; M; 8-1882; F; M; Head
1452; 1435;  Youngbear, Cora; F; 7-1888[?]; M; M; Wife [Birth year 1890. 1904-1919.]
1453; 1436;  Youngbear, Arthur; M; 8-1913; M; S; Son

Census of the __Northern Cheyenne__ tribe of the __Tongue River Agency__ jurisdiction as of __June 30, 1929__ taken by __C.B. Lohmiller__, Superintendent.

**Key:** Present Number; Last Number; Indian Name; English Name; Sex; Month, Year, of Birth; Degree of Blood "F-Fullblood, M-Mixed Blood"; Marital Status; Relationship;

1454; 1437;    Youngbear, Ralph; M; 10-1921[sic]; M; S; Son [Shows up in 1920. Born 1919.]
1455; 1438;    Youngbear, Mary; F; 12-20-1927; M; S; Dau
                Youngbear, Baby; F; 9-25-1928; M; S; Dau Died 9-26-1928

1456; 1439;    Youngbird, James; M; 9-1857; F; M; Head
1457; 1440;    Youngbird, Clara; F; 5-1863; F; M; Wife

1458; 1441;    Youngbird, John; M; 9-1884; F; M; Head
1459; 1442;    Youngbird, Anne; F; 2-1885; F; M; Wife [Looksbehind]
1460; 1443;    Youngbird, Carl James; M; 4-1912; F; S; Son [Birth year 1923 in 1926.]

1261; 1444;    Schaffer, Letha E.; F; 4-1913; M; M; Head [Son, Carl in 1916 Census. Eastman in 1927]

CENSUS OF NORTHERN CHEYENNE

-of-

TONGUE RIVER RESERVATION, MONT.

April 1, 1930,

TONGUE RIVER AGENCY,

C. B. Lohmiller, Superintendent.

CENSUS OF THE
TONGUE RIVER RESERVATION
OF the
TONGUE RIVER JURISDICTION
AS OF
APRIL 1, 1930

Original

Schedule 1029 drp

Cheyenne

Census of the __Tongue River__ reservation of the __Tongue River__ jurisdiction, as of __April 1__, 1930, taken by __C. B. Lohmiller__, Superintendent.

**Key:** Number; NAME: Surname, Given; Sex; Age At Last Birthday; Tribe; Degree of Blood; Marital Status; Relationship To Head of Family; At Jurisdiction Where Enrolled (Yes or No); At Another Jurisdiction; ELSEWHERE: Post office, County, State; Ward (Yes or No); Allotment, Annuity, and Identification Numbers.

1; Americanhorse, Austin; M; 58; Cheyenne; F; M; Head; Yes; Yes; No Al #, No An #, No Id #
2; Americanhorse, Maude; F; 47; Cheyenne; F; M; Wife; Yes; Yes
3; Americanhorse, Lucy May; F; 19; Cheyenne; F; S; Dau; Yes; Yes
4; Americanhorse, George; M; 15; Cheyenne; F; S; Son; Yes; Yes [Texas]

5; Americanhorse, George; M; 48; Cheyenne; F; Wd[sic]; Head; Yes; Yes
6; Americanhorse, Bessie; F; 24; Cheyenne; F; S; Dau; Yes; Yes
7; Americanhorse, James; M; 18; Cheyenne; M; S; Son; Yes; Yes
8; Americanhorse, Marie; F; 15; Cheyenne; F; S; Dau; Yes; Yes
9; Americanhorse, Lucy; F; 11; Cheyenne; F; S; Dau; Yes; Yes

10; Americanhorse, Walter; M; 39; Cheyenne; F; M; Head; No; Cheyenne & Arap. Ag, Okla; Yes

11; Americanhorse, Willis; M; 37; Cheyenne; F; M; Head; Yes; Yes
12; Americanhorse, Margaret; F; 37; Cheyenne; F; M; Wife; Yes; Yes
13; Americanhorse, Ernest; M; 18; Cheyenne; F; S; Son; Yes; Yes
14; Americanhorse, Martha L.; F; 15; Cheyenne; F; S; Dau; Yes; Yes
15; Americanhorse, Madge; F; 13; Cheyenne; F; S; Dau; Yes; Yes
16; Americanhorse, Grace J.; F; 11; Cheyenne; F; S; Dau; Yes; Yes
17; Twomoons, Austin; M; 2; Cheyenne; F; S; S-Son; Yes; Yes

18; Ant, James; M; 26; Cheyenne; F; M; Head; Yes; Yes
19; Ant, Hannah; F; 29; Cheyenne; F; M; Wife; Yes; Yes [Highwalking]
20; Ant, Bertha; F; 5; Cheyenne; F; S; Dau; Yes; Yes
21; Ant, Thelma; F; 1; Cheyenne; F; S; Dau; Yes; Yes

22; Ant, Walter; M; 50; Cheyenne; F; M; Head; Yes; Yes
23; Ant, Helen; F; 47; Cheyenne; F; M; Wife; Yes; Yes
24; Ant, June; F; 10; Cheyenne; F; S; Dau; Yes; Yes

25; Atwood, James; M; 39; Cheyenne; F; M; Head; Yes; Yes [Twentystands]
26; Atwood, Cecelia; F; 32; Cheyenne; F; M; Wife; Yes; Yes
27; Atwood, Mary; F; 15; Cheyenne; F; S; Dau; Yes; Yes
28; Atwood, Herbert; M; 7; Cheyenne; F; S; Son; Yes; Yes
29; Atwood, David; M; 8/12; Cheyenne; F; S; Son; Yes; Yes

30; Baldeagle, Hugh; M; 71; Cheyenne; F; M; Head; Yes; Yes
31; Baldeagle, Minnie; F; 70; Cheyenne; F; M; Wife; Yes; Yes

32; Bearchum, Frank; M; 29; Cheyenne; 1/4; S; Head; Yes; Yes

33; Bearcomesout, Charles; M; 49; Cheyenne; F; M; Head; Yes; Yes
34; Bearcomesout, Mary; F; 23; Cheyenne; F; M; Wife; Yes; Yes

Census of the **Tongue River** reservation of the **Tongue River** jurisdiction, as of **April 1**, 1930, taken by **C. B. Lohmiller**, Superintendent.

**Key:** Number; NAME: Surname, Given; Sex; Age At Last Birthday; Tribe; Degree of Blood; Marital Status; Relationship To Head of Family; At Jurisdiction Where Enrolled (Yes or No); At Another Jurisdiction; ELSEWHERE: Post office, County, State; Ward (Yes or No); Allotment, Annuity, and Identification Numbers.

35; Bearcomesout, Harold; M 22; Cheyenne; F; S; Son; Yes; Yes
36; Bearcomesout, Pius; M; 14; Cheyenne; F; S; Son; Yes; Yes
37; Bearcomesout, Herbert; M; 1; Cheyenne; F; S; Son; Yes; Yes

38; Bearquiver, Edward; M; 48; Cheyenne; F; Wd[sic]; Head; Yes; Yes
39; Bearquiver, Claude; M; 13; Cheyenne; F; S; Son; Yes; Yes
40; Bearquiver, James; M; 9; Cheyenne; F; S; Son; Yes; Yes
41; Bearquiver, Martin; M; 7; Cheyenne; F; S; Son; Yes; Yes

42; Beartusk, Jerome; M; 44; Cheyenne; F; M; Head; Yes; Yes
43; Beartusk, Ida S.; F; 31; Cheyenne; F; M; Wife; Yes; Yes

44; Beartusk, Lucy; F; 39; Cheyenne; -1/4; D; Head; No; Lodgegrass ~~Town~~, Big Horn, Mont.; Yes
45; Beartusk, Alice; F; 12; Cheyenne; 1/4+; S; Dau; No; Lodgrass[sic] ~~town~~; Big Horn, Mont; Yes
46; Beartusk, Gladys; F; 11; Cheyenne; 1/4+; S; Dau; No; Lodgrass ~~town~~; Big Horn, Mont; Yes [Nellie]
47; Beartusk, Kenneth; M; 9; Cheyenne; 1/4+; S; Son; No; Lodgegrass ~~town~~; Big Horn, Mont; Yes
48; Beartusk, Bertha; F; 6; Cheyenne; 1/4+; S; Dau; No; Lodgegrass ~~town~~; Big Horn, Mont; Yes
49; Beartusk, Jerome, Jr; M; 4; Cheyenne; 1/4+; S; Son; No; Lodgegrass ~~town~~; Big Horn, Mont; Yes

50; Beaverheart, Thomas; M; 66; Cheyenne; F; M; Head; Yes; Yes
51; Beaverheart, Nellie; F; 73; Cheyenne; F; M; Wife; Yes; Yes
52; Beaverheart, David; M; 40; Cheyenne; F; S; Son; Yes; Yes [Name Davis in 1926.]

53; Beirdneau, Adeline; F; 31; Cheyenne; -1/4; Wd; Head; Yes; Yes
54; Beirdneau, Betty B.; F; 7; Cheyenne; -1/4; S; Dau; Yes; Yes
55; Beirdneau, Barbara M.; F; 4; Cheyenne; -1/4; S; Dau; Yes; Yes
56; Beirdneau, Albert L.; M; 2; Cheyenne; -1/4; S; Son; Yes; Yes

57; BeMent, Emma; F; 28; Cheyenne; -1/4; M; Head; Yes; Yes [Burns]
58; BeMent, Jacqueline; F; 7; Cheyenne; -1/4; S; Dau; Yes; Yes
59; BeMent, Jessie; M; 5; Cheyenne; -1/4; S; Son; Yes; Yes [Joseph in 1925]
60; BeMent, Geraldine; F; 3; Cheyenne; -1/4; S; Dau; Yes; Yes
61; BeMent, Celia C.; F; 2; Cheyenne; -1/4; S; Dau; Yes; Yes

62; Bigback, Charles; M; 67; Cheyenne; F; M: Head; Yes; Yes
63; Bigback, Clara; F; 60; Cheyenne; F; M; Wife; Yes; Yes
64; Bigback, Stephen; M; 38; Cheyenne; F; S; Son; Yes; Yes
65; Redowl, Mabel; F; 83; Cheyenne; F; Wd; Mother-in-law; Yes; Yes

Census of the **Tongue River** reservation of the **Tongue River** jurisdiction, as of **April 1**, 1930, taken by **C. B. Lohmiller**, Superintendent.

**Key:** Number; NAME: Surname, Given; Sex; Age At Last Birthday; Tribe; Degree of Blood; Marital Status; Relationship To Head of Family; At Jurisdiction Where Enrolled (Yes or No); At Another Jurisdiction; ELSEWHERE: Post office, County, State; Ward (Yes or No); Allotment, Annuity, and Identification Numbers.

66; Bigback, James; M; 35; Cheyenne; F; M; Head; Yes; Yes
67; Bigback, Jennie; F; 31; Cheyenne; F; M; Wife; Yes; Yes
68; Bigback, Gladys; F; 9; Cheyenne; F; S; Dau; Yes; Yes
69; Bigback, Robert; M; 6; Cheyenne; F; S; Son; Yes; Yes
70; Bigback, Marie; F; 7/12; Cheyenne; F; S; Dau; Yes; Yes

71; Bigback, John; M; 26; Cheyenne; F; M; Head; Yes; Yes [Henry in 1919.]
72; Bigback, Nina S.E.; F; 23; Cheyenne; F; M; Wife; Yes; Yes

73; Bigbeaver, August; M; 69; Cheyenne; F; Wd[sic]; Head; Yes; Yes

74; Bigcrow, Andrew; M; 76; Cheyenne; F; M; Head; Yes; Yes
75; Bigcrow, Jennie; F; 41; Cheyenne; F; M; Wife; Yes; Yes

76; Bigfoot, Davis; M; 31; Cheyenne; F; M; Head; Yes; Yes
77; Bigfoot, Lucy; F; 29; Cheyenne; F; M; Wife; Yes; Yes
78; Bigfoot, Alice; F; 9; Cheyenne; F; S; Dau; Yes; Yes [Martha in 1925 & 1926.]
79; Bigfoot, May; F; 6; Cheyenne; F; S; Dau; Yes; Yes [Mary in 1929]

80; Bigfoot, John; M; 49; Cheyenne; F; M; Head; No; Cheyenne & Arap Ag, Okla; Yes

81; Bigfoot, White; M; 54; Cheyenne; F; M; Head; Yes; Yes
82; Bigfoot, Louisa; F; 44; Cheyenne; F; M; Wife; Yes; Yes
83; Bigfoot, Louis Paul; M; 18; Cheyenne; F; S; Son; Yes; Yes

84; Bigheadman, Benjamin; M; 40; Cheyenne; F; M; Head; Yes; Yes
85; Bigheadman, Julia; F; 35; Cheyenne; F; M; Wife; Yes; Yes
86; Bigheadman, Gladys; F; 11; Cheyenne; F; S; Dau; Yes; Yes [Lucille in 1926]
87; Bigheadman, Laura; F; 2; Cheyenne; F; S; Dau; Yes; Yes

88; Bigheadman, Blair; M; 37; Cheyenne; F; M; Head; Yes; Yes
89; Bigheadman, Clara; F; 29; Cheyenne; F; M; Wife; Yes; Yes
90; Bigheadman, Wm. Grover; M; 10; Cheyenne; F; S; Son; Yes; Yes
91; Bigheadman, August; M; 7; Cheyenne; F; S; Son; Yes; Yes
92; Bigheadman, Julia; F; 5; Cheyenne; F; S; Dau; Yes; Yes
93; Bigheadman, James; M; 2/12; Cheyenne; F; S; Son; Yes; Yes

94; Bigheadman, John; M; 80; Cheyenne; F; M; Head; Yes; Yes
95; Bigheadman, Nellie; F; 76; Cheyenne; F; M; Wife; Yes; Yes

96; Bigheadman, William; M; 43; Cheyenne; F; M; Head; Yes; Yes [Whitehorse]
97; Bigheadman, Nellie; F; 38; Cheyenne; F; M; Wife; Yes; Yes

Census of the **Tongue River** reservation of the **Tongue River** jurisdiction, as of **April 1**, 1930, taken by **C. B. Lohmiller**, Superintendent.

**Key:** Number; NAME: Surname, Given; Sex; Age At Last Birthday; Tribe; Degree of Blood; Marital Status; Relationship To Head of Family; At Jurisdiction Where Enrolled (Yes or No); At Another Jurisdiction; ELSEWHERE: Post office, County, State; Ward (Yes or No); Allotment, Annuity, and Identification Numbers.

98; Bigheadman, Richard; M; 20; Cheyenne; F; S; Son; Yes; Yes [Richard Rowland]
99; Bigheadman, Grace M; F; 11; Cheyenne; F; S; Dau; Yes; Yes
100; Bigheadman, Marjorie; F; 4; Cheyenne; F; S; Dau; Yes; Yes
101; Bigheadman, Susie D.; F; 3; Cheyenne; F; S; Dau; Yes; Yes
102; Bigheadman, Helen E.; F; 2; Cheyenne; F; S; Dau; Yes; Yes

103; Bigleg, Hinton; M; 42; Cheyenne; F; M; Head; Yes; Yes
104; Bigleg, Annie; F; 51; Cheyenne; 1/4+; M; Wife; Yes; Yes
105; Rowland, Claude; M; 26; Cheyenne; 1/4+; S; Step-son; Yes; Yes
106; Rowland, Benjamin; M; 21; Cheyenne; 1/4+; S; Step-son; Yes; Yes

107; Bignose, James; M; 66; Cheyenne; F; Wd; Head; Yes; Yes
108; Bignose, Samuel; M; 38; Cheyenne; F; S; Son; Yes; Yes
109; Bignose, George; M; 31; Cheyenne; F; S; Son; Yes; Yes

110; Bites, James; M; 29; Cheyenne; F; M; Head; Yes; Yes
111; Bites, Sally; F; 29; Cheyenne; F; M; Wife; Yes; Yes [Crazymule]
112; Bites, Florence; F; 3; Cheyenne; F; S; Dau; Yes; Yes
113; Bites, James Jr.; M; 11/12; Cheyenne; F; S; Son; Yes; Yes

114; Bites, Sally; F; 66; Cheyenne; F; Wd; Head; Yes; Yes
115; Russell, Clara; F; 7; Cheyenne; F; S; G-Dau; Yes; Yes
116; Russell, Herman; M; 4; Cheyenne; F; S; G-Son; Yes; Yes

117; Bixby, Benjamin; M; 42; Cheyenne; 1/4+; M; Head; Yes; Yes
118; Bixby, Gertrude; F; 36; Cheyenne; 1/4+; M; Wife; Yes; Yes [Whitepowder 1904-07; Tallwhiteman 1908; Bixby 1909-1929]
119; Bixby, Annie; F; 16; Cheyenne; 1/4+; S; Dau; Yes; Yes
120; Bixby, James; M; 14; Cheyenne; 1/4+; S; Son; Yes; Yes

121; Bixby, Edward; M; 39; Cheyenne; 1/4-; M; Head; Yes; Yes
122; Bixby, Edward G.; M; 7; Cheyenne; -1/4; S; Son; Yes; Yes [1924 Clara, dau; F. 1925-26 Jack.]
123; Bixby, Elsie V.; F; 6; Cheyenne; -1/4; S; Dau; Yes; Yes [Vianne 1925-26.]
124; Bixby, Wm. L.; M; 5; Cheyenne; -1/4; S; Son; Yes; Yes
125; Bixby, Hattie C.; F; 1; Cheyenne; -1/4; S; Dau; Yes; Yes

125; Blackbird, Isaac; M; 66; Cheyenne; F; Wd[sic]; Head; Yes; Yes

127; Blackeagle, William; M; 41; Cheyenne; F; Wd[sic]; Head; Yes; Yes

128; Blackhorse, Alex; M; 32; Cheyenne; F; M; Head; Yes; Yes
129; Blackhorse, Mary; F; 26; Cheyenne; F; M; Wife; Yes; Yes

Census of the **Tongue River** reservation of the **Tongue River** jurisdiction, as of **April 1**, 1930, taken by **C. B. Lohmiller**, Superintendent.

**Key:** Number; NAME: Surname, Given; Sex; Age At Last Birthday; Tribe; Degree of Blood; Marital Status; Relationship To Head of Family; At Jurisdiction Where Enrolled (Yes or No); At Another Jurisdiction; ELSEWHERE: Post office, County, State; Ward (Yes or No); Allotment, Annuity, and Identification Numbers.

130; Blackhorse, Francis; M; 7; Cheyenne; F; S; Son; Yes; Yes [1923-26 name Merton.]
131; Blackhorse, Lafe C.; M; 8/12; Cheyenne; F; S; Son; Yes; Yes

132; Blackhorse, Rueben[sic]; M; 76; Cheyenne; F; M; Head; Yes; Yes
133; Blackhorse, Lena; F; 53; Cheyenne; F; M; Wife; Yes; Yes
134; Blackhorse, Anna; F; 16; Cheyenne; F; S; Dau; Yes; Yes [#135, Son, Arthur in 1913-14 Censuses. Name Ada 1915-19. Name Ida 1920-26.]
135; Seminole, Delbert; M; 18; Cheyenne; 1/4-; S; G-Dau[sic]; Yes; Yes
136; Seminole, Hannah; F; 17; Cheyenne; 1/4-; S; G-Dau; Yes; Yes

137; Blackree, Paul; M; 51; Cheyenne; F; M; Head; Yes; Yes
138; Blackree, Jennie; F; 48; Cheyenne; F; M; Wife; Yes; Yes
139; Blackree, Alice; F; 20; Cheyenne; F; D; Dau; Yes; Yes
140; Blackree, Anna; F; 6; Cheyenne; F; S; 6-Dau; Yes; Yes
141; Star, May; F; 27; Cheyenne; F; M; Dau; Yes; Yes
142; Star, Charles; M; 3; Cheyenne; F; S; G-son; Yes; Yes
143; Ironshirt, Nora; F; 79; Cheyenne; F; Wd; S-Mother; Yes; Yes

144; Blackstone, Charles; M; 69; Cheyenne; F; Wd[sic]; Head; Yes; Yes
145; Blackstone, Lena; F; 51; Cheyenne; F; S; S-Dau; Yes; Yes [7/8 blood in 1928.]
146; Blackstone, Arthur; M; 37; Cheyenne; F; M; Son; Yes; Yes
147; Blackstone, Anna K.; F; 19; Cheyenne; F; M; Daughter-in-law; Yes; Yes

148; Blackwolf, Bennie; M; 32; Cheyenne; F; M; Head; Yes; Yes [1904-1923 name Alex.]
149; Blackwolf, Ella; F; 29; Cheyenne; F; M; Wife; Yes; Yes
150; Blackwolf, Henry; M; 10; Cheyenne; F; S; Son; Yes; Yes [1925 Census Thomas.]
151; Blackwolf, James; M; 6; Cheyenne; F; S; Son; Yes; Yes [1925 Census Alfred.]
152; Blackwolf, Ruth; F; 3; Cheyenne; F; S; Dau; Yes; Yes

153; Blackwolf, John; M; 59; Cheyenne; F; M; Head; Yes; Yes
154; Blackwolf, Nellie; F; 55; Cheyenne; F; M; Wife; Yes; Yes
155; Blackwolf, Alex; M; 23; Cheyenne; F; S; Son; Yes; Yes [#156, Name Busby, a brother Alex born 1897 in 1916 census, married in 1917.]
156; Blackwolf, Mary; F; 16; Cheyenne; F; S; Dau; Yes; Yes
157; Wolfname, Martha; F; 19; Cheyenne; F; S; G-Dau; Yes; Yes
158; Wolfname, Henry; M; 17; Cheyenne; F; S; G-son; Yes; Yes
159; Wolfname, Wilbur P.; M; 8; Cheyenne; F; S; G-son; Yes; Yes

160; Blindman, Arthur; M; 61; Cheyenne; F; Wd[sic]; Head; Yes; Yes

Census of the __Tongue River__ reservation of the __Tongue River__ jurisdiction, as of __April 1__, 1930, taken by __C. B. Lohmiller__, Superintendent.

**Key:** Number; NAME: Surname, Given; Sex; Age At Last Birthday; Tribe; Degree of Blood; Marital Status; Relationship To Head of Family; At Jurisdiction Where Enrolled (Yes or No); At Another Jurisdiction; ELSEWHERE: Post office, County, State; Ward (Yes or No); Allotment, Annuity, and Identification Numbers.

161; Bluehawk, Louis; M; 79; Cheyenne; 1/4+; Wd[sic]; Head; Yes; Yes; No Al #, No An #, No Id #

162; Bobtailhorse, Thomas; M; 79; Cheyenne; F; M; Head; Yes; Yes
163; Bobtailhorse, Gertrude; F; 78; Cheyenne; F; M; Wife; Yes; Yes

164; Boxelder, Laura; F; 58; Cheyenne; F; Wd; Head; No; Shoshone Ag & Arap, Wy; Yes

165; Brady, Alex; M; 31; Cheyenne; F; M; Head; Yes; Yes
166; Brady, Josie; F; 27; Cheyenne; F; M; Wife; Yes; Yes [Pine]
167; Brady, Charles; M; 6; Cheyenne; F; S; Son; Yes; Yes

168; Brady, Arthur; M; 89; Cheyenne; F; M; Head; Yes; Yes
169; Brady, Ellen; F; 76; Cheyenne; F; M; Wife; Yes; Yes

170; Brady, George; M; 48; Cheyenne; F; M; Head; Yes; Yes
171; Brady, Flossie; G; 33; Cheyenne; 1/4+; M; Wife; Yes; Yes
172; Brady, Elmore; M; 23; Cheyenne; F; S; Son; Yes; Yes
173; Brady, James H.; M; 17; Cheyenne; F; S; Son; Yes; Yes
174; Brady, Howard; M; 14; Cheyenne; F; S; Son; Yes; Yes
175; Brady, Ramona; F; 12; Cheyenne; F; S; Dau; Yes; Yes
176; Brady, Wilson; M; 11; Cheyenne; F; S; Son; Yes; Yes
177; Brady, Martha; F; 9; Cheyenne; 1/4+; S; Dau; Yes; Yes
178; Brady, Roy; M; 5; Cheyenne; 1/4+; S; Son; Yes; Yes
179; Brady, Pearl; F; 1; Cheyenne; 1/4+; S; Dau; Yes; Yes
180; Flying, Pauline; F; 13; Cheyenne; 1/4+; S; Dau; Yes; Yes [Male, Paul in 1920 #150 under Brady.]

181; Braidedlocks, William; M; 77; Cheyenne; F; Wd[sic]; Head; Yes; Yes

182; Brein, Margaret; F; 25; Cheyenne; -1/4; M; Head; Yes; Yes
183; Brein, Myron; M; 5/12; Cheyenne; 1/4-; S; Son; Yes; Yes

184; Brownbird, Joseph; M; 64; Cheyenne; F; M; Head; Yes; Yes
185; Brownbird, Anna; F; 64; Cheyenne; F; M; Wife; Yes; Yes

186; Buffalohorn, John; M; 68; Cheyenne; F; M; Head; Yes; Yes
187; Buffalohorn, Lena; F; 59; Cheyenne; F; M; Wife; Yes; Yes

188; Buffalochump, Samuel; M; 84; Cheyenne; F; M; Head; Yes; Yes [Buffalohump in 1929]
189; Buffalochump, Nora; F; 81; Cheyenne; F; M; Wife; Yes; Yes

190; Burns, George; M; 35; Cheyenne; -1/4; M; Head; Yes; Yes

Census of the **Tongue River** reservation of the **Tongue River** jurisdiction, as of **April 1**, 1930, taken by **C. B. Lohmiller**, Superintendent.

**Key:** Number; NAME: Surname, Given; Sex; Age At Last Birthday; Tribe; Degree of Blood; Marital Status; Relationship To Head of Family; At Jurisdiction Where Enrolled (Yes or No); At Another Jurisdiction; ELSEWHERE: Post office, County, State; Ward (Yes or No); Allotment, Annuity, and Identification Numbers.

191; Burns, Julia; F; 58; Cheyenne; 1/4+; Wd; Head; Yes; Yes
192; Burns, James C.; M; 21; Cheyenne; -1/4; S; Son; Yes; Yes
193; Burns, Margaret; F; 18; Cheyenne; -1/4; S; Dau; Yes; Yes
194; Burns, Anna G.; F; 16; Cheyenne; -1/4; S; Dau; Yes; Yes
195; BeMent, Clarence; M; 6; Cheyenne; -1/4; S; G-Son; Yes; Yes [Max in 1925. Mickie in 1926.]

196; Burns, Lizzie; F; 57; Cheyenne; -1/4; M; Head; Yes; Yes
197; Burns, Josephine; F; 11; Cheyenne; 1/4-; S; A-Dau; Yes; Yes [Had a Kitty Small in 1925. Adopt-dau., in 1925-26.]

198; Burns, Robert; M; 32; Cheyenne; -1/4; M; Head; Yes; Yes
199; Burns, Phyllis R.; F; 4; Cheyenne; -1/4; S; Dau; Yes; Yes
200; Burns, George E.; M; 7/12; Cheyenne; -1/4; S; Dau; Yes; Yes

201; Cain, Edith S.; F; 20; Cheyenne; -1/4; M; Head; Yes; Yes

202; Callsfirst, Andrew; M; 41; Cheyenne; F; M; Head; Yes; Yes
203; Callsfirst, Jennie; F; 57; Cheyenne; 1/4+; M; Wife; Yes; Yes
204; Woodenleg, Mabel; F; 3; Cheyenne; F; S; Niece; Yes; Yes

205; Chasingbear, Willis; M; 35; Cheyenne; F; M; Head; Yes; Yes
206; Chasingbear, Madge; F; 31; Cheyenne; F; M; Wife; Yes; Yes [Powderface]

207; Chubby, John; M; 54; Cheyenne; F; M; Head; Yes; Yes
208; Chubby, Anne; F; 44; Cheyenne; F; M; Wife; Yes; Yes
209; Chubby, Rhoda; F; 10; Cheyenne; F; S; Dau; Yes; Yes
210; Hairlessbear, Hilda; F; 18; Cheyenne; F; S; S-Dau; Yes; Yes

211; Clubfoot, Floyd; M; 42; Cheyenne; F; M; Head; Yes; Yes
212; Clubfoot, Stella; F; 34; Cheyenne; F; M; Wife; Yes; Yes [Weaselbear]
213; Clubfoot, Norman; M; 13; Cheyenne; F; S; Son; Yes; Yes [1917 shows Norman died in 1916. In 1918-23 Census as born 1916 and alive?]
214; Clubfoot, Flossie; F; 4; Cheyenne; F; S; Dau; Yes; Yes

215; Clubfoot, Frank; M; 39; Cheyenne; F; M; Head; Yes; Yes
216; Clubfoot, Lucy A.; F; 37; Cheyenne; F; M; Wife; Yes; Yes
217; Clubfoot, James; M; 7; Cheyenne; F; S; Son; Yes; Yes
218; Clubfoot, Frank Jr.; M; 3; Cheyenne; F; S; Son; Yes; Yes

219; Clubfoot, John; M; 69; Cheyenne; F; M; Head; Yes; Yes
220; Clubfoot, Minnie; F; 59; Cheyenne; F; M; Wife; Yes; Yes
221; Clubfoot, Willis; M; 38; Cheyenne; F; S; Son; Yes; Yes
222; Clubfoot, Joseph; M; 29; Cheyenne; F; S; Son; Yes; Yes

Census of the __Tongue River__ reservation of the __Tongue River__ jurisdiction, as of __April 1__, 1930, taken by __C. B. Lohmiller__, Superintendent.

**Key:** Number; NAME: Surname, Given; Sex; Age At Last Birthday; Tribe; Degree of Blood; Marital Status; Relationship To Head of Family; At Jurisdiction Where Enrolled (Yes or No); At Another Jurisdiction; ELSEWHERE: Post office, County, State; Ward (Yes or No); Allotment, Annuity, and Identification Numbers.

223; Colhoff, Emma; F; 35; Cheyenne; 1/4+; M; Head; No; Pine Ridge, S.D.; Yes
224; Colhoff, Maxine; F; 13; Cheyenne; 1/4+; S; Dau; No; Pine Ridge, S.D.; Yes
225; Colhoff, Edward; M; 11; Cheyenne; 1/4+; S; Son; No; Pine Ridge, S.D.; Yes
226; Colhoff, Annie G.; F; 9; Cheyenne; 1/4+; S; Dau; No; Pine Ridge, S.D.; Yes
227; Colhoff, William; M; 6; Cheyenne; 1/4+; S; Son; No; Pine Ridge, S.D.; Yes
228; Colhoff, George; M; 3; Cheyenne; 1/4+; S; Son; No; Pine Ridge, S.D.; Yes

229; Cooley, Julia; F; 38; Cheyenne; -1/4; M; Head; Yes; Yes
230; Cooley, Violet; F; 16; Cheyenne; -1/4; S; Dau; Yes; Yes
231; Cooley, Junior; M; 13; Cheyenne; -1/4; S; Son; Yes; Yes
232; Cooley, Francis; M; 7; Cheyenne; -1/4; S; Son; Yes; Yes
233; Cooley, Vera; F; 5; Cheyenne; -1/4; S; Dau; Yes; Yes

234; Crawling, Charles; M; 45; Cheyenne; F; M; Head; Yes; Yes
235; Crawling, Flora; F; 48; Cheyenne; F; M; Wife; Yes; Yes
236; Crawling, Martha; F; 13; Cheyenne; F; S; Dau; Yes; Yes
237 Chasingbear, Laura; F; 13; Cheyenne; F; S; S-dau; Yes; Yes
238; Chasingbear, Robert; M; 5; Cheyenne; F; S; S-dau[sic]; Yes; Yes

239; Crazymule, Eva; F; 20; Cheyenne; F; S; Head; No; Cheyenne & Arap. Ag Okla; Yes [Wyoming in 1926.]

240; Crazymule, James; M; 19; Cheyenne; F; S; Son; Yes; Yes
241; Crazymule, Chas R.; M; 10; Cheyenne; F; S; Son; Yes; Yes [Raymond in 1926.]
242; Crazymule, Xavier; M; 8; Cheyenne; F; S; Son; Yes; Yes

243; Crazymule, John; M; 60; Cheyenne; F; M; Head; Yes; Yes [#234; In 1919 name Joseph, previous #220, birth year 1881. Mixed with another family not in 1920 census.] [Between 1920-22 Census takers mixed up #218 John and #220 Joseph's names and wifes and names.]
244; Crazymule, Jennie; F; 73; Cheyenne; F; M; Wife; Yes; Yes [Issues]

245; Crazymule, Joseph; M; 49; Cheyenne; F; M; Head; Yes; Yes
246; Crazymule, Sarah; F; 56; Cheyenne; F; M; Wife; Yes; Yes
247; Greasydog, Fannie; F; 32; Cheyenne; F; S; S-Dau; Yes; Yes

248; Crook, George; M; 64; Cheyenne; F; M; Head; Yes; Yes
249; Crook, Theresa; F; 64; Cheyenne; F; M; Wife; Yes; Yes

250; Crook, Rosa; F; 64; Cheyenne; F; Wd; Head; Yes; Yes
251; Crook, Albert; M; 29; Cheyenne; F; S; Son; Yes; Yes

252; Crookednose, Nicholas; M; 62; Cheyenne; F; M; Head; Yes; Yes
253; Crookednose, Susie; F; 57; Cheyenne; F; M; Wife; Yes; Yes

Census of the **Tongue River** reservation of the **Tongue River** jurisdiction, as of **April 1**, 1930, taken by **C. B. Lohmiller**, Superintendent.

**Key:** Number; NAME: Surname, Given; Sex; Age At Last Birthday; Tribe; Degree of Blood; Marital Status; Relationship To Head of Family; At Jurisdiction Where Enrolled (Yes or No); At Another Jurisdiction; ELSEWHERE: Post office, County, State; Ward (Yes or No); Allotment, Annuity, and Identification Numbers.

254; Curley, Thomas; M; 40; Cheyenne; F; M; Head; Yes; Yes
255; Curley, Esther; F; 34; Cheyenne; F; M: Wife; Yes; Yes
256; Curley, Ella; F; 5; Cheyenne; F; M[sic]; Dau; Yes; Yes
257; Curley, Hattie; F; 73; Cheyenne; F; Wd; Mother; Yes; Yes

258; Deafy, David; M; 31; Cheyenne; F; M; Head; Yes; Yes [Americanhorse]
259; Deafy; Anna; F; 34; Cheyenne; F; M; Wife; Yes; Yes [Horseroads]
260; Deafy; Willie; M; 12; Cheyenne; F; S; Son; Yes; Yes
261; Deafy, Elsie; F; 4; Cheyenne; F; S; Dau; Yes; Yes
262; Deafy, Irene; F; 9/12; Cheyenne; F; S; Dau; Yes; Yes

263; Deafy, James; M; 59; Cheyenne; F; Wd; Head; Yes; Yes
264; Deafy, Carrie; F; 19; Cheyenne; F; S; Dau; Yes; Yes [Jessie in 1926.]

265; Divesbackward, John; M; 60; Cheyenne; F; Wd[sic]; Head; Yes; Yes [Depending the on census taker they spell Divesbackwards at the end with or without an "s".]
266; Lonebull, Louis; M; 78; Cheyenne; F; Wd[sic]; Brother; Yes; Yes

267; Divesbackward, Rufus; M; 40; Cheyenne; F; M; Head; Yes; Yes
268; Divesbackward, Nancy; F; 48; Cheyenne; F; M; Wife; Yes; Yes
269; Divesbackward, Sam; M; 11; Cheyenne; F; S; Son; Yes; Yes
270; Divesbackward, Strane; M; 9; Cheyenne; F; S; Son; Yes; Yes
271; Divesbackward, Grace; F; 5; Cheyenne; F S; Dau; Yes; Yes
272; Redcherries, Anna; F; 19; Cheyenne; F; S; S-Dau; Yes; Yes
273; Redcherries, Wallace; M; 1; Cheyenne; F; S; G-Son; Yes; Yes
274; Standsout, Sallie; F; 82; Cheyenne; F; Wd; Mother; Yes; Yes

275; Dog, Louis; M; 74; Cheyenne; F; M; Head; Yes; Yes
276; Dog, Maude; F; 64; Cheyenne; F; M; Wife; Yes; Yes

277; Duster, Albert; M; 41; Cheyenne; F; M; Head; Yes; Yes
278; Duster, Vinnie; F; 33; Cheyenne; F; M; Wife; Yes; Yes
279; Duster, Annie; F; 9; Cheyenne; F; S; Dau; Yes; Yes
280; Duster, Bessie; F; 5; Cheyenne; F; S; Dau; Yes; Yes

281; Eaglefeathers, Jacob; M; 55; Cheyenne; F; Wd; Head; Yes; Yes
282; Eaglefeathers, Mildred; F; 9; Cheyenne; F; S; Dau; Yes; Yes

283; Eaglefeathers, Oliver; M; 34; Cheyenne; F; M; Head; Yes; Yes
284; Eaglefeathers, Julia; F; 34; Cheyenne; 1/4+; M; Wife; Yes; Yes
285; Eaglefeathers, Simon; M; 8; Cheyenne; 1/4+; S; Son; Yes; Yes
286; Eaglefeathers, Rosie; F; 4; Cheyenne; 1/4+; S; Dau; Yes; Yes
287; Eaglefeathers, Milton; M; 1; Cheyenne; 1/4+; S; Son; Yes; Yes

Census of the **Tongue River** reservation of the **Tongue River** jurisdiction, as of **April 1**, 19**30**, taken by **C. B. Lohmiller**, Superintendent.

**Key:** Number; NAME: Surname, Given; Sex; Age At Last Birthday; Tribe; Degree of Blood; Marital Status; Relationship To Head of Family; At Jurisdiction Where Enrolled (Yes or No); At Another Jurisdiction; ELSEWHERE: Post office, County, State; Ward (Yes or No); Allotment, Annuity, and Identification Numbers.

288; Littlehead, Rena; F; 10; Cheyenne; 1/4+; S; S-Dau; Yes; Yes [Mildred in 1926.]

289; Eastman, Mary G.; F; 53; Cheyenne; 1/4+; M; Head; No; Lodgegrass town, Big Horn, Mont.; Yes
290; Eastman, Chas.; M; 29; Cheyenne; -1/4; Wd; Son; No; Lodgegrass town, Big Horn, Mont.; Yes
291; Eastman, Robert; M; 19; Cheyenne; -1/4; S; Son; No; Lodgegrass town, Big Horn, Mont.; Yes
292; Eastman, Rose; F; 14; Cheyenne; -1/4; S Dau; No; Lodgegrass town, Big Horn, Mont.; Yes
293; Eastman, Louisa; F; 11; Cheyenne; -1/4; S; Dau; No; Lodgegrass town, Big Horn, Mont.; Yes
294; Eastman, Myrtle; F; 16; Cheyenne; -1/4; S; G-Dau; No; Lodgegrass town, Big Horn, Mont.; Yes [Julia 1926. Lucy Beartusk, mother.]

295; Eastman, Perry; M; 34; Cheyenne; -1/4; M; Head; Yes; Yes
296; Eastman, Mary; F; 37; Cheyenne; F; M; Wife; Yes; Yes
297; Beartusk, Edith; F; 14; Cheyenne; 1/4+; S; Niece; Yes; Yes

298; Elkshoulder, Henry; M; 35; Cheyenne; F; M; Head; Yes; Yes
299; Elkshoulder, Bessie; F; 36; Cheyenne; F; M; Wife; Yes; Yes
300; Elkshoulder, Curtis; M; 22; Cheyenne; F; S; Son; Yes; Yes
301; Elkshoulder, Lucy; F; 13; Cheyenne; F; S Dau; Yes; Yes
302; Elkshoulder, Sylvia; F; 7; Cheyenne; F; S; Dau; Yes; Yes
303; Elkshoulder, George; M; 4; Cheyenne; F; S; Son; Yes; Yes [Adolph in 1926.]
304; Elkshoulder, Calvin; M; 1; Cheyenne; F; S; Son; Yes; Yes

305; Elliot, Elizabeth; F; 23; Cheyenne; 1/4+; M; Head; Yes; Yes
306; Elliot, Edwin F.; M; 2; Cheyenne; -1/4; S; Son; Yes; Yes
307; Elliot, Loretta M; F; 1; Cheyenne; -1/4; S; Dau; Yes; Yes

308; Eyesyellow, Wilbur; M; 61; Cheyenne; F; M; Head; Yes; Yes
309; Eyesyellow, Daisy; F; 73; Cheyenne; F; M; Wife; Yes; Yes

310; Fightingbear, Edgar; M; 55; Cheyenne; F; M; Head; Yes; Yes
311; Fightingbear, Alice; F; 36; Cheyenne; F; M; Wife; Yes; Yes
312; Fightingbear, Elmer; M; 8; Cheyenne; F; S; Son; Yes; Yes
313; Fightingbear, Herbert; M; 6; Cheyenne; F; S; Son; Yes; Yes
314; Fightingbear, Emma; F; 3; Cheyenne; F; S Dau; Yes; Yes

315; Fingers, Otis; M; 41; Cheyenne; F; Wd; Head; Yes; Yes
316; Fingers, Joseph; M; 15; Cheyenne; F; S; Son; Yes; Yes [1917 Census Daughter, Josie 1915-20.]

Census of the **Tongue River** reservation of the **Tongue River** jurisdiction, as of **April 1**, 1930, taken by **C. B. Lohmiller**, Superintendent.

**Key:** Number; NAME: Surname, Given; Sex; Age At Last Birthday; Tribe; Degree of Blood; Marital Status; Relationship To Head of Family; At Jurisdiction Where Enrolled (Yes or No); At Another Jurisdiction; ELSEWHERE: Post office, County, State; Ward (Yes or No); Allotment, Annuity, and Identification Numbers.

317; Firecrow, Peter; M; 43; Cheyenne; F; Wd; Head; Yes; Yes
318; Firecrow, Joseph; M; 6; Cheyenne; F; S; Son; Yes; Yes [Josephine; dau; F., in 1926]

319; Firewolf, John; M; 53; Cheyenne; F; M; Head; Yes; Yes
320; Firewolf, Josephine; F; 55; Cheyenne; F; M; Wife; Yes; Yes
321; Tallwhiteman, Agnes; F; 5; Cheyenne; F; S; G-Dau; Yes; Yes

322; Fisher, Eugene; M; 51; Cheyenne; 1/4+; M; Head; Yes; Yes
323; Fisher, Kitty; F; 40; Cheyenne; -1/4; M; Wife; Yes; Yes
324; Fisher, Eugene Jr.; M; 17; Cheyenne; 1/4+; S; Son; Yes; Yes
325; Fisher, Langburn; M; 14; Cheyenne; 1/4+; S; Son; Yes; Yes
326; Fisher, James A.; M; 13; Cheyenne; 1/4+; S; Son; Yes; Yes [1917 Census name Ira.]
327; Fisher, Alliwitchie; F; 10; Cheyenne; 1/4+; S; Dau; Yes; Yes [1919 Census name Pearl.]
328; Fisher, Calleaus; F[sic]; 10; Cheyenne; 1/4+; S; Son; Yes; Yes [1919 Census name Earl.]
329; Fisher, Russell; M; 8; Cheyenne; 1/4+; S; Son; Yes; Yes
330; Fisher, Helen; F; 6; Cheyenne; 1/4+; S; Dau; Yes; Yes
331; Fisher, Bernidine; M; 3; Cheyenne; 1/4+; S; Son; Yes; Yes

332; Fisher, Henry; M; 24; Cheyenne; F; M; Head; Yes; Yes
333; Fisher, Lucy; F; 22; Cheyenne; 1/4+; M; Wife; Yes; Yes

334; Fisher, John; M; 28; Cheyenne; F; M; Head; Yes; Yes
335; Fisher, Mary P.; F; 19; Cheyenne; F; M; Wife; Yes; Yes [Playingbear]
336; Fisher, Burton; M; 9/12; Cheyenne; F; S; Son; Yes; Yes

337; Fliesabout, William; M; 51; Cheyenne; F; M; Head; Yes; Yes
338; Fliesabout, Minnie; F; 47; Cheyenne; F; M; Wife; Yes; Yes
339; Fliesabout, June; F; 6; Cheyenne; F; S; Dau; Yes; Yes [Martin; son; F[sic], in 1926.]

340; Flying, Debs; M; 44; Cheyenne; F; Wd[sic]; Head; Yes; Yes
341; Flying, Frank; M; 14; Cheyenne; F; S; Son; Yes; Yes
342; Flying, Parker; M; 12; Cheyenne; F; S; Son; Yes; Yes
343; Flying, Myra; F; 62; Cheyenne; F; S; Mother; Yes; Yes
344; Killsnight, Ruth; F; 13; Cheyenne; F; S; Sister; Yes; Yes

345; Flying, Thomas; M; 61; Cheyenne; F; Wd[sic]; Head; Yes; Yes

346; Fontenelle, Francis[sic]; F; 21; Cheyenne; -1/4; M[sic]; Head; Yes; Yes [Sherman]

Census of the __Tongue River__ reservation of the __Tongue River__ jurisdiction, as of __April 1__, 1930, taken by __C. B. Lohmiller__, Superintendent.

**Key:** Number; NAME: Surname, Given; Sex; Age At Last Birthday; Tribe; Degree of Blood; Marital Status; Relationship To Head of Family; At Jurisdiction Where Enrolled (Yes or No); At Another Jurisdiction; ELSEWHERE: Post office, County, State; Ward (Yes or No); Allotment, Annuity, and Identification Numbers.

347; Foot, Ruth Y.; F; 51; Cheyenne; F; M; Head; Yes; Yes
348; Foot, Thelma; F; 16; Cheyenne; 1/4+; S; S-Dau; Yes; Yes [1917 Census name Daisy.]
349; Foot, Edward; F[sic]; 12; Cheyenne; 1/4+; S; S-Son; Yes; Yes
350; Foot, Bertha; F; 10; Cheyenne; 1/4+; S; S-Dau; Yes; Yes
351; Foot, Eva; F; 6; Cheyenne; 1/4+; S; S-Dau; Yes; Yes
352; Foot, Sylvia; F; 1; Cheyenne; 1/4+; S; Dau; Yes; Yes
353; Hardrobe, Margaret; F; 12; Cheyenne; F; S; Dau; Yes; Yes

354; Ghostbull, Arthur; M; 60; Cheyenne; F; Wd[sic]; Head; Yes; Yes
355; Ghostbull, Eva; F; 22; Cheyenne; F; S; Dau; Yes; Yes

356; Gillispie, May P.; F; 42; Cheyenne; 1/4+; M; Head; No; Pine Ridge Ag., S.D. Pine Ridge

357; Grasshopper, Isaac; M; 79; Cheyenne; F; Wd[sic]; Head; Yes; Yes
358; Grasshopper, Frank; M; 23; Cheyenne; F; S; G-Son; Yes; Yes [Son of Mrs. Stanley Lamewoman.] [Arthur in 1926.]

359; Gray, Bessie; F; 25; Cheyenne; F; D; Head; Yes; Yes [1920 #917, name Sandcrane.]
360; Gray, Rose Marie; F; 6; Cheyenne; F; S; Dau; Yes; Yes
361; Sandcrane, Peter; M; 1; Cheyenne; F; S; Son; Yes; Yes

362; Gray, Edward; M; 57; Cheyenne; F; M; Head; Yes; Yes
363; Gray, Nellie; F; 55; Cheyenne; F; M; Wife; Yes; Yes
364; Gray, Teddy; M; 14; Cheyenne; F; S; Son; Yes; Yes

365; Gray, John; M; 27; Cheyenne; F; M; Head; Yes; Yes
366; Gray, Kate; F; 30; Cheyenne; F; M; Wife; Yes; Yes [Wolfname] [Ida in 1926.]

367; Hairyhand, Henry; M; 74; Cheyenne; F; Wd[sic]; Head; Yes; Yes
368; Fightingbear, Willie; M; 30; Cheyenne; F; S; G-Son; Yes; Yes

369; Hardground, Ernest; M; 33; Cheyenne; F; M; Head; Yes; Yes
370; Hardground, Mary; F; 34; Cheyenne; F; M; Wife; Yes; Yes
371; Hardground, Ethel; F; 9; Cheyenne; F; S; Dau; Yes; Yes
372; Hardground, Katie; F; 6; Cheyenne; F; S; Dau; Yes; Yes
373; Hardground, Susan; F; 3/12; Cheyenne; F; S; Dau; Yes; Yes

374; Hardground, Robert; M; 53; Cheyenne; F; M; Head; Yes; Yes
375; Hardground, Patty B.L.; F; 54; Cheyenne; F; M; Wife; Yes; Yes
376; Hardground, Albert; M; 30; Cheyenne; F; Wd[sic]; Son; Yes; Yes
377; Hardground, George; M; 29; Cheyenne; F; S; Son; Yes; Yes
378; Hardground, Lucy; F; 19; Cheyenne; F; S; Dau; Yes; Yes [Rena in 1926.]

Census of the **Tongue River** reservation of the **Tongue River** jurisdiction, as of **April 1**, 1930, taken by **C. B. Lohmiller**, Superintendent.

**Key:** Number; NAME: Surname, Given; Sex; Age At Last Birthday; Tribe; Degree of Blood; Marital Status; Relationship To Head of Family; At Jurisdiction Where Enrolled (Yes or No); At Another Jurisdiction; ELSEWHERE: Post office, County, State; Ward (Yes or No); Allotment, Annuity, and Identification Numbers.

379; Hardground, Lyla; F; 15; Cheyenne; F; S; Dau; Yes; Yes
380; Biglefthand, Rapheal[sic]; M; 17; Cheyenne; F; S; S-Son; Yes; Yes [1915-#72 was Daisy, female.]

381; Hardrobe, Colonel; M; 74; Cheyenne; F; Wd[sic]; Head; Yes; Yes
382; Hardrobe, Fannie; f; 49; Cheyenne; F; S; Dau; Yes; Yes
383; Hardrobe, Albert J.; M; 33; Cheyenne; F; S; Son; Yes; Yes

384; Harris, Bryan; M; 31; Cheyenne; 1/4+; M; Head; Yes; Yes
385; Harris, Ruth; F; 23; Cheyenne; F; M; Wife; Yes; Yes [Spottedhawk, Medicinebird]
386; Harris, Carl; M; 8; Cheyenne; 1/4+; S; Son; Yes; Yes
387; Harris, Elmer F.; M; 8/12; Cheyenne; 1/4+; S; Son; Yes; Yes
388; Harris, Sallie; F; 79; Cheyenne; 1/4+; Wd; Mother; Yes; Yes [Allie in 1928]

389; Harris, Edward; M; 43; Cheyenne; 1/4+; Cheyenne; Head; Yes; Yes
390; Harris, Bessie; F; 40; Cheyenne; F; M: Wife; Yes; Yes
391; Harris, May; F; 18; Cheyenne; 1/4+; S; Dau; Yes; Yes
392; Harris, Nellie; F; 15; Cheyenne; 1/4+; S; Dau; Yes; Yes
393; Harris, Dorothy; F; 10; Cheyenne; 1/4+; S; Dau; Yes; Yes
394; Harris, Hubert; F[sic]; 7; Cheyenne; 1/4+; S; Dau; Yes; Yes [Lawrence Edw. In 1926.]
395; Harris, Inez R.; F; 2; Cheyenne; 1/4+; S; Dau; Yes; Yes

396; Harris, William; M; 53; Cheyenne; 1/4+; M; Head; Yes; Yes
397; Harris, Margaret; F; 45; Cheyenne; 1/4+; M; Wife; Yes; Yes
398; Harris, George; M; 22; Cheyenne; 1/4+; S; Son; Yes; Yes
399; Harris, Julia; F; 19; Cheyenne; 1/4+; S; Dau; Yes; Yes
400; Harris, Agnes; F; 17; Cheyenne; 1/4+; S; Dau; Yes; Yes
401; Harris, Raymond; M; 15; Cheyenne; 1/4+; S; Son; Yes; Yes
402; Harris, Mary; F; 11; Cheyenne; 1/4+; S; Dau; Yes; Yes [1920 name Leota.]
403; Harris, Florence; F; 6; Cheyenne; 1/4+; S; Dau; Yes; Yes [1925 son Joseph, M.]

404; Hart, Charles; M; 49; Cheyenne; F; M; Head; Yes; Yes
405; Hart, Louisa; F; 44; Cheyenne; 1/4+; M; Wife; Yes; Yes
406; Hart, Mattie L.; F; 18; Cheyenne; 1/4+; S; Dau; No; Billings Town, Yellowstone, Mont; Yes
407; Hart, Eva; F; 16; Cheyenne; 1/4+; S; Dau; Yes; Yes
408; Hart, Jessie D.; F; 14; Cheyenne; 1/4+; S; Dau; Yes; Yes

409; Hart, Frank; M; 31; Cheyenne; 1/4+; M; Head; Yes; Yes
410; Hart, Alice; F; 22; Cheyenne; F; M; Wife; Yes; Yes [Hairlessbear]
411; Hart, Edna; F; 2; Cheyenne; 1/4+; S; Dau; Yes; Yes

Census of the **Tongue River** reservation of the **Tongue River** jurisdiction, as of **April 1**, 1930, taken by **C. B. Lohmiller**, Superintendent.

**Key:** Number; NAME: Surname, Given; Sex; Age At Last Birthday; Tribe; Degree of Blood; Marital Status; Relationship To Head of Family; At Jurisdiction Where Enrolled (Yes or No); At Another Jurisdiction; ELSEWHERE: Post office, County, State; Ward (Yes or No); Allotment, Annuity, and Identification Numbers.

412; Headswift, Charles; M; 63; Cheyenne; F; Wd[sic]; Head; Yes; Yes
413; Headswift, Frank; M; 18; Cheyenne; F; S; Son; Yes; Yes

414; Highbear, William; M; 42; Cheyenne; F; M; Head; Yes; Yes
415; Highbear, Minnie; F; 38; Cheyenne; F; M; Wife; Yes; Yes

416; Highwalking, Floyd; M; 42; Cheyenne; F; M; Head; Yes; Yes
417; Highwalking, Belle; F; 36; Cheyenne; F; M; Wife; Yes; Yes
418; Highwalking, George; M; 17; Cheyenne; F; S; Son; Yes; Yes [David in 1926.]
419; Highwalking, Max; M; 13; Cheyenne; F; S; Son; Yes; Yes; Yes
420; Highwalking, Nellie; F; 71; Cheyenne; F; Wd; Mother; Yes; Yes

421; Hisbadhorse, Willis; M; 21; Cheyenne; F; M; Head; Yes; Yes
422; Hisbadhorse, Ernest; M; 12; Cheyenne; F; S; Son; Yes; Yes [1924 s-son. Eugene in 1926.]
423; Hisbadhorse, Medaris; M; 8; Cheyenne; F; S; Son; Yes; Yes [Bird; son; 1917; in 1926.]
424; Hisbadhorse, Fannie; F; 7; Cheyenne; F; S; Dau; Yes; Yes [Josephine in 1926.]
425; Rowland, Carrie; F; 3; Cheyenne; 1/4-; S; S-Dau; Yes; Yes
426; Hisbadhorse, Rhoda; F; 73; Cheyenne; F; Wd; Mother; Yes; Yes
427; Americanhorse, Albert M.; M; 17; Cheyenne; F; S; Nephew; Yes; Yes

428; Hollowbreast, Hubert; M; 54; Cheyenne; F; M; Head; Yes; Yes
429; Hollowbreast, Mary; F; 34; Cheyenne; F; M; Wife; Yes; Yes [Previous censuses name Hattie Hisbadhorses. 1926 Hisbadhorses, wdw. #426.]
430; Hollowbreast, Donald; M; 12; Cheyenne; F; S; Son; Yes; Yes
431; Hollowbreast, Jack; M; 5; Cheyenne; F; S; Son; Yes; Yes
432; Hollowbreast, Edward; M; 1; Cheyenne; F; S; Son; Yes; Yes

433; Hollowbreast, William; M; 29; Cheyenne; F; M; Head; Yes; Yes
434; Hollowbreast, Mary; F; 26; Cheyenne; F; S; Wife; Yes; Yes [Littlewolf]

435; Hollowwood, Richard; M; 73; Cheyenne; M; Wd[sic]; Head; Yes; Yes

436; Horn, Annie W.; F; 29; Cheyenne; F; M; Head; Yes; Yes [Name Alice 1904-20.]
437; Horn, Rose; F; 8; Cheyenne; F; S; Dau; Yes; Yes
438; Horn, Wilena; F; 7; Cheyenne; F; S; Dau; Yes; Yes
439; Horn, Margaret; F; 3; Cheyenne; F; S; Dau; Yes; Yes
440; Horn, Celia M.; F; 1; Cheyenne; F; S; Dau; Yes; Yes

441; Horseroads, Thomas; M; 51; Cheyenne; F; M; Head; Yes; Yes
442; Horseroads, Lucy; F; 42; Cheyenne; F; M; Wife; Yes; Yes
443; Horseroads, Ida; F; 6; Cheyenne; F; S; Dau; Yes; Yes

Census of the **Tongue River** reservation of the **Tongue River** jurisdiction, as of **April 1**, 1930, taken by **C. B. Lohmiller**, Superintendent.

**Key:** Number; NAME: Surname, Given; Sex; Age At Last Birthday; Tribe; Degree of Blood; Marital Status; Relationship To Head of Family; At Jurisdiction Where Enrolled (Yes or No); At Another Jurisdiction; ELSEWHERE: Post office, County, State; Ward (Yes or No); Allotment, Annuity, and Identification Numbers.

444; Horseroads, Cora; F; 3; Cheyenne; F; S; Dau; Yes; Yes

445; Howlingantelope, Albert; M; 56; Cheyenne; F; M; Head; Yes; Yes
446; Howlingantelope, Eva; F; 45; Cheyenne; F; M; Wife; Yes; Yes
447; Fasthorse, Clara; F; 16; Cheyenne; F; S; G-Dau; Yes; Yes

448; Huff, Pearl; F; 22; Cheyenne; -1/4; M; Head; Yes; Yes [Eastman]
449; Huff, Elsie M.; F; 2; Cheyenne; 1/4+; S; Dau; Yes; Yes
450; Huff, Percy; M; 1; Cheyenne; 1/4+; S; Son; Yes; Yes

451; Ironhand, William; M; 47; Cheyenne; F; M; Head; Yes; Yes
452; Ironhand, Sally; F; 45; Cheyenne; F; M; Wife; Yes; Yes
453; Ironhand, Henry; M; 19; Cheyenne; F; S; Son; Yes; Yes
454; Ironhand, Willis; M; 15; Cheyenne; F; S; Son; Yes; Yes
455; Ironhand, Jane; F; 3; Cheyenne; F; S; Dau; Yes; Yes

456; Issues, Francis; M; 33; Cheyenne; F; M; Head; Yes; Yes
457; Issues, Mamie L.; F; 22; Cheyenne; 1/4-; M; Wife; Yes; Yes
458; Issues, Ira; M; 10; Cheyenne; F; S; Son; Yes; Yes [1919 name Ira, 1920-23, George.]
459; Issues, Irene; F; 8; Cheyenne; F; S; Dau; Yes; Yes

460; Issues, John; M; 66; Cheyenne; F; M; Head; Yes; Yes
461; Issues, Clara; F; 60; Cheyenne; F; M; Wife; Yes; Yes [Blackmedicine; 1904-17, she becomes Issues 1915]

462; Killsback, James; M; 66; Cheyenne; F; M; Head; Yes; Yes [Census #461, name Joseph Killsacross in 1926.]
463; Killsback, Amelia; F; 51; Cheyenne; F; M; Wife; Yes; Yes

464; Killsnight, Charles; M; 39; Cheyenne; F; M; Head; Yes; Yes
465; Killsnight, Rose L.W.; F; 39; Cheyenne; F; M; Wife; Yes; Yes
466; Killsnight, Rose; F; 14; Cheyenne; F; S; Dau; Yes; Yes
467; Killsnight, Hubert; M; 10; Cheyenne; F; S; Son; Yes; Yes [Brighton in 1926.]
468; Lonewolf, James; M; 14; Cheyenne; F; S; S-Son; Yes; Yes
469; Lonewolf, Ella; F; 4; Cheyenne; F; S; S-Dau; Yes; Yes

470; Killsnight, Hugh; M; 63; Cheyenne; F; M; Head; Yes; Yes
471; Killsnight, Clara; F; 57; Cheyenne; F; M; Wife; Yes; Yes

472; Killsnight, Martin; M; 23; Cheyenne; F; Wd[sic]; Head; Yes; Yes
473; Killsnight, Kitty B.; F; 1; Cheyenne; 1/4+; S; Dau; Yes; Yes

474; Killsnight, Rose; F; 31; Cheyenne; F; D; Head; Yes; Yes
475; Killsnight, Margaret; F; 6; Cheyenne; F; S; Dau; Yes; Yes

Census of the __Tongue River__ reservation of the __Tongue River__ jurisdiction, as of __April 1__, 1930, taken by __C. B. Lohmiller__, Superintendent.

**Key:** Number; NAME: Surname, Given; Sex; Age At Last Birthday; Tribe; Degree of Blood; Marital Status; Relationship To Head of Family; At Jurisdiction Where Enrolled (Yes or No); At Another Jurisdiction; ELSEWHERE: Post office, County, State; Ward (Yes or No); Allotment, Annuity, and Identification Numbers.

476; Killsnight, Dorothy; F; 3; Cheyenne; F; S; Dau; Yes; Yes
477; Killsnight, Jennie; F; 1; Cheyenne; F; S; Dau; Yes; Yes

478; Killsnight, William; M; 74; Cheyenne; F; M; Head; Yes; Yes
479; Killsnight, Cora; F; 69; Cheyenne; F; M; Wife; Yes; Yes
480; Killsnight, Cole; M; 25; Cheyenne; F; S; Son; Yes; Yes
481; Killsnight, William Jr.; M; 25; Cheyenne; F; S; G-Son; Yes; Yes

482; Killsnight, Willis; M; 35; Cheyenne; F; M; Head; Yes; Yes [Rutherford in 1926.]
483; Killsnight, Carrie; F; 39; Cheyenne; F; S[sic]; Wife; Yes; Yes [Whitemoon]
484; Killsnight, Flossie; F; 7; Cheyenne; F; S; Dau; Yes; Yes [Sage in 1926.]
485; Killsnight, James; M; 4; Cheyenne; F; S; Son; Yes; Yes
486; Killsnight, Ralph; M; 2; Cheyenne; F; S; Son; Yes; Yes

487; Killsnightwoman; F; 71; Cheyenne; F; Wd; Head; Yes; Yes

488; Killsontop, John; M; 23; Cheyenne; F; M; Head; Yes; Yes
489; Killsontop, Mary; F; 21; Cheyenne; F; S[sic]; Wife; Yes; Yes [Strangeowl]
490; Killsontop, June; F; 3; Cheyenne; F; S; Dau; Yes; Yes
491; Killsontop, Levern; M; 1; Cheyenne; F; S; Son; Yes; Yes

492; Kingfisher, Carrie; F; 53; Cheyenne; F; Wd; Head; Yes; Yes

493; Kingfisher, Willis J.; M; 33; Cheyenne; F; M; Head; Yes; Yes
494; Kingfisher, Minnie; F; 33; Cheyenne; F; M; Wife; Yes; Yes
495; Kingfisher, Isabelle; F; 11; Cheyenne; F; S; Dau; Yes; Yes
496; Kingfisher, Charles; M; 8; Cheyenne; F; S; Dau[sic]; Yes; Yes
497; Kingfisher, Louise; F; 7; Cheyenne; F; S; Dau; Yes; Yes
498; Kingfisher, Ellen; F; 3 Cheyenne; F; S; Dau; Yes; Yes
499; Kingfisher, Angela; F; 11/12; Cheyenne; F; S; Dau; Yes; Yes

500; Kinsel, Alice; F; 37; Cheyenne; 1/4+; M; Head; Yes; Yes
501; Kinsel, Emma L.; F; 12; Cheyenne; -1/4; S; Dau; Yes; Yes
502; Kinsel, Helen L.; F; 10; Cheyenne; -1/4; S; Dau; Yes; Yes
503; Kinsel, Cecelia L; F; 5; Cheyenne; -1/4; S; Dau; Yes; Yes
504; Kinsel, Virgil B.; M; 2; Cheyenne; -1/4; S; Son; Yes; Yes

505; Knows-his-gun, Frances; F; 25; Cheyenne; F; M; Head; Yes; Yes
506; Knows-his-gun, Sylvester; M; 3; Cheyenne; F; S; Son; Yes; Yes
507; Knows-his-gun, Edith; F; 1; Cheyenne; F; S; Dau; Yes; Yes

508; LaFever, Rena; F; 33; Cheyenne; -1/4; M; Head; No; Lodgegrass T~~own~~, Big Horn, Mont.; Yes

Census of the **Tongue River** reservation of the **Tongue River** jurisdiction, as of **April 1**, 1930, taken by **C. B. Lohmiller**, Superintendent.

**Key:** Number; NAME: Surname, Given; Sex; Age At Last Birthday; Tribe; Degree of Blood; Marital Status; Relationship To Head of Family; At Jurisdiction Where Enrolled (Yes or No); At Another Jurisdiction; ELSEWHERE: Post office, County, State; Ward (Yes or No); Allotment, Annuity, and Identification Numbers.

509; Bolson, Gail; F; 14; Cheyenne; -1/4; S; Dau; No; Lodgegrass T̶o̶w̶n̶, Big Horn, Mont.; Yes
510; Bolson, Frank; M; 12; Cheyenne; -1/4; S; Son; No; Lodgegrass T̶o̶w̶n̶, Big Horn, Mont.; Yes
511; Bolson, Roy; M; 10; Cheyenne; -1/4; S; Son; No; Lodgegrass Town, Big Horn, Mont.; Yes
512; LaFever, Kenneth; M; 4; Cheyenne; -1/4; S; Son; No; Lodgegrass Town, Big Horn, Mont.; Yes [#501; Herman; son; birth year 1925 in 1926.]

513; Lamebear, Benjamin; M; 35; Cheyenne; F; M; Head; Yes; Yes
514; Lamebear, Clara; F; 35; Cheyenne; F; M; Wife; Yes; Yes
515; Lamebear, Eva; F; 19; Cheyenne; F; S; Dau; Yes; Yes
516; Lamebear, Cora; F; 11; Cheyenne; F; S; Dau; Yes; Yes
517; Lamebear, Charles; M; 8; Cheyenne; F; S; Son; Yes; Yes
518; Lamebear, Susie; F; 2/12; Cheyenne; F; S; Dau; Yes; Yes

519; Lamewoman, Sam; M; 17; Cheyenne; F; M; Head; Yes; Yes [Sam Littlebear; 1928]
520; Lamewoman, Alice; F; 19; Cheyenne; 1/4+; M; Wife; Yes; Yes [Rowland; 7/8 [Birth year 1912 in 1926.]
521; Lamewoman, Ruth; F; 6/12; Cheyenne; 1/4+; S; Dau; Yes; Yes

522; Lamewoman, Stanley; M; 40; Cheyenne; F; M; Head; Yes; Yes
523; Lamewoman, Augusta; F; 44; Cheyenne; F; M; Wife; Yes; Yes
524; Lamewoman, Jessie; F; 15; Cheyenne; F; S; Dau; Yes; Yes
525; Lamewoman, Virgil; M; 7; Cheyenne; F; S; Son; Yes; Yes
526; Grasshopper, Mary; F; 15; Cheyenne; F; S; S-Dau; Yes; Yes
527; Lamewoman, Nellie; F; 75; Cheyenne; F; Wd; Mother; Yes; Yes

528; Lastbull, Fred; M; 41; Cheyenne; F; M; Head; Yes; Yes

529; Lennon, Mary B.; F; 23; Cheyenne; -1/4; M; Head; No; Columbine, Natrone[sic], Wyo.; Yes
530; Lennon, Arthur G.; M; 3; Cheyenne; -1/4; S; Son; No; Columbine, Natrone[sic], Wyo.; Yes

531; Lightning, Frank; M; 58; Cheyenne; F; Wd[sic]; Head; Yes; Yes

532; Limberhand, Nathan; M; 53; Cheyenne; F; M; Head; Yes; Yes
533; Limberhand, Artie; F; 43; Cheyenne; F; M; Wife; Yes; Yes
534; Limberhand, James; M; 27; Cheyenne; F; S; Son; Yes; Yes
535; Limberhand, Elmore; M; 20; Cheyenne; F; S; Son; Yes; Yes
536; Limberhand, Bennie; M; 18; Cheyenne; F; S; Son; Yes; Yes
537; Limberhand, Jennie; F; 14; Cheyenne; F; S; Dau; Yes; Yes
538; Limberhand, Doris; F; 7; Cheyenne; F; S; Dau; Yes; Yes

Census of the **Tongue River** reservation of the **Tongue River** jurisdiction, as of **April 1**, 1930, taken by **C. B. Lohmiller**, Superintendent.

**Key:** Number; NAME: Surname, Given; Sex; Age At Last Birthday; Tribe; Degree of Blood; Marital Status; Relationship To Head of Family; At Jurisdiction Where Enrolled (Yes or No); At Another Jurisdiction; ELSEWHERE: Post office, County, State; Ward (Yes or No); Allotment, Annuity, and Identification Numbers.

539; Limpy, Henry; M; 10; Cheyenne; 1/4+; G-Son; Yes; Yes

540; Limberhand, Richard; M; 24; Cheyenne; F; M; Head; No; Billings Town, Yellowstone, Mont; Yes
541; Limberhand, Jessie; F; 24; Cheyenne; F; M; Wife; Yes; Yes [Rockroads (Rhoda) all numbers past and present coincide, shows up in 1915, birth year 1913. 1926 last name Russell, wife, husband Frank, separated.]
542; Limberhand, Doris; F; 2; Cheyenne; F; S; Dau; Yes; Yes

543; Limpy, Benjamin; F[sic]; 37; Cheyenne; F; M; Head; Yes; Yes
544; Limpy, Hattie; F; 35; Cheyenne; F; M; Wife; Yes; Yes [#540; Hallie Killsacross #271, 1914 census. 1915-16 Hallie Limpy.]
545; Limpy, Anna; F; 15; Cheyenne; F; S; Dau; Yes; Yes [Son, Jack 1916-19; Jean in 1926.]
546; Limpy, Rosa; F; 10; Cheyenne; F; S; Dau; Yes; Yes [#530 Elnora in 1926.]
547; Limpy, Bessie; F; 7; Cheyenne; F; S; Dau; Yes; Yes
548; Limpy, Eunice; F; 2; Cheyenne; F; S; Dau; Yes; Yes
549; Dullknife, Bessie; F; 80; Cheyenne; F; Wd; Mother-in-law; Yes; Yes

550; Limpy, Charles; M; 72; Cheyenne; F; M; Head; Yes; Yes
551; Limpy, Nellie; F; 74; Cheyenne; F; M; Wife; Yes; Yes

552; Limpy, Fred; M; 46; Cheyenne; 1/4+; M; Head; No; Forsyth Town, Rosebud, Mont; Yes
553; Limpy, Amelia; F; 44; Cheyenne; F; M; Wife; Yes; Yes [Womanleggins]
554; Limpy, Frank; M; 19; Cheyenne; 1/4+; S; Son; Yes; Yes
555; Limpy, Mary; F; 14; Cheyenne; 1/4+; S; Dau; Yes; Yes [#506, Limpy, Mary; D.; 6 Mo; in 1909. #538 May Limpy birth year 1913 in 1926.]
556; Limpy, Cora; M; 4; Cheyenne; 1/4+; S; Dau; Yes; Yes
557; Limpy, Fred Jr.; M; 10/12; Cheyenne; 1/4+; S; Son; Yes; Yes

558; Littlebear, Paul; M; 42; Cheyenne; F; M; Head; Yes; Yes
559; Littlebear, Rose; F; 42; Cheyenne; F; M; Wife; Yes; Yes
560; Littlebear, Flossie; F; 18; Cheyenne; F; S; Dau; Yes; Yes [Mary in 1926.]
561; Littlebear, Clara; G; 14; Cheyenne; F; S; Dau; Yes; Yes
562; Littlebear, Peter T.; M; 6; Cheyenne; F; S; Son; Yes; Yes
563; Littlebear, Lucille; F; 3; Cheyenne; F; S; Dau; Yes; Yes
564; Littlebear, Lester; M; 6/12; Cheyenne; F; S; Son; Yes; Yes
565; Littlebear, May; F; 21; Cheyenne; F; S; Dau; Yes; Yes [Anne in 1926.]
566; Littlebear, Lenora C.; F; 1; Cheyenne; F; S; G-Dau; Yes; Yes

567; Littlebird, Peter; M; 59; Cheyenne; F; M; Head; Yes; Yes
568; Littlebird, Jennie; F; 37; Cheyenne; F; M; Wife; Yes; Yes
569; Littlebird, Joseph; M; 17; Cheyenne; F; S; Son; Yes; Yes
570; Littlebird, Julia; F; 7; Cheyenne; F; S; Dau; Yes; Yes

Census of the __Tongue River__ reservation of the __Tongue River__ jurisdiction, as of __April 1__, 1930, taken by __C. B. Lohmiller__, Superintendent.

**Key:** Number; NAME: Surname, Given; Sex; Age At Last Birthday; Tribe; Degree of Blood; Marital Status; Relationship To Head of Family; At Jurisdiction Where Enrolled (Yes or No); At Another Jurisdiction; ELSEWHERE: Post office, County, State; Ward (Yes or No); Allotment, Annuity, and Identification Numbers.

571; Littlebird, James Wm.; M; 4; Cheyenne; F; S; Son; Yes; Yes
572; Littlebird, Theresa; F; 4/12; Cheyenne; F; S; Dau; Yes; Yes

573; Littlechief, Victor; M; 53; Cheyenne; F; M; Head; Yes; Yes
574; Littlechief, Louisa; F; 55; Cheyenne; F; M; Wife; Yes; Yes
575; Littlechief, Lucille; F; 19; Cheyenne; F; S; Dau; Yes; Yes

576; Littlecoyote, Henry; M; 54; Cheyenne; F; M; Head; Yes; Yes
577; Littlecoyote, Julia; F; 53; Cheyenne; F; M; Wife; Yes; Yes
578; Littlecoyote, Daniel E.; M; 19; Cheyenne; F; S; Son; Yes; Yes
579; Whitefrog, Nellie; F; 68; Cheyenne; F; S; S-Mother; Yes; Yes

580; Littleeagle, Charles; M; 62; Cheyenne; F; M; Head; Yes; Yes
581; Littleeagle, Mary; F; 51; Cheyenne; F; M; Wife; Yes; Yes
582; Littleeagle, Clara; F; 24; Cheyenne; F; S; Dau; Yes; Yes

583; Littlehawk, Dora; F; 60; Cheyenne; F; Wd; Head; Yes; Yes
584; Medicineelk, Jennie; F; 25; Cheyenne; F; M; Other; Yes; Yes [Eaglefeathers]
585; Medicineelk, Sarah A.; F; 2; Cheyenne; F; S; Other; Yes; Yes
586; Woodpecker, Donald Chas.; M; 20; Cheyenne; F; S; Nephew; Yes; Yes

587; Littlehead, Charles; M; 60; Cheyenne; F; M; Head; Yes; Yes
588; Littlehead, Nellie; F; 47; Cheyenne; F; M; Wife; Yes; Yes
589; Littlehead, Frank; M; 20; Cheyenne; F; S; Son; Yes; Yes
590; Littlehead, George; M; 9; Cheyenne; F; S; Son; Yes; Yes [1920 name John.]
591; Blackstone, Gladys; F; 29; Cheyenne; F; D; Dau; Yes; Yes
592; Blackstone, Louis; M; 2; Cheyenne; F; S; G-Son; Yes; Yes
593; Blackstone, Joseph; M; 10/12; Cheyenne; F; S; G-Son; Yes; Yes

594; Littlehead, John; M; 35; Cheyenne; F; M; Head; No; Cheyenne & Arap Ag, Okla; Yes

595; Littlemouth, John; M; 35; Cheyenne; F; M; Head; Yes; Yes
596; Littlemouth, Jennie; F; 31; Cheyenne; F; M; Wife; Yes; Yes
597; Littlemouth, Evelyn; F; 8; Cheyenne; F; S; Dau; Yes; Yes
598; Littlemouth, James; M; 7; Cheyenne; F; S; Son; Yes; Yes
599; Littlemouth, Mary; F; 2; Cheyenne; F; S; Dau; Yes; Yes
600; Littlemouth, Clara; F; 70; Cheyenne; F; Wd; Mother; Yes; Yes

601; Littlesun, Frank; M; 45; Cheyenne; F; M; Head; Yes; Yes
602; Littlesun, Anna; F; 37; Cheyenne; F; M; Wife; Yes; Yes
603; Littlesun, Alfred; M; 17; Cheyenne; F; S; Son; Yes; Yes
604; Littleoldman, Thomas; M; 16; Cheyenne; F; S; S-Son; Yes; Yes

605; Littlesun, Samuel; M; 71; Cheyenne; F; M; Head; Yes; Yes

Census of the __Tongue River__ reservation of the __Tongue River__ jurisdiction, as of __April 1__, 1930, taken by __C. B. Lohmiller__, Superintendent.

**Key:** Number; NAME: Surname, Given; Sex; Age At Last Birthday; Tribe; Degree of Blood; Marital Status; Relationship To Head of Family; At Jurisdiction Where Enrolled (Yes or No); At Another Jurisdiction; ELSEWHERE: Post office, County, State; Ward (Yes or No); Allotment, Annuity, and Identification Numbers.

606; Littlesun, Cora; F; 65; Cheyenne; F; M; Wife; Yes; Yes
607; Littlesun, Jack; M; 9; Cheyenne; F; S; G-Son; Yes; Yes
608; Littlesun, Horace; M; 7; Cheyenne; F; S; G-Son; Yes; Yes

609; Littlewhirlwind, George; M; 28; Cheyenne; F; M; Head; Yes; Yes
610; Littlewhirlwind, Martha; F; 20; Cheyenne; F; M; Wife; Yes; Yes [Fannie Walksalong in 1926.]
611; Littlewhirlwind, Anna; F; 1; Cheyenne; F; S; Dau; Yes; Yes

612; Littlewhiteman, Aaron; M; 67; Cheyenne; 1/4+; M; Head; Yes; Yes
613; Littlewhiteman, Sadie; F; 65; Cheyenne; F; M; Wife; Yes; Yes
614; Littlewhiteman, Wesley; M; 32; Cheyenne; 1/4+; S; Son; Yes; Yes
615; Powderface, Julia; F; 16; Cheyenne; 1/4+; S; G-Dau; Yes; Yes

616; Littlewhiteman, David; M; 61; Cheyenne; 1/4+; M; Head; Yes; Yes
617; Littlewhiteman, Agnes; F; 57; Cheyenne; F; M; Wife; Yes; Yes
618; Littlewhiteman, Peter; M; 24; Cheyenne; F; S; Son; Yes; Yes

619; Littlewhiteman, Frank; M; 28; Cheyenne; 1/4+; M; Head; Yes; Yes
620; Littlewhiteman, Emma F; F; 29; Cheyenne; F; M; Wife; Yes; Yes [#964 in 1919 shows as Lightning, Emma; g dt; 1901; F. Grandparents Shortsioux in census as birth year 1901 starting in 1912 or 11 years old.]
621; Littlewhiteman, Leon; M; 9; Cheyenne; 1/4+; S; Son; Yes; Yes [John in 1926.]
622; Littlewhiteman, Margaret; F; 7; Cheyenne; 1/4+; S; Dau; Yes; Yes
623; Littlewhiteman, John; M; 4; Cheyenne; 1/4+; S; Son; Yes; Yes
624; Littlewhiteman, Philip; M; 3; Cheyenne; 1/4+; S; Son; Yes; Yes

625; Littlewhiteman, Henry; M; 39; Cheyenne; 1/4+; M; Head; Yes; Yes
626; Littlewhiteman, Josie; F; 33; Cheyenne; F; M; Wife; Yes; Yes [Weaselbear; Prev. Marriage Woodenlegs.]
627; Littlewhiteman, Edith; F; 17; Cheyenne; 1/4+; S; Dau; Yes; Yes
628; Littlewhiteman, Rosa; F; 15; Cheyenne; 1/4+; S; Dau; Yes; Yes
629; Littlewhiteman, Agnes; F; 8; Cheyenne; 1/4+; S; Dau; Yes; Yes
630; Littlewhiteman, Bessie; F; 3; Cheyenne; 1/4+; S; Dau; Yes; Yes

631  Littlewhiteman, James; M; 34; Cheyenne; 1/4+; M; Head; Yes; Yes
632; Littlewhiteman, Gusta; F; 32; Cheyenne; F; M; Wife; Yes; Yes [Littlesun]
633; Littlewhiteman, Kitty; F; 6; Cheyenne; 1/4+; S; Dau; Yes; Yes
634; Littlewhiteman, Winn; M; 2; Cheyenne; 1/4+; S; Son; Yes; Yes
635; Littlewhiteman, Mona F.: F; 1/12; Cheyenne; 1/4+; S; Dau; Yes; Yes

636; Littlewhiteman, Milton; M; 45; Cheyenne; 1/4+; M; Head; Yes; Yes
637; Littlewhiteman, Rose; F; 47; Cheyenne; F; M; Wife; Yes; Yes
638; Yellowhorse, Julia; F; 16; Cheyenne; F; S; Dau; Yes; Yes

Census of the **Tongue River** reservation of the **Tongue River** jurisdiction, as of **April 1**, 1930, taken by **C. B. Lohmiller**, Superintendent.

**Key:** Number; NAME: Surname, Given; Sex; Age At Last Birthday; Tribe; Degree of Blood; Marital Status; Relationship To Head of Family; At Jurisdiction Where Enrolled (Yes or No); At Another Jurisdiction; ELSEWHERE: Post office, County, State; Ward (Yes or No); Allotment, Annuity, and Identification Numbers.

639; Littlewhiteman, Stanley; M; 41; Cheyenne; 1/4+; M; Head; Yes; Yes
640; Littlewhiteman, Grace; F; 36; Cheyenne; F; S[sic]; Wife; Yes; Yes [1920-#1300, name Walkingbear.]
641; Littlewhiteman, Milton; M; 17; Cheyenne; 1/4+; S; Son; Yes; Yes
642; Littlewhiteman, Aaron; M; 8; Cheyenne; 1/4+; S; Son; Yes; Yes
643; Littlewhiteman, Adrain; F[sic]; 5; Cheyenne; 1/4+; S; Son; Yes; Yes [Name Hillman in 1926.]
644; Littlewhiteman, Sadie; F; 3; Cheyenne; 1/4+; S; Dau; Yes; Yes
645; Littlewhiteman, Warren; F[sic]; 1; Cheyenne; 1/4+; S; Son; Yes; Yes

646; Littlewolf, Frank; M; 53; Cheyenne; F; M; Head; Yes; Yes
647; Littlewolf, Kate; F; 47; Cheyenne; F; M; Wife; Yes; Yes
648; Littlewolf, Susan; F; 15; Cheyenne; F; S; Dau; Yes; Yes
649; Littlewolf, Mary; F; 8; Cheyenne; F; S; Dau; Yes; Yes

650; Littlewolf, Laura; F; 77; Cheyenne; F; Wd; Head; Yes; Yes
651; Littlewolf, Lena; F; 51; Cheyenne; F; S; Dau; Yes; Yes

652; Littlewolf, Robert; M; 47; Cheyenne; F; M; Head; Yes; Yes
653; Littlewolf, May; F; 35; Cheyenne; F; M; Wife; Yes; Yes [Name Harris in 1920.]
654; Littlewolf, Charles; M; 21; Cheyenne; F; S; Son; Yes; Yes
655; Littlewolf, Geraldine; F; 8; Cheyenne; F; S; Dau; Yes; Yes
656; Littlewolf, Eva; F; 5; Cheyenne; F; S; Dau; Yes; Yes
657; Littlewolf, Laban; M; 1; Cheyenne; F; S; Son; Yes; Yes
658; Littlewolf, Herbert; M; 1/12; Cheyenne; F; S; Son; Yes; Yes

659; Littlewolf, William; M; 46; Cheyenne; F; M; Head; Yes; Yes
660; Littlewolf, May; F; 39; Cheyenne; F; M; Wife; Yes; Yes
661; Littlewolf, Mamie; F; 18; Cheyenne; F; S; Dau; Yes; Yes
662; Littlewolf, William Jr.; M; 15; Cheyenne; F; S; Son; Yes; Yes
663; Littlewolf, Claude; F[sic]; 13; Cheyenne; F; S; Son; Yes; Yes

664; Littleyellowman, Eddie; M; 38; Cheyenne; F; M; Head; No; Cheyenne & Arap Ag, Okla; Yes
665; Littleyellowman, Susie; F; 9; Cheyenne; F; S; Dau; No; Cheyenne & Arap Ag, Okla; Yes
666; Littleyellowman, Rose; F; 7; Cheyenne; F; S; Dau; No; Cheyenne & Arap Ag, Okla; Yes

667; Littleyellowman, Hugh; M; 45; Cheyenne; F; M; Head; No; Cheyenne & Arap Ag, Okla; Yes
668; Littleyellowman, May; F; 13; Cheyenne; F; S; Dau; No; Cheyenne & Arap Ag, Okla; Yes

Census of the **Tongue River** reservation of the **Tongue River** jurisdiction, as of **April 1**, 1930, taken by **C. B. Lohmiller**, Superintendent.

**Key:** Number; NAME: Surname, Given; Sex; Age At Last Birthday; Tribe; Degree of Blood; Marital Status; Relationship To Head of Family; At Jurisdiction Where Enrolled (Yes or No); At Another Jurisdiction; ELSEWHERE: Post office, County, State; Ward (Yes or No); Allotment, Annuity, and Identification Numbers.

669; Littleyellowman, Jake; M; 48; Cheyenne; F; M; Head; Yes; Yes
670; Littleyellowman, Lena; F; 53; Cheyenne; F; S[sic]; Wife; No; Warm Springs, Deer Lodge, Mont; Yes
671; Fisher, Alice; F; 31; Cheyenne; F; S; S-Dau; Yes; Yes
672; Fisher, Isabelle; F; 21; Cheyenne; F; S; S-Dau; Yes; Yes
673; Fisher, Richard; M; 17; Cheyenne; F; S; S-Dau[sic]; Yes; Yes
674; Fisher, Harold; M; 9; Cheyenne; F; S; S-Son; Yes; Yes

675; Littleyellowman, Richard; M; 39; Cheyenne; F; S; Head; Yes; Yes

676; Loneelk, Wilson; M; 19; Cheyenne; F; M; Head; Yes; Yes
677; Loneelk, Sarah A.; F; 17; Cheyenne; F; M; Wife; Yes; Yes

278[sic];Lonewolf, Charles; M; 46; Cheyenne; F; M; Head; Yes; Yes

679; Longjaw, Charles; M; 84; Cheyenne; F; M; Head; Yes; Yes
680; Longjaw, Clara; F; 68; Cheyenne; F; M; Wife; Yes; Yes
681; Longjaw, Charles Jr.; M; 14; Cheyenne; F; S; G-Son; Yes; Yes

682; Longjaw, Elmer; M; 46; Cheyenne; F; M; Head; Yes; Yes
683; Longjaw, Lena; F; 43; Cheyenne; F; M; Wife; Yes; Yes
684; Longjaw, Albert; M; 17; Cheyenne; F; S; Son; Yes; Yes
685; Longjaw, Henry; M; 14; Cheyenne; F; S; Son; Yes; Yes
686; Longjaw, Clara; F; 11; Cheyenne; F; S; Dau; Yes; Yes

687; Longjaw, Frank; M; 30; Cheyenne; F; M; Head; Yes; Yes
688; Longjaw, Bernice M.; F; 20; Cheyenne; F; M; Wife; Yes; Yes [Medicineflying; Jennie in 1928.]
689; Longjaw, Robert; M; 3; Cheyenne; F; S; Son; Yes; Yes

690; Longjaw, James; M; 48; Cheyenne; F; M; Head; Yes; Yes
691; Longjaw, Nellie; F; 34; Cheyenne; F; M; Wife; Yes; Yes
692; Longjaw, Donald; M; 1; Cheyenne; F; S; Son; Yes; Yes

693; Longroach, George; M; 48; Cheyenne; F; M; Head; Yes; Yes
694; Longroach, Nellie; F; 41; Cheyenne; F; M; Wife; Yes; Yes
695; Longroach, Harry; M; 19; Cheyenne; F; S; Son; Yes; Yes
696; Longroach, James; M; 15; Cheyenne; F; S; Son; Yes; Yes
697; Longroach, Mary; F; 13; Cheyenne; F; S; Dau; Yes; Yes [Name Vita 1917-26.]
698; Longroach, Frank; M; 10; Cheyenne; F; S; Son; Yes; Yes
699; Longroach, Regina; F; 6; Cheyenne; F; S; Dau; Yes; Yes [Veria in 1923.]

700; Looksatbareground, James; M; 51; Cheyenne; F; M; Head; Yes; Yes

Census of the __Tongue River__ reservation of the __Tongue River__ jurisdiction, as of __April 1__, 1930, taken by __C. B. Lohmiller__, Superintendent.

**Key:** Number; NAME: Surname, Given; Sex; Age At Last Birthday; Tribe; Degree of Blood; Marital Status; Relationship To Head of Family; At Jurisdiction Where Enrolled (Yes or No); At Another Jurisdiction; ELSEWHERE: Post office, County, State; Ward (Yes or No); Allotment, Annuity, and Identification Numbers.

701; Looksatbareground, Julia; F; 77; Cheyenne; F; M; Wife; Yes; Yes [1924 wd., Elkshoulders.]

702; Looksbehind, Charles; M; 69; Cheyenne; F; M; Head; Yes; Yes

703; Looksbehind, James; M; 45; Cheyenne; F; M; Head; No; Cheyenne & Arap. Ag, Okla; Yes [James Nightwalking]
704; Looksbehind, Roy; M; 9; Cheyenne; F; S; Son; No; Cheyenne & Arap. Ag, Okla; Yes
705; Looksbehind, Camilla; F; 6; Cheyenne; F; S; Dau; No; Cheyenne & Arap. Ag, Okla; Yes
706; Looksbehind, James Jr.; M; 2; Cheyenne; F; S; Son; No; Cheyenne & Arap. Ag, Okla; Yes

707; Looksbehind, Sallie; F; 70; Cheyenne; F; Wd; Head; Yes; Yes
708; Redneck, Pius; M; 18; Cheyenne; F; S; G-Son; Yes; Yes

709; Lostleg, Nelson; M; 38; Cheyenne; F; Wd[sic]; Head; Yes; Yes
710; Lostleg, James; M; 14; Cheyenne; F; S; Son; Yes; Yes [Ernest George in 1926.]
711; Lostleg, Virgina[sic]; F; 11; Cheyenne; F; S; Dau; Yes; Yes [Son Theodore in 1920.]

712; Magpie, Albert; M; 44; Cheyenne; F; Wd[sic]; Head; Yes; Yes [Prev. censuses from 1904-15 name is Youngmagpie with same birth year, none in 1913, Magpie in 1916. As early as 1907 a first wife Julia born 1887. Anne is a second wife starting in 1919. Anne is not in 1925.]
713; Magpie, Anna Mary; F; 10; Cheyenne; F; S; Dau; Yes; Yes [Minnie in 1926.]
714; Magpie, Gilbert; M; 7; Cheyenne; F; S; Son; Yes; Yes

715; Magpie, Louis; M; 44; Cheyenne; F; M; Head; Yes; Yes
716; Magpie, Mira; F; 35; Cheyenne; F; M; Wife; Yes; Yes
717; Magpie, Eddie; M; 20; F; S; Son; No; Warm Springs-Town, Deer Lodge, Mont, Yes
718; Hardrobe, Mollie; F; 14; Cheyenne; F; S; S-Dau; Yes; Yes

719; Manbear, Lena; F; 62; Cheyenne; F; Wd; Head; Yes; Yes
720; Manbear, Lizzie; F; 28; Cheyenne; F; S; Dau; Yes; Yes
721; Walters, Coolidge; M; 4; Cheyenne; 1/4+; S; G-Son; Yes; Yes

722; Marrowbone, Jessie; F; 41; Cheyenne; F; M; Head; No; Pine Ridge Ag. S.D.; Yes [Children enrolled at Pine Ridge.]

723; Medicine, Sampson; M; 53; Cheyenne; F; M; Head; Yes; Yes
724; Medicine, Anna; F; 51; Cheyenne; F; M; Wife; Yes; Yes

Census of the __Tongue River__ reservation of the __Tongue River__ jurisdiction, as of __April 1__, 1930, taken by __C. B. Lohmiller__, Superintendent.

**Key:** Number; NAME: Surname, Given; Sex; Age At Last Birthday; Tribe; Degree of Blood; Marital Status; Relationship To Head of Family; At Jurisdiction Where Enrolled (Yes or No); At Another Jurisdiction; ELSEWHERE: Post office, County, State; Ward (Yes or No); Allotment, Annuity, and Identification Numbers.

725; Medicine, Jennie; F; 28; Cheyenne; F; S; Dau; Yes; Yes
726; Redeagle, Jennie; F; 88; Cheyenne; F; Wd; Mother; Yes; Yes

727; Medicinebird, Nelson; M; 54; Cheyenne; F; M; Head; Yes; Yes
728; Medicinebird, Ella; F; 47; Cheyenne; F; M; Wife; Yes; Yes
729; Medicinebird, Homer J.; M; 16; Cheyenne; F; S; Son; Yes; Yes

730; Medicinebull, Robert; M; 69; Cheyenne; F; M; Head; Yes; Yes
731; Medicinebull, Maggie; F; 67; Cheyenne; F; M; Wife; Yes; Yes

732; Medicinebull, Willis; M; 43; Cheyenne; F; M; Head; Yes; Yes
733; Medicinebull, Anne; F; 27; Cheyenne; F; M; Wife; Yes; Yes [Swallow]
734; Medicinebull, James; M; 19; Cheyenne; F; S; Son; Yes; Yes
735; Medicinebull, Ruth; F; 16; Cheyenne; F; S; Dau; Yes; Yes
736; Medicinebull, Fred; M; 4; Cheyenne; F; S; Son; Yes; Yes
737; Medicinebull, Bert; M; 3; Cheyenne; f; S; Son; Yes; Yes

738; Medicineelk, Andrew; M; 31; Cheyenne; F; M; Head; Yes; Yes
739; Medicineelk, Maggie B.; F; 27; Cheyenne; F; M; Wife; Yes; Yes [Bearquiver]
740; Medicineelk, Peter; M; 4; Cheyenne; F; S; Son; Yes; Yes
741; Medicineelk, Margaret; F; 2/12; Cheyenne; F; S; Dau; Yes; Yes

742; Medicineelk, Basil; M; 36; Cheyenne; F; M; Head; Yes; Yes

743; Medicineelk, Harold; M; 64; Cheyenne; F; Wd[sic]; Head; Yes; Yes
744; Medicineelk, John; M; 19; Cheyenne; F; S; Son; Yes; Yes [Sandwoman; G-son in 1928]

745; Medicineelk, James; M; 28; Cheyenne; F; S; Head; No; Cheyenne & Arap. Ag, Okla; Yes

746; Medicineelk, Thomas; M; 23; Cheyenne; F; D; Head; Yes; Yes

747; Medicineflying, John; M; 47; Cheyenne; F; M; Head; Yes; Yes
748; Medicineflying, Bertha; F; 45; Cheyenne; F; M; Wife; Yes; Yes
749; Medicineflying, Helen J.; F; 13; Cheyenne; F; S; Dau; Yes; Yes
750; Medicineflying, Agnes A.; F; 9; Cheyenne; F; S; Dau; Yes; Yes
751; Medicineflying, Phyllis A.; F; 5; Cheyenne; F; S; Dau; Yes; Yes
752; Standingelk, Annie; F; 22; Cheyenne; F; D; Dau; Yes; Yes
753; Standingelk, Roy; F; 3; Cheyenne; F; S; G-Son; Yes; Yes

754; Medicinetop, James; M; 68; Cheyenne; F; Wd[sic]; Head; Yes; Yes

755; Medicinetop, John; M; 45; Cheyenne; F; M; Head; Yes; Yes

Census of the **Tongue River** reservation of the **Tongue River** jurisdiction, as of **April 1**, 1930, taken by **C. B. Lohmiller**, Superintendent.

**Key:** Number; NAME: Surname, Given; Sex; Age At Last Birthday; Tribe; Degree of Blood; Marital Status; Relationship To Head of Family; At Jurisdiction Where Enrolled (Yes or No); At Another Jurisdiction; ELSEWHERE: Post office, County, State; Ward (Yes or No); Allotment, Annuity, and Identification Numbers.

756; Medicinetop, Ida; F; 39; Cheyenne; F; M; Wife; Yes; Yes
757; Medicinetop, Clarence; M; 19; Cheyenne; F; S; Son; Yes; Yes
758; Medicinetop, Majorie[sic]; F; 15; Cheyenne; F; S; Dau; Yes; Yes
759; Medicinetop, Phyllis; F; 7; Cheyenne; F; S; Dau; Yes; Yes
760; Medicinetop, Roy; M; 5; Cheyenne; F; S; Son; Yes; Yes
761; Medicinetop, Lena; F; 2; Cheyenne; F; S; Dau; Yes; Yes
762; Medicinetop, Edward; M; 1; Cheyenne; F; S; Son; Yes; Yes

763; Merritt, Wesley; M; 53; Cheyenne; F; M; Head; Yes; Yes
764; Merritt, Josie; F; 66; Cheyenne; F; M; Wife; Yes; Yes
765; Walkingbear, Mannie; F; 32; Cheyenne; F; D; S-Dau; Yes; Yes
766; Twomoons, George; M; 9; Cheyenne; F; S; G-Son; Yes; Yes

767; ~~Mexicancheyenne~~ King, Ernest; M; 40; Cheyenne; 1/4+; M; Head; Yes; Yes King - Letter dated 5/13/31
768; ~~Mexicancheyenne~~ King, Mary; F; 30; Cheyenne; F; M; Wife; Yes; Yes
769; ~~Mexicancheyenne~~ King, Harriet; F; 11; Cheyenne; 1/4+; S; Dau; Yes; Yes [Hilda in 1928.]
770; ~~Mexicancheyenne~~ King, M. Victoria; F; 8; Cheyenne; 1/4+; S; Dau; Yes; Yes
771; ~~Mexicancheyenne~~ King, Rudolph; M; 5; Cheyenne; 1/4+; S; Son; Yes; Yes [Anabelle; dau; 1925.]
772; ~~Mexicancheyenne~~ King, Anna Joyce; F; 1; Cheyenne; 1/4+; S; Dau; Yes; Yes

773; ~~Mexicancheyenne~~ King, Marion; M; 42; Cheyenne; 1/4+; M; Head; Yes; Yes
774; ~~Mexicancheyenne~~ King, Emma; F; 36; Cheyenne; F; M; Wife; Yes; Yes
775; ~~Mexicancheyenne~~ King, James; M; 15; Cheyenne; 1/4+; S; Son; Yes; Yes
776; ~~Mexicancheyenne~~ King, Rosa; F; 11; Cheyenne; 1/4+; S; Dau; Yes; Yes
777; ~~Mexicancheyenne~~ King, Margaret; F; 9; Cheyenne; 1/4+; S; Dau; Yes; Yes [Ethel in 1926.]
778; ~~Mexicancheyenne~~ King, Mary; F; 4; Cheyenne; 1/4+; S; Dau; Yes; Yes
779; ~~Mexicancheyenne~~ King, Mabel Ann; F; 2; Cheyenne; 1/4+; S; Dau; Yes; Yes

780; Oldbull, Daniel; M; 59; Cheyenne; F; Wd[sic]; Head; Yes; Yes
781; Oldbull, Thomas; F[sic]; 19; Cheyenne; F; S; Son; Yes; Yes

782; Onebear, James; M; 29; Cheyenne; 1/4+; M; Head; Yes; Yes
783; Onebear, Maggie; F; 27; Cheyenne; 1/4+; M; Wife; Yes; Yes [Seminole]
784; Onebear, Robert; M; 4; Cheyenne; 1/4+; S; Son; Yes; Yes
785; Onebear, Louise; F; 5/12; Cheyenne; 1/4+; S; Dau; Yes; Yes

786; Parker, Alvin O.; M; 50; Cheyenne; 1/4+; M; Head; Yes; Yes
787; Parker, Clyde S.; M; 7; Cheyenne; -1/4; S; Son; Yes; Yes
788; Parker, Verda F.; F; 5; Cheyenne; -1/4; S; Dau; Yes; Yes
789; Parker, Shirley R.; M; 3; Cheyenne; -1/4; S; Son; Yes; Yes
790; Parker, Donald E.; M; 1; Cheyenne; -1/4; S; Son; Yes; Yes

Census of the __Tongue River__ reservation of the __Tongue River__ jurisdiction, as of __April 1__, 1930, taken by __C. B. Lohmiller__, Superintendent.

**Key:** Number; NAME: Surname, Given; Sex; Age At Last Birthday; Tribe; Degree of Blood; Marital Status; Relationship To Head of Family; At Jurisdiction Where Enrolled (Yes or No); At Another Jurisdiction; ELSEWHERE: Post office, County, State; Ward (Yes or No); Allotment, Annuity, and Identification Numbers.

791; Parker, Charles A.; M; 44; Cheyenne; 1/4+; M; Head; Yes; Yes
792; Parker, Theresa; F; 18; Cheyenne; 1/4+; S; Dau; Yes; Yes
793; Parker, Gabriel; M; 3; Cheyenne; 1/4+; S; Son; Yes; Yes

794; Parker, Edwin; M; 35; Cheyenne; 1/4+; S; Head; Yes; Yes

795; Parker, Guy; M; 38; Cheyenne; 1/4+; M; Head; Yes; Yes
796; Parker, Winfred; M; 15; Cheyenne; 1/4+; Son; Yes; Yes
797; Parker, Alice; F; 13; Cheyenne; 1/4+; S; Dau; Yes; Yes
798; Parker, Stella; F; 10; Cheyenne; 1/4+; S; Dau; Yes; Yes
799; Parker, Charlotte; F; 8/12; Cheyenne; 1/4+; S; Dau; Yes; Yes

800; Pease, Ida; F; 23; Cheyenne; -1/4; M; Head; No; Lodgegrass town, Big Horn, Mont; Yes [Eastman]

801; Pine, Frank; M; 66; Cheyenne; F; M; Head; Yes; Yes
802; Pine, Nora W.; F; 66; Cheyenne; F; M; Wife; Yes; Yes

803; Pine, Rutherford; M; 43 Cheyenne; F; M; Head; Yes; Yes
804; Pine, Julia; F; 33; Cheyenne; F; M; Wife; Yes; Yes [In 1916 marries Julia Blackcrane nee Kingfisher; in 1912 she is 18 years old, birth year is 1894 from 1904-16. Gave birth year as 1884 from 1917-26.]
805; Pine, Cecelia; F; 14; Cheyenne; F; S; Dau; Yes; Yes
806; Pine, Daniel; F[sic]; 6; Cheyenne; F; S; Son; Yes; Yes

807; Pine, Wilson; M; 43; Cheyenne; F; M; Head; Yes; Yes
808; Pine, Nora; F; 41; Cheyenne; F; M; Wife; Yes; Yes
809; Pine, Alexander; M; 12; Cheyenne; F; S; Son; Yes; Yes
810; Pine, John; M; 8; Cheyenne; F; S; Son; Yes; Yes
811; Pine, Sarah; F; 5; Cheyenne; F; S; Dau; Yes; Yes
812; Powderface, Fern; F; 11; Cheyenne; F; S; S-Dau; Yes; Yes

813; Playingbear, Henry; M; 53; Cheyenne; F; M; Head; Yes; Yes
814; Playingbear, Mildred; F; 50; Cheyenne; F; M; Wife; Yes; Yes

815; Powderface, John; M; 63; Cheyenne; F; Wd[sic]; Head; No; Shoshone Ag & Arap., Wyo.; Yes

816; Powell, Clay; M; 25; Cheyenne; -1/4; M; Head; No; Sheridan Town, Big Horn, Wyo.; Yes

817; Powell, Mary; F; 48; Cheyenne; 1/4+; M; Head; Yes; Yes
818; Powell, Deyo; M; 22; Cheyenne; -1/4; S; Son; Yes; Yes
819; Powell, Howard; M; 18; Cheyenne; -1/4; S; Son; Yes; Yes

Census of the **Tongue River** reservation of the **Tongue River** jurisdiction, as of **April 1**, 1930, taken by **C. B. Lohmiller**, Superintendent.

**Key:** Number; NAME: Surname, Given; Sex; Age At Last Birthday; Tribe; Degree of Blood; Marital Status; Relationship To Head of Family; At Jurisdiction Where Enrolled (Yes or No); At Another Jurisdiction; ELSEWHERE: Post office, County, State; Ward (Yes or No); Allotment, Annuity, and Identification Numbers.

820; Prairiebear, Arthur; M; 48; Cheyenne; F; M; Head; Yes; Yes
821; Prairiebear, Sallie; F; 44; Cheyenne; F; M; Wife; Yes; Yes
822; Prairiebear, Louis; M; 1; Cheyenne; F; S; Son; Yes; Yes

823; Redbead, John; M; 58; Cheyenne; F; M; Head; Yes; Yes
824; Redbead, Nancy; F; 52; Cheyenne; F; M; Wife; Yes; Yes
825; Redbead, Susie; F; 16; Cheyenne; F; S; Dau; Yes; Yes
826; Redbead, Clara; F; 14; Cheyenne; F; S; Dau; Yes; Yes
827; Redbead, Georgia; F; 12; Cheyenne; F; S; Dau; Yes; Yes [Name Gloria 1917-20.]

828; Redbird, Joseph; M; 30; Cheyenne; F; D; Head; Yes; Yes [Middle name Francis in 1910.]
829; Redbird, William; M; 7; Cheyenne; F; S; Son; No; Cheyenne & Arap. Ag, Okla; Yes
830; Redbird, Allen; M; 4; Cheyenne; F; S; Son; No; Cheyenne & Arap. Ag, Okla; Yes [First shows in 1925 with birth in 1924. Same Prev. #, Helena; dau; 1925, F. in 1926.]

831; Redbird, William; M; 53; Cheyenne; F; M; Head; Yes; Yes
832; Redbird, Florence; F; 52; Cheyenne; 1/4+; M; Wife; Yes; Yes
833; Redbird, Lena; F; 9; Cheyenne; 1/4+; S; Dau; Yes; Yes [Susie in 1926.]
834; Redbird, Samuel; M; 1; Cheyenne; 1/4+; S; Son; Yes; Yes
835; Rowland, Elizabeth; F; 16; Cheyenne; 1/4-; S; S-Dau; Yes; Yes
836; Rowland, Lillian; F; 13; Cheyenne; 1/4-; S; S-Dau; Yes; Yes
837; Tangledhornelk, Nellie; F; 77; Cheyenne; F; Wd; Mother; Yes; Yes

838; Redbreath, Charles; M; 50; Cheyenne; F; M; Head; Yes; Yes

839; Redbreath, Betty; F; 22; Cheyenne; F; M; Head[sic]; Yes; Yes [Yellownose]
840; Redbreath, Elina J.; F; 4; Cheyenne; F; S; Dau; Yes; Yes [Elina June in 1926.]
841; Redbreath, George; M; 2; Cheyenne; F; S; Son; Yes; Yes

842; Redcherries, Teddy; M; 41; Cheyenne; F; M; Head; No; Cheyenne & Arap. Ag, Okla; Yes
843; Redcherries, Miller; M; 9; Cheyenne; F; S; Son; No; Cheyenne & Arap. Ag, Okla; Yes

844; Redcherries, William; M; 39; Cheyenne; F; M; Head; Yes; Yes
845; Redcherries, Bessie; F; 36; Cheyenne; F; M; Wife; Yes; Yes
846; Redcherries, Alice; F; 17; Cheyenne; F; S; Dau; Yes; Yes
847; Redcherries, Rose; F; 14; Cheyenne; F; S; Dau; Yes; Yes
848; Redcherries, Frank; M; 10; Cheyenne; F; S; Son; Yes; Yes
849; Redcherries, Margaret; F; 6; Cheyenne; F; M[sic]; Dau; Yes; Yes
850; Redcherries, Katie; F; 2; Cheyenne; F; S; Dau; Yes; Yes

Census of the __Tongue River__ reservation of the __Tongue River__ jurisdiction, as of __April 1__, 1930, taken by __C. B. Lohmiller__, Superintendent.

**Key:** Number; NAME: Surname, Given; Sex; Age At Last Birthday; Tribe; Degree of Blood; Marital Status; Relationship To Head of Family; At Jurisdiction Where Enrolled (Yes or No); At Another Jurisdiction; ELSEWHERE: Post office, County, State; Ward (Yes or No); Allotment, Annuity, and Identification Numbers.

851; Stumphorn, Anna; F; 78; Cheyenne; F; Wd; Mother; Yes; Yes

852; Redeagle, Nellie; F; 57; Cheyenne; F; Wd; Head; Yes; Yes
853; Redeagle, Willis; M; 28; Cheyenne; F; S; Son; Yes; Yes

854; Redfox, James; M; 64; Cheyenne; F; M; Head; Yes; Yes
855; Redfox, Cora; F; 62; Cheyenne; F; M; Wife; Yes; Yes

856; Redfox, Jennie; F; 56; Cheyenne; F; Wd; Head; Yes; Yes

857; Redfox, Robert; M; 30; Cheyenne; F; M; Head; Yes; Yes
858; Redfox, Cecelia; F; 35; Cheyenne; F; M; Wife; Yes; Yes
859; Redfox, Edna S.; F; 2; Cheyenne; F; S; Dau; Yes; Yes
860; Redfox, Ralph; M; 5/12; Cheyenne; F; S; Son; Yes; Yes
861; Sanchez, Pauline; F; 15; Cheyenne; 1/4+; S; S-Dau; Yes; Yes
862; Sanchez, Cecelia; F; 7; Cheyenne; 1/4+; S; S-Dau; Yes; Yes

863; Redneck, Curtis; M; 42; Cheyenne; F; M; Head; Yes; Yes
864; Redneck, Josie; F; 33; Cheyenne; F; M; Wife; Yes; Yes

865; Redneck, David; M; 38; Cheyenne; F; M; Head; No; Cheyenne & Arap. Ag, Okla; Yes
866; Redneck, Minnie; F; 9; Cheyenne; F; S; Dau; No; Cheyenne & Arap. Ag, Okla; Yes

867; Redneck, Henry; M; 47; Cheyenne; F; M; Head; Yes; Yes
868; Redneck, Fannie; F; 45; Cheyenne; F; M; Wife; Yes; Yes
869; Redneck, Dora; F; 15; Cheyenne; F; S; Dau; Yes; Yes
870; Redneck, Homer; M; 12; Cheyenne; F; S; Son; Yes; Yes
871; Redneck, Florence; F; 9; Cheyenne; F; S; Dau; Yes; Yes
872; Redneck, John; M; 4; Cheyenne; F; s; Son; Yes; Yes

873; Rednose, Paul; M; 53; Cheyenne; F; M; Head; Yes; Yes
874; Rednose, Lucy; F; 59; Cheyenne; F; M; Wife; Yes; Yes [1/2 in 1928.]

875; Redrobe, Fred; M; 62; Cheyenne; F; M; Head; Yes; Yes
876; Redrobe, Nora; F; 60; Cheyenne; F; M; Wife; Yes; Yes
877; Redrobe, Louis; M; 37; Cheyenne; F; S; Son; Yes; Yes
878; Whistlingelk, Flora; F; 23; Cheyenne; F; D; Dau; Yes; Yes
879; Whistlingelk, May; F; 4; Cheyenne; F; S; G-Dau; Yes; Yes

880; Redrobe, Jasper; M; 29; Cheyenne; F; S; Head; No; Dear Lodge town, Deer Lodge, Mont; Yes

881; Redrobe, William; M; 32; Cheyenne; F; M; Head; Yes; Yes

Census of the __Tongue River__ reservation of the __Tongue River__ jurisdiction, as of __April 1__, 1930, taken by __C. B. Lohmiller__, Superintendent.

**Key:** Number; NAME: Surname, Given; Sex; Age At Last Birthday; Tribe; Degree of Blood; Marital Status; Relationship To Head of Family; At Jurisdiction Where Enrolled (Yes or No); At Another Jurisdiction; ELSEWHERE: Post office, County, State; Ward (Yes or No); Allotment, Annuity, and Identification Numbers.

882; Redrobe, Alice; F; 45; Cheyenne; F; M; Wife; Yes; Yes [1907-19, birth year 1884-5. 1904 nee-Killsnight; 1905-6 Risingsun, 1907-19 Shell, 1920-28 Redrobe.

883; Weaselbear, Stella C[?]; F; 12; Cheyenne; F; S; Niece; Yes; Yes [s-dau-Henry Littlewhiteman. Clarice in 1926.]

884; Redwater, Cecelia; F; 57; Cheyenne; F; D; Head; Yes; Yes

885; Redwater, Thaddeus; M; 54; Cheyenne; F; M; Head; Yes; Yes

886; Redwoman, Frank; M; 41; Cheyenne; F; Wd[sic]; Head; Yes; Yes
887; Redwoman, Flossie A.; F; 18; Cheyenne; F; S; Dau; Yes; Yes
888; Redwoman, Eugene; M; 7; Cheyenne; F; S; Son; Yes; Yes
889; Redwoman, Joe; M; 4; Cheyenne; F; S; Son; Yes; Yes

890; Redwoman, Manuel; M; 48; Cheyenne; F; M; Head; Yes; Yes
891; Redwoman, Olive; F; 38; Cheyenne; F; M; Wife; Yes; Yes
892; Redwoman, Edna; F; 3; Cheyenne; F; S; Dau; Yes; Yes
893; Redwoman, Donald; M; 1; Cheyenne; F; S; Dau[sic]; Yes; Yes
894; Redwoman, John; M; 27; Cheyenne; F; Wd; Son; Yes; Yes
895; Redneck, Clyde; M; 17; Cheyenne; F; S; Nephew; Yes; Yes

896; Ridgebear, Charles; M; 47; Cheyenne; F; M; Head; No; Cheyenne & Arap. Ag, Okla; Yes

897; Ridgebear, Willis; M; 42; Cheyenne; F; M; Head; Yes; Yes
898; Ridgebear, Rilla; F; 32; Cheyenne; F; M; Wife; Yes; Yes
899; Ridgebear, Bessie A.; F 11; Cheyenne; F; S; Dau; Yes; Yes
900; Ridgebear, Carrie; F; 8; Cheyenne; F S; Dau; Yes; Yes [Katie in 1926.]
901; Ridgebear, Anna; F; 2; Cheyenne; F; S; Dau; Yes; Yes
902; Ridgebear, James; M; 1; Cheyenne; F; S; Son; Yes; Yes

903; Ridgewalker, Robert; M; 69; Cheyenne; F; M; Head; Yes; Yes
904; Ridgewalker, Ethel; F; 59; Cheyenne; 1/4+; M; Wife; Yes; Yes
905; Ridgewalker, Frank; M; 21; Cheyenne; 1/4+; S; Son; Yes; Yes

906; Risingfire, Bessie; F; 73; Cheyenne; F; Wd; Head; Yes; Yes
907; Fightingbear, Julia; F; 18; Cheyenne; F; S; G-Dau; Yes; Yes
908; Fightingbear, Dora; F; 15; Cheyenne; F; S; G-Dau; Yes; Yes

909; Risingsun, Oliver; M; 29; Cheyenne; F; M; Head; Yes; Yes
910; Risingsun, Elizabeth; F; 22; Cheyenne; F; M; Wife; Yes; Yes [Flying]
911; Risingsun, Teddy; M; 3; Cheyenne; F; S; Son; Yes; Yes

912; Risingsun, Peter; M; 42; Cheyenne; F; Wd; Head; Yes; Yes
913; Risingsun, Maude; F; 16; Cheyenne; F; S; Dau; Yes; Yes

Census of the __Tongue River__ reservation of the __Tongue River__ jurisdiction, as of __April 1__, 1930, taken by __C. B. Lohmiller__, Superintendent.

**Key:** Number; NAME: Surname, Given; Sex; Age At Last Birthday; Tribe; Degree of Blood; Marital Status; Relationship To Head of Family; At Jurisdiction Where Enrolled (Yes or No); At Another Jurisdiction; ELSEWHERE: Post office, County, State; Ward (Yes or No); Allotment, Annuity, and Identification Numbers.

914; Risingsun, Harry; M; 8; Cheyenne; F; S; Son; Yes; Yes
915; Risingsun, Lyman; M; 6; Cheyenne; F; S; Son; Yes; Yes
916; Risingsun, James; M; 4; Cheyenne; F; S; Son; Yes; Yes

917; Risingsun, Philip; M; 67; Cheyenne; F; M; Head; Yes; Yes
918; Risingsun, Nora; F; 61; Cheyenne; F; M; Wife; Yes; Yes
919; Risingsun, John; M; 34; Cheyenne; F; S; Son; Yes; Yes
920; Risingsun, Pearl; F; 1; Cheyenne; F; S; Niece; Yes; Yes

921; Risingsun, William; M; 25; Cheyenne; F; M; Head; Yes; Yes
922; Risingsun, Edna Josie; F; 17; Cheyenne; F; M; Wife; Yes; Yes

923; Robinson, Nellie; F; 32; Cheyenne; -1/4; M; Head; Yes; Yes
924; Robinson, David C.; M; 11; Cheyenne; -1/4; S; Son; Yes; Yes
925; Robinson, Cornelius; M; 9; Cheyenne; -1/;4; S; Son; Yes; Yes
926; Robinson, Eloise E.; F; 8; Cheyenne; -1/4; S; Dau; Yes; Yes
927; Robinson, Buell D.; M; 1; Cheyenne; -1/4; S; Son; Yes; Yes

928; Rockroads, Mack; M; 36; Cheyenne; F; M; Head; Yes; Yes
929; Rockroads, Nellie; F; 36; Cheyenne; F; M; Wife; Yes; Yes
930; Rockroads, Thomas; M; 12; Cheyenne; F; S; Son; Yes; Yes    [1918 Census #902; Name is Lettie, female.]
931; Rockroads, Flossie; F; 8/12; Cheyenne; F; S; Dau; Yes; Yes
932; Rockroads, Nora; F; 59; Cheyenne; F; Wd; Mother; Yes; Yes
933; Rockroads, Mary; F; 16; Cheyenne; F; S; Sister; Yes; Yes

934; Romannose, Louis; M; 47; Cheyenne; F; M; Head; Yes; Yes
935; Romannose, Mary; F; 39; Cheyenne; F; M; Wife; Yes; Yes
936; Romannose, George; M; 19; Cheyenne; F; S; Son; Yes; Yes
937; Romannose, Blanche; F; 15; Cheyenne; F; S; Dau; Yes; Yes [Helen in 1926.]
938; Romannose, Julia; F; 13; Cheyenne; F; S; Dau; Yes; Yes [May in 1926.]
939; Romannose, Willeatte; F; 8; Cheyenne; F; S; Dau; Yes; Yes
940; Romannose, Montana; F; 6; Cheyenne; F; S; Dau; Yes; Yes
941; Romannose, Eva L.; F; 1; Cheyenne; F; S; Dau; Yes; Yes

942; Rondeau, Antoine; M; 42; Cheyenne; 1/4+; M; Head; Yes; Yes
943; Rondeau, Louise; F; 40; Cheyenne; 1/4+; M; Wife; Yes; Yes
944; Rondeau, Clara; F; 17; Cheyenne; 1/4+; S; Dau; Yes; Yes
945; Rondeau, Charles; M; 9; Cheyenne; 1/4+; S; Son; Yes; Yes
946; Bixby, Jessie; F; 74; Cheyenne; 1/4+; Wd; Mother-in-law; Yes; Yes

947; Rondeau, William; M; 46; Cheyenne; 1/4+; Wd[sic]; Head; Yes; Yes
948; Rondeau, Henry; M; 19; Cheyenne; 1/4+; S; Son; Yes; Yes
949; Rondeau, John; M; 18; Cheyenne; 1/4+; S; Son; Yes; Yes

Census of the __Tongue River__ reservation of the __Tongue River__ jurisdiction, as of __April 1__, 1930, taken by __C. B. Lohmiller__, Superintendent.

**Key:** Number; NAME: Surname, Given; Sex; Age At Last Birthday; Tribe; Degree of Blood; Marital Status; Relationship To Head of Family; At Jurisdiction Where Enrolled (Yes or No); At Another Jurisdiction; ELSEWHERE: Post office, County, State; Ward (Yes or No); Allotment, Annuity, and Identification Numbers.

950; Roundstone, Flora; F; 41; Cheyenne; F; M; Head; Yes; Yes [Twobulls]
951; Roundstone, Martin; M; 18; Cheyenne; F; S; Son; Yes; Yes
952; Roundstone, Sarah; F; 9; Cheyenne; F; S; Dau; Yes; Yes
953; Roundstone, Paul; M; 7; Cheyenne; F; S; Son; Yes; Yes
954; Roundstone, Ruth; F; 3; Cheyenne; F; S; Dau; Yes; Yes

955; Rowland, Benton; M; 31; Cheyenne; 1/4+; M; Head; No; Pine Ridge Ag., S.D.; Yes
956; Rowland, Marie; F; 3; Cheyenne; 1/4+; S; Dau; No; Pine Ridge Ag., S.D.; Yes
957; Rowland, Eugene; M; 3; Cheyenne; 1/4+; S; Son; No; Pine Ridge Ag., S.D.; Yes

958; Rowland, Clay T.; M; 50; Cheyenne; 1/4+; M; Head; Yes; Yes

959; Rowland, Joe; M; 27; Cheyenne; 1/4+; M; Head; No; Pine Ridge; Yes [In 1926 #935; Jose; son; birth year 1900.]

960; Rowland, Thomas; M; 37; Cheyenne; 1/4+; M; Head; Yes; Yes
961; Rowland, Daisy; F; 29; Cheyenne; F; M; Wife; Yes; Yes [Fightingbear, Ellen in 1924.]
962; Rowland, Blanche; F; 4; Cheyenne; 1/4+; S; Dau; Yes; Yes
963; Rowland, Don; M; 2; Cheyenne; 1/4+; S; Son; Yes; Yes

964; Rowland, William; M; 34; Cheyenne; 1/4+; M; Head; Yes; Yes
965; Rowland, Chester C.; M; 9; Cheyenne; 1/4+; S; Son; No; Pine Ridge Ag., S.D.; Yes
966; Rowland, Allen E.; M; 4; Cheyenne; 1/4+; S; Son; Yes; Yes
967; Rowland, Ardeth F.; F; 1; Cheyenne; 1/4+; S; Dau; Yes; Yes

968; Rowland, Willis; M; 67; Cheyenne; 1/4+; M; Head; Yes; Yes
969; Rowland, Helen; F; 61; Cheyenne; F; M; Wife; Yes; Yes [Sarah 1908-1919.]
970; Rowland, Jessie; M; 46; Cheyenne; 1/4+; S; Nephew; Yes; Yes [Name Frank and previous #932 in 1926.]
971; Rowland, Grace; F; 15; Cheyenne; 1/4+; S; A-Dau; Yes; Yes
972; Rowland, Frank; M; 5; Cheyenne; 1/4+; S; G-Son; Yes; Yes
973; Rowland, Zac; M; 61; Cheyenne; 1/4+; M; Head; Yes; Yes
974; Rowland, Edna; F; 53; Cheyenne; F; M; Wife; Yes; Yes

975; Russell, Frank; M; 31; Cheyenne; 1/4+; M; Head; Yes; Yes
976; Russell, Ellen; F; 32; Cheyenne; F; M; Wife; Yes; Yes [Sweetmedicine]

977; Russell, John; M; 36; Cheyenne; 1/4+; M; Head; Yes; Yes
978; Russell, Alice R.; F; 20; Cheyenne; F; SM; Wife; Yes; Yes
979; Russell, Stella; F; 14; Cheyenne; 1/4+; S; Dau; No; Superior ~~Town~~, Douglas, Wis.; Yes

Census of the **Tongue River** reservation of the **Tongue River** jurisdiction, as of **April 1**, 1930, taken by **C. B. Lohmiller**, Superintendent.

**Key:** Number; NAME: Surname, Given; Sex; Age At Last Birthday; Tribe; Degree of Blood; Marital Status; Relationship To Head of Family; At Jurisdiction Where Enrolled (Yes or No); At Another Jurisdiction; ELSEWHERE: Post office, County, State; Ward (Yes or No); Allotment, Annuity, and Identification Numbers.

980; Russell, May; F; 5; Cheyenne; 1/4+; S; Dau; No; Cheyenne & Arap. Ag, Okla; Yes
981; Russell, Inez I.; F; 3; Cheyenne; 1/4+; S; Dau; No; Cheyenne & Arap. Ag, Okla; Yes
982; Russell, John Jr.; M; 1; Cheyenne; 1/4+; S; Son; No; Cheyenne & Arap. Ag, Okla; Yes
983; Russell, William; M; 56; Cheyenne; F; M; Head; Yes; Yes
984; Russell, Fred; M; 21; Cheyenne; F; S; Son; Yes; Yes
985; Russell, Earl; M; 14; Cheyenne; F; S; Son; Yes; Yes
986; Russell, Mary; F; 11; Cheyenne; F; S; Dau; Yes; Yes [Mildred in 1926.]

987; Sandcrane, Henry; M; 40; Cheyenne; F; Wd[sic]; Head; Yes; Yes
988; Sandcrane, Margaret; F; 9; Cheyenne; F; S; Dau; Yes; Yes

989; Sandcrane, John; M; 57; Cheyenne; F; M; Head; Yes; Yes
990; Sandcrane, Ruth; F; 51; Cheyenne; F; M; Wife; Yes; Yes
991; Sandcrane, Isabelle; F; 15; Cheyenne; F; S; Dau; Yes; Yes
992; Littleoldman, Fern; F; 12; Cheyenne; F; S; G-Dau; Yes; Yes [s.-dau. Chas. Sharpnose, #569; Littleman, Julia; s-dau; 1915; F. (s-dau Fred Limpy) in 1926.]

993; Sansaver, Lillian; F; 23; Cheyenne; 1/4+; S; Head; No; Kansas City, Jackson, Mo.; Yes [dau-Rhoda Seminole; Sansover mother was a Miles in 1915. Sansover in 1917 #741.]

994; Scalpcane, August; M; 24; Cheyenne; F; S; Head; Yes; Yes
995; Scalpcane, Otto; M; 15; Cheyenne; F; S; Brother; Yes; Yes
996; Scalpcane, Henry; M; 10; Cheyenne; F; S; Brother; Yes; Yes [Rudolph in 1926.]

997; Schaffer, Letha; F; 16; Cheyenne; -1/4; M; Head; No; Crow Ag, Mont; ~~Crow Agency, Big Horn, Mont;~~ Yes [Son, Carl in 1916 Census. Eastman in 1927]

998; Seminole, Dan; M; 35; Cheyenne; 1/4+; M; Head; Yes; Yes
999; Seminole, Jennie; F; 33; Cheyenne; F; M; Wife; Yes; Yes
1000; Seminole, Anna; F; 9; Cheyenne; 1/4+; S; Dau; Yes; Yes
1001; Seminole, Margaret; F; 8; Cheyenne; 1/4+; S; Dau; Yes; Yes
1002; Seminole, Alfred; M; 6; Cheyenne; 1/4+; S; Son; Yes; Yes
1003; Seminole, Beatrice; F; 1; Cheyenne; 1/4+; S; Dau; Yes; Yes
1004; Littlewhiteman, Charles; M; 15; Cheyenne; 1/4+; S; S-Son; Yes; Yes

1005; Seminole, John; M; 51; Cheyenne; 1/4+; M; Head; Yes; Yes
1006; Seminole, Mary R.; F; 32; Cheyenne; F; M; Wife; Yes; Yes
1007; Seminole, Fred; M; 14; Cheyenne; 1/4+; S; Son; No; Cheyenne & Arap. Ag, Okla; Yes

Census of the **Tongue River** reservation of the **Tongue River** jurisdiction, as of **April 1**, 19**30**, taken by **C. B. Lohmiller**, Superintendent.

**Key:** Number; NAME: Surname, Given; Sex; Age At Last Birthday; Tribe; Degree of Blood; Marital Status; Relationship To Head of Family; At Jurisdiction Where Enrolled (Yes or No); At Another Jurisdiction; ELSEWHERE: Post office, County, State; Ward (Yes or No); Allotment, Annuity, and Identification Numbers.

1008; Seminole, Max; M; 5; Cheyenne; 1/4+; S; Son; Yes; Yes [son-Mary Redbird, 1926 #813 entry; Redbird, Maxine; g-g-son; 1924; M.; g-g-son Joseph Tangledhornelk]
1009; Fox, Margaret; F; 11; Cheyenne; F; S; S-Dau; Yes; Yes [Jessie in 1927.]
1010; Fox, Marie; F; 7; Cheyenne; F; S; S-Dau; Yes; Yes [Max, M., 1922-25.]

1011; Seminole, Josephine; F; 38; Cheyenne; 1/4+; S; Head; Yes; Yes
1012; Seminole, Lawrence; F[sic]; 18; Cheyenne; 1/4+; S; Son; Yes; Yes

1013; Seminole, Louis; M; 45; Cheyenne; 1/4+; Wd[sic]; Head; Yes; Yes

1014; Seminole, Miles; M; 60 Cheyenne; 1/4+; M; Head; Yes; Yes

1015; Sharpnose, Josephine; F; 27; Cheyenne; F; Wd; Head; Yes; Yes [Hisbadhorses]

1016; Shavedhead, James; M; 30; Cheyenne; F; M; Head; Yes; Yes
1017; Shavedhead, Alice; F; 23; Cheyenne; F; M; Wife; Yes; Yes [Medicineflying; age 3 in 1910. Birth 1906-07.]
1018; Shavedhead, Anna; F; 4; Cheyenne; F; S; Dau; Yes; Yes [Hyacinth in 1926.]
1019; Shavedhead, Mabel; F; 3/12; Cheyenne; F; S; Dau; Yes; Yes
1020; Shavedhead, Mary; F; 64; Cheyenne; F; S; Mother; Yes; Yes
1021; Divesbackward, Louisa; F; 12; Cheyenne; F; S; Niece; Yes; Yes [States 7/8 blood in 1928.]

1022; Shavedhead, Jean S.; F; 28; Cheyenne; F; M; Head; No; Shoshone Ag Wyo & Arapaho; Yes [Swallow]
1023; Shavedhead, Charles; M; 5; Cheyenne; F; S; Son; No; Shoshone Ag Wyo & Arapaho; Yes [Jeffrey, Jr. and birth year 1925 in 1926.]
1024; Shavedhead, Anna M.; F; 3; Cheyenne; F; S; Dau; No; Shoshone Ag Wyo & Arapaho; Yes

1025; Shell, Joseph; M; 49; Cheyenne; F; M; Head; Yes; Yes
1026; Shell, Julia; F; 28; Cheyenne; F; M; Wife; Yes; Yes [Previous #530 in 1906, censuses 1906-19, wife Alice [Risingsun] Shell, birth year 1885.] [Julia starts census 1920.]

1027; Shepherd, Mollie; F; 34; Cheyenne; 1/4+; M; Head; No; Cheyenne & Arapaho Ag, Okla; Yes

1028; Sherman, Ethel; F; 46; Cheyenne; 1/4+; M; Head; Yes; Yes
1029; Sherman, George; M; 18; Cheyenne; -1/4; S; Son; Yes; Yes
1030; Sherman, Otto; M; 16; Cheyenne; -1/4; S; Son; Yes; Yes
1031; Sherman, Wretha; F; 14; Cheyenne; -1/4; S; Dau; Yes; Yes
1032; Sherman, Carl; M; 11; Cheyenne; -1/4; S; Son; Yes; Yes

Census of the __Tongue River__ reservation of the __Tongue River__ jurisdiction, as of __April 1__, 1930, taken by __C. B. Lohmiller__, Superintendent.

**Key:** Number; NAME: Surname, Given; Sex; Age At Last Birthday; Tribe; Degree of Blood; Marital Status; Relationship To Head of Family; At Jurisdiction Where Enrolled (Yes or No); At Another Jurisdiction; ELSEWHERE: Post office, County, State; Ward (Yes or No); Allotment, Annuity, and Identification Numbers.

1033; Sherman, Clarence; M; 7; Cheyenne; -1/4; S; Son; Yes; Yes
1034; Shortsioux, Mary; F; 15; Cheyenne; F; S; Dau; Yes; Yes; Crow Agency, Mont. [Dau Longears,]

1035; Shoulderblade, Benedict; M; 55; Cheyenne; F; M; Head; Yes; Yes
1036; Shoulderblade, Fannie; F; 5; Cheyenne; F; S; Dau; Yes; Yes

1037; Shoulderblade, Fred; M; 68; Cheyenne; F; M; Head; Yes; Yes
1038; Shoulderblade, Richard; M; 19; Cheyenne; F; S; Son; Yes; Yes

1039; Shoulderblade, Pius; M; 40; Cheyenne; F; M; Head; Yes; Yes
1040; Shoulderblade, Ethel; F; 36; Cheyenne; 1/4+; M; Wife; Yes; Yes
1041; Shoulderblade, Thomas; F; 14; Cheyenne; 1/4+; S; Son; Yes; Yes
1042; Shoulderblade, Francis; F; 13; Cheyenne; 1/4+; S; Son; Yes; Yes [1917 Census William]
1043; Shoulderblade, Wendel; M; 9; Cheyenne; 1/4+; S; Son; Yes; Yes
1044; Shoulderblade, Everett J.; M; 6; Cheyenne; 1/4+; S; Son; Yes; Yes
1045; Shoulderblade, Fern; F; 2; Cheyenne; 1/4+; S; Dau; Yes; Yes

1046; Silloway, Veta; F; 25; Cheyenne; -1/4; M; Head; No; Miles City ~~Town~~, Custer, Mont; Yes

1047; Sioux, Thomas; M; 59; Cheyenne; F; M; Head; Yes; Yes
1048; Sioux, Jane W.; F; 63; Cheyenne; F; M; Wife; Yes; Yes
1049; Sioux, Henry; M; 18; Cheyenne; F; S; Son; Yes;
1050; Lonetravelingwolf, Mabel; F; 19; Cheyenne; F; S; S-Dau; Yes; Yes
1051; Risingsun, Ruby; F; 1; Cheyenne; F; S; A-Dau; Yes; Yes

1052; Sittingman, Charles; M; 63; Cheyenne; F; M; Head; Yes; Yes
1053; Sittingman, Lucy; F; 63; Cheyenne; F; M; Wife; Yes; Yes
1054; Sittingman, Edward; M; 29; Cheyenne; F; D; Son; Yes; Yes [Edward in 1927. Was Edwin in 1926.]

1055; Small, Josephine; F; 38; Cheyenne; 1/4+; M; Head; Yes; Yes
1056; Small, Victor; M; 17; Cheyenne; 1/4+; S; Son; Yes; Yes
1057; Small, Edward; M; 16; Cheyenne; 1/4+; S; Son; No; Deer Lodge ~~Town~~, Deer Lodge, Mont; Yes
1058; Small, Max J.; M; 14; Cheyenne; 1/4+; S; Son; Yes; Yes
1059; Small, Ivan; M; 9; Cheyenne; 1/4+; S; Son; Yes; Yes
1060; Small, Thomas; M; 8; Cheyenne; 1/4+; S; Son; Yes; Yes
1061; Small, Horace; M; 6; Cheyenne; 1/4+; S; Son; Yes; Yes
1062; Small, Melvin; M; 5; Cheyenne; 1/4+; S; Son; Yes; Yes
1063; Small, Worth; M; 3; Cheyenne; 1/4+; S; Son; Yes; Yes
1064; Small, Clinton; M; 4/12; Cheyenne; 1/4+; S; Son; Yes; Yes

Census of the __Tongue River__ reservation of the __Tongue River__ jurisdiction, as of __April 1__, 1930, taken by __C. B. Lohmiller__, Superintendent.

**Key:** Number; NAME: Surname, Given; Sex; Age At Last Birthday; Tribe; Degree of Blood; Marital Status; Relationship To Head of Family; At Jurisdiction Where Enrolled (Yes or No); At Another Jurisdiction; ELSEWHERE: Post office, County, State; Ward (Yes or No); Allotment, Annuity, and Identification Numbers.

1065; Smith, John; M; 54; Cheyenne; F; M; Head; Yes; Yes
1066; Smith, Blanche; F; 50; Cheyenne; F; M; Wife; Yes; Yes
1067; Americanhorse, Rueben[sic]; M; 12; Cheyenne; F; S; A-Son; Yes; Yes

1068; Soldierwolf, John; M; 46; Cheyenne; F; M; Head; Yes; Yes
1069, Soldierwolf, Mary K.; F; 41; Cheyenne; F; M; Wife; Yes; Yes
1070; Soldierwolf, Thomas; M; 19; Cheyenne; F; S; Son; Yes; Yes
1071; Soldierwolf, Josie A.; F; 14; Cheyenne; F; S; Son[sic]; Yes; Yes
1072; Soldierwolf, Bessie L.; F; 12; Cheyenne; F; S; Dau; Yes; Yes
1073; Soldierwolf, James K.; M; 9; Cheyenne; F; S; Son; Yes; Yes
1074; Soldierwolf, Annie K.; F; 7; Cheyenne; F; S; Son[sic]; Yes; Yes

1075; Spang, Alban; M; 37; Cheyenne; -1/4; M; Head; Yes; Yes
1076; Spang, Edward; F[sic]; 1; Cheyenne; -1/4; S; Son; Yes; Yes

1077; Spang, Alfonso; M; 43; Cheyenne; 1/4+; M; Head; Yes; Yes
1078; Spang, Mary C.; F; 18; Cheyenne; 1/4+; M; Wife; Yes; Yes [1924 Annie. Callsfirst in 1928.]

1079; Spang, Deyo; M; 41; Cheyenne; -1/4; M; Head; No; Poplar-~~Town~~, Roosevelt, Mont; Yes
1080; Spang, Bruce S.; M; 5; Cheyenne; -1/4; S; Son; No; Poplar-~~Town~~, Roosevelt, Mont; Yes
1081; Spang, Dale C.; M; 3; Cheyenne; -1/4; S; Son; No; Poplar-~~Town~~, Roosevelt, Mont; Yes

1082; Spang, James; M; 30; Cheyenne; -1/4; M; Head; Yes; Yes
1083; Spang, James R.; M; 2; Cheyenne; -1/4; S; Son; Yes; Yes
1084; Spang, Shirley A.; F; 1; Cheyenne; -1/4; S; Dau; Yes; Yes

1085; Spang, Lucy; F; 60; Cheyenne; 1/4+; M; Head; Yes; Yes
1086; Spang, Harriet; F; 24; Cheyenne; -1/4; S; Dau; Yes; Yes
1087; Spang, Cash; M; 18; Cheyenne; -1/4; S; Son; Yes; Yes

1088; Spang, Roy; M; 33; Cheyenne; -1/4; M; Head; Yes; Yes
1089; Spang, Viola; F; 22; Cheyenne; F; M; Wife; Yes; Yes [Wildhog]
1090; Spang, Regina S.; F; 7; Cheyenne; 1/4+; S; Dau; Yes; Yes [Regina Rosetta in 1926.]
1091; Spang, Lyman; M; 6; Cheyenne; 1/4+; S; Son; Yes; Yes

1092; Spang, Wilfred; M; 28; Cheyenne; -1/4; Wd[sic]; Head; Yes; Yes
1093; Spang, Norman; M; 2; Cheyenne; 1/4+; S; Son; Yes; Yes

1094; Speelman, Jessie F.; F; 41; Cheyenne; 1/4+; M; Head; Yes; Yes
1095; Farr, Evelyn; F; 15; Cheyenne; -1/4; S; Dau; Yes; Yes

Census of the __Tongue River__ reservation of the __Tongue River__ jurisdiction, as of __April 1__, 1930, taken by __C. B. Lohmiller__, Superintendent.

**Key:** Number; NAME: Surname, Given; Sex; Age At Last Birthday; Tribe; Degree of Blood; Marital Status; Relationship To Head of Family; At Jurisdiction Where Enrolled (Yes or No); At Another Jurisdiction; ELSEWHERE: Post office, County, State; Ward (Yes or No); Allotment, Annuity, and Identification Numbers.

1096; Farr, Frank; M; 12; Cheyenne; -1/4; S; Son; Yes; Yes
1097; Speelman, William L.; M; 9/12; Cheyenne; -1/4; S; Son; Yes; Yes

1098; Sponge, Alfred; M; 33; Cheyenne; F; M; Head; Yes; Yes
1099; Sponge, Josie; F; 28; Cheyenne; F; M: Wife; Yes; Yes [Shoulderblade] [1922 was #958, Scott.]

1100; Sponge, Oliver; M; 32; Cheyenne; F; M; Head; Yes; Yes
1101; Sponge, Clara; F; 24; Cheyenne; F; M; Wife; Yes; Yes [Tangleyellowhair]
1102; Sponge, Paul; M; 2; Cheyenne; F; S; Son; Yes; Yes
1103; Sponge, Lena; F; 7/12; Cheyenne; F; S; Dau; Yes; Yes

1104; Spottedblackbird, Lee; M; 70; Cheyenne; F; M; Head; Yes; Yes [Birth year 1854 in 1926. #1082. Didn't pickup a first name until 1915 name, Lee; or Leo.]
1105; Spottedblackbird, Clara; F; 55; Cheyenne; F; M; Wife; Yes; Yes
1106; Hardground, Jane; F; 14; Cheyenne; F; S; G-Dau; Yes; Yes

1107; Spottedelk, Charles; M; 67; Cheyenne; F; Wd[sic]; Head; Yes; Yes
1108; Spottedelk, August; M; 32; Cheyenne; F; S; Son; Yes; Yes
1109; Spottedelk, Alex; M; 29; Cheyenne; F; M; Son; Yes; Yes
1110; Spottedelk, Nellie T.; F; 17; Cheyenne; F; M; Daughter-in-law; Yes; Yes
1111; Medicineelk, William; M; 1; Cheyenne; F; S; G-Son; Yes; Yes

1112; Spottedwolf, Charles; M; 37; Cheyenne; F; M; Head; Yes; Yes
1113; Spottedwolf, Lena; F; 37; Cheyenne; F; M; Wife; Yes; Yes
1114; Spottedwolf, Julia E.; 16; Cheyenne; F; S; Dau; Yes; Yes
1115; Spottedwolf, Martha P.; F; 8; Cheyenne; F; S; Dau; Yes; Yes
1116; Spottedwolf, John; M; 6; Cheyenne; F; S; Son; Yes; Yes
1117; Spottedwolf, Della; F; 2/12; Cheyenne; F; S; Dau; Yes; Yes
1118; Littlewhiteman, Florence; F; 14; Cheyenne; 1/4+; S; S-Dau; Yes; Yes

1119; Spottedwolf, Patrick; M; 42; Cheyenne; F; M; Head; Yes; Yes
1120; Spottedwolf, Jean; F; 28; Cheyenne; 1/4+; M; Wife; Yes; Yes
1121; Spottedwolf, Ruby; F; 9; Cheyenne; 1/4+; S; Dau; Yes; Yes
1122; Spottedwolf, Phyllis; F; 6; Cheyenne; 1/4+; S; Dau; Yes; Yes
1123; Spottedwolf, Eugene; M; 4; Cheyenne; 1/4+; S; Son; Yes; Yes
1124; Spottedwolf, Mollie; F; 2; Cheyenne; 1/4+; S; Dau; Yes; Yes

1125; Squinteye, Josie; F; 45; Cheyenne; F; M; Head; Yes; Yes [Whistlingelk]
1126; Whistlingelk, Alfred; M; 13; Cheyenne; F; S; Son; Yes; Yes

1127; Standingelk, Alex; M; 33; Cheyenne; F; M; Head; Yes; Yes
1128; Standingelk, Nora; F; 26; Cheyenne; F; M; Wife; Yes; Yes
1129; Standingelk, Geneva S.; F; 8; Cheyenne; F; S; Dau; Yes; Yes
1130; Standingelk, Margaret; F; 5; Cheyenne; F; S; Dau; Yes; Yes

Census of the **Tongue River** reservation of the **Tongue River** jurisdiction, as of **April 1**, 1930, taken by **C. B. Lohmiller**, Superintendent.

**Key:** Number; NAME: Surname, Given; Sex; Age At Last Birthday; Tribe; Degree of Blood; Marital Status; Relationship To Head of Family; At Jurisdiction Where Enrolled (Yes or No); At Another Jurisdiction; ELSEWHERE: Post office, County, State; Ward (Yes or No); Allotment, Annuity, and Identification Numbers.

1131; Standingelk, Wayne; M; 11/12; Cheyenne; F; S; Son; Yes; Yes

1132; Standingelk, Francis; M; 28; Cheyenne; F; D; Head; Yes; Yes

1133; Standingelk, Frank; M; 55; Cheyenne; F; M; Head; Yes; Yes
1134; Standingelk, Fannie; F; 51; Cheyenne; F; M; Wife; Yes; Yes
1135; Standingelk, Flora; F; 8; Cheyenne; F; S; Dau; Yes; Yes

1136; Standingelk, Henry; M; 38; Cheyenne; F; M; Head; Yes; Yes
1137; Standingelk, Mary S.; F; 22; Cheyenne; F; M; Wife; Yes; Yes
1138; Standingelk, Aiden; F[sic]; 1; Cheyenne; F; S; Son; Yes; Yes
1139; Standingelk, Benno; M; 1/12; Cheyenne; F; S; Son; Yes; Yes

1140; Standingelk, Robert B.; M; 59; Cheyenne; F; M; Head; Yes; Yes
1141; Standingelk, Sally; F; 34; Cheyenne; F; M; Wife; Yes; Yes
1142; Standingelk, Ella J.; F; 11; Cheyenne; F; S; Dau; Yes; Yes
1143; Standingelk, Jennie; F; 2; Cheyenne; F; S; Dau; Yes; Yes
1144; Standingelk, Lockwood; M; 39; Cheyenne; F; Wd[sic]; Son; Yes; Yes

1145; Standsintimber, John; M; 44; Cheyenne; F; M; Head; Yes; Yes [Family Part Blood in 1928.]
1146; Standsintimber, Josie; F; 32; Cheyenne; F; M; Wife; Yes; Yes
1147; Standsintimber, Josephine; F; 9; Cheyenne; F; S; Dau; Yes; Yes
1148; Standsintimber, John Jr.; M; 8; Cheyenne; F; S; Son; Yes; Yes
1149; Standsintimber, Elva; F; 11/12; Cheyenne; F; S; Dau; Yes; Yes

1150; Strangeowl, James; M; 25; Cheyenne; F; M; Head; Yes; Yes
1151; Strangeowl, Grace R.; F; 20; Cheyenne; F; M; Wife; Yes; Yes

1152; Strangeowl, John; M; 57; Cheyenne; F; M; Head; Yes; Yes
1153; Strangeowl, Gertie; F; 61; Cheyenne; F; M; Wife; Yes; Yes

1154; Starvingbear, James; M; 53; Cheyenne; F; Wd[sic]; Head; Yes; Yes
1155; Starvingbear, Jack; M; 16; Cheyenne; F; S; Son; Yes; Yes [Rosco in 1926.]

1156; Stumphorn, Frank; M; 86; Cheyenne; F; M; Head; Yes; Yes
1157; Stumphorn, Annie; F; 75; Cheyenne; F; M; Wife; Yes; Yes [Shortsioux]

1158; Sunbear, Micheal[sic]; M; 38; Cheyenne; F; M; Head; No; Kiowa Agency, Okla; Yes
1159; Sunbear, Herman; M; 6; Cheyenne; F; M[sic]; Son; No; Kiowa Agency, Okla; Yes
1160; Sunbear, Deyo; M; 5; Cheyenne; F; M[sic]; Son; No; Kiowa Agency, Okla; Yes

Census of the __Tongue River__ reservation of the __Tongue River__ jurisdiction, as of __April 1__, 1930, taken by __C. B. Lohmiller__, Superintendent.

**Key:** Number; NAME: Surname, Given; Sex; Age At Last Birthday; Tribe; Degree of Blood; Marital Status; Relationship To Head of Family; At Jurisdiction Where Enrolled (Yes or No); At Another Jurisdiction; ELSEWHERE: Post office, County, State; Ward (Yes or No); Allotment, Annuity, and Identification Numbers.

1161; Sunroads, David; M; 48; Cheyenne; F; M; Head; Yes; Yes
1162; Sunroads, Lizzie; F; 47; Cheyenne; F; M; Wife; Yes; Yes

1163; Sunroads, John; M; 86; Cheyenne; F; M; Head; Yes; Yes
1164; Sunroads, Lena; F; 85; Cheyenne; F; M; Wife; Yes; Yes

1165; Swallow, William; M; 56; Cheyenne; F; M; Head; Yes; Yes
1166; Swallow, Gertrude; F; 34; Cheyenne; F; M; Wife; Yes; Yes [Redbreath]
1167; Swallow, Oliver; M; 30; Cheyenne; F; S; Son; Yes; Yes
1168; Swallow, Edward; M; 28; Cheyenne; F; S; Son; Yes; Yes
1169; Swallow, Percy R.; M; 10; Cheyenne; F; S; Son; Yes; Yes

1170; Sweetmedicine, David; M; 67; Cheyenne; F; M; Head; Yes; Yes
1171; Sweetmedicine, Clara; F; 59; Cheyenne; F; M; Wife; Yes; Yes
1172; Sweetmedicine, Jacob; M; 35; Cheyenne; F; S; Son; Yes; Yes
1173; Sweetmedicine, Joseph; M; 31; Cheyenne; F; S; Son; Yes; Yes

1174; Sweetmedicine, William; M; 41; Cheyenne; F; M; Head; No; Cheyenne & Arap. Ag, Okla; Yes
1175; Sweetmedicine, Alta; F; 16; Cheyenne; F; S; Dau; No; No; Cheyenne & Arap. Ag, Okla; Yes [1915-Son, Thomas; M.]

1176; Tallbull, Albert; M; 23; Cheyenne; F; S; Head; Yes; Yes

1177; Tallbull, Charles; M; 42; Cheyenne; F; M; Head; Yes; Yes
1178; Tallbull, Mary; F; 36; Cheyenne; F; M; Wife; Yes; Yes
1179; Tallbull, Joseph; M; 14; Cheyenne; F; S; Son; Yes; Yes
1180; Tallbull, Henry; M; 12; Cheyenne; F; S; Son; Yes; Yes
1181; Tallbull, William; M; 9; Cheyenne; F; S; Son; Yes; Yes
1182; Tallbull, Nelson; M; 6; Cheyenne; F; S; Son; Yes; Yes
1183; Tallbull, Cecil R.; M; 3; Cheyenne; F; S; Son; Yes; Yes
1184; Tallbull, Nellie; F; 1; Cheyenne; F; S; Dau; Yes; Yes

1185; Tallbull, Nora; F; 71; Cheyenne; F; Wd; Head; Yes; Yes

1186; Tallwhiteman, Jasper; M; 36; Cheyenne; F; Wd[sic]; Head; Yes; Yes

1187; Tallwhiteman, John; M; 43; Cheyenne; F; M; Head; Yes; Yes
1188; Tallwhiteman, Eleanor; F; 32; Cheyenne; F; M; Wife; Yes; Yes
1189; Tallwhiteman, Clarence; M; 17; Cheyenne; F; S; Son; Yes; Yes
1190; Tallwhiteman, Florence; F; 15; Cheyenne; F; S; Dau; Yes; Yes
1191; Tallwhiteman, Jasper; M; 13; Cheyenne; F; S; Son; Yes; Yes
1192; Tallwhiteman, Alice; F; 9; Cheyenne; F; S; Dau; Yes; Yes
1193; Tallwhiteman, Tug; M; 6; Cheyenne; F; S; Song[sic]; Yes; Yes
1194; Tallwhiteman, Agnes; F; 4; Cheyenne; F; S; Dau; Yes; Yes

Census of the **Tongue River** reservation of the **Tongue River** jurisdiction, as of **April 1**, 1930, taken by **C. B. Lohmiller**, Superintendent.

**Key:** Number; NAME: Surname, Given; Sex; Age At Last Birthday; Tribe; Degree of Blood; Marital Status; Relationship To Head of Family; At Jurisdiction Where Enrolled (Yes or No); At Another Jurisdiction; ELSEWHERE: Post office, County, State; Ward (Yes or No); Allotment, Annuity, and Identification Numbers.

1195; Tangledyellowhair, Chas.; M; 38; Cheyenne; F; M; Head; Yes; Yes
1196; Tangledyellowhair, Georgia; F; 38; Cheyenne; F; M; Wife; Yes; Yes [Talks]
1197; Tangledyellowhair, Roberta; F; 5; Cheyenne; F; S; Dau; Yes; Yes
1198; Tangledyellowhair, Marie; F; 1; Cheyenne; F; S; Dau; Yes; Yes

1199; Tangledyellowhair, David; M; 31; Cheyenne; F; M; Head; Yes; Yes [1904-18 no "d" in last name. Birth year 1894 in 1926.]
1200; Tangledyellowhair, Florence; F; 29; Cheyenne; F; M; Wife; Yes; Yes [Tallwhiteman]
1201; Tangledyellowhair, Clara; F; 10; Cheyenne; F; S; Dau; Yes; Yes
1202; Tangledyellowhair, Winona; F; 7; Cheyenne; F; S; Dau; Yes; Yes
1203; Tallwhiteman, Alice; F; 13; Cheyenne; F; S; S-Dau; Yes; Yes
1204; Tallwhiteman, Regina; F; 6; Cheyenne; F; S; S-Dau; Yes; Yes

1205; Tangledyellowhair, James; M; 61; Cheyenne; F; M; Head; Yes; Yes [1904-18 no "d" in last name.]
1206; Tangledyellowhair, Minnie; F; 59; Cheyenne; F; M; Wife; Yes; Yes
1207; Tangledyellowhair, Josie; F; 81; Cheyenne; F; Wd; Mother; Yes; Yes

1208; Teeth, Charles; M; 67; Cheyenne; F; Wd[sic]; Head; Yes; Yes

1209; Teeth, Franklin; M; 20; Cheyenne; F; M; Head; Yes; Yes
1210; Teeth, Mabel D.; F; 16; Cheyenne; F; M; Wife; Yes; Yes

1211; Teeth, John; M; 40; Cheyenne; F; M; Head; Yes; Yes
1212; Teeth, Edith; F; 27; Cheyenne; F; M; Wife; Yes; Yes
1213; Teeth, Earl; M; 13; Cheyenne; F; S; Son; Yes; Yes
1214; Teeth, Montana; F; 7; Cheyenne; F; S; Dau; Yes; Yes
1215; Teeth, Elsie; F; 4; Cheyenne; F; S; Dau; Yes; Yes
1216; Teeth, Logan; M; 1; Cheyenne; F; S; Son; Yes; Yes
1217; Americanhorse, Flora; F; 69; Cheyenne; F; Wd; G-Mother; Yes; Yes

1218; Threefingers, John; M; 68; Cheyenne; F; M; Head; Yes; Yes
1219; Threefingers, Pansy; F; 53; Cheyenne; F; M; Wife; Yes; Yes
1220; Threefingers, William; M; 28; Cheyenne; F; Wd[sic]; Son; Yes; Yes
1221; Walkingbear, David; M; 32; Cheyenne; F; D; S-Son; Yes; Yes

1222; Turkeylegs, John; M; 70; Cheyenne; F; M; Head; Yes; Yes
1223; Turkeylegs, Lydia; F; 55; Cheyenne; F; M: Wife; Yes; Yes
1224; Turkeylegs, Lawrence; M; 23; Cheyenne; F; S; Son; Yes; Yes [Name James in 1926.]
1225; Redbird, Dorothy M.; F; 21; Cheyenne; 1/4+; D; G-Dau; Yes; Yes
1226; Redbird, David; M; 1; Cheyenne; 1/4+; S; G G-Son; Yes; Yes

1227; Twin, Louis James; M; 42; Cheyenne; F; M; Head; Yes; Yes

Census of the **Tongue River** reservation of the **Tongue River** jurisdiction, as of **April 1**, 1930, taken by **C. B. Lohmiller**, Superintendent.

**Key:** Number; NAME: Surname, Given; Sex; Age At Last Birthday; Tribe; Degree of Blood; Marital Status; Relationship To Head of Family; At Jurisdiction Where Enrolled (Yes or No); At Another Jurisdiction; ELSEWHERE: Post office, County, State; Ward (Yes or No); Allotment, Annuity, and Identification Numbers.

1228; Twin, Bessie; F; 44; Cheyenne; F; M; Wife; Yes; Yes
1229; Twin, Margaret; F; 11; Cheyenne; F; S; Dau; Yes; Yes

1230; Twobirds, Peter; F[sic]; 51; Cheyenne; F; M; Head; Yes; Yes
1231; Twobirds, Lenora; F; 57; Cheyenne; F; M; Wife; Yes; Yes
1232; Twobirds, Jacob; M; 28; Cheyenne; F; S; Son; Yes; Yes

1233; Twobulls, Martin; M; 38; Cheyenne; F; M; Head; Yes; Yes
1234; Twobulls, Eleanor; F; 29; Cheyenne; F; M; Wife; Yes; Yes
1235; Twobulls, William; M; 9; Cheyenne; F; S; Son; Yes; Yes
1236; Twobulls, Alice; F; 2; Cheyenne; F; S; Dau; Yes; Yes

1237; Twofeathers, John; M; 72; Cheyenne; F; M; Head; Yes; Yes
1238; Twofeathers, Clara; F; 59; Cheyenne; F; M; Wife; Yes; Yes
1239; Twofeathers, Ethel; F; 21; Cheyenne; F; S; Dau; Yes; Yes

1240; Twomoons, Bert, M; 42; Cheyenne; F; M; Head; Yes; Yes

1241; Twomoons, John; M; 74; Cheyenne; F; Wd[sic]; Head; Yes; Yes
1241; Bigheadman, Betty N.; F; 15; Cheyenne; F; S; G-Dau; Yes; Yes
1242; Bigheadman, Frank B.; M; 12; Cheyenne; F; S; G-Son; Yes; Yes

1243; Twomoons, William; M; 45; Cheyenne; F; M; Head; Yes; Yes
1245; Twomoons, Emma Bites; F; 34; Cheyenne; F; M; Wife; Yes; Yes [Rowland]

1246; Vassau, Jessie; F; 22; Cheyenne; F; M; Head; No; Forsyth-Town, Rosebud, Mont; Yes

1247; Walkingbear, Charles; M; 53; Cheyenne; F; M; Head; Yes; Yes
1248; Walkingbear, Jennie; F; 57; Cheyenne; F; M; Wife; Yes; Yes

1249; Walkinghorse, John; M; 72; Cheyenne; F; M; Head; Yes; Yes
1250; Walkinghorse, Olive; F; 63; Cheyenne; F; M; Wife; Yes; Yes

1251; Walksalong, Hugh; M; 44; Cheyenne; F; M; Head; Yes; Yes
1252; Walksalong, Mamie; F; 32; Cheyenne; F; M; Wife; Yes; Yes
1253; Walksalong, Flora; F; 14; Cheyenne; F; S; Dau; Yes; Yes [Previous census 1916-19, Fred son.]
1254; Walksalong, Mary E.; F; 9; Cheyenne; F; S; Dau; Yes; Yes
1255; Walksalong, Carol; F; 1; Cheyenne; F; S; Dau; Yes; Yes
1256; Killsontop, Ida; F; 5; Cheyenne; F; S; S-Dau; Yes; Yes

1257; Walkslast, Frank; M; 22; Cheyenne; F; M; Head; Yes; Yes
1258; Walkslast, Carrie; F; 18; Cheyenne; F; M; Wife; Yes; Yes

Census of the **Tongue River** reservation of the **Tongue River** jurisdiction, as of **April 1**, 1930, taken by **C. B. Lohmiller**, Superintendent.

**Key:** Number; NAME: Surname, Given; Sex; Age At Last Birthday; Tribe; Degree of Blood; Marital Status; Relationship To Head of Family; At Jurisdiction Where Enrolled (Yes or No); At Another Jurisdiction; ELSEWHERE: Post office, County, State; Ward (Yes or No); Allotment, Annuity, and Identification Numbers.

1259; Walkslast, James; M; 24; Cheyenne; F; M; Head; Yes; Yes [Clement in 1926.]
1260; Walkslast, May L.; F; 19; Cheyenne; F; M; Wife; Yes; Yes

1261; Walkslast, Richard; M; 74; Cheyenne; F; M; Head; Yes; Yes
1262; Walkslast, Anne; F; 67; Cheyenne; F; M; Wife; Yes; Yes

1263; Walksnice, Adolph; M; 51; Cheyenne; F; M; Head; Yes; Yes
1264; Walksnice, Flora; F; 44; Cheyenne; F; M; Wife; Yes; Yes
1265; Walksnice, Dick; M; 18; Cheyenne; F; S; Son; Yes; Yes
1266; Wolfchum, Lily; F; 13; Cheyenne; F; S; G-Dau; Yes; Yes [1917 Census name Betty.]

1267; Walksnice, John; M; 24; Cheyenne; F; M; Head; Yes; Yes
1268; Walksnice, Mary; F; 27; Cheyenne; F; M; Wife; Yes; Yes [Crookednose]
1269; Walksnice, Mae; F; 5/12; Cheyenne; F; S; Dau; Yes; Yes

1270; Wallowing, Rufus; M; 42; Cheyenne; F; M; Head; Yes; Yes [Dustybuffalo, Rollingbull] Name changed to "Wallowing" see 57750-26. [First name Rutherford misspelled starting in 1918.]
1271; Wallowing, Stella; F; 44; Cheyenne; 1/4+; M; Wife; Yes; Yes
1272; Redwoman, George P.; M; 1; Cheyenne; F; S; A-Dau[sic]; Yes; Yes

1273; Walters, George; M; 32; Cheyenne; 1/4+; M; Head; Yes; Yes

1274; Wanderingmedicine, Wm.; M; 61; Cheyenne; F; M; Head; Yes; Yes
1275; Wanderingmedicine, Gertrude; F; 50; Cheyenne; F; M; Wife; Yes; Yes [Littleyellowman]

1276; Waters[sic], Frank; M; 55; Cheyenne; F; M; Head; Yes; Yes [1904-20, name is Water.]
1277; Waters, Joseph; F; 7; Cheyenne; F; S; A-Son; Yes; Yes [1346; 1377; Woodenlegs, Martin; son; 1922; in 1926. S-son in 1928.]

1278; Weaselbear, Frank; M; 68; Cheyenne; F; M; Head; Yes; Yes
1279; Weaselbear, Mary; F; 60; Cheyenne; F; M; Wife; Yes; Yes
1280; Looksbehind, Sarah; F; 16; Cheyenne; F; Wd; Dau; Yes; Yes
1281; Looksbehind, Inez; F; 7/12; Cheyenne; F; S; G-Dau; Yes; Yes

1282; Weaselbear, Hugh; M; 40; Cheyenne; F; M; Head; No; Cheyenne & Arap. Ag, Okla; Yes
1283; Weaselbear, Andrew; M; 14; Cheyenne; F; S; Son; No; Cheyenne & Arap. Ag, Okla; Yes
1284; Weaselbear, Busby; M; 7; Cheyenne; F; S; Son; No; Cheyenne & Arap. Ag, Okla; Yes

Census of the __Tongue River__ reservation of the __Tongue River__ jurisdiction, as of __April 1__, 1930, taken by __C. B. Lohmiller__, Superintendent.

**Key:** Number; NAME: Surname, Given; Sex; Age At Last Birthday; Tribe; Degree of Blood; Marital Status; Relationship To Head of Family; At Jurisdiction Where Enrolled (Yes or No); At Another Jurisdiction; ELSEWHERE: Post office, County, State; Ward (Yes or No); Allotment, Annuity, and Identification Numbers.

1285; Wheeler, Dewitt C.; M; 37; Sioux[?]; 1/4-; M; Head; Yes; Yes
1286; Wheeler, Dewitt P.; M; 13; Sioux; 1/4+; S; Son; Yes; Yes

1287; Whirlwind, Thomas; M; 53; Cheyenne; F; M; Head; Yes; Yes
1288; Whirlwind, Minnie S.; F; 47; Cheyenne; F; M; Wife; Yes; Yes
1289; Killsnight, Susan; F; 12; Cheyenne; F; S; S-Dau; Yes; Yes
1290; Killsnight, Bessie; F; 10; Cheyenne; F; S; S-Dau; Yes; Yes
1291; Ironshirt, Jennie; F; 71; Cheyenne; F; Wd; Mother-in-law; Yes; Yes

1292; Whistlingelk, John; M; 25; Cheyenne; F; M; Head; Yes; Yes

1293; White, Stamper; M; 31; Cheyenne; F; M; Head; Yes; Yes
1294; White, Lottie; F; 27; Cheyenne; 1/4-; M; Wife; Yes; Yes [Rowland]
1295; White, Pearl; F; 6; Cheyenne; 1/4-; S; Dau; Yes; Yes
1296; White, Willis; M; 1 da.; Cheyenne; 1/4-; S; Son; Yes; Yes

1297; Whitebear, Joseph; M; 33; Cheyenne; F; D; Head; Yes; Yes

1298; Whitebird, Frank; M; 28; Cheyenne; F; M; Head; Yes; Yes
1299; Whitebird, Julia R.; F; 20; Cheyenne; F; M; Wife; Yes; Yes [1926 Nicetalker, Clarice; s-dau; 1909; F. Also s-dau John Chubby.]
1300; Whitebird, Edward; M; 1/12; Cheyenne; F; S; Son; Yes; Yes

1301; Whitebuffalo, John; M; 59; Cheyenne; F; M; Head; Yes; Yes
1302; Whitebuffalo, Ella; F; 62; Cheyenne; F; M; Wife; Yes; Yes
1303; Woundedeye, Paul; M; 18; Cheyenne; F; S; G-son; Yes; Yes
1304; Medicineelk, Spencer; M; 12; Cheyenne; F; S; G-son; Yes; Yes

1305; Whitecrane, Leo; M; 34; Cheyenne; F; M; Head; Yes; Yes
1306; Whitecrane, Ella; F; 28; Cheyenne; F; M; Wife; Yes; Yes [Littlebird]
1307; Whitecrane, Victor; M; 5; Cheyenne; F; S; Son; Yes; Yes
1308; Whitecrane, Eva; F; 1; Cheyenne; F; S; Son[sic]; Yes; Yes
1309; Littlebird, Harry; M; 11; Cheyenne; F; S; S-Son; Yes; Yes
1310; Littlebird, James; M; 10; Cheyenne; F; S; S-Son; Yes; Yes [Previous #1274; Littlebird, Elsie; s-dau; birth year 1920; F in 1926.]

1311; Whitecrow, Alfred; M; 19; Cheyenne; F; S; Head; No; Cheyenne & Arap. Ag, Okla; Yes [Teddy Redcherries- Fthr.]

1312; Whitedirt, Charlie; M; 24; Cheyenne; F; M; Head; Yes; Yes
1313; Whitedirt, Julia W.; F; 20; Cheyenne; F; M; Wife; Yes; Yes [Whistlingelk]
1314; Whitedirt, Leona; F; 1; Cheyenne; F; S; Dau; Yes; Yes
1315; Whitedirt, Maggie; F; 52; Cheyenne; F; Wd; Mother; Yes; Yes
1316; Whitedirt, Jennie; F; 19; Cheyenne; F; S; Sister; Yes; Yes

Census of the __Tongue River__ reservation of the __Tongue River__ jurisdiction, as of __April 1__, 1930, taken by __C. B. Lohmiller__, Superintendent.

**Key:** Number; NAME: Surname, Given; Sex; Age At Last Birthday; Tribe; Degree of Blood; Marital Status; Relationship To Head of Family; At Jurisdiction Where Enrolled (Yes or No); At Another Jurisdiction; ELSEWHERE: Post office, County, State; Ward (Yes or No); Allotment, Annuity, and Identification Numbers.

1317; Whistlingelk, Charles; M; 54; Cheyenne; F; M; Head; Yes; Yes
1318; Whistlingelk, Rose; F; 37; Cheyenne; F; M; Wife; Yes; Yes
1319; Whitebird, Lena; F; 74; Cheyenne; F; Wd; Mother-in-law; Yes; Yes

1320; Whitehawk, Charles J.; M; 30; Cheyenne; F; M; Head; Yes; Yes
1321; Whitehawk, Alice C.; F; 22; Cheyenne; F; M; Wife; Yes; Yes
1322; Whitehawk, Mary; F; 10; Cheyenne; f; S; Dau; Yes; Yes
1323; Whitehawk, Marguerite; F; 9; Cheyenne; F; S; Dau; Yes; Yes [Same #1251 John, 1922-25, son, M.; Same prev., #1289 Emma; dau; 1922 in 1926.]
1324; Whitehawk, Andrew; M; 3; Cheyenne; F; S; Son; Yes; Yes
1325; Whitehawk, James; M; 1; Cheyenne; F; S; Son; Yes; Yes

1326; Whitehawk, Emma; F; 46; Cheyenne; F; Wd; Head; Yes; Yes
1327; Whitehawk, Verlie; F; 12; Cheyenne; F; S; Dau; Yes; Yes
1328; Whitehawk, Theresa; F; 2; Cheyenne; F; S; Dau; Yes; Yes

1329; Whitehawk, Mary; F; 71; Cheyenne; F; Wd; Head; Yes; Yes

1330; Whitemoon, George; M; 75; Cheyenne; F; M; Head; Yes; Yes
1331; Whitemoon, Kate T.; F; 64; Cheyenne; F; M; Wife; Yes; Yes
1332; Whitemoon, Hugh; M; 48; Cheyenne; F; S[sic]; Son; Yes; Yes
1333; Whitemoon, Eva; F; 36; Cheyenne; F; S[sic]; Daughter-in-law; Yes; Yes

1334; Whitewolf, Charles I.; M; 39; Cheyenne; F; M; Head; Yes; Yes
1335; Whitewolf, Belle; F; 27; Cheyenne; F; M; Wife; Yes; Yes
1336; Whitewolf, Joseph; M; 9; Cheyenne; F; S; Son; Yes; Yes
1337; Whitewolf, George; M; 6; Cheyenne; F; S; Son; Yes; Yes
1338; Whitewolf, Fred; M; 1; Cheyenne; F; S; Son; Yes; Yes

1339; Whitewolf, Everett; M; 16; Cheyenne; F; S; Son; Yes; Yes
1340; Whitewolf, Carrie; F; 14; Cheyenne; F; S; Dau; Yes; Yes [Philip son, M., 1920 census.]
1341; Whitewolf, Wilson; M; 10; Cheyenne; F; S; Son; Yes; Yes
1342; Whitewolf, Thomas; M; 8; Cheyenne; F; S; Son; Yes; Yes
1343; Whitewolf, Martin O.; M; 7; Cheyenne; F; S; Son; Yes; Yes
1344; Whitewolf, Calvin M.; M; 5; Cheyenne; F; S; Son; Yes; Yes [Clara dau, F., 1925 census, same #.]

1345; Whitewolf, Frank; M; 83; Cheyenne; F; M; Head; Yes; Yes
1346; Whitewolf, Julia; F; 75; Cheyenne; F; M; Wife; Yes; Yes

1347; Whitewolf, Susie G.; F; 20; Cheyenne; F; M; Head; Yes; Yes [Grasshopper; Dau. of Mrs. Stanley Lamewoman.]
1348; Whitewolf, Leo; M; 3/12; Cheyenne; F; S; Son; Yes; Yes

Census of the **Tongue River** reservation of the **Tongue River** jurisdiction, as of **April 1**, 1930, taken by **C. B. Lohmiller**, Superintendent.

**Key:** Number; NAME: Surname, Given; Sex; Age At Last Birthday; Tribe; Degree of Blood; Marital Status; Relationship To Head of Family; At Jurisdiction Where Enrolled (Yes or No); At Another Jurisdiction; ELSEWHERE: Post office, County, State; Ward (Yes or No); Allotment, Annuity, and Identification Numbers.

1349; Whitright, Rhoda S.; F; 48; Cheyenne; 1/4+; M; Head; Yes; Yes
1350; Seminole, Lorraine; F; 13; Cheyenne; 1/4+; S; Dau; Yes; Yes
1351; Seminole, David; M; 10; Cheyenne; 1/4+; S; Son; Yes; Yes

1352; Wildhog, Bird; M; 60; Cheyenne; F; M; Head; Yes; Yes
1353; Wildhog, Lydia; F; 57; Cheyenne; F; M; Wife; Yes; Yes
1354; Wildhog, Anne; F; 34; Cheyenne; F; S; Dau; Yes; Yes
1355; Wildhog, John; M; 31; Cheyenne; F; S; Son; Yes; Yes
1356; Wildhog, Mary; F; 26; Cheyenne; F; S; Dau; Yes; Yes
1357; Wildhog, Vida; F; 25; Cheyenne; F; S; Dau; Yes; Yes [Viola in 1906-25. Shows as 2 months old in 1906 yet majority of census years show the year of birth as 1907.]
1358; Wildhog, Julia; F; 16; Cheyenne; F; S; Dau; Yes; Yes [Susie in 1926.]
1359; Wildhog, Opal; F; 5; Cheyenne; F; S; G-Dau; Yes; Yes

1360; Wilson, Martha; F; 35; Cheyenne; 1/4+; M; Head; Yes; Yes
1361; Wilson, Arthur; M; 11; Cheyenne; 1/4+; S; Son; Yes; Yes [1919 name James Jr.]
1362; Wilson, Esther M.; F; 9; Cheyenne; 1/4+; S; Dau; Yes; Yes
1363; Wilson, Alice; F; 8; Cheyenne; 1/4+; S; Dau; Yes; Yes [#1324 in 1926 was Josephine.]
1364; Wilson, Florence; F; 7; Cheyenne; 1/4+; S; Dau; Yes; Yes
1365; Wilson, Josephine; F; 5; Cheyenne; 1/4+; S; Dau; Yes; Yes
1366; Wilson, James Jr.; M; 3; Cheyenne; 1/4+; S; Dau[sic]; Yes; Yes
1367; Wilson, George; M; 10/12; Cheyenne; 1/4+; S; Son; Yes; Yes

1368; Windsor, Sarah; F; 25; Cheyenne; -1/4; M; Head; Yes; Yes

1369; Wolf, Rosa; F; 52; Cheyenne; F; Wd; Head; Yes; Yes [nee Crow / Bigbeaver.]
1370; Wolf, Fannie L.; F; 14; Cheyenne; F; S; Dau; Yes; Yes

1371; Wolfblack, Dallas; M; 47; Cheyenne; F; M; Head; Yes; Yes
1372; Wolfblack, Rose; F; 39; Cheyenne; F; M; Wife; Yes; Yes [Whitemoon]
1373; Wolfblack, Gladys; F; 14; Cheyenne; F; S; Dau; Yes; Yes
1374; Wolfblack, Oran; M; 5; Cheyenne; F; S; Son; Yes; Yes
1375; Wolfblack, Mary; F; 1; Cheyenne; F; S; Dau; Yes; Yes

1376; Wolfchief, Harshey; M; 77; Cheyenne; F; M; Head; Yes; Yes
1377; Wolfchief, Anna; F; 68; Cheyenne; F; S[sic]; Wife; Yes; Yes [Whiteelk]
1378; Wolfchief, Richard; M; 37; Cheyenne; F; M; Head; Yes; Yes
1379; Wolfchief, Flora; F; 28; Cheyenne; F; M; Wife; Yes; Yes
1380; Wolfchief, Ann; F; 2; Cheyenne; F; S; Dau; Yes; Yes
1381; Wolfchief, Norman; F[sic]; 1; Cheyenne; F; S; Son; Yes; Yes

Census of the __Tongue River__ reservation of the __Tongue River__ jurisdiction, as of __April 1__, 1930, taken by __C. B. Lohmiller__, Superintendent.

**Key:** Number; NAME: Surname, Given; Sex; Age At Last Birthday; Tribe; Degree of Blood; Marital Status; Relationship To Head of Family; At Jurisdiction Where Enrolled (Yes or No); At Another Jurisdiction; ELSEWHERE: Post office, County, State; Ward (Yes or No); Allotment, Annuity, and Identification Numbers.

1382; Wolfchum, Paul; M; 36; Cheyenne; F; M; Head; Yes; Yes
1383; Wolfchum, Bessie L.; F; 39; Cheyenne; F; M; Wife; Yes; Yes [Littlesun in 1927.]
1384; Wolfchum, Walker; M; 3; Cheyenne; F; S; Son; Yes; Yes
1385; Wolfchum, John; M; 1; Cheyenne; F; S; Son; Yes; Yes
1386; Wolfchum, Espy; M; 1 da.; Cheyenne; F; S; Son; Yes; Yes

1387; Wolfear, Willis; M; 46; Cheyenne; F; M; Head; Yes; Yes
1388; Wolfear, Sophia; F; 57; Cheyenne; F; M; Wife; Yes; Yes

1389; Wolfname, William; M; 76; Cheyenne; F; M; Head; Yes; Yes
1390; Wolfname, Bessie; F; 75; Cheyenne; F; M; Wife; Yes; Yes
1391; Wolfname, Grace; F; 13; Cheyenne; F; S; G-Dau; Yes; Yes

1392; Wolfroads, Mack; M; 52; Cheyenne; F; Wd[sic]; Head; Yes; Yes
1393; Wolfroads, Maude; F; 19; Cheyenne; F; S; Dau; Yes; Yes
1394; Wolfroads, Leo; M; 2/12; Cheyenne; F; S; G-Son; Yes; Yes

1395; Wolftooth, Young; M; 48; Cheyenne; F; M; Head; Yes; Yes
1396; Wolftooth, Mary; F; 11; Cheyenne; F; S; Dau; Yes; Yes
1397; Wolftooth, Norman; M; 9; Cheyenne; F; S; Son; Yes; Yes
1398; Wolftooth, Doris; F; 4; Cheyenne; F; S; Dau; Yes; Yes
1399; Wolftooth, Wayne; M; 1; Cheyenne; F; S; Son; Yes; Yes

1400; Wolfvoice, Grover; M; 29; Cheyenne; F; M; Head; Yes; Yes
1401; Wolfvoice, Jennie; F; 47; Cheyenne; F; M; Wife; Yes; Yes
1402; Wolfvoice, Anne; F; 12; Cheyenne; F; S; Dau; Yes; Yes
1403; Wolfvoice, Dewey; M; 3; Cheyenne; F; S; Son; Yes; Yes
1404; Bearquiver, Grace; F; 3; Cheyenne F; S; A-Dau; Yes; Yes
1405; Blackcrane, Clara; F; 63; Cheyenne; F; Wd; Mother-in-law; Yes; Yes

1406; Womanleggins, Edward; M; 41; Cheyenne; F; M; Head; Yes; Yes
1407; Womanleggins, Mannie[sic]; F; 38; Cheyenne; F; M; Wife; Yes; Yes [Lamewoman]
1408; Badhorse, Mabel; F; 14; Cheyenne; F; S; S-Dau; Yes; Yes [1917-20 son, Junior, M.; Name is June in 1926. Womanleggins in 1929.]
1409; LameWoman, Mary; F; 12; Cheyenne; F; S; S-Dau; Yes; Yes
1410; Bearchum, Benjamin; M; 10; Cheyenne; 1/4+; S; S-Son; Yes; Yes

1411; Woodenlegs[sic], Richard; M; 70; Cheyenne; F; M; Head; Yes; Yes
1412; Woodenlegs, Sophia; F; 70; Cheyenne; F; M; Wife; Yes; Yes

1413; Woodenlegs[sic], Tom; M; 42; Cheyenne; F; M; Head; Yes; Yes [Seminole]
1414; Woodenlegs, Alice; F; 16; Cheyenne; F; M; Wife; Yes; Yes
1415; Woodenlegs, John; M; 20; Cheyenne; F; S; Son; Yes; Yes

Census of the **Tongue River** reservation of the **Tongue River** jurisdiction, as of **April 1**, 1930, taken by **C. B. Lohmiller**, Superintendent.

**Key:** Number; NAME: Surname, Given; Sex; Age At Last Birthday; Tribe; Degree of Blood; Marital Status; Relationship To Head of Family; At Jurisdiction Where Enrolled (Yes or No); At Another Jurisdiction; ELSEWHERE: Post office, County, State; Ward (Yes or No); Allotment, Annuity, and Identification Numbers.

1416; Woodenthigh, Arthur; M; 46; Cheyenne; F; M; Head; Yes; Yes
1417; Woodenthigh, Eva; F; 42; Cheyenne; F; M; Wife; Yes; Yes
1418; Woodenthigh, Esther C.; F; 19; Cheyenne; F; S; Dau; Yes; Yes
1419; Woodenthigh, Alice M.; F; 16; Cheyenne; F; S; Dau; Yes; Yes
1420; Woodenthigh, Peter; M; 11; Cheyenne; F; S; A-Son; Yes; Yes

1421; Woodenthigh, Chester; M; 45; Cheyenne; F; M; Head; Yes; Yes
1422; Woodenthigh, Lena; F; 39; Cheyenne; F; M; Wife; Yes; Yes
1423; Woodenthigh, Philip; M; 14; Cheyenne; F; S; Son; Yes; Yes
1424; Woodenthigh, John; M; 13; Cheyenne; F; S; Son; Yes; Yes
1425; Woodenthigh, Melvin; M; 6; Cheyenne; F; S; Son; Yes; Yes

1426; Woodpecker, James; M; 29; Cheyenne; F; M; Head; Yes; Yes
1427; Woodpecker, Mary; F; 25; Cheyenne; F; M; Wife; Yes; Yes [Littlewhiteman]

1428; Woundedeye, Davis; M; 34; Cheyenne; F; M; Head; Yes; Yes
1429; Woundedeye, Susie; F; 26; Cheyenne; F; M; Wife; Yes; Yes
1430; Woundedeye, Milton; M; 9; Cheyenne; F; S; Son; Yes; Yes
1431; Woundedeye, Veta E.; F; 3; Cheyenne; F; S; Dau; Yes; Yes
1432; Woundedeye, Waldo; M; 7/12; Cheyenne; F; S; Son; Yes; Yes

1433; Woundedeye, Ford; M; 47; Cheyenne; F; M; Head; Yes; Yes
1434; Woundedeye, Florence; F; 39; Cheyenne; F; M; Wife; Yes; Yes
1435; Woundedeye, Victoria; F; 8; Cheyenne; F; S; Dau; Yes; Yes
1436; Woundedeye, Ruth; F; 2; Cheyenne; F; S; Dau; Yes; Yes
1437; Goggles, Laura; F; 20; Cheyenne; F; M; Dau; Yes; Yes
1438; Goggles, Hayes; M; 1; Cheyenne; F; S; G-Son; Yes; Yes

1439; Woundedeye, Winfield; M; 21; Cheyenne; F; M; Head; Yes; Yes
1440; Woundedeye, Alice; F; 17; Cheyenne; F; M; Wife; Yes; Yes

1441; Yelloweagle, Kate; F; 77; Cheyenne; F; Wd; Head; Yes; Yes
1442; Rednose, Sarah Mae; F; 15; Cheyenne; F; S; G-Dau; Yes; Yes

1443; Yelloweyes, Abram; M; 55; Cheyenne; F; M; Head; Yes; Yes
1444; Yelloweyes, Nora; F; 52; Cheyenne; F; M; Wife; Yes; Yes

1445; Yelloweyes, Oliver; M; 28; Cheyenne; F; M; Head; Yes; Yes
1446; Yelloweyes, Gertrude; F; 24; Cheyenne; F; M; Wife; Yes; Yes [Brownbird]
1447; Yelloweyes, Mary; F; 5; Cheyenne; F; S; Dau; Yes; Yes
1448; Yelloweyes, David; M; 3/12; Cheyenne; F; S; Son; Yes; Yes

1449; Yellowfox, Robert; M; 54; Cheyenne; F; M; Head; Yes; Yes
1450; Yellowfox, Carrie; F; 47; Cheyenne; F; M; Wife; Yes; Yes
1451; Yellowfox, Frank; M; 28; Cheyenne; F; S; Son; Yes; Yes

Census of the **Tongue River** reservation of the **Tongue River** jurisdiction, as of **April 1**, 1930, taken by **C. B. Lohmiller**, Superintendent.

**Key:** Number; NAME: Surname, Given; Sex; Age At Last Birthday; Tribe; Degree of Blood; Marital Status; Relationship To Head of Family; At Jurisdiction Where Enrolled (Yes or No); At Another Jurisdiction; ELSEWHERE: Post office, County, State; Ward (Yes or No); Allotment, Annuity, and Identification Numbers.

1452; Yellowfox, Charles; M; 21; Cheyenne; F; S; Son; Yes; Yes

1453; Yellowfox, William; M; 29; Cheyenne; F; M; Head; Yes; Yes
1454; Yellowfox, Margaret Y.; F; 25; Cheyenne; F; M; Wife; Yes; Yes [Yellownose]
1455; Yellowfox, Mary J.; F; 1/12; Cheyenne; F; S; Dau; Yes; Yes

1456; Yellownose, George; M; 33; Cheyenne; F; M; Head; Yes; Yes
1457; Yellownose, Marie; F; 18; Cheyenne; F; M; Wife; Yes; Yes
1458; Yellownose, Mary; F; 2; Cheyenne; F; S; Dau; Yes; Yes

1459; Yellownose, Robert; M; 52; Cheyenne; F; M; Head; Yes; Yes

1460; Yellowrobe, Charles; M; 37; Cheyenne; F; M; Head; Yes; Yes
1461; Yellowrobe, Alice; F; 31; Cheyenne; F; M; Wife; Yes; Yes
1462; Yellowrobe, Ruth; F 12; Cheyenne; F; S; Dau; Yes; Yes [Name Ruana in 1926.]
1463; Yellowrobe, Martha; F; 4; Cheyenne; F; S; Dau; Yes; Yes

1464; Yellowrobe, Jasper; M; 35; Cheyenne; F; M; Head; Yes; Yes
1465; Yellowrobe, Jean W.S.; F; 30; Cheyenne; F; M; Wife; Yes; Yes [Whiteshirt]
1466; Whiteshirt, Caroline; F; 8; Cheyenne; F; S; S-Dau; Yes; Yes [Name Alice in 1926.]
1467; Yellowrobe, Moses; M; 1; Cheyenne; F; S; Son; Yes; Yes

1468; Yellowrobe, William; M; 64; Cheyenne; F; M; Head; Yes; Yes
1469; Yellowrobe, Minnie; F; 73; Cheyenne; F; M; Wife; Yes; Yes

1470; Youngbear, George; M; 47; Cheyenne; F; M; Head; Yes; Yes
1471; Youngbear, Cora; F; 41; Cheyenne; F; M; Wife; Yes; Yes
1472; Youngbear, Arthur; M; 16; Cheyenne; F; S; Son; Yes; Yes
1473; Youngbear, Ralph H.; M; 8; Cheyenne; F; S; Son; Yes; Yes

1474; Youngbird, James; M; 72; Cheyenne; F; M; Head; Yes; Yes
1475; Youngbird, Clara; F; 66; Cheyenne; F; M; Wife; Yes; Yes

1476; Youngbird, John; M; 45; Cheyenne; F; M; Head; Yes; Yes
1477; Youngbird, Anne; F; 45; Cheyenne; F; M; Wife; Yes; Yes [Looksbehind]
1478; Youngbird, Carl J.; M; 13; Cheyenne; F; S; Son; Yes; Yes

CENSUS OF NORTHERN CHEYENNE

-of-

TONGUE RIVER RESERVATION, MONT.

April 1, 1931.

TONGUE RIVER AGENCY,

C. B. Lohmiller, Superintendent.

CENSUS OF THE
NORTHERN CHEYENNE INDIANS
OF
TONGUE RIVER AGENCY
LAME DEER, MONTANA

April 1, 1931

Census of the __Tongue River__ reservation of the __Tongue River__ jurisdiction, as of __April 1__, 1931, taken by __C. B. Lohmiller__, Superintendent.

**Key:** Number; NAME: Surname, Given; Sex; Birthdate, Age At Last Birthday; Tribe; Degree of Blood; Marital Status; Relationship To Head of Family; At Jurisdiction Where Enrolled (Yes or No); At Another Jurisdiction; ELSEWHERE: Post office, County, State; Ward (Yes or No); Allotment, Annuity, and Identification Numbers.

1; Americanhorse, Austin; M; 10-71, 58; Cheyenne; F; M; Head; Yes; Yes
2; Americanhorse, Maude; F; 4-83, 48; Cheyenne; F; M; Wife; Yes; Yes
3; Americanhorse, Lucy May; F; 11-10, 20; Cheyenne; F; S; Dau; Yes; Yes
4; Americanhorse, George; M; 9-14, 16; Cheyenne; F; S; Son; Yes; Yes [Texas]

5; Americanhorse, George; M; 10-81, 49; Cheyenne; F; Wd[sic]; Head; Yes; Yes
6; Americanhorse, Bessie; F; 11-05, 25; Cheyenne; F; S; Dau; Yes; Yes
7; Americanhorse, James; M; 11-11, 19; Cheyenne; M; S; Dau[sic]; Yes; Yes
8; Americanhorse, Marie; F; 6-14, 16; Cheyenne; F; S; Dau; Yes; Yes
9; Americanhorse, Lucy; F; 8-18, 12; Cheyenne; F; S; Dau; Yes; Yes

10; Americanhorse, Walter; M; 10-90, 40; Cheyenne; F; M; Head; Yes; Yes
11; Americanhorse, Ruth; F; 8-11/25, 5; Cheyenne; F; S; Dau; Yes[sic]; Cheyenne & Arap. Okla, ~~Cheyenne~~; Yes
12; Americanhorse, Ella; F; 6/21/27, 3; Cheyenne; F; S; Dau; Yes[sic]; Cheyenne & Arap. Okla, ~~Cheyenne~~; Yes
13; Americanhorse, Esther; F; 3/22/30, 1; Cheyenne; F; S; Dau; Yes[sic]; Cheyenne & Arap. Okla, ~~Cheyenne~~; Yes

14; Americanhorse, Willis; M; 10/92, 38; Cheyenne; F; M; Head; Yes; Yes
15; Americanhorse, Margaret; F; 8/92, 38; Cheyenne; F; M; Wife; Yes; Yes
16; Americanhorse, Ernest; M; 11/11, 19; Cheyenne; F; S; Son; Yes; Yes
17; Americanhorse, Martha; F; 6/14, 16; Cheyenne; F; S; Dau; Yes; Yes
18; Americanhorse, Madge L.; F; 12/16, 14; Cheyenne; F; S; Dau; Yes; Yes
19; Americanhorse, Grace J.; F; 4/18, 12; Cheyenne; F; S; Dau; Yes; Yes
20; Twomoons, Austin; M; 2/27, 4; Cheyenne; F; S; Dau[sic]; Yes; Yes;

21; Ant, James; M; 2/03, 28; Cheyenne; F; M; Head; Yes; Yes
22; Ant, Hannah; F; 5/00, 30; Cheyenne; F; M; Wife; Yes; Yes [Highwalking]
23; Ant, Bertha; F; 1/25, 6; Cheyenne; F; S; Dau; Yes; Yes
24; Ant, Thelma; F; 10/18/28, 2; Cheyenne; F; S; Dau; Yes; Yes
25; Ant, Francis; M; 7/15/30, [?]; Cheyenne; F; S; Son; Yes; Yes

26; Ant, Walter; M; 1/80, 51; Cheyenne; F; M; Head; Yes; Yes
27; Ant, Helen; F; 5/82, 48; Cheyenne; F; M; Wife; Yes; Yes
28; Ant, June; F; 1/20, 11; Cheyenne; F; S; Dau; Yes; Yes

29; Atwood, James; M; 3-91, 40; Cheyenne; F; M; Head; Yes; Yes [Twentystands]
30; Atwood, Cecelia; F; 1/98, 33; Cheyenne; F; M; Wife; Yes; Yes
31; Atwood, Mary; F; 5/14, 16; Cheyenne; F; S; Dau; Yes; Yes
32; Atwood, Herbert W.; M; 8/22, 8; Cheyenne; F; S; Son; Yes; Yes
33; Atwood, David; M; 8/16/29, 1; Cheyenne; F; S; Son; Yes; Yes

Census of the  Tongue River  reservation of the Tongue River  jurisdiction, as of
 April 1   , 1931, taken by  C. B. Lohmiller  , Superintendent.

**Key:** Number; NAME: Surname, Given; Sex; Birthdate, Age At Last Birthday; Tribe; Degree of Blood; Marital Status; Relationship To Head of Family; At Jurisdiction Where Enrolled (Yes or No); At Another Jurisdiction; ELSEWHERE: Post office, County, State; Ward (Yes or No); Allotment, Annuity, and Identification Numbers.

34; Baldeagle, Hugh; M; 5/58, 72; Cheyenne; F; M; Head; Yes; Yes
35; Baldeagle, Minnie; F; 9/59, 71; Cheyenne; F; M; Wife; Yes; Yes

36; Bearchum, Frank; M; 3/01, 30; Cheyenne; F; M; Head; Yes; Yes
37; Bearchum, Anna R. C.; F; 5/10, 20; Cheyenne; F; M; Wife; Yes; Yes
38; Bearchum, Wallace; M; 2/4/29, 2; Cheyenne; F; S; S-Son; Yes; Yes

39; Bearquiver, Edward; M; 9/81, 49; Cheyenne; F; Wd; Head; Yes; Yes
40; Bearquiver, Claude; M; 11/16, 14; Cheyenne; F; S; Son; Yes; Yes
41; Bearquiver, James; M; 6/20, 10; Cheyenne; F; S; Son; Yes; Yes
42; Bearquiver, Martin Frank; M; 8/22, 8; Cheyenne; F; S; Son; Yes; Yes

43; Bearcomesout, Charles; M; 10/80, 50; Cheyenne; F; M; Head; Yes; Yes
44; Bearcomesout, Mary; F; 3/07, 24; Cheyenne; F; M; Wife; Yes; Yes
45; Bearcomesout, Harold; M; 3/08, 23; Cheyenne; F; S; Son; Yes; Yes
46; Bearcomesout, Pius; M; 9/15, 15; Cheyenne; F; S; Son; Yes; Yes
47; Bearcomesout, Herbert; M; 9/12/28, 2; Cheyenne; F; S; Son; Yes; Yes

48; Beartusk, Jerome; M; 8/85, 45; Cheyenne; F; M; Head; Yes; Yes
49; Beartusk, Ida S.; F; 6/98, 32; Cheyenne; F; M; Wife; Yes; Yes

50; Beaverheart, Thomas; M; 5/63, 67; Cheyenne; F; M; Head; Yes; Yes
51; Beaverheart, Nellie; F; 3/57, 74; Cheyenne; F; M; Wife; Yes; Yes
52; Beaverheart, David; M; 4/90, 41; Cheyenne; F; S; Son; Yes; Yes [Name Davis in 1926.]

53; Beirdneau, Adeline; F; 2/99, 32; Cheyenne; -1/4; Wd; Head; Yes; Yes
54; Beirdneau, Betty B.; F; 4/23, 8; Cheyenne; -1/4; S; Dau; Yes; Yes
55; Beirdneau, Barbara M.; F; 4/26, 5; Cheyenne; -1/4; S; Dau; Yes; Yes
56; Beirdneau, Albert L.; M; 2/16/28, 3; Cheyenne; -1/4; S; Son; Yes; Yes

57; BeMent, Emma; F; 6/01, 29; Cheyenne; -1/4; M; Head; Yes; Yes [Burns]
58; BeMent, Jacqueline; F; 10/22, 8; Cheyenne; -1/4; S; Dau; Yes; Yes
59; BeMent, Jesse; M; 3/25, 6; Cheyenne; -1/4; W; Son; Yes; Yes [Joseph in 1925.]
60; BeMent, Geraldine; F; 2/1/27, 4; Cheyenne; -1/4; S; Dau; Yes; Yes
61; BeMent, Celia C.; F; 1/19/28, 3; Cheyenne; -1/4; S; Dau; Yes; Yes

62; Bigback, Charles; M; 3/63, 68; Cheyenne; F; M; Head; Yes; Yes
63; Bigback, Clara; F; 7/69, 61; Cheyenne; F; M; Wife; Yes; Yes
---; ~~Bigback, Stephen; M; 4/92, 39; Cheyenne; F; S; Son; Yes; Yes Died August 3, 1930.~~
64; Redowl, Mabel; F; 7/46, 84; Cheyenne; F; Wd; Mother-in-law; Yes; Yes

Census of the __Tongue River__ reservation of the __Tongue River__ jurisdiction, as of __April 1__, 1931, taken by __C. B. Lohmiller__, Superintendent.

**Key:** Number; NAME: Surname, Given; Sex; Birthdate, Age At Last Birthday; Tribe; Degree of Blood; Marital Status; Relationship To Head of Family; At Jurisdiction Where Enrolled (Yes or No); At Another Jurisdiction; ELSEWHERE: Post office, County, State; Ward (Yes or No); Allotment, Annuity, and Identification Numbers.

65; Bigback, James; M; 8/94, 36; Cheyenne; F; M; Head; Yes; Yes
66; Bigback, Jennie; F; 5/98, 32; Cheyenne; F; M; Wife; Yes; Yes
67; Bigback, Gladys; F; 7/20, 10; Cheyenne; F; S; Dau; Yes; Yes
68; Bigback, Robert; M; 12/23, 7; Cheyenne; F; S; Son; Yes; Yes
69; Bigback, Marie; F; 9/8/29, 1; Cheyenne; F; S; Dau; Yes; Yes

70; Bigback, John; M; 2/04, 27; Cheyenne; F; M; Head; Yes; Yes [Henry in 1919.]
71; Bigback, Nina S. E.; F; 6/07, 24; Cheyenne; F; M; Wife; Yes; Yes
72; Bigback, Eugene; M; 5/7/30, 11/12; Cheyenne; F; S; Son; Yes; Yes

73; Bigbeaver, August; M; 3/16, 70; Cheyenne; F; Wd[sic]; Head; Yes; Yes

74; Bigcrow, Andrew; M; 4/54, 77; Cheyenne; F; M; Head; Yes; Yes
75; Bigcrow, Jennie; F; 11/88, 42; Cheyenne; F; M; Wife; Yes; Yes

76; Bigfoot, Davis; M; 5/98, 31; Cheyenne; F; M; Head; Yes; Yes
77; Bigfoot, Lucy; F; 10/00, 30; Cheyenne; F; M; Wife; Yes; Yes
78; Bigfoot, Alice; F; 1/21, 10; Cheyenne; F; S; Dau; Yes; Yes [Martha in 1925 & 1926.]
79, Bigfoot, Mary; F; 4/24, 7; Cheyenne; F; S; Dau; Yes; Yes
80; Bigfoot, Hoover; M; 6/10/30, 11/12; Cheyenne; F; S; Son; Yes; Yes

81; Bigfoot, John; M; [sic], 50; Cheyenne; F; M; Head; Yes; Yes

82; Bigfoot, White; M; 10/75, 55; Cheyenne; F; M: Head; Yes; Yes
83; Bigfoot, Louisa; F; 9/85, 45; Cheyenne; F; M; Wife; Yes; Yes
84; Bigfoot, Louis Paul; M; 6/11, 19; Cheyenne; F; S; Son; Yes; Yes

85; Bigheadman, Benjamin; M; 7/89, 41; Cheyenne; F; M; Head; Yes; Yes
86; Bigheadman, Julia; F; 7/94, 36; Cheyenne; F; M; Wife; Yes; Yes
87; Bigheadman, Gladys; F; 9/18, 12; Cheyenne; F; S; Dau; Yes; Yes [Lucille in 1926]
88; Bigheadman, Laura; F; 7/27, 3; Cheyenne; F; S; Dau; Yes; Yes
89; Bigheadman, [sic]; F; 3/13/31, [?]; Cheyenne; F; S; Dau; Yes; Yes

90; Bigheadman, Blair; M; 6/92, 38; Cheyenne; F; M; Head; Yes; Yes
91; Bigheadman, Clara; F; 4/01, 30; Cheyenne; F; M; Wife; Yes; Yes
92; Bigheadman, Wm. Grover; M; 7/19, 11; Cheyenne; S; Son; Yes; Yes
93; Bigheadman, August; M; 8/22, 8; Cheyenne; F; S; Son; Yes; Yes
94; Bigheadman, Julia; F; 12/24, 6; Cheyenne; F; S; Dau; Yes; Yes
95; Bigheadman, James; M; 2/24/29, 1; Cheyenne; F; S; Son; Yes; Yes
96; Bigheadman, [sic]; 3/6/31, [sic]; Cheyenne; F; S; Dau; Yes; Yes

Census of the **Tongue River** reservation of the **Tongue River** jurisdiction, as of **April 1**, 1931, taken by **C. B. Lohmiller**, Superintendent.

**Key:** Number; NAME: Surname, Given; Sex; Birthdate, Age At Last Birthday; Tribe; Degree of Blood; Marital Status; Relationship To Head of Family; At Jurisdiction Where Enrolled (Yes or No); At Another Jurisdiction; ELSEWHERE: Post office, County, State; Ward (Yes or No); Allotment, Annuity, and Identification Numbers.

97; Bigheadman, John; M; 6/49, 81; Cheyenne; F; M; Head; Yes; Yes
98; Bigheadman, Nellie; F; 10/53, 77; Cheyenne; F; M; Wife; Yes; Yes

99; Bigheadman, William; M; 12/86, 44; Cheyenne; F; M; Head; Yes; Yes [Whitehorse]
100; Bigheadman, Nellie; F; 6/91, 39; Cheyenne; F; M; Wife; Yes; Yes
101; Bigheadman, Richard; M; 4/09, 21; Cheyenne; F; S; Son; Yes; Yes [Richard Rowland]
102; Bigheadman, Grace M.; F; 5/18, 12; Cheyenne; F; S; Dau; Yes; Yes
103; Bigheadman, Marjorie; F; 3/25, 5; Cheyenne; F S; Dau; Yes; Yes
104; Bigheadman, Susie D.; F; 6/26, 4; Cheyenne; F; S; Dau; Yes; Yes
105; Bigheadman, Helen E.; F; 11/28, 2; Cheyenne; F; S; Dau; Yes; Yes
--- Bigheadman, Anthony; M; 1/9/31, [sic]; Cheyenne; F; S; Dau[sic]; Yes; Yes Died March 18, 1931.

106; Bigleg, Hinton; M; 5/87, 43; Cheyenne; F; S; Head; Yes; Yes
107; Bigleg, Annie; F; 1/79, 52; Cheyenne; 1/4+; M; Wife; Yes; Yes
108; Rowland, Claude; M; 4/04, 27; Cheyenne; 1/4+; S; S-Son; Yes; Yes
109; Rowland, Benjamin; M; 7/08, 22; Cheyenne; 1/4+; S; S-Son; Yes; Yes

110; Bignose, James; M; 10/63, 67; Cheyenne; F; Wd[sic]; Head; Yes; Yes
111; Bignose, Samuel; M; 5/91, 39; Cheyenne; F; S; Son; Yes; Yes
112; Bignose, George; M; 8/97, 32; Cheyenne; F; S; Son; Yes; Yes

113; Bites, James; M; 9/00, 30; Cheyenne; F; M; Head; Yes; Yes
114; Bites, Sally; F; 1/05, 26; Cheyenne; F; M; Wife; Yes; Yes [Crazymule]
115; Bites, Florence; F; 7/26, 4; Cheyenne; F; S; Dau; Yes; Yes
116; Bites, James Jr.; M; 5/5/29, 1; Cheyenne; F; S; Son; Yes; Yes

117; Bites, Sally; F; 10/66, 67; Cheyenne; F; Wd; Head; Yes; Yes
118; Bites, Clara; F; 5/22, 8; Cheyenne; F; S; G-Dau; Yes; Yes
119; Bites, Herman; M; 5/25, 5; Cheyenne; F; S; G-Son; Yes; Yes

120; Bixby, Benjamin; M; 10/87, 43; Cheyenne; 1/4-; M; Head; Yes; Yes
121; Bixby, Gertrude; F; 5/92, 37; Cheyenne; 1/4-; M; Wife; Yes; Yes [Whitepowder 1904-07; Tallwhiteman 1908; Bixby 1909-1931]
122; Bixby, Annie; F; 9/13, 17; Cheyenne; 1/4-; S; Dau; Yes; Yes
123; Bixby, James; M; 12/15, 15; Cheyenne; 1/4-; S; Son; Yes; Yes

124; Bixby, Edward; M; 3/91, 40; Cheyenne; 1/4+; M; Head; Yes; Yes
125; Bixby, Edward G.; M; 7/22, 8; Cheyenne; -1/4; S; Son; Yes; Yes [1924 Clara, dau; F. 1925-26 Jack.]
126; Bixby, Elsie V.; F; 12/23, 7; Cheyenne; -1/4; S; Dau; Yes; Yes [Vianne 1925-26.]

Census of the __Tongue River__ reservation of the __Tongue River__ jurisdiction, as of __April 1__, 1931, taken by __C. B. Lohmiller__, Superintendent.

**Key:** Number; NAME: Surname, Given; Sex; Birthdate, Age At Last Birthday; Tribe; Degree of Blood; Marital Status; Relationship To Head of Family; At Jurisdiction Where Enrolled (Yes or No); At Another Jurisdiction; ELSEWHERE: Post office, County, State; Ward (Yes or No); Allotment, Annuity, and Identification Numbers.

127; Bixby, Wm. L.; M; 3/25, 6; Cheyenne; -1/4; S; Son; Yes; Yes
128; Bixby, Hattie C.; F; 7/24/28, 2; Cheyenne; -1/4; S; Dau; Yes; Yes
129; Bixby, Juanita; F; 5/24/30, 10/12; Cheyenne; -1/4; S; Dau; Yes; Yes

130; Blackbird, Isaac; M; 6/63, 67; Cheyenne; F; Wd[sic]; Head; Yes; Yes

131; Blackeagle, William; M; 6/88, 42; Cheyenne; F; Wd[sic]; Head; Yes; Yes

132; Blackhorse, Alex; M; 10/97, 33; Cheyenne; F; M; Head; Yes; Yes
133; Blackhorse, Mary; F; 6/03, 27; Cheyenne; F; M; Wife; Yes; Yes
134; Blackhorse, Francis; M; 7/22, 8; Cheyenne; F; S; Son; Yes; Yes [1923-26 name Merton.]
135; Blackhorse, Lafe C.; M; 7/18/29, 1; Cheyenne; F; S; Son; Yes; Yes

136; Blackhorse, Rueben[sic]; M; 7/53, 77; Cheyenne; F; M; Head; Yes; Yes
137; Blackhorse, Lena; F; 12/76, 54; Cheyenne; F; M; Wife; Yes; Yes
138; Seminole, Delbert; M; 6/11, 19; Cheyenne; 1/4+; G-Son; Yes; Yes
139; Seminole, Hannah; F; 11/12, 18; Cheyenne; 1/4+; S; G-Son[sic]; Yes; Yes

140; Blackree, Paul; M; 10/78, 52; Cheyenne; F; M; Head; Yes; Yes
141; Blackree, Jennie; F; 5/81, 49; Cheyenne; F; M; Wife; Yes; Yes
142; Star, May; F; 12/04, 28; Cheyenne; F; M; Dau; Yes; Yes
143; Star, Charles; M; 3/29/27, 4; Cheyenne; F; S; G-Son; Yes; Yes
144; Ironshirt, Nora; F; 8/50, 80; Cheyenne; F; Wd; Step-Mother; Yes; Yes

145; Blackstone, Charles; M; 12/60, 70; Cheyenne; F; Wd[sic]; Head; Yes; Yes
146; Blackstone, Lena; F; 7/78, 52; Cheyenne; F; S; Step-Dau; Yes; Yes [7/8 blood in 1928.]
147; Blackstone, Arthur; M; 12/92, 38; Cheyenne; F; M; Son; Yes; Yes
148; Blackstone, Anna K.; F; 3/11, 20; Cheyenne; F; M; Dau-in-Law; Yes; Yes
149; Blackstone, Leo; M; 10/22/20[sic], 6/12; Cheyenne; F; S; G-Son; Yes; Yes

150; Blackwolf, Bennie; M; 6/97, 33; Cheyenne; F; M; Head; Yes; Yes [1904-1923 name Alex.]
151; Blackwolf, Ella; F; 12/00, 30; Cheyenne; F; M; Wife; Yes; Yes
152; Blackwolf, Henry; M; 10/19, 11; Cheyenne; F; S; Son; Yes; Yes [1925 Census Thomas.]
153; Blackwolf, James; M; 8/23, 7; Cheyenne; F; S; Son; Yes; Yes
154; Blackwolf, Ruth; F; 1/27, 4; Cheyenne; F; S; Dau; Yes; Yes

155; Blackwolf, John; M; 8/70, 60; Cheyenne; F; M; Head; Yes; Yes
156; Blackwolf, Nellie; F; 7/74, 56; Cheyenne; M; Wife; Yes; Yes
157; Blackwolf, Alex; M; 5/06, 24; Cheyenne; F; S; Son; Yes; Yes [#156, Name Busby, a brother Alex born 1897 in 1916 census, married in 1917.]

Census of the **Tongue River** reservation of the **Tongue River** jurisdiction, as of **April 1**, 1931, taken by **C. B. Lohmiller**, Superintendent.

**Key:** Number; NAME: Surname, Given; Sex; Birthdate, Age At Last Birthday; Tribe; Degree of Blood; Marital Status; Relationship To Head of Family; At Jurisdiction Where Enrolled (Yes or No); At Another Jurisdiction; ELSEWHERE: Post office, County, State; Ward (Yes or No); Allotment, Annuity, and Identification Numbers.

158; Blackwolf, Mary; F; 1/14, 17; Cheyenne; F; S; Dau; Yes; Yes
159; Wolfname, Henry; M; 9/12, 18; Cheyenne; F; S; G-Son; Yes; Yes
160; Wolfname, Wilbur P.; M; 10/20, 9; Cheyenne; F; S; G-Son; Yes; Yes

161; Blindman, Arthur; M; 11/68, 62; Cheyenne; F; Wd[sic]; Head; Yes; Yes

162; Bluehawk, Louis; M; [sic], 79; Cheyenne; 1/4+; Wd[sic]; Head; Yes; Yes

163; Bobtailhorse, Thomas; M; 7/50, 80; Cheyenne; F; M; Head; Yes; Yes
164; Bobtailhorse, Gertrude; F; 12/51, 79; Cheyenne; F; M; Wife; Yes; Yes

165; Boxelder, Laura; F; 1/72, 59; Cheyenne; F; Wd; Head; No; Shoshone & Arap. Okla; Yes

166; Brady, Alex; M; 12/98, 32; Cheyenne; F; M; Head; Yes; Yes
167; Brady, Josie; F; 12/02, 28; Cheyenne; F; M; Wife; Yes; Yes [Pine]
168; Brady, Charles; M; 11/23, 7; Cheyenne; F; S; Son; Yes; Yes
169; Brady, Clifford; M; 10/10/30, 5/12; Cheyenne; F; S; Son; Yes; Yes

170; Brady, Arthur; M; 12/40, 90; Cheyenne; F; M; Head; Yes; Yes
171; Brady, Ellen; F; 12/53, 77; Cheyenne; F; M; Wife; Yes; Yes

172; Brady, George; M; 7/81, 49; Cheyenne; F; M; Head; Yes; Yes
173; Brady, Flossie; F; 2/97, 34; Cheyenne; 1/4+; M; Wife; Yes; Yes
174; Brady, Elmore; M; 3/07, 24; Cheyenne; F; S; Son; Yes; Yes
175; Brady, James H.; M; 4/13, 18; Cheyenne; F; S; Son; Yes; Yes
176; Brady, Howard; M; 11/15, 15; Cheyenne; F; S; Son; Yes; Yes
177; Brady, Ramona; F; 12/17, 13; Cheyenne; F; S; Dau; Yes; Yes
178; Brady, Wilson; M; 10/18, 12; Cheyenne; F; S; Son; Yes; Yes
179; Brady, Martha; F; 2/21, 10; Cheyenne; 1/4+; S; Dau; Yes; Yes
180; Brady, Roy; M; 1/25, 6; Cheyenne; 1/4+; S; Son; Yes; Yes
181; Brady, Pearl; F; 7/14/28, 2; Cheyenne; 1/4+; S; Dau; Yes; Yes
182; Flying, Pauline; F; 6/16, 14; Cheyenne; 1/4+; S; Step-Daughter; Yes; Yes
[Male, Paul in 1920 #150 under Brady.]

183; Braidedlocks, William; M; 10/51, 78; Cheyenne; F; Wd[sic]; Head; Yes; Yes

184; Brein, Margaret; F; 5/03, 27; Cheyenne; -1/4; M; Head; Yes; Yes
185; Brein, Myron; M; 10/12/29, 1; Cheyenne; 1/4+; S; Son; Yes; Yes

186; Brownbird, Joseph; M; 9/65, 65; Cheyenne; F; M; Head; Yes; Yes
187; Brownbird, Anna; F; 5/70, 65; Cheyenne; F; M; Wife; Yes; Yes

188; Buffalohorn, John; M; 4/62, 69; Cheyenne; F; M; Head; Yes; Yes

Census of the  Tongue River  reservation of the Tongue River  jurisdiction, as of   April 1  , 19**31**, taken by  C. B. Lohmiller  , Superintendent.

**Key:** Number; NAME: Surname, Given; Sex; Birthdate, Age At Last Birthday; Tribe; Degree of Blood; Marital Status; Relationship To Head of Family; At Jurisdiction Where Enrolled (Yes or No); At Another Jurisdiction; ELSEWHERE: Post office, County, State; Ward (Yes or No); Allotment, Annuity, and Identification Numbers.

189; Buffalohorn, Lena; F; 5/70, 60; Cheyenne; F; M; Wife; Yes; Yes

190; Buffalochump, Samuel; M; 7/45, 85; Cheyenne; F; M; Head; Yes; Yes
191; Buffalochump, Nora; F; 8/48, 82; Cheyenne; F; M; Wife; Yes; Yes

192; Burns, George; M; 3/96, 36; Cheyenne; -1/4; M; Head; Yes; Yes

193; Burns, Julia; F; 2/72, 59; Cheyenne; 1/4-; Wd; Head; Yes; Yes
194; Burns, James C.; M; 7/08, 22; Cheyenne; -1/4; S; Son; Yes; Yes
195; Burns, Margaret; F; 9/11, 19; Cheyenne; -1/4; S; Dau; Yes; Yes
196; Burns, Anna G; F; 8/13, 17; Cheyenne; -1/4; S; Dau; Yes; Yes
197; BeMent, Clarence; M; 11/23, 7; Cheyenne; -1/4; S; G-Son; Yes; Yes [Max in 1925. Mickie in 1926.]

198; Burns, Lizzie; F; 1/73. 59; Cheyenne; -1/4; M; Head; Yes; Yes
199; Burns, Josephine; F; 7/18, 12; Cheyenne; 1/4+; S; Adopted Dau; Yes; Yes [Had a Kitty Small in 1925. Adopt-dau., in 1925-26.]

200; Burns, Robert; M; 9/97; Cheyenne; -1/4; M; Head; Yes; Yes
201; Burns, Phyllis R.; F; 3/26, 5; Cheyenne; -1/4; S; Dau; Yes; Yes
202; Burns, George E.; M; 8/13/29, 1; Cheyenne; -1/4; S; Son; Yes; Yes

203; Cain, Edith S.; F; 12/09, 20; Cheyenne; -1/4; M; Head; Yes; Yes

204; Callsfirst, Andrew; M; 6/88, 42; Cheyenne; F; M; Head; Yes; Yes
205; Callsfirst, Jennie; F; 7/72, 58; Cheyenne; 1/4+; M; Wffe[sic]; Yes; Yes
206; Woodenleg, Mabel; F; 3/27, 4; Cheyenne; F; S; Niece; Yes; Yes

207; Chasingbear, Willis; M; 3/95, 36; Cheyenne; F; M; Head; Yes; Yes
208; Chasingbear, Madge; F; 4/98, 32; Cheyenne; F; M; Wife; Yes; Yes [Powderface]

209; Chubby, John; M; 11/75, 55; Cheyenne; F; M; Head; Yes; Yes
210; Chubby, Anne; F; 12/85, 45; Cheyenne; F; M; Wife; Yes; Yes
211; Chubby, Rhoda; F; 1/20, 11; Cheyenne; F; S; Dau; Yes; Yes
212; Hairlessbear, Hilda; F; 3/12, 19; Cheyenne; F; S; Step-Dau; Yes; Yes

---; ~~Clubfoot, Floyd; M; 3/88, 43; Cheyenne; F; M; Head; Yes; Died April 2, 1930.~~

213; Clubfoot, Frank; M; 3/91, 40; Cheyenne; F; M; Head; Yes; Yes
214; Clubfoot, Lucy A.; F; 2/93, 38; Cheyenne; F; M; Wife; Yes; Yes
215; Clubfoot, James; M; 10/22, 8; Cheyenne; F; S; Son; Yes; Yes
216; Clubfoot, Frank Jr.; M; 3/27, 4; Cheyenne; F; S; Son; Yes; Yes

Census of the __Tongue River__ reservation of the __Tongue River__ jurisdiction, as of __April 1__, 1931, taken by __C. B. Lohmiller__, Superintendent.

**Key:** Number; NAME: Surname, Given; Sex; Birthdate, Age At Last Birthday; Tribe; Degree of Blood; Marital Status; Relationship To Head of Family; At Jurisdiction Where Enrolled (Yes or No); At Another Jurisdiction; ELSEWHERE: Post office, County, State; Ward (Yes or No); Allotment, Annuity, and Identification Numbers.

217; Clubfoot, John; M; 12/60, 70; Cheyenne; F; M; Head; Yes; Yes
218; Clubfoot, Minnie; F; 7/70, 60; Cheyenne; F; M; Wife; Yes; Yes
219; Clubfoot, Joseph; M; 7/00, 30; Cheyenne; F; S; Son; Yes; Yes

220; Clubfoot, Willis; M; 3/91, 39; Cheyenne; F; M; Head; Yes; Yes
221; Clubfoot, Stella Mary; F; 4/96, 35; Cheyenne; F; M; Wife; Yes; Yes [Weaselbear]
222; Clubfoot, Norman; M; 11/16, 14; Cheyenne; F; S; Step-Son; Yes; Yes [1917 shows Norman died in 1916. In 1918-23 Census as born 1916 and alive?]
223; Clubfoot, Flossie; F; 12/25, 5; Cheyenne; F; S; Step-Son[sic]; Yes; Yes

224; Colhoff, Emma; F; 9/94, 36; Cheyenne; 1/4+; M; Head; No; Pine Ridge, S.D.; Yes
225; Colhoff, Maxine; F; 5/16, 14; Cheyenne; 1/4+; S; Dau; No; Pine Ridge, S.D.; Yes
226; Colhoff, Edward; M; 5/18, 12; Cheyenne; 1/4+; S; Son; No; Pine Ridge, S.D.; Yes
227; Colhoff, Annie G.; F; 3/21, 10; Cheyenne; 1/4+; S; Dau; No; Pine Ridge, S.D.; Yes
228; Colhoff, William; M; 4/24/7; Cheyenne; 1/4+; S; Son; No; Pine Ridge, S.D.; Yes
229; Colhoff, George; M; 1/27, 4; Cheyenne; 1/4+; S; Son; No; Pine Ridge, S.D.; Yes

230; Cooley, Julia; F; 11/91, 39; Cheyenne; -1/4; M; Head; Yes; Yes
231; Cooley, Violet; F; 3/14, 17; Cheyenne; -1/4; S; Dau; Yes; Yes
232; Cooley, Junior; M; 5/16, 14; Cheyenne; -1/4; S; Son; Yes; Yes
233; Cooley, Francis; M; 10/22, 8; Cheyenne; -1/4; S; Son; Yes; Yes
234; Cooley, Vera; F; 1/25, 5; Cheyenne; -1/4; S; Dau; Yes; Yes

235; Crawling, Charles; M; 8/84, 46; Cheyenne; F; M; Head; Yes; Yes
236; Crawling, Flora; F; [sic], 49; Cheyenne; F; M; Wife; Yes; Yes
237; Crawling, Martha; F; 1/17, 14; Cheyenne; F; S; Dau; Yes; Yes
238; Chasingbear, Laura; F; 5/16, 14; Cheyenne; F; S; Step-Dau; Yes; Yes
239; Chasingbear, Robert; M; 7/24, 6; Cheyenne; F; S; Step-Son; Yes; Yes

240; Crazymule, Eva; F; 5/09, 21; Cheyenne; F; S; Head; No; Cheyenne & Arap. Okla; Yes [Wyoming in 1926.]

XXX; ~~Crazymule, John; M; 3/70, 61; Cheyenne; F; M; Head; Yes; Died August 12, 1930.~~
241; Crazymule, Jennie; F; 2/57, 74; Cheyenne; F; M; Wife; Yes; Yes [Issues]

242; Crazymule, James; M; 11/10. 20; Cheyenne; F; S; Head; Yes; Yes

Census of the **Tongue River** reservation of the **Tongue River** jurisdiction, as of **April 1**, 19**31**, taken by **C. B. Lohmiller**, Superintendent.

**Key:** Number; NAME: Surname, Given; Sex; Birthdate, Age At Last Birthday; Tribe; Degree of Blood; Marital Status; Relationship To Head of Family; At Jurisdiction Where Enrolled (Yes or No); At Another Jurisdiction; ELSEWHERE: Post office, County, State; Ward (Yes or No); Allotment, Annuity, and Identification Numbers.

243; Crazymule, Chas R.; M; 11/19, 11; Cheyenne; F; S; Brother; Yes; Yes [Raymond in 1926.]
244; Crazymule, Xavier; M; 11/21, 9; Cheyenne; F; S; Brother; Yes; Yes

245; Crazymule, Joseph; M; 3/81, 50; Cheyenne; F; M; Head; Yes; Yes
246; Crazymule, Sarah; F; 7/73, 57; Cheyenne; F; M; Wife; Yes; Yes
247; Greasydog, Fannie; F; 6/97, 33; Cheyenne; F; S; Step-Dau; Yes; Yes

248; Crook, George; M; 1/64, 67; Cheyenne; F; M; Head; Yes; Yes
249; Crook, Theresa; F; 11/66, 64; Cheyenne; F; M; Wife; Yes; Yes

250; Crook, Rosa; F; 8/65, 65; Cheyenne; F; Wd; Head; Yes; Yes
251; Crook, Albert; M; 4/01, 30; Cheyenne; F; S; Son; Yes; Yes

252; Crookednose, Nicholas; M; 6/67, 63; Cheyenne; F; M; Head; Yes; Yes
253; Crookednose, Susie; F; 9/72, 58; Cheyenne; F; M; Wife; Yes; Yes

254; Curley, Thomas; M; 11/89, 41; Cheyenne; F; M; Head; Yes; Yes
255; Curley, Esther; F; 12/95, 35; Cheyenne; F; M: Wife; Yes; Yes
256; Curley, Ella; F; 4/25, 6; Cheyenne; F; S; Dau; Yes; Yes

257; Deafy, David; M; 5/98, 32; Cheyenne; F; M; Head; Yes; Yes [Americanhorse]
258; Deafy; Anna; F; 12/95, 35; Cheyenne; F; M; Wife; Yes; Yes [Horseroads]
259; Deafy; Willie; M; 11/17, 13; Cheyenne; F; S; Son; Yes; Yes
260; Deafy, Elsie; F; 7/25, 5; Cheyenne; F; S; Dau; Yes; Yes
261; Deafy, Irene; F; 7/15/29, 1; Cheyenne; F; S; Dau; Yes; Yes

262; Divesbackward, John; M; 1/70, 61; Cheyenne; F; Wd[sic]; Head; Yes; Yes [Depending the on census taker they spell Divesbackwards at the end with or without an "s".]
263; Lonebull, Louis; M; 6/58, 79; Cheyenne; F; Wd[sic]; Brother; Yes; Yes

264; Divesbackward, Rufus; M; 2/90, 41; Cheyenne; F; M; Head; Yes; Yes
265; Divesbackward, Nancy; F; 3/82, 49; Cheyenne; F; M; Wife; Yes; Yes
266; Divesbackward, Sam; M; 4/18, 12; Cheyenne; F; S; Son; Yes; Yes
267; Divesbackward, Strane; M; 5/20, 10; Cheyenne; F; S; Son; Yes; Yes
268; Divesbackward, Grace; F; 2/25, 6; Cheyenne; F S; Dau; Yes; Yes
269; Standsout, Sallie; F; 8/47, 83; Cheyenne; F; Wd; Mother; Yes; Yes

270; Dog, Louis; M; 5/55, 75; Cheyenne; F; M; Head; Yes; Yes
271; Dog, Maude; F; 3/66,65; Cheyenne; F; M; Wife; Yes; Yes

272; Duster, Albert; M; 4/89, 42; Cheyenne; F; M; Head; Yes; Yes
273; Duster, Vinnie; F; 9/96, 34; Cheyenne; F; M; Wife; Yes; Yes

Census of the __Tongue River__ reservation of the __Tongue River__ jurisdiction, as of __April 1__, 1931, taken by __C. B. Lohmiller__, Superintendent.

**Key:** Number; NAME: Surname, Given; Sex; Birthdate, Age At Last Birthday; Tribe; Degree of Blood; Marital Status; Relationship To Head of Family; At Jurisdiction Where Enrolled (Yes or No); At Another Jurisdiction; ELSEWHERE: Post office, County, State; Ward (Yes or No); Allotment, Annuity, and Identification Numbers.

274; Duster, Annie; F; 12/20, 10; Cheyenne; F; S; Dau; Yes; Yes
275; Duster, Bessie; F; 7/24, 6; Cheyenne; F; S; Dau; Yes; Yes

276; Eaglefeathers, Jacob; M; 9/74, 56; Cheyenne; F; Wd[sic]; Head; Yes; Yes
277; Eaglefeathers, Mildred; F; 5/20, 10; Cheyenne; F; S; Dau; Yes; Yes

278; Eaglefeathers, Oliver; M; 9/95, 35; Cheyenne; F; M; Head; Yes; Yes
279; Eaglefeathers, Julia; F; 6/95, 35; Cheyenne; 1/4+; M; Wife; Yes; Yes
280; Eaglefeathers, Simon; M; 3/22, 9; Cheyenne; 1/4+; S; Son; Yes; Yes
281; Eaglefeathers, Rosie; F; 7/25,5; Cheyenne; 1/4+; S; Dau; Yes; Yes
282; Eaglefeathers, Milton; M; 1/12/29, 2; Cheyenne; 1/4+; S; Son; Yes; Yes
283; Littlehead, Rena; F; 11/19, 11; Cheyenne; 1/4+; S; Step-Dau; Yes; Yes [Mildred in 1926.]

284; Eastman, Charles; M; 2/01, 30; Cheyenne; -1/4; M; Head; No; Lodgegrass Town, Big Horn, Mont.; Yes

285; Eastman, Mary G.; F; 12/76, 54; Cheyenne; 1/4+; M; Head; No; Lodgegrass Town, Big Horn, Mont.; Yes
286; Eastman, Robert; M; 3/11, 20; Cheyenne; -1/4; S; Son; No; Lodgegrass Town, Big Horn, Mont.; Yes
287; Eastman, Rose; F; 9/15, 15; Cheyenne; -1/4; S Dau; No; Lodgegrass Town, Big Horn, Mont.; Yes
288; Eastman, Louisa; F; 3/18, 12; Cheyenne; -1/4; S; Dau; No; Lodgegrass Town, Big Horn, Mont.; Yes
289; Eastman, Myrtle; F; 8/13, 17; Cheyenne; -1/4; S; G-Dau; No; Lodgegrass Town, Big Horn, Mont.; Yes [Julia 1926. Lucy Beartusk, mother.]

290; Eastman, Perry; M; 11/95, 35; Cheyenne; -1/4; M: Head; Yes; Yes
291; Eastman, Mary; F; 372/93, 38; Cheyenne; F; M; Wife; Yes; Yes
292; Beartusk, Edith; F; 4/16, 15; Cheyenne; 1/4+; S; Niece; Yes; Yes

293; Elkshoulder, Henry; M; 7/94, 36; Cheyenne; F; M; Head; Yes; Yes
294; Elkshoulder, Bessie; F; 8/93, 37; Cheyenne; F; M; Wife; Yes; Yes
295; Elkshoulder, Curtis; M; 2/08, 23; Cheyenne; F; S; Son; Yes; Yes
296; Elkshoulder, Lucy; F; 3/17, 14; Cheyenne; F; S Dau; Yes; Yes
297; Elkshoulder, Sylvia; F; 7/22, 8; Cheyenne; F; S; Dau; Yes; Yes
298; Elkshoulder, George; M; 12/25, 5; Cheyenne; F; S; Son; Yes; Yes [Adolph in 1926.]
299; Elkshoulder, Calvin; M; 8/5/28, 2; Cheyenne; F; S; Son; Yes; Yes

300; Elliott, Elizabeth; F; 4/06, 24; Cheyenne; 1/4+; M; Head; Yes; Yes
301; Elliott, Edwin F.; M; 1/8/28, 3; Cheyenne; -1/4; S; Son; Yes; Yes
302; Elliott, Loretta M.; F; 4/13/29, 2; Cheyenne; -1/4; S; Dau; Yes; Yes

Census of the  Tongue River  reservation of the Tongue River  jurisdiction, as of
 April 1  , 1931, taken by  C. B. Lohmiller  , Superintendent.

**Key:** Number; NAME: Surname, Given; Sex; Birthdate, Age At Last Birthday; Tribe; Degree of Blood; Marital Status; Relationship To Head of Family; At Jurisdiction Where Enrolled (Yes or No); At Another Jurisdiction; ELSEWHERE: Post office, County, State; Ward (Yes or No); Allotment, Annuity, and Identification Numbers.

303; Elliott, Myron L.; M; 11/3/30, 5/12; Cheyenne; -1/4; S; Son; Yes; Yes

304; Eyesyellow, Wilbur; M; 8/68, 62; Cheyenne; F; M; Head; Yes; Yes
305; Eyesyellow, Daisy; F; 9.56, 74; Cheyenne; F; M; Wife; Yes; Yes

306; Fightingbear, Edgar; M; 10/74, 56; Cheyenne; F; M; Head; Yes; Yes
307; Fightingbear, Alice; F; 6/93, 37; Cheyenne; F; M; Wife; Yes; Yes
308; Fightingbear, Elmer; M; 4/21, 9; Cheyenne; F; S; Son; Yes; Yes
309; Fightingbear, Herbert; M; 11/21/23, 7; Cheyenne; F; S; Son; Yes; Yes
310; Fightingbear, Emma; F; 5/26, 4; Cheyenne; F; S Dau; Yes; Yes

311; Fingers, Otis; M; 10/68, 62; Cheyenne; F; Wd; Head; Yes; Yes
312; Fingers, Joseph; M; 8/14, 16; Cheyenne; F; S; Son; Yes; Yes [1917 Census Daughter, Josie 1915-20.]

313; Firecrow, Peter; M; 4/87, 44; Cheyenne; F; Wd; Head; Yes; Yes
314; Firecrow, Joseph; M; 10/23, 7; Cheyenne; F; S; Son; Yes; Yes [Josephine; dau; F., in 1926]

315; Firewolf, John; M; 4/77, 54; Cheyenne; F; M; Head; Yes; Yes
316; Firewolf, Josephine; F; 1/75, 56; Cheyenne; F; M; Wife; Yes; Yes
317; Tallwhiteman, Agnes; F; 4/24, 6; Cheyenne; F; S; G-Dau; Yes; Yes

318; Fisher, Eugene; M; 7/78, 52; Cheyenne; 1/4+; M; Head; Yes; Yes
319; Fisher, Kitty; F; 4/90, 41; Cheyenne; -1/4; M; Wife; Yes; Yes
320; Fisher, Eugene Jr.; M; 12/12, 18; Cheyenne; 1/4+; S; Son; Yes; Yes
321; Fisher, Langburn; M; 7/15, 15; Cheyenne; 1/4+; S; Son; Yes; Yes
322; Fisher, James A.; M; 3/17, 14; Cheyenne; 1/4+; S; Son; Yes; Yes [1917 Census name Ira.]
323; Fisher, Alliwitchie; F; 5/19, 11; Cheyenne; 1/4+; S; Dau; Yes; Yes [1919 Census name Pearl.]
324; Fisher, Calleaus; M; 5/19, 11; Cheyenne; 1/4+; S; Son; Yes; Yes [1919 Census name Earl.]
325; Fisher, Russell; M; 11/21, 9; Cheyenne; 1/4+; S; Son; Yes; Yes
326; Fisher, Helen; F; 3/24, 7; Cheyenne; 1/4+; S; Dau; Yes; Yes
327; Fisher, Bernidine; M; 12/26, 4; Cheyenne; 1/4+; S; Son; Yes; Yes
328; Fisher, Virginia; F; 12/14/30, 3/12; Cheyenne; 1/4+; S; Dau; Yes; Yes

329; Fisher, Henry; M; 8/05, 25; Cheyenne; F; M; Head; Yes; Yes
330; Fisher, Lucy; F; 1/08, 23; Cheyenne; 1/4+; M; Wife; Yes; Yes

331; Fisher, John; M; 7/01, 29; Cheyenne; F; M; Head; Yes; Yes
332; Fisher, Mary P.; F; 2/11, 20; Cheyenne; F; M; Wife; Yes; Yes [Playingbear]
333; Fisher, Burton; M; 7/27/29, 1; Cheyenne; F; S; Son; Yes; Yes

Census of the  Tongue River  reservation of the Tongue River  jurisdiction, as of
 April 1   , 1931, taken by  C. B. Lohmiller  , Superintendent.

**Key:** Number; NAME: Surname, Given; Sex; Birthdate, Age At Last Birthday; Tribe; Degree of Blood; Marital Status; Relationship To Head of Family; At Jurisdiction Where Enrolled (Yes or No); At Another Jurisdiction; ELSEWHERE: Post office, County, State; Ward (Yes or No); Allotment, Annuity, and Identification Numbers.

334;   Fliesabout, William; M; 2/79, 52; Cheyenne; F; M; Head; Yes; Yes
335;   Fliesabout, Minnie; F; 12/82, 48; Cheyenne; F; M; Wife; Yes; Yes
336;   Fliesabout, June; F; 6/23, 7; Cheyenne; F; S; Dau; Yes; Yes [Martin; son; F[sic], in 1926.]

337;   Flying, Debs; M; 2/86, 45; Cheyenne; F; Wd[sic]; Head; Yes; Yes
338;   Flying, Frank; M; 10/15, 15; Cheyenne; F; S; Son; Yes; Yes
339;   Flying, Parker; M; 4/18, 12; Cheyenne; F; S; Son; Yes; Yes
340;   Flying, Myra; F; 6/67, 63; Cheyenne; F; S; Mother; Yes; Yes
341;   Killsnight, Ruth; F; 12/16, 14; Cheyenne; F; S; Sister; Yes; Yes

342;   Flying, Thomas; M; 3/69, 62; Cheyenne; F; Wd[sic]; Head; Yes; Yes

343;   Fontenelle, Francis; F; 12/08, 22; Cheyenne; -1/4; M; Head; Yes; Yes [Sherman]

344;   Foot, Ruth Y.; F; 9/98, 32; Cheyenne; F; M; Head; Yes; Yes
345;   Foot, Thelma; F; 6/13, 17; Cheyenne; 1/4+; S; S-Dau; Yes; Yes [1917 Census name Daisy.]
346;   Foot, Edward; M; 4/18, 13; Cheyenne; 1/4+; S; Step-Son; Yes; Yes
347;   Foot, Bertha; F; 12/19, 11; Cheyenne; 1/4+; S; Step-Dau; Yes; Yes
348;   Foot, Eva; F; 5/23, 7; Cheyenne; 1/4+; S; Step-Dau; Yes; Yes
349;   Foot, Sylvia; F; 11/19/28, 2; Cheyenne; 1/4+; S; Dau; Yes; Yes
350;   Hardrobe, Margaret; F; 4/18, 13; Cheyenne; F; S; Dau; Yes; Yes

351;   Ghostbull, Arthur; M; 2/70, 61; Cheyenne; F; Wd[sic]; Head; Yes; Yes
352;   Ghostbull, Eva; F; 3/08, 23; Cheyenne; F; S; Dau; Yes; Yes

353;   Gillispie, May P.; F; 5/88, 43; Cheyenne; 1/4+; M; Head; No; Pine Ridge, S.D.

354;   Grasshopper, Isaac; M; 6/50, 80; Cheyenne; F; Wd[sic]; Head; Yes; Yes
355;   Grasshopper, Frank; M; 9/06, 24; Cheyenne; F; S; G-Son; Yes; Yes [Son of Mrs. Stanley Lamewoman.] [Arthur in 1926.]

356;   Gray, Bessie; F; 7/04, 26; Cheyenne; F; D; Head; Yes; Yes [1920 #917, name Sandcrane.]
357;   Gray, Rose Marie; F; 11/23, 7; Cheyenne; F; S; Dau; Yes; Yes
358;   Sandcrane, Peter; M; 11/29/28, 2; Cheyenne; F; S; Son; Yes; Yes

359;   Gray, Edward; M; 4/73, 58; Cheyenne; F; M; Head; Yes; Yes
360;   Gray, Nellie; F; 9/74, 56; Cheyenne; F; M; Wife; Yes; Yes
361;   Gray, Teddy; M; 8/15, 15; Cheyenne; F; S; Son; Yes; Yes

362;   Gray, John; M; 8/02,28; Cheyenne; F; M; Head; Yes; Yes

Census of the __Tongue River__ reservation of the __Tongue River__ jurisdiction, as of __April 1__, 1931, taken by __C. B. Lohmiller__, Superintendent.

**Key:** Number; NAME: Surname, Given; Sex; Birthdate, Age At Last Birthday; Tribe; Degree of Blood; Marital Status; Relationship To Head of Family; At Jurisdiction Where Enrolled (Yes or No); At Another Jurisdiction; ELSEWHERE: Post office, County, State; Ward (Yes or No); Allotment, Annuity, and Identification Numbers.

363; Gray, Kate; F; 3/00, 31; Cheyenne; F; M; Wife; Yes; Yes [Wolfname] [Ida in 1926.]
364; Gray, Buddy; M; 11/9/30, 4/12; Cheyenne; F; S; Yes; Yes

365; Hairyhand, Henry; M; 10/55, 75; Cheyenne; F; Wd[sic]; Head; Yes; Yes
366; Fightingbear, Willie; M; 6/99, 31; Cheyenne; F; S; G-Son; Yes; Yes

367; Hardground, Ernest; M; 7/96, 34; Cheyenne; F; M; Head; Yes; Yes
--- ~~Hardground, Mary; F; 8/95, 35; Cheyenne; F; M; Wife; Yes; Yes Died April 12, 1930~~
368; Hardground, Ethel; F; 2/21, 10; Cheyenne; F; S; Dau; Yes; Yes
369; Hardground, Katie; F; 9/23, 7; Cheyenne; F; S; Dau; Yes; Yes
370; Hardground, Nancy Susan; F; 1/30, 1; Cheyenne; F; S; Dau; Yes; Yes

371; Hardground, George; M; 4/01, 30; Cheyenne; F; M; Head; Yes; Yes
372; Hardground, Thomas; M; 4/26/30, 11/12; Cheyenne; F; S; Son; Yes; Yes

373; Hardground, Robert; M; 11/76, 54; Cheyenne; F; M; Head; Yes; Yes
374; Hardground, Patty B.L.; F; 12/75, 55; Cheyenne; F; M; Wife; Yes; Yes
375; Hardground, Albert; M; 6/99, 31; Cheyenne; F; Wd[sic]; Son; Yes; Yes
376; Hardground, Lyla; F; 2/14, 16; Cheyenne; F; S; Dau; Yes; Yes
377; Biglefthand, Rapheal[sic]; M; 9/12, 18; Cheyenne; F; S; S-Son; Yes; Yes [1915-#72 was Daisy, female.]

378; Hardrobe, Colonel; M; 2/56, 75; Cheyenne; F; Wd[sic]; Head; Yes; Yes
379; Hardrobe, Albert J.; M; 7/96, 34; Cheyenne; F; S; Son; Yes; Yes

380; Harris, Bryan; M; 4/98, 32; Cheyenne; 1/4+; M; Head; Yes; Yes
381; Harris, Ruth M.B.; F; 12/07, 24; Cheyenne; F; M; Wife; Yes; Yes [Spottedhawk, Medicinebird]
382; Harris, Carl; M; 10/21, 9; Cheyenne; 1/4+; S; Son; Yes; Yes
383; Harris, Francis E.; M; 9/1/29, 1; Cheyenne; 1/4+; S; Son; Yes; Yes [Elmer F. in 1930]
384; Harris, Chester; M; 2/25/31, 1/12; Cheyenne; 1/4+; S; Son; Yes; Yes
385; Harris, Sallie; F; 79; Cheyenne; 1/4+; Wd; Mother; Yes; Yes [Allie in 1928]

386; Harris, Edward; M; 1/87, 44; Cheyenne; 1/4+; Cheyenne; Head; Yes; Yes
387; Harris, Bessie; F; 5/89, 41; Cheyenne; F; M: Wife; Yes; Yes
388; Harris, May; F; 5/11, 19; Cheyenne; 1/4+; S; Dau; Yes; Yes
389; Harris, Nellie; F; 5/14, 16; Cheyenne; 1/4+; S; Dau; Yes; Yes
390; Harris, Dorothy; F; 5/19, 11; Cheyenne; 1/4+; S; Dau; Yes; Yes
391; Harris, Hubert; M; 1/22, 8; Cheyenne; 1/4+; S; Dau; Yes; Yes [Lawrence Edw. in 1926.]
392; Harris, Inez R.; F; 12/9/27, 3; Cheyenne; 1/4+; S; Dau; Yes; Yes

Census of the __Tongue River__ reservation of the __Tongue River__ jurisdiction, as of __April 1__, 1931, taken by __C. B. Lohmiller__, Superintendent.

**Key:** Number; NAME: Surname, Given; Sex; Birthdate, Age At Last Birthday; Tribe; Degree of Blood; Marital Status; Relationship To Head of Family; At Jurisdiction Where Enrolled (Yes or No); At Another Jurisdiction; ELSEWHERE: Post office, County, State; Ward (Yes or No); Allotment, Annuity, and Identification Numbers.

393: Harris, George; M; 9/07, 23; Cheyenne; 1/4+; M; Head; Yes; Yes
394; Harris, Anna; F; 7/13, 17; Cheyenne; F; M; Wife; Yes; Yes

395; Harris, William; M; 1/77, 54; Cheyenne; 1/4+; M; Head; Yes; Yes
396; Harris, Margaret; F; 5/84, 46; Cheyenne; 1/4+; M; Wife; Yes; Yes
397; Harris, Julia; F; 12/10, 20; Cheyenne; 1/4+; S; Dau; Yes; Yes
398; Harris, Agnes; F; 9/12, 18; Cheyenne; 1/4+; S; Dau; Yes; Yes
399; Harris, Raymond; M; 4/15, 16; Cheyenne; 1/4+; S; Son; Yes; Yes
400; Harris, Mary; F; 4/19, 12; Cheyenne; 1/4+; S; Dau; Yes; Yes [1920 name Leota.]
401; Harris, Florence; F; 9/23, 7; Cheyenne; 1/4+; S; Dau; Yes; Yes [1925 son Joseph, M.]

402; Hart, Charles; M; 49; Cheyenne; F; M; Head; Yes; Yes
403; Hart, Louisa; F; 44; Cheyenne; 1/4+; M; Wife; Yes; Yes
404; Hart, Eva; F; 16; Cheyenne; 1/4+; S; Dau; Yes; Yes
405; Hart, Jessie D.; F; 14; Cheyenne; 1/4+; S; Dau; Yes; Yes
406; Aikin, Mattie L.; F; 7/11, 19; Cheyenne; 1/4+; M; Dau; Yes; Yes

407; Hart, Frank; M; 7/98, 31; Cheyenne; 1/4+; M; Head; Yes; Yes
408; Hart, Alice; F; 5/07, 23; Cheyenne; F; M; Wife; Yes; Yes [Hairlessbear]
409; Hart, Edna; F; 11/16/27, 3; Cheyenne; 1/4+; S; Dau; Yes; Yes
410; Hart, Hilda; F; 8/29/30, 7/12; Cheyenne; 1/4+; S; Dau; Yes; Yes

411; Headswift, Charles; M; 3/67, 64; Cheyenne; F; Wd[sic]; Head; Yes; Yes
412; Headswift, Frank; M; 6/11, 19; Cheyenne; F; S; Son; Yes; Yes

413; Highbear, William; M; 3/88, 43; Cheyenne; F; M; Head; Yes; Yes
414; Highbear, Minnie; F; 5/97, 33; Cheyenne; F; M; Wife; Yes; Yes

415; Highwalking, Floyd; M; 4/88, 42; Cheyenne; F; M; Head; Yes; Yes
416; Highwalking, Belle; F; 6/93, 37; Cheyenne; F; M; Wife; Yes; Yes
417; Highwalking, George; M; 3/13, 18; Cheyenne; F; S; Son; Yes; Yes [David in 1926.]
418; Highwalking, Max; M; 1/17, 14; Cheyenne; F; S; Son; Yes; Yes
419; Highwalking, Nellie; F; 4/59, 72; Cheyenne; F; Wd; Mother; Yes; Yes

422; Hisbadhorse, Willis; M; 8/98, 32; Cheyenne; F; M; Head; Yes; Yes
421; Hisbadhorse, Ernest; M; 5/17, 13; Cheyenne; F; S; Son; Yes; Yes [1924 s-son. Eugene in 1926.]
422; Hisbadhorse, Medaris; M; 8/21, 9; Cheyenne; F; S; Son; Yes; Yes [Bird; son; 1917; in 1926.]
423; Hisbadhorse, Fannie; F; 10/22, 7; Cheyenne; F; S; Dau; Yes; Yes [Josephine in 1926.]

Census of the **Tongue River** reservation of the **Tongue River** jurisdiction, as of **April 1**, 19**31**, taken by **C. B. Lohmiller**, Superintendent.

**Key:** Number; NAME: Surname, Given; Sex; Birthdate, Age At Last Birthday; Tribe; Degree of Blood; Marital Status; Relationship To Head of Family; At Jurisdiction Where Enrolled (Yes or No); At Another Jurisdiction; ELSEWHERE: Post office, County, State; Ward (Yes or No); Allotment, Annuity, and Identification Numbers.

424; Rowland, Carrie; F; 11/26, 4; Cheyenne; 1/4-; S; Step-Dau; Yes; Yes
425; Hisbadhorse, Esther; F; 8/19/30, 7/12; Cheyenne; F; S; Dau; Yes; Yes
426; Hisbadhorse, Rhoda; F; 6/56, 74; Cheyenne; F; Wd; Mother; Yes; Yes
427; Americanhorse, Albert M.; M; 7/12, 18; Cheyenne; F; S; Nephew; Yes; Yes

428; Hollowbreast, Hubert; M; 5/75, 55; Cheyenne; F; M; Head; Yes; Yes
429; Hollowbreast, Mary; F; 4/96, 35; Cheyenne; F; M; Wife; Yes; Yes [Previous censuses name Hattie Hisbadhorses. 1926 Hisbadhorses, wdw. #426.]
430; Hollowbreast, Donald; M; 5/17, 13; Cheyenne; F; S; Son; Yes; Yes
431; Hollowbreast, Jack Richard; M; 25, 6; Cheyenne; F; S; Son; Yes; Yes
432; Hollowbreast, Edward; M; 4/7/29, 2; Cheyenne; F; S; Son; Yes; Yes

433; Hollowbreast, William; M; 3/00, 30; Cheyenne; F; M; Head; Yes; Yes
434; Hollowbreast, Mary; F; 11/03, 27; Cheyenne; F; M; Wife; Yes; Yes [Littlewolf]

435; Hollowwood, Richard; M; 7/56, 75; Cheyenne; M; M; Head; Yes; Yes
436; Hollowwood, Hattie; F; 8/56, 74; Cheyenne; M; M; Wife; Yes; Yes

437; Horn, Annie W.; F; 5/00, 30; Cheyenne; F; M; Head; Yes; Yes [Name Alice 1904-20.]
438; Horn, Rose; F; 6/21, 9; Cheyenne; F; S; Dau; Yes; Yes
439; Horn, Wilena; F; 3/23, 8; Cheyenne; F; S; Dau; Yes; Yes
440; Horn, Margaret; F; 7/26, 4; Cheyenne; F; S; Dau; Yes; Yes
441; Horn, Celia M.; F; 5/7/28, 2; Cheyenne; F; S; Dau; Yes; Yes
442; Horn, Denver S.; M; 12/13/30, 3/12; Cheyenne; F; S; Son; Yes; Yes

443; Horseroads, Thomas; M; 9/78, 52; Cheyenne; F; M; Head; Yes; Yes
444; Horseroads, Lucy; F; 8/87, 43; Cheyenne; F; M; Wife; Yes; Yes
445; Horseroads, Ida; F; 1/24, 7; Cheyenne; F; S; Dau; Yes; Yes
446; Horseroads, Cora; F; 11/26, 4; Cheyenne; F; S; Dau; Yes; Yes

447; Howe, Lucy; F; 1/93, 40; Cheyenne; -1/4; M; Head; No; Lodgegrass Town, Big Horn, Mont; Yes
448; Beartusk, Alice; F; 4/16, 13; Cheyenne; 1/4+; S; Dau; Yes; Yes
449; Beartusk, Gladys; F; 1/19, 12; Cheyenne; 1/4+; S; Dau; Yes; Yes [Nellie]
450; Beartusk, Kenneth; M; 12/20, 10 Cheyenne; 1/4+; S; Son; Yes; Yes
451; Beartusk, Bertha; F; 3/23, 7; Cheyenne; 1/4+; S; Dau; Yes; Yes
452; Beartusk, Jerome, Jr; M; 12/25, 4; Cheyenne; 1/4+; S; Son; Yes; Yes

453; Howlingantelope, Albert; M; 4/74, 57; Cheyenne; F; M; Head; Yes; Yes
454; Howlingantelope, Eva; F; 5/80, 46; Cheyenne; F; M; Wife; Yes; Yes
455; Fasthorse, Clara; F; 5/13, 17; Cheyenne; F; S; G-Dau; Yes; Yes

Census of the **Tongue River** reservation of the **Tongue River** jurisdiction, as of **April 1**, 1931, taken by **C. B. Lohmiller**, Superintendent.

**Key:** Number; NAME: Surname, Given; Sex; Birthdate, Age At Last Birthday; Tribe; Degree of Blood; Marital Status; Relationship To Head of Family; At Jurisdiction Where Enrolled (Yes or No); At Another Jurisdiction; ELSEWHERE: Post office, County, State; Ward (Yes or No); Allotment, Annuity, and Identification Numbers.

456; Huff, Pearl; F; 6/07, 23; Cheyenne; -1/4; M; Head; No; Lodgegrass town, Big Horn, Mont; Yes [Eastman]
457; Huff, Elsie; F; 12/23/27, 3; Cheyenne; 1/4+; S; Dau; No; Lodgegrass town, Big Horn, Mont; Yes
458; Huff, Percy; M; 8/29, 2; Cheyenne; 1/4+; S; Son; No; Lodgegrass town, Big Horn, Mont; Yes

459; Ironhand, Henry; M; 6/10, 20; Cheyenne; F; M; Head; Yes; Yes
460; Ironhand, Mamie; F; 7/12, 19; Cheyenne; F; M; Wife; Yes; Yes

461; Ironhand, William; M; 11/82, 48; Cheyenne; F; M; Head; Yes; Yes
462; Ironhand, Sally; F; 7/84, 46; Cheyenne; F; M; Wife; Yes; Yes
463; Ironhand, Willis; M; 1/15, 16; Cheyenne; F; S; Son; Yes; Yes
464; Ironhand, Jane; F; 2/27, 4; Cheyenne; F; S; Dau; Yes; Yes

465; Issues, Francis; M; 3/97, 34; Cheyenne; F; M; Head; Yes; Yes
466; Issues, Mamie L.; F; 12/07, 23; Cheyenne; 1/4+; M; Wife; Yes; Yes [1930 1/4-]
467; Issues, Ira; M; 2/20, 11; Cheyenne; F; S; Son; Yes; Yes [1919 name Ira, 1920-23, George.]
468; Issues, Irene; F; 5/21, 9; Cheyenne; F; S; Dau; Yes; Yes

469; Issue, John; M; 1863, 67; Cheyenne; F; M; Head; Yes; Yes [1930 name Issues]
470; Issue, Clara; F; 3/70, 61; Cheyenne; F; M; Wife; Yes; Yes [Blackmedicine; 1904-17, she becomes Issues 1915]

471; Killsback, James; M; 7/63, 67; Cheyenne; F; M; Head; Yes; Yes [Census #461, name Joseph Killsacross in 1926.]
472; Killsback, Amelia; F; 12/78, 52; Cheyenne; F; M; Wife; Yes; Yes

473; Killsnight, Charles; M; 6/90, 40; Cheyenne; F; M; Head; Yes; Yes
474; Killsnight, Rose L.W.; F; 12/90, 40; Cheyenne; F; M; Wife; Yes; Yes
475; Killsnight, Rose; F; 4/15, 15; Cheyenne; F; S; Dau; Yes; Yes
476; Killsnight, Hubert; M; 2/19, 11; Cheyenne; F; S; Son; Yes; Yes [Brighton in 1926.]
477; Lonewolf, James; M; 7/15, 15; Cheyenne; F; S; Step-Son; Yes; Yes
478; Lonewolf, Ella; F; 5/25, 5; Cheyenne; F; S; Step-Dau; Yes; Yes

479; Killsnight, Hugh; M; 8/66, 64; Cheyenne; F; M; Head; Yes; Yes
480; Killsnight, Clara; F; 9/72, 58; Cheyenne; F; M; Wife; Yes; Yes

481; Killsnight, Martin; M; 1/07, 24; Cheyenne; F; Wd[sic]; Head; Yes; Yes

Census of the __Tongue River__ reservation of the __Tongue River__ jurisdiction, as of __April 1__, 1931, taken by __C. B. Lohmiller__, Superintendent.

**Key:** Number; NAME: Surname, Given; Sex; Birthdate, Age At Last Birthday; Tribe; Degree of Blood; Marital Status; Relationship To Head of Family; At Jurisdiction Where Enrolled (Yes or No); At Another Jurisdiction; ELSEWHERE: Post office, County, State; Ward (Yes or No); Allotment, Annuity, and Identification Numbers.

482; Killsnight, Kitty B.; F; 11/9/28, 2; Cheyenne; 1/4-; S; Dau; Yes; Yes [1930 1/4+]

483; Killsnight, Rose; F; 2/99, 32; Cheyenne; F; D; Head; Yes; Yes
484; Killsnight, Margaret; F; 2/24, 7; Cheyenne; F; S; Dau; Yes; Yes
--- Killsnight, Dorothy; F; 2/27, 4; Cheyenne; F; S; Dau; Yes; Yes Died February 16, 1931.
485; Killsnight, Jennie; F; 3/12/29, 2; Cheyenne; F; S; Dau; Yes; Yes

486; Killsnight, William; M; 4/56, 75; Cheyenne; F; M; Head; Yes; Yes
487; Killsnight, Cora; F; 6/60, 70; Cheyenne; F; M; Wife; Yes; Yes
488; Killsnight, William Jr.; M; 10/04, 26; Cheyenne; F; S; G-Son; Yes; Yes
489; Killsnight, Cole; M; 2/05, 26; Cheyenne; F; S; Son; Yes; Yes
490; Killsnight, Mabel L.; F; 6/10, 20; Cheyenne; F; M; Dau-in-law; Yes; Yes

491; Killsnight, Willis; M; 3/95, 36; Cheyenne; F; M; Head; Yes; Yes [Rutherford in 1926.]
492; Killsnight, Carrie; F; 5/90, 40; Cheyenne; F; S[sic]; Wife; Yes; Yes [Whitemoon]
493; Killsnight, Mary Flossie; F; 2/23, 8; Cheyenne; F; S; Dau; Yes; Yes [Sage in 1926.]
494; Killsnight, James; M; 4/26, 5; Cheyenne; F; S; Son; Yes; Yes
495; Killsnight, Ralph; M; 4/7/28, 3; Cheyenne; F; S; Son; Yes; Yes

496; Killsnightwoman; F; 72; Cheyenne; F; Wd; Head; Yes; Yes

497; Killsontop, John; M; 8/06, 24; Cheyenne; F; M; Head; Yes; Yes
498; Killsontop, Mary; F; 2/09, 22; Cheyenne; F; S[sic]; Wife; Yes; Yes [Strangeowl]
499; Killsontop, June; F; 4/27, 4; Cheyenne; F; S; Dau; Yes; Yes
500; Killsontop, Levern; M; 1/1/29, 2; Cheyenne; F; S; Son; Yes; Yes
501; Killsontop, Harold; M; 6/21/30, 9/12; Cheyenne; F; S; Son; Yes; Yes

502; Kingfisher, Carrie; F; 54; Cheyenne; F; Wd; Head; Yes; Yes

503; Kingfisher, Willis J.; M; 9/96, 35; Cheyenne; F; M; Head; Yes; Yes
504; Kingfisher, Minnie; F; 7/96, 34; Cheyenne; F; M; Wife; Yes; Yes
505; Kingfisher, Isabelle; F; 9/18, 12; Cheyenne; F; S; Dau; Yes; Yes
506; Kingfisher, Charles; M; 6/21, 9; Cheyenne; F; S; Dau[sic]; Yes; Yes
507; Kingfisher, Louise; F; 10/22, 8; Cheyenne; F; S; Dau; Yes; Yes
508; Kingfisher, Ellen; F; 6/26, 4 Cheyenne; F; S; Dau; Yes; Yes
509; Kingfisher, Angela; F; 5/23/28, 1; Cheyenne; F; S; Dau; Yes; Yes

510; Kinsel, Alice; F; 3/93,38; Cheyenne; 1/4-; M; Head; Yes; Yes [1/4+ 1930]

Census of the **Tongue River** reservation of the **Tongue River** jurisdiction, as of **April 1**, 1931, taken by **C. B. Lohmiller**, Superintendent.

**Key:** Number; NAME: Surname, Given; Sex; Birthdate, Age At Last Birthday; Tribe; Degree of Blood; Marital Status; Relationship To Head of Family; At Jurisdiction Where Enrolled (Yes or No); At Another Jurisdiction; ELSEWHERE: Post office, County, State; Ward (Yes or No); Allotment, Annuity, and Identification Numbers.

511; Kinsel, Emma L.; F; 6/17, 13; Cheyenne; -1/4; S; Dau; Yes; Yes
512; Kinsel, Helen L.; F; 3/20, 11; Cheyenne; -1/4; S; Dau; Yes; Yes
513; Kinsel, Cecelia L; F; 7/24, 6; Cheyenne; -1/4; S; Dau; Yes; Yes
514; Kinsel, Virgil B.; M; 10/9/27, 3; Cheyenne; -1/4; S; Son; Yes; Yes

515; Knows-his-gun, Frances; F; 10/04, 26; Cheyenne; F; M; Head; Yes; Yes
516; Knows-his-gun, Sylvester; M; 9/26, 4; Cheyenne; F; S; Son; Yes; Yes
517; Knows-his-gun, Edith; F; 5/11/28, 2; Cheyenne; F; S; Dau; Yes; Yes

518; LaFever, Rena; F; 8/96, 34; Cheyenne; -1/4; M; Head; No; [None given.]; Yes
519; Bolson, Frank; M; 8/17, 13; Cheyenne; -1/4; S; Son; *Yes*; Yes
520; Bolson, Roy; M; 12/19, 11; Cheyenne; -1/4; S; Son; *Yes*; Yes
521; LaFever, Kenneth; M; 12/25, 5; Cheyenne; -1/4; S; Son; *No*; [None given.]; Yes

522; Lamebear, Benjamin; M; 36; Cheyenne; F; M; Head; Yes; Yes
523; Lamebear, Clara; F; 26; Cheyenne; F; M; Wife; Yes; Yes [Age 35 1930]
524; Lamebear, Eva; F; 20; Cheyenne; F; S; Dau; Yes; Yes
525; Lamebear, Cora; F; 12; Cheyenne; F; S; Dau; Yes; Yes
526; Lamebear, Charles; M; 9; Cheyenne; F; S; Son; Yes; Yes
527; Lamebear, Susie; F; 1; Cheyenne; F; S; Dau; Yes; Yes

528; Lamewoman, Sam; M; 10/12, 18; Cheyenne; F; M; Head; Yes; Yes [Sam Littlebear; 1928]
529; Lamewoman, Maude; F; 6/13, 17; Cheyenne; F; M; Wife; Yes; Yes

530; Lamewoman, Alice; F; 7/10, 20; Cheyenne; 1/4+; M; Head; Yes; Yes [Rowland; 7/8 [Birth year 1912 in 1926.]
531; Lamewoman, Ruth; F; 10/15/30, 1; Cheyenne; 1/4+; S; Dau; Yes; Yes

532; Lamewoman, Stanley; M; 8/89, 41; Cheyenne; F; M; Head; Yes; Yes
533; Lamewoman, Augusta; F; 7/85, 45; Cheyenne; F; M; Wife; Yes; Yes
534; Lamewoman, Jessie; F; 6/14, 16; Cheyenne; F; S; Dau; Yes; Yes
535; Lamewoman, Virgil; M; 2/22, 8; Cheyenne; F; S; Son; Yes; Yes
536; Lamewoman, Nellie; F; 7/54, 76; Cheyenne; F; Wd; Mother; Yes; Yes

537; Lastbull, Fred; M; 1/88, 42; Cheyenne; F; M; Head; Yes; Yes

538; Lennon, Mary B.; F; 6/06, 24; Cheyenne; -1/4; M; Head; Yes; Yes
539; Lennon, Arthur G.; M; 11/26, 4; Cheyenne; -1/4; S; Son; Yes; Yes

540; Lightning, Frank; M; 8/71, 59; Cheyenne; F; Wd[sic]; Head; Yes; Yes

541; Limberhand, Nathan; M; 3/76, 54; Cheyenne; F; M; Head; Yes; Yes
542; Limberhand, Artie; F; 9/83, 44; Cheyenne; F; M; Wife; Yes; Yes

Census of the **Tongue River** reservation of the **Tongue River** jurisdiction, as of **April 1**, 19**31**, taken by **C. B. Lohmiller**, Superintendent.

**Key:** Number; NAME: Surname, Given; Sex; Birthdate, Age At Last Birthday; Tribe; Degree of Blood; Marital Status; Relationship To Head of Family; At Jurisdiction Where Enrolled (Yes or No); At Another Jurisdiction; ELSEWHERE: Post office, County, State; Ward (Yes or No); Allotment, Annuity, and Identification Numbers.

543; Limberhand, James; M; 10/02, 28; Cheyenne; F; S; Son; Yes; Yes
544; Limberhand, Elmore; M; 1/09, 21; Cheyenne; F; S; Son; Yes; Yes
545; Limberhand, Bennie; M; 1/12, 20; Cheyenne; F; S; Son; Yes; Yes
546; Limberhand, Doris; F; 5/22, 18; Cheyenne; F; S; Dau; Yes; Yes
547; Limpy, Henry; M; 8/19, 10; Cheyenne; 1/4+; G-Son; Yes; Yes

548; Limberhand, Richard; M; 8/05, 25; Cheyenne; F; M; Head; Yes; Yes
549; Limberhand, Jessie; F; 10/05, 25; Cheyenne; F; M; Wife; Yes; Yes
[Rockroads (Rhoda) all numbers past and present coincide, shows up in 1915, birth year 1913. 1926 last name Russell, wife, husband Frank, separated.]
550; Limberhand, Doris; F; 10/15/28, 3; Cheyenne; F; S; Dau; Yes; Yes

551; Limpy, Benjamin; M; 10/92, 38; Cheyenne; F; M; Head; Yes; Yes
552; Limpy, Hattie; F; 6/94, 36; Cheyenne; F; M; Wife; Yes; Yes [#540; Hallie Killsacross #271, 1914 census. 1915-16 Hallie Limpy.]
553; Limpy, Anna; F; 1/15, 16; Cheyenne; F; S; Dau; Yes; Yes [Son, Jack 1916-19; Jean in 1926.]
554; Limpy, Rosa; F; 8/19, 11; Cheyenne; F; S; Dau; Yes; Yes [#530 Elnora in 1926.]
555; Limpy, Jessie; F; 11/22, 8; Cheyenne; F; S; Dau; Yes; Yes [Name Bessie 1930]
556; Limpy, Eunice; F; 9/23/27, 3; Cheyenne; F; S; Dau; Yes; Yes
557; Dullknife, Bessie; F; 3/70, 81; Cheyenne; F; Wd; Mother-in-law; Yes; Yes

558; Limpy, Charles; M; 10/57, 73; Cheyenne; F; M; Head; Yes; Yes
559; Limpy, Nellie; F; 7/54, 75; Cheyenne; F; M; Wife; Yes; Yes

560; Limpy, Fred; M; 4/84, 47; Cheyenne; 1/4+; M; Head; Yes; Yes
561; Limpy, Amelia; F; 5/85, 45; Cheyenne; F; M; Wife; Yes; Yes [Womanleggins]
562; Limpy, Frank; M; 5/11, 20; Cheyenne; 1/4+; S; Son; Yes; Yes
563; Limpy, Mary; F; 5/13, 15; Cheyenne; 1/4+; S; Dau; Yes; Yes [#506, Limpy, Mary; D.; 6 Mo; in 1909. May Limpy 1926.]
564; Limpy, Cora; F; 11/25, 5; Cheyenne; 1/4+; S; Dau; Yes; Yes
---  Limpy, Fred Jr.; M; 6/10/29, 1; Cheyenne; 1/4+; S; Son; Yes; Yes Died October 15, 1930.

565; Littlebear, Paul; M; 7/87, 43; Cheyenne; F; M; Head; Yes; Yes
567[sic]; Littlebear, Rose; F; 8/87, 43; Cheyenne; F; M; Wife; Yes; Yes
567; Littlebear, Flossie; F; 4/12, 19; Cheyenne; F; S; Dau; Yes; Yes [Mary in 1926.]
568; Littlebear, Clara; F; 4/16, 15; Cheyenne; F; S; Dau; Yes; Yes
569; Littlebear, Peter T.; M; 12/23, 6; Cheyenne; F; S; Son; Yes; Yes
570; Littlebear, Lucille; F; 7/26, 4; Cheyenne; F; S; Dau; Yes; Yes

Census of the **Tongue River** reservation of the **Tongue River** jurisdiction, as of **April 1**, 1931, taken by **C. B. Lohmiller**, Superintendent.

**Key:** Number; NAME: Surname, Given; Sex; Birthdate, Age At Last Birthday; Tribe; Degree of Blood; Marital Status; Relationship To Head of Family; At Jurisdiction Where Enrolled (Yes or No); At Another Jurisdiction; ELSEWHERE: Post office, County, State; Ward (Yes or No); Allotment, Annuity, and Identification Numbers.

571; Littlebear, Lester; M; 9/16/29, 1; Cheyenne; F; S; Son; Yes; Yes
572; Littlebear, May; F; 5/08, 22; Cheyenne; F; S; Dau; Yes; Yes [Anne in 1926.]
573; Littlebear, Lenora C.; F; 12/2/28, 2; Cheyenne; F; S; G-Dau; Yes; Yes

574; Littlebird, Peter; M; 5/70, 60; Cheyenne; F; M; Head; Yes; Yes
575; Littlebird, Jennie; F; 7/92, 38; Cheyenne; F; M; Wife; Yes; Yes
576; Littlebird, Joseph; M; 9/12, 18; Cheyenne; F; S; Son; Yes; Yes
577; Littlebird, Julia; F; 6/22, 8; Cheyenne; F; S; Dau; Yes; Yes
578; Littlebird, James Wm.; M; 6/25, 5; Cheyenne; F; S; Son; Yes; Yes
579; Littlebird, Theresa; F; 12/8/29, 1; Cheyenne; F; S; Dau; Yes; Yes

580; Littlechief, Victor; M; 1/77, 54; Cheyenne; F; M; Head; Yes; Yes
581; Littlechief, Louisa; F; 3/75, 56; Cheyenne; F; M; Wife; Yes; Yes

582; Littlecoyote, Henry; M; 9/76, 55; Cheyenne; F; M; Head; Yes; Yes
583; Littlecoyote, Julia P.; F; 4/76, 54; Cheyenne; F; M; Wife; Yes; Yes
584; Littlecoyote, Daniel E.; M; 10/10, 20; Cheyenne; F; S; Son; Yes; Yes
585; Whitefrog, Nellie; F; 5/61, 69; Cheyenne; F; S; Step-Mother; Yes; Yes

586; Littleeagle, Charles; M; 5/67, 63; Cheyenne; F; M; Head; Yes; Yes
587; Littleeagle, Mary; F; 6/78, 52; Cheyenne; F; M; Wife; Yes; Yes
588; Littleeagle, Clara; F; 8/05, 25; Cheyenne; F; S; Dau; Yes; Yes

589; Littlehawk, Dora; F; 1/69, 61; Cheyenne; F; Wd; Head; Yes; Yes
590; Medicineelk, Jennie; F; 9/04, 26; Cheyenne; F; M; Niece; Yes; Yes [Eaglefeathers]
591; Medicineelk, Sarah A.; F; 4/20/28, 3; Cheyenne; F; S; G-Niece; Yes; Yes
---   Woodpecker, Donald C.; M; 7/09, 21; Cheyenne; F; S; Nephew; Yes; Yes Died February 12, 1931.

592; Littlehead, Charles; M; 6/69, 61; Cheyenne; F; M; Head; Yes; Yes
593; Littlehead, Nellie; F; 12/82, 48; Cheyenne; F; M; Wife; Yes; Yes
594; Littlehead, Frank; M; 11/09, 21; Cheyenne; F; S; Son; Yes; Yes
595; Littlehead, George; M; 5/20, 10; Cheyenne; F; S; Son; Yes; Yes [1920 name John.]
596; Blackstone, Gladys; F; 8/00, 30; Cheyenne; F; D; Dau; Yes; Yes
597; Blackstone, Louis; M; 10/21/27, 3; Cheyenne; F; S; G-Son; Yes; Yes
598; Blackstone, Joseph; M; 6/20/29, 1; Cheyenne; F; S; G-Son; Yes; Yes

599; Littlehead, John; M; 10/94, 36; Cheyenne; F; M; Head; No; Cheyenne & Arap. Okla; Yes

600; Littlemouth, John; M; 10/94, 36; Cheyenne; F; M; Head; Yes; Yes
601; Littlemouth, Jennie; F; 9/98, 32; Cheyenne; F; M; Wife; Yes; Yes

Census of the __Tongue River__ reservation of the __Tongue River__ jurisdiction, as of __April 1__, 1931, taken by __C. B. Lohmiller__, Superintendent.

**Key:** Number; NAME: Surname, Given; Sex; Birthdate, Age At Last Birthday; Tribe; Degree of Blood; Marital Status; Relationship To Head of Family; At Jurisdiction Where Enrolled (Yes or No); At Another Jurisdiction; ELSEWHERE: Post office, County, State; Ward (Yes or No); Allotment, Annuity, and Identification Numbers.

602; Littlemouth, Evelyn; F; 5/21, 9; Cheyenne; F; S; Dau; Yes; Yes
603; Littlemouth, James; M; 6/22, 8; Cheyenne; F; S; Son; Yes; Yes
604; Littlemouth, Mary; F; 4/24, 3; Cheyenne; F; S; Dau; Yes; Yes
605; Littlemouth, Clara; F; 7/59, 71; Cheyenne; F; Wd; Mother; Yes; Yes

---  ~~Littlesun, Frank; M; 10/84, 46; Cheyenne; F; M; Yes; Yes~~
~~Died December 11, 1930~~

606; Littlesun, Samuel; M; 7/58, 72; Cheyenne; F; M; Head; Yes; Yes
607; Littlesun, Cora; F; 9/64, 66; Cheyenne; F; M; Wife; Yes; Yes
608; Littlesun, Jack; M; 8/20, 10; Cheyenne; F; S; G-Son; Yes; Yes
609; Littlesun, Horace; M; 9/22, 8; Cheyenne; F; S; G-Son; Yes; Yes

610; Littlewhirlwind, George; M; 1/01, 30; Cheyenne; F; M; Head; Yes; Yes
611; Littlewhirlwind, Martha; F; 10/09, 21; Cheyenne; F; M; Wife; Yes; Yes
[Fannie Walksalong in 1926.]
612; Littlewhirlwind, Anna; F; 11/30/28, 2; Cheyenne; F; S; Dau; Yes; Yes

613; Littlewhiteman, Aaron; M; 12/62, 68; Cheyenne; 1/4+; M; Head; Yes; Yes
614; Littlewhiteman, Sadie; F; 4/66, 64; Cheyenne; F; M; Wife; Yes; Yes
615; Littlewhiteman, Wesley; M; 8/97, 32; Cheyenne; 1/4+; S; Son; Yes; Yes
616; Powderface, Julia; F; 8/13, 17; Cheyenne; 1/4+; S; G-Dau; Yes; Yes

617; Littlewhiteman, David; M; 2/69, 62; Cheyenne; 1/4+; M; Head; Yes; Yes
618; Littlewhiteman, Agnes; F; 7/72, 58; Cheyenne; F; M; Wife; Yes; Yes
619; Littlewhiteman, Peter; M; 4/06, 25; Cheyenne; M; S; Son; Yes; Yes

620; Littlewhiteman, Frank; M; 11/01, 29; Cheyenne; 1/4+; M; Head; Yes; Yes
621; Littlewhiteman, Emma F; F; 10/00, 30; Cheyenne; F; M; Wife; Yes; Yes
[#964 in 1919 shows as Lightning, Emma; g dt; 1901; F. Grandparents Shortsioux in census as birth year 1901 starting in 1912 or 11 years old.]
622; Littlewhiteman, Leon; M; 8/20, 10; Cheyenne; 1/4+; S; Son; Yes; Yes [John in 1926.]
623; Littlewhiteman, Margaret; F; 7/22, 8; Cheyenne; 1/4+; S; Dau; Yes; Yes
624; Littlewhiteman, John; M; 10/25, 5; Cheyenne; 1/4+; S; Son; Yes; Yes
625; Littlewhiteman, Philip; M; 3/29/27, 4; Cheyenne; 1/4+; S; Son; Yes; Yes

626; Littlewhiteman, Henry; M; 1/91, 40; Cheyenne; 1/4+; M; Head; Yes; Yes
627; Littlewhiteman, Mary R.; F; 5/90, 40; Cheyenne; F; M; Wife; Yes; Yes
628; Littlewhiteman, Edith; F; 12/12, 18; Cheyenne; 1/4+; S; Dau; Yes; Yes
629; Littlewhiteman, Rosa; F; 9/15, 16; Cheyenne; 1/4+; S; Dau; Yes; Yes
630; Littlewhiteman, Agnes; F; 10/21, 9; Cheyenne; 1/4+; S; Dau; Yes; Yes

--- ~~Littlewhiteman, Elmer; M; 10/28/29, 1; Cheyenne; 1/4 [sic]; S; Son; Yes; Yes~~
~~Died April 15, 1930.~~

Census of the **Tongue River** reservation of the **Tongue River** jurisdiction, as of **April 1**, 1931, taken by **C. B. Lohmiller**, Superintendent.

**Key:** Number; NAME: Surname, Given; Sex; Birthdate, Age At Last Birthday; Tribe; Degree of Blood; Marital Status; Relationship To Head of Family; At Jurisdiction Where Enrolled (Yes or No); At Another Jurisdiction; ELSEWHERE: Post office, County, State; Ward (Yes or No); Allotment, Annuity, and Identification Numbers.

631; Romannose, Eva L.; 7/26/28, 2; Cheyenne; F; S; Step-Dau; Yes; Yes

632; Littlewhiteman, James; M; 6/95, 34; Cheyenne; 1/4+; M; Head; Yes; Yes
633; Littlewhiteman, Gusta; F; 9/97, 33; Cheyenne; F; M; Wife; Yes; Yes [Littlesun]
634; Littlewhiteman, Kitty; F; 9/23, 7; Cheyenne; 1/4+; S; Dau; Yes; Yes
635; Littlewhiteman, Winn; M; 11/28, 3; Cheyenne; 1/4+; S; Son; Yes; Yes
636; Littlewhiteman, Mona F.: F; 3/31/30, 1; Cheyenne; 1/4+; S; Dau; Yes; Yes

637; Littlewhiteman, Milton; M; 9/84, 46; Cheyenne; 1/4+; M; Head; Yes; Yes
638; Littlewhiteman, Rose; F; 9/82, 48; Cheyenne; F; M; Wife; Yes; Yes
639; Yellowhorse, Julia; F; 5/13, 17; Cheyenne; F; S; Step-Dau; Yes; Yes

640; Littlewhiteman, Stanley; M; 7/88, 42; Cheyenne; 1/4+; M; Head; No; Yes; Penitentiary
641; Littlewhiteman, Grace; F; 1894, 37; Cheyenne; F; M; Wife; Yes; Yes [1920-#1300, name Walkingbear.]
642; Littlewhiteman, Milton; M; 12/25/12, 18; Cheyenne; 1/4+; S; Son; Yes; Yes
643; Littlewhiteman, Aaron; M; 12/21, 9; Cheyenne; 1/4+; S; Son; Yes; Yes
644; Littlewhiteman, Adrain; M; 12/23, 6; Cheyenne; 1/4+; S; Son; Yes; Yes [Name Hillman in 1926.]
645; Littlewhiteman, Sadie; F; 1/27, 4; Cheyenne; 1/4+; S; Dau; Yes; Yes
646; Littlewhiteman, Willis Warren; M; 8/9/28, 2; Cheyenne; 1/4+; S; Son; Yes; Yes
--- Littlewhiteman, Mabel; F; 12/9/30, 10/12; Cheyenne; 1/4+; S; Dau; Yes; Yes Died August 16, 1930

647; Littlewolf, Frank; M; 2/77, 54; Cheyenne; F; M; Head; Yes; Yes
648; Littlewolf, Kate; F; 3/83, 48; Cheyenne; F; M; Wife; Yes; Yes
649; Littlewolf, Susan; F; 6/14, 16; Cheyenne; F; S; Dau; Yes; Yes
650; Littlewolf, Mary; F; 2/22, 9; Cheyenne; F; S; Dau; Yes; Yes

--- Littlewolf, Laura; F; 11/52, 78; Cheyenne; F; Wd; Head; Yes; Yes Died March 27, 1931
651; Littlewolf, Lena; F; 12/78, 52; Cheyenne; F; S; Dau; Yes; Yes

652; Littlewolf, Robert; M; 6/82, 48; Cheyenne; F; M; Head; Yes; Yes
653; Littlewolf, May; F; 6/94, 36; Cheyenne; F; M; Wife; Yes; Yes [Name Harris in 1920.]
654; Littlewolf, Charles; M; 7/08, 22; Cheyenne; F; S; Son; Yes; Yes
655; Littlewolf, Esther Geraldine; F; 12/21, 9; Cheyenne; F; S; Dau; Yes; Yes
656; Littlewolf, Eva; F; 4/25, 6; Cheyenne; F; Dau; Yes; Yes
657; Littlewolf, Laban; M; 6/4/28, 2; Cheyenne; F; S; Son; Yes; Yes
658; Littlewolf, Herbert; M; 3/19/30, 1; Cheyenne; F; S; Son; Yes; Yes

Census of the **Tongue River** reservation of the **Tongue River** jurisdiction, as of **April 1**, 1931, taken by **C. B. Lohmiller**, Superintendent.

**Key:** Number; NAME: Surname, Given; Sex; Birthdate, Age At Last Birthday; Tribe; Degree of Blood; Marital Status; Relationship To Head of Family; At Jurisdiction Where Enrolled (Yes or No); At Another Jurisdiction; ELSEWHERE: Post office, County, State; Ward (Yes or No); Allotment, Annuity, and Identification Numbers.

659; Littlewolf, William; M; 8/83, 47; Cheyenne; F; M; Head; Yes; Yes
660; Littlewolf, May; F; 12/90, 40; Cheyenne; F; M; Wife; Yes; Yes
661; Littlewolf, William Jr.; M; 10/14, 16; Cheyenne; F; S; Son; Yes; Yes
662; Littlewolf, Claude; M; 12/16, 14; Cheyenne; F; S; Son; Yes; Yes

663; Littleyellowman, Eddie; M; 1892, 39; Cheyenne; F; M; Head; No; Cheyenne & Arap. Okla; Yes
664; Littleyellowman, Susie; F; 2/21, 10; Cheyenne; F; S; Dau; No; Cheyenne & Arap. Okla; Yes
665; Littleyellowman, Rose; F; 3/23, 7; Cheyenne; F; S; Dau; No; Cheyenne & Arap. Okla; Yes

666; Littleyellowman, Hugh; M; 1885, 46; Cheyenne; F; M; Head; No; Cheyenne & Arap. Okla; Yes
667; Littleyellowman, May; F; 1916, 14; Cheyenne; F; S; Dau; No; Cheyenne & Arap. Okla; Yes

668; Littleyellowman, Jake; M; 10/61, 49; Cheyenne; F; M; Head; Yes; Yes
669; Littleyellowman, Lena; F; 5/76, 54; Cheyenne; F; M; Wife; Yes; Yes
670; Fisher, Alice; F; 8/98, 32; Cheyenne; F; S; Step-Dau; Yes; Yes
671; Fisher, Isabelle; F; 6/08, 22; Cheyenne; F; S; Step-Dau; Yes; Yes
672; Fisher, Richard; M; 11/12, 18; Cheyenne; F; S; Step-Son; Yes; Yes
673; Fisher, Harold; M; 1/20, 10; Cheyenne; F; S; Step-Son; Yes; Yes

674; Littleyellowman, Richard; M; 39; Cheyenne; F; S; Head; Yes; Yes

675; Livingston, Gail Bolson; F; 7/15, 15; Cheyenne; -1/4; M; Head; No; Ekalaka town, Carter, Mont; Yes

676; Loneelk, Wilson; M; 3/11, 20; Cheyenne; F; M; Head; Yes; Yes
677; Loneelk, Sarah A.; F; 8/12, 18; Cheyenne; F; M; Wife; Yes; Yes
678; Loneelk, George; M; 3/17/31, 1/12; Cheyenne; F; S; Son; Yes; Yes

679; Lonewolf, Charles; M; 47; Cheyenne; F; M; Head; Yes; Yes

680; Longjaw, Charles; M; 3/46, 85; Cheyenne; F; M; Head; Yes; Yes
681; Longjaw, Clara; F; 4/62, 69; Cheyenne; F; M; Wife; Yes; Yes
682; Longjaw, Charles Jr.; M; 7/15, 15; Cheyenne; F; S; G-Son; Yes; Yes

683; Longjaw, Elmer; M; 12/83, 47; Cheyenne; F; M; Head; Yes; Yes
684; Longjaw, Lena; F; 8/86, 44; Cheyenne; F; M; Wife; Yes; Yes
685; Longjaw, Albert; M; 6/12, 18; Cheyenne; F; S; Son; Yes; Yes
686; Longjaw, Henry; M; 1/16, 15; Cheyenne; F; S; Son; Yes; Yes
687; Longjaw, Clara; F; 1/19, 12; Cheyenne; F; S; Dau; Yes; Yes

Census of the __Tongue River__ reservation of the __Tongue River__ jurisdiction, as of __April 1__, 1931, taken by __C. B. Lohmiller__, Superintendent.

Key: Number; NAME: Surname, Given; Sex; Birthdate, Age At Last Birthday; Tribe; Degree of Blood; Marital Status; Relationship To Head of Family; At Jurisdiction Where Enrolled (Yes or No); At Another Jurisdiction; ELSEWHERE: Post office, County, State; Ward (Yes or No); Allotment, Annuity, and Identification Numbers.

688; Longjaw, Frank; M; 4/00, 31; Cheyenne; F; M; Head; Yes; Yes
689; Longjaw, Bernice M.; F; 2/10, 21; Cheyenne; F; M; Wife; Yes; Yes [Medicineflying, Jennie in 1928.]
690; Longjaw, Robert; M; 3/27, 4; Cheyenne; F; S; Son; Yes; Yes

691; Longjaw, James; M; 5/81, 49; Cheyenne; F; M; Head; Yes; Yes
692; Longjaw, Nellie; F; 1/96, 35; Cheyenne; F; M; Wife; Yes; Yes
693; Longjaw, Donald; M; 11/27/27, 2; Cheyenne; F; S; Son; Yes; Yes
694; Longjaw, Claudia; F; 10/7/30, 6/12; Cheyenne; F; S; Dau; Yes; Yes

695; Longroach, George; M; 4/82, 49; Cheyenne; F; M; Head; Yes; Yes
696; Longroach, Nellie; F; 6/88, 42; Cheyenne; F; M; Wife; Yes; Yes
697; Longroach, Harry; M; 1/11, 20; Cheyenne; F; S; Son; Yes; Yes
698; Longroach, James; M; 11/14, 16; Cheyenne; F; S; Son; Yes; Yes
699; Longroach, Mary; F; 4/17, 14; Cheyenne; F; S; Dau; Yes; Yes [Name Vita 1917-26.]
700; Longroach, Frank; M; 2/20, 11; Cheyenne; F; S; Son; Yes; Yes
701; Longroach, Regina; F; 9/23, 7; Cheyenne; F; S; Dau; Yes; Yes [Veria in 1923.]

702; Looksatbareground, James; M; 5/78, 52; Cheyenne; F; M; Head; Yes; Yes
703; Looksatbareground, Julia; F; 5/52, 78; Cheyenne; F; M; Wife; Yes; Yes [1924 wd., Elkshoulders.]

704; Looksbehind, Charles; M; 10/60, 70; Cheyenne; F; M; Head; Yes; Yes

705; Looksbehind, James; M; 1885, 46; Cheyenne; F; M; Head; No; Cheyenne & Arap. Okla; Yes [James Nightwalking]
706; Looksbehind, Roy; M; 1921, 10; Cheyenne; F; S; Son; No; Cheyenne & Arap. Okla; Yes
707; Looksbehind, Camilla; F; 8/23, 7; Cheyenne; F; S; Dau; No; Cheyenne & Arap. Okla; Yes
708; Looksbehind, James Jr.; M; 5/27, 3; Cheyenne; F; S; Son; No; Cheyenne & Arap. Okla; Yes

709; Looksbehind, Sallie; F; 10/59, 79; Cheyenne; F; Wd; Head; Yes; Yes
710; Looksbehind, Pius; M; 3/12, 19; Cheyenne; F; S; G-Son; Yes; Yes [Redneck, Pius 1930]

---- Lostleg, Nelson; M; 7/91, 39; Cheyenne; F; Wd[sic]; Head; Yes; Yes Died June 3, 1930
711; Lostleg, James; M; 12/15, 15; Cheyenne; F; S; Son; Yes; Yes [Ernest George in 1926.]

Census of the **Tongue River** reservation of the **Tongue River** jurisdiction, as of **April 1**, 1931, taken by **C. B. Lohmiller**, Superintendent.

**Key:** Number; NAME: Surname, Given; Sex; Birthdate, Age At Last Birthday; Tribe; Degree of Blood; Marital Status; Relationship To Head of Family; At Jurisdiction Where Enrolled (Yes or No); At Another Jurisdiction; ELSEWHERE: Post office, County, State; Ward (Yes or No); Allotment, Annuity, and Identification Numbers.

712; Lostleg, Virginia; F; 2/19, 12; Cheyenne; F; S; Dau; Yes; Yes [Son Theodore in 1920.]

713; Magpie, Albert; M; 4/86, 44; Cheyenne; F; Wd[sic]; Head; Yes; Yes [Prev. censuses from 1904-15 name is Youngmagpie with same birth year, none in 1913, Magpie in 1916. As early as 1907 a first wife Julia born 1887. Anne is a second wife starting in 1919. Anne is not in 1925.]
714; Magpie, Anna Mary; F; 12/19, 10; Cheyenne; F; S; Dau; Yes; Yes [Minnie in 1926.]
715; Magpie, Gilbert; M; 8/22, 8; Cheyenne; F; S; Son; Yes; Yes

716; Magpie, Louis; M; 10/85, 45; Cheyenne; F; M; Head; Yes; Yes
717; Magpie, Mira; F; 7/94, 36; Cheyenne; F; M; Wife; Yes; Yes
718; Magpie, Eddie; M; 4/10, 21; F; S; Son; No; Warm Springs-town, Deer Lodge, Mont, Yes
719; Hardrobe, Mollie; F; 10/19, 15; Cheyenne; F; S; Step-Dau; Yes; Yes

720; Manbear, Lena; F; 8/67, 63; Cheyenne; F; Wd; Head; Yes; Yes
721; Manbear, Lizzie; F; 4/02, 29; Cheyenne; F; S; Dau; Yes; Yes
722; Walters, Coolidge; M; 2/26, 5; Cheyenne; 1/4+; S; G-Son; Yes; Yes

723; Marrowbone, Jessie; F; 1888, 42; Cheyenne; F; M; Head; No; Pine Ridge, S.D.; Yes [Children enrolled at Pine Ridge.]

724; Medicine, Sampson; M; 9/76, 54; Cheyenne; F; M; Head; Yes; Yes
725; Medicine, Anna; F; 2/79, 52; Cheyenne; F; M; Wife; Yes; Yes
726; Medicine, Jennie; F; 3/02, 29; Cheyenne; F; S; Dau; Yes; Yes
727; Redeagle, Jennie; F; 9/41, 89; Cheyenne; F; Wd; Mother; Yes; Yes

728; Medicinebird, Nelson; M; 8/75, 55; Cheyenne; F; M; Head; Yes; Yes
729; Medicinebird, Ella; F; 2/83, 48; Cheyenne; F; M; Wife; Yes; Yes
730; Medicinebird, Homer J.; M; 3/14, 17; Cheyenne; F; S; Son; Yes; Yes

731; Medicinebull, Robert; M; 8/60, 70; Cheyenne; F; M; Head; Yes; Yes
732; Medicinebull, Maggie; F; 7/62, 68; Cheyenne; F; M; Wife; Yes; Yes

733; Medicinebull, Willis; M; 4/87, 44; Cheyenne; F; M; Head; Yes; Yes
734; Medicinebull, Anne; F; 5/02, 28; Cheyenne; F; M; Wife; Yes; Yes [Swallow]
735; Medicinebull, James; M; 8/10, 20; Cheyenne; F; S; Son; Yes; Yes
736; Medicinebull, Ruth; F; 6/13, 17; Cheyenne; F; S; Dau; Yes; Yes
737; Medicinebull, Fred; M; 10/25, 5; Cheyenne; F; S; Son; Yes; Yes
738; Medicinebull, Bert; M; 1/31/27, 4; Cheyenne; F; S; Son; Yes; Yes
739; Medicinebull, Mae; F; 4/30/30, 11/12; Cheyenne; F; S; Dau; Yes; Yes

Census of the **Tongue River** reservation of the **Tongue River** jurisdiction, as of **April 1**, 1931, taken by **C. B. Lohmiller**, Superintendent.

**Key:** Number; NAME: Surname, Given; Sex; Birthdate, Age At Last Birthday; Tribe; Degree of Blood; Marital Status; Relationship To Head of Family; At Jurisdiction Where Enrolled (Yes or No); At Another Jurisdiction; ELSEWHERE: Post office, County, State; Ward (Yes or No); Allotment, Annuity, and Identification Numbers.

740; Medicineelk, Andrew; M; 5/98, 32; Cheyenne; F; M; Head; Yes; Yes
741; Medicineelk, Maggie B.; F; 1/03, 28; Cheyenne; F; M; Wife; Yes; Yes
[Bearquiver]
742; Medicineelk, Peter; M; 3/26, 5; Cheyenne; F; S; Son; Yes; Yes
743; Medicineelk, Margaret; F; 2/2/30, 1; Cheyenne; F; S; Dau; Yes; Yes

744; Medicineelk, Basil; M; 1/94, 37; Cheyenne; F; M; Head; Yes; Yes

--- Medicineelk, Harold; M; 7/65, 65; Cheyenne; F; Wd[sic]; Head; Yes; Yes Died October 31, 1931.
745; Medicineelk, John; M; 10/10, 20; Cheyenne; F; S; G-Son; Yes; Yes
[Sandwoman; G-son in 1928 and 1930]

746; Medicineelk, James; M; 4/02, 29; Cheyenne; F; S; Head; No; Cheyenne & Arap. Okla; Yes

747; Medicineelk, Thomas; M; 7/06, 24; Cheyenne; F; S; Head; Yes; Yes
[Divorced in 1930]

748; Medicineflying, John; M; 9/82, 48; Cheyenne; F; M; Head; Yes; Yes
749; Medicineflying, Bertha; F; 2/85, 46; Cheyenne; F; M; Wife; Yes; Yes
750; Medicineflying, Helen J.; F; 8/16, 14; Cheyenne; F; S; Dau; Yes; Yes
751; Medicineflying, Agnes S.; F; 5/20, 10; Cheyenne; F; S; Dau; Yes; Yes
752; Medicineflying, Phyllis A.; F; 7/24, 6; Cheyenne; F; S; Dau; Yes; Yes

753; Medicinetop, James; M; 5/61, 69; Cheyenne; F; Wd[sic]; Head; Yes; Yes

754; Medicinetop, John; M; 1/85, 46; Cheyenne; F; M; Head; Yes; Yes
755; Medicinetop, Ida; F; 5/90, 40; Cheyenne; F; M; Wife; Yes; Yes
756; Medicinetop, Clarence; M; 10/10, 20; Cheyenne; F; S; Son; Yes; Yes
757; Medicinetop, Majorie[sic]; F; 4/14, 16; Cheyenne; F; S; Dau; Yes; Yes
758; Medicinetop, Phyllis; F; 9/22, 8; Cheyenne; F; S; Dau; Yes; Yes
759; Medicinetop, Roy; M; 8/24, 6; Cheyenne; F; S; Son; Yes; Yes
760; Medicinetop, Lena; F; 10/24/27, 3; Cheyenne; F; S; Dau; Yes; Yes
761; Medicinetop, Edward; M; 3/15/29, 2; Cheyenne; F; S; Son; Yes; Yes

762; Merritt, Wesley; M; 10/76, 54; Cheyenne; F; M; Head; Yes; Yes
763; Merritt, Josie; F; 5/63, 67; Cheyenne; F; M; Wife; Yes; Yes
764; Walkingbear, Mannie; F; 8/97, 33; Cheyenne; F; D; Step-Dau; Yes; Yes
765; Twomoons, George; M; 1/20, 10; Cheyenne; F; S; G-Son; Yes; Yes

766; Mexicancheyenne, Ernest; M; 12/89, 41; Cheyenne; 1/4 -; M; Head; Yes; Yes
King - Letter dated 5/13/31 [King in 1930; 1/4+]

Census of the  Tongue River  reservation of the Tongue River  jurisdiction, as of  April 1  , 19**31**, taken by  **C. B. Lohmiller**  , Superintendent.

**Key:** Number; NAME: Surname, Given; Sex; Birthdate, Age At Last Birthday; Tribe; Degree of Blood; Marital Status; Relationship To Head of Family; At Jurisdiction Where Enrolled (Yes or No); At Another Jurisdiction; ELSEWHERE: Post office, County, State; Ward (Yes or No); Allotment, Annuity, and Identification Numbers.

767; Mexicancheyenne, Mary; F; 7/99, 31; Cheyenne; F; M; Wife; Yes; Yes [King in 1930]
768; Mexicancheyenne, Harriet; F; 6/19, 12; Cheyenne; 1/4-; S; Dau; Yes; Yes [Hilda in 1928.] [King in 1930; 1/4+]
769; Mexicancheyenne, M. Victoria; F; 8/21, 9; Cheyenne; 1/4-; S; Dau; Yes; Yes [King in 1930; 1/4+]
770; Mexicancheyenne, Rudolph; M; 2/25, 6; Cheyenne; 1/4-; S; Son; Yes; Yes [Anabelle; dau; 1925.] [King in 1930; 1/4+]
771; Mexicancheyenne, Anna Joyce; F; 8/15/28, 2; Cheyenne; 1/4-; S; Dau; Yes; Yes [King in 1930; 1/4+]

772; Mexicancheyenne, Marion; M; 7/87, 43; Cheyenne; 1/4-; M; Head; Yes; Yes [King in 1930; 1/4+]
773; Mexicancheyenne, Emma; F; 6/93, 37; Cheyenne; F; M; Wife; Yes; Yes [King in 1930]
774; Mexicancheyenne, James; M; 6/8/14, 16; Cheyenne; 1/4-; S; Son; Yes; Yes [King in 1930; 1/4+]
775; Mexicancheyenne, Rosa; F; 11/18, 12; Cheyenne; 1/4-; S; Dau; Yes; Yes [King in 1930; 1/4+]
776; Mexicancheyenne, Margaret; F; 12/20, 10; Cheyenne; 1/4-; S; Dau; Yes; Yes [Ethel in 1926.] [King in 1930; 1/4+]
777; Mexicancheyenne, Mary; F; 7/25, 5; Cheyenne; 1/4+; S; Dau; Yes; Yes
778; Mexicancheyenne, Mabel Ann; F; 2/2/28, 3; Cheyenne; 1/4+; S; Dau; Yes; Yes

779; Oldbull, Daniel; M; 10/70, 60; Cheyenne; F; Wd[sic]; Head; Yes; Yes
780; Oldbull, Thomas; M; 11/10, 20; Cheyenne; F; S; Wife[sic]; Yes; Yes

781; Onebear, James; M; 7/00, 30; Cheyenne; 1/4+; M; Head; Yes; Yes
782; Onebear, Maggie; F; 3/03, 28; Cheyenne; 1/4+; M; Wife; Yes; Yes [Seminole]
783; Onebear, Robert; M; 12/25, 5; Cheyenne; 1/4+; S; Son; Yes; Yes
784; Onebear, Louise; F; 10/18/29, 1; Cheyenne; 1/4+; S; Dau; Yes; Yes

785; Parker, Alvin O.; M; 6/79, 51; Cheyenne; 1/4+; M; Head; Yes; Yes
786; Parker, Clyde S.; M; 11/22, 8; Cheyenne; -1/4; S; Son; Yes; Yes
787; Parker, Verda F.; F; 9/24, 6; Cheyenne; -1/4; S; Dau; Yes; Yes
788; Parker, Shirley R.; M; 1/27, 4; Cheyenne; -1/4; S; Son; Yes; Yes
789; Parker, Donald E.; M; 8/25, 28, 2; Cheyenne; -1/4; S; Son; Yes; Yes
790; Parker, Lyle Neal; M; 9/8/30, 7/12; Cheyenne; -1/4; S; Son; Yes; Yes

791; Parker, Charles A.; M; 7/85, 45; Cheyenne; 1/4+; M; Head; Yes; Yes
792; Parker, Theresa; F; 3/12, 19; Cheyenne; 1/4+; S; Dau; Yes; Yes
793; Parker, Gabriel; M; 10/26, 4; Cheyenne; 1/4+; S; Son; Yes; Yes

Census of the **Tongue River** reservation of the **Tongue River** jurisdiction, as of **April 1**, 1931, taken by **C. B. Lohmiller**, Superintendent.

**Key:** Number; NAME: Surname, Given; Sex; Birthdate, Age At Last Birthday; Tribe; Degree of Blood; Marital Status; Relationship To Head of Family; At Jurisdiction Where Enrolled (Yes or No); At Another Jurisdiction; ELSEWHERE: Post office, County, State; Ward (Yes or No); Allotment, Annuity, and Identification Numbers.

794; Parker, Edwin; M; 4/95, 36; Cheyenne; 1/4+; S; Head; Yes; Yes

795; Parker, Guy; M; 9/91, 39; Cheyenne; 1/4+; M; Head; Yes; Yes
796; Parker, Winfred; M; 4/14, 16; Cheyenne; 1/4+; Son; Yes; Yes
797; Parker, Alice; F; 2/17, 14; Cheyenne; 1/4+; S; Dau; Yes; Yes
798; Parker, Stella; F; 4/19, 11; Cheyenne; 1/4+; S; Dau; Yes; Yes
799; Parker, Charlotte; F; 7/23/29, 1; Cheyenne; 1/4+; S; Dau; Yes; Yes

800; Pease, Ida; F; 2/06, 24; Cheyenne; -1/4; M; Head; No; Crow Agency, Mont; Yes [Eastman]

801; Pine, Frank; M; 7/64, 67; Cheyenne; F; M; Head; Yes; Yes
802; Pine, Nora W.; F; 67; Cheyenne; F; M; Wife; Yes; Yes

803; Pine, Rutherford; M; 6/86, 44 Cheyenne; F; M; Head; Yes; Yes
804; Pine, Julia; F; 8/96, 34; Cheyenne; F; M; Wife; Yes; Yes [In 1916 marries Julia Blackcrane nee Kingfisher; in 1912 she is 18 years old, birth year is 1894 from 1904-16. Gave birth year as 1884 from 1917-26.]
805; Pine, Cecelia; F; 1/16, 15; Cheyenne; F; S; Dau; Yes; Yes
806; Pine, Daniel; M; 9/23, 7; Cheyenne; F; S; Son; Yes; Yes

807; Pine, Wilson; M; 6/86, 44; Cheyenne; F; M; Head; Yes; Yes
808; Pine, Nora; F; 7/88, 42; Cheyenne; F; M; Wife; Yes; Yes
809; Pine, Alexander; M; 11/17, 13; Cheyenne; F; S; Son; Yes; Yes
810; Pine, John; M; 4/22, 9; Cheyenne; F; S; Son; Yes; Yes
811; Pine, Sarah; F; 8/24, 6; Cheyenne; F; S; Dau; Yes; Yes
812; Powderface, Fern; F; 7/18, 12; Cheyenne; F; S; Step-Dau; Yes; Yes

813; Playingbear, Henry; M; 1/77, 54; Cheyenne; F; M; Head; Yes; Yes
814; Playingbear, Mildred; F; 4/80, 51; Cheyenne; F; M; Wife; Yes; Yes

815; Powderface, John; M; 5/66, 64; Cheyenne; F; Wd[sic]; Head; No; Shoshone & Arap. Okla; Yes

816; Powell, Clay; M; 11/04, 26; Cheyenne; -1/4+[sic]; M; Head; No; Sheridantown, Sheridan, Wyo.; Yes

817; Powell, Mary; F; 11/81, 49; Cheyenne; 1/4+; M; Head; Yes; Yes
818; Powell, Deyo; M; 6/07, 23; Cheyenne; 1/4+; S; Son; Yes; Yes [-1/4 1930]
819; Powell, Howard; M; 2/12, 19; Cheyenne; 1/4+; S; Son; Yes; Yes [-1/4 1930]

820; Prairiebear, Arthur; M; 3/82, 49; Cheyenne; F; M; Head; Yes; Yes
821; Prairiebear, Sallie; F; 10/85, 45; Cheyenne; F; M; Wife; Yes; Yes
822; Prairiebear, A. Louis; M; 11/2/28, 2; Cheyenne; F; S; Son; Yes; Yes

Census of the __Tongue River__ reservation of the __Tongue River__ jurisdiction, as of __April 1__, 1931, taken by __C. B. Lohmiller__, Superintendent.

**Key:** Number; NAME: Surname, Given; Sex; Birthdate, Age At Last Birthday; Tribe; Degree of Blood; Marital Status; Relationship To Head of Family; At Jurisdiction Where Enrolled (Yes or No); At Another Jurisdiction; ELSEWHERE: Post office, County, State; Ward (Yes or No); Allotment, Annuity, and Identification Numbers.

823; Redbead, John; M; 11/71, 59; Cheyenne; F; M; Head; Yes; Yes
824; Redbead, Nancy; F; 4/78, 23; Cheyenne; F; M; Wife; Yes; Yes
825; Redbead, Susie; F; 5/13, 17; Cheyenne; F; S; Dau; Yes; Yes
826; Redbead, Clara; F; 6/15, 15; Cheyenne; F; S; Dau; Yes; Yes
827; Redbead, Georgia; F; 7/17, 13; Cheyenne; F; S; Dau; Yes; Yes
[Name Gloria 1917-20.]

828; Redbird, Joseph; M; 10/99, 31; Cheyenne; F; D; Head; Yes; Yes
[Middle name Francis in 1910.]
829; Redbird, Lucille; F; 2/11, 20; Cheyenne; F; M; Wife; Yes; Yes
830; Redbird, William; M; 6/22, 8; Cheyenne; F; S; Son; No; Cheyenne & Arap. Okla; Yes
831; Redbird, Allen; M; 5/25/25, 5; Cheyenne; F; S; Son; No; Cheyenne & Arap. Okla; Yes [First shows in 1925 with birth in 1924. Same Prev. #, Helena; dau; 1925, F. in 1926.]
832; Redbird, Diva; F; 12/8/30, 4/12; Cheyenne; F; S; Dau; Yes; Yes

833; Redbird, William; M; 7/76, 54; Cheyenne; F; M; Head; Yes; Yes
834; Redbird, Florence; F; 6/77, 53; Cheyenne; 1/4+; M; Wife; Yes; Yes
835; Redbird, Lena; F; 11/20, 10; Cheyenne; 1/4+; S; Dau; Yes; Yes
[Susie in 1926.]
836; Redbird, Samuel; M; 11/22/28, 2; Cheyenne; 1/4+; S; Son; Yes; Yes
837; Rowland, Elizabeth; F; 11/13, 17; Cheyenne; 1/4+; S; S-Dau; Yes; Yes
[1/4- 1930]
838; Rowland, Lillian; F; 11/16, 14; Cheyenne; 1/4+; S; S-Dau; Yes; Yes
[1/4- 1930]
839; Tangledhornelk, Nellie; F; 1853, 78; Cheyenne; F; Wd; Mother; Yes; Yes

840; Redbreath, Charles; M; 4/79, 51; Cheyenne; F; M; Head; Yes; Yes
841; Redbreath, Betty; F; 1/08, 23; Cheyenne; F; M; Wife; Yes; Yes [Yellownose]
842; Redbreath, Elina J.; F; 6/25, 5; Cheyenne; F; S; Dau; Yes; Yes
[Elina June in 1926.]
843; Redbreath, George; M; 7/27, 3; Cheyenne; F; S; Son; Yes; Yes

844; Redcherries, Teddy; M; 1888, 42; Cheyenne; F; M; Head; No; Cheyenne & Arap. Okla; Yes
845; Redcherries, Miller; M; 11/18/20, 10; Cheyenne; F; S; Son; No; Cheyenne & Arap. Okla; Yes

846; Redcherries, William; M; 6/90, 40; Cheyenne; F; M; Head; Yes; Yes
847; Redcherries, Bessie; F; 2/94, 37; Cheyenne; F; M; Wife; Yes; Yes
848; Redcherries, Alice; F; 8/12, 18; Cheyenne; F; S; Dau; Yes; Yes
849; Redcherries, Rose; F; 4/16, 15; Cheyenne; F; S; Dau; Yes; Yes
850; Redcherries, Frank; M; 5/19, 11; Cheyenne; F; S; Son; Yes; Yes

Census of the __Tongue River__ reservation of the __Tongue River__ jurisdiction, as of __April 1__, 1931, taken by __C. B. Lohmiller__, Superintendent.

**Key:** Number; NAME: Surname, Given; Sex; Birthdate, Age At Last Birthday; Tribe; Degree of Blood; Marital Status; Relationship To Head of Family; At Jurisdiction Where Enrolled (Yes or No); At Another Jurisdiction; ELSEWHERE: Post office, County, State; Ward (Yes or No); Allotment, Annuity, and Identification Numbers.

851; Redcherries, Margaret; F; 9/23, 7; Cheyenne; F; S; Dau; Yes; Yes
852; Redcherries, Katie; F; 9/3/27, 3; Cheyenne; F; S; Dau; Yes; Yes
853; Redcherries, Della; F; 5/18/30, 11/12; Cheyenne; F; S; Dau; Yes; Yes
854; Stumphorn, Anna; F; 9/51, 79; Cheyenne; F; Wd; Mother; Yes; Yes

855; Redeagle, Nellie; F; 8/72, 58; Cheyenne; F; Wd; Head; Yes; Yes
856; Redeagle, Willis; M; 12/01, 29; Cheyenne; F; S; Son; Yes; Yes

857; Redfox, James; M; 4/65, 65; Cheyenne; F; M; Head; Yes; Yes
--- ~~Redfox, Cora; F; 7/67, 63; Cheyenne; F; M; Wife; Yes; Yes~~
~~Died April 15, 1930~~

858; Redfox, Jennie; F; 12/73, 57; Cheyenne; F; Wd; Head; Yes; Yes

859; Redfox, Robert; M; 3/00, 31; Cheyenne; F; M; Head; Yes; Yes
860; Redfox, Cecelia; F; 6/94, 36; Cheyenne; F; M; Wife; Yes; Yes
861; Redfox, Edna S.; F; 3/27, 3; Cheyenne; F; S; Dau; Yes; Yes
862; Redfox, Ralph; M; 9/24/29, 1; Cheyenne; F; S; Son; Yes; Yes
863; Sanchez, Pauline; F; 3/15, 16; Cheyenne; 1/4+; S; Step-Dau; Yes; Yes
864; Sanchez, Cecelia; F; 4/22, 8; Cheyenne; 1/4+; S; Step-Dau; Yes; Yes

865; Redneck, Curtis; M; 1/88, 42; Cheyenne; F; M; Head; Yes; Yes
866; Redneck, Josie; F; 12/96, 34; Cheyenne; F; M; Wife; Yes; Yes
867; Redneck, Clyde; M; 8/12, 18; Cheyenne; F; S; Son; Yes; Yes

868; Redneck, David; M; 9/81, 39; Cheyenne; F; M; Head; No; Cheyenne & Arap. Okla; Yes
869; Redneck, Minnie; F; 8/10/20, 10; Cheyenne; F; S; Dau; No; Cheyenne & Arap. Okla; Yes

870; Redneck, Henry; M; 8/82, 48; Cheyenne; F; M; Head; Yes; Yes
871; Redneck, Fannie; F; 7/84, 46; Cheyenne; F; M; Wife; Yes; Yes
872; Redneck, Dora; F; 10/14, 16; Cheyenne; F; S; Dau; Yes; Yes
873; Redneck, Homer; M; 7/17, 13; Cheyenne; F; S; Son; Yes; Yes
874; Redneck, Florence; F; 4/21, 10; Cheyenne; F; S; Dau; Yes; Yes
875; Redneck, John; M; 5/25, 5; Cheyenne; F; S; Son; Yes; Yes

876; Rednose, Paul; M; 6/76, 54; Cheyenne; F; M; Head; Yes; Yes
877; Rednose, Lucy; F; 5/70, 60; Cheyenne; F; M; Wife; Yes; Yes [1/2 in 1928.]

878; Redrobe, Fred; M; 63; Cheyenne; F; M; Head; Yes; Yes
879; Redrobe, Nora; F; 61; Cheyenne; F; M; Wife; Yes; Yes
880; Redrobe, Louis; M; 11/92, 38; Cheyenne; F; S; Son; Yes; Yes
881; Redrobe, Jasper; M; 7/00, 30; Cheyenne; F; S; Son; No; Penitentiary; Yes

Census of the **Tongue River** reservation of the **Tongue River** jurisdiction, as of **April 1**, 1931, taken by **C. B. Lohmiller**, Superintendent.

**Key:** Number; NAME: Surname, Given; Sex; Birthdate, Age At Last Birthday; Tribe; Degree of Blood; Marital Status; Relationship To Head of Family; At Jurisdiction Where Enrolled (Yes or No); At Another Jurisdiction; ELSEWHERE: Post office, County, State; Ward (Yes or No); Allotment, Annuity, and Identification Numbers.

882; Redrobe, William; M; 8/97, 33; Cheyenne; F; M; Head; Yes; Yes
883; Redrobe, Alice; F; 5/84, 46; Cheyenne; F; M; Wife; Yes; Yes [1907-19, birth year 1884-5. 1904 nee-Killsnight; 1905-6 Risingsun, 1907-19 Shell, 1920-28 Redrobe.]
884; Weaselbear, Stella C.; F; 5/17, 13; Cheyenne; F; S; Niece; Yes; Yes [s-dau-Henry Littlewhiteman. Clarice in 1926.]

885; Redwater, Cecelia; F; 2/72, 58; Cheyenne; F; D; Head; Yes; Yes

886; Redwater, Thaddeus; M; 4/75, 55; Cheyenne; F; M; Head; Yes; Yes

887; Redwoman, Frank; M; 2/89, 42; Cheyenne; F; Wd[sic]; Head; Yes; Yes
888; Redwoman, Flossie A.; F; 9/11, 19; Cheyenne; F; S; Dau; Yes; Yes
889; Redwoman, Eugene; M; 2/23, 8; Cheyenne; F; S; Son; Yes; Yes
890; Redwoman, Joe; M; 5/24, 6; Cheyenne; F; S; Son; Yes; Yes

891; Redwoman, John; M; 7/02, 28; Cheyenne; F; Wd; Son; Yes; Yes (Robert Ironshirt)

--- Redwoman, Manuel; M; 7/81, 49; Cheyenne; F; M; Head; Yes; Yes Died December 9, 1930
892; Redwoman, Olive; F; 8/91, 39; Cheyenne; F; M; Wife; Yes; Yes
893; Redwoman, Edna; F; 7/3/26, 4; Cheyenne; F; S; Dau; Yes; Yes
894; Redwoman, Donald; M; 7/10/28, 2; Cheyenne; F; S; Dau[sic]; Yes; Yes

895; Ridgebear, Charles; M; 1882, 48; Cheyenne; F; M; Head; No; Cheyenne & Arap. Okla; Yes

896; Ridgebear, Willis; M; 7/87, 43; Cheyenne; F; M; Head; Yes; Yes
897; Ridgebear, Rilla; F; 7/98, 33; Cheyenne; F; M; Wife; Yes; Yes
898; Ridgebear, Bessie A.; F; 11/18, 12; Cheyenne; F; S; Dau; Yes; Yes
899; Ridgebear, Carrie; F; 4/21, 9; Cheyenne; F S; Dau; Yes; Yes [Katie in 1926.]
900; Ridgebear, Anna; F; 11/22/27, 3; Cheyenne; F; S; Dau; Yes; Yes
901; Ridgebear, James; M; 3/2/29, 2; Cheyenne; F; S; Son; Yes; Yes

902; Ridgewalker, Robert; M; 6/60, 70; Cheyenne; F; M; Head; Yes; Yes
903; Ridgewalker, Ethel; F; 6/70, 60; Cheyenne; 1/4+; M; Wife; Yes; Yes
904; Ridgewalker, Frank; M; 4/08, 22; Cheyenne; 1/4+; S; Son; Yes; Yes

905; Risingfire, Bessie; F; 11/56, 74; Cheyenne; F; Wd; Head; Yes; Yes
906; Fightingbear, Julia; F; 7/11, 19; Cheyenne; F; S; G-Dau; Yes; Yes
907; Fightingbear, Dora; F; 3/15, 16; Cheyenne; F; S; G-Dau; Yes; Yes

908; Risingsun, Oliver; M; 5/00, 30; Cheyenne; F; M; Head; Yes; Yes

Census of the **Tongue River** reservation of the **Tongue River** jurisdiction, as of **April 1**, 1931, taken by **C. B. Lohmiller**, Superintendent.

**Key:** Number; NAME: Surname, Given; Sex; Birthdate, Age At Last Birthday; Tribe; Degree of Blood; Marital Status; Relationship To Head of Family; At Jurisdiction Where Enrolled (Yes or No); At Another Jurisdiction; ELSEWHERE: Post office, County, State; Ward (Yes or No); Allotment, Annuity, and Identification Numbers.

909; Risingsun, Elizabeth; F; 8/07, 23; Cheyenne; F; M; Wife; Yes; Yes [Flying]
910; Risingsun, Teddy; M; 10/26, 4; Cheyenne; F; S; Son; Yes; Yes

911; Risingsun, Peter; M; 8/87, 43; Cheyenne; F; Wd; Head; Yes; Yes
912; Risingsun, Harry; M; 4/21, 9; Cheyenne; F; S; Son; Yes; Yes
913; Risingsun, Lyman; M; 7/23, 7; Cheyenne; F; S; Son; Yes; Yes
914; Risingsun, James; M; 12/25, 5; Cheyenne; F; S; Son; Yes; Yes

915; Risingsun, Philip; M; 8/62, 68; Cheyenne; F; M; Head; Yes; Yes
916; Risingsun, Nora; F; 1/68, 62; Cheyenne; F; M; Wife; Yes; Yes
917; Risingsun, John; M; 6/95, 35; Cheyenne; F; S; Son; Yes; Yes
918; Risingsun, Pearl; F; 9/19/28, 2; Cheyenne; F; S; Dau; Yes; Yes
[Niece in 1930]

919; Risingsun, William; M; 6/04, 26; Cheyenne; F; M; Head; Yes; Yes
920; Risingsun, Edna Josie; F; 12/12, 18; Cheyenne; F; M; Wife; Yes; Yes

921; Robinson, Nellie; F; 10/97, 33; Cheyenne; -1/4; M; Head; Yes; Yes
922; Robinson, David C.; M; 8/18, 12; Cheyenne; -1/4; S; Son; Yes; Yes
923; Robinson, Cornelius; M; 6/20, 10; Cheyenne; -1/4; S; Son; Yes; Yes
924; Robinson, Eloise E.; F; 3/22, 9; Cheyenne; -1/4; S; Dau; Yes; Yes
925; Robinson, Buell D.; M; 7/30/28, 2; Cheyenne; -1/4; S; Son; Yes; Yes

926; Rockroads, Mack; M; 4/93, 37; Cheyenne; F; M; Head; Yes; Yes
927; Rockroads, Nellie; F; 11/93, 37; Cheyenne; F; M; Wife; Yes; Yes
928; Rockroads, Thomas; M; 4/17, 13; Cheyenne; F; S; Son; Yes; Yes
[1918 Census #902; Name is Lettie, female.]
929; Rockroads, Flossie; F; 7/10/29, 1; Cheyenne; F; S; Dau; Yes; Yes
930; Rockroads, Nora; F; 12/70, 60; Cheyenne; F; Wd; Mother; Yes; Yes
931; Rockroads, Mary; F; 8/13, 17; Cheyenne; F; S; Sister; Yes; Yes

932; Romannose, Louis; M; 9/82, 48; Cheyenne; F; M; Head; Yes; Yes
933; Romannose, George; M; 7/10, 20; Cheyenne; F; S; Son; Yes; Yes
934; Romannose, Blanche; F; 9/14, 16; Cheyenne; F; S; Dau; Yes; Yes [Helen in 1926.]
935; Romannose, Julia; F; 4/16, 14; Cheyenne; F; S; Dau; Yes; Yes [May in 1926.]
936; Romannose, Willeatte; F; 10/21, 9; Cheyenne; F; S; Dau; Yes; Yes
937; Romannose, Montana; F; 11/23, 7; Cheyenne; F; S; Dau; Yes; Yes

938; Rondeau, Antoine; M; 4/87, 43; Cheyenne; 1/4+; M; Head; Yes; Yes
939; Rondeau, Louise; F; 6/89, 41; Cheyenne; 1/4+; M; Wife; Yes; Yes
940; Rondeau, Clara; F; 12/12, 18; Cheyenne; 1/4+; S; Dau; Yes; Yes
941; Rondeau, Charles; M; 5/20, 10; Cheyenne; 1/4+; S; Son; Yes; Yes
942; Bixby, Jessie; F; 5/53, 75; Cheyenne; 1/4+; Wd; Mother-in-law; Yes; Yes

Census of the **Tongue River** reservation of the **Tongue River** jurisdiction, as of **April 1**, 1931, taken by **C. B. Lohmiller**, Superintendent.

Key: Number; NAME: Surname, Given; Sex; Birthdate, Age At Last Birthday; Tribe; Degree of Blood; Marital Status; Relationship To Head of Family; At Jurisdiction Where Enrolled (Yes or No); At Another Jurisdiction; ELSEWHERE: Post office, County, State; Ward (Yes or No); Allotment, Annuity, and Identification Numbers.

943; Rondeau, William; M; 3/66, 47; Cheyenne; 1/4+; Wd[sic]; Head; Yes; Yes
944; Rondeau, Henry; M; 3/11, 20; Cheyenne; 1/4+; S; Son; Yes; Yes
945; Rondeau, John; M; 3/12, 19; Cheyenne; 1/4+; S; Son; Yes; Yes

946; Roundstone, Flora; F; 4/88, 42; Cheyenne; F; M; Head; Yes; Yes [Twobulls]
947; Roundstone, Sarah; F; 5/20, 10; Cheyenne; F; S; Dau; Yes; Yes
948; Roundstone, Paul; M; 4/22, 8; Cheyenne; F; S; Son; Yes; Yes
949; Roundstone, Ruth; F; 7/26, 4; Cheyenne; F; S; Dau; Yes; Yes

950; Roundstone, Martin; M; 11/11, 19; Cheyenne; F; M; Son; Yes; Yes
951; Roundstone, Mary G.; F; 8/14, 16; Cheyenne; F; M; Wife; Yes; Yes

952; Rowland, Benton; M; 32; Cheyenne; 1/4+; M; Head; No; Pine Ridge SD; Yes
953; Rowland, Marie; F; 4; Cheyenne; 1/4+; S; Dau; No; Pine Ridge SD; Yes
954; Rowland, Eugene; M; 3; Cheyenne; 1/4+; S; Son; No; Pine Ridge SD; Yes

955; Rowland, Clay T.; M; 2/80, 51; Cheyenne; 1/4+; M; Head; Yes; Yes

956; Rowland, Joe; M; 12/02, 28; Cheyenne; 1/4+; M; Head; No; Pine Ridge SD; Yes [In 1926 #935; Jose; son; birth year 1900.]

957; Rowland, Thomas; M; 12/18/92, 38; Cheyenne; 1/4+; M; Head; Yes; Yes
958; Rowland, Daisy; F; 4/1900, 30; Cheyenne; F; M; Wife; Yes; Yes [Fightingbear, Ellen in 1924.]
959; Rowland, Blanche; F; 8/29/25, 5; Cheyenne; 1/4+; S; Dau; Yes; Yes
960; Rowland, Don; M; 1/22/28, 3; Cheyenne; 1/4+; S; Son; Yes; Yes
961; Rowland, Julia; F; 9/11/30, 7/12; Cheyenne; 1/4+; S; Dau; Yes; Yes

962; Rowland, William; M; 9/14/95, 35; Cheyenne; 1/4+; M; Head; Yes; Yes
963; Rowland, Chester C.; M; 6/20, 10; Cheyenne; 1/4+; S; Son; No; Pine Ridge SD; Yes
964; Rowland, Allen E.; M; 2/9/26, 5; Cheyenne; 1/4+; S; Son; Yes; Yes
965; Rowland, Ardeth F.; F; 4/30/28, 2; Cheyenne; 1/4+; S; Dau; Yes; Yes

966; Rowland, Willis; M; 4/8/62, 68; Cheyenne; 1/4+; M; Head; Yes; Yes
---    ~~Rowland, Helen; F; 5/68, 62; Cheyenne; F; M; Wife; Yes; Yes~~
~~Died January 15, 1931~~
967; Rowland, Jessie; M; 2/84, 47; Cheyenne; 1/4+; S; Nephew; Yes; Yes [Name Frank and previous #932 in 1926.]
968; Rowland, Grace; F; 11/14, 16; Cheyenne; 1/4+; S; A-Dau; Yes; Yes
969; Rowland, Frank; M; 5/24, 6; Cheyenne; 1/4+; S; G-Son; Yes; Yes

970; Rowland, Zac; M; 12/68, 62; Cheyenne; 1/4+; M; Head; Yes; Yes
971; Rowland, Edna; F; 10/76, 54; Cheyenne; F; M; Wife; Yes; Yes

Census of the **Tongue River** reservation of the **Tongue River** jurisdiction, as of **April 1**, 1931, taken by **C. B. Lohmiller**, Superintendent.

**Key:** Number; NAME: Surname, Given; Sex; Birthdate, Age At Last Birthday; Tribe; Degree of Blood; Marital Status; Relationship To Head of Family; At Jurisdiction Where Enrolled (Yes or No); At Another Jurisdiction; ELSEWHERE: Post office, County, State; Ward (Yes or No); Allotment, Annuity, and Identification Numbers.

972; Russell, Frank; M; 12/98, 32; Cheyenne; 1/4+; M; Head; Yes; Yes
973; Russell, Ellen; F; 8/97, 33; Cheyenne; F; M; Wife; Yes; Yes  [Sweetmedicine]

974; Russell, John; M; 9/93, 37; Cheyenne; 1/4+; M; Head; Yes; Yes
975; Russell, Alice R.; F; 12/09, 21; Cheyenne; F; M; Wife; Yes; Yes
976; Russell, Stella; F; 2/16, 15; Cheyenne; 1/4+; S; Dau; Yes No; Flandreau, I.S.; Yes
--- Russell, May; F; 5/24, 6; Cheyenne; 1/4+; S; Dau; No; Cheyenne & Arap.; Yes Died July 5, 1930
--- Russell, Inez I.; F; 3; Cheyenne; 1/4+; S; Dau; No; Cheyenne & Arap.; Yes Died March 5, 1931
--- Russell, John Jr.; M; 1; Cheyenne; 1/4+; S; Son; No; Cheyenne & Arap.; Yes Died March 2, 1931
977; Russell, Clifford; M; 9/17/30, 6/12; Cheyenne; 1/4+; S; Son; Yes; Yes

978; Russell, William; M; 5/73, 57; Cheyenne; F; M; Head; Yes; Yes
979; Russell, Fred; M; 7/08, 22; Cheyenne; F; S; Son; Yes; Yes
980; Russell, Earl; M; 8/15, 15; Cheyenne; F; S; Son; Yes; Yes
981; Russell, Mary; F; 9/19, 12; Cheyenne; F; S; Dau; Yes; Yes  [Mildred in 1926.]

982; Sandcrane, Henry; M; 10/89, 41; Cheyenne; F; M; Head; Yes; Yes
983; Sandcrane, Anna; F; 6/92, 38; Cheyenne; F; M; Wife; Yes; Yes
984; Sandcrane, Margaret; F; 10/20, 10; Cheyenne; F; S; Dau; Yes; Yes
985; Littlesun, Alfred; M; 12/12, 18; Cheyenne; F; S; Step-Son; Yes; Yes
986; Littleoldman, Thomas; M; 12/13, 17; Cheyenne; F; S; Step-Son; Yes; Yes

987; Sandcrane, John; M; 1/73, 58; Cheyenne; F; M; Head; Yes; Yes
988; Sandcrane, Ruth; F; 12/78, 52; Cheyenne; F; M; Wife; Yes; Yes
989; Sandcrane, Isabelle; F; 5/14, 16; Cheyenne; F; S; Dau; Yes; Yes
990; Littleoldman, Fern; F; 8/17, 13; Cheyenne; F; S; G-Dau; Yes; Yes  [s.-dau. Chas. Sharpnose, #569; Littleman, Julia; Step-dau; 1915; F. (s-dau Fred Limpy) in 1926.]

991; Sansaver, Lillian; F; 7/06, 24; Cheyenne; 1/4+; S; Head; Yes; Yes  [dau-Rhoda Seminole; Sansover mother was a Miles in 1915. Sansover in 1917 #741.]

992; Scalpcane, August; M; 2/06, 25; Cheyenne; F; S; Head; Yes; Yes
993; Scalpcane, Otto; M; 11/14, 16; Cheyenne; F; S; Brother; Yes; Yes
994; Scalpcane, Henry; M; 11/19, 11; Cheyenne; F; S; Brother; Yes; Yes  [Rudolph in 1926.]

995; Schaffer, Letha; F; 4/13, 17; Cheyenne; -1/4; M; Head; No; Crow Agency, Mont; Yes  [Son, Carl in 1916 Census. Eastman in 1927]

Census of the __Tongue River__ reservation of the __Tongue River__ jurisdiction, as of __April 1__, 1931, taken by __C. B. Lohmiller__, Superintendent.

**Key:** Number; NAME: Surname, Given; Sex; Birthdate, Age At Last Birthday; Tribe; Degree of Blood; Marital Status; Relationship To Head of Family; At Jurisdiction Where Enrolled (Yes or No); At Another Jurisdiction; ELSEWHERE: Post office, County, State; Ward (Yes or No); Allotment, Annuity, and Identification Numbers.

996; Seminole, Dan; M; 8/94, 36; Cheyenne; 1/4+; M; Head; Yes; Yes
997; Seminole, Jennie; F; 7/96, 35; Cheyenne; F; M; Wife; Yes; Yes
998; Seminole, Anna; F; 6/20, 10; Cheyenne; 1/4+; S; Dau; Yes; Yes
999; Seminole, Margaret; F; 1/22, 9; Cheyenne; 1/4+; S; Dau; Yes; Yes
1000; Seminole, Alfred; M; 3/23, 7; Cheyenne; 1/4+; S; Son; Yes; Yes
1001; Seminole, Beatrice; F; 8/27/28, 2; Cheyenne; 1/4+; S; Dau; Yes; Yes
1002; Littlewhiteman, Charles; M; 2/15, 16; Cheyenne; 1/4+; S; Step-Son; Yes; Yes

1003; Seminole, John; M; 2/79, 52; Cheyenne; 1/4+; M; Head; Yes; Yes
1004; Seminole, Mary R.; F; 8/97, 33; Cheyenne; F; M; Wife; Yes; Yes
1005; Seminole, Fred; M; 6/15, 15; Cheyenne; 1/4+; S; Son; Yes; Yes
1006; Seminole, Max; M; 11/24, 6; Cheyenne; 1/4+; S; Son; Yes; Yes [son-Mary Redbird, 1926 #813 entry; Redbird, Maxine; g-g-son; 1924; M.; g-g-son Joseph Tangledhornelk]
1007; Fox, Margaret; F; 8/18, 12; Cheyenne; F; S; Step-Dau; Yes; Yes [Jessie in 1927.]
1008; Fox, Marie; F; 10/22, 8; Cheyenne; F; S; Step-Dau; Yes; Yes [Max, M., 1922-25.]

1009; Seminole, Josephine; F; 4/91, 39; Cheyenne; 1/4+; S; Head; Yes; Yes
1010; Seminole, Lawrence; M; 12/11, 19; Cheyenne; 1/4+; S; Son; Yes; Yes

1011; Seminole, Louis; M; 6/84, 46; Cheyenne; 1/4+; Wd[sic]; Head; Yes; Yes

1012; Seminole, Miles; M; 4/69, 61 Cheyenne; 1/4+; M; Head; Yes; Yes
1013; Seminole, Mary R.; F; 5/06, 24; Cheyenne; F; M; Wife; Yes; Yes
1014; Seminole, Lucille; F; 2/24/31, 1/12; Cheyenne; F; S; Dau; Yes; Yes
1015; Whistlingelk, May; F; 3/26, 5; Cheyenne; F; S; Step-Dau; Yes; Yes

1016; Sharpnose, Josephine; F; 6/02, 28; Cheyenne; F; Wd; Head; Yes; Yes [Hisbadhorses]

1017; Shavedhead, James; M; 11/99, 31; Cheyenne; F; M; Head; Yes; Yes
1018; Shavedhead, Alice; F; 2/07, 24; Cheyenne; F; M; Wife; Yes; Yes [Medicineflying; age 3 in 1910. Birth 1906-07.]
1019; Shavedhead, Anna; F; 9/25, 5; Cheyenne; F; S; Dau; Yes; Yes [Hyacinth in 1926.]
1020; Shavedhead, Mabel; F; 1/23/30, 1; Cheyenne; F; S; Dau; Yes; Yes
1021; Shavedhead, Mary; F; 6/65, 65; Cheyenne; F; Wd; Mother; Yes; Yes
1022; Divesbackward, Louisa; F; 8/17, 13; Cheyenne; F; S; Niece; Yes; Yes [7/8 blood in 1928.]

1023; Shavedhead, Jean S.; F; 28; Cheyenne; F; M; Head; No; Shoshone & Arap. Okla; Yes [Swallow]

Census of the **Tongue River** reservation of the **Tongue River** jurisdiction, as of **April 1**, 1931, taken by **C. B. Lohmiller**, Superintendent.

**Key:** Number; NAME: Surname, Given; Sex; Birthdate, Age At Last Birthday; Tribe; Degree of Blood; Marital Status; Relationship To Head of Family; At Jurisdiction Where Enrolled (Yes or No); At Another Jurisdiction; ELSEWHERE: Post office, County, State; Ward (Yes or No); Allotment, Annuity, and Identification Numbers.

1024; Shavedhead, Charles; M; 5; Cheyenne; F; S; Son; No; Shoshone & Arap. Okla; Yes [Jeffrey, Jr. and birth year 1925 in 1926.]
1025; Shavedhead, Anna M.; F; 3; Cheyenne; F; S; Dau; No; Shoshone & Arap. Okla; Yes

1026; Shell, Joseph; M; 2/81, 50; Cheyenne; F; M; Head; Yes; Yes
1027; Shell, Julia; F; 9/01, 29; Cheyenne; F; M; Wife; Yes; Yes [Previous #530 in 1906, censuses 1906-19, wife Alice [Risingsun] Shell, birth year 1885.] [Julia starts census 1920.]

1028; Shepherd, Mollie; F; 4/95, 35; Cheyenne; 1/4+; M; Head; No; Cheyenne & Arap. Okla; Yes

1029; Sherman, Ethel; F; 5/83, 47; Cheyenne; 1/4-; M; Head; Yes; Yes [1/4+ 1930]
1030; Sherman, George; M; 10/11, 19; Cheyenne; -1/4; S; Son; Yes; Yes
1031; Sherman, Otto; M; 6/13, 17; Cheyenne; -1/4; S; Son; Yes; Yes
1032; Sherman, Wretha; F; 8/15, 15; Cheyenne; -1/4; S; Dau; Yes; Yes
1033; Sherman, Carl; M; 12/18, 12; Cheyenne; -1/4; S; Son; Yes; Yes
1034; Sherman, Clarence; M; 7/22, 8; Cheyenne; -1/4; S; Son; Yes; Yes

1035; Shortsioux, Mary; F; 6/14, 16; Cheyenne; F; S; Dau; No; Crow Agency, Mont; Yes [Dau Longears, Crow Agency, Mont.]

1036; Shoulderblade, Benedict; M; 9/74, 56; Cheyenne; F; M; Head; Yes; Yes
1037; Shoulderblade, Fannie; F; 7/23/24, 6; Cheyenne; 1/4+; S; Dau; Yes; Yes [Full in 1930]

1038; Shoulderblade, Fred; M; 10/61, 69; Cheyenne; F; M; Head; Yes; Yes
1039; Shoulderblade, Richard; M; 8/11, 20; Cheyenne; F; S; Son; Yes; Yes

---- Shoulderblade, Pius; M; 5/89, 41; Cheyenne; F; M; Head; Yes; Yes Died January 3, 1931.
1040; Shoulderblade, Ethel; F; 8/93, 37; Cheyenne; 1/4+; M; Wife; Yes; Yes
1041; Shoulderblade, Thomas; M; 10/15, 15; Cheyenne; 1/4+; S; Son; Yes; Yes
1042; Shoulderblade, Francis; F[sic]; 3/17, 14; Cheyenne; 1/4+; S; Son; Yes; Yes [1917 Census William]
1043; Shoulderblade, Wendel; M; 8/20, 10; Cheyenne; 1/4+; S; Son; Yes; Yes
---- Shoulderblade, Everett J.; M; 6/23, 7; Cheyenne; 1/4+; S; Son; Yes; Yes Died June 17, 1930.
1044; Shoulderblade, Fern; F; 3; Cheyenne; 1/4+; S; Dau; Yes; Yes
1045; Shoulderblade, Claudia; F; 7/8/30, 9/12; Cheyenne; 1/4+; S; Dau; Yes; Yes

1046; Silloway, Veta; F; 11/04, 26; Cheyenne; -1/4; M; Head; No; Miles City-town, Custer, Mont; Yes

Census of the __Tongue River__ reservation of the __Tongue River__ jurisdiction, as of __April 1__, 1931, taken by __C. B. Lohmiller__, Superintendent.

**Key:** Number; NAME: Surname, Given; Sex; Birthdate, Age At Last Birthday; Tribe; Degree of Blood; Marital Status; Relationship To Head of Family; At Jurisdiction Where Enrolled (Yes or No); At Another Jurisdiction; ELSEWHERE: Post office, County, State; Ward (Yes or No); Allotment, Annuity, and Identification Numbers.

1047; Sioux, Thomas; M; 11/70, 60; Cheyenne; F; M; Head; Yes; Yes
1048; Sioux, Jane W.; F; 3/67, 64; Cheyenne; F; M; Wife; Yes; Yes
1049; Sioux, Henry; M; 6/11, 19; Cheyenne; F; S; Son; Yes;
1050; Risingsun, Ruby; F; 9/19/28, 2; Cheyenne; F; S; A-Dau; Yes; Yes

1051; Sittingman, Charles; M; 10/66, 64; Cheyenne; F; M; Head; Yes; Yes
1052; Sittingman, Lucy; F; 5/66, 64; Cheyenne; F; M; Wife; Yes; Yes
1053; Sittingman, Edward; M; 6/00, 30; Cheyenne; F; D; Son; Yes; Yes
[Edward in 1927. Was Edwin in 1926.]

1054; Small, Josephine; F; 2/92, 39; Cheyenne; 1/4+; M; Head; Yes; Yes
1055; Small, Victor; M; 8/12, 18; Cheyenne; 1/4+; S; Son; Yes; Yes
1056; Small, Edward; M; 11/13, 17; Cheyenne; 1/4+; S; Son; Yes; Yes
1057; Small, Max J.; M; 4/15, 15; Cheyenne; 1/4+; S; Son; Yes; Yes
1058; Small, Ivan; M; 4/20, 10; Cheyenne; 1/4+; S; Son; Yes; Yes
1059; Small, Thomas; M; 12/21, 9; Cheyenne; 1/4+; S; Son; Yes; Yes
1060; Small, Horace; M; 7/23, 7; Cheyenne; 1/4+; S; Son; Yes; Yes
1061; Small, Melvin; M; 2/24, 6; Cheyenne; 1/4+; S; Son; Yes; Yes
1062; Small, Worth; M; 2/27, 4; Cheyenne; 1/4+; S; Son; Yes; Yes
1063; Small, Clinton; M; 11/19/29, 1; Cheyenne; 1/4+; S; Son; Yes; Yes

1064; Smith, John; M; 6/75, 55; Cheyenne; F; M; Head; Yes; Yes
1065; Smith, Blanche; F; 3/80, 51; Cheyenne; F; M; Wife; Yes; Yes
1066; Americanhorse, Rueben[sic]; M; 11/17, 13; Cheyenne; F; S; A-Son; Yes; Yes

1067; Soldierwolf, John; M; 4/83, 47; Cheyenne; F; M; Head; Yes; Yes
1068, Soldierwolf, Mary K.; F; 4/88, 42; Cheyenne; F; M; Wife; Yes; Yes
1069; Soldierwolf, Thomas; M; 6/10, 20; Cheyenne; F; S; Son; Yes; Yes
1070; Soldierwolf, Josie A.; F; 1/15, 15; Cheyenne; F; S; Dau; Yes; Yes
1071; Soldierwolf, Bessie L.; F; 10/17, 13; Cheyenne; F; S; Dau; Yes; Yes
1072; Soldierwolf, James K.; M; 7/20, 10; Cheyenne; F; S; Son; Yes; Yes
1073; Soldierwolf, Annie K.; F; 5/22, 8; Cheyenne; F; S; Dau; Yes; Yes
1074; Soldierwolf, Doris; F; 4/5/30, 1; Cheyenne; F; S; Dau; Yes; Yes

1075; Spang, Alban; M; 9/1892, 38; Cheyenne; -1/4; M; Head; Yes; Yes
1076; Spang, Edward F.; M; 3/16/29, 2; Cheyenne; -1/4; S; Son; Yes; Yes
1077; Spang, Peter A.; M; 2/24/31, 1/12; Cheyenne; -1/4; S; Son; Yes; Yes

1078; Spang, Alfonso; M; 1/87, 44; Cheyenne; -1/4+[sic]; M; Head; Yes; Yes
1079; Spang, Mary C.; F; 9/11, 19; Cheyenne; 1/4+; M; Wife; Yes; Yes
[1924 Annie. Callsfirst in 1928.]

1080; Spang, Deyo; M; 12/88, 42; Cheyenne; -1/4; M; Head; Yes; Yes
1081; Spang, Bruce S.; M; 6/24, 6; Cheyenne; -1/4; S; Son; Yes; Yes

Census of the **Tongue River** reservation of the **Tongue River** jurisdiction, as of **April 1**, 1931, taken by **C. B. Lohmiller**, Superintendent.

**Key:** Number; NAME: Surname, Given; Sex; Birthdate, Age At Last Birthday; Tribe; Degree of Blood; Marital Status; Relationship To Head of Family; At Jurisdiction Where Enrolled (Yes or No); At Another Jurisdiction; ELSEWHERE: Post office, County, State; Ward (Yes or No); Allotment, Annuity, and Identification Numbers.

1082; Spang, Dale C.; M; 7/26, 4; Cheyenne; -1/4; S; Son; Yes; Yes
1083; Spang, Darrel Dean; M; 8/9/30, 7/12; Cheyenne; -1/4; S; Son; Yes; Yes

1084; Spang, James; M; 7/99, 31; Cheyenne; -1/4; M; Head; Yes; Yes
1085; Spang, James R.; M; 5/13/27, 3; Cheyenne; -1/4; S; Son; Yes; Yes
1086; Spang, Shirley A.; F; 5/29/28, 2; Cheyenne; -1/4; S; Dau; Yes; Yes

1087; Spang, Lucy; F; 5/69, 61; Cheyenne; 1/4-; M; Head; Yes; Yes [Fullblood in 1930]
1088; Spang, Harriet; F; 10/05, 25; Cheyenne; -1/4; S; Dau; Yes; Yes
1089; Spang, Cash; M; 10/11, 19; Cheyenne; -1/4; S; Son; Yes; Yes
1090; Spang, Joyce; F; 1/5/31, 3/12; Cheyenne; -1/4; S; G-Son; Yes; Yes

1091; Spang, Roy; M; 9/96, 34; Cheyenne; -1/4; M; Head; Yes; Yes
1092; Spang, Viola; F; 1/07, 23; Cheyenne; F; M; Wife; Yes; Yes [Wildhog]
1093; Spang, Regina S.; F; 6/22, 8; Cheyenne; 1/4+; S; Dau; Yes; Yes [Regina Rosetta in 1926.]
1094; Spang, Lyman; M; 8/23, 7; Cheyenne; 1/4+; S; Son; Yes; Yes

1095; Spang, Wilfred; M; 5/01, 29; Cheyenne; -1/4; M; Head; Yes; Yes
1096; Spang, Jennie L.; F; 11/15, 15; Cheyenne; F; M; Wife; Yes; Yes
1097; Spang, Norman; M; 9/27, 3; Cheyenne; 1/4+; S; Son; Yes; Yes

1098; Speelman, Jessie F.; F; 1/89, 42; Cheyenne; 1/4+; M; Head; Yes; Yes
1099; Farr, Evelyn; F; 12/14, 16; Cheyenne; -1/4; S; Dau; Yes; Yes
1100; Farr, Frank; M; 7/17, 13; Cheyenne; -1/4; S; Son; Yes; Yes
1101; Speelman, William L.; M; 7/26/29, 1; Cheyenne; -1/4; S; Son; Yes; Yes

1102; Sponge, Alfred; M; 7/96, 34; Cheyenne; F; M; Head; Yes; Yes
1103; Sponge, Josie; F; 9/01, 29; Cheyenne; F; M: Wife; Yes; Yes [Shoulderblade] [1922 was #958, Scott.]

1104; Sponge, Oliver; M; 3/98, 33; Cheyenne; F; M; Head; Yes; Yes
1105; Sponge, Clara; F; 5/05, 25; Cheyenne; F; M; Wife; Yes; Yes [Tangleyellowhair]
1106; Sponge, Paul; M; 12/10/27, 3; Cheyenne; F; S; Son; Yes; Yes
1107; Sponge, Lena; F; 8/28/29, 1; Cheyenne; F; S; Dau; Yes; Yes

1108; Spottedblackbird, Lee; M; 6/59, 71; Cheyenne; F; M; Head; Yes; Yes [Birth year 1854 in 1926. #1082. Didn't pickup a first name until 1915 name, Lee; or Leo.]
1109; Spottedblackbird, Clara; F; 10/74, 56; Cheyenne; F; M; Wife; Yes; Yes
     ----  ~~Hardground, Jane; F; 3/15, 15; Cheyenne; F; S; G-Dau; Yes; Yes~~
~~Died May 5, 1930~~

Census of the  Tongue River  reservation of the Tongue River  jurisdiction, as of
 April 1   , 1931, taken by  C. B. Lohmiller , Superintendent.

**Key:** Number; NAME: Surname, Given; Sex; Birthdate, Age At Last Birthday; Tribe; Degree of Blood; Marital Status; Relationship To Head of Family; At Jurisdiction Where Enrolled (Yes or No); At Another Jurisdiction; ELSEWHERE: Post office, County, State; Ward (Yes or No); Allotment, Annuity, and Identification Numbers.

1110; Spottedelk, Alex; M; 11/00, 30; Cheyenne; F; M; Head; Yes; Yes
1111; Spottedelk, Nellie T.; F; 10/12, 18; Cheyenne; F; M; Wife; Yes; Yes
1112; Medicineelk, William; M; 3/5/28, 2; Cheyenne; F; S; Step-Son; Yes; Yes

1113; Spottedelk, Charles; M; 3/63, 68; Cheyenne; F; Wd[sic]; Head; Yes; Yes
1114; Spottedelk, August; M; 7/97, 33; Cheyenne; F; S; Son; Yes; Yes

1115; Spottedwolf, Charles; M; 10/92, 38; Cheyenne; F; M; Head; Yes; Yes
1116; Spottedwolf, Lena; F; 9/92, 38; Cheyenne; F; M; Wife; Yes; Yes
1117; Spottedwolf, Julia E.; 4/13, 17; Cheyenne; F; S; Dau; Yes; Yes
1118; Spottedwolf, Martha P.; F; 9/21, 9; Cheyenne; F; S; Dau; Yes; Yes
1119; Spottedwolf, John; M; 10/23, 7; Cheyenne; F; S; Son; Yes; Yes
----   Spottedwolf, Della; F; 1/7/30, 1; Cheyenne; F; S; Dau; Yes; Yes
Died October 6, 1930
1120; Littlewhiteman, Florence; F; 2/15, 15; Cheyenne; 1/4+; S; Step-Dau; Yes; Yes

1121; Spottedwolf, Patrick; M; 11/87, 43; Cheyenne; F; M; Head; Yes; Yes
1122; Spottedwolf, Jean; F; 10/01, 29; Cheyenne; 1/4+; M; Wife; Yes; Yes
1123; Spottedwolf, Ruby; F; 9/20, 10; Cheyenne; 1/4+; S; Dau; Yes; Yes
1124; Spottedwolf, Eldora Phyllis; F; 10/23, 7; Cheyenne; 1/4+; S; Dau; Yes; Yes
1125; Spottedwolf, Clarence Eugene; M; 8/25, 5; Cheyenne; 1/4+; S; Son; Yes; Yes
1126; Spottedwolf, Mollie; F; 9/28/27, 3; Cheyenne; 1/4+; S; Dau; Yes; Yes

1127; Squinteye, Josie; F; 6/84, 46; Cheyenne; F; M; Head; Yes; Yes [Whistlingelk]
1128; Whistlingelk, Alfred; M; 1/17, 14; Cheyenne; F; S; Son; Yes; Yes

1129; Standingelk, Alex; M; 4/96, 34; Cheyenne; F; M; Head; Yes; Yes
1130; Standingelk, Nora; F; 7/03, 27; Cheyenne; F; M; Wife; Yes; Yes
1131; Standingelk, Geneva S.; F; 3/22, 9; Cheyenne; F; S; Dau; Yes; Yes
1132; Standingelk, Margaret; F; 11/24, 6; Cheyenne; F; S; Dau; Yes; Yes
1133; Standingelk, Wayne; M; 5/29, 1; Cheyenne; F; S; Son; Yes; Yes

1134; Standingelk, Annie; F; 5/07, 23; Cheyenne; F; D; Head; Yes; Yes
1135; Standingelk, Roy; M; 8/26, 4; Cheyenne; F; S; Son; Yes; Yes
1136; Swallow, Elsie; F; 4/12/30, 1; Cheyenne; F; S; Son; Yes; Yes

1137; Standingelk, Francis; M; 4/01, 29; Cheyenne; F; D; Head; Yes; Yes

1138; Standingelk, Frank; M; 6/74, 56; Cheyenne; F; M; Head; Yes; Yes
1139; Standingelk, Fannie; F; 4/78, 52; Cheyenne; F; M; Wife; Yes; Yes
1140; Standingelk, Flora; F; 4/21, 9; Cheyenne; F; S; Dau; Yes; Yes

1141; Standingelk, Henry; M; 6/91, 39; Cheyenne; F; M; Head; Yes; Yes
1142; Standingelk, Mary S.; F; 5/07, 23; Cheyenne; F; M; Wife; Yes; Yes

Census of the __Tongue River__ reservation of the __Tongue River__ jurisdiction, as of __April 1__, 1931, taken by __C. B. Lohmiller__, Superintendent.

**Key:** Number; NAME: Surname, Given; Sex; Birthdate, Age At Last Birthday; Tribe; Degree of Blood; Marital Status; Relationship To Head of Family; At Jurisdiction Where Enrolled (Yes or No); At Another Jurisdiction; ELSEWHERE: Post office, County, State; Ward (Yes or No); Allotment, Annuity, and Identification Numbers.

1143; Standingelk, Aiden; M; 5/17/28, 2; Cheyenne; F; S; Son; Yes; Yes
1144; Standingelk, Benno; M; 2/21/30, 1; Cheyenne; F; S; Son; Yes; Yes

1145; Standingelk, Robert B.; M; 10/70, 60; Cheyenne; F; M; Head; Yes; Yes
1146; Standingelk, Sally; F; 9/95, 35; Cheyenne; F; M; Wife; Yes; Yes
1147; Standingelk, Ella J.; F; 12/18, 12; Cheyenne; F; S; Dau; Yes; Yes
1148; Standingelk, Jennie; F; 5/27, 3; Cheyenne; F; S; Dau; Yes; Yes
1149; Standingelk, Lockwood; M; 6/90, 40; Cheyenne; F; Wd[sic]; Son; Yes; Yes

1150; Standsintimber, John; M; 3/86, 45; Cheyenne; F; M; Head; Yes; Yes [Family Part Blood in 1928.]
1151; Standsintimber, Josie; F; 3/98, 33; Cheyenne; F; M; Wife; Yes; Yes
1152; Standsintimber, Josephine; F; 6/20, 10; Cheyenne; F; S; Dau; Yes; Yes
1153; Standsintimber, John Jr.; M; 10/21, 9; Cheyenne; F; S; Son; Yes; Yes
1154; Standsintimber, Elva; F; 4/21/28, 1; Cheyenne; F; S; Dau; Yes; Yes
1155; Standsintimber, Gilbert; M; 10/24/30, 5/12; Cheyenne; F; S; Son; Yes; Yes

1156; Strangeowl, James; M; 6/24, 26; Cheyenne; F; M; Head; Yes; Yes
1157; Strangeowl, Grace R.; F; 3/10, 20; Cheyenne; F; M; Wife; Yes; Yes

1158; Strangeowl, John; M; 9/72, 58; Cheyenne; F; M; Head; Yes; Yes
1159; Strangeowl, Gertie; F; 11/68, 62; Cheyenne; F; M; Wife; Yes; Yes

1160; Starvingbear, James; M; 4/76, 54; Cheyenne; F; Wd[sic]; Head; Yes; Yes
1161; Starvingbear, Jack; M; 2/14, 17; Cheyenne; F; S; Son; Yes; Yes [Rosco in 1926.]

1162; Stumphorn, Frank; M; 10/43, 87; Cheyenne; F; M; Head; Yes; Yes
1163; Stumphorn, Annie; F; 7/55, 76; Cheyenne; F; M; Wife; Yes; Yes [Shortsioux]

1164; Sunbear, Micheal[sic]; M; 1891, 39; Cheyenne; F; M; Head; No; Kiowa Agency Okla; Yes
1165; Sunbear, Herman; M; 3/23, 7; Cheyenne; F; M[sic]; Son; No; Kiowa Agency Okla; Yes
1166; Sunbear, Deyo; M; 1924, 6; Cheyenne; F; M[sic]; Son; No; Kiowa Agency Okla; Yes

1167; Sunroads, David; M; 9/81, 49; Cheyenne; F; M; Head; Yes; Yes
1168; Sunroads, Lizzie; F; 3/83, 48; Cheyenne; F; M; Wife; Yes; Yes

1169; Sunroads, John; M; 7/43, 87; Cheyenne; F; M; Head; Yes; Yes
1170; Sunroads, Lena; F; 3/45, 86; Cheyenne; F; M; Wife; Yes; Yes

1171; Swallow, William; M; 2/74, 57; Cheyenne; F; M; Head; Yes; Yes

Census of the __Tongue River__ reservation of the __Tongue River__ jurisdiction, as of __April 1__, 1931, taken by __C. B. Lohmiller__, Superintendent.

**Key:** Number; NAME: Surname, Given; Sex; Birthdate, Age At Last Birthday; Tribe; Degree of Blood; Marital Status; Relationship To Head of Family; At Jurisdiction Where Enrolled (Yes or No); At Another Jurisdiction; ELSEWHERE: Post office, County, State; Ward (Yes or No); Allotment, Annuity, and Identification Numbers.

1172; Swallow, Gertrude; F; 3/96, 35; Cheyenne; F; M; Wife; Yes; Yes [Redbreath]
1173; Swallow, Oliver; M; 4/99, 31; Cheyenne; F; S; Son; Yes; Yes
1174; Swallow, Edward; M; 3/02, 29; Cheyenne; F; S; Son; Yes; Yes
---- Swallow, Percy R.; M; 11/19, 11; Cheyenne; F; S; Son; Yes; Yes Died August 22, 1930

1175; Sweetmedicine, David; M; 3/64, 68; Cheyenne; F; M; Head; Yes; Yes
1176; Sweetmedicine, Clara; F; 12/70, 60; Cheyenne; F; M; Wife; Yes; Yes
1177; Sweetmedicine, Jacob; M; 4/94, 36; Cheyenne; F; S; Son; Yes; Yes
1178; Sweetmedicine, Joseph; M; 12/98, 32; Cheyenne; F; S; Son; Yes; Yes

1179; Sweetmedicine, William; M; 42; Cheyenne; F; M; Head; No; Cheyenne & Arap. Okla; Yes
1180; Sweetmedicine, Alta; F; 17; Cheyenne; F; S; Dau; No; Cheyenne & Arap. Okla; Yes [1915-Son, Thomas; M.]

1181; Tallbear, Josie; F; 34; Cheyenne; F; M; Head; Yes; Yes
1182; Tallbear, Ermajean; F; 2/17/31, 1/12; Cheyenne; F; S; Dau; Yes; Yes
1183; Littlewhiteman, Bessie; F; 5/26, 4; Cheyenne; F; S; Dau; Yes; Yes

1184; Tallbull, Albert; M; 4/06, 24; Cheyenne; F; S; Head; Yes; Yes

1185; Tallbull, Charles; M; 10/87, 43; Cheyenne; F; M; Head; Yes; Yes
1186; Tallbull, Mary; F; 5/93, 37; Cheyenne; F; M; Wife; Yes; Yes
1187; Tallbull, Joseph; M; 6/15, 15; Cheyenne; F; S; Son; Yes; Yes
1188; Tallbull, Henry; M; 12/17, 13; Cheyenne; F; S; Son; Yes; Yes
1189; Tallbull, William; M; 1/21, 10; Cheyenne; F; S; Son; Yes; Yes
1190; Tallbull, Nelson; M; 10/23, 7; Cheyenne; F; S; Son; Yes; Yes
1191; Tallbull, Cecil R.; M; 1/27, 4; Cheyenne; F; S; Son; Yes; Yes
1192; Tallbull, Nellie; F; 1/5/29, 2; Cheyenne; F; S; Dau; Yes; Yes

1193; Tallbull, Nora; F; 6/58, 72; Cheyenne; F; Wd; Head; Yes; Yes

1194; Tallwhiteman, Jasper; M; 7/93, 37; Cheyenne; F; M; Head; Yes; Yes [Wd[sic] in 1930]

1195; Tallwhiteman, John; M; 4/86, 44; Cheyenne; F; M; Head; Yes; Yes
1196; Tallwhiteman, Eleanor; F; 3/98, 33; Cheyenne; F; M; Wife; Yes; Yes
1197; Tallwhiteman, Clarence; M; 7/12, 18; Cheyenne; F; S; Son; Yes; Yes
1198; Tallwhiteman, Florence; F; 5/14, 16; Cheyenne; F; S; Dau; Yes; Yes
1199; Tallwhiteman, Jasper; M; 7/16, 14; Cheyenne; F; S; Son; Yes; Yes
1200; Tallwhiteman, Elsie; F; 5/20, 10; Cheyenne; F; S; Dau; Yes; Yes [Alice in 1930]
1201; Tallwhiteman, Tug; M; 6/22, 7; Cheyenne; F; S; Son; Yes; Yes

Census of the __Tongue River__ reservation of the __Tongue River__ jurisdiction, as of __April 1__, 1931, taken by __C. B. Lohmiller__, Superintendent.

**Key:** Number; NAME: Surname, Given; Sex; Birthdate, Age At Last Birthday; Tribe; Degree of Blood; Marital Status; Relationship To Head of Family; At Jurisdiction Where Enrolled (Yes or No); At Another Jurisdiction; ELSEWHERE: Post office, County, State; Ward (Yes or No); Allotment, Annuity, and Identification Numbers.

1202; Tallwhiteman, Agnes Virginia; F; 7/25, 5; Cheyenne; F; S; Dau; Yes; Yes

1203; Tangledyellowhair, Chas.; M; 2/92, 39; Cheyenne; F; M; Head; Yes; Yes
1204; Tangledyellowhair, Georgia; F; 9/91, 39; Cheyenne; F; M; Wife; Yes; Yes [Talks]
1205; Tangledyellowhair, Roberta; F; 9/24, 6; Cheyenne; F; S; Dau; Yes; Yes
1206; Tangledyellowhair, Marie; F; 3/31/29, 2; Cheyenne; F; S; Dau; Yes; Yes

1207; Tangledyellowhair, David; M; 6/98, 32; Cheyenne; F; M; Head; Yes; Yes [1904-18 no "d" in last name. Birth year 1894 in 1926.]
1208; Tangledyellowhair, Florence; F; 7/00, 30; Cheyenne; F; M; Wife; Yes; Yes [Tallwhiteman]
1209; Tangledyellowhair, Clara; F; 10/19, 11; Cheyenne; F; S; Dau; Yes; Yes
1210; Tangledyellowhair, Winona; F; 1/22, 8; Cheyenne; F; S; Dau; Yes; Yes
1211; Tallwhiteman, Alice; F; 1/16, 14; Cheyenne; F; S; Step-Dau; Yes; Yes
1212; Tallwhiteman, Regina; F; 6/23, 7; Cheyenne; F; S; Step-Dau; Yes; Yes

1213; Tangledyellowhair, James; M; 1/69, 62; Cheyenne; F; M; Head; Yes; Yes [1904-18 no "d" in last name.]
1214; Tangledyellowhair, Minnie; F; 12/70, 60; Cheyenne; F; M; Wife; Yes; Yes
1215; Tangledyellowhair, Josie; F; 3/48, 81; Cheyenne; F; Wd; Mother; Yes; Yes

1216; Teeth, Charles; M; 3/63, 68; Cheyenne; F; M; Head; Yes; Yes
1217; Teeth, Fannie; F; 10/80, 50; Cheyenne; F; M; Wife; Yes; Yes

1218; Teeth, Franklin; M; 10/09, 21; Cheyenne; F; M; Head; Yes; Yes
1219; Teeth, Mabel D.; F; 7/13, 17; Cheyenne; F; M; Wife; Yes; Yes

1220; Teeth, John; M; 5/89, 41; Cheyenne; F; M; Head; Yes; Yes
1221; Teeth, Edith; F; 10/02, 28; Cheyenne; F; M; Wife; Yes; Yes
1222; Teeth, Earl; M; 6/16, 14; Cheyenne; F; S; Son; Yes; Yes
1223; Teeth, Montana; F; 4/22, 8; Cheyenne; F; S; Dau; Yes; Yes
1224; Teeth, Elsie; F; 9/25, 5; Cheyenne; F; S; Dau; Yes; Yes
1225; Teeth, Logan; M; 11/15/28, 2; Cheyenne; F; S; Son; Yes; Yes
1226; Americanhorse, Flora; F; 1861, 70; Cheyenne; F; Wd; G-Mother; Yes; Yes

1227; Threefingers, John; M; 3/62, 69; Cheyenne; F; M; Head; Yes; Yes
1228; Threefingers, Pansy; F; 7/76, 54; Cheyenne; F; M; Wife; Yes; Yes
1229; Walkingbear, David; M; 6/97, 33; Cheyenne; F; D; Step-Son; Yes; Yes

1230; Threefingers, William; M; 9/01, 29; Cheyenne; F; M; Head; Yes; Yes
1231; Threefingers, Lucy; F; 9/11, 20; Cheyenne; F; M; Wife; Yes; Yes
1232; Threefingers, Isaac; M; 1/22/31, 2/12; Cheyenne; F; S; Son; Yes; Yes

Census of the **Tongue River** reservation of the **Tongue River** jurisdiction, as of **April 1**, 1931, taken by **C. B. Lohmiller**, Superintendent.

**Key:** Number; NAME: Surname, Given; Sex; Birthdate, Age At Last Birthday; Tribe; Degree of Blood; Marital Status; Relationship To Head of Family; At Jurisdiction Where Enrolled (Yes or No); At Another Jurisdiction; ELSEWHERE: Post office, County, State; Ward (Yes or No); Allotment, Annuity, and Identification Numbers.

1233;  Turkeylegs, John; M; 7/59, 71; Cheyenne; F; M; Head; Yes; Yes
1234;  Turkeylegs, Lydia; F; 8/74, 56; Cheyenne; F; M: Wife; Yes; Yes
1235;  Redbird, Dorothy; F; 7/08, 22; Cheyenne; 1/4+; D; G-Dau; Yes; Yes
1236;  Redbird, David; M; 5/22/28, 2; Cheyenne; 1/4+; S; G G-Son; Yes; Yes

1237;  Turkeylegs, Lawrence; M; 7/06, 24; Cheyenne; F; S; Head; No; Pine Ridge SD; Yes [Name James in 1926.]

1238;  Twin, Louis J.; M; 12/87, 43; Cheyenne; F; M; Head; Yes; Yes [Name Louis James in 1930]
1239;  Twin, Bessie; F; 3/86, 45; Cheyenne; F; M; Wife; Yes; Yes
1240;  Twin, Margaret; F; 4/18, 12; Cheyenne; F; S; Dau; Yes; Yes

1241;  Twobirds, Peter; M; 5/78, 52; Cheyenne; F; M; Head; Yes; Yes
1242;  Twobirds, Lenora; F; 7/72, 57; Cheyenne; F; M; Wife; Yes; Yes
1243;  Twobirds, Jacob; M; 1/01, 29; Cheyenne; F; S; Son; Yes; Yes

1244;  Twobulls, Martin; M; 7/91, 39; Cheyenne; F; M; Head; Yes; Yes
1245;  Twobulls, Eleanor; F; 5/00, 30; Cheyenne; F; M; Wife; Yes; Yes
1246;  Twobulls, William; M; 9/20, 10; Cheyenne; F; S; Son; Yes; Yes
1247;  Twobulls, Alice; F; 8/27, 3; Cheyenne; F; S; Dau; Yes; Yes
1248;  Twobulls, Ruth; F; 1/15/21, 2/12; Cheyenne; F; S; Dau; Yes; Yes

1249;  Twofeathers, John; M; 4/57, 73; Cheyenne; F; M; Head; Yes; Yes
1250;  Twofeathers, Clara; F; 5/70, 60; Cheyenne; F; M; Wife; Yes; Yes
1251;  Twofeathers, Ethel; F; 9/07, 22; Cheyenne; F; S; Dau; Yes; Yes

1252;  Twomoons, Bert, M; 11/87, 43; Cheyenne; F; M; Head; Yes; Yes

1253;  Twomoons, John; M; 4/55, 75; Cheyenne; F; Wd[sic]; Head; Yes; Yes
1254;  Bigheadman, Betty N.; F; 1/15, 16; Cheyenne; F; S; G-Dau; Yes; Yes
1255;  Bigheadman, Frank B.; M; 8/17, 13; Cheyenne; F; S; G-Son; Yes; Yes

1256;  Twomoons, William; M; 5/84, 46; Cheyenne; F; M; Head; Yes; Yes
1257;  Twomoons, Emma Bites; F; 7/95, 35; Cheyenne; F; M; Wife; Yes; Yes [Rowland]

1258;  Vassau, Jessie; F; 5/07, 23; Cheyenne; F; M; Head; No; Miles City-town, Custer, Mont; Yes

1259;  Walkingbear, Charles; M; 5/76, 54; Cheyenne; F; M; Head; Yes; Yes
1260;  Walkingbear, Jennie; F; 9/72, 58; Cheyenne; F; M; Wife; Yes; Yes

1261;  Walkinghorse, John; M; 8/57, 73; Cheyenne; F; M; Head; Yes; Yes

Census of the **Tongue River** reservation of the **Tongue River** jurisdiction, as of **April 1**, 1931, taken by **C. B. Lohmiller**, Superintendent.

**Key:** Number; NAME: Surname, Given; Sex; Birthdate, Age At Last Birthday; Tribe; Degree of Blood; Marital Status; Relationship To Head of Family; At Jurisdiction Where Enrolled (Yes or No); At Another Jurisdiction; ELSEWHERE: Post office, County, State; Ward (Yes or No); Allotment, Annuity, and Identification Numbers.

1262; Walkinghorse, Olive; F; 9/66, 64; Cheyenne; F; M; Wife; Yes; Yes

1263; Walksalong, Hugh; M; 4/85, 45; Cheyenne; F; M; Head; Yes; Yes
1264; Walksalong, Mamie; F; 3/97, 33; Cheyenne; F; M; Wife; Yes; Yes
1265; Walksalong, Flora; F; 5/15, 15; Cheyenne; F; S; Dau; Yes; Yes
[Previous censuses 1916-19, Fred, son.]
1266; Walksalong, Mary E.; F; 6/20, 10; Cheyenne; F; S; Dau; Yes; Yes
1267; Walksalong, Carol; F; 1/10/28, 2; Cheyenne; F; S; Dau; Yes; Yes
1268; Killsontop, Ida; F; 10/24, 6; Cheyenne; F; S; S-Dau; Yes; Yes

1269; Walkslast, Frank; M; 3/08, 23; Cheyenne; F; M; Head; Yes; Yes
1270; Walkslast, Carrie; F; 5/11, 19; Cheyenne; F; M; Wife; Yes; Yes
1271; Walkslast, Lloyd; M; 9/2/30, 7/12; Cheyenne; F; S; Son; Yes; Yes

1272; Walkslast, James; M; 9/05, 25; Cheyenne; F; M; Head; Yes; Yes [Clement in 1926.]
1273; Walkslast, May L.W.; F; 3/11, 20; Cheyenne; F; M; Wife; Yes; Yes
1274; Walkslast, Gilbert; M; 3/13/21, 1/12; Cheyenne; F; S; Yes; Yes

1275; Walkslast, Richard; M; 3/56, 75; Cheyenne; F; M; Head; Yes; Yes
1276; Walkslast, Anne; F; 7/62, 68; Cheyenne; F; M; Wife; Yes; Yes

1277; Walksnice, Adolph; M; 4/78, 52; Cheyenne; F; M; Head; Yes; Yes
1278; Walksnice, Flora; F; 10/84, 45; Cheyenne; F; M; Wife; Yes; Yes
1279; Walksnice, Dick; M; 15/11, 19; Cheyenne; F; S; Son; Yes; Yes
1280; Wolfchum, Lily; F; 5/16, 14; Cheyenne; F; S; G-Dau; Yes; Yes [1917 Census name Betty.]

1281; Walksnice, John; M; 9/05, 25; Cheyenne; F; M; Head; Yes; Yes
1282; Walksnice, Mary; F; 1/03, 28; Cheyenne; F; M; Wife; Yes; Yes [Crookednose]
1283; Walksnice, Mae; F; 11/1/29, 1; Cheyenne; F; S; Dau; Yes; Yes

1284; Wallowing, Rufus; M; 11/87, 43; Cheyenne; F; M; Head; Yes; Yes [Dustybuffalo, Rollingbull] Name changed to "Wallowing" see 57750-26. [First name Rutherford misspelled starting in 1918.]
1285; Wallowing, Stella; F; 7/85, 45; Cheyenne; 1/4+; M; Wife; Yes; Yes
1286; Redwoman, George P.; M; 4/4/28, 2; Cheyenne; F; S; A-Dau[sic]; Yes; Yes

1287; Walters, George; M; 9/97, 33; Cheyenne; 1/4+; M; Head; Yes; Yes

---- Wanderingmedicine, Wm.; M; 4/69, 62; Cheyenne; F; M; Head; Yes; Yes Died April 25, 1930
1288; Wanderingmedicine, Gertrude; F; 4/75, 51; Cheyenne; F; M; Wife; Yes; Yes [Littleyellowman]

Census of the __Tongue River__ reservation of the __Tongue River__ jurisdiction, as of __April 1__, 1931, taken by __C. B. Lohmiller__, Superintendent.

**Key:** Number; NAME: Surname, Given; Sex; Birthdate, Age At Last Birthday; Tribe; Degree of Blood; Marital Status; Relationship To Head of Family; At Jurisdiction Where Enrolled (Yes or No); At Another Jurisdiction; ELSEWHERE: Post office, County, State; Ward (Yes or No); Allotment, Annuity, and Identification Numbers.

1289; Waters[sic], Frank; M; 53/75, 56; Cheyenne; F; M; Head; Yes; Yes [1904-20, name is Water.]
1290; Waters, Joseph; F; 7/22, 8; Cheyenne; F; S; A-Son; Yes; Yes [1346; 1377; Woodenlegs, Martin; son; 1922; in 1926. Step-son in 1928.]

1291; Weaselbear, Frank; M; 9/61, 69; Cheyenne; F; M; Head; Yes; Yes
1292; Weaselbear, Mary; F; 2/70, 61; Cheyenne; F; M; Wife; Yes; Yes
---- Looksbehind, Inez; F; 8/19/29, 1; Cheyenne; F; S; G-Dau; Yes; Yes Died April 12, 1930

1293; Weaselbear, Hugh; M; 1889, 41; Cheyenne; F; M; Head; Yes; Yes
1294; Weaselbear, Andrew; M; 4/15, 15; Cheyenne; F; S; Son; Yes; Yes
1295; Weaselbear, Busby; M; 7/22, 8; Cheyenne; F; S; Son; Yes; Yes

1296; Weaselbear, Martha W.; F; 6/10, 20; Cheyenne; F; M; Head; Yes; Yes

1297; Wheeler, Dewitt C.; M; 12/92, 38; Sioux[?]; 1/4+; M; Head; Yes; Yes [Listed as Sioux in 1930; 1/4- in 1930]
1298; Wheeler, Dewitt P.; M; 11/16, 14; Sioux; 1/4+; S; Son; Yes; Yes [Listed as Sioux in 1930]

1299; Whirlwind, Thomas; M; 10/76, 54; Cheyenne; F; M; Head; Yes; Yes
1300; Whirlwind, Minnie S.; F; 6/82, 47; Cheyenne; F; M; Wife; Yes; Yes
1301; Killsnight, Susan; F; 5/17, 13; Cheyenne; F; S; Step-Dau; Yes; Yes
1302; Killsnight, Bessie; F; 2/20, 11; Cheyenne; F; S; Step-Dau; Yes; Yes
1303; Ironshirt, Jennie; F; 7/58, 72; Cheyenne; F; Wd; Mother-in-law; Yes; Yes

1304; Whistlingelk, John; M; 4/04, 26; Cheyenne; F; M; Head; Yes; Yes
1305; Whistlingelk, Carrie D.; F; 6/10, 20; Cheyenne; F; M; Wife; Yes; Yes

1306; White, Stamper; M; 4/98, 32; Cheyenne; F; M; Head; Yes; Yes
1307; White, Lottie; F; 3/03, 28; Cheyenne; 1/4+; M; Wife; Yes; Yes [Rowland] [1/4- 1930]
1308; White, Pearl; F; 8/23, 7; Cheyenne; 1/4+; S; Dau; Yes; Yes [1/4- 1930]
1309; White, Willis; M; 3/31/30, 1; Cheyenne; 1/4+; S; Son; Yes; Yes [1/4- 1930]

1310; Whitebear, Joseph; M; 1896, 34; Cheyenne; F; M; Head; Yes; Yes
1311; Whitebear, Alice; F; 3/09, 21; Cheyenne; F; M; Wife; Yes; Yes
1312; Whitebear, Anna; F; 8/23, 7; Cheyenne; F; S; Dau; Yes; Yes

1313; Whitebird, Frank; M; 2/02, 29; Cheyenne; F; M; Head; Yes; Yes
1314; Whitebird, Julia R.; F; 7/09, 21; Cheyenne; F; M; Wife; Yes; Yes [1926 Nicetalker, Clarice; s-dau; 1909; F. Also s-dau John Chubby.]
1315; Whitebird, Edward; M; 3/4/30, 1; Cheyenne; F; S; Son; Yes; Yes

Census of the __Tongue River__ reservation of the __Tongue River__ jurisdiction, as of __April 1__, 1931, taken by __C. B. Lohmiller__, Superintendent.

**Key:** Number; NAME: Surname, Given; Sex; Birthdate, Age At Last Birthday; Tribe; Degree of Blood; Marital Status; Relationship To Head of Family; At Jurisdiction Where Enrolled (Yes or No); At Another Jurisdiction; ELSEWHERE: Post office, County, State; Ward (Yes or No); Allotment, Annuity, and Identification Numbers.

1316; Whitebuffalo, John; M; 3/71, 60; Cheyenne; F; M; Head; Yes; Yes
---- ~~Whitebuffalo, Ella; F; 8/67, 63; Cheyenne; F; M; Wife; Yes; Yes Died May 11, 1930~~
1317; Woundedeye, Paul; M; 6/11, 19; Cheyenne; F; S; G-son; Yes; Yes
1318; Medicineelk, Spencer; M; 7/17, 13; Cheyenne; F; S; G-son; Yes; Yes

1319; Whitecrane, Leo; M; 6/95, 35; Cheyenne; F; M; Head; Yes; Yes
1320; Whitecrane, Ella; F; 7/01, 29; Cheyenne; F; M; Wife; Yes; Yes [Littlebird]
1321; Whitecrane, Victor; M; 6/24, 6; Cheyenne; F; S; Son; Yes; Yes
1322; Whitecrane, Eva; F; 12/5/28, 2; Cheyenne; F; S; Son[sic]; Yes; Yes
1323; Whitecrane, Anna; F; 2/6/31, 1/12; Cheyenne; F; S; Son[sic]; Yes; Yes
1324; Littlebird, Harry; M; 8/18, 12; Cheyenne; F; S; Step-Son; Yes; Yes
1325; Littlebird, James; M; 7/19, 11; Cheyenne; F; S; Step-Son; Yes; Yes [Previous #1274; Littlebird, Elsie; s-dau; birth year 1920; F in 1926.]

1326; Whitecrow, Alfred; M; 12/10, 20; Cheyenne; F; S; Head; No; Cheyenne & Arap. Okla; Yes [Teddy Redcherries- Fthr.]

1327; Whitedirt, Charlie; M; 6/05, 25; Cheyenne; F; M; Head; Yes; Yes
1328; Whitedirt, Julia W.; F; 7/09, 21; Cheyenne; F; M; Wife; Yes; Yes [Whistlingelk]
1329; Whitedirt, Leona; F; 12/7/28, 2; Cheyenne; F; S; Dau; Yes; Yes
1330; Whitedirt, May; F; 5/26/30; Cheyenne; F; S; Dau; Yes; Yes
1331; Whitedirt, Maggie; F; 6/75, 53[sic]; Cheyenne; F; Wd; Mother; Yes; Yes
1332; Whitedirt, Jennie; F; 2/11, 20; Cheyenne; F; S; Sister; Yes; Yes

1333; Whistlingelk, Charles; M; 1/76, 55; Cheyenne; F; M; Head; Yes; Yes
1334; Whistlingelk, Rose; F; 12/92, 38; Cheyenne; F; M; Wife; Yes; Yes
1335; Whitebird, Lena; F; 10/55, 75; Cheyenne; F; Wd; Mother-in-law; Yes; Yes

1336; Whitehawk, Charles J.; M; 4/99, 31; Cheyenne; F; M; Head; Yes; Yes
1337; Whitehawk, Alice C.; F; 1/08, 23; Cheyenne; F; M; Wife; Yes; Yes
1338; Whitehawk, Mary; F; 9/19, 11; Cheyenne; F; S; Dau; Yes; Yes
1339; Whitehawk, Marguerite; F; 11/20, 10; Cheyenne; F; S; Dau; Yes; Yes [Same #1251 John, 1922-25, son, M.; Same prev., #1289 Emma; dau; 1922 in 1926.]
1340; Whitehawk, Andrew; M; 12/20/27, 4; Cheyenne; F; S; Son; Yes; Yes
1341; Whitehawk, James; M; 7/3/29, 2; Cheyenne; F; S; Son; Yes; Yes
1342; Whitehawk, George; M; 12/6/30, 4/12; Cheyenne; F; S; Son; Yes; Yes

1343; Whitehawk, Emma; F; 9/83, 47; Cheyenne; F; Wd; Head; Yes; Yes
1344; Whitehawk, Verlie; F; 3/18, 13; Cheyenne; F; S; Dau; Yes; Yes
1345; Whitehawk, Theresa; F; 8/3/27, 3; Cheyenne; F; S; Dau; Yes; Yes

1346; Whitehawk, Mary; F; 7/58, 72; Cheyenne; F; Wd; Head; Yes; Yes

Census of the __Tongue River__ reservation of the __Tongue River__ jurisdiction, as of __April 1__, 1931, taken by __C. B. Lohmiller__, Superintendent.

**Key:** Number; NAME: Surname, Given; Sex; Birthdate, Age At Last Birthday; Tribe; Degree of Blood; Marital Status; Relationship To Head of Family; At Jurisdiction Where Enrolled (Yes or No); At Another Jurisdiction; ELSEWHERE: Post office, County, State; Ward (Yes or No); Allotment, Annuity, and Identification Numbers.

1347; Whitemoon, George; M; 11/54, 76; Cheyenne; F; M; Head; Yes; Yes
1348; Whitemoon, Kate T.; F; 8/65, 65; Cheyenne; F; M; Wife; Yes; Yes

1349; Whitemoon, Hugh; M; 4/81, 49; Cheyenne; F; M; Head; Yes; Yes
1350; Whitemoon, Eva L.E.; F; 7/93, 37; Cheyenne; F; M; Wife; Yes; Yes
1351; Whitemoon, Clarence; M; 8/8/30, 8/12; F; S; Son; Yes; Yes

---- Whitewolf, Charles I.; M; 8/90, 40; Cheyenne; F; M; Head; Yes; Yes Died April 11, 1930
1352; Whitewolf, Belle; F; 5/02, 28; Cheyenne; F; M; Wife; Yes; Yes
1353; Whitewolf, Joseph; M; 3/21, 10; Cheyenne; F; S; Son; Yes; Yes
1354; Whitewolf, George; M; 6/23, 7; Cheyenne; F; S; Son; Yes; Yes
1355; Whitewolf, Fred; M; 2/20/28, 2; Cheyenne; F; S; Son; Yes; Yes

1356; Whitewolf, Everett; M; 3/14, 17; Cheyenne; F; S; Son; Yes; Yes
1357; Whitewolf, Carrie; F; 6/16, 15; Cheyenne; F; S; Dau; Yes; Yes [Philip son, M., 1920 census.]
1358; Whitewolf, Wilson; M; 5/19, 11; Cheyenne; F; S; Son; Yes; Yes
1359; Whitewolf, Thomas; M; 11/21, 9; Cheyenne; F; S; Son; Yes; Yes
1360; Whitewolf, Martin O.; M; 2/23, 8; Cheyenne; F; S; Son; Yes; Yes
1361; Whitewolf, Calvin M.; M; 1/25, 6; Cheyenne; F; S; Son; Yes; Yes [Clara dau, F., 1925 census, same #.]

1362; Whitewolf, Frank; M; 3/47, 84; Cheyenne; F; M; Head; Yes; Yes
1363; Whitewolf, Julia; F; 7/54, 76; Cheyenne; F; M; Wife; Yes; Yes

1364; Whitewolf, Susie G.; F; 4/09, 21; Cheyenne; F; M; Head; Yes; Yes [Grasshopper; Dau. of Mrs. Stanley Lamewoman.]
1365; Whitewolf, Leo; M; 12/18/29, 1; Cheyenne; F; S; Son; Yes; Yes

1366; Whitright, Rhoda S.; F; 3/82, 49; Cheyenne; 1/4+; M; Head; Yes; Yes
1367; Seminole, Lorraine; F; 6/16, 14; Cheyenne; 1/4+; S; Dau; Yes; Yes
1368; Seminole, David; M; 4/19, 11; Cheyenne; 1/4+; S; Son; Yes; Yes

1369; Wildhog, Bird; M; 6/69, 61; Cheyenne; F; M; Head; Yes; Yes
1370; Wildhog, Lydia; F; 10/72, 58; Cheyenne; F; M; Wife; Yes; Yes
1371; Wildhog, Anne; F; 9/95, 35; Cheyenne; F; S; Dau; Yes; Yes
1372; Wildhog, John; M; 10/98, 32; Cheyenne; F; S; Son; Yes; Yes
1373; Wildhog, Mary; F; 12/03, 27; Cheyenne; F; S; Dau; Yes; Yes
1374; Wildhog, Vida; F; 3/05, 26; Cheyenne; F; S; Dau; Yes; Yes [Viola in 1906-25. Shows as 2 months old in 1906 yet majority of census years show the year of birth as 1907.]
1375; Wildhog, Julia; F; 7/13, 17; Cheyenne; F; S; Dau; Yes; Yes [Susie in 1926.]
1376; Wildhog, Opal; F; 1/25, 6; Cheyenne; F; S; G-Dau; Yes; Yes

Census of the __Tongue River__ reservation of the __Tongue River__ jurisdiction, as of __April 1__, 1931, taken by __C. B. Lohmiller__, Superintendent.

**Key:** Number; NAME: Surname, Given; Sex; Birthdate, Age At Last Birthday; Tribe; Degree of Blood; Marital Status; Relationship To Head of Family; At Jurisdiction Where Enrolled (Yes or No); At Another Jurisdiction; ELSEWHERE: Post office, County, State; Ward (Yes or No); Allotment, Annuity, and Identification Numbers.

1377; Wilson, Martha; F; 5/94, 36; Cheyenne; F; M; Head; Yes; Yes [1/4+ 1930]
1378; Wilson, Arthur; M; 9/18, 12; Cheyenne; 1/4-; S; Son; Yes; Yes [1919 name James Jr.] [1/4+ 1930]
1379; Wilson, Esther M.; F; 8/20, 10; Cheyenne; 1/4-; S; Dau; Yes; Yes [1/4+ 1930]
1380; Wilson, Alice; F; 7/21, 9; Cheyenne; 1/4-; S; Dau; Yes; Yes [#1324 in 1926 was Josephine.] [1/4+ 1930]
1381; Wilson, Florence; F; 9/22, 8; Cheyenne; 1/4-; S; Dau; Yes; Yes [1/4+ 1930]
1382; Wilson, Josephine; F; 11/24, 6; Cheyenne; 1/4-; S; Dau; Yes; Yes [1/4+ 1930]
1384; [sic] Wilson, James Jr.; M; 12/26, 4; Cheyenne; 1/4-; S; Son; Yes; Yes [1/4+ 1930]
1385; [sic] Wilson, George; M; 5/24/29, 1; Cheyenne; 1/4-; S; Son; Yes; Yes [1/4+ 1930]

1386; [sic] Windsor, Sarah; F; 8/4, 26; Cheyenne; -1/4; M; Head; Yes; Yes
1387; [sic] Windsor, Lee Roland; M; 5/23/30, 10/12; Cheyenne; -1/4; S; Son; Yes; Yes

1387; Wolfblack, Dallas; M; 4/82, 48; Cheyenne; F; M; Head; Yes; Yes
1388; Wolfblack, Rose; F; 6/90, 40; Cheyenne; F; M; Wife; Yes; Yes [Whitemoon]
1389; Wolfblack, Gladys; F; 12/15, 15; Cheyenne; F; S; Dau; Yes; Yes
1390; Wolfblack, Oran; M; 4/24, 5; Cheyenne; F; S; Son; Yes; Yes
1391; Wolfblack, Harry; M; 1/26, 5; Cheyenne; F; S; Son; Yes; Yes
1392; Wolfblack, Mary; F; 4/8/29, 2; Cheyenne; F; S; Dau; Yes; Yes

1393; Wolfchief, Harshey; M; 8/52, 78; Cheyenne; F; M; Head; Yes; Yes
----   ~~Wolfchief, Anna; F; 7/61, 69; Cheyenne; F; S[sic]; Wife; Yes; Yes Died June 22, 1930.~~ [Whiteelk]

----   ~~Wolfchief, Richard; M; 4/92, 28; Cheyenne; F; M; Head; Yes; Yes Died February 8, 1931.~~
1394; Wolfchief, Flora; F; 9/91, 29; Cheyenne; F; M; Wife; Yes; Yes
1395; Wolfchief, Ann; F; 5/27, 3; Cheyenne; F; S; Dau; Yes; Yes
1396; Wolfchief, Norman; M; 3/7/29, 2; Cheyenne; F; S; Son; Yes; Yes
1397; Wolfchief, Mary; F; 3/1/31, 1/12; Cheyenne; F; S; Dau; Yes; Yes

1398; Wolfchum, Paul; M; 10/93, 37; Cheyenne; F; M; Head; Yes; Yes
1399; Wolfchum, Bessie L.; F; 6/90, 40; Cheyenne; F; M; Wife; Yes; Yes [Littlesun in 1927.]
1400; Wolfchum, Walker; M; 12/26, 4; Cheyenne; F; S; Son; Yes; Yes
1401; Wolfchum, John; M; 11/10/28, 2; Cheyenne; F; S; Son; Yes; Yes
1402; Wolfchum, Espy; M; 4/1/30, 1; Cheyenne; F; S; Son; Yes; Yes

1403; Wolfear, Willis; M; 1/84, 47; Cheyenne; F; M; Head; Yes; Yes
1404; Wolfear, Sophia; F; 5/72, 58; Cheyenne; F; M; Wife; Yes; Yes

Census of the **Tongue River** reservation of the **Tongue River** jurisdiction, as of **April 1**, 1931, taken by **C. B. Lohmiller**, Superintendent.

**Key:** Number; NAME: Surname, Given; Sex; Birthdate, Age At Last Birthday; Tribe; Degree of Blood; Marital Status; Relationship To Head of Family; At Jurisdiction Where Enrolled (Yes or No); At Another Jurisdiction; ELSEWHERE: Post office, County, State; Ward (Yes or No); Allotment, Annuity, and Identification Numbers.

---- ~~Wolfname, William; M; 1/54, 77; Cheyenne; F; M; Head; Yes; Yes Died January 15, 1931.~~

1405; Wolfname, Bessie; F; 5/54, 76; Cheyenne; F; M; Wife; Yes; Yes
1406; Wolfname, Grace; F; 6/16, 14; Cheyenne; F; S; G-Dau; Yes; Yes

1407; Wolfroads, Mack; M; 7/78, 52; Cheyenne; F; Wd[sic]; Head; Yes; Yes
1408; Wolfroads, Maude; F; 7/10, 20; Cheyenne; F; S; Dau; Yes; Yes
1409; Medicineelk, Leo; M; 9/6/29, 1; Cheyenne; F; S; G-Son; Yes; Yes [Wolfroads in 1930]

1410; Wolftooth, Young; M; 11/81, 49; Cheyenne; F; M; Head; Yes; Yes
1411; Wolftooth, Mary; F; 5/18, 12; Cheyenne; F; S; Dau; Yes; Yes
1412; Wolftooth, Norman; M; 7/20, 10; Cheyenne; F; S; Son; Yes; Yes
1413; Wolftooth, Doris; F; 11/25, 5; Cheyenne; F; S; Dau; Yes; Yes
---- ~~Wolftooth, Wayne; M; 5/30/28, 2; Cheyenne; F; S; Son; Yes; Yes Died June 1, 1930.~~

1414; Wolfvoice, Grover; M; 4/90, 40; Cheyenne; F; M; Head; Yes; Yes
1415; Wolfvoice, Jennie; F; 5/82, 48; Cheyenne; F; M; Wife; Yes; Yes
1416; Wolfvoice, Anne; F; 2/28, 13; Cheyenne; F; S; Dau; Yes; Yes
1417; Wolfvoice, Dewey; M; 3/27, 4; Cheyenne; F; S; Son; Yes; Yes
1418; Bearquiver, Grace; F; 5/27, 4; Cheyenne F; S; A-Dau; Yes; Yes
1419; Blackcrane, Clara; F; 12/66, 64; Cheyenne; F; Wd; Mother-in-law; Yes; Yes

1420; Womanleggins, Edward; M; 4/88, 42; Cheyenne; F; M; Head; Yes; Yes
1421; Womanleggins, Mannie; F; 11/91, 39; Cheyenne; F; M; Wife; Yes; Yes [Lamewoman]
1422; Badhorse, Mabel; F; 8/15, 15; Cheyenne; F; S; Step-Dau; Yes; Yes [1917-20 son, Junior, M.; Name is June in 1926. Womanleggins in 1929.]
1423; Lamewoman, Mary; F; 8/17, 13; Cheyenne; F; S; Step-Dau; Yes; Yes
1424; Bearchum, Benjamin; M; 3/19, 11; Cheyenne; 1/4+; S; Step-Son; Yes; Yes

1425; Woodenlegs[sic], Richard; M; 8/59, 71; Cheyenne; F; M; Head; Yes; Yes
1426; Woodenlegs, Sophia; F; 5/59, 70; Cheyenne; F; M; Wife; Yes; Yes

1427; Woodenlegs[sic], Tom; M; 7/87, 43; Cheyenne; F; M; Head; Yes; Yes [Seminole]
1428; Woodenlegs, Alice; F; 6/13, 17; Cheyenne; F; M; Wife; Yes; Yes
1429; Woodenlegs, John; M; 11/09, 21; Cheyenne; F; S; Son; Yes; Yes

1430; Woodenthigh, Arthur; M; 11/83, 47; Cheyenne; F; M; Head; Yes; Yes
1431; Woodenthigh, Eva; F; 12/87, 43; Cheyenne; F; M; Wife; Yes; Yes
1431; Woodenthigh, Esther C.; F; 4/10, 20; Cheyenne; F; S; Dau; Yes; Yes
1431; Woodenthigh, Alice M.; F; 2/14, 17; Cheyenne; F; S; Dau; Yes; Yes

Census of the **Tongue River** reservation of the **Tongue River** jurisdiction, as of **April 1**, 1931, taken by **C. B. Lohmiller**, Superintendent.

**Key:** Number; NAME: Surname, Given; Sex; Birthdate, Age At Last Birthday; Tribe; Degree of Blood; Marital Status; Relationship To Head of Family; At Jurisdiction Where Enrolled (Yes or No); At Another Jurisdiction; ELSEWHERE: Post office, County, State; Ward (Yes or No); Allotment, Annuity, and Identification Numbers.

1431; Woodenthigh, Peter; M; 5/18, 12; Cheyenne; F; S; A-Son; Yes; Yes

1435; Woodenthigh, Chester; M; 9/84, 46; Cheyenne; F; M; Head; Yes; Yes
1436; Woodenthigh, Lena; F; 9/90, 40; Cheyenne; F; M; Wife; Yes; Yes
1437; Woodenthigh, Philip; M; 5/15, 15; Cheyenne; F; S; Son; Yes; Yes
1438; Woodenthigh, John; M; 6/16, 14; Cheyenne; F; S; Son; Yes; Yes
1439; Woodenthigh, Melvin; M; 11/23, 7; Cheyenne; F; S; Son; Yes; Yes

1440; Woodpecker, James; M; 3/01, 30; Cheyenne; F; M; Head; Yes; Yes
1441; Woodpecker, Mary; F; 5/04, 26; Cheyenne; F; M; Wife; Yes; Yes
[Littlewhiteman]

1442; Woundedeye, Davis; M; 6/95, 35; Cheyenne; F; M; Head; Yes; Yes
1443; Woundedeye, Susie; F; 8/03, 27; Cheyenne; F; M; Wife; Yes; Yes
1444; Woundedeye, Milton; M; 4/20, 10; Cheyenne; F; S; Son; Yes; Yes
1445; Woundedeye, Veta E.; F; 1/27, 4; Cheyenne; F; S; Dau; Yes; Yes
1446; Woundedeye, Waldo; M; 8/22/29, 1; Cheyenne; F; S; Son; Yes; Yes

1447; Woundedeye, Ford; M; 4/82, 48; Cheyenne; F; M; Head; Yes; Yes
1448; Woundedeye, Florence; F; 5/90, 40; Cheyenne; F; M; Wife; Yes; Yes
1449; Woundedeye, Victoria; F; 1/22, 9; Cheyenne; F; S; Dau; Yes; Yes
1450; Woundedeye, Ruth; F; 4/27, 3; Cheyenne; F; S; Dau; Yes; Yes
1451; Goggles, Laura; F; 11/09, 21; Cheyenne; F; M; Dau; Yes; Yes
1452; Goggles, Hayes; M; 6/26/28, 2; Cheyenne; F; S; G-Son; Yes; Yes

1453; Woundedeye, Winfield; M; 4/08, 22; Cheyenne; F; M; Head; Yes; Yes
1454; Woundedeye, Alice; F; 11/12, 18; Cheyenne; F; M; Wife; Yes; Yes
1455; Woundedeye, Iva Ruth; F; 10/18/30, 5/12; Cheyenne; F; S; Dau; Yes; Yes

1456; Yelloweagle, Kate; F; 4/52, 78; Cheyenne; F; Wd; Head; Yes; Yes
1457; Rednose, Sarah Mae; F; 11/14, 16; Cheyenne; F; S; G-Dau; Yes; Yes

1458; Yelloweyes, Abram; M; 7/74, 56; Cheyenne; F; M; Head; Yes; Yes
1459; Yelloweyes, Nora; F; 2/77, 53; Cheyenne; F; M; Wife; Yes; Yes

1460; Yelloweyes, Oliver; M; 7/01, 29; Cheyenne; F; M; Head; Yes; Yes
1461; Yelloweyes, Gertrude; F; 5/05, 25; Cheyenne; F; M; Wife; Yes; Yes
[Brownbird]
1462; Yelloweyes, Mary; F; 11/24, 6; Cheyenne; F; S; Dau; Yes; Yes
1463; Yelloweyes, David; M; 12/26/29, 1; Cheyenne; F; S; Son; Yes; Yes

1464; Yellowfox, Robert; M; 7/75, 55; Cheyenne; F; M; Head; Yes; Yes
1465; Yellowfox, Carrie; F; 11/82, 48; Cheyenne; F; M; Wife; Yes; Yes
1466; Yellowfox, Frank; M; 7/01, 29; Cheyenne; F; S; Son; Yes; Yes

Census of the **Tongue River** reservation of the **Tongue River** jurisdiction, as of **April 1**, 1931, taken by **C. B. Lohmiller**, Superintendent.

**Key:** Number; NAME: Surname, Given; Sex; Birthdate, Age At Last Birthday; Tribe; Degree of Blood; Marital Status; Relationship To Head of Family; At Jurisdiction Where Enrolled (Yes or No); At Another Jurisdiction; ELSEWHERE: Post office, County, State; Ward (Yes or No); Allotment, Annuity, and Identification Numbers.

1467; Yellowfox, Charles; M; 10/08, 22; Cheyenne; F; S; Son; Yes; Yes
1468; Yellowfox, Sarah W.; F; 6/13, 17; Cheyenne; F; M; Dau-in-law; Yes; Yes

1469; Yellowfox, William; M; 5/00, 30; Cheyenne; F; M; Head; Yes; Yes
1470; Yellowfox, Margaret Y.; F; 3/05, 26; Cheyenne; F; M; Wife; Yes; Yes [Yellownose]
1471; Yellowfox, Mary J.; F; 3/1/30, 1; Cheyenne; F; S; Dau; Yes; Yes

1472; Yellownose, George; M; 11/96, 34; Cheyenne; F; M; Head; Yes; Yes
1473; Yellownose, Marie B.; F; 6/11, 19; Cheyenne; F; M; Wife; Yes; Yes
1474; Yellownose, Mary; F; 7/27, 3; Cheyenne; F; S; Dau; Yes; Yes
1475; Yellownose, Lena; F; 11/24/30, 4/12; Cheyenne; F; S; Dau; Yes; Yes

1476; Yellownose, Robert; M; 9/57, 53; Cheyenne; F; M; Head; Yes; Yes
1477; Yellownose, Rosa; F; 5/77, 53; Cheyenne; F; M; Wife; Yes; Yes
1478; Wolf, Fannie L.; F; 3/16, 15; Cheyenne; F; S; Step-Dau; Yes; Yes

1479; Yellowrobe, Charles; M; 6/92, 38; Cheyenne; F; M; Head; Yes; Yes
1480; Yellowrobe, Alice; F; 5/98, 32; Cheyenne; F; M; Wife; Yes; Yes
1481; Yellowrobe, Ruth; F 3/17, 13; Cheyenne; F; S; Dau; Yes; Yes [Name Ruana in 1926.]
1482; Yellowrobe, Martha; F; 1/26, 5; Cheyenne; F; S; Dau; Yes; Yes
1483; Yellowrobe, Theordore[sic]; M; 7/5/30, 8/12; Cheyenne; F; S; Son; Yes; Yes

1484; Yellowrobe, Jasper; M; 12/94, 36; Cheyenne; F; M; Head; Yes; Yes
1485; Yellowrobe, Jean W.S.; F; 7/99, 31; Cheyenne; F; M; Wife; Yes; Yes [Whiteshirt]
1486; Yellowrobe, Moses; M; 2/7/29, 2; Cheyenne; F; S; Son; Yes; Yes
---- Yellowrobe, Hilda; F; 4/7/30; Cheyenne; F; S; Dau; Yes; Yes Died November 10, 1930.
1487; Whiteshirt, Caroline; F; 11/21, 9; Cheyenne; F; S; Step-Dau; Yes; Yes [Name Alice in 1926.]

1488; Yellowrobe, William; M; 10/65, 65; Cheyenne; F; M; Head; Yes; Yes
1489; Yellowrobe, Minnie; F; 1/57, 74; Cheyenne; F; M; Wife; Yes; Yes

1490; Youngbear, George; M; 8/82, 48; Cheyenne; F; M; Head; Yes; Yes
1491; Youngbear, Cora; F; 7/88, 42; Cheyenne; F; M; Wife; Yes; Yes
1492; Youngbear, Arthur; M; 8/13, 17; Cheyenne; F; S; Son; Yes; Yes
1493; Youngbear, Ralph H.; M; 10/21, 9; Cheyenne; F; S; Son; Yes; Yes

1494; Youngbird, James; M; 9/57, 73; Cheyenne; F; M; Head; Yes; Yes
1495; Youngbird, Clara; F; 5/63, 67; Cheyenne; F; M; Wife; Yes; Yes

Census of the __Tongue River__ reservation of the __Tongue River__ jurisdiction, as of __April 1__, 1931, taken by __C. B. Lohmiller__, Superintendent.

**Key:** Number; NAME: Surname, Given; Sex; Birthdate, Age At Last Birthday; Tribe; Degree of Blood; Marital Status; Relationship To Head of Family; At Jurisdiction Where Enrolled (Yes or No); At Another Jurisdiction; ELSEWHERE: Post office, County, State; Ward (Yes or No); Allotment, Annuity, and Identification Numbers.

1496; Youngbird, John; M; 9/84, 46; Cheyenne; F; M; Head; Yes; Yes
1497; Youngbird, Anne; F; 2/85, 46; Cheyenne; F; M; Wife; Yes; Yes [Looksbehind]
1498; Youngbird, Carl J.; M; 4/16, 14; Cheyenne; F; S; Son; Yes; Yes

# CENSUS OF NORTHERN CHEYENNE

-of-

TONGUE RIVER RESERVATION, MONT.

as of April 1, 1931.

TONGUE RIVER AGENCY,

C. B. Lohmiller, Superintendent.

-- BIRTHS --

-- DEATHS --

-- ADDITIONS --

Census of the  Tongue River  reservation of the Tongue River  jurisdiction, as of
  April 1  , 1931, taken by  C. B. Lohmiller  , Superintendent.

**Key:** Present Census Roll Number; NAME: Surname, Given; Sex; Birthdate, Age At Last Birthday; Tribe; Degree of Blood; Marital Status; At Jurisdiction Where Enrolled (Yes or No); Ward (Yes or No); Allotment, Annuity, and Identification Numbers.

- - BIRTHS - -

25; Ant, Francis; M; 7/15/30, 10/12; Cheyenne; F; S; Yes; Yes; Yes; None
72; Bigback, Eugene; M; 5/7/30, 11/12; Cheyenne; F; S; Yes; Yes; Yes; None
80; Bigfoot, Hoover; M; 6/10/30, 10/12; Cheyenne; F; S; Yes; Yes; Yes; None
89; Bigheadman, [Blank]; F; 3/13/31, 1/12; Cheyenne; F; S; Yes; Yes; Yes; None
96; Bigheadman, [Blank]; F; 3/6/31, 1/12; Cheyenne; F; S; Yes; Yes; Yes; None
-- Bigheadman, Anthony; M; 1/9/31; Cheyenne; F; S; Yes; Yes; Yes; None
129; Bixby, Juanita; F; 5/24/30, 10/12; Cheyenne; 1/4; S; Yes; Yes; Yes; None
149; Blackstone, Leo; M; 10/22/30, 6/12; Cheyenne; F; S; Yes; Yes; Yes; None
169; Brady, Clifford; M; 10/10/30, 5/12; Cheyenne; F; S; Yes; Yes; Yes; None
303; Elliott, Myron L.; M; 11/3/30, 5/12; Cheyenne; 1/4; S; Yes; Yes; Yes; None
328; Fisher, Virginia Mae; F; 12/14/30, 3/12; Cheyenne; 1/4; S; Yes; Yes; Yes; None
364; Gray, Buddy; M; 11-9-30, 4/12; Cheyenne; F; S; Yes; Yes; Yes; None
372; Hardground, Thomas; M; 4/26/30, 11/12; Cheyenne; F; S; Yes; Yes; Yes; None
384; Harris, Chester; M; 2/25/31, 2/12; Cheyenne; 1/4; S; Yes; Yes; Yes; None
410; Hart, Hilda; F; 8-29-30, 7/12; Cheyenne; 1/4; S; Yes; Yes; Yes; None
425; Hisbadhorse, Esther; F; 8/19/30, 7/12; Cheyenn3[sic]; F; S; Yes; Yes; Yes; None
442; Horn, Denver S.; M; 12/13/30, 3/12; Cheyenne; F; S; Yes; Yes; Yes; None
501; Killsontop, Harold; M; 6/21/30, 9-12; Cheyenne; F; S; Yes; Yes; Yes; None
--- Littlewhiteman, Mabel; F; 10/12; Cheyenne; 1/4; S; Yes; Yes; Yes; None
678; Loneelk, George; M; 3/17/31, 1/12; Cheyenne; F; S; Yes; Yes; Yes; None
694; Lonejaw[sic], Claudia; F; 10-7-30, 6/12; Cheyenne; F; S; Yes; Yes; Yes; None
739; Medicinebull, Mae; F; 4/30/30, 11/12; Cheyenne; F; S; Yes; Yes; Yes; None
790; Parker, Lyle Neal; M; 9/18/30, 7/12; Cheyenne; 1/4; S; Yes; Yes; Yes; None
832; Redbird, Diva; F; 12/8/30, 4/12; Cheyenne; F; S; Yes; Yes; Yes; None
853; Redcherries, Della; F; 5/18/30, 11/12; Cheyenne; F; S; Yes; Yes; Yes; None
961; Rowland, Julia; F; 9/11/30, 7/12; Cheyenne; 1/4; S; Yes; Yes; Yes; None
977; Russell, Clifford; M; 9/17/30, 7/12; Cheyenne; F; S; Yes; Yes; Yes; None
1045; Shoulderblade, Claudia; F; 4/5/30, 8/12; Cheyenne; 1/4; S; Yes; Yes; Yes; None
1074; Soldierwolf, Doris; F; 4/5/30, 1; Cheyenne; F; S; Yes; Yes; Yes; None
1083; Spang, Darrel D.; M; 8/9/30, 7/12; Cheyenne; 1/4; S; Yes; Yes; Yes; None
1077; Spang, Peter A.; M; 2/24/31, 1/12; Cheyenne; 1/4; S; Yes; Yes; Yes; None
1090; Spang, Joyce; F; 1/5/31, 3/12; Cheyenne; 1/4; S; Yes; Yes; Yes; None
1014; Seminole, Lucille; F; 2/24/31, 1/12; Cheyenne; F; S; Yes; Yes; Yes; None
1155; Standsintimber, Gilbert; M; 10-24-30, 5/12; Cheyenne; F; S; Yes; Yes; Yes; None
1136; Swallow, Elsie; F; 4/12/30, 1; Cheyenne; F; S; Yes; Yes; Yes; None
1271; Walkslast, Lloyd; M; 9/2/30, 7/12; Cheyenne; F; S; Yes; Yes; Yes; None
1274; Walkslast, Gilbert; M; 3/13/31, 1/12; Cheyenne; F; S; Yes; Yes; Yes; None
1182; Tallbear, Erma Jean; F; 2/17/31, 1/12; Cheyenne; F; S; Yes; Yes; Yes; None

Census of the __Tongue River__ reservation of the __Tongue River__ jurisdiction, as of __April 1__, 19**31**, taken by __C. B. Lohmiller__, Superintendent.

**Key:** Present Census Roll Number; NAME: Surname, Given; Sex; Birthdate, Age At Last Birthday; Tribe; Degree of Blood; Marital Status; At Jurisdiction Where Enrolled (Yes or No); Ward (Yes or No); Allotment, Annuity, and Identification Numbers.

1232;  Threefingers, Isaac; M; 1/22/31, 2/12; Cheyenne; F; S; Yes; Yes; Yes; None
1248;  Twobulls, Ruth; F; 1/15/31, 2/12; Cheyenne; F; S; Yes; Yes; Yes; None
1323;  Whitecrane, Anna; F; 2/6/31, 1/12; Cheyenne; F; S; Yes; Yes; Yes; None
1330;  Whitedirt, May; F; 5/26/30, 10/12; Cheyenne; F; S; Yes; Yes; Yes; None
1342;  Whitehawk, George; M; 12/6/30, 4/12; Cheyenne; F; S; Yes; Yes; Yes; None
1351;  Whitemoon, Clarence; M; 8-8-30, 8/12; Cheyenne; F; S; Yes; Yes; Yes; None
1386;  Windsor, Lee Roland; M; 5/23/30, 10/12; Cheyenne; 1/4; S; Yes; Yes; Yes; None
1397;  Wolfchief, Mary; F; 3/1/31, 1/12; Cheyenne; F; S; Yes; Yes; Yes; None
1455;  Woundedeye, Iva Ruth; F; 10/18/30, 5/12; Cheyenne; F; S; Yes; Yes; Yes; None
1475;  Yellownose, Lena; F; 11-24-30, 4/12; Cheyenne; F; S; Yes; Yes; Yes; None
1483;  Yellowrobe, Theadore[sic]; M; 7/5/30, 8/12; Cheyenne; F; S; Yes; Yes; Yes; None
---    Yellowrobe, Hilda; F; 4/7/30; Cheyenne; F; S; Yes; Yes; Yes; None

Census of the **Tongue River** reservation of the **Tongue River** jurisdiction, as of **April 1**, 1931, taken by **C. B. Lohmiller**, Superintendent.

**Key:** Previous Census Roll Number; NAME: Surname, Given; Sex; Birthdate, Age At Last Birthday; Tribe; Degree of Blood; Marital Status; Relationship To Head of Family; At Jurisdiction Where Enrolled (Yes or No); At Another Jurisdiction (Yes or No); ELSEWHERE: Post office, County, State; Date of Death; Ward (Yes or No); Allotment, Annuity, and Identification Numbers.

- - DEATHS - -

64; Bigback, Stephen; M; 4/92, 39; Cheyenne; F; S; Yes; Died Aug. 18, 1930; Yes; None

-- Bigheadman, Anthony; M; 1/9/31, 3/12; Cheyenne; F; S; Yes; Died March li[sic], 1931 Yes; None

211; Clubfoot, Floyd; M; 3/88, 43; Cheyenne; F; M; Yes; Died April 2, 1930; Yes; None

243; Crazymule, John; M; 3/70, 61; Cheyenne; F; M; Yes; Died Aug. 12, 1931; Yes; None

1106; Hardground, Jane; F; 3/15, 15; Cheyenne; F; S; Yes; Died May 5, 1930; Yes; None

370; Hardground, Mary; F; 8/95, 35; Cheyenne; F; M; Yes; Died April 12, 1931; Yes; None

476; Killsnight, Dorothy; F; 2/27, 4; Cheyenne; F; S; Yes; Died Feb. 16, 1931; Yes; None

357; Limpy, Fred Jr.; M; 6/10/29, 1; Cheyenne; 1/4; S; Yes; Died Oct. 15, 1930; Yes; None

601; Littlesun, Frank; M; 10/84, 46; Cheyenne; F; M; Yes; Died Dec. 11, 1930; Yes; None

--- Littlewhiteman, Elmer; M; 10/28/29, 1; Cheyenne; 1/4; S; Yes; Died April 15, 1930; Yes; None

--- Littlewhiteman, Mabel; F; 10/11; Cheyenne; 1/4; S; Yes; Died Aug. 16, 1930; Yes; None

650; Littlewolf, Laura; F; 11/52, 78; Cheyenne; F; Wd; Yes; Died March 27, 1931; Yes; None

1281; Looksbehind, Inez; F; 8/19/29, 1; Cheyenne F; S; Yes; Died April 12, 1930; Yes; None

709; Lostleg, Nelson; M; 7/91, 39; Cheyenne; F; Wd[sic]; Yes; Died June 3, 1930; Yes; None

743; Medicineelk, Harold; M; 7/65, 65; Cheyenne; F; Wd[sic]; Yes; Died Oct. 31, 1931; Yes; None

855; Redfox, Cora; F; 7/67, 63; Cheyenne; F; Wd; Yes; Died April 15, 1930; Yes; None

890; Redwoman, Manuel; M; 7/81, 49; Cheyenne; F; M; Yes; Died Dec. 9, 1930; Yes; None

969; Rowland, Helen; F; 5/68, 62 Cheyenne; F; M; Yes; Died Jan. 15, 1931; Yes; None

980; Russell, May; F; 5/24, 6; Cheyenne; 1/4; S; No; Yes; Chey. & Arap. Okla; Died July 30, 1930; Yes; None

981; Russell, Inez I.; F; 3/27, 4; Cheyenne; 1/4; S; No; Yes; Chey. & Arap. Okla; Died Mar. 5, 1931; Yes; None

982; Russell, John Jr.; M; 3/31/29, 2; Cheyenne; 1/4; S; No; Yes; Chey. & Arap. Okla; Died Mar. 2, 1931; Yes; None

Census of the __Tongue River__ reservation of the __Tongue River__ jurisdiction, as of __April 1__, 1931, taken by __C. B. Lohmiller__, Superintendent.

**Key:** Previous Census Roll Number; NAME: Surname, Given; Sex; Birthdate, Age At Last Birthday; Tribe; Degree of Blood; Marital Status; Relationship To Head of Family; At Jurisdiction Where Enrolled (Yes or No); At Another Jurisdiction (Yes or No); ELSEWHERE: Post office, County, State; Date of Death; Ward (Yes or No); Allotment, Annuity, and Identification Numbers.

1039; Shoulderblade, Pius; M; 5/89, 41; Cheyenne; F; M; Yes; Died Jan. 3, 1931; Yes; None

1044; Shoulderblade, Everett J.; M; 6/23, 7; Cheyenne; 1/4; S; Yes; Died June 17, 1930; Yes; None

1117; Spottedwolf, Della; F; 1/7/30, 1; Cheyenne; F; S; Yes; Died Oct. 6, 1930; Yes; None

1169; Swallow, Percy R.; M; 11/19, 11; Cheyenne; F; S; Yes; Died Aug. 22, 1930; Yes; None

1274; Wanderingmedicine, William; M; 4/69, 62; Cheyenne; F; M; Yes; Died April 25, 1930; Yes; None

1302; Whitebuffalo, Ella; F; 8/67, 63; Cheyenne; F; M; Yes; Died May 11, 1930; Yes; None

1334; Whitewolf, Charles I.; M; 8/90, 40; Cheyenne; F; M; Yes; Died April 11, 1930; Yes; None

1377; Wolfchief, Anna; F; 7/61, 69; Cheyenne; F; M; Yes; Died June 22, 1930; Yes; None

1378; Wolfchief, Richard; M; 4/92, 38; Cheyenne; F; M; Yes; Died Feb. 8, 1931; Yes; None

1399; Wolftooth, Wayne; M; 3/30/28, 2; Cheyenne; F; S; Yes; Died June 1, 1930; Yes; None

586; Woodpecker, Donald C.; M; 7/09, 21; Cheyenne; F; S; Yes; Died Jan. 12. 1931; Yes; None

--- Yellowrobe, Hilda; F; 4/7/30, 9/12; Cheyenne; F; S; Yes; Died Nov. 10, 1930; Yes; None

Census of the __Tongue River__ reservation of the __Tongue River__ jurisdiction, as of __April 1__, 1931, taken by __C. B. Lohmiller__, Superintendent.

**Key:** Present Census Roll Number; NAME: Surname, Given; Sex; Birthdate, Age At Last Birthday; Tribe; Degree of Blood; Marital Status; At Jurisdiction Where Enrolled (Yes or No); Reason for Addition; Ward (Yes or No); Allotment, Annuity, and Identification Numbers.

- - ADDITIONS - -

1391; Wolfblack, Harry; M; 1/16, 5; Cheyenne; F; S; Yes; Erroneously reported dead & dropped on prior roll; Yes; None

11; Americanhorse, Ruth; F; 8/11/25, 5; Cheyenne; F; S; Yes; Not reported on prior rolls; Yes; None

12; Americanhorse, Ella; F; 6/21/27, 3; Cheyenne; S; Yes; Not reported on prior rolls; Yes; None

13; Americanhorse, Esther; F; 3/22/30, 1; Cheyenne; F; S; Yes; Not reported on prior rools[sic]; Yes; None

(All of above are additions to present census roll)

No deductions

CENSUS OF NORTHERN CHEYENNE

-of-

TONGUE RIVER RESERVATION, MONT.

April 1, 1932.

TONGUE RIVER AGENCY,

W. R. Centerwall, Superintendent.

CENSUS ROLL
NORTHERN CHEYENNE INDIANS
TONGUE RIVER AGENCY
TONGUE RIVER RESERVATION
MONTANA
APRIL 1, 1932

Census of the **Tongue River** reservation of the **Tongue River** jurisdiction, as of **April 1**, **1932**, taken by **W. R. Centerwall**, Superintendent.

**Key:** Number; NAME: Surname, Given; Sex; Birthdate, Age At Last Birthday; Tribe; Degree of Blood; Marital Status; Relationship To Head of Family; Last Census Roll Number; At Jurisdiction Where Enrolled (Yes or No); At Another Jurisdiction; ELSEWHERE: Post office, County, State; Ward (Yes or No); Allotment, Annuity, and Identification Numbers.

1; Americanhorse, Austin; M; 10/78, 60; Cheyenne; F; M; Head; 1; Yes; Yes; None [1931 Birthdate 10/71]
2; Americanhorse, Maude; F; 4/82, 49; Cheyenne; F; M; Wife; 2; Yes; Yes; None (Littlechief, Maude) [1931 Birthdate 4/83]
3; Americanhorse, Lucy May; F; 11/10, 21; Cheyenne; F; S; Dau; 3; Yes; Yes; None
4; Americanhorse, George; M; 9/14, 17; Cheyenne; F; S; Son; 4; Yes; Yes; None [Texas]

5; Americanhorse, George; M; 10/81, 50; Cheyenne; F; Wd[sic]; Head; 5; Yes; Yes; None
6; Americanhorse, James; M; 11-11, 19; Cheyenne; M; S; Son; 7; Yes; Yes; None
7; Americanhorse, Marie; F; 6/14, 17; Cheyenne; F; S; Dau; 8; Yes; Yes; None
8; Americanhorse, Lucy; F; 8/18, 13; Cheyenne; F; S; Dau; 9; Yes; Yes; None

9; Americanhorse, Walter; M; 10/15/90, 41; Cheyenne; F; M; Head; 10; No; Chey. & Arap. Agency, Okla.; Yes; None
10; Americanhorse, Ruth; F; 8/11/25, 6; Cheyenne; F; S; Dau; 11; No; Chey. & Arap. Agency, Okla.; Yes; None
11; Americanhorse, Ella; F; 6/21/27, 4; Cheyenne; F; S; Dau; 12; No; Chey. & Arap. Agency, Okla.; Yes; None
12; Americanhorse, Esther; F; 3/22/30, 1; Cheyenne; F; S; Dau; 13; No; Chey. & Arap. Agency, Okla.; Yes; None

13; Americanhorse, Willis; M; 10/92, 39; Cheyenne; F; M; Head; 14; Yes; Yes; None
14; Americanhorse, Margaret (Risingsun, Margaret); F; 8/92, 39; Cheyenne; F; M; Wife; 15; Yes; Yes; None
15; Americanhorse, Ernest; M; 11/11, 20; Cheyenne; F; S; Son; 16; Yes; Yes; None
16; Americanhorse, Martha; F; 6/14, 17; Cheyenne; F; S; Dau; 17; Yes; Yes; None
17; Americanhorse, Madge L.; F; 12/16, 15; Cheyenne; F; S; Dau; 18; Yes; Yes; None
18; Americanhorse, Grace J.; F; 4/18, 13; Cheyenne; F; S; Dau; 19; Yes; Yes; None
19; Twomoons, Austin; M; 2/2/27, 5; Cheyenne; F; S; S-Son; 20; Yes; Yes; None

20; Ant, James; M; 2/03, 28; Cheyenne; F; M; Head; 21; Yes; Yes; None
21; Ant, Hannah (Highwalking, Hannah); F; 5/00, 31; Cheyenne; F; M; Wife; 22; Yes; Yes; None
---; ~~Ant, Bertha; F; 1/1/25, 6; Cheyenne; F; S; Dau; 23; Yes; Yes; None Died September 24, 1931.~~
22; Ant, Thelma; F; 10/18/28, 3; Cheyenne; F; S; 24; Dau; Yes; Yes; None

Census of the __Tongue River__ reservation of the __Tongue River__ jurisdiction, as of __April 1__, 1932, taken by __W. R. Centerwall__, Superintendent.

**Key:** Number; NAME: Surname, Given; Sex; Birthdate, Age At Last Birthday; Tribe; Degree of Blood; Marital Status; Relationship To Head of Family; Last Census Roll Number; At Jurisdiction Where Enrolled (Yes or No); At Another Jurisdiction; ELSEWHERE: Post office, County, State; Ward (Yes or No); Allotment, Annuity, and Identification Numbers.

23; Ant, Francis; M; 7/15/30, 1; Cheyenne; F; S; 25; Son; Yes; Yes; None

24; Ant, Walter; M; 1/80, 52; Cheyenne; F; M; Head; 26; Yes; Yes; None
25; Ant, Helen (Blackwolf, Helen); F; 5/82, 49; Cheyenne; F; M; Wife; 27; Yes; Yes; None
26; Ant, June; F; 1/20, 12; Cheyenne; F; S; Dau; 28; Yes; Yes; None

27; Atwood, James; M; 3/91, 41; Cheyenne; F; M; Head; 29; Yes; Yes; None [Twentystands]
28; Atwood, Cecelia (Yellowfox, Cecelia); F; 1/98, 34; Cheyenne; F; M; Wife; 30; Yes; Yes; None
29; Atwood, Mary; F; 5/14, 17; Cheyenne; F; S; Dau; 31; Yes; Yes; None
30; Atwood, Herbert W.; M; 8/22, 9; Cheyenne; F; S; Son; 32; Yes; Yes; None
31; Atwood, David; M; 8/16/29, 2; Cheyenne; F; S; Son; 33; Yes; Yes; None

32; Baldeagle, Hugh; M; 5/58, 73; Cheyenne; F; M; Head; 34; Yes; Yes; None
33; Baldeagle, Minnie; F; 5/59, 72; Cheyenne; F; M; Wife; 35; Yes; Yes; None [1931 Birthdate 9/59]

34; Bearchum, Frank; M; 3/01, 31; Cheyenne; 3/4; M; Head; 36; Yes; Yes; None [Fullblood in 1931]
35; Bearchum, Anna (Redcherries, Anna); F; 5/10, 21; Cheyenne; F; M; Wife; 38; Yes; Yes; None
36; Bearchum, Wallace; M; 2/4/29, 3; Cheyenne; F; S; S-Son; 38; Yes; Yes; None
37; Bearchum, Frank Jr.; M; 9/26/31, 6/12; Cheyenne; 7/8; S; Son; --; Yes; Yes; None

38; Bearquiver, Edward; M; 9/81, 50; Cheyenne; F; M; Head; 39; Yes; Yes; None
39; Bearquiver, Minnie; F; 12/82, 49; Cheyenne; F; M; Wife; 335; Yes; Yes; None
40; Bearquiver, Claud; M; 11/16, 14; Cheyenne; F; S; Son; 40; Yes; Yes; None [Claude 1931]
41; Bearquiver, James; M; 6/20, 11; Cheyenne; F; S; Son; 41; Yes; Yes; None
42; Bearquiver, Martin F.; M; 8/22, 9; Cheyenne; F; S; Son; 42; Yes; Yes; None [1931 Martin Frank]
43; Fliesabout, June; F; 6/23, 8; Cheyenne; F; S; S-Dau; 336; Yes; Yes; None

44; Bearcomesout, Charles; M; 10/80, 51; Cheyenne; F; M; Head; 43; Yes; Yes; None
45; Bearcomesout, Mary; F; 3/07, 25; Cheyenne; F; M; Wife; 44; Yes; Yes; None
46; Bearcomesout, Harold; M; 3/08, 24; Cheyenne; F; S; Son; 45; Yes; Yes; None
47; Bearcomesout, Pius; M; 9/15, 16; Cheyenne; F; S; Son; 46; Yes; Yes; None
48; Bearcomesout, Herbert; M; 9/12/28, 3; Cheyenne; F; S; Son; 47; Yes; Yes; None

Census of the **Tongue River** reservation of the **Tongue River** jurisdiction, as of **April 1**, **1932**, taken by **W. R. Centerwall**, Superintendent.

**Key:** Number; NAME: Surname, Given; Sex; Birthdate, Age At Last Birthday; Tribe; Degree of Blood; Marital Status; Relationship To Head of Family; Last Census Roll Number; At Jurisdiction Where Enrolled (Yes or No); At Another Jurisdiction; ELSEWHERE: Post office, County, State; Ward (Yes or No); Allotment, Annuity, and Identification Numbers.

49; Beartusk, Jerome; M; 8/85, 46; Cheyenne; F; M; Head; 48; Yes; Yes; None
50; Beartusk, Ida S. (Littleyellowman, Ida); F; 6/98, 33; Cheyenne; F; M; Wife; 49; Yes; Yes; None
51; Beartusk, Alice; F; 4/16, 14; Cheyenne; 9/16; S; Dau; 448; Yes; Yes; None
52; Beartusk, Gladys; F; 1/19, 13; Cheyenne; 9/16; S; Dau; 449; Yes; Yes; None
53; Beartusk, Kenneth; M; 12/20, 11; Cheyenne; 9/16; S; Son; 450; Yes; Yes; None
54; Beartusk, Bertha; F; 3/23, 8; Cheyenne; 9/16; S; Dau; 451; Yes; Yes; None
55: Beartusk, Jerome Jr.; M; 12/23/25, 6; Cheyenne; 9/16; S; Son; 452; Yes; Yes; None

56; Beaverheart, Thomas; M; 5/63, 68; Cheyenne; F; M; Head; 50; Yes; Yes; None
57; Beaverheart, Nellie; F; 3/57, 75; Cheyenne; F; M; Wife; 51; Yes; Yes; None
58; Beaverheart, David; M; 4/90, 42; Cheyenne; F; S; Son; 52; Yes; Yes; None [Name Davis in 1926.]

59; Bement (Burns), Emma; F; 6/01, 30; Cheyenne; 1/8; M; Head; 57; Yes; Yes; None
60; Bement, Jacqueline; F; 10/22, 9; Cheyenne; 1/16; S; Wife[sic]; 58; Yes; Yes; None
61; Bement, Jesse; M; 3/14/25, 7; Cheyenne; 1/16; S; Son; 59; Yes; Yes; None [Joseph in 1925.]
62; Bement, Geraldine; F; 2/1/27, 5; Cheyenne; 1/16; S; Dau; 60; Yes; Yes; None
63; Bement, Celia C.; F; 1/19/28, 4; Cheyenne; 1/16; S; Dau; 61; Yes; Yes; None
64; Bement, Albert R.; M; 4/14/31, 11/12; Cheyenne; 1/16; S; Son; [--]; Yes; Yes; None

65; Bigback, Charles; M; 3/63, 69; Cheyenne; F; M; Head; 62; Yes; Yes; None
66; Bigback, Clara; F; 7/69, 62; Cheyenne; F; M; Wife; 63; Yes; Yes; None
67; Redowl, Mabel; F; 7/46, 85; Cheyenne; F; Wd; Mother-in-law; 64; Yes; Yes; None

68; Bigback, James; M; 8/94, 37; Cheyenne; F; M; Head; 65; Yes; Yes; None
69; Bigback, Jennie (Risingsun, Jennie); F; 5/98, 33; Cheyenne; F; M; Wife; 66; Yes; Yes; None
70; Bigback, Gladys; F; 7/20, 11; Cheyenne; F; S; Dau; 67; Yes; Yes; None
71; Bigback, Robert; M; 12/23, 8; Cheyenne; F; S; Son; 68; Yes; Yes; None
72; Bigback, Marie; F; 9/8/29, 2; Cheyenne; F; S; Dau; 69; Yes; Yes; None

73; Bigback, John; M; 2/04, 28; Cheyenne; F; M; Head; 70; Yes; Yes; None [Henry in 1919.]
74; Bigback, Nina (Standingelk, Nina); F; 6/07, 25; Cheyenne; F; M; Wife; 71; Yes; Yes; None

Census of the **Tongue River** reservation of the **Tongue River** jurisdiction, as of **April 1**, 19**32**, taken by **W. R. Centerwall**, Superintendent.

**Key:** Number; NAME: Surname, Given; Sex; Birthdate, Age At Last Birthday; Tribe; Degree of Blood; Marital Status; Relationship To Head of Family; Last Census Roll Number; At Jurisdiction Where Enrolled (Yes or No); At Another Jurisdiction; ELSEWHERE: Post office, County, State; Ward (Yes or No); Allotment, Annuity, and Identification Numbers.

75; Bigback, Eugene; M; 5/7/30, 1; Cheyenne; F; S; Son; 72; Yes; Yes; None

76; Bigbeaver, August; M; 71; Cheyenne; F; Wd; Head; 73; Yes; Yes; None

77; Bigcrow, Andrew; M; 4/54, 77; Cheyenne; F; M; Head; 74; Yes; Yes; None
78; Bigcrow, Jennie (Redrobe, Jennie); F; 11/88, 43; Cheyenne; F; M; Wife; 75; Yes; Yes; None

79; Bigfoot, Davis; M; 5/98, 32; Cheyenne; F; M; Head; 76; Yes; Yes; None
80; Bigfoot, Lucy (Scabby, Lucy); F; 10/00, 31; Cheyenne; F; M; Wife; 77; Yes; Yes; None
81; Bigfoot, Alice; F; 1/21, 11; Cheyenne; F; S; Dau; 78; Yes; Yes; None [Martha in 1925 & 1926.]
82; Bigfoot, Mary; F; 4/24, 8; Cheyenne; F; S; Dau; 79; Yes; Yes; None
83; Bigfoot, Hoover; M; 6/10/30, 1; Cheyenne; F; S; Son; 80; Yes; Yes; None

84; Bigfoot, John; M; 4-1881, 51; Cheyenne; F; M; Head; 81; No; Cheyenne & Arap. Okla; Yes; None
85; Bigfoot, White; M; 7/2/31, 9/12; Cheyenne; F; S; Son; --; No; Cheyenne & Arap. Okla; Yes; None

86; Bigfoot, White; M; 10/75, 56; Cheyenne; F; M; Head; 82; Yes; Yes; None
87; Bigfoot, Louisa (Sunbear, Louisa); F; 9/85, 46; Cheyenne; F; M; Wife; 83; Yes; Yes; None
88; Bigfoot, Louis Paul; M; 6/11, 20; Cheyenne; F; S; Son; 84; Yes; Yes; None

89; Bigheadman, Benjamin; M; 7/89, 42; Cheyenne; F; M; Head; 85; Yes; Yes; None
90; Bigheadman, Julia (Swallow, Julia); F; 7/94, 37; Cheyenne; F; M; Wife; 86; Yes; Yes; None
91; Bigheadman, Gladys; F; 9/18, 13; Cheyenne; F; S; Dau; 87; Yes; Yes; None [Lucille in 1926]
92; Bigheadman, Laura; F; 7/27/27, 4; Cheyenne; F; S; Dau; 88; Yes; Yes; None
93; Bigheadman, Julia; 3/13/31, 1; Cheyenne; F; S; Dau; 89; Yes; Yes; None

94; Bigheadman, Blair; M; 6/92, 39; Cheyenne; F; M; Head; 90; Yes; Yes; None
95; Bigheadman, Cora[sic] (Oldbull, Clara); F; 4/01, 30; Cheyenne; F; M; Wife; 91; Yes; Yes; None
96; Bigheadman, Wm. Grover; M; 7/19, 12; Cheyenne; F; S; Son; 92; Yes; Yes; None
97; Bigheadman, August; M; 8/22, 8; Cheyenne; F; S; Son; 93; Yes; Yes; None
98; Bigheadman, Julia; F; 12/14, 7; Cheyenne; F; S; Dau; 94; Yes; Yes; None
99; Bigheadman, James; M; 2/24/29, 2; Cheyenne; F; S; Son; 95; Yes; Yes; None

Census of the **Tongue River** reservation of the **Tongue River** jurisdiction, as of **April 1**, 1932, taken by **W. R. Centerwall**, Superintendent.

**Key:** Number; NAME: Surname, Given; Sex; Birthdate, Age At Last Birthday; Tribe; Degree of Blood; Marital Status; Relationship To Head of Family; Last Census Roll Number; At Jurisdiction Where Enrolled (Yes or No); At Another Jurisdiction; ELSEWHERE: Post office, County, State; Ward (Yes or No); Allotment, Annuity, and Identification Numbers.

100; Bigheadman, Esther Stella; F; 3/6/31, 1; Cheyenne; F; S; Dau; 96; Yes; Yes; None

101; Bigheadman, John; M; 6/49, 82; Cheyenne; F; M; Head; 97; Yes; Yes; None
102; Bigheadman, Nellie; F; 78; Cheyenne; F; M; Wife; 98; Yes; Yes; None

103; Bigheadman, William; M; 12/86, 45; Cheyenne; F; M; Head; 99; Yes; Yes; None
104; Bigheadman, Nellie (Yellownose, Nellie); F; 6/91, 40; Cheyenne; F; M; Wife; 100; Yes; Yes; None
105; Bigheadman, Richard; M; 4/09, 22; Cheyenne; F; S; Son; 101; Yes; Yes; None [Richard Rowland]
106; Bigheadman, Grace M.; F; 5/18, 13; Cheyenne; F; S; Dau; 102; Yes; Yes; None
107; Bigheadman, Majorie[sic]; F; 3/25, 7; Cheyenne; F; S; Dau; 103; Yes; Yes; None
108; Bigheadman, Susie D.; F; 6/30/26, 5; Cheyenne; F; S; Dau; 104; Yes; Yes; None
109; Bigheadman, Helen E.; F; 11/16/28, 3; Cheyenne; F; S; Dau; 105; Yes; Yes; None

110; Bigleg, Hinton; M; 5/87, 44; Cheyenne; F; M; Head; 106; Yes; Yes; None
111; Bigleg, Annie (Bixby, Annie); F; 1/79, 53; Cheyenne; 1/4; M; Wife; 107; Yes; Yes; None
112; Rowland, Claude; M; 4/04, 28; Cheyenne; 3/8; S; S-son; 108; Yes; Yes; None
113; Rowland, Benjamin; M; 7/08, 23; Cheyenne; 3/8; S; S-son; 109; Yes; Yes; None

114; Bignose, James; M; 10/63, 68; Cheyenne; F; Wd; Head; 110; Yes; Yes; None
115; Bignose, Samuel; M; 5/91, 40; Cheyenne; F; S; Son; 111; Yes; Yes; None
116; Bignose, George; M; 8/97, 33; Cheyenne; F; S; Son; 112; Yes; Yes; None

Bird, James & family – see under "Woodpecker" (name changed Office authority 12-13-32

117; Bites, James; M; 9/00, 31; Cheyenne; F; M; Head; 113; Yes; Yes; None
118; Bites, Sally (Crazymule, Sally); F; 1/05, 27; Cheyenne; F; M; Wife; 114; Yes; Yes; None
119; Bites, Florence; F; 7/16/26, 5; Cheyenne; F; S; Dau; 115; Yes; Yes; None
120; Bites, James Jr.; M; 5/5/29, 2; Cheyenne; F; S; Son; 116; Yes; Yes; None
121; Bites, Mamie; F; 11/10/31, 4/12; Cheyenne; F; S; Dau; --; Yes; Yes; None

122; Bites, Sally; F; 10/66, 68; Cheyenne; F; Wd; Head; 117; Yes; Yes; None
123; Bites, Clara; F; 5/22, 9; Cheyenne; F; S; G-Dau; 118; Yes; Yes; None

Census of the **Tongue River** reservation of the **Tongue River** jurisdiction, as of **April 1**, 1932, taken by **W. R. Centerwall**, Superintendent.

**Key:** Number; NAME: Surname, Given; Sex; Birthdate, Age At Last Birthday; Tribe; Degree of Blood; Marital Status; Relationship To Head of Family; Last Census Roll Number; At Jurisdiction Where Enrolled (Yes or No); At Another Jurisdiction; ELSEWHERE: Post office, County, State; Ward (Yes or No); Allotment, Annuity, and Identification Numbers.

124; Bites, Herman; M; 5/25, 6; Cheyenne; F; S; G-Son; 119; Yes; Yes; None

125; Bixby, Benjamin; M; 10/87, 44; Cheyenne; 1/4; M; Head; 120; Yes; Yes; None
126; Bixby, Gertrude (Seminole, Gertrude); F; 5/93, 38; Cheyenne; 3/4; M; Wife; 121; Yes; Yes; None [Whitepowder 1904-07; Tallwhiteman 1908; Bixby 1909-1932]
127; Bixby, Annie; F; 9/13, 18; Cheyenne; 1/2; S; Dau; 122; Yes; Yes; None
128; Bixby, James; M; 12/15, 16; Cheyenne; 1/2; S; Son; 123; Yes; Yes; None

129; Bixby, Edward; M; 3/91, 41; Cheyenne; 1/4; M; Head; 124; Yes; Yes; None [1/4+ 1931]
130; Bixby, Edward G.; M; 7/22, 9; Cheyenne; 1/8; S; Son; 125; Yes; Yes; None [1924 Clara, dau; F. 1925-26 Jack.]
131; Bixby, Elsie V.; F; 12/23, 8; Cheyenne; 1/8; S; Dau; 126; Yes; Yes; None [Vianne 1925-26.]
132; Bixby, Wm. L.; M; 3/3/25, 7; Cheyenne; 1/8; S; Son; 127; Yes; Yes; None
133; Bixby, Hattie C.; F; 7/24/28, 3; Cheyenne; 1/8; S; Son[sic]; 128; Yes; Yes; None
134; Bixby, Juanita; F; 5/24/30, 1; Cheyenne; 1/8; S; Dau; 129; Yes; Yes; None
135; Bixby, Loyd James; M; 3/18/32; Cheyenne; 1/8; S; Son; --; Yes; Yes; None

136; Blackbird, Isaac; M; 6/63, 68; Cheyenne; F; Wd[sic]; Head; 130; Yes; Yes; None

137; Blackeagle, William; M; 6/88, 43; Cheyenne; F; Wd[sic]; Head; 131; Yes; Yes; None

138; Blackhorse, Alex; M; 10/97, 34; Cheyenne; F; M; Head; 132; Yes; Yes; None
139; Blackhorse, Mary (Whistlingelk, Mary); F; 6/03, 28; Cheyenne; F; M; Wife; 133; Yes; Yes; None
140; Blackhorse, Francis; M; 7/22, 9 Cheyenne; F; S; Son; 134; Yes; Yes; None [1923-26 name Merton.]
141; Blackhorse, Lafe C.; M; 7/18/29, 2; Cheyenne; F; S; Son; 135; Yes; Yes; None
--   Blackhorse, Ruben Jr.; M; 12/18/31; Cheyenne; F; S; Son; --; Yes; Yes; None

142; Blackhorse, Rueben[sic]; M; 7/53, 78; Cheyenne; F; M; Head; 136; Yes; Yes; None
143; Blackhorse, Lena; F; 12/76, 55; Cheyenne; F; M; Wife; 137; Yes; Yes; None
144; Seminole, Delbert; M; 20; Cheyenne; 7/8; S; G-son; 138; Yes; Yes; None

145; Blackree, Paul; M; 10/78, 53; Cheyenne; F; M; Head; 140; Yes; Yes; None
146; Blackree, Jennie; F; 5/81, 50; Cheyenne; F; M; Wife; 141; Yes; Yes; None
147; Star, May; F; 12/04, 26; Cheyenne; F; M; Dau; 142; Yes; Yes; None

Census of the **Tongue River** reservation of the **Tongue River** jurisdiction, as of **April 1**, 1932, taken by **W. R. Centerwall**, Superintendent.

**Key:** Number; NAME: Surname, Given; Sex; Birthdate, Age At Last Birthday; Tribe; Degree of Blood; Marital Status; Relationship To Head of Family; Last Census Roll Number; At Jurisdiction Where Enrolled (Yes or No); At Another Jurisdiction; ELSEWHERE: Post office, County, State; Ward (Yes or No); Allotment, Annuity, and Identification Numbers.

148; Star, Charles; M; 3/28/27, 5; Cheyenne; F; S; G-Son; 143; Yes; Yes; None
-- ~~Ironshirt, Nora; F; 8/50, 81; Cheyenne; F; Wd; Step-Mother; 144; Yes; Yes; None Died Sept. 27, 1931~~

-- ~~Blackstone, Charles; M; 12/60, 71; Cheyenne; F; Wd[sic]; Head; 145; Yes; Yes; None Died August 18, 1931~~
149; Blackstone, Lena; F; 7/78, 53; Cheyenne; F; S; Step-Dau; 146; Yes; Yes; None [7/8 blood in 1928.]
150; Blackstone, Arthur; M; 12/92, 39; Cheyenne; F; M; Son; 147; Yes; Yes; None
-- ~~Blackstone, Anna (Killsnight); F; 3/11, 20; Cheyenne; F; M; Dau-in-Law; 148; Yes; Yes; None Died January 11, 1932~~
151; Blackstone, Leo; ; 10/22/30, 1; Cheyenne; F; S; G-Son; 149; Yes; Yes; None

152; Blackwolf, Bennie; M; 6/97, 34; Cheyenne; F; M; Head; 150; Yes; Yes; None [1904-1923 name Alex.]
153; Blackwolf, Ella (Walkslast, Ella); F; 12/00, 31; Cheyenne; F; M; Wife; 151; Yes; Yes; None
154; Blackwolf, Henry; M; 10/19, 12; Cheyenne; F; S; Son; 152; Yes; Yes; None [1925 Census Thomas.]
155; Blackwolf, James; M; 8/23, 8; Cheyenne; F; S; Son; 153; Yes; Yes; None
156; Blackwolf, Ruth; F; 1/22/27, 5; Cheyenne; F; S; Dau; 154; Yes; Yes; None

157; Blackwolf, John; M; 8/70, 61; Cheyenne; F; M; Head; 155; Yes; Yes; None
158; Blackwolf, Nellie (Bravewolf, Nellie); F; 7/74, 57; Cheyenne; F; M; Wife; 156; Yes; Yes; None
159; Blackwolf, Alex; M; 5/06, 25; Cheyenne; F; S; Son; 157; Yes; Yes; None
[#156, Name Busby, a brother Alex born 1897 in 1916 census, married in 1917.]
160; Wolfname, Henry; M; 9/12, 19; Cheyenne; F; S; G-Son; 159; Yes; Yes; None
161; Wolfname, Wilbur P.; M; 10/21, 10; Cheyenne; F; S; G-son; 160; Yes; Yes; None

162; Blindman, Arthur; M; 63; Cheyenne; F; Wd[sic]; Head; 161; Yes; Yes; None

163; Bluehawk, Louis; M; 6/1850, 80; Cheyenne; F; Wd[sic]; Head; 162; Yes; Yes; None [1/4+ 1931]

164; Bobtailhorse, Thomas; M; 7/50, 81; Cheyenne; F; Wd[sic]; Head; 163; Yes; Yes; None
-- Bobtailhorse, Gertrude; F; 12/51, 80; Cheyenne; F; M; Wife; 164; Yes; Yes; None ~~Died August 17, 1931~~

165; Boxelder, Laura; F; 1/-72, 60; Cheyenne; F; Wd; Head; 165; No; Shoshone & Arap. Wyo.; Yes; None

Census of the **Tongue River** reservation of the **Tongue River** jurisdiction, as of **April 1**, 1932, taken by **W. R. Centerwall**, Superintendent.

**Key:** Number; NAME: Surname, Given; Sex; Birthdate, Age At Last Birthday; Tribe; Degree of Blood; Marital Status; Relationship To Head of Family; Last Census Roll Number; At Jurisdiction Where Enrolled (Yes or No); At Another Jurisdiction; ELSEWHERE: Post office, County, State; Ward (Yes or No); Allotment, Annuity, and Identification Numbers.

166; Brady, Alex; M; 12/98, 33; Cheyenne; F; M; Head; 166; Yes; Yes; None
167; Brady, Josie (Pine, Josie); F; 12/02, 29; Cheyenne; F; M; Wife; Yes; Yes; None
168; Brady, Charles; M; 11/23, 8; Cheyenne; F; S; Son; 168; Yes; Yes; None
169; Brady, Clifford; M; 10/10/30, 1; Cheyenne; F; S; Son; 169; Yes; Yes; None

170; Brady, Arthur; M; 12/40, 91; Cheyenne; F; M; Head; 170; Yes; Yes; None
171; Brady, Ellen; F; 12/53,78; Cheyenne; F; M; Wife; 171; Yes; Yes; None

172; Brady, George; M; 7/81, 50; Cheyenne; F; M; Head; 172; Yes; Yes; None
173; Brady, Flossie (Bearchum, Flossie); F; 2/97, 35; Cheyenne; 3/4; M; Wife; 173; Yes; Yes; None [1/4+ 1931]
174; Brady, Elmore; M; 3/07, 25; Cheyenne; F; S; Son; 174; Yes; Yes; None
175; Brady, James H.; M; 4/13, 19; Cheyenne; F; S; Son; 175; Yes; Yes; None
176; Brady, Howard; M; 11/15, 16; Cheyenne; F; S; Son; 175; Yes; Yes; None
177; Brady, Ramona; F; 12/17, 14; Cheyenne; F; S; Dau; 177; Yes; Yes; None
178; Brady, Wilson; M; 10/18, 13; Cheyenne; F; S; Son; 178; Yes; Yes; None
179; Brady, Martha; F; 2/21, 11; Cheyenne; 7/8; S; Dau; 179; Yes; Yes; None
180; Brady, Roy; M; 1/25, 7; Cheyenne; 7/8; S; Son; 180; Yes; Yes; None
181; Brady, Pearl; F; 7/14/28, 3; Cheyenne; 7/8; S; Dau; 181; Yes; Yes; None
182; Flying, Pauline; F; 15; Cheyenne; 7/8; S; S-Dau; 182; Yes; Yes; None
[Male, Paul in 1920 #150 under Brady.]

183; Braidedlocks, William; M; 79; Cheyenne; F; Wd[sic]; Head; 183; Yes; Yes; None

N.E. Brein, Frederick; M; [--]; Cree; 1/2; M; Head; --
184; Brein, Margaret (Eastman, Margaret); F; 5/03, 28; Cheyenne; 1/8; M; Wife; 184; Yes; Yes; None
185; Brein, Myron; M; 10/12/29, 2; Cheyenne; 5/16; S; Son; 185; Yes; Yes; None [1/4+ 1931]
186; Brein, Lorraine; F; 1/19/32, 2/12; Cheyenne; 5/16; S; Dau; --; Yes; Yes; None

187; Brownbird, Joseph; M; 9/65, 66; Cheyenne; F; M; Head; 186; Yes; Yes; None
188; Brownbird, Anna (Low Brow, Anna); F; 5/70, 63; Cheyenne; F; M; Wife; 187; Yes; Yes; None

189; Buffalohorn, John; M; 4/62, 70; Cheyenne; F; M; Head; 188; Yes; Yes; None
190; Buffalohorn, Lena (Plentycrows, Lena); F; 5/70, 61; Cheyenne; F; M; Wife; 189; Yes; Yes; None

~~--; Buffalohump, Samuel; M; 7/45, 86; Cheyenne; F; M; Head; 190; Yes; Yes; None Died February 2, 1932.~~
191; Buffalohump, Nora; F; 8/48, 83; Cheyenne; F; M; Wife; 191; Yes; Yes; None

Census of the **Tongue River** reservation of the **Tongue River** jurisdiction, as of **April 1**, 1932, taken by **W. R. Centerwall**, Superintendent.

**Key:** Number; NAME: Surname, Given; Sex; Birthdate, Age At Last Birthday; Tribe; Degree of Blood; Marital Status; Relationship To Head of Family; Last Census Roll Number; At Jurisdiction Where Enrolled (Yes or No); At Another Jurisdiction; ELSEWHERE: Post office, County, State; Ward (Yes or No); Allotment, Annuity, and Identification Numbers.

192; Burns, George; M; 3/95, 37; Cheyenne; -1/4; M; Head; 192; Yes; Yes; None

193; Burns (Harris), Julia; F; 2/72, 60; Cheyenne; 1/4; Wd; Head; 193; Yes; Yes; None [1/4- 1931]

194; Burns, James C.; M; 7/08, 23; Cheyenne; 1/8; S; Son; 194; Yes; Yes; None [-1/4 1931]

195; Burns, Margaret; F; 9/11, 20; Cheyenne; 1/8; S; Dau; 195; Yes; Yes; None [-1/4 1931]

196; Burns, Anna G.; F; 8/13, 18; Cheyenne; 1/8; S; Dau; 196; Yes; Yes; None [-1/4 1931]

197; Bement, Clarence; M; 11/23, 8; Cheyenne; 1/16; S; G-Son; 197; Yes; Yes; None [Max in 1925. Mickie in 1926.] [-1/4 1931]

198 Burns (Harris), Lizzie; F; 1/73, 59; Cheyenne; 1/4; Wd; Head; 198; Yes; Yes; None [-1/4 1931]

199; Burns (Small), Josephine; F; 7/18, 13; Cheyenne; 1/4; S; A-Dau; 199; Yes; Yes; None [Had a Kitty Small in 1925. Adopt-dau., in 1925-26.] [1/4+ 1931]

200; Burns, Robert; M; 9/97, 34; Cheyenne; 1/8; M; Head; 200; Yes; Yes; None [-1/4 1931]

201; Burns, Phyllis R.; G; 3/21/26, 6; Cheyenne; 1/16; S; Dau; 201; Yes; Yes; None [-1/4 1931]

202; Burns, George E.; M; 8/13/29, 2; Cheyenne; 1/16; S; Son; 202; Yes; Yes; None [-1/4 1931]

N.E. Cain, Leslie; M; [--]; Sioux; [--]; M; Head; --
203; Cain, Edith (Spang, Edith); F; 12/09, 21; Cheyenne; 1/8; M; Wife; 203; Yes; Yes; None [-1/4 1931]

204; Callsfirst, Andrew; M; 6/88, 43; Cheyenne; F; M; Head; 204; Yes; Yes; None
205; Callsfirst, Jennie (Seminole, Jennie); F; 7/72, 59; Cheyenne; 3/4; M; Wife; 205; Yes; Yes; None [1/4+ 1931]
206; Woodenleg, Mabel; F; 5; Cheyenne; 3/4; S; Niece; 206; Yes; Yes; None [Full blood 1931]

207; Chasingbear, Willis; M; 3/95, 37; Cheyenne; F; M; Head; 207; Yes; Yes; None
208; Chasingbear, Madge (Redrobe, Madge); F; 4/98, 33; Cheyenne; F; M; Wife; 208; Yes; Yes; None [Powderface]

209; Chubby, John; M; 11/75, 56; Cheyenne; F; M; Head; 209; Yes; Yes; None
210; Chubby, Anne (Redcherries, Anne); F; 12/85, 46; Cheyenne; F; M; Wife; 210; Yes; Yes; None
211; Chubby, Rhoda; F; 1/20, 12; Cheyenne; F; S; Dau; 211; Yes; Yes; None
212; Hairlessbear, Hilda; F; 3/12, 20; Cheyenne; F; S; S-Dau; 212; Yes; Yes; None

Census of the **Tongue River** reservation of the **Tongue River** jurisdiction, as of **April 1**, 1932, taken by **W. R. Centerwall**, Superintendent.

**Key:** Number; NAME: Surname, Given; Sex; Birthdate, Age At Last Birthday; Tribe; Degree of Blood; Marital Status; Relationship To Head of Family; Last Census Roll Number; At Jurisdiction Where Enrolled (Yes or No); At Another Jurisdiction; ELSEWHERE: Post office, County, State; Ward (Yes or No); Allotment, Annuity, and Identification Numbers.

213; Clubfoot, Frank; M; 3/91, 41; Cheyenne; F; M; Head; 213; Yes; Yes; None
214; Clubfoot, Lucy (Oldbull, Lucy); F; 2/93, 39; Cheyenne; F; M; Wife; 214; Yes; Yes; None
215; Clubfoot, James; M; 10/22, 9; Cheyenne; F; S; Son; 215; Yes; Yes; None
216; Clubfoot, Frank Jr.; M; 3/25/27, 5; Cheyenne; F; S; Son; 216; Yes; Yes; None

217; Clubfoot, John; M; 12/60, 71; Cheyenne; F; M; Head; 217; Yes; Yes; None
218; Clubfoot, Minnie; F; 7/70, 61; Cheyenne; F; M; Wife; 218; Yes; Yes; None
219; Clubfoot, Joseph; M; 7/00, 31; Cheyenne; F; S; Son; 219; Yes; Yes; None

220; Clubfoot, Willis; M; 3/91, 40; Cheyenne; F; M; Head; 220; Yes; Yes; None
221; Clubfoot, Stella M. (Weaselbear, Stella); F; 4/95, 36; Cheyenne; F; M; Wife; 221; Yes; Yes; None
222; Clubfoot, Norman; M; 11/16, 15; Cheyenne; F; S; Step-Son; 222; Yes; Yes; None [1917 shows Norman died in 1916. In 1918-23 Census as born 1916 and alive?]
223; Clubfoot, Flossie; F; 12/25, 6; Cheyenne; F; S; Step-Dau; 223; Yes; Yes; None

N.E. Colhoff, William; M; [--]; Sioux; 1/2; M; Head; --; Pine Ridge, S.D.; No
224; Colhoff, Emma (Rowland, Emma); F; 9/94, 37; Cheyenne; 3/4; M; Wife; 224; No; Pine Ridge, S.D.; Yes; None [1/4+ 1931]
225; Colhoff, Maxine; F; 5/16, 15; Cheyenne; 5/8; S; Dau; 225; No; Pine Ridge, S.D.; Yes; None [1/4+ 1931]
226; Colhoff, Edward; M; 5/18, 13; Cheyenne; 5/8; W; Son; 226; No; Pine Ridge, S.D.; Yes; None [1/4+ 1931]
227; Colhoff, Annie G.; F; 3/21, 11; Cheyenne; 5/8; S; Dau; 227; No; Pine Ridge, S.D.; Yes; None [1/4+ 1931]
228; Colhoff, William R.; M; 4/24, 8; Cheyenne; 5/8; S; Son; 228; No; Pine Ridge, S.D.; Yes; None [1/4+ 1931]
229; Colhoff, George; M; 1/29/27, 5; Cheyenne; 5/8; S; Son; 229; No; Pine Ridge, S.D.; Yes; None [1/4+ 1931]

230; Cooley (Spang), Julia; F; 11/91, 40; Cheyenne; 1/8; M; Head; 230; Yes; Yes; None [-1/4 1931]
231; Cooley, Violet; F; 3/14, 18; Cheyenne; 1/16; S; Dau; 231; Yes; Yes; None [-1/4 1931]
232; Cooley, Junior; M; 5/16, 15; Cheyenne; 1/16; S; Son; 232; Yes; Yes; None [-1/4 1931]
233; Cooley, Francis; M; 10/22, 9; Cheyenne; 1/16; S; Son; 233; Yes; Yes; None [-1/4 1931]
234; Cooley, Rachel V.; F; 1/25, 7; Cheyenne; 1/16; S; Dau; 234; Yes; Yes; None [-1/4 1931; Vera 1931]
235; Cooley, Charlotte; F; 2/15/27, 5; Cheyenne; 1/16; S; Dau; --; Yes; Yes; None

Census of the **Tongue River** reservation of the **Tongue River** jurisdiction, as of **April 1**, 1932, taken by **W. R. Centerwall**, Superintendent.

**Key:** Number; NAME: Surname, Given; Sex; Birthdate, Age At Last Birthday; Tribe; Degree of Blood; Marital Status; Relationship To Head of Family; Last Census Roll Number; At Jurisdiction Where Enrolled (Yes or No); At Another Jurisdiction; ELSEWHERE: Post office, County, State; Ward (Yes or No); Allotment, Annuity, and Identification Numbers.

236; Cooley, Odessa M.; F; 11/6/31, 4/12; Cheyenne; 1/16; S; Dau; --; Yes; Yes; None

N.E. Crawford, Francis; M; [--]; Sioux; 1/2; M; Head; --;
237; Crawford, Lillian (Sansaver, Lillian); F; 7/06, 25; Cheyenne; 3/8; F; Wife; 991; Yes; Yes; None
238; Crawford, Lyman E.; M; 4/30/31, 11/12; Cheyenne; 7/16; S; Son; --; Yes; Yes; None

239; Crawling, Charles; M; 8/84, 47; Cheyenne; F; M; Head; 235; Yes; Yes; None
240; Crawling, Flora (Hollowwood, Flora); F; 3/82, 50; Cheyenne; F; M; Wife; 236; Yes; Yes; None
241; Crawling, Martha; F; 1/17, 15; Cheyenne; F; S; Dau; 237; Yes; Yes; None
242; Chasingbear, Laura; F; 5/16, 15; Cheyenne; F; S; S-Dau; 238; Yes; Yes; None
243; Chasingbear, Robert; M; 7/24, 7; Cheyenne; F; S; S-Son; 239; Yes; Yes; None

-- Crazymule, Eva; F; 5/09, 22; Cheyenne; F; S; Head; 240; No; Cheyenne & Arap. Okla. Dropped Auth. L-C 53963-31 10/9/31 on 1930 roll-Other deductions [Wyoming in 1926.]

244; Crazymule, Jennie; F; 2/57, 75; Cheyenne; F; Wd; Head; 241; Yes; Yes; None [Issues]

245; Crazymule, James; M; 11/10, 21; Cheyenne; F; S; Head; 242; Yes; Yes; None
246; Crazymule, Charles R.; M; 11/19, 12; Cheyenne; F; S; Bro.; 243; Yes; Yes; None [Raymond in 1926.]
247; Crazymule, Xavier; M; 11/21, 10; Cheyenne; F; S; Bro.; 244; Yes; Yes; None

248; Crazymule, Joseph; M; 3/81, 51; Cheyenne; F; M; Head; 245; Yes; Yes; None
249; Crazymule, Sarah; F; 7/72, 58; Cheyenne; F; M; Wife; 246; Yes; Yes; None
250; Greasydog, Fannie; F; 6/97, 34; Cheyenne; F; S; S-Dau; 247; Yes; Yes; None

251; Crook, George; M; 1/64, 68; Cheyenne; F; M; Head; 248; Yes; Yes; None
252; Crook, Theresa; F; 11/66, 65; Cheyenne; F; M; Wife; 249; Yes; Yes; None

253; Crook, Rosa; F; 8/65, 66; Cheyenne; F; Wd; Head; 250; Yes; Yes; None
-- Crook, Albert; M; 4/01, 30; Cheyenne; F; S; Son; 251; Yes; [--]; [--] Died March 28, 1932.

254; Crookednose, Nicholas; M; 6/67, 64; Cheyenne; F; M: Head; 252; Yes; Yes; None
255; Crookednose, Susie; F; 9/72, 59; Cheyenne; F; M; Wife; 253; Yes; Yes; None

256; Curley, Thomas; M; 11/89, 42; Cheyenne; F; M; Head; 254; Yes; Yes; None

Census of the **Tongue River** reservation of the **Tongue River** jurisdiction, as of **April 1**, 1932, taken by **W. R. Centerwall**, Superintendent.

**Key:** Number; NAME: Surname, Given; Sex; Birthdate, Age At Last Birthday; Tribe; Degree of Blood; Marital Status; Relationship To Head of Family; Last Census Roll Number; At Jurisdiction Where Enrolled (Yes or No); At Another Jurisdiction; ELSEWHERE: Post office, County, State; Ward (Yes or No); Allotment, Annuity, and Identification Numbers.

257; Curley, Esther (Bullard, Esther); F; 12/95, 36; Cheyenne; F; M; Wife; 255; Yes; Yes; None
258; Curley, Joseph; M; 4/25, 7; Cheyenne; F; S; Son; 256; Yes; Yes; None

259; Dahle (Burns), Adeline; F; 2/99, 33; Cheyenne; 1/8; M; Head; 53; Yes; Yes; None [Beirdneau, Adeline 1931] [-1/4 1931]
260; Beirdneau, Betty B.; F; 4/23, 9; Cheyenne; 1/16; S; Dau; 54; Yes; Yes; None [-1/4 1931]
261; Beirdneau, Barbara M.; F; 4/21/26, 6; Cheyenne; 1/16; S; Dau; 55; Yes; Yes; None [-1/4 1931]
262; Beirdneau, Albert L.; M; 2/16/28, 4; Cheyenne; 1/16; S; Son; 56; Yes; Yes; None [-1/4 1931]

263; Deafy, David; M; 5/98, 33; Cheyenne; F; M; Head; 257; Yes; Yes; None [Americanhorse]
264; Deafy, Anna (Horseroads, Anna); F; 12/95, 36; Cheyenne; F; M; Wife; 258; Yes; Yes; None
265; Deafy, Willis; M; 11/17, 14; Cheyenne; F; S; Son; 259; Yes; Yes; None
266; Deafy, Elsie; F; 7/17/25, 6; Cheyenne; F; S; Dau; 260; Yes; Yes; None
267; Deafy, Irene; F; 7/15/29, 2; Cheyenne; F; S; Dau; 261; Yes; Yes; None

268; Deafy, James; M; 8/70, 61; Cheyenne; F; Wd[sic]; Head; --; Yes; Yes; None

269; Divesbackward, John; M; 1/70, 62; Cheyenne; F; Wd[sic]; Head; 262; Yes; Yes; None [Depending the on census taker they spell Divesbackwards at the end with or without an "s".]
270; Lonebull, Louis; M; 7/58, 80; Cheyenne; F; Wd[sic]; Bro.; 263; Yes; Yes; None

271; Divesbackward, Rufus; M; 2/90, 42; Cheyenne; F; M; Head; 264; Yes; Yes; None
272; Divesbackward, Nancy; F; 3/82, 50; Cheyenne; F; M; Wife; 265; Yes; Yes; None
273; Divesbackward, Sam; M; 4/18, 13; Cheyenne; F; S; Step-Son; 266; Yes; Yes; None
274; Divesbackward, Strane; M; 5/20,11; Cheyenne; F; S; Son; 267; Yes; Yes; None
275; Divesbackward, Grace; F; 2/22/25, 7; Cheyenne; F; S; Dau; 268; Yes; Yes; None
276; Standsout, Sallie; F; 8/47, 84; Cheyenne; F; Wd; Mother; 269; Yes; Yes; None

277; Dog, Louis; M; 5/55, 76; Cheyenne; F; M; Head; 270; Yes; Yes; None
278; Dog, Maude (Blackbear, Maude); F; 3/66, 66; Cheyenne; F; M; Wife; 271; Yes; Yes; None

Census of the __Tongue River__ reservation of the __Tongue River__ jurisdiction, as of __April 1__, 1932, taken by __W. R. Centerwall__, Superintendent.

**Key:** Number; NAME: Surname, Given; Sex; Birthdate, Age At Last Birthday; Tribe; Degree of Blood; Marital Status; Relationship To Head of Family; Last Census Roll Number; At Jurisdiction Where Enrolled (Yes or No); At Another Jurisdiction; ELSEWHERE: Post office, County, State; Ward (Yes or No); Allotment, Annuity, and Identification Numbers.

279; ~~Duster~~, Albert; M; 4/89, 43; Cheyenne; F; M; Head; 272; Yes; Yes; None Monothy changed see letter 4/1/1933
280; Duster, Vinnie (Redfox, Vinnie); F; 9/96, 35; Cheyenne; F; M; Wife; 273; Yes; Yes; None
281; Duster, Annie; F; 12/20, 11; Cheyenne; F; S; Dau; 274; Yes; Yes; None
282; Duster, Bessie; F; 7/12/24, 7; Cheyenne; F; S; Dau; 275; Yes; Yes; None

283; Eaglefeathers, Jacob; M; 9/74, 57; Cheyenne; F; Wd[sic]; Head; 276; Yes; Yes; None
284; Eaglefeathers, Mildred; F; 5/20, 11; Cheyenne; F; S; Dau; 277; Yes; Yes; None

285; Eaglefeathers, Oliver; M; 9/95, 36; Cheyenne; F; M; Head; 278; Yes; Yes; None
286; Eaglefeathers, Julia (Seminole, Julia); F; 6/95, 36; Cheyenne; 3/4; M; Wife; 279; Yes; Yes; None [1/4+ 1931]
287; Eaglefeathers, Simon; M; 3/22, 10; Cheyenne; 7/8; S; Son; 280; Yes; Yes; None [1/4+ 1931]
288; Eaglefeathers, Rosie; F; 7/5/25, 6; Cheyenne; 7/8; S; Dau; 281; Yes; Yes; None [1/4+ 1931]
289; Eaglefeathers, Milton; M; 1/12/29, 3; Cheyenne; 7/8; S; Son; 282; Yes; Yes; None [1/4+ 1931]
290; Littlehead, Rena; F; 11/19, 12; Cheyenne; 7/8; S; S-Dau; 283; Yes; Yes; None [1/4+ 1931] [Mildred in 1926.]

291; Eastman, Charles; M; 2/01, 31; Cheyenne; 1/8; M; Head; 284; No; Crow Agency, Mont. – elsewhere on 1930 Roll; Yes; None [-1/4 1931]
292; Eastman (Bixby), Mary G.; F; 12/76, 55; Cheyenne; 1/4; M; Head; 285; No; Lodgegrass, town, Big Horn, Mont.; Yes; None [1/4+ 1931]
293; Eastman, Robert; M; 3/11, 21; Cheyenne; 1/8; S; Son; 286; No; Lodgegrass, town, Big Horn, Mont.; Yes; None [-1/4 1931]
294; Eastman, Rose; F; 9/15, 16; Cheyenne; 1/8; S; Dau; 287; No; Lodgegrass, town, Big Horn, Mont.; Yes; None [-1/4 1931]
295; Eastman, Louisa; F; 3/18, 13; Cheyenne; 1/8; S; Dau; 288; No; Lodgegrass, town, Big Horn, Mont.; Yes; None [-1/4 1931]
296; Eastman, Myrtle; F; 3/13, 18; Cheyenne; 1/16; S; G-Dau; 289; no; Lodgegrass, town, Big Horn, Mont.; Yes; None [-1/4 1931]

297; Eastman, Perry; M; 11/95, 36; Cheyenne; 1/8; M; Head; 290; Yes; Yes; None [-1/4 1931]
298; Eastman, Mary (Beartusk, Mary); F; 2/93, 39; Cheyenne; F; M; Wife; 291; Yes; Yes; None

Census of the __Tongue River__ reservation of the __Tongue River__ jurisdiction, as of __April 1__, 1932, taken by __W. R. Centerwall__, Superintendent.

**Key:** Number; NAME: Surname, Given; Sex; Birthdate, Age At Last Birthday; Tribe; Degree of Blood; Marital Status; Relationship To Head of Family; Last Census Roll Number; At Jurisdiction Where Enrolled (Yes or No); At Another Jurisdiction; ELSEWHERE: Post office, County, State; Ward (Yes or No); Allotment, Annuity, and Identification Numbers.

299; Beartusk, Edith; F; 4/16, 16; Cheyenne; F; S; Niece; 292; Yes; Yes; None [1/4+ 1931]

300; Elkshoulder, Henry; M; 7/94, 37; Cheyenne; F; M; Head; 293; Yes; Yes; None
301; Elkshoulder, Bessie (Wanderingmed[sic], Bessie); F; 8/93, 38; Cheyenne; F; M; Wife; 294; Yes; Yes; None
302; Elkshoulder, Curtis; M; 2/08, 24; Cheyenne; F; S; Son; 295; Yes; Yes; None
303; Elkshoulder, Lucy; F; 3/17, 15; Cheyenne; F; S; Dau; 296; Yes; Yes; None
304; Elkshoulder, Sylvia; F; 7/22, 9; Cheyenne; F; S; Dau; 297; Yes; Yes; None
305; Elkshoulder, George; M; 12/8/25, 6; Cheyenne; F; S; Son; 298; Yes; Yes; None [Adolph in 1926.]
--- Elkshoulder, Calvin; M; 8/5/28, 3; Cheyenne; F; S; Son; 299; Yes; Yes; None Died December 21, 1931.
306; Elkshoulder, Fred; M; 7/9/31, 9/12; Cheyenne; F; S; Son; --; Yes; Yes; None

307; Elliott, Elizabeth (Harris, Elizabeth); F; 4/06, 25; Cheyenne; 3/8; M; Head; 300; Yes; Yes; None [1/4+ 1931]
308; Elliott, Edwin F.; M; 1/8/28, 4; Cheyenne; 3/16; S; Son; 301; Yes; Yes; None [-1/4 1931]
309; Elliott, Loretta M.; F; 4/13/29, 3; Cheyenne; 3/16; S; Dau; 302; Yes; Yes; None [-1/4 1931]
310; Elliott, Myron L.; M; 11/3/30, 1; Cheyenne; 3/16; S; Son; 303; Yes; Yes; None [-1/4 1931]

311; Eyesyellow, Wilbur; M; 8/68, 63; Cheyenne; F; Wd[sic]; Head; 304; Yes; Yes; None
--; Eyesyellow, Daisy; F; 9/56, 75; Cheyenne; F; M; Wife; 305; Yes; Yes; None Died June 22, 1931

312; Fightingbear, Edgar; M; 10/74, 57; Cheyenne; F; M; Head; 306; Yes; Yes; None
--- Fightingbear, Alice; F; 6/93, 38; Cheyenne; F; M; Wife; 307; Yes; Yes; None Died December 31, 1931
313; Fightingbear, Elmer; M; 4/21, 10; Cheyenne; F; S; Son; 308; Yes; Yes; None
314; Fightingbear, Herbert; M; 11/21/23, 8; Cheyenne; F; S; Son; 309; Yes; Yes; None
-- Fightingbear, Emma; F; 5/19/26, 5; Cheyenne; F; S; Dau; 310; Yes; Yes; None Died November 1928
-- Fightingbear, Francis; M; 11/13/31, 4/12; Cheyenne; F; S; Son; --; Yes; Yes; None Died March 16, 1932

315; Fingers, Otis; M; 10/68, 63; Cheyenne; F; M; Head; 311; Yes; Yes; None
316; Fingers, Nellie (Roundstone, Nellie); F; 6/88, 43; Cheyenne; F; M; Wife; 696; Yes; Yes; None

Census of the **Tongue River** reservation of the **Tongue River** jurisdiction, as of **April 1**, 1932, taken by **W. R. Centerwall**, Superintendent.

**Key:** Number; NAME: Surname, Given; Sex; Birthdate, Age At Last Birthday; Tribe; Degree of Blood; Marital Status; Relationship To Head of Family; Last Census Roll Number; At Jurisdiction Where Enrolled (Yes or No); At Another Jurisdiction; ELSEWHERE: Post office, County, State; Ward (Yes or No); Allotment, Annuity, and Identification Numbers.

317; Fingers, Joseph; M; 8/14, 17; Cheyenne; F; S; Son; 312; Yes; Yes; None [1917 Census Daughter, Josie 1915-20.]
318; Longroach, Harry; M; 1/11, 21; Cheyenne; F S; S-Son; 697; Yes; Yes; None
319; Longroach, James; M; 11/14, 17; Cheyenne; F; S; S-Son; 698; Yes; Yes; None
320; Longroach, Mary; F; 4/17, 15; Cheyenne; F; S; S-Dau; 699; Yes; Yes; None [Name Vita 1917-26.]
321; Longroach, Frank; M; 2/20, 12; Cheyenne; F; S; S-Son; 700; Yes; Yes; None
322; Longroach, Regina; F; 9/23, 8; Cheyenne; F; S; S-Dau; 701; Yes; Yes; None [Veria in 1923.]

323; Firecrow, Peter; M; 4/87, 45; Cheyenne; F; Wd[sic]; Head; 313; Yes; Yes; None
324; Firecrow, Joseph; M; 10/23, 8; Cheyenne; F; S; Son; 314; Yes; Yes; None [Josephine; dau; F., in 1926]

325; Firewolf, John; M; 4/77, 54; Cheyenne; F; M; Head; 315; Yes; Yes; None
326; Firewolf, Josephine; F; 1/75, 57; Cheyenne; F; M; Wife; 316; Yes; Yes; None
327; Tallwhiteman, Agnes; F; 4/24, 7; Cheyenne; F; S; g-Dau; 317; Yes; Yes; None

328; Fisher, Eugene; M; 7/78, 53; Cheyenne; 1/2; M; Head; 318; Yes; Yes; None [+1/4 1931]
329; Fisher, Kitty (Spang, Kitty); F; 4/90, 42; Cheyenne; 1/8; M; Wife; 319; Yes; Yes; None [-1/4 1931]
330; Fisher, Eugene Jr.; M; 12/12, 19; Cheyenne; 5/16; S; Son; 320; Yes; Yes; None
331; Fisher, Langburn; M; 7/15, 16; Cheyenne; 5/16; S; Son; 321; Yes; Yes; None
332; Fisher, James A.; M; 3/17, 15; Cheyenne; 5/16; S; Son; 322; Yes; Yes; None [1917 Census name Ira.]
333; Fisher, Alliwitchie; F; 5/19, 12; Cheyenne; 5/16; S; Dau; 323; Yes; Yes; None [1919 Census name Pearl.]
334; Fisher, Calleaus; M; 5/19, 12; Cheyenne; 5/16; S; Son; 324; Yes; Yes; None [+1/4 1931] [1919 Census name Earl.]
335; Fisher, Russell; M; 11/21, 10; Cheyenne; 5/16; S; Son; 325; Yes; Yes; None [+1/4 1931]
336; Fisher, Helen; F; 3/24, 8; Cheyenne; 5/16; S; Dau; 326; Yes; Yes; None [+1/4 1931]
337; Fisher, Bernidine; M; 12/29/26, 6; Cheyenne; 5/16; S; Son; 327; Yes; Yes; None [+1/4 1931]
338; Fisher, Virginia; F; 12/14/30, 1; Cheyenne; 5/16; S; Dau; 328; Yes; Yes; None [+1/4 1931]

339; Fisher, Henry; M; 8/05, 26; Cheyenne; F; M; Head; 329; Yes; Yes; None
340; Fisher, Lucy (Harris, Lucy); F; 1/08, 24; Cheyenne; 3/8; M; Wife; 320; Yes; Yes; None

Census of the __Tongue River__ reservation of the __Tongue River__ jurisdiction, as of __April 1__, 19**32**, taken by __W. R. Centerwall__, Superintendent.

**Key:** Number; NAME: Surname, Given; Sex; Birthdate, Age At Last Birthday; Tribe; Degree of Blood; Marital Status; Relationship To Head of Family; Last Census Roll Number; At Jurisdiction Where Enrolled (Yes or No); At Another Jurisdiction; ELSEWHERE: Post office, County, State; Ward (Yes or No); Allotment, Annuity, and Identification Numbers.

341; Fisher, Emeline; F; 2/10/31, 1; Cheyenne; 11/16; S; Dau; --; Yes; Yes; None

342; Fisher, John; M; 7/01, 30; Cheyenne; F; M; Head; 331; Yes; Yes; None
343; Fisher, Mary (Playingbear, Mary); F; 2/11, 21; Cheyenne; F; M; Wife; 332; Yes; Yes; None
344; Fisher, Burton; M; 7/27/29, 2; Cheyenne; F; S; Son; 333; Yes; Yes; None
345; Fisher, Floyd; M; 3/30/32; Cheyenne; F; S; Son; --; Yes; Yes; None

346; Fliesabout, William; M; 2/79, 53; Cheyenne; F; D; Head; 334; Yes; Yes; None

347; Flying, Debs; M; 2/86, 46; Cheyenne; F; Wd[sic]; Head; 337; Yes; Yes; None
348; Flying, Frank; M; 10/15, 16; Cheyenne; F; S; Son; 338; Yes; Yes; None
349; Flying, Parker; M; 4/18, 13; Cheyenne; F; S; Son; 339; Yes; Yes; None
350; Flying, Myra; F; 6/67, 64; Cheyenne; F; S; Mother; 340; Yes; Yes; None
351; Killsnight, Ruth; F; 12/16, 15; Cheyenne; F; S; Sister; 341; Yes; Yes; None

352; Flying, Thomas; M; 3/69, 63; Cheyenne; F; Wd[sic]; Head; 342; Yes; Yes; None

353; Fontenelle, Frances; F; 23; Cheyenne; 1/8; M; Head; 343; Yes; Yes; None [-1/4 1931, Sherman]

N.E. Foot, Albert; M; [--]; Sioux; 1/2; Wd[sic]; Head; --
---- Foot, Ruth (Yellownose, Ruth); F; 9/98, 32; Cheyenne; F; M; Wife; 344; Yes; Yes; None  Died July 28, 1931
354; Foot, Edward; M; 4/18, 14; Cheyenne; 5/8; S; Son; 346; Yes; Yes; None [1/4+ 1931]
355; Foot, Bertha; F; 12/19, 12; Cheyenne; 5/8; S; Dau; 347; Yes; Yes; None [1/4+ 1931]
356; Foot, Eva; F; 5/23, 8; Cheyenne; 5/8; S; Dau; 348; Yes; Yes; None [1/4+ 1931]
357; Foot, Sylvia; F; 11/19/28, 3; Cheyenne; 3/4; S; Dau; 349; Yes; Yes; None [1/4+ 1931]
358; Foot, Joseph; M; 4/30/31, 11/12; Cheyenne; 3/4; S; Son; --; No; Ft. Peck Agency, Mont. not on 1930 roll – a birth; Yes; None
359; Hardrobe, Margaret; F; 4/18, 14; Cheyenne; F; S; S-Dau; 350; Yes; Yes; None

360; Ghostbull, Arthur; M; 62; Cheyenne; F; Wd[sic]; Head; 351; Yes; Yes; None

-- Gillispie, George; M; [--]; Sioux; [--]; M; Head; --
361; Gillispie, Mary (Parker, May); F; 5/88, 44; Cheyenne; 1/4; M; Wife; [--]; No; Pine Ridge, S.Dak.; Yes; None [1/4+ 1931]

Census of the **Tongue River** reservation of the **Tongue River** jurisdiction, as of **April 1**, 1932, taken by **W. R. Centerwall**, Superintendent.

**Key:** Number; NAME: Surname, Given; Sex; Birthdate, Age At Last Birthday; Tribe; Degree of Blood; Marital Status; Relationship To Head of Family; Last Census Roll Number; At Jurisdiction Where Enrolled (Yes or No); At Another Jurisdiction; ELSEWHERE: Post office, County, State; Ward (Yes or No); Allotment, Annuity, and Identification Numbers.

362; Grasshopper, Isaac; M; 6/50, 44; Cheyenne; F; Wd[sic]; Head; 354; Yes; Yes; None
363; Grasshopper, Frank; M; 9/06, 25; Cheyenne; F; S; G-Son; 355; Yes; Yes; None [Son of Mrs. Stanley Lamewoman.] [Arthur in 1926.]

364; Gray, Bessie; F; 7/04, 27; Cheyenne; F; D; Head; 356; Yes; Yes; None [1920 #917, name Sandcrane.]
365; Gray, Rose Marie; F; 11/23, 8; Cheyenne; F; S; Dau; 357; Yes; Yes; None
366; Sandcrane, Peter; M; 11/29/28, 3; Cheyenne; F; S; Son; 358; Yes; Yes; None
367; Gray, Joseph; M; 7/11/31, 9/12; Cheyenne; F; S; Son; [--]; Yes; Yes; None

368; Gray, Edward; M; 4/73, 59; Cheyenne; F; M; Head; 359; Yes; Yes; None
369; Gray, Nellie; F; 9/74, 57; Cheyenne; F; M; Wife; 360; Yes; Yes; None
370; Gray, Teddy; M; 8/15, 16; Cheyenne; F; S; Son; 361; Yes; Yes; None

371; Gray, John; M; 8/02, 29; Cheyenne; F; M; Head; 362; Yes; Yes; None
372; Gray, Kate (Wolfname, Kate); F; 3/00, 32; Cheyenne; F; M; Wife; 363; Yes; Yes; None [Ida in 1926.]
373; Gray, Buddy; M; 11/9/30, 1; Cheyenne; F; S; Son; 364; Yes; Yes; None

374; Hairyhand, Henry; M; 10/56, 76; Cheyenne; F; Wd[sic]; Head; 365; Yes; Yes; None
375; Fightingbear, Willie; M; 6/99, 32; Cheyenne; F; S; G-Son; 366; Yes; Yes; None

376; Hardground, Ernest; M; 7/96, 35; Cheyenne; F; M: Head; 367; Yes; Yes; None
377; Hardground, Ethel; F; 2/21, 11; Cheyenne; F; S; Dau; 368; Yes; Yes; None
378; Hardground, Katie; F; 9/23, 8; Cheyenne; F; S; Dau; 369; Yes; Yes; None
379; Hardground, Nancy Susan; F; 1/30, 2; Cheyenne; F; S; Dau; 370; Yes; Yes; None

380; Hardground, George; M; 4/01, 31; Cheyenne; F; M; Head; 371; Yes; Yes; None
381; Hardground, Thomas; M; 4/26/30, 1; Cheyenne; F; S; Son; 372; Yes; Yes; None

382; Hardground, Robert; M; 11/76, 55; Cheyenne; F; M; Head; 373; Yes; Yes; None
383; Hardground, Patty; F; 6/99, 56; Cheyenne; F; M; Wife; 374; Yes; Yes; None
384; Hardground, Albert; M; 6/99, 32; Cheyenne; F; Wd[sic]; Son; 375; Yes; Yes; None
385; Hardground, Lyla; F 2/14, 17; Cheyenne; F; S; Dau; 376; Yes; Yes; None
386; Biglefthand, Rapheal[sic]; M; 2/19, 19; Cheyenne; F; S; S-Son; 377; Yes; Yes; None [1915-#72 was Daisy, female.]

Census of the **Tongue River** reservation of the **Tongue River** jurisdiction, as of **April 1**, 1932, taken by **W. R. Centerwall**, Superintendent.

**Key:** Number; NAME: Surname, Given; Sex; Birthdate, Age At Last Birthday; Tribe; Degree of Blood; Marital Status; Relationship To Head of Family; Last Census Roll Number; At Jurisdiction Where Enrolled (Yes or No); At Another Jurisdiction; ELSEWHERE: Post office, County, State; Ward (Yes or No); Allotment, Annuity, and Identification Numbers.

387; Hardrobe, Colonel; M; 2/56, 76; Cheyenne; F; Wd[sic]; Head; 378; Yes; Yes; None
388; Hardrobe, Albert; M; 7/96, 35; Cheyenne; F; S; Son; 379; Yes; Yes; None

389; Harris, Bryan; M; 4/98, 33; Cheyenne; 1/4; M; Head; 380; Yes; Yes; None [1/4+ 1931]
390; Harris, Ruth (Medicinebird, Ruth); F; 12/07, 25; Cheyenne; F; M; Wife; 381; Yes; Yes; None [Spottedhawk]
391; Harris, Carl; M; 10/21, 10; Cheyenne; 5/8; S; Son; 382; Yes; Yes; None [1/4+ 1931]
392; Harris, Francis E.; M; 9/1/29, 2; Cheyenne; 5/8; S; Son; 383; Yes; Yes; None [Elmer F. in 1930] [1/4+ 1931]
393; Harris, Chester; M; 2/25/31, 1; Cheyenne; 5/8; S; Son; 384; Yes; Yes; None [1/4+ 1931]
-- Harris, Sallie; F; 9/50, 81; Cheyenne; 1/2; Wd; Mother; 385; Yes; Yes; None Died February 23, 1932

394; Harris, Edward; M; 1/24/87, 45; Cheyenne; 1/4; M; Head; 386; Yes; Yes; None [1/4+ 1931]
395; Harris, Bessie (Standingelk, Bessie); F; 5/89, 42; Cheyenne; F; M; Wife; 387; Yes; Yes; None
396; Harris, Nellie; F; 5/14, 17; Cheyenne; 5/8; S; Dau; 388; Yes; Yes; None [1/4+ 1931]
397; Harris, Dorothy; F; 5/19, 12; Cheyenne; 5/8; S; Dau; 390; Yes; Yes; None [1/4+ 1931]
398; Harris, Hubert; M; 1/22, 10; Cheyenne; 5/8; S; Son; 391; Yes; Yes; None [Lawrence Edw. in 1926] [1/4+ 1931]
399; Harris, Inez R.; F 12/9/27, 4; Cheyenne; 5/8; S; Dau; 392; Yes; Yes; None [1/4+ 1931]
400; Beckman, May; F; 5/11, 20; Cheyenne; 5/8; M; Dau; 388; Yes; Yes; None [1/4+ 1931]
401; Beckman, Eugene V.; M; 12/29/31, 3/12; Cheyenne; 5/16; S; G-Son; --; Yes; Yes; None

402; Harris, George; M; 9/07, 24; Cheyenne; 3/8; Wd[sic]; Head; 393; Yes; Yes; None
--- Harris, Anna (Blackhorse, Anna); F; 7/13, 18; Cheyenne; F; M; Wife; 394; Yes; Yes; None Died December 10, 1931

403; Harris, William; M; 1/77, 55; Cheyenne; 1/4; M; Head; 395; Yes; Yes; None [1/4+ 1931]
404; Harris, Margaret (Twentystands, Margaret); F; 5/84, 47; Cheyenne; 1/2; M; Wife; 396; Yes; Yes; None [1/4+ 1931]

Census of the **Tongue River** reservation of the **Tongue River** jurisdiction, as of **April 1**, 19**32**, taken by **W. R. Centerwall**, Superintendent.

**Key:** Number; NAME: Surname, Given; Sex; Birthdate, Age At Last Birthday; Tribe; Degree of Blood; Marital Status; Relationship To Head of Family; Last Census Roll Number; At Jurisdiction Where Enrolled (Yes or No); At Another Jurisdiction; ELSEWHERE: Post office, County, State; Ward (Yes or No); Allotment, Annuity, and Identification Numbers.

405; Harris, Julia; F; 12/10, 21; Cheyenne; 3/8; S; Dau; 397; Yes; Yes; None [1/4+ 1931]
406; Harris, Agnes; F; 9/12, 19; Cheyenne; 3/8; S; Dau; 398; Yes; Yes; None [1/4+ 1931]
407; Harris, Raymond; M; 4/15, 17; Cheyenne; 3/8; S; Son; 399; Yes; Yes; None [1/4+ 1931]
408; Harris, Mary; F; 4/19, 13; Cheyenne; 3/8; S; Dau; 400; Yes; Yes; None [1920 name Leota.] [1/4+ 1931]
409; Harris, Florence; F; 9/23, 8; Cheyenne; 3/8; S; Dau; 401; Yes; Yes; None [1925 son Joseph, M.] [1/4+ 1931]

410; Hart, Charles; M; 5/80, 51; Cheyenne; F; M; Head; 402; Yes; Yes; None
411; Hart, Louisa (Harris, Louisa); F; 9/85, 46; Cheyenne; 1/4; M; Wife; 403; Yes; Yes; None [1/4+ 1931]
412; Hart, Eva; F; 12/13, 18; Cheyenne; 5/8; S; Dau; 404; Yes; Yes; None [1/4+ 1931]
413; Hart, Jessie; F; 4/17, 15; Cheyenne; 5/8; S; Dau; 405; Yes; Yes; None [1/4+ 1931]
414; Akin, Mattie L.; F; 7/11, 20; Cheyenne; 5/8; M; Dau; 406; Yes; Yes; None [1/4+ 1931]
415; Akin, Vernon H.; M; 6/28/31, 9/12; Cheyenne; 5/16; S; G-Son; --; Yes; Yes; None

416; Hart, Frank; M; 7/98, 43; Cheyenne; 7/8; M; Head; 407; Yes; Yes; None [1/4+ 1931]
417; Hart, Alice (Hairlessbear, Alice); F; 5/07, 24; Cheyenne; F; M; Wife; 408; Yes; Yes; None
418; Hart, Edna; F; 11/16/27, 4; Cheyenne; 15/16; S; Dau; 409; Yes; Yes; None [1/4+ 1931]
419; Hart, Hilda; F; 8/29/30, 1; Cheyenne; 15/16; S; Dau; 410; Yes; Yes; None [1/4+ 1931]

N.E. Hawk, Nelson; M; [--]; Cheyenne[sic]; F; M; Head; --;
420; Hawk, Hannah (Seminole, Hannah); F; 11/12, 19; Cheyenne; 7/8; M; Wife; 139; Yes; Yes; None [1/4+ 1931]

421; Headswift, Charles; M; 3/67, 54; Cheyenne; F; Wd[sic]; Head; 411; Yes; Yes; None
422; Headswift, Frank; M; 6/11, 20; Cheyenne; F; S; Son; 412; Yes; Yes; None

423; Highbear, William; M; 3/88, 44; Cheyenne; F; M; Head; 413; Yes; Yes; None
424; Highbear, Minnie (Blindman, Minnie); F; 5/97, 34; Cheyenne; F; M; Wife; 414; Yes; Yes; None

Census of the **Tongue River** reservation of the **Tongue River** jurisdiction, as of **April 1**, 1932, taken by **W. R. Centerwall**, Superintendent.

Key: Number; NAME: Surname, Given; Sex; Birthdate, Age At Last Birthday; Tribe; Degree of Blood; Marital Status; Relationship To Head of Family; Last Census Roll Number; At Jurisdiction Where Enrolled (Yes or No); At Another Jurisdiction; ELSEWHERE: Post office, County, State; Ward (Yes or No); Allotment, Annuity, and Identification Numbers.

425; Highwalking, Floyd; M; 4/88, 43; Cheyenne; F; M; Head; 415; Yes; Yes; None
426; Highwalking, Belle (Teeth, Belle); F; 6/93, 38; Cheyenne; F; M; Wife; 416; Yes; Yes; None
427; Highwalking, George; M; 3/13, 29; Cheyenne; F; S; Son; 417; Yes; Yes; None [David in 1926.]
428; Highwalking, Max; M; 1/17, 15; Cheynne[sic]; F; S; Son; 418; Yes; Yes; None
429; Highwalking, Nellie; F; 4/59, 73; Cheyenne; F; Wd; Mother; 419; Yes; Yes; None

430; Hisbadhorse, Willis; M; 8/98, 34; Cheyenne; F; M; Head; 420; Yes; Yes; None
431; Hisbadhorse, Ernest; M; 5/17, 14; Cheyenne; F; S; Son; 421; Yes; Yes; None [1924 s-son. Eugene in 1926.]
432; Hisbadhorse, Medaris; M; 8/21, 10; Cheyenne; F; S; Son; 422; Yes; Yes; None [Bird; son; 1917; in 1926.]
433; Hisbadhorse, Fannie; F; 10/22, 8; Cheyenne; F; S; Dau; 423; Yes; Yes; None [Josephine in 1926.]
434; Hisbadhorse, Esther; F; 8/19/30, 1; Cheyenne; F; S; Dau; 425; Yes; Yes; None
435; Hisbadhorse, Rhoda; F; 6/56, 75; Cheyenne; F; S; Mother; 426; Yes; Yes; None
436; Rowland, Carrie; F; 11/26, 5; Cheyenne; 7/8; S; S-Dau; 424; Yes; Yes; None [1/4- 1931]

437; Hollowbreast, Hubert; M; 5/75, 56; Cheyenne; F; M; Head; 428; Yes; Yes; None
438; Hollowbreast, Mary (Bites, Mary); F; 4/96, 36; Cheyenne; F; M; Wife; 429; Yes; Yes; None [Previous censuses name Hattie Hisbadhorses. 1926 Hisbadhorses, wdw. #426.]
439; Hollowbreast, Donald; M; 5/17, 14; Cheyenne; F; S; Son; 430; Yes; Yes; None
440; Hollowbreast, Jack R.; M; 10/25, 7; Cheyenne; F; S; Son; 431; Yes; Yes; None [Jack Richard 1931]
441; Hollowbreast, Edward; M; 4/7/29, 3; Cheyenne; F; S; Son; 432; Yes; Yes; None
442; Hollowbreast, Fern; F; 9/1/31, 7/12; Cheyenne; F; S; Dau; --; Yes; Yes; None

443; Hollowbreast, William; M; 3/1900, 31; Cheyenne; F; M; Head; 433; Yes; Yes; None
444; Hollowbreast, Mary (Littlewolf, Mary); F; 11/03, 28; Cheyenne; F; M; Wife; 434; Yes; Yes; None

445; Hollowwood, Richard; M; 7/56, 75; Cheyenne; F; M; Head; 435; Yes; Yes; None

Census of the __Tongue River__ reservation of the __Tongue River__ jurisdiction, as of __April 1__, 1932, taken by __W. R. Centerwall__, Superintendent.

**Key:** Number; NAME: Surname, Given; Sex; Birthdate, Age At Last Birthday; Tribe; Degree of Blood; Marital Status; Relationship To Head of Family; Last Census Roll Number; At Jurisdiction Where Enrolled (Yes or No); At Another Jurisdiction; ELSEWHERE: Post office, County, State; Ward (Yes or No); Allotment, Annuity, and Identification Numbers.

446; Hollowwood, Hattie C.; F; 8/56, 75; Cheyenne; F; M; Wife; 436; Yes; Yes; None

N.E. Horn, Miles; M; [--]; Arickaree; F; M; Head; --
447; Horn, Anna (Chubby, Anna); F; 5/90, 31; Cheyenne; F; M; Wife; 437; Yes; Yes; None  [1931 Horn, Annie W.]  [Name Alice 1904-20.]
448; Horn, Rose; F; 6/21, 10; Cheyenne; F; S; Dau; 438; Yes; Yes; None
449; Horn, Wilena; F; 3/23, 9; Cheyenne; F; S; Dau; 439; Yes; Yes; None
450; Horn, Margaret; F; 7/18/26, 5; Cheyenne; F; S; Dau; 440; Yes; Yes; None
451; Horn, Celia M.; F; 5/7/28, 3; Cheyenne; F; S; Dau; 441; Yes; Yes; None
452; Horn, Denver S.; M; 12/13/30, 1; Cheyenne; F; S; Son; 442; Yes; Yes; None

453; Horseroads, Thomas; M; 9/78, 53; Cheyenne; F; M; Head; 443; Yes; Yes; None
454; Horseroads, Lucy (Shortsioux, Lucy); F; 8/87, 44; Cheyenne; F; M; Wife; 444; Yes; Yes; None
455; Horseroads, Ida; F; 1/24, 8; Cheyenne; F; S; Dau; 445; Yes; Yes; None
456; Horseroads, Cora; F; 11/26/26, 5; Cheyenne; F; S; Dau; 446; Yes; Yes; None

457; Howe, Lucy (Eastman, Lucy); F; 1/93, 41; Cheyenne; 1/8; M; Head; 447; No; Crow Agency, Mont.; not on 1930 roll  [-1/4 1931]

458; Howlingantelope, Albert; M; 4/74, 58; Cheyenne; F; M; Head; 453; Yes; Yes; None
459; Howlingantelope, Eva (Redbird, Eva); F; 5/80, 47; Cheyenne; F; M; Wife; 454; Yes; Yes; None
460; Fasthorse, Clara; F; 5/13, 18; Cheyenne; F; S; G-Dau; 455; Yes; Yes; None
461; Redbird, Ellen; F; 12/15/25, 6; Cheyenne; F; S; A-Dau; --; Yes; Yes; None

N.E. ~~Huff, Patrick; M; [--]; Sioux; 1/2; M; Head; [--]~~
462; Huff, Pearl (Eastman, Pearl); F; 6/07, 24; Cheyenne; 1/8; M; Wife; 456; No; Lodgegrass, town, Big Horn, Mont.; Yes; None  [-1/4 1931]
463; Huff, Elsie; F; 10/23/27, 4; Cheyenne; 5/16; S; Dau; 457; No; Lodgegrass, town, Big Horn, Mont.; Yes; None  [1/4+ 1931]
464; Huff, Percy; M; 8/29, 3; Cheyenne; 5/16; S; Son; 458; No; Lodgegrass, town, Big Horn, Mont.; Yes; None  [1/4+ 1931]

465; Ironhand, Henry; M; 6/10, 21; Cheyenne; F; M; Head; 359; Yes; Yes; None
466; Ironhand, Mamie (Littlewolf, Mamie); F; 7/12, 20; Cheyenne; F; M; Wife; 360; Yes; Yes; None
467; Ironhand, Rufus Grant; M; 2/19/32, 1/12; Cheyenne; F; S; Son; --; Yes; Yes; None

468; Ironhand, William; M; 11/82, 49; Cheyenne; F; M; Head; 461; Yes; Yes; None

Census of the **Tongue River** reservation of the **Tongue River** jurisdiction, as of **April 1**, 1932, taken by **W. R. Centerwall**, Superintendent.

Key: Number; NAME: Surname, Given; Sex; Birthdate, Age At Last Birthday; Tribe; Degree of Blood; Marital Status; Relationship To Head of Family; Last Census Roll Number; At Jurisdiction Where Enrolled (Yes or No); At Another Jurisdiction; ELSEWHERE: Post office, County, State; Ward (Yes or No); Allotment, Annuity, and Identification Numbers.

469; Ironhand, Sally (Lamewoman, Sally); F; 7/84, 47; Cheyenne; F; M; Wife; 462; Yes; Yes; None
470; Ironhand, Willis; M; 1/15, 17; Cheyenne; F; S; Son; 463; Yes; Yes; None
471; Ironhand, Jane; F; 2/21/27, 5; Cheyenne; F; S; Dau; 464; Yes; Yes; None

472; Issues, Francis; M; 3/97, 35; Cheyenne; F; M; Head; 465; Yes; Yes; None
473; Issues, Mamie (Limpy, Mamie); F; 12/07, 24; Cheyenne; 3/4; M; Wife; 466; Yes; Yes; None [1/4+ 1931]
474; Issues, Ira; M; 2/28/20, 12; Cheyenne; F; S; Son; 467; Yes; Yes; None [1919 name Ira, 1920-23, George.]
475; Issues, Irene; F; 5/21, 10; Cheyenne; F; S; Dau; 468; Yes; Yes; None

476; Issues, John; M; 1863, 68; Cheyenne; F; M; Head; 469; Yes; Yes; None
477; Issues, Clara; F; 3/70, 62; Cheyenne; F; M; Wife; 470; Yes; Yes; None [Blackmedicine; 1904-17, she becomes Issues 1915]

478; Killsback, James; M; 7/63; Cheyenne; F; M; Head; 471; Yes; Yes; None [Census #461, name Joseph Killsacross in 1926.]
479; Killsback, Amelia; F; 12/78, 53; Cheyenne; F; M; Wife; 472; Yes; Yes; None

480; Killsnight, Charles; M; 6/90, 41; Cheyenne; F; M; Head; 473; Yes; Yes; None
481; Killsnight, Rose (Blackmedicine, Rose); F; 12/90, 41; Cheyenne; F; M; Wife; 474; Yes; Yes; None
482; Killsnight, Rose; F; 4/15, 16; Cheyenne; F; S; Dau; 475; Yes; Yes; None
483; Killsnight, Hubert; M; 2/19, 12; Cheyenne; F; S; Son; 476; Yes; Yes; None [Brighton in 1926.]
484; Lonewolf, James; M; 7/15, 16; Cheyenne; F; S; S-Son; 477; Yes; Yes; None
485; Lonewolf, Ella; F; 5/10/25, 6; Cheyenne; F; S; S-Dau; 478; Yes; Yes; None

486; Killsnight, Hugh; M; 8/66, 64; Cheyenne; F; M; Head; 479; Yes; Yes; None
487; Killsnight, Clara; F; 9/72, 59; Cheyenne; F; M; Wife; 480; Yes; Yes; None

488; Killsnight, Martin; M; 1/07, 25; Cheyenne; F; M; Head; 481; Yes; Yes; None
489; Killsnight, Flossie A. (Redwoman, Flossie); F; 20; Cheyenne; F; M; Wife; 888; Yes; Yes; None

490; Killsnight, Rose; F; 2/99, 33; Cheyenne; F; D; Head; 483; Yes; Yes; None
491; Killsnight, Margaret; F; 2/24, 8; Cheyenne; F; S; Dau; 484; Yes; Yes; None
492; Killsnight, Jennie; F; 3/12/29, 3; Cheyenne; F; S; Dau; 485; Yes; Yes; None

493; Killsnight, William; M; 4/56, 76; Cheyenne; F; M; Head; 486; Yes; Yes; None
494; Killsnight, Cora; F; 6/60, 71; Cheyenne; F; M; Wife; 487; Yes; Yes; None
495; Killsnight, William Jr.; M; 10/04, 27; Cheyenne; F; S; G-Son; 488; Yes; Yes; None

Census of the **Tongue River** reservation of the **Tongue River** jurisdiction, as of **April 1**, 1932, taken by **W. R. Centerwall**, Superintendent.

**Key:** Number; NAME: Surname, Given; Sex; Birthdate, Age At Last Birthday; Tribe; Degree of Blood; Marital Status; Relationship To Head of Family; Last Census Roll Number; At Jurisdiction Where Enrolled (Yes or No); At Another Jurisdiction; ELSEWHERE: Post office, County, State; Ward (Yes or No); Allotment, Annuity, and Identification Numbers.

496; Killsnight, Cole; M; 2/05, 27; Cheyenne; F; M; Son; 489; Yes; Yes; None
497; Killsnight, Mabel (Lonetravelingwolf, Mabel); F; 6/10, 21; Cheyenne; F; M; Dau-in-Law; 490; Yes; Yes; None

498; Killsnight, Willis; M; 3/95, 37; Cheyenne; F; M; Head; 491; Yes; Yes; None [Rutherford in 1926.]
499; Killsnight, Carrie (Redrobe, Carrie); F; 5/90, 41; Cheyenne; F; M; Wife; 492; Yes; Yes; None [Whitemoon]
500; Killsnight, Mary Flossie; F; 2/23, 9; Cheyenne; F; S; Dau; 493; Yes; Yes; None [Sage in 1926.]
501; Killsnight, James; M; 4/2/26, 6; Cheyenne; F; S; Son; 494; Yes; Yes; None
502; Killsnight, Ralph; M; 4/7/28, 4; Cheyenne; F; S; Son; 495; Yes; Yes; None

503; Killsnightwoman; F; 8/58, 72; Cheyenne; F; Wd; Head; 496; Yes; Yes; None

504; Killsontop, John; M; 8/06, 25; Cheyenne; F; M; Head; 497; Yes; Yes; None
505; Killsontop, Mary (Strangeowl, Mary); F; 2/09, 23; Cheyenne; F; M; Wife; 498; Yes; Yes; None
506; Killsnight[sic], June; F; 4/1/27, 5; Cheyenne; F; S; Dau; 499; Yes; Yes; None [Last name should be Killsontop]
507; Killsnight[sic], Levern; M; 1/1/29, 3; Cheyenne; F; S; Son; 500; Yes; Yes; None [Last name should be Killsontop]
508; Killsnight[sic], Harold; M; 6/21/31, 1; Cheyenne; F; S; Son; 501; Yes; Yes; None [Last name should be Killsontop]
509; Killsnight[sic], Paul; M; 3/4/32, 27 da.; Cheyenne; F; S; Son; [--]; Yes; Yes; None [Last name should be Killsontop]

510; King, Ernest; M; 12/89, 42; Cheyenne; 1/2; M; Head; 766; Yes; Yes; None [Mexicancheyenne, Ernest 1931; 1/4- 1931] [King in 1930]
511; King, Mary (Issues, Mary); F; 7/99, 32; Cheyenne; F; M; Wife; 767; Yes; Yes; None [Mexicancheyenne, Mary 1931] [King in 1930]
512; King, Harriet; F; 6/19, 13; Cheyenne; 3/4; S; Dau; 768; Yes; Yes; None [Mexicancheyenne, Harriet 1931; 1/4- 1931] [King in 1930; 1/4+] [Hilda in 1928.]
513; King, M. Victoria; F; 8/21, 10; Cheyenne; 3/4; S; Dau; 769; Yes; Yes; None [Mexicancheyenne, M. Victoria 1931; 1/4- 1931] [King in 1930; 1/4+]
514; King, Rudolph; M; 2/25, 7; Cheyenne; 3/4; S; Son; 770; Yes; Yes; None [Mexicancheyenne, Rudolph 1931, 1/4-] [King in 1930; 1/4+] [Anabelle; dau; 1925.]
515; King, Anna Joyce; F; 8/15/28, 3; Cheyenne; 3/4; S; Dau; 771; Yes; Yes; None [Mexicancheyenne, Anna Joyce 1931, 1/4- 1931] [King in 1930; 1/4+]
516; King, Stephen; M; 3/8/32, 23 da.; Cheyenne; 3/4; S; Son; --; Yes; Yes; None

517; King, Marion; M; 7/87, 44; Cheyenne; 1/2; M; Head; 772; Yes; Yes; None [Mexicancheyenne, Marion 1931, 1/4- 1931] [King 1930; 1/4+ 1930]

Census of the **Tongue River** reservation of the **Tongue River** jurisdiction, as of **April 1**, 1932, taken by **W. R. Centerwall**, Superintendent.

**Key:** Number; NAME: Surname, Given; Sex; Birthdate, Age At Last Birthday; Tribe; Degree of Blood; Marital Status; Relationship To Head of Family; Last Census Roll Number; At Jurisdiction Where Enrolled (Yes or No); At Another Jurisdiction; ELSEWHERE: Post office, County, State; Ward (Yes or No); Allotment, Annuity, and Identification Numbers.

518; King, Emma (Rollingbull, Emma); F; 6/93, 38; Cheyenne; F; M; Wife; 773; Yes; Yes; None [Mexicancheyenne, Emma 1931] [King in 1930]
519; King, James; M; 6/8/14, 17; Cheyenne; 3/4; S; Son; 774; Yes; Yes; None [Mexicancheyenne, James 1931; 1/4- 1931] [King in 1930; 1/4- 1930]
520; King, Rosa; F; 11/18, 13; Cheyenne; 3/4; S; Dau; 775; Yes; Yes; None [Mexicancheyenne, Rosa; 1/4- 1931] [King in 1930; 1/4+ 1930]
521; King, Margaret; F; 12/20, 11; Cheyenne; 3/4; S; Dau; 776; Yes; Yes; None [Mexicancheyenne, Margaret 1931; 1/4- 1931] [King in 1930, 1/4+ 1930] [Ethel in 1926]
522; King, Mary; F; 76/25, 6; Cheyenne; 3/4; S; Dau; 777; Yes; Yes; None [Mexicancheyenne, Mary 1931; 1/4+ 1931]
523; King, Mabel Ann; F; 2/2/28, 4; Cheyenne; 3/4; S; Dau; 778; Yes; Yes; None [Mexicancheyenne, Mabel Ann 1931; 1/4+ 1931]

524; Kingfisher, Carrie; F; 8/76, 55; Cheyenne; F; Wd; Head; 502; Yes; Yes; None

525; Kingfisher, James W.; M; 9/96, 35; Cheyenne; F; M; Head; 503; Yes; Yes; None [Kingfisher, Willis J. 1931]
526; Kingfisher, Minnie (Twobirds, Minnie); F; 7/96, 35; Cheyenne; F; M; Wife; 504; Yes; Yes; None
527; Kingfisher, Isabelle; F; 9/18, 13; Cheyenne; F; S; Dau; 505; Yes; Yes; None
528; Kingfisher, Charles; M; 6/21, 10; Cheyenne; F; S; Son; 506; Yes; Yes; None
529; Kingfisher, Louise; F; 10/22, 9; Cheyenne; F; S; Dau; 507; Yes; Yes; None
530; Kingfisher, Ellen; F; 6/17/26, 5; Cheyenne; F; S; Dau; 508; Yes; Yes; None
531; Kingfisher, Angela; F; 5/23/28, 2; Cheyenne; F; S; Dau; 509; Yes; Yes; None
532; Kingfisher, Elizabeth; F; 8/1/30, 8/12; Cheyenne; F; S; Dau; xxx; Yes; Yes; None

533; Kinzel (Harris), Alice; F; 3/93, 39; Cheyenne; 1/4; M; Head; 510; Yes; Yes; None [Kinsel 1931; 1/4- 1931]
534; Kinzel, Emma L.; F; 6/17, 14; Cheyenne; 1/8; S; Dau; 511; Yes; Yes; None [Kinsel 1931; -1/4 1931]
535; Kinzel, Helen L.; F; 3/20, 12; Cheyenne; 1/8; S; Dau; 512; Yes; Yes; None [Kinsel 1931; -1/4 1931]
536; Kinzel, Celia L.; F; 7/23/24, 7; Cheyenne; 1/8; S; Dau; 513; Yes; Yes; None [Kinsel 1931; -1/4 1931]
537; Kinzel; Virgil B.; M 10/9/27, 4; Cheyenne; 1/8; S; Son; 514; Yes; Yes; None [Kinsel 1931; -1/4 1931]
---- Kinzel, [--]; M; 6/26/31; Cheyenne; 1/8; S; Son; --; Stillbirth

N.E. Knows-his-gun, Hector; M; [--]; Crow; F; M; Head;
538; Knows-his-gun, Frances (Twobirds, Frances); F; 10/04, 27; Cheyenne; F; M; Wife; 515; Yes; Yes; None

Census of the **Tongue River** reservation of the **Tongue River** jurisdiction, as of **April 1**, 1932, taken by **W. R. Centerwall**, Superintendent.

**Key:** Number; NAME: Surname, Given; Sex; Birthdate, Age At Last Birthday; Tribe; Degree of Blood; Marital Status; Relationship To Head of Family; Last Census Roll Number; At Jurisdiction Where Enrolled (Yes or No); At Another Jurisdiction; ELSEWHERE: Post office, County, State; Ward (Yes or No); Allotment, Annuity, and Identification Numbers.

539; Knows-his-gun, Sylvester; M; 9/26, 5; Cheyenne; F; S; Son; 516; Yes; Yes; None
540; Knows-his-gun, Edith; F; 5/11/28, 3; Cheyenne; F; S; Dau; 517; Yes; Yes; None
---- Knows-his-gun, Genevieve; F; 7/13/30, 1; Cheyenne; F; S; Dau; ---; Yes; Yes; None  Died May 14, 1931
541; Knows-his-gun, Hector Jr.; M; 3/5/32, 26 da.; Cheyenne; F; S; Son; ---; Yes; Yes; None

542; LaFever, Rena (Eastman, Rena); F; 8/96, 35; Cheyenne; 1/8; M; Head; 518; No; Lodgegrass, town, Big Horn, Mont.; Yes; None
543; Bolson, Frank; M; 8/17, 14; Cheyenne; 1/16; S; Son; 519; No; Lodgegrass, town, Big Horn, Mont.; Yes; None
544; Bolson, Roy; M; 12/19, 12; Cheyenne; 1/16; S; Son; 520; No; Lodgegrass, town, Big Horn, Mont.; Yes; None
545; LaFever, Kenneth; M; 12/25, 6; Cheyenne; 1/16; S Son; 521; No; Lodgegrass, town, Big Horn, Mont.; Yes; None

546; Lamebear, Benjamin; M; 7/94, 37; Cheyenne; F; M; Head; 522; Yes; Yes; None
547; Lamebear, Clara (Standingelk, Clara); F; 5/94, 37; Cheyenne; F; M; Wife; 523; Yes; Yes; None
548; Lamebear, Eva; F; 11/10, 21; Cheyenne; F; S; Dau; 524; Yes; Yes; None
549; Lamebear, Cora; F; 4/19, 13; Cheyenne; F; S; Dau; 525; Yes; Yes; None
550; Lamebear, Charles; M; 10/21, 10; Cheyenne; F; S; Son; 526; Yes; Yes; None
551; Lamebear, Susie; F; 2/12/30, 2; Cheyenne; F; S; Dau; 527; Yes; Yes; None
--- Lamebear, Ethel; F; 9/20/31; Cheyenne; F; S; Dau; 528; Yes; Yes; None Died September 20, 1931

552; Lamewoman, Alice; F; 7/10, 21; Cheyenne; 3/4; D; Head 530; Yes; Yes; None [1/4+ 1931] [Rowland; 7/8 [Birth year 1912 in 1926.]
---- Lamewoman, Ruth; F; 10/15/30, 2; Cheyenne; 7/8; S; Dau; 531; Yes; Yes; None  Died March 7, 1932.

553; Lamewoman, Sam; M; 10/12, 19; Cheyenne; F; M; Head; 528; Yes; Yes; None [Sam Littlebear; 1928]
554; Lamewoman, Maude (Risingsun, Maude); F; 6/13, 18; Cheyenne; F; M; Wife; 529; Yes; Yes; None
555; Lamewoman, Sam Jr.; M; 5/14/31, 10/12; Cheyenne; F; S; Son; [--]; Yes; Yes; None

556; Lamewoman, Stanley; M; 8/89, 42; Cheyenne; F; M; Head; 532; Yes; Yes; None

Census of the **Tongue River** reservation of the **Tongue River** jurisdiction, as of **April 1**, 1932, taken by **W. R. Centerwall**, Superintendent.

**Key:** Number; NAME: Surname, Given; Sex; Birthdate, Age At Last Birthday; Tribe; Degree of Blood; Marital Status; Relationship To Head of Family; Last Census Roll Number; At Jurisdiction Where Enrolled (Yes or No); At Another Jurisdiction; ELSEWHERE: Post office, County, State; Ward (Yes or No); Allotment, Annuity, and Identification Numbers.

557; Lamewoman, Augusta; F; 7/85, 46; Cheyenne; F; M; Wife; 533; Yes; Yes; None
558; Lamewoman, Jessie; F; 6/14. 17; Cheyenne; F; S; Dau; 534; Yes; Yes; None
559; Lamewoman, Virgil; M; 2/22, 9; Cheyenne; F; S; Dau[sic]; 535; Yes; Yes; None
560; Lamewoman, Nellie; F; 7/54, 77; Cheyenne; F; Wd; Mother; 536; Yes; Yes; None

561; Lastbull, Fred; M; 1/88, 43; Cheyenne; F; M; Head; 537; Yes; Yes; None

562; Lennon (Burns), Mary; F; 6/06, 25; Cheyenne; 1/8; M; Head; 538; No; Columbine-town, Natrone[sic], WYO.; Yes; None
563; Lennon, Arthur G.; M; 11/26, 5; Cheyenne; 1/16; S; Son; 539; No; Columbine-town, Natrone[sic], WYO.; Yes; None

564; Lightning, Frank; M; 8/71, 60; Cheyenne; F; wd[sic]; Head; 540; Yes; Yes; None

565; Limberhand, Elmore; M; 1/09, 22; Cheyenne; F; M; Head; 544; yes;
566; Limberhand, Bessie (Americanhorse, Bessie); F; 24; Cheyenne; F; M; Wife; 6; Yes; Yes; None [Birthdate 11-05, 25 in 1931]

567; Limberhand, Nathan; M; 3/76, 55; Cheyenne F; M; Head; 541; Yes; Yes; None
568; Limberhand, Artie (Wolfchief, Artie); F; 45; Cheyenne; F; M; Wife; 542; Yes; Yes; None
569; Limberhand, James; M; 10/02, 29; Cheyenne; F; S; Son; 543; Yes; Yes; None
570; Limberhand, Bennie; M; 1/12, 21; Cheyenne; F; S; Son; 545; Yes; Yes; None
571; Limberhand, Doris; F; 5/22, 9; Cheyenne; F; S; Dau; 546; Yes; Yes; None
572; Limpy, Henry; M; 9/19, 11; Cheyenne; 3/4; S; G-Son; 547; Yes; Yes; None

573; Limberhand, Richard; M; 8/05, 26; Cheyenne; F; M; Head; 548; Yes; Yes; None
574; Limberhand, Jessie (Rockroads, Jessie); F; 10/05, 25; Cheyenne; F; M; Wife; 549; Yes; Yes; None
575; Limberhand, Doris; F; 10/15/28, 4; Cheyenne; F; S; Dau; 550; Yes; Yes; None
---   Limberhand, George; M; 3/23/31, 1; Cheyenne; F; S; Son; ---; Yes; Yes; None Died October 23, 1931.

576; Limpy, Benjamin; M; 10/92, 39; Cheyenne; F; M; Head; 551; Yes; Yes; None
577; Limpy, Hattie (Killsback, Hattie); F; 6/94, 37; Cheyenne; F; M; Wife; 552; Yes; Yes; None [#540; Hallie Killsacross #271, 1914 census. 1915-16 Hallie Limpy.]

Census of the **Tongue River** reservation of the **Tongue River** jurisdiction, as of **April 1**, 1932, taken by **W. R. Centerwall**, Superintendent.

**Key:** Number; NAME: Surname, Given; Sex; Birthdate, Age At Last Birthday; Tribe; Degree of Blood; Marital Status; Relationship To Head of Family; Last Census Roll Number; At Jurisdiction Where Enrolled (Yes or No); At Another Jurisdiction; ELSEWHERE: Post office, County, State; Ward (Yes or No); Allotment, Annuity, and Identification Numbers.

578; Limpy, Anna; F; 1/15, 17; Cheyenne; F; S; Dau; 553; Yes; Yes; None [Son, Jack 1916-19; Jean in 1926.]
579; Limpy, Rosa; F; 8/19, 12; Cheyenne; F; S; Dau; 554; Yes; Yes; None [#530 Elnora in 1926.]
580; Limpy, Jessie; F; 11/22, 9; Cheyenne; F; S; Dau; 555; Yes; Yes; None [Name Bessie 1930]
581; Limpy, Eunice; F; 9/23/27, 4; Cheyenne; F; S; Dau; 556; Yes; Yes; None
582; Dullknife, Bessie; F; 3/70, 82; Cheyenne; F; Wd; Mother-in-law; 557; Yes; Yes; None

583; Limpy, Charles; M; 10/57, 74; Cheyenne; F; M; Head; 558; Yes; Yes; None
584; Limpy, Nellie (Blackbear, Nellie); F; 7/54, 76; Cheyenne; F; M; Wife; 559; Yes; Yes; None

585; Limpy, Fred; M; 4/84, 48; Cheyenne; 1/2; M; Head; 560; Yes; Yes; None [1/4+ 1931]
--- Limpy, Amelia (Blackwhetstone, Amelia); F; 5/85, 46; Cheyenne; F; M; Wife; 561; Yes; Yes; None Died April 20, 1931 [Womanleggins]
586; Limpy, Frank; M; 5/11, 21; Cheyenne; 3/4; S; Son; 562; Yes; Yes; None [1/4+ 1931]
587; Limpy, Mary; F; 5/13, 18; Cheyenne; 3/4; S; Dau; 563; Yes; Yes; None [#506, Limpy, Mary; D.; 6 Mo; in 1909. May Limpy 1926.] [1/4+ 1931]
588; Limpy, Cora Eva; F; 11/8/25, 6; Cheyenne; 3/4; S; Dau; 564; Yes; Yes; None [1/4+ 1931]

589; Littlebear, Paul; M; 7/87, 44; Cheyenne; F; M; Head; 565; Yes; Yes; None
590; Littlebear, Rose; F; 887, 44; Cheyenne; F; M; Wife; 566; Yes; Yes; None
591; Littlebear, Flossie; F; 4/12, 21; Cheyenne; F; S; Dau; 567; Yes; Yes; None [Mary in 1926.]
592; Littlebear, Clara; F; 4/16, 16; Cheyenne; F; S; Dau; 568; Yes; Yes; None
593; Littlebear, Peter T.; M; 12/23, 7; Cheyenne; F; S; Son; 569; Yes; Yes; None
594; Littlebear, Lucille; F; 7/14/26, 5; Cheyenne; F; S; Dau; 570; Yes; Yes; None
595; Littlebear, Lester; M; 9/16/29, 2; Cheyenne; F; S; Son; 571; Yes; Yes; None
596; Americanhorse, Albert M.; M; 7/12, 19; Cheyenne; F; M; Son-in-Law; 427; Yes; Yes; None
597; Americanhorse, Mae; F; 5/08, 23; Cheyenne; F; M; Dau; 572; Yes; Yes; None
598; Littlebear, Lenora C.; 12/2/28, 3; Cheyenne; F; S; G-Dau; 573; Yes; Yes; None
---- Littlebear, (Unnamed); F; 11/27/31; Cheyenne; F; S; G-Dau; ---; Yes; Yes; None Died November 27, 1931.

599; Littlebird, Peter; M; 5/70, 62; Cheyenne; F; M; Head; 574; Yes; Yes; None
600; Littlebird, Jennie (Brownbird, Jennie); F; 7/92, 39; Cheyenne; F; M; Wife; 575; Yes; Yes; None

Census of the **Tongue River** reservation of the **Tongue River** jurisdiction, as of **April 1**, 1932, taken by **W. R. Centerwall**, Superintendent.

**Key:** Number; NAME: Surname, Given; Sex; Birthdate, Age At Last Birthday; Tribe; Degree of Blood; Marital Status; Relationship To Head of Family; Last Census Roll Number; At Jurisdiction Where Enrolled (Yes or No); At Another Jurisdiction; ELSEWHERE: Post office, County, State; Ward (Yes or No); Allotment, Annuity, and Identification Numbers.

602; Littlebird, Joseph; M; 9/12, 19; Cheyenne; F; S; Son; 576; Yes; Yes; None
603; Littlebird, James Wm.; M; 6/25/25, 6; Cheyenne; F; S; Son; 578; Yes; Yes; None
604; Littlebird, Theresa; F; 12/8/29, 2; Cheyenne; F; S; Dau; 579; Yes; Yes; None

605; Littlechief, Victor; M; 1/77, 55; Cheyenne; F; M; Head; 580; Yes; Yes; None
606; Littlechief, Louisa (Deafy, Louisa); F; 3/75, 57; Cheyenne; F; M; Wife; 581; Yes; Yes; None

607; Littlecoyote, Henry; M; 9/76, 56; Cheyenne; F; M; Head; 582; Yes; Yes; None
608; Littlecoyote, Julia (Howlingwolf, Julia); F; 4/76, 55; Cheyenne; F; M; Wife; 583; Yes; Yes; None [Littlecoyote, Julia P. 1931]
609; Littlecoyote, Daniel E.; M; 10/10, 21; Cheyenne; F; S; Son; 584; Yes; Yes; None
610; Whitefrog, Nellie; F; 5/16, 70; Cheyenne; F; S; S-Mother; 585; Yes; Yes; None

611; Littleeagle, Charles; M; 5/67, 64; Cheyenne; F; M; Head; 586; Yes; Yes; None
612; Littleeagle, Mary; F; 6/78, 54; Cheyenne; F; M; Wife; 587; Yes; Yes; None

613; Littlehawk, Dora; F; 1/69, 62; Cheyenne; F; Wd; Head; 589; Yes; Yes; None
614; Medicineelk, Jennie; F; 9/04, 27; Cheyenne; F; M; Niece; 590; Yes; Yes; None [Eaglefeathers]
615; Medicineelk, Sarah A.; F; 4/20/28, 4; Cheyenne; F; S; Niece[sic]; 591; Yes; Yes; None [G-Niece 1931]

616; Littlehead, Charles; M; 6/69, 62; Cheyenne; F; M; Head; Yes; Yes; None
617; Littlehead, Nellie (Sioux, Nellie); F; 12/82, 49; Cheyenne; F; M; Wife; 593; Yes; Yes; None
618; Littlehead, Frank; M; 11/09, 22; Cheyenne; F; S; Son; 594; Yes; Yes; None
619; Littlehead, George; M; 5/20, 11; Cheyenne; F; S; Son; 595; Yes; Yes; None [1920 name John.]

620; Littlehead, John; M; 10/94, 37; Cheyenne; F; M; Head; 599; No; Cheyenne & Arap., Okla.; Yes; Yes; None

621; Littlemouth, John; M; 10/94, 37; Cheyenne; F; M; Head; 600; Yes; Yes; None
622; Littlemouth, Jennie (Littlehead, Jennie); F; 9/98, 33; Cheyenne; F; M; Wife; 601; Yes; Yes; None
623; Littlemouth, Evelyn; F; 5/21, 10; Cheyenne; F; S; Dau; 602; Yes; Yes; None
624; Littlemouth, James; M; 6/22, 9; Cheyenne; F; S; Son; 603; Yes; Yes; None
625; Littlemouth, Mary; F; 4/24, 8; Cheyenne; F; S; Dau; 604; Yes; Yes; None
626; Littlemouth, Clara; F; 7/59, 72; Cheyenne; F; Wd; Mother; 605; Yes; Yes; None

Census of the **Tongue River** reservation of the **Tongue River** jurisdiction, as of **April 1**, 1932, taken by **W. R. Centerwall**, Superintendent.

Key: Number; NAME: Surname, Given; Sex; Birthdate, Age At Last Birthday; Tribe; Degree of Blood; Marital Status; Relationship To Head of Family; Last Census Roll Number; At Jurisdiction Where Enrolled (Yes or No); At Another Jurisdiction; ELSEWHERE: Post office, County, State; Ward (Yes or No); Allotment, Annuity, and Identification Numbers.

--- Littlemouth, Fred; M; 1/27/31, 9/12; Cheyenne; F; S; Son; ---; Yes; Yes; None Died October 12, 1931.

--- Littlesun, Samuel; M; 7/58, 73; Cheyenne; F; M; Head; 606; Yes; Yes; None Died May 17, 1931
--- Littlesun, Cora; F; 9/64, 66; Cheyenne; F; M; Wife; 607; Yes; Yes; None Died Dec. 21, 1931
627; Littlesun, Jack; M; 8/20, 11; Cheyenne; F; S; G-Son; 608; Yes; Yes; None
628; Littlesun, Horace; M; 9/22, 9; Cheyenne; F; S; G-Son; 609; Yes; Yes; None

629; Littlewhirlwind, George; M; 1/01, 31; Cheyenne; F; M; Head; 610; Yes; Yes; None
630; Littlewhirlwind, Martha (Whirlwind, Martha); F; 10/09, 22; Cheyenne; F; M; Wife; 611; Yes; Yes; None [Fannie Walksalong in 1926.]
631; Littlewhirlwind, Anna; F; 11/30/28, 3; Cheyenne; F; S; Dau; 612; Yes; Yes; None
632; Littlewhirlwind, Levi; M; 9/6/31, 6/12; Cheyenne; F; S; Son; ---; Yes; Yes; None

--- Littlewhiteman, Aaron; M; 1/57, 74; Cheyenne; 1/2; M; Head; 613; Yes; Yes; None Died December 13, 1931. [1/4+ 1931]
633; Whiteman, Sadie (Low Brow, Sadie); F; 4/62, 69; Cheyenne; F; M; Wife; 614; Yes; Yes; None
634; Whiteman, Wesley; M; 8/97, 33; Cheyenne; 3/4; S; Son; 615; Yes; Yes; None [1/4+ 1931]
635; Powderface, Julia; F; 8/13, 18; Cheyenne; F; S; G-Dau; 616; Yes; Yes; None [1/4+ 1931]
    Family Name changed to Whiteman  Letter May 5, 1933

--- Littlewhiteman, David; M; 2/69, 63; Cheyenne; 1/2; M; Head; 617; Yes; Yes; None Died October 15, 1931. [1/4+ 1931]
636; Littlewhiteman, Agnes (Twomoon, Agnes); F; 7/72, 59; Cheyenne; F; M; Wife; 618; Yes; Yes; None
637; Littlewhiteman, Peter; M; 4/06, 26; Cheyenne; 3/4; S; Son; 619; Yes; Yes; None [Mixed 1931]

638; Littlewhiteman, Frank; M; 11/01, 30; Cheyenne; 3/4; M; Head; 620; Yes; Yes; None [1/4+ 1931]
639; Littlewhiteman, Emma (Lightning, Emma); F; 10/00, 31; Cheyenne; F; M; Wife; 621; Yes; Yes; None [#964 in 1919 shows as Lightning, Emma; g dt; 1901; F. Grandparents Shortsioux in census as birth year 1901 starting in 1912 or 11 years old.]
640; Littlewhiteman, Leon; M; 8/20, 11; Cheyenne; 7/8; S; Son; 622; Yes; Yes; None [1/4+ 1931]

Census of the **Tongue River** reservation of the **Tongue River** jurisdiction, as of **April 1**, **1932**, taken by **W. R. Centerwall**, Superintendent.

**Key:** Number; NAME: Surname, Given; Sex; Birthdate, Age At Last Birthday; Tribe; Degree of Blood; Marital Status; Relationship To Head of Family; Last Census Roll Number; At Jurisdiction Where Enrolled (Yes or No); At Another Jurisdiction; ELSEWHERE: Post office, County, State; Ward (Yes or No); Allotment, Annuity, and Identification Numbers.

641; Littlewhiteman, Margaret; F; 7/22, 9; Cheyenne; 7/8; S; Dau; 623; Yes; Yes; None [1/4+ 1931]
642; Littlewhiteman, John; M; 10/6/25, 6; Cheyenne; 7/8; S; Son; 624; Yes; Yes; None [1/4+ 1931]
643; Littlewhiteman, Philip; M; 3/29/27, 5; Cheyenne; 7/8; S; Son; 625; Yes; Yes; None [1/4+ 1931]

644; Littlewhiteman, Henry; M; 1/91, 41; Cheyenne; 3/4; M; Head; 626; Yes; Yes; None [1/4+ 1931]
645; Littlewhiteman, Mary (Taylor, Mary); F; 5/90, 41; Cheyenne; F; M; Wife; 627; Yes; Yes; None [Littlewhiteman, Mary R. 1931]
646; Littlewhiteman, Edith; F; 12/12, 19; Cheyenne; 7/8; S; Dau; 628; Yes; Yes; None [1/4+ 1931]
647; Littlewhiteman, Rose; F; 9/15, 17; Cheyenne; 7/8; S; Dau; 629; Yes; Yes; None [1/4+ 1931]
648; Littlewhiteman, Agnes; F; 10/21, 10; Cheyenne; 7/8; S; Dau; 630; Yes; Yes; None [1/4+ 1931]
649; Littlewhiteman, Clara; F; 3/24/32, 7 das; Cheyenne; 7/8; S; Dau; ---; Yes; Yes; None
650; Romannose, Eva L.; F; 7/26/28, 3; Cheyenne; F; S; S-Dau; 631; Yes; Yes; None

651; Littlewhiteman, James; M; 6/95, 36; Cheyenne; 3/4; M; Head; 632; Yes; Yes; None [1/4+ 1931]
652; Littlewhiteman, Gusta (Littlesun, Gusta); F; 9/97, 34; Cheyenne; F; M; Wife; 633; Yes; Yes; None
653; Littlewhiteman, Kitty; F; 9/23, 8; Cheyenne; 7/8; S; Dau; 634; Yes; Yes; None [1/4+ 1931]
654; Littlewhiteman, Winn; M; 11/28, 4; Cheyenne; 7/8; S; Son; 635; Yes; Yes; None [1/4+ 1931]
655; Littlewhiteman, Mona F.; F; 3/31/30, 2; Cheyenne; 7/8; S; Dau; 636; Yes; Yes; None [1/4+ 1931]

656; Littlewhiteman, Milton; M; 9/84, 47; Cheyenne; 3/4; M; Head; 637; Yes; Yes; None [1/4+ 1931]
657; Littlewhiteman, Rose (Bearcoal, Rose); F; 9/82, 49; Cheyenne; F; M; Wife; 638; Yes; Yes; None
658; Yellowhorse, Julia; F; 5/13, 18; Cheyenne; F; S; S-Dau; 639; Yes; Yes; None
659; Spang, Norman; M; 9/20/27, 4; Cheyenne; F; S; G-Son; 1097; Yes; Yes; None

660; Littlewhiteman, Stanley; M; 7/88, 43; Cheyenne; 3/4; M; Head; 640; Yes; Yes; None [1/4+ 1931] [Penitentiary 1931]
661; Littlewhiteman, Grace (Walkingbear, Grace); F; 1894, 38; Cheyenne; F; M; Wife; 641; Yes; Yes; None

Census of the __Tongue River__ reservation of the __Tongue River__ jurisdiction, as of __April 1__, 1932, taken by __W. R. Centerwall__, Superintendent.

**Key:** Number; NAME: Surname, Given; Sex; Birthdate, Age At Last Birthday; Tribe; Degree of Blood; Marital Status; Relationship To Head of Family; Last Census Roll Number; At Jurisdiction Where Enrolled (Yes or No); At Another Jurisdiction; ELSEWHERE: Post office, County, State; Ward (Yes or No); Allotment, Annuity, and Identification Numbers.

662; Littlewhiteman, Milton; M; 12/25/12, 19; Cheyenne; 7/8; S; Son; 642; Yes; Yes; None [1/4+ 1931]
663; Littlewhiteman, Aaron; M; 12/21, 10; Cheyenne; 7/8; S; Son; 643; Yes; Yes; None [1/4+ 1931]
664; Littlewhiteman, Adrain; M; 12/23, 7; Cheyenne; 7/8; S; Son; 644; Yes; Yes; None [1/4+ 1931] [Name Hillman in 1926.]
665; Littlewhiteman, Sadie; F; 1/23/27, 5; Cheyenne; 7/8; S; Dau; 645; Yes; Yes; None [1/4+ 1931]
666; Littlewhiteman, Willis Warren; M; 8/9/28, 3; Cheyenne; 7/8; S; Son; 646; Yes; Yes; None [1/4+ 1931]
667; Littlewhiteman, Richard; M; 5/3/31, 11/12; Cheyenne; 7/8; S; Son; xxx; Yes; Yes; None;

668; Littlewolf, Frank; M; 2/77, 55; Cheyenne; F; M; Head; 647; Yes; Yes; None
669; Littlewolf, Kate (Redsleeves, Kate); F; 3/83, 49; Cheyenne; F; M; Wife; 648; Yes; Yes; None
670; Littlewolf, Susan; F; 6/14, 17; Cheyenne; F; S; Dau; 639; Yes; Yes; None
671; Littlewolf, Anna Mary; F; 2/22, 10; Cheyenne; F; S; Dau; 650; Yes; Yes; None

672; Littlewolf, Lena; F; 12/78, 52; Cheyenne; F; S; Head; 651; Yes; Yes; None

673; Littlewolf, Robert; M; 6/82, 49; Cheyenne; F; M; Head; 652; Yes; Yes; None
674; Littlewolf, May (Onebear, May); F; 6/94, 37; Cheyenne; F; M; Wife; 653; Yes; Yes; None [Name Harris in 1920.]
675; Littlewolf, Charles; M; 7/08, 23; Cheyenne; F; S; Son; 654; Yes; Yes; None
676; Littlewolf, Esther G.; F; 12/21, 10; Cheyenne; F; S; Dau; 655; Yes; Yes; None
677; Littlewolf, Eva; F; 4/5/25, 3; Cheyenne; F; S; Dau; 656; Yes; Yes; None
678; Littlewolf, Laban; M; 6/4/28, 3; Cheyenne; F; S; Son; 657; Yes; Yes; None
679; Littlewolf, Herbert; M; 3/19/30, 2; Cheyenne; F; S; Son; 658; Yes; Yes; None

680; Littlewolf, William; M; 8/83, 48; Cheyenne; F; M; Head; 659; Yes; Yes; None
681; Littlewolf, May (Womanleggins, May); F; 12/90, 41; Cheyenne; F; M; Wife; 660; Yes; Yes; None
682; Littlewolf, William Jr.; M; 10/14, 17; Cheyenne; F; S; Son; 661; Yes; Yes; None
683; Littlewolf, Claude; M; 12/16, 15; Cheyenne; F; S; Son; 662; Yes; Yes; None

684; Littleyellowman, Eddie; M; 1892, 40; Cheyenne; F; M; Head; 663; No; Cheyenne & Arap., Okla.; Yes; None
685; Littleyellowman, Susie; F; 1/4/22, 11; Cheyenne; F; S; Dau; 664; No.; Cheyenne & Arap., Okla.; Yes; None
--- Littleyellowman, Rose; F; 3/23/24, 8; Cheyenne; F; S; Dau; 665; No; Cheyenne & Arap., Okla.; Yes; None Died August 7, 1930

Census of the __Tongue River__ reservation of the __Tongue River__ jurisdiction, as of __April 1__, 19__32__, taken by __W. R. Centerwall__, Superintendent.

**Key:** Number; NAME: Surname, Given; Sex; Birthdate, Age At Last Birthday; Tribe; Degree of Blood; Marital Status; Relationship To Head of Family; Last Census Roll Number; At Jurisdiction Where Enrolled (Yes or No); At Another Jurisdiction; ELSEWHERE: Post office, County, State; Ward (Yes or No); Allotment, Annuity, and Identification Numbers.

686; Littleyellowman, Hugh E.; M; 6/19/31, 10/12; Cheyenne; F; S; Son; ---; No; Cheyenne & Arap., Okla.; Yes; None

687; Littleyellowman, Hugh; M; 1885, 47; Cheyenne; F; M; Head; 666; No; Cheyenne & Arap., Okla.; Yes; None
688; Littleyellowman, May; F; 1916, 15; Cheyenne; F; S; Dau; 667; No; Cheyenne & Arap., Okla.; Yes; None

689; Littleyellowman, Jake; M; 10/61, 50; Cheyenne; F; M; Head; 668; Yes; Yes; None
---   Littleyellowman, Lena (Oldbull, Lena); F; 5/76, 55; Cheyenne; F; M; Wife; 669; Yes; Yes; None   Died November 15, 1931.
690; Fisher, Alice; F; 8/98, 33; Cheyenne; F; S; Step-Dau; 670; Yes; Yes; None
691; Fisher, Isabelle; F; 6/08, 23; Cheyenne; F; S; Step-Dau; 671; Yes; Yes; None
692; Fisher, Richard; M; 11/12, 19; Cheyenne; F; S; Step-Son; 672; Yes; Yes; None
693; Fisher, Harold; M; 1/20, 11; Cheyenne; F; S; Step-Son; 673; Yes; Yes; None

694; Littleyellowman, Richard; M; 7/90, 41; Cheyenne; F; S; Head; 674; Yes; Yes; None

695; Livingston, Gail (Bolson); F; 7/15, 16; Cheyenne; 1/16; M; Head; 675; No; Ekalaka, town, Carter, Mont.; Yes; None   [-1/4 1931]

696; Loneelk, Wilson; M; 3/11, 21; Cheyenne; F; M; Head; 676; Yes; Yes; None
697; Loneelk, Sarah A. (Bigcrow, Sarah A.); F; 8/12, 19; Cheyenne; F; M; Wife; 677; Yes; Yes; None
698; Loneelk, George; M; 3/17/31, 1; Cheyenne; F; S; Son; 678; Yes; Yes; None

699; Lonewolf, Charles; M; 6/83, 48; Cheyenne; F; D; Head; 679; Yes; Yes; None

700; Longjaw, Charles; M; 3/46, 85; Cheyenne; F; Wd[sic]; Head; 680; Yes; Yes; None
---   Longjaw, Clara; F; 4/62, 70; Cheyenne; F; M; Wife; 681; Yes; Yes; None   Died December 6, 1931
701; Longjaw, Charles Jr.; M; 7/15, 16; Cheyenne; F; S; G-Son; 682; Yes; Yes; None

702; Longjaw, Elmer; M; 12/83, 48; Cheyenne; F; M; Head; 683; Yes; Yes; None
703; Longjaw, Lena (Limpy, Lena); F; 8/86, 45; Cheyenne; F; M; Wife; 684; Yes; Yes; None
704; Longjaw, Albert; M; 6/12, 19; Cheyenne; S[sic]; S; Son; 685; Yes; Yes; None
705; Longjaw, Henry; M; 1/16, 16; Cheyenne; S[sic]; S; Son; 686; Yes; Yes; None
706; Longjaw, Clara; F; 1/19, 13; Cheyenne; S[sic]; S; Dau; 687; Yes; Yes; None

Census of the __Tongue River__ reservation of the __Tongue River__ jurisdiction, as of __April 1__, 1932, taken by __W. R. Centerwall__, Superintendent.

**Key:** Number; NAME: Surname, Given; Sex; Birthdate, Age At Last Birthday; Tribe; Degree of Blood; Marital Status; Relationship To Head of Family; Last Census Roll Number; At Jurisdiction Where Enrolled (Yes or No); At Another Jurisdiction; ELSEWHERE: Post office, County, State; Ward (Yes or No); Allotment, Annuity, and Identification Numbers.

707; Longjaw, Frank; M; 4/00, 32; Cheyenne; F; M; Head; 688; Yes; Yes; None
708; Longjaw, Bernice (Medicineflying, Bernice); F; 2/10, 22; Cheyenne; F; M; Wife; 689; Yes; Yes; None [Medicineflying, Jennie in 1928.]
709; Longjaw, Robert; M; 3/25/27, 5; Cheyenne; F; S; Son; 690; Yes; Yes; None

710; Longjaw, James; M; 5/81, 50; Cheyenne; F; M; Head; 691; Yes; Yes; None
711; Longjaw, Nellie (Rockroads, Nellie); F; 1/96, 36; Cheyenne; F; M; Wife; 692; Yes; Yes; None
712; Longjaw, Donald; M; 11/27/27, 3; Cheyenne; F; S; Son; 693; Yes; Yes; None
713; Longjaw, Claudia; F; 10/7/30, 1; Cheyenne; F; S; Dau; 694; Yes; Yes; None

714; Longroach, George; M; 4/82, 50; Cheyenne; F; M; Head; 695; Yes; Yes; None
715; Longroach, Emma (Bigheadman, Emma); F; 9/83, 48; Cheyenne; F; M; Wife; 1343; Yes; Yes; None [Whitehawk, Emma; Wd; in 1931]
716; Whitehawk, Verlie; F; 3/18, 14; Cheyenne; F; S; S-Dau; 1344; Yes; Yes; None
--- Whitehawk, Theresa; F; 8/3/27, 4; Cheyenne; F; S; S-Dau; 1345; Yes; Yes; None Died December 13, 1931

717; Looksatbareground, James; M; 5/78, 53; Cheyenne; F; M; Head; 702; Yes; Yes; None
--- Looksatbareground, Julia; F; 5/52, 79; Cheyenne; F; M; Wife; 703; Yes; Yes; None Died February 13, 1932

718; Looksbehind, Charles; M; 10/60, 71; Cheyenne; F; M; Head; 704; Yes; Yes; None

719; Looksbehind, James; M; 1885, 46; Cheyenne; F; M; Head; 705; No; Cheyenne & Arap., Okla; Yes; None [James Nightwalking]
720; Looksbehind, Roy; M; 1921, 11; Cheyenne; F; S; Son; 706; No; Cheyenne & Arap., Okla; Yes; None
721; Looksbehind, Camilla; F; 8/23, 8; Cheyenne; F; S; Dau; 707; No; Cheyenne & Arap., Okla; Yes; None
722; Looksbehind, James Jr.; M; 5/27, 4; Cheyenne; F; S; Son; 708; No; Cheyenne & Arap., Okla; Yes; None

723; Looksbehind, Sallie (Bearcoal, Sallie); F; 10/59, 80; Cheyenne; F; D; Head; 709; Yes; Yes; None
724; Looksbehind, Pius; M; 3/12, 20; Cheyenne; F; S; G-Son; 710; Yes; Yes; None [Redneck, Pius 1930]

725; Lostleg, James; M; 12/15, 16; Cheyenne; F; S; Alone; 711; Yes; Yes; None [Ernest George in 1926.]
726; Lostleg, Virginia; F; 2/19, 13; Cheyenne; F; S; Alone; 712; Yes; Yes; None [Son Theodore in 1920.]

Census of the __Tongue River__ reservation of the __Tongue River__ jurisdiction, as of __April 1__, 1932, taken by __W. R. Centerwall__, Superintendent.

**Key:** Number; NAME: Surname, Given; Sex; Birthdate, Age At Last Birthday; Tribe; Degree of Blood; Marital Status; Relationship To Head of Family; Last Census Roll Number; At Jurisdiction Where Enrolled (Yes or No); At Another Jurisdiction; ELSEWHERE: Post office, County, State; Ward (Yes or No); Allotment, Annuity, and Identification Numbers.

727; Magpie, Albert; M; 4/86, 45; Cheyenne; F; Wd[sic]; Head; 713; Yes; Yes; None [Prev. censuses from 1904-15 name is Youngmagpie with same birth year, none in 1913, Magpie in 1916. As early as 1907 a first wife Julia born 1887. Anne is a second wife starting in 1919. Anne is not in 1925.]
728; Magpie, Anna Mary; F; 12/19, 11; Cheyenne; F; S; Dau; 714; Yes; Yes; None [Minnie in 1926.]
729; Magpie, Gilbert; M; 8/22, 9; Cheyenne; F; S; Son; 715; Yes; Yes; None

730; Magpie, Louis; M; 10/85, 46; Cheyenne; F; M; Head; 716; Yes; Yes; None
731; Magpie, Mira (Hardrobe, Mira); F; 7/94, 37; Cheyenne; F; M; Wife; 717; Yes; Yes; None
732; Magpie, Eddie; M; 4/10, 22; Cheyenne; F; S; Son; 718; Yes; Yes; None
733; Hardrobe, Mollie; F; 10/19, 16; Cheyenne; F; S; Step-Dau; 719; Yes; Yes; None

734; Manbear, Lena; F; 8/67, 64; Cheyenne; F; Wd; Head; 720; Yes; Yes; None
735; Manbear, Lizzie; F; 4/02, 30; Cheyenne; F; S; Dau; 721; Yes; Yes; None
736; Walters, Coolidge; M; 2/6/26, 6; Cheyenne; 11/16; S; G-Son; 722; Yes; Yes; None [1/4+ 1931]

737; Marrowbone, Jessie; F; 1888, 43; Cheyenne; F; M; Head; 723; No; Pine Ridge, S. Dak.; Yes; None [Children enrolled at Pine Ridge.]

738; Medicine, Sampson; M; 9/76, 55; Cheyenne; F; M; Head; 724; Yes; Yes; None
739; Medicine, Anna; F; 2/79, 53; Cheyenne; F; M; Wife; 725; Yes; Yes; None
740; Medicine, Jennie; F; 3/02, 30; Cheyenne; F; S; Dau; 726; Yes; Yes; None
741; Redeagle, Jennie; F; 9/41, 90; Cheyenne; F; S; Mother; 727; Yes; Yes; None [Wd 1931]

742; Medicinebird, Nelson; M; 8/75, 56; Cheyenne; F; M; Head; 728; Yes; Yes; None
743; Medicinebird, Ella (Spottedwolf, Ella); F; 2/83, 49; Cheyenne; F; M; Wife; 729; Yes; Yes; None
744; Medicinebird, Homer J.; M; 3/14, 18; Cheyenne; F; S; Son; 730; Yes; Yes; None

745; Medicinebull, Robert; M; 8/60, 70; Cheyenne; F; M; Head; 731; Yes; Yes; None
746; Medicinebull, Maggie; F; 7/62, 68; Cheyenne; F; M; Wife; 732; Yes; Yes; None
747; Medicinebull, Willis; M; 4/87, 45; Cheyenne; F; M; Head; 733; Yes; Yes; None

Census of the **Tongue River** reservation of the **Tongue River** jurisdiction, as of **April 1**, 1932, taken by **W. R. Centerwall**, Superintendent.

**Key:** Number; NAME: Surname, Given; Sex; Birthdate, Age At Last Birthday; Tribe; Degree of Blood; Marital Status; Relationship To Head of Family; Last Census Roll Number; At Jurisdiction Where Enrolled (Yes or No); At Another Jurisdiction; ELSEWHERE: Post office, County, State; Ward (Yes or No); Allotment, Annuity, and Identification Numbers.

748; Medicinebull, Anne (Swallow, Anne); F; 5/02, 29; Cheyenne; F; M; Wife; 734; Yes; Yes; None

--- Medicinebull, James; M; 8/10, 21; Cheyenne; F; S; Son; 735; Yes; Yes; None Died June 28, 1931

749; Medicinebull, Fred; M; 10/28/25, 6; Cheyenne F; S; Son; 737; Yes; Yes; None
750; Medicinebull, Bert; M; 1/31/27, 5; Cheyenne; F; S; Son; 738; Yes; Yes; None
751; Medicinebull, Mae; F; 4/30/30, 1; Cheyenne; F; S; Dau; 739; Yes; Yes; None

752; Medicineelk, Andrew; M; 5/98, 33; Cheyenne; F; M; Head; 740; Yes; Yes; None
753; Medicineelk, Maggie (Bearquiver, Maggie); F 1/03, 29; Cheyenne; F; M; Wife; 741; Yes; Yes; None
754; Medicineelk, Peter; M; 3/12/26, 6; Cheyenne; F; S; Son; 742; Yes; Yes; None
755; Medicineelk, Margaret; F; 2/2/30, 2; Cheyenne; F; S; Dau; 743; Yes; Yes; None

756; Medicineelk, Basil; M; 1/94, 38; Cheyenne; F; M; Head; 744; Yes; Yes; None

757; Medicineelk, James; M; 4/02, 30; Cheyenne; F; S; Head; 746; No; Chey. & Arap. Agency, Okla; Yes; None

758; Medicineelk, John; M; 10/10, 21; Cheyenne; F; S; Head; 745; Yes; Yes; None [Sandwoman; G-son in 1928 and 1930]

--- Medicineelk, Thomas; M; 25; Cheyenne; F; S; Head; 747; Yes; Yes; None Died September 13, 1931

759; Medicineflying, John; M; 9/82, 49; Cheyenne; F; M; Head; 748; Yes; Yes; None
760; Medicineflying, Bertha (Littleoldman, Bertha); F; 2/85, 47; Cheyenne; F; M; Wife; 749; Yes; Yes; None
761; Medicineflying, Helen J.; F; 8/16, 15; Cheyenne; F; S; Dau; 750; Yes; Yes; None
762; Medicineflying, Agnes S.; F; 5/20, 11; Cheyenne; F; S; Dau; 751; Yes; Yes; None
763; Medicineflying, Phyllis A.; F; 7/24, 7; Cheyenne; F; S; Dau; 752; Yes; Yes; None

764; Medicinetop, James; M; 5/61, 70; Cheyenne; F; Wd; Head; 753; Yes; Yes; None

765; Medicinetop, John; M; 1/85, 47; Cheyenne; F; M; Head; 754; Yes; Yes; None
766; Medicinetop, Ida (Littleoldman, Ida); F; 5/90, 41; Cheyenne; F; M; Wife; 755; Yes; Yes; None

Census of the __Tongue River__ reservation of the __Tongue River__ jurisdiction, as of __April 1__, 1932, taken by __W. R. Centerwall__, Superintendent.

**Key:** Number; NAME: Surname, Given; Sex; Birthdate, Age At Last Birthday; Tribe; Degree of Blood; Marital Status; Relationship To Head of Family; Last Census Roll Number; At Jurisdiction Where Enrolled (Yes or No); At Another Jurisdiction; ELSEWHERE: Post office, County, State; Ward (Yes or No); Allotment, Annuity, and Identification Numbers.

767; Medicinetop, Clarence; M; 10/10, 21; Cheyenne; F; S; Son; 756; Yes; Yes; None
768; Medicinetop, Majorie[sic]; F; 4/14, 17; Cheyenne; F; S; Dau; 757; Yes; Yes; None
769; Medicinetop, Phyllis; F; 9/22, 9; Cheyenne; F; S; Dau; 758; Yes; Yes; None
770; Medicinetop, Roy; M; 8/19/24, 7; Cheyenne; F; S; Son; 759; Yes; Yes; None
771; Medicinetop, Lena; 10/24/27, 4; Cheyenne; F; S; Dau; 760; Yes; Yes; None
772; Medicinetop, Edward; M; 3/15/29, 3; Cheyenne; F; S; 761; Yes; Yes; None

773; Meritt, Wesley; M; 10/75, 55; Cheyenne; F; M; Head; 762; Yes; Yes; None [Name spelled Merritt in 1931]
774; Meritt, Josie; F; 5/63, 68; Cheyenne; F; M; Wife; 763; Yes; Yes; None
775; Walkingbear, Nannie; F; 8/97, 34; Cheyenne; F; S; S-Dau; 764; Yes; Yes; None
776; Twomoons, George; M; 1/20, 11; Cheyenne; F; S; G-Son; 765; Yes; Yes; None

[---] Monothy, Albert; M; 4/89, 43; Cheyenne; F; M; Head; 272; Yes; Yes; None [See Page [297] Albert Duster changed to Monothy]

777; Oldbull, Daniel; M; 10/70, 61; Cheyenne; F; M; Head; 779; Yes; Yes; None [Wd[sic] 1931]
778; Oldbull, Gertrude (Blackwolf, Gertrude); F; 4/75, 52; Cheyenne; F; M; Wife; 1288; Yes; Yes; None [Wanderingmedicine, Gertrude 1931]
779; Oldbull, Thomas; M; 11/10, 21; Cheyenne; F; S; Son; 780; Yes; Yes; None

780; Onebear, James; M; 7/00, 32; Cheyenne; 7/8; M; Head; 781; Yes; Yes; None [1/4+ 1931]
781; Onebear, Maggie (Seminole, Maggie); F; 3/03, 29; Cheyenne; 3/4; M; Wife; 782; Yes; Yes; None [1/4+ 1931]
782; Onebear, Robert; M; 12/5/25, 6; Cheyenne; 13/16; S; Son; 783; Yes; Yes; None [1/4+ 1931]
783; Onebear, Louise; F; 10/18/29, 2; Cheyenne; 13/16; S; Dau; 784; Yes; Yes; None [1/4+ 1931]
784; Onebear, Wayne; M; 6/10/31, 10/12; Cheyenne; 13/16; W; Son; ---; Yes; Yes; None

785; Parker, Alvin O.; M; 6/79, 52; Cheyenne; 1/4; M; Head; 785; Yes; Yes; None
786; Parker, Clyde S.; M; 11/22, 9; Cheyenne; 1/8; S; Son; 786; Yes; Yes; None [-1/4 1931]
787; Parker, Verda; F; 9/2/24, 7; Cheyenne; 1/8; S; Dau; 787; Yes; Yes; None [-1/4 1931]
788; Parker, Shirley R.; M; 1/8/27, 5; Cheyenne; 1/8; S; Son; 788; Yes; Yes; None [-1/4 1931]

Census of the **Tongue River** reservation of the **Tongue River** jurisdiction, as of **April 1**, 19**32**, taken by **W. R. Centerwall**, Superintendent.

**Key:** Number; NAME: Surname, Given; Sex; Birthdate, Age At Last Birthday; Tribe; Degree of Blood; Marital Status; Relationship To Head of Family; Last Census Roll Number; At Jurisdiction Where Enrolled (Yes or No); At Another Jurisdiction; ELSEWHERE: Post office, County, State; Ward (Yes or No); Allotment, Annuity, and Identification Numbers.

789; Parker, Donald E.; M; 8/25/28, 3; Cheyenne; 1/8; S; Son; 789; Yes; Yes; None [-1/4 1931]
790; Parker, Lyle Neal; M; 9/8/30, 1; Cheyenne; 1/8; S; Son; 790; Yes; Yes; None [-1/4 1931]

791; Parker, Charles A.; M; 7/85 46; Cheyenne; 1/4; M; Head; 791; Yes; Yes; None [1/4+ 1931]
792; Parker, Theresa; F; 3/12, 20; Cheyenne; 1/4; S; Dau; 792; Yes; Yes; None [1/4+ 1931]
793; Parker, Gabriel; M; 10/22/26, 5; Cheyenne; 1/4; S; Son; 793; Yes; Yes; None [1/4+ 1931]

794; Parker, Edwin; M; 4/95, 37; Cheyenne; 1/4; S; Head; 794; Yes; Yes; None [1/4+ 1931]

795; Parker, Guy; M; 9/91, 40; Cheyenne; 1/4; M; Head; 795; Yes; Yes; None [1/4+ 1931]
796; Parker, Winfred; M; 4/14, 17; Cheyenne; 1/4; M; Wife; 796; Yes; Yes; None [1/4+ 1931]
797; Parker, Alice; F; 2/2/17, 15; Cheyenne; 1/4; S; Dau; 797; Yes; Yes; None [1/4+ 1931]
798; Parker, Stella; F; 4/30/19, 12; Cheyenne; 1/4; S; Dau; 798; Yes; Yes; None [1/4+ 1931]
799; Parker, Charlotte; F; 7/23/29, 2; Cheyenne; 1/4; S; Dau; 799; Yes; Yes; None [1/4+ 1931]

800; Pease, Ida; F; 2/06, 25; Cheyenne; 1/8; M; Head; 800; No; Crow Agency, Mont.; Yes; None [-1/4 1931]

801; Pine, Frank; M; 7/63, 68; Cheyenne; F; M; Head; 801; Yes; Yes; None
802; Pine, Nora; F; 3/64, 68; Cheyenne; F M; Wife; 802; Yes; Yes; None

803; Pine, Rutherford; M; 6/86, 45; Cheyenne; F; M; Head; 803; Yes; Yes; None
804; Pine, Julia (Kingfisher, Julia); F; 8/96, 35; Cheyenne; F; M; Wife; 804; Yes; Yes; None [In 1916 marries Julia Blackcrane nee Kingfisher; in 1912 she is 18 years old, birth year is 1894 from 1904-16. Gave birth year as 1884 from 1917-26.]
805; Pine, Cecelia; F; 1/16, 16; Cheyenne; F; S; Dau; 805; Yes; Yes; None
806; Pine, Daniel; M; 9/23, 8; Cheyenne; F; S; Son; 806; Yes; Yes; None

807; Pine, Wilson; M; 6/86, 45; Cheyenne; F; M; Head; 807; Yes; Yes; None
808; Pine, Nora (Bignose, Nora); F; 7/88, 43; Cheyenne; F; M; Wife; 808; Yes; Yes; None
809; Pine, Alexander; M; 11/17/14; Cheyenne; F; S; Son; 809; Yes; Yes; None
810; Pine, John; M; 4/22, 10; Cheyenne; F; S; Son; 810; Yes; Yes; None

Census of the **Tongue River** reservation of the **Tongue River** jurisdiction, as of **April 1**, 1932, taken by **W. R. Centerwall**, Superintendent.

**Key:** Number; NAME: Surname, Given; Sex; Birthdate, Age At Last Birthday; Tribe; Degree of Blood; Marital Status; Relationship To Head of Family; Last Census Roll Number; At Jurisdiction Where Enrolled (Yes or No); At Another Jurisdiction; ELSEWHERE: Post office, County, State; Ward (Yes or No); Allotment, Annuity, and Identification Numbers.

811; Pine, Sarah Mary; F; 8/4/24, 7; Cheyenne; F; S; Dau; 811; Yes; Yes; None
812; Powderface, Fern; F; 7/18, 13; Cheyenne; F; S; Dau; 812; Yes; Yes; None [Step-Dau 1931]

813; Playingbear, Henry; M; 1/77, 55; Cheyenne; F; M; Head; 813; Yes; Yes; None
814; Playingbear, Mildred; F; 4/80, 52; Cheyenne; F; M; Wife; 814; Yes; Yes; None

815; Powderface, John; M; 5/66, 65; Cheyenne; F; Wd[sic]; Head; 815; Yes; Yes; None

816; Powell, Clay; M; 11/04, 27; Cheyenne; 1/4; M; Head; 816; No; Sheridan, town, Sheridan, Wyo.; Yes; None

817; Powell, Mary (Rowland, Mary); F; 11/81, 50; Cheyenne; 1/2; M; Head; 817; Yes; Yes; None [1/4+ 1931]
818; Powell, Deyo; M; 6/07, 24; Cheyenne; 1/4; M; Son; 818; Yes; Yes; None [1/4+ 1931; -1/4 1930]
819; Powell, Howard; M; 2/12, 20; Cheyenne; 1/4; S; Son; 819; Yes; Yes; None [-1/4 1931 & 1930]

820; Prairiebear, Arthur; M; 3/82, 50; Cheyenne; F; M; Head; 820; Yes; Yes; None
821; Prairiebear, Sallie (Roundstone, Sallie); F; 10/85, 46; Cheyenne; F; M; Wife; 821; Yes; Yes; None
822; Prairiebear, A. Louis; M; 11/2/28, 3; Cheyenne; F; S; Son; 822; Yes; Yes; None

823; Redbeads, John; M; 11/71, 60; Cheyenne; F; M; Head; 823; Yes; Yes; None [Redbead 1931]
824; Redbeads, Nancy; F; 4/78, 54; Cheyenne; F; M; Wife; 824; Yes; Yes; None [Redbead 1931]
825; Redbeads, Susie; F; 6/15, 18; Cheyenne; F; S; Dau; 825; Yes; Yes; None [Redbead 1931]
826; Redbeads, Clara; F; 6/15, 16; Cheyenne; F; S; Dau; 826; Yes; Yes; None [Redbead 1931]
827; Redbeads, Georgia; F; 7/17, 14; Cheyenne; F; S; Dau; 827; Yes; Yes; None [Redbead 1931] [Name Gloria 1917-20.]

828; Redbird, Joseph; M; 10/99, 32; Cheyenne; F; M; Head; 828; Yes; Yes; None [Middle name Francis in 1910.]
829; Redbird, Lucille (Littlechief, Lucille); F; 2/11, 21; Cheyenne; F; M; Wife; 829; Yes; Yes; None
830; Redbird, William; M; 6/22, 9; Cheyenne; F; S; Son; 830; No; Cheyenne & Arap. Okla.; Yes; None

Census of the **Tongue River** reservation of the **Tongue River** jurisdiction, as of **April 1**, 1932, taken by **W. R. Centerwall**, Superintendent.

**Key:** Number; NAME: Surname, Given; Sex; Birthdate, Age At Last Birthday; Tribe; Degree of Blood; Marital Status; Relationship To Head of Family; Last Census Roll Number; At Jurisdiction Where Enrolled (Yes or No); At Another Jurisdiction; ELSEWHERE: Post office, County, State; Ward (Yes or No); Allotment, Annuity, and Identification Numbers.

831; Redbird, Allen; M; 5/25/25, 6; Cheyenne; F; S; Son; 831; No; Cheyenne & Arap. Okla.; Yes; None [First shows in 1925 with birth in 1924. Same Prev. #, Helena; dau; 1925, F. in 1926.]
832; Redbird, Diva; F; 12/8/30, 1; Cheyenne; F; S; Dau; 832; Yes; Yes; None

833; Redbird, William; M; 7/76, 55; Cheyenne; F; M; Head; 833; Yes; Yes; None
--- Redbird, Flornce[sic] (Littlewhiteman, Florence); F; 6/77, 54; Cheyenne; 3/4; M; Wife; 834; Yes; Yes; None Died January 19, 1932
834; Redbird, Lena; F; 11/20, 11; Cheyenne; 7/8; S; Dau; 835; Yes; Yes; None [1/4+ 1931]
835; Redbird, Samuel; M; 11/22/26, 3; Cheyenne; 7/8; S; Son; 836; Yes; Yes; None [1/4+ 1931]
836; Tangledhornelk, Nellie; F; 1853, 79; Cheyenne; F; Wd; Mother; 839; Yes; Yes; None

837; Redbreath, Charles; M; 4/79, 52; Cheyenne; F; M; Head; 840; Yes; Yes; None
838; Redbreath, Betty (Yellownose, Betty); F; 1/08, 24; Cheyenne; F; M; Wife; 841; Yes; Yes; None
839; Redbreath, Elina J; F; 5/25, 6; Cheyenne; F; S; Dau; 842; Yes; Yes; None [Elina June in 1926.]
840; Redbreath, George; M; 7/8/27, 4; Cheyenne; F; S; Son; 843; Yes; Yes; None

841; Redcherries, Teddy; M; 1888, 43; Cheyenne; F; M; Head; 844; No; Cheyenne & Arap., Okla.; Yes; None
842; Redcherries, Miller; M; 11/18/20, 11; Cheyenne; F; S; Son; 845; No; Cheyenne & Arap., Okla.; Yes; None

843; Redcherries, William; M; 6/90, 41; Cheyenne; F; M; Head; 846; Yes; Yes; None
844; Redcherries, Bessie (Wildhog, Bessie); F; 2/94, 38; Cheyenne; F; M; Wife; 847; Yes; Yes; None
845; Redcherries, Alice; F; 8/12, 19; Cheyenne; F; S; Dau; 848; Yes; Yes; None
846; Redcherries, Rose; F; 4/9/16, 16; Cheyenne; F; S; Dau; 849; Yes; Yes; None
847; Redcherries, Frank; M; 5/19, 12; Cheyenne; F; S; Son; 850; Yes; Yes; None
848; Redcherries, Margaret; F; 9/23, 8; Cheyenne; F; S; Dau; 851; Yes; Yes; None
849; Redcherries, Katie; F; 9/3/27, 4; Cheyenne; F; S; Dau; 852; Yes; Yes; None
850; Redcherries, Della; F; 5/18/30, 1; Cheyenne; F; S; Dau; 853; Yes; Yes; None
851; Stumphorn, Anna; F; 9/51, 80; Cheyenne; F; Wd; Mother; 854; Yes; Yes; None

852; Redeagle, Nellie (Bravewolf, Nellie); F; 8/72, 59; Cheyenne; F; Wd; Head; 855; Yes; Yes; None
853; Redeagle, Willis; M; 12/01, 30; Cheyenne; F; S; Son; 856; Yes; Yes; None

Census of the **Tongue River** reservation of the **Tongue River** jurisdiction, as of **April 1**, 1932, taken by **W. R. Centerwall**, Superintendent.

**Key:** Number; NAME: Surname, Given; Sex; Birthdate, Age At Last Birthday; Tribe; Degree of Blood; Marital Status; Relationship To Head of Family; Last Census Roll Number; At Jurisdiction Where Enrolled (Yes or No); At Another Jurisdiction; ELSEWHERE: Post office, County, State; Ward (Yes or No); Allotment, Annuity, and Identification Numbers.

854; Redfox, James; M; 4/65, 66; Cheyenne; F; M; Head; 857; Yes; Yes; None
855; Redfox, Nora; F; 6/58, 73; Cheyenne; F; M; Wife; 1193; Yes; Yes; None

--- Redfox, Jennie; F; 12/73, 58; Cheyenne; F; Wd; Head; 858; Yes; Yes; None Died August 9, 1931
856; Redfox, Robert; M; 3/00, 32; Cheyenne; F; M; Head; 859; Yes; Yes; None
857; Redfox, Cecelia (Whitemoon, Cecelia); F; 6/94, 37; Cheyenne; F; M; Wife; 860; Yes; Yes; None
858; Redfox, Edna S.; F; 3/13/27, 4; Cheyenne; F; S; Dau; 861; Yes; Yes; None
859; Redfox, Ralph; M; 9/24/29, 2; Cheyenne; F; S; Son; 862; Yes; Yes; None
860; Sanchez, Pauline; F; 3/15, 17; Cheyenne; 3/4; S; S-Dau; 863; Yes; Yes; None [1/4+ 1931]
861; Sanchez, Cecelia; F; 4/22, 9; Cheyenne; 3/4; S; S-Dau; 864; Yes; Yes; None [1/4+ 1931]

862; Redneck, Curtis; M; 1/88, 43; Cheyenne; 3/4; M; Head; 865; Yes; Yes; None [Fullblood 1931]
863; Redneck, Josie (Wolfear, Josie); F; 12/96, 35; Cheyenne; F; M; Wife; 866; Yes; Yes; None
864; Redneck, Clyde; M; 8/12, 19; Cheyenne; 7/8; S; Son; 867; Yes; Yes; None [Fullblood 1931]

865; Redneck, David; M; 9/81, 40; Cheyenne; 3/4; M; Head; 868; Yes; Yes; None [Fullblood 1931]
866; Redneck, Minnie; F; 8/10/20, 11; Cheyenne; 7/8; S; Dau; 869; Yes; Yes; None [Fullblood 1931]

867; Redneck, Henry; M; 8/82, 49; Cheyenne; F; M; Head; 870; Yes; Yes; None
868; Redneck, Fannie (Looksbehind, Fannie); F; 7/84, 47; Cheyenne; F; M; Wife; 871; Yes; Yes; None
869; Redneck, Dora; F; 10/14, 17; Cheyenne; F; S; Dau; 872; Yes; Yes; None
870; Redneck, Homer; M; 7/17, 14; Cheyenne; F; S; Son; 873; Yes; Yes; None
871; Redneck, Florence; F; 4/21, 11; Cheyenne; F; S; Dau; 874; Yes; Yes; None
872; Redneck, John; M; 5/25, 6; Cheyenne; F; S; Son; 875; Yes; Yes; None

873; Rednose, Paul; M; 6/76, 55; Cheyenne; F; M; Head; 876; Yes; Yes; None
874; Rednose, Lucy; F; 5/70, 61; Cheyenne; F; M; Wife; 877; Yes; Yes; None [1/2 in 1928]

875; Redrobe, Fred; M; 10/67, 64; Cheyenne; F; M; Head; 878; Yes; Yes; None
876; Redrobe, Nora (Nicetalker, Nora); F; 4/69, 62; Cheyenne; F; M; Wife; 879; Yes; Yes; None
877; Redrobe, Louis; M; 11/92, 39; Cheyenne; F; S; Son; 880; Yes; Yes; None
878; Redrobe, Jasper; M; 7/00, 31; Cheyenne; F; S; Son; 881; Yes; Yes; None

Census of the __Tongue River__ reservation of the __Tongue River__ jurisdiction, as of __April 1__, 1932, taken by __W. R. Centerwall__, Superintendent.

**Key:** Number; NAME: Surname, Given; Sex; Birthdate, Age At Last Birthday; Tribe; Degree of Blood; Marital Status; Relationship To Head of Family; Last Census Roll Number; At Jurisdiction Where Enrolled (Yes or No); At Another Jurisdiction; ELSEWHERE: Post office, County, State; Ward (Yes or No); Allotment, Annuity, and Identification Numbers.

879; Redrobe, William; M; 8/97, 34; Cheyenne; F; M; Head; 882; Yes; Yes; None
880; Redrobe, Alice (Killsnight, Alice); F; 5/84, 47; Cheyenne; F; M; Wife; 883; Yes; Yes; None [1907-19, birth year 1884-5. 1904 nee-Killsnight; 1905-6 Risingsun, 1907-19 Shell, 1920-28 Redrobe.]
881; Weaselbear, Stella C.; F; 5/17, 14; Cheyenne; F; S; Niece; 884; Yes; Yes; None [s-dau-Henry Littlewhiteman. Clarice in 1926.]

882; Redwater, Cecelia; F; 2/72, 59; Cheyenne; F; D; Head; 885; Yes; Yes; None

883; Redwater, Thaddeus; M; 4/75, 56; Cheyenne; F; M; Head; 886; Yes; Yes; None

884; Redwoman, Frank; M; 2/89, 43; Cheyenne; F; Wd[sic]; Head; 887; Yes; Yes; None
885; Redwoman, Eugene; M; 2/23, 9; Cheyenne; F; S; Son; 888, Yes; Yes; None
886; Redwoman, Joe; M; 5/24, 7; Cheyenne; F; S; Son; 890; Yes; Yes; None

887; Redwoman, John; M; 7/02, 29; Cheyenne; F; Wd[sic]; Head; 891; Yes; Yes; None [Robert Ironshirt]

888; Ridgebear, Charles; M; 1882, 49; Cheyenne; F; M; Head; 895; No; Cheyenne & Arap., Okla.; Yes; None

889; Ridgebear, Willis; M; 7/87, 44; Cheyenne; F; M; Head; 896; Yes; Yes; None
890; Ridgebear, Rilla (Killsnight, Rilla); F; 7/98, 34; Cheyenne; F; M; Wife; 897; Yes; Yes; None
891; Ridgebear, Bessie A.; F; 11/18, 13; Cheyenne; F; S; Dau; 898; Yes; Yes; None
892; Ridgebear, Carrie; F; 4/21, 10; Cheyenne; F; S; Dau; 899; Yes; Yes; None
893; Ridgebear, Anna; F; 1/22/27, 4; Cheyenne; F; S; Dau; 900; Yes; Yes; None
894; Ridgebear, James; M; 3/2/29, 3; Cheyenne; F; S; Son; 901; Yes; Yes; None
895; Ridgebear, Jerry K.; M; 11/12/31, 5/12; Cheyenne; F; S; Son; xxx; Yes; Yes; None

896; Ridgewalker, Robert; M; 6/60, 71; Cheyenne; F; M; Head; 902; Yes; Yes; None
897; Ridgewalker, Ethel; F; 6/70, 61; Cheyenne; 3/4; M; Wife; 903; Yes; Yes; None
898; Ridgewalker, Frank; M; 4/08, 23; Cheyenne; 7/8; S; Son; 904; Yes; Yes; None

899; Risingfire, Bessie; F; 11/56, 75; Cheyenne; F; Wd; Head; Yes; Yes; None
--- ~~Fightingbear, Julia; F; 7/11, 20; Cheyenne; F; S; G-Dau; 906; Yes; Yes; None Died March 27, 1932~~
900; Fightingbear, Dora; F; 17; Cheyenne; F; S; G-Dau; 907; Yes; Yes; None

Census of the __Tongue River__ reservation of the __Tongue River__ jurisdiction, as of __April 1__, 19__32__, taken by __W. R. Centerwall__, Superintendent.

**Key:** Number; NAME: Surname, Given; Sex; Birthdate, Age At Last Birthday; Tribe; Degree of Blood; Marital Status; Relationship To Head of Family; Last Census Roll Number; At Jurisdiction Where Enrolled (Yes or No); At Another Jurisdiction; ELSEWHERE: Post office, County, State; Ward (Yes or No); Allotment, Annuity, and Identification Numbers.

901; Risingsun, Oliver; M; 5/00, 31; Cheyenne; F; M; Head; 908; Yes; Yes; None
902; Risingsun, Elizabeth (Flying, Elizabeth); F; 8/07, 24; Cheyenne; F; M; Wife; 909; Yes; Yes; None
903; Risingsun, Teddy; M; 10/26/26, 6; Cheyenne; F; S; Son; 910; Yes; Yes; None
904; Risingsun, Jordan; M; 5/13/31, 10/12; Cheyenne; F; S; Son; ---; Yes; Yes; None

905; Risingsun, Peter; M; 8/87, 44; Cheyenne; F; Wd; Head; 911; Yes; Yes; None
906; Risingsun, Harry; S[sic]; 4/21, 10; Cheyenne; F; S; Son; 912; Yes; Yes; None
907; Risingsun, Lyman; M; 7/23, 8; Cheyenne; F; S; Son; 913; Yes; Yes; None
908; Risingsun, James; M; 12/25, 6; Cheyenne; F; S; Son; 914; Yes; Yes; None

909; Risingsun, Philip; M; 8/62, 69; Cheyenne; F; M; Head; 915; Yes; Yes; None
910; Risingsun, Nora; F; 1/68, 62; Cheyenne; F; M; Wife; 916; Yes; Yes; None
911; Risingsun, John; M; 6/95, 36; Cheyenne; F; S; Son; 917; Yes; Yes; None
912; Risingsun, Pearl; F; 9/19/28, 3; Cheyenne; F; S; G-Dau; 918; Yes; Yes; None

913; Risingsun, William; M; 6/04, 27; Cheyenne; F; M; Head; 919; Yes; Yes; None
914; Risingsun, Edna Josie (Bearquiver, Edna Josie); F; 12/12, 19; Cheyenne; F; M; Wife; 920; Yes; Yes; None
915; Risingsun, Irvin Wm.; M; 8/25/31, 8/12; Cheyenne; F; M; Son; ---; Yes; Yes; None

N.E. Robinson, James M.; M; 34; Sioux; 1/8; M; Head; ---; ---
916; Robinson, Nellie (Spang, Nellie); F; 10/97, 34; Cheyenne; 1/8; M; Wife; 921; Yes; Yes; None [-1/4 1931]
917; Robinson, David C.; M; 8/18, 13; Cheyenne; 1/8; S; Son; 922; Yes; Yes; None [-1/4 1931]
918; Robinson, Cornelius D.; M; 6/20, 11; Cheyenne; 1/8; S; Son; 923; Yes; Yes; None [-1/4 1931]
919; Robinson, Eloise E.; F; 3/22, 10; Cheyenne; 1/8; S; Dau; 924; Yes; Yes; None [-1/4 1931]
920; Robinson, Buell D.; M; 7/30/28, 3; Cheyenne; 1/8; S; Son; 925; Yes; Yes; None [-1/4 1931]
921; Robinson, James M.; M; 2/16/32, 1/12; Cheyenne; 1/8; S; Son; ---; Yes; Yes; None

922; Rockroads, Mack; M; 4/93, 38; Cheyenne; F; M; Head; 926; Yes; Yes; None
923; Rockroads, Nellie (Bearchum, Nellie); F; 11/93, 38; Cheyenne; 3/4; M; Wife; 927; Yes; Yes; None [Fullblood 1931]
924; Rockroads, Thomas; M; 4/17, 14; Cheyenne; 7/8; S; Son; 928; Yes; Yes; None [Fullblood 1931] [1918 Census #902; Name is Lettie, female.]
925; Rockroads, Flossie; F; 7/10/29, 2; Cheyenne; 7/8; S; Dau; 929; Yes; Yes; None [Fullblood 1931]

Census of the **Tongue River** reservation of the **Tongue River** jurisdiction, as of **April 1**, 1932, taken by **W. R. Centerwall**, Superintendent.

**Key:** Number; NAME: Surname, Given; Sex; Birthdate, Age At Last Birthday; Tribe; Degree of Blood; Marital Status; Relationship To Head of Family; Last Census Roll Number; At Jurisdiction Where Enrolled (Yes or No); At Another Jurisdiction; ELSEWHERE: Post office, County, State; Ward (Yes or No); Allotment, Annuity, and Identification Numbers.

[Note: The following Census Numbers are incorrect, they should read 926 - 952]
726;[sic] Rockroads, Nora; F; 12/70, 61; Cheyenne; F; Wd; Head; 930; Yes; Yes; None
727; Rockroads, Mary; F; 8/13, 18; Cheyenne; F; S; Dau; 931; Yes; Yes; None

728; Romannose, Louis; M; 9/82, 49; Cheyenne; F; D; Head; 932; Yes; Yes; None
729; Romannose, George; M; 7/10, 21; Cheyenne; F; S; Son; 933; Yes; Yes; None
730; Romannose, Julia; F; 4/16, 15; Cheyenne; F; S; Dau; 935; Yes; Yes; None
[May in 1926.]
731; Romannose, Willette; F; 10/21, 10; Cheyenne; F; S; Dau; 936; Yes; Yes; None
[Name spelled Willeatte 1931]
732; Romannose, Montana; F; 11/23, 8; Cheyenne; F; S; Dau; 937; Yes; Yes; None
733; Romannose, Blanche; F; 9/14, 17; Cheyenne; F; S; Dau; 934; Yes; Yes; None
[Helen in 1926.]
734; Limpy, Lee; M; 11/14/31, 4/12; Cheyenne; F; S; G-Son; ---; Yes; Yes; None

735; Rondeau, Antoine; M; 4/87, 44; Cheyenne; 1/2; M; Head; 938; Yes; Yes; None [1/4+ 1931]
736; Rondeau, Louise (Bixby, Louise); F; 6/89, 42; Cheyenne; 1/4; M; Wife; 939; Yes; Yes; None [1/4+ 1931]
737; Rondeau, Charles; M; 5/20, 11; Cheyenne; 3/8; S; Son; 941; Yes; Yes; None [1/4+ 1931]
738; Ballard, Clara; F; 12/12, 19; Cheyenne; 3/8; M; Dau; 940; Yes; Yes; None [1/4+ 1931]
--- Zettle, Frank; M; 11/7/31; Cheyenne; 3/16; S; G-Son; ---; Yes; Yes; None Died November 13, 1931
739; Bixby, Jessie; F; 5/53, 75; Cheyenne; 1/2; Wd; Mother-in-law; 942; Yes; Yes; None [1/4+ 1931]

740; Rondeau, William; M; 3/66, 48; Cheyenne; 1/2; M; Head; 943; Yes; Yes; None [1/4+ 1931]
741; Rondeau, Henry; M; 3/11, 21; Cheyenne; 3/8; S; Son; 944; Yes; Yes; None [1/4+ 1931]
942; Rondeau, John; M; 3/12, 21; Cheyenne; 3/8; S; Son; 945; Yes; Yes; None [1/4+ 1931]

N.E. Roundstone, Fred; M; [---]; Cheyenne; F; M; Head; ---
743; Roundstone, Flora (Plentycamps, Flora); F; 4/88, 43; Cheyenne; F; M; Wife; 946; Yes; Yes; None [Twobulls]
744; Roundstone, Sarah; F; 5/20, 11; Cheyenne; F; S; Dau; 947; Yes; Yes; None
745; Roundstone, Paul; M; 4/22, 9; Cheyenne; F; S; Son; 948; Yes; Yes; None
746; Roundstone, Ruth; F; 7/16/26, 5; Cheyenne; F; S; Dau; 949; Yes; Yes; None

747; Roundstone, Martin; M; 11/11, 20; Cheyenne; F; M; Head; 950; Yes; Yes; None

Census of the __Tongue River__ reservation of the __Tongue River__ jurisdiction, as of __April 1__, 1932, taken by __W. R. Centerwall__, Superintendent.

**Key:** Number; NAME: Surname, Given; Sex; Birthdate, Age At Last Birthday; Tribe; Degree of Blood; Marital Status; Relationship To Head of Family; Last Census Roll Number; At Jurisdiction Where Enrolled (Yes or No); At Another Jurisdiction; ELSEWHERE: Post office, County, State; Ward (Yes or No); Allotment, Annuity, and Identification Numbers.

748; Roundstone, Mary (Grasshopper, Mary); F; 8/14, 17; Cheyenne; F; M; Wife; 951; Yes; Yes; None [Roundstone, Mary G. 1931]
749; Roundstone, Victoria; F; 8-20-31, 9/12; Cheyenne; F; S; Dau; xxx; Yes; Yes; None

750; Rowland, Benton; M; 12/98, 33; Cheyenne; 3/4; M; Head; 952; No; Pine Ridge, S. Dak.; Yes; None [1/4+ 1931]
751; Rowland, Marie; F; 5/26, 5; Cheyenne; 7/8; S; Dau; 953; No; Pine Ridge, S. Dak.; Yes; None [1/4+ 1931]
752; Rowland, Eugene; M; 8/13/27, 4; Cheyenne; 7/8; S; Son; 954; No; Pine Ridge, S. Dak.; Yes; None [1/4+ 1931]

953; Rowland, Clay T.; M; 2/80, 52; Cheyenne; 3/4; M; Head; 955; Yes; Yes; None [1/4+ 1931]

954; Rowland, Joe; M; 12/02, 29; Cheyenne; 3/4; M; Head; 956; No; Pine Ridge, S. Dak.; Yes; None [1/4+ 1931] [In 1926 #935; Jose; son; birth year 1900.]

955; Rowland, Thomas; M; 12/92, 29; Cheyenne; 3/4; M; Head; 957; Yes; Yes; None [1/4+ 1931]
956; Rowland, Daisy (Fightingbear, Daisy); F; 4/00, 31; Cheyenne; F; M; Wife; 958; Yes; Yes; None [Fightingbear, Ellen in 1924.]
957; Rowland, Elizabeth; F; 11/13, 18; Cheyenne; 3/4; S; Dau; 837; Yes; Yes; None [1/4+ 1931] [1/4- 1930]
958; Rowland, Lillian; F; 11/16, 15; Cheyenne; 3/4; S; Dau; 838; Yes; Yes; None [1/4+ 1931] [1/4- 1930]
959; Rowland, Blanche; F; 8/29/25, 6; Cheyenne; 7/8; S; Dau; 959; Yes; Yes; None [1/4+ 1931]
960; Rowland, Don; M; 1/22/28, 4; Cheyenne; 7/8; S; Son; 960; Yes; Yes; None [1/4+ 1931]
961; Rowland, Julia; F; 9/11/30, 1; Cheyenne; 7/8; S; Dau; 961; Yes; Yes; None [1/4+ 1931]

962; Rowland, William; M; 9/14/95, 36; Cheyenne; 3/4; M; Head; 962; Yes; Yes; None [1/4+ 1931]
963; Rowland, Chester C.; M; 6/20, 11; Cheyenne; 5/8; S; Son; 963; No; Pine Ridge, S. Dak.; Yes; None [1/4+ 1931]
964; Rowland, Allen E.; M; 2/9/26, 6; Cheyenne; 5/8; S; Son; 964; Yes; Yes; None [1/4+ 1931]
965; Rowland, Ardeth F.; F; 4/30/28, 3; Cheyenne; 5/8; S; Dau; 965; Yes; Yes; None [1/4+ 1931]

966; Rowland, Willis; M; 4/8/62, 69; Cheyenne; 1/2; Wd[sic]; Head; 966; Yes; Yes; None [1/4+ 1931]

Census of the __Tongue River__ reservation of the __Tongue River__ jurisdiction, as of __April 1__, 1932, taken by __W. R. Centerwall__, Superintendent.

**Key:** Number; NAME: Surname, Given; Sex; Birthdate, Age At Last Birthday; Tribe; Degree of Blood; Marital Status; Relationship To Head of Family; Last Census Roll Number; At Jurisdiction Where Enrolled (Yes or No); At Another Jurisdiction; ELSEWHERE: Post office, County, State; Ward (Yes or No); Allotment, Annuity, and Identification Numbers.

967; Rowland, Jesse; M; 2/84, 48; Cheyenne; 3/4; S; Nephew; 967; Yes; Yes; None [1/4+ 1931]
968; Rowland, Grace; F; 11/18/14, 17; Cheyenne; 3/4; S; A-Dau; 968; Yes; Yes; None [1/4+ 1931]
969; Rowland, Frank; M; 5/24, 7; Cheyenne; 7/8; S; G-Son; 969; Yes; Yes; None [1/4+ 1931]

970; Rowland, Zac; M; 12/68, 63; Cheyenne; 1/2; M; Head; 970; Yes; Yes; None [1/4+ 1931]
971; Rowland, Edna (Crazyhead, Edna); F; 10/76, 55; Cheyenne; F; M; Wife; 971; Yes; Yes; None

972; Russell, Frank; M; 12/98, 33; Cheyenne; 7/8; M; Head; 972; Yes; Yes; None [1/4+ 1931]
973; Russell, Ellen (Howlingantelope, Ellen); F; 8/97, 34; Cheyenne; F; M; Wife; 973; Yes; Yes; None [Sweetmedicine]

974; Russell, John; M; 9/93, 38; Cheyenne; 7/8; M; Head; 974; Yes; Yes; None
975; Russell, Alice (Risingsun, Alice); F; 12/09, 22; Cheyenne; F; M; Wife; 975; Yes; Yes; None
976; Russell, Stella; F; 2/16, 16; Cheyenne; 15/16; S; Dau; 976; No; Superior, town, Douglas, Wis.; Yes; None [1/4+ 1931]
977; Russell, Clifford; M; 9/17/30, 1; Cheyenne; 15/16; S; Son; 977; Yes; Yes; None [1/4+ 1931]

978; Russell, Fred; M; 7/08, 23; Cheyenne; F; M; Head; 976; Yes; Yes; None
979; Russell, Mary (Blackwolf, Mary); F; 1/14, 18; Cheyenne; F; M; Wife; 158; Yes; Yes; None
980; Russell, Hubert; M; 10/5/31, 5/12; Cheyenne; F; S; Son; Yes; Yes; None

981; Russell, William; M; 5/73, 56; Cheyenne; F; M; Head; 978; Yes; Yes; None
982; Russell, Earl; M; 10/15/15, 16; Cheyenne; F; S; Son; 979; Yes; Yes; None
983; Russell, Mary; F; 9/19, 13; Cheyenne; F; S; Dau; 980; Yes; Yes; None [Mildred in 1926.]

984; Sandcrane, Henry; M; 10/89, 42; Cheyenne; F; M; Head; 982; Yes; Yes; None
985; Sandcrane, Anna (Snowbird, Anna); F; 6/92, 39; Cheyenne; F; M; Wife; 983; Yes; Yes; None
986; Sandcrane, Margaret; F; 10/20, 11; Cheyenne; F; S; Dau; 984; Yes; Yes; None
987; Littlesun, Alfred; M; 12/12, 19; Cheyenne; F; S; S-Son; 985; Yes; Yes; None
--- Littleoldman, Thomas; M; 12/13, 18; Cheyenne; F; S; S-Son; Yes; Yes; None Died December 17, 1931.

988; Sandcrane, John; M; 1/73, 59; Cheyenne; F; M; Head; 987; Yes; Yes; None

Census of the __Tongue River__ reservation of the __Tongue River__ jurisdiction, as of __April 1__, 19**32**, taken by __W. R. Centerwall__, Superintendent.

**Key:** Number; NAME: Surname, Given; Sex; Birthdate, Age At Last Birthday; Tribe; Degree of Blood; Marital Status; Relationship To Head of Family; Last Census Roll Number; At Jurisdiction Where Enrolled (Yes or No); At Another Jurisdiction; ELSEWHERE: Post office, County, State; Ward (Yes or No); Allotment, Annuity, and Identification Numbers.

989; Sandcrane, Ruth (Arapaho, Ruth); F; 12/78, 53; Cheyenne; F; M; Wife; 988; Yes; Yes; None
990; Sandcrane, Isabelle; F; 5/14, 17; Cheyenne; F; S; Dau; 989; Yes; Yes; None

991; Littleoldman, Fern; F; 12/13, 14; Cheyenne; F; S; G-Dau; 990; Yes; Yes; None [s.-dau. Chas. Sharpnose, #569; Littleman, Julia; Step-dau; 1915; F. (s-dau Fred Limpy) in 1926.]

992; Scalpcane, August; M; 2/06, 26; Cheyenne; F; S; Head; 992; Yes; Yes; None
993; Scalpcane, Otto; M; 11/14, 17; Cheyenne; F; S; Bro.; 993; Yes; Yes; None
994; Scalpcane, Henry; M; 11/19, 12; Cheyenne; F; S; Bro.; 994; Yes; Yes; None [Rudolph in 1926.]

N.E. Schaffer, George; M; [---]; Crow; [---]; M; Head; [---]
995; Schaffer, Letha (Eastman, Letha); F; 4/13, 18; Cheyenne; 1/8; M; Wife; 995; No; Crow Agency, Mont.; Yes; None [-1/4 1931] [Son, Carl in 1916 Census.]

996; Seminole, Dan; M; 8/94, 37; Cheyenne; 3/4; M; Head; 996; Yes; Yes; None [1/4+ 1931]
997; Seminole, Jennie (Blackhorse, Jennie); F; 7/96, 36; Cheyenne; F; M; Wife; 997; Yes; Yes; None
998; Seminole, Anna; F; 6/20, 11; Cheyenne; 7/8; S; Dau; 998; Yes; Yes; None [1/4+ 1931]
999; Seminole, Margaret; F; 1/11, 10; Cheyenne; 7/8; S; Dau; 999; Yes; Yes; None [1/4+ 1931]
1000; Seminole, Alfred; M; 3/24, 8; Cheyenne; 7/8; S; Son; 1000; Yes; Yes; None [1/4+ 1931]
1001; Seminole, Beatrice; F; 8/27/28, 3; Cheyenne; 7/8; S; Dau; 1001; Yes; Yes; None [1/4+ 1931]
1002; Seminole, Eva; F; 8/24/31, 7/12; Cheyenne; 7/8; S; Dau; ---; Yes; Yes; None
---- ~~Littlewhiteman, Charles; M; 2/25, 17; Cheyenne; 7/8; S; S-Son; 1002; Yes; Yes; None Died February 14, 1932~~

1003; Seminole, John; M; 2/79, 53; Cheyenne; 3/4; M; Head; 1003; Yes; Yes; None [1/4+ 1931]
1004; Seminole, Mary (Redbird, Mary); F; 8/97, 34; Cheyenne; F; M; Wife; 1004; Yes; Yes; None
1005; Seminole, Fred; M; 6/15, 16; Cheyenne; 7/8; S; Son; 1005; Yes; Yes; None [1/4+ 1931]
1006; Seminole, Max; M; 11/24, 7; Cheyenne; 7/8; S; Son; 1006; Yes; Yes; None [1/4+ 1931] [son-Mary Redbird, 1926 #813 entry; Redbird, Maxine; g-g-son; 1924; M.; g-g-son Joseph Tangledhornelk]
1007; Seminole, Jule; M; 12/15/31, 3/12; Cheyenne; 7/8; S; Son; xxx; Yes; Yes; None

Census of the **Tongue River** reservation of the **Tongue River** jurisdiction, as of **April 1**, 1932, taken by **W. R. Centerwall**, Superintendent.

**Key:** Number; NAME: Surname, Given; Sex; Birthdate, Age At Last Birthday; Tribe; Degree of Blood; Marital Status; Relationship To Head of Family; Last Census Roll Number; At Jurisdiction Where Enrolled (Yes or No); At Another Jurisdiction; ELSEWHERE: Post office, County, State; Ward (Yes or No); Allotment, Annuity, and Identification Numbers.

1008; Fox, Margaret; F; 8/18, 13; Cheyenne; F; S; S-Dau; 1007; Yes; Yes; None [Jessie in 1927.]
1009; Fox, Marie; F; 10/22, 9; Cheyenne; F; S; S-Dau; 1008; Yes; Yes; None [Max, M., 1922-25.]

1010; Seminole, Josephine; F; 4/91, 40; Cheyenne; 3/4; S; Head; 1009; Yes; Yes; None [1/4+ 1931]
1011; Seminole, Lawrence; M; 12/11, 21; Cheyenne; 7/8; S; Son; 1010; Yes; Yes; None [1/4+ 1931]

1012; Seminole, Louis; M; 6/84, 47; Cheyenne; 3/4; Wd[sic]; Head; 1011; Yes; Yes; None [1/4+ 1931]

1013; Seminole, Miles; M; 4/69, 62; Cheyenne; 3/4; M; Head; 1012; Yes; Yes; None [1/4+ 1931]
1014; Seminole, Flora (Redrobe, Flora); F; 5/06, 25; Cheyenne; F; M; Wife; 1013; Yes; Yes; None
1015; Seminole, Lucille; F; 2/24/31, 1; Cheyenne; 7/8; S; Dau; 1014; Yes; Yes; None [Fullblood 1931]
1016; Whistlingelk, May; F; 3/9/26, 6; Cheyenne; F; S; S-Dau; 1015; Yes; Yes; None

1017; Sharpnose, Josephine; F; 6/02, 29; Cheyenne; F; Wd.; Head; 1016; Yes; Yes; None [Hisbadhorses]

1018; Shavedhead, James; M; 11/99, 32; Cheyenne; F; M; Head; 1017; Yes; Yes; None
1019; Shavedhead, Alice (Medicineflying, Alice); F; 2/07, 25; Cheyenne; F; M; Wife; 1018; Yes; Yes; None [age 3 in 1910. Birth 1906-07.]
1020; Shavedhead, Anna; F; 9/6/25, 6; Cheyenne; F; S; Dau; 1019; Yes; Yes; None [Hyacinth in 1926.]
1021; Shavedhead, Mabel; F; 1/23/30, 2; Cheyenne; F; S; Dau; 1020; Yes; Yes; None
1022; Divesbackward, Mary; F; 6/65, 66; Cheyenne; F; Wd; Mother; 1021; Yes; Yes; None [Shavedhead, Mary in 1931]
1023; Divesbackward, Louisa; F; 8/17; Cheyenne; F; S; Niece; 1022; Yes; Yes; None [7/8 blood in 1928.]

1024; Shavedhead, Jean; F; 6/01, 30; Cheyenne; F; M; Head; 1023; No; Shoshone & Arap. Wyo.; Yes; None [Swallow]
1025; Shavedhead, Charles; M; 6/23/24, 7; Cheyenne; F; S; Son; 1024; No; Shoshone & Arap. Wyo.; Yes; None [Jeffrey, Jr. and birth year 1925 in 1926.]
1026; Shavedhead, Marjorie A.; F; 9/30/26, 5; Cheyenne; F; S; Dau; 1025; No; Shoshone & Arap. Wyo.; Yes; None [Shavedhead, Anna M. in 1931]

Census of the **Tongue River** reservation of the **Tongue River** jurisdiction, as of **April 1**, 1932, taken by **W. R. Centerwall**, Superintendent.

**Key:** Number; NAME: Surname, Given; Sex; Birthdate, Age At Last Birthday; Tribe; Degree of Blood; Marital Status; Relationship To Head of Family; Last Census Roll Number; At Jurisdiction Where Enrolled (Yes or No); At Another Jurisdiction; ELSEWHERE: Post office, County, State; Ward (Yes or No); Allotment, Annuity, and Identification Numbers.

1027; Shell, Joseph; M; 2/81, 51; Cheyenne; F; M; Head; 1026; Yes; Yes; None
1028; Shell, Julia (Killsnight, Julia); F; 9/01, 30; Cheyenne; F; M; Wife; 1027; Yes; Yes; None [Previous #530 in 1906, censuses 1906-19, wife Alice [Risingsun] Shell, birth year 1885.] [Julia starts census 1920.]

N.E. Shepherd, Clarence; M; [--]; Cheyenne; F; M; Head; [--]; --
1029; Shepherd, Mollie (Seminole, Mollie); F; 4/95, 36; Cheyenne; 7/8; M; Wife; 1028; No; Cheyenne & Arap., Okla; Yes; None [1/4+ 1931]

1030; Sherman, Ethel (Parker, Ethel); F; 5/83, 48; Cheyenne; 1/4; M; Head; 1029; Yes; Yes; None [1/4+ 1930; 1/4- 1931]
1031; Sherman, George; M; 10/11, 20; Cheyenne; 1/8; S; Son; 1030; Yes; Yes; None [-1/4 1931]
1032; Sherman, Otto; M; 6/12, 18; Cheyenne; 1/8; S; Son; 1031; Yes; Yes; None [-1/4 1931]
1033; Sherman, Wretha; F; 8/15, 16; Cheyenne; 1/8; S; Dau; 1032; Yes; Yes; None [-1/4 1931]
1034; Sherman, Carl; M; 12/18, 13; Cheyenne; 1/8; S; Son; 1033; Yes; Yes; None [-1/4 1931]
1035; Sherman, Clarence; M; 7/22, 9; Cheyenne; 1/8; S; Son; 1034; Yes; Yes; None [-1/4 1931]

1036; Shortsioux, Mary; F; 6/14, 17; Cheyenne; 7/8; S; Alone; 1035; No; Crow Agency, Mont.; Yes; None [Dau Longears, Crow Agency, Mont.]

1037; Shoulderblade, Benedict; M; 9/74, 57; Cheyenne; F; M; Head; 1036; Yes; Yes; None
1038; Shoulderblade, Fannie; F; 7/23/24, 7; Cheyenne; 3/4; S; Dau; 1037; Yes; Yes; None [1/4+ 1931; Full 1930]

1039; Shoulderblade, Fred; M; 10/61, 70; Cheyenne; F; M; Head; 1038; Yes; Yes; None
1040; Shoulderblade, Richard; M; 8/11, 21; Cheyenne; F; S; Son; 1039; Yes; Yes; None

1041; Shoulderblade, Ethel (Woodenleg, Ethel); F; 8/93, 38; Cheyenne; 1/2; Wd; Head; 1040; Yes; Yes; None [1/4+ 1931]
1042; Shoulderblade, Thomas; M; 10/15, 16; Cheyenne; 3/4; S; Son; 1041; Yes; Yes; None [1/4+ 1931]
1043; Shoulderblade, Francis; F[sic]; 3/17, 15; Cheyenne; 3/4; S; Son; 1042; Yes; Yes; None [1/4+ 1931] [1917 Census William]
1044; Shoulderblade, Wendel; M; 8/20, 11; Cheyenne; 3/4; S; Son; 1033; Yes; Yes; None [1/4+ 1931]

Census of the __Tongue River__ reservation of the __Tongue River__ jurisdiction, as of __April 1__, 1932, taken by __W. R. Centerwall__, Superintendent.

**Key:** Number; NAME: Surname, Given; Sex; Birthdate, Age At Last Birthday; Tribe; Degree of Blood; Marital Status; Relationship To Head of Family; Last Census Roll Number; At Jurisdiction Where Enrolled (Yes or No); At Another Jurisdiction; ELSEWHERE: Post office, County, State; Ward (Yes or No); Allotment, Annuity, and Identification Numbers.

1045; Shoulderblade, Fern; F; 2/23/28, 4; Cheyenne; 3/4; S; Dau; 1044; Yes; Yes; None [1/4+ 1931]
1046; Shoulderblade, Claudia; F; 7/8/30, 1; Cheyenne; 3/4; S; Dau; 1045; Yes; Yes; None [1/4+ 1931]

1047; Silloway (Burns), Veta; F; 11/04, 27; Cheyenne; 1/8; M; Head; 1046; No; Miles City, town, Custer, Mont.; Yes; None [-1/4 1931]

1048; Sioux, Thomas; M; 11/70, 61; Cheyenne; F; M; Head; 1047; Yes; Yes; None
--- Sioux, Jane W.; F; 3/67, 64; Cheyenne; F; M; Wife; 1048; Yes; Yes; None Died August 18, 1931.
1049; Sioux, Henry; M; 6/11, 20; Cheyenne; F; S; Son; 1049; Yes; Yes; None
1050; Risingsun, Ruby; F; 9/19/28, 3; Cheyenne; F; S; A-Dau; 1050; Yes; Yes; None

1051; Sittingman, Charles; M; 10/66, 65; Cheyenne; F; M; Head; 1051; Yes; Yes; None
1052; Sittingman, Lucy (Crazyhead, Lucy); F; 5/66, 65; Cheyenne; F; M; Wife; 1052; Yes; Yes; None
1053; Sittingman, Edw. Chas.; M; 6/00, 31; Cheyenne; F; D; Son; 1053; Yes; Yes; None [Edward in 1927 & 1931. Was Edwin in 1926.]

1054; Small, Josephine; F; 2/92, 40; Cheyenne; 1/2; M; Head; 1054; Yes; Yes; None [1/4+ 1931]
1055; Small, Victor; M; 8/12, 19; Cheyenne; 1/4; S; Son; 1055; Yes; Yes; None [1/4+ 1931]
1056; Small, Edward; M; 11/5/13, 18; Cheyenne; 1/4; S; Son; 1056; Yes; Yes; None [1/4+ 1931]
1057; Small, Max J.; M; 4/15, 16; Cheyenne; 1/4; S; Son; 1057; Yes; Yes; None [1/4+ 1931]
1058; Small, Ivan; M; 4/20, 11; Cheyenne; 1/4; S; Son; 1058; Yes; Yes; None [1/4+ 1931]
1059; Small, Thomas; M; 12/21, 10; Cheyenne; 1/4; S; Son; 1059; Yes; Yes; None [1/4+ 1931]
1060; Small, Horace; M; 7/23, 8; Cheyenne; 1/4; S; Son; 1060; Yes; Yes; None [1/4+ 1931]
1061; Small, Melvin; M; 2/25, 7; Cheyenne; 1/4; S; Son; 1061; Yes; Yes; None [1/4+ 1931]
1062; Small, Worth; M; 2/2/27, 5; Cheyenne; 1/4; S; Son; 1062; Yes; Yes; None [1/4+ 1931]
1063; Small, Clinton; M; 11/19/29, 2; Cheyenne; 1/4; S; Son; 1062; Yes; Yes; None [1/4+ 1931]

1064; Smith, John; M; 6/75, 56; Cheyenne; F; M; Head; 1064; Yes; Yes; None

Census of the **Tongue River** reservation of the **Tongue River** jurisdiction, as of **April 1**, 1932, taken by **W. R. Centerwall**, Superintendent.

**Key:** Number; NAME: Surname, Given; Sex; Birthdate, Age At Last Birthday; Tribe; Degree of Blood; Marital Status; Relationship To Head of Family; Last Census Roll Number; At Jurisdiction Where Enrolled (Yes or No); At Another Jurisdiction; ELSEWHERE: Post office, County, State; Ward (Yes or No); Allotment, Annuity, and Identification Numbers.

1065; Smith, Blanche (Shebear, Blanche); F; 3/80, 52; Cheyenne; F; M; wife; 1065; Yes; Yes; None

1066; Americanhorse, Rueben[sic]; M; 11/17, 14; Cheyenne; F; S; A-Son; 1066; Yes; Yes; None

1067; Soldierwolf, John; M; 4/83, 48; Cheyenne; F; M; Head; 1067; Yes; Yes; None
1068; Soldierwolf, Mary K. (Killsnight, Mary); F; 4/88, 43; Cheyenne; F; M; Wife; 1068; Yes; Yes; None
1069; Soldierwolf, Thomas; M; 6/10, 21; Cheyenne; F; S; Son; 1069; Yes; Yes; None
1070; Soldierwolf, Josie A.; F; 1/15, 16; Cheyenne; F; S; Dau; 1070; Yes; Yes; None
1071; Soldierwolf, Bessie L.; F; 10/17, 14; Cheyenne; F; S; Dau; 1071; Yes; Yes; None
1072; Soldierwolf, James K.; M; 7/20, 11; Cheyenne; F; S; Son; 1072; Yes; Yes; None
1073; Soldierwolf, Annie K.; F; 5/22, 9; Cheyenne; F; S; Dau; 1073; Yes; Yes; None
1074; Soldierwolf, Doris; F; 4/5/30, 2; Cheyenne; F; S; Dau; 1074; Yes; Yes; None

1075; Sooktis, Josie (Americanhorse, Josie); F; 1889; Cheyenne; F; M; Head; ---; No; Cheyenne & Arap., Okla. (L-C 34875-26 23276-31); Yes; None
1076; Sooktis, Andrew; M; 3/12/26, 6; Cheyenne; F; S; Son; ---; No; Cheyenne & Arap., Okla; Yes; None

1077; Spang, Alban D.; M; 9/92, 39; Cheyenne; 1/8; M; Head; 1075; Yes; Yes; None [-1/4 1931]
1078; Spang, Edward F.; M; 3/16/29, 3; Cheyenne; 1/16; S; Son; 1076; Yes; Yes; None [-1/4 1931]
1079; Spang, Peter A.; M; 2/24/31, 1; Cheyenne; 1/16; S; Son; 1077; Yes; Yes; None [-1/4 1931]

1080; Spang, Alfonso; M; 1/87, 45; Cheyenne; 1/8; M; Head; 1078; Yes; Yes; None [-1/4+[sic] 1931]
1081; Spang, Mary (Callsfirst, Mary); F; 9/11, 20; Cheyenne; 7/8; M; Wife; 1079; Yes; Yes; None [1/4+ 1931] [1924 Annie.]
1082; Spang, Alfonso Jr.; M; 8/15/31, 5/12; Cheyenne; 1/2; S; Son; xxxx; Yes; Yes; None

1083; Spang, Deyo; M; 12/88, 43; Cheyenne; 1/8; M; Head; 1080; No; Poplar-town, Roosevelt, Mont.; Yes; None [-1/4 1931]
1084; Spang, Bruce S.; M; 6/24, 7; Cheyenne; 1/16; S; Son; 1081; No; Poplar-town, Roosevelt, Mont.; Yes; None [-1/4 1931]
1085; Spang, Dale C.; M; 7/8/26, 5; Cheyenne; 1/16; S; Son; 1082; No; Poplar-town, Roosevelt, Mont.; Yes; None [-1/4 1931]

Census of the **Tongue River** reservation of the **Tongue River** jurisdiction, as of **April 1**, 1932, taken by **W. R. Centerwall**, Superintendent.

**Key:** Number; NAME: Surname, Given; Sex; Birthdate, Age At Last Birthday; Tribe; Degree of Blood; Marital Status; Relationship To Head of Family; Last Census Roll Number; At Jurisdiction Where Enrolled (Yes or No); At Another Jurisdiction; ELSEWHERE: Post office, County, State; Ward (Yes or No); Allotment, Annuity, and Identification Numbers.

1086; Spang, Darrel D.; M; 8/9/30, 1; Cheyenne; 1/16; S; Son; 1083; No; Poplartown, Roosevelt, Mont.; Yes; None   [-1/4 1931]

1087; Spang, James; M; 7/99, 32; Cheyenne; 1/8; M; Head; 1084; Yes; Yes; None [-1/4 1931]
1088; Spang, James R.; M; 5/13/27, 4; Cheyenne; 1/16; S; Son; 1085; Yes; Yes; None   [-1/4 1931]
1089; Spang, Shirley A.; F; 5/19/28, 3; Cheyenne; 1/16; S; Dau; 1086; Yes; Yes; None   [-1/4 1931]

1090; Spang, Lucy; F; 5/69, 62; Cheyenne; 1/4; M; Head; 1087; Yes; Yes; None [1/4- 1931; Fullblood 1930]
1091; Spang, Harriet; F; 10/05, 26; Cheyenne; 1/8; S; Dau; 1088; Yes; Yes; None [-1/4 1931]
1092; Spang, Cash; M; 10/11, 20; Cheyenne; 1/8; M; Son; 1089; Yes; Yes; None [-1/4 1931]
1093; Spang, Joyce; F; 1/5/31, 1; Cheyenne; 1/16; S; G-Dau; 1090; Yes; Yes; None [-1/4 1931]

1094; Spang, Roy; M; 9/96, 35; Cheyenne; 1/8; M; Head; 1091; Yes; Yes; None [-1/4 1931]
1095; Spang, Viola (Wildhog, Viola); F; 1/07,24; Cheyenne; F; M; Wife; 1092; Yes; Yes; None
1096; Spang, Regina S.; F; 6/22, 9; Cheyenne; 9/16; S; Dau; 1093; Yes; Yes; None [1/4+ 1931] [Regina Rosetta in 1926.]
1097; Spang, Lyman; M; 8/23, 8; Cheyenne; 9/16; S; Son; 1094; Yes; Yes; None [1/4+ 1931]

1098; Spang, Wilfred; M; 5/01, 30; Cheyenne; 1/8; M; Head; 1095; Yes; Yes; None [-1/4 1931]
1099; Spang, Jennie (Limberhand, Jennie); F; 11/15, 16; Cheyenne; F; M; Wife; 1096; Yes; Yes; None
1100; Spang, Lawrence R.; M; 7/6/31, 9/12; Cheyenne; 9/16; S; Son; 1097; Yes; Yes; None   [1/4+ 1931]

1101; Speelman, Jessie; F; 1/89, 43; Cheyenne; 1/4; M; Head; 1098; Yes; Yes; None [1/4+ 1931]
1102; Farr, Evelyn; F; 12/14, 17; Cheyenne; 1/8; S; Dau; 1099; Yes; Yes; None [-1/4 1931]
1103; Farr, Frank; M; 7/17, 14; Cheyenne; 1/8; S; Son; 1100; Yes; Yes; None [-1/4 1931]
1104; Speelman, William L.; M; 7/26/29, 2; Cheyenne; 1/8; S; Son; 1101; Yes; Yes; None   [-1/4 1931]

Census of the __Tongue River__ reservation of the __Tongue River__ jurisdiction, as of __April 1__, 1932, taken by __W. R. Centerwall__, Superintendent.

**Key:** Number; NAME: Surname, Given; Sex; Birthdate, Age At Last Birthday; Tribe; Degree of Blood; Marital Status; Relationship To Head of Family; Last Census Roll Number; At Jurisdiction Where Enrolled (Yes or No); At Another Jurisdiction; ELSEWHERE: Post office, County, State; Ward (Yes or No); Allotment, Annuity, and Identification Numbers.

1105; Speelman, Orville; M; 7/26/29, 11/12; Cheyenne; 1/8; S; Son; 1102[sic]; Yes; Yes; None
1106; Killsnight, Kitty B.; F; 11/9/28, 3; Cheyenne; 9/16; S; G-Dau; 482; Yes; Yes; None [-1/4 1931; 1/4+ 1930]

1107; Sponge, Alfred; M; 7/96, 35; Cheyenne; F; M; Head; 1102; Yes; Yes; None
1108; Sponge, Mary Josie (Shoulderblade, Mary Josie); F; 9/01, 30; Cheyenne; F; M; Wife; 1103; Yes; Yes; None [1922 was #958, Scott.]

1109; Sponge, Oliver; M; 3/98, 34; Cheyenne; F; M; Head; 1104; Yes; Yes; None
1110; Sponge, Clara (Tangledyellowhair, Clara); F; 5/05, 26; Cheyenne; F; M; Wife; 1105; Yes; Yes; None
1111; Sponge, Paul; M; 12/10/27, 4; Cheyenne; F; S; Son; 1106; Yes; Yes; None
1112; Sponge, Lena; F; 8/28/29, 2; Cheyenne; F; S; Dau; 1107; Yes; Yes; None
1113; Sponge, Charles; M; 7/1/31, 9/12; Cheyenne; F; S; Son; xxxx; Yes; Yes; None

1114; Spottedblackbird, Lee; M; 6/59, 72; Cheyenne; F; M; Head; 1108; Yes; Yes; None [Birth year 1854 in 1926. #1082. Didn't pickup a first name until 1915 name, Lee; or Leo.]
1115; Spottedblackbird, Clara (Oldbull, Clara); F; 10/74, 57; Cheyenne; F; M; Wife; 1109; Yes; Yes; None

1116; Spottedelk, Alex; M; 11/00, 31; Cheyenne; F; M; Head; 1110; Yes; Yes; None
1117; Spottedelk, Nellie (Teeth, Nellie); F; 10/12, 19; Cheyenne; F; M; Wife; 1111; Yes; Yes; None [Spottedelk, Nellie T. in 1931]
1118; Spottedelk, Eugene; M; 1/28/31, 1; Cheyenne; F; S; Son; ---; Yes; Yes; None
1119; Medicineelk, William; M; 3/5/28, 3; Cheyenne; F; S; S-Son; 1112, Yes; Yes; None

1120; Spottedelk, Charles; M; 3/63, 69; Cheyenne; F; Wd[sic]; Head; 1113; Yes; Yes; None
1121; Spottedelk, August; M; 7/97, 34; Cheyenne; F; S; Son; 1114; Yes; Yes; None

1122; Spottedwolf, Charles; M; 10/92, 39; Cheyenne; F; M; Head; 1115; Yes; Yes; None
1123; Spottedwolf, Lena (Standingwolf, Lena); F; 9/92, 39; Cheyenne; F; M; Wife; 1116; Yes; Yes; None
1124; Spottedwolf, Julia E.; F; 4/13, 18; Cheyenne; F; S; Dau; 1117; Yes; Yes; None
1125; Spottedwolf, Martha P.; F; 9/21, 10; Cheyenne; F; S; Dau; 1118; Yes; Yes; None
1126; Spottedwolf, John; M; 10/23, 8; Cheyenne; F; S; Son; 1119; Yes; Yes; None
1127; Littlewhiteman, Florence; F; 2/15, 16; Cheyenne; 7/8; S; S-Dau; 1120; Yes; Yes; None [1/4+ 1931]

Census of the **Tongue River** reservation of the **Tongue River** jurisdiction, as of **April 1**, 19**32**, taken by **W. R. Centerwall**, Superintendent.

**Key:** Number; NAME: Surname, Given; Sex; Birthdate, Age At Last Birthday; Tribe; Degree of Blood; Marital Status; Relationship To Head of Family; Last Census Roll Number; At Jurisdiction Where Enrolled (Yes or No); At Another Jurisdiction; ELSEWHERE: Post office, County, State; Ward (Yes or No); Allotment, Annuity, and Identification Numbers.

1128; Spottedwolf, Patrick; M; 11/87, 44; Cheyenne; F; M; Head; 1121; Yes; Yes; None
1129; Spottedwolf, Jean (Walters, Jean); F; 10/01, 30; Cheyenne; 3/8; M; Wife; 1122; Yes; Yes; None [1/4+ 1931]
1130; Spottedwolf, Ruby; F; 9/20, 11; Cheyenne; 11/16; S; Dau; 1123; Yes; Yes; None [1/4+ 1931]
1131; Spottedwolf, Eldora P.; F; 10/23, 8; Cheyenne; 11/16; S; Dau; 1124; Yes; Yes; None [Spottedwolf, Eldora Phyllis; 1/4+ 1931]
1132; Spottedwolf, Eugene C.; M; 8/25, 6; Cheyenne; 11/16; S; Son; 1125; Yes; Yes; None [Spottedwolf, Clarence Eugene; 1/4+ 1931]
1133; Spottedwolf, Mollie; F; 9/28/27, 4; Cheyenne; 11/16; S; Dau; 1126; Yes; Yes; None [1/4+ 1931]
1134; Spottedwolf, James; M; 3/15/31, 9/12; Cheyenne; 11/16; S; Son; ----; Yes; Yes; None

N.E. Squinteye, John; M; [--]; Cheyenne; F; M; Head
1135; Squinteye, Josie (Stronglefthand, Josie); F; 6/84, 47; Cheyenne; F; M; Wife; 1127; Yes; Yes; None [Whistlingelk]
1136; Whistlingelk, Alfred; M; 1/17, 15; Cheyenne; F; S; Son; 1128; Yes; Yes; None

1137; Standingelk, Alex; M; 4/96, 35; Cheyenne; F; M; Head; 1129; Yes; Yes; None
1138; Standingelk, Nora (Redneck, Nora); F; 7/03, 28; Cheyenne; F; M; wife; 1130; Yes; Yes; None
1139; Standingelk, Geneva S.; F; 3/22, 10; Cheyenne; F; S; Dau; 1131; Yes; Yes; None
1140; Standingelk, Margaret; F; 11/10/24, 7; Cheyenne; F; S; Dau; 1132; Yes; Yes; None
1141; Standingelk, Wayne; M; 5/29, 2; Cheyenne; F; S; Son; 1133; Yes; Yes; None
1142; Standingelk, Jordan; M; 9/1/31, 8/12; Cheyenne; F; S; Son; ----; Yes; Yes; None

1143; Standingelk, Annie; F; 5/07, 24; Cheyenne; F; D; Head; 1134; Yes; Yes; None
1144; Standingelk, Roy; M; 8/26, 5; Cheyenne; F; S; Son; 1135; Yes; Yes; None
1145; Swallow, Elsie; F; 4/12/30, 2; Cheyenne; F; S; Son; 1136; Yes; Yes; None

1146; Standingelk, Francis; M; 4/01, 30; Cheyenne; F; M; Head; 1137; Yes; Yes; None
1147; Standingelk, Ruth (Medicinebull, Ruth); F; 6/13, 19; Cheyenne; F; M; Wife; 736; Yes; Yes; None
1148; Standingelk, Isaac; M; 11/27/31, 4/12; Cheyenne; F; S; Son; ----; Yes; Yes; None

1149; Standingelk, Frank; M; 6/74, 57; Cheyenne; F; M; Head; 1138; Yes; Yes; None

Census of the **Tongue River** reservation of the **Tongue River** jurisdiction, as of **April 1**, 1932, taken by **W. R. Centerwall**, Superintendent.

**Key:** Number; NAME: Surname, Given; Sex; Birthdate, Age At Last Birthday; Tribe; Degree of Blood; Marital Status; Relationship To Head of Family; Last Census Roll Number; At Jurisdiction Where Enrolled (Yes or No); At Another Jurisdiction; ELSEWHERE: Post office, County, State; Ward (Yes or No); Allotment, Annuity, and Identification Numbers.

1150; Standingelk, Fannie; F; 4/78, 53; Cheyenne; F; M; Wife; 1139; Yes; Yes; None

1151; Standingelk, Flora; F; 4/21, 10; Cheyenne; F; S; Dau; 1140; Yes; Yes; None

1152; Standingelk, Henry; M; 6/91, 40; Cheyenne; F; M; Head; 1141; Yes; Yes; None

1153; Standingelk, Mary (Swallow, Mary); F; 5/07, 24; Cheyenne; F; M; Wife; 1142; Yes; Yes; None

--- Standingelk, Aiden; M; 5/17/28, 3; Cheyenne; F; S; Son; 1143; Yes; Yes; None  Died August 25, 1931

1154; Standingelk, Benno; M; 2/21/30, 2; Cheyenne; F; S; Son; 1144; Yes; Yes; None

1155; Standingelk, George; M; 2/22/32, 1/12; Cheyenne; F; S; Son; ----; Yes; Yes; None

1156; Standingelk, Robert B.; M; 10/70, 61; Cheyenne; F; M; Head; 1145; Yes; Yes; None

1157; Standingelk, Sally (Lostleg, Sally); F; 9/95, 36; Cheyenne; F; M; Wife; 1146; Yes; Yes; None

--- Standingelk, Ella J.; F; 12/18, 13; Cheyenne; F; S; Dau; 1147; Yes; Yes; None Died November 12, 1931

1158; Standingelk, Jennie; F; 5/27, 4; Cheyenne; F; S; Dau; 1148; Yes; Yes; None

1159; Standingelk, Lockwood; M; 6/90, 41; Cheyenne; F; Wd[sic]; Son; 1149; Yes; Yes; None

1160; Standsintimber Timber, John; M; 3/86, 46; Cheyenne; F; M; Head; 1150; Yes; Yes; None  Name changed to John Timber  Letter May 11/1933  [Family Part Blood in 1928.]

1161; Standsintimber Timber, Josie (Onebear, Josie); F; 3/98, 34; Cheyenne; 3/4; M; Wife; 1151; Yes; Yes; None

1162; Standsintimber Timber, Josephine; F; 6/20, 11; Cheyenne; 7/8; S; Dau; 1152; Yes; Yes; None

1163; Standsintimber Timber, John Jr.; M; 10/21, 10; Cheyenne; 7/8; S; Son; 1153; Yes; Yes; None

1164; Standsintimber Timber, Elva; F; 4/21/28, 2; Cheyenne; 7/8; S; Dau; 1154; Yes; Yes; None

1165; Standsintimber Timber, Gilbert; M; 10/24/30, 1; Cheyenne; 7/8; S; Son; 1155; Yes; Yes; None

1166; Strangeowl, James; M; 6/04, 27; Cheyenne; F; M; Head; 1156; Yes; Yes; None

1167; Strangeowl, Grace (Redneck, Grace); F; 3/10, 21; Cheyenne; F; M; Wife; 1157; Yes; Yes; None  [Strangeowl, Grace R. in 1931]

Census of the **Tongue River** reservation of the **Tongue River** jurisdiction, as of **April 1**, 1932, taken by **W. R. Centerwall**, Superintendent.

**Key:** Number; NAME: Surname, Given; Sex; Birthdate, Age At Last Birthday; Tribe; Degree of Blood; Marital Status; Relationship To Head of Family; Last Census Roll Number; At Jurisdiction Where Enrolled (Yes or No); At Another Jurisdiction; ELSEWHERE: Post office, County, State; Ward (Yes or No); Allotment, Annuity, and Identification Numbers.

1168; Strangeowl, John; M; 9/72, 59; Cheyenne; F; M; Head; 1158; Yes; Yes; None
1169; Strangeowl, Gertie; F; 11/68, 63; Cheyenne; F; M; Wife; 1159; Yes; Yes; None

1170; Starvingbear, James; M; 4/76, 55; Cheyenne; F; Wd[sic]; Head; 1160; Yes; Yes; None
1171; Starvingbear, Jack J.; M; 2/14, 18; Cheyenne; F; S; Son; 1161; Yes; Yes; None [Rosco in 1926.]

1172; Stumphorn, Frank; M; 10/43, 87; Cheyenne; F; M; Head; 1162; Yes; Yes; None
1173; Stumphorn, Annie; F; 7/55, 77; Cheyenne; F; M; Wife; 1163; Yes; Yes; None [Shortsioux]

1174; Sunbear, Micheal[sic]; M; 1891, 40; Cheyenne; F; M; Head; 1164; No; Kowa[sic] Agency, Okla.; Yes; None
1175; Sunbear, Herman; M; 3/23, 8; Cheyenne; F; M[sic]; Wife[sic]; 1165; No; Kiowa Agency, Okla.; Yes; None
1176; Sunbear, Deyo; M; 1924, 7; Cheyenne; F; M[sic]; Son; 1166; No; Kiowa Agency, Okla.; Yes; None

1177; Sunroads, David; M; 9/81, 50; Cheyenne; F; M; Head; 1167; Yes; Yes; None
1178; Sunroads, Lizzie (Crazyhead, Lizzie); F; 3/83, 49; Cheyenne; F; M; Wife; 1168; Yes; Yes; None

1179; Sunroads, John; M; 7/43, 88; Cheyenne; F; M; Head; 1169; Yes; Yes; None
1180; Sunroads, Lena; F; 87; Cheyenne; F; M; Wife; 1170; Yes; Yes; None

N.E. ~~Swallow, Johnnie; M; [--]; Cheyenne; F; M; Head~~
1181; Swallow, Mae (Rednose, Mae); F; 11/14, 17; Cheyenne; F; M; Wife; 1457; Yes; Yes; None  [Rednose, Sarah Mae in 1931]
1182; Swallow, Herbert; M; 11/11/31, 4/12; Cheyenne; F; S; Son; ----; Yes; Yes; None

1183; Swallow, William; M; 2/74, 58; Cheyenne; F; M; Head; 1171; Yes; Yes; None
1184; Swallow, Gertrude (Yellownose, Gertrude); F; 3/96, 36; Cheyenne; F; M; Wife; 1172; Yes; Yes; None
1185; Swallow, Oliver; M; 4/99, 32; Cheyenne; F; S; Son; 1173; Yes; Yes; None
--- ~~Swallow, Edward; M; 3/02, 30; Cheyenne; F; S; Son; 1174; Yes; Yes; None Died April 13, 1931~~

1186; Sweetmedicine, David; M; 3/63, 69; Cheyenne; F; M; Head; 1175; Yes; Yes; None

Census of the **Tongue River** reservation of the **Tongue River** jurisdiction, as of **April 1**, 1932, taken by **W. R. Centerwall**, Superintendent.

**Key:** Number; NAME: Surname, Given; Sex; Birthdate, Age At Last Birthday; Tribe; Degree of Blood; Marital Status; Relationship To Head of Family; Last Census Roll Number; At Jurisdiction Where Enrolled (Yes or No); At Another Jurisdiction; ELSEWHERE: Post office, County, State; Ward (Yes or No); Allotment, Annuity, and Identification Numbers.

1187; Sweetmedicine, Clara (Bearcoal, Clara); F; 12/70, 61; Cheyenne; F; M; Wife; 1176; Yes; Yes; None
1188; Sweetmedicine, Jacob; M; 4/94, 37; Cheyenne; F; S; Son; 1177; Yes; Yes; None
1189; Sweetmedicine, Joseph; M; 12/98, 33; Cheyenne; F; S; Son; 1178; Yes; Yes; None

1190; Sweetmedicine, William; M; 1889, 42; Cheyenne; F; M; Head; 1179; Yes; Yes; None
1191; Salzer, Alta; F; 1913, 18; Cheyenne; F; M; Dau; 1180; No; Cheyenne & Arap., Okla.; Yes; None  [Sweetmedicine, Alta in 1931]  [1915-Son, Thomas; M.]
1192; Salzer, Frances; F; 8/4/31, 8/12; Cheyenne; 1/2; S; G-Dau; ----; No; Cheyenne & Arap., Okla.; Yes; None

N.E.  Tallbear, DeForest; M; [--]; Cheyenne; F; M; Head;
1193; Tallbear, Josie; F; 2/97, 35; Cheyenne; F; M; Wife; 1181, Yes; Yes; None
1194; Tallbear, Ermajean; F; 2/17/31, 1; Cheyenne; F; S; Dau; 1182; Yes; Yes; None
1195; Littlewhiteman, Bessie; F; 5/26, 26; Cheyenne; 7/8; S; S-Dau; 1183; Yes; Yes; None  [Fullblood in 1931; Dau 1931]

1196; Tallbull, Albert; M; 4/06, 25; Cheyenne; F; S; Head; 1184; Yes; Yes; None

----  ~~Tallbull, Charles; M; 10/87, 44; Cheyenne; F; M; Head; 1185; Yes; Yes; None Died May 15, 1931~~
1197; Tallbull, Mary (Brady, Mary); F; 5/93, 38; Cheyenne; F; M; Wife; 1186; Yes; Yes; None
1198; Tallbull, Joseph; M; 6/15, 16; Cheyenne; F; S; Son; 1187; Yes; Yes; None
1199; Tallbull, Henry; M; 12/17, 14; Cheyenne; F; S; Son; 1188; Yes; Yes; None
1200; Tallbull, William; M; 1/21, 11; Cheyenne; F; S; Son; 1189; Yes; Yes; None
1201; Tallbull, Nelson; M; 10/23; 8; Cheyenne; F; S; Son; 1190; Yes; Yes; None
1202; Tallbull, Cecil R.; M; 1/1/27, 5; Cheyenne; F; S; Son; 1191; Yes; Yes; None
1203; Tallbull, Nellie; F; 1/5/29, 3; Cheyenne; F; S; Dau; 1192; Yes; Yes; None
1204; Tallbull, Charles Jr.; 9/11/31, 7/12; Cheyenne; F; S; Son; xxx; Yes; Yes; None

1205; Tallwhiteman, Jasper; M; 7/93, 38; Cheyenne; F; M; Head; 1194; Yes; Yes; None  [Wd[sic] in 1930]

1206; Tallwhiteman, John; M; 4/86, 45; Cheyenne; F; M; Head; 1195; Yes; Yes; None
1207; Tallwhiteman, Eleanor (Whitecrane, Eleanor); F; 3/98, 34; Cheyenne; F; M; Wife; 1196; Yes; Yes; None
1208; Tallwhiteman, Clarence; M; 7/12, 19; Cheyenne; F; S; Son; 1197; Yes; Yes; None

Census of the __Tongue River__ reservation of the __Tongue River__ jurisdiction, as of __April 1__, 1932, taken by __W. R. Centerwall__, Superintendent.

**Key:** Number; NAME: Surname, Given; Sex; Birthdate, Age At Last Birthday; Tribe; Degree of Blood; Marital Status; Relationship To Head of Family; Last Census Roll Number; At Jurisdiction Where Enrolled (Yes or No); At Another Jurisdiction; ELSEWHERE: Post office, County, State; Ward (Yes or No); Allotment, Annuity, and Identification Numbers.

1209; Tallwhiteman, Florence; F; 5/14, 17; Cheyenne; F; S; Dau; 1198; Yes; Yes; None
1210; Tallwhiteman, Jasper; M; 7/16, 15; Cheyenne; F; S; Son; 1199; Yes; Yes; None
1211; Tallwhiteman, Elsie; F; 5/20, 11; Cheyenne; F; S; Dau; 1200; Yes; Yes; None [Alice in 1930]
1212; Tallwhiteman, Tug; M; 6/22, 8; Cheyenne; F; S; Son; 1201; Yes; Yes; None
1213; Tallwhiteman, Agnes V.; F; 7/25, 6; Cheyenne; F; S; Dau; 1202; Yes; Yes; None [Tallwhiteman, Agnes Virginia 1931]

1214; Tangleyellowhair, Chas.; M; 2/92, 40; Cheyenne; F; M; Head; 1203; Yes; Yes; None
1215; Tangleyellowhair, Georgia (Littlewhirlwind, Georgia); F; 9/91, 40; Cheyenne; F; M; Wife; 1204; Yes; Yes; None [Talks]
1216; Tangleyellowhair, Roberta; F; 9/24, 7; Cheyenne; F; S; Dau; 1205; Yes; Yes; None
1217; Tangleyellowhair, Marie; F; 3/31/29, 3; Cheyenne; F; S; Dau; 1206; Yes; Yes; None
1218; Tangleyellowhair, Ruth; F; 2/12; Cheyenne; F; S; Dau; ----; Yes; Yes; None [Tangledyellowhair with a "d" in 1930 - the whole family]

1219; Tangleyellowhair, David P.; M; 6/98, 33; Cheyenne; F; M; Head; 1207; Yes; Yes; None [1904-18 no "d" in last name. Birth year 1894 in 1926.]
1220; Tangleyellowhair, Florence (Sunbear, Florence); F; 7/00, 31; Cheyenne; F; M; Wife; 1208; Yes; Yes; None [Tallwhiteman]
1221; Tangleyellowhair, Clara; F; 10/19, 12; Cheyenne; F; S; Dau; 1209, Yes; Yes; None
1222; Tangleyellowhair, Winona; F; 1/22, 9; Cheyenne; F; S; Dau; 1210; Yes; Yes; None [Tangledyellowhair with a "d" in 1930 - the whole family]
1223; Tallwhiteman, Alice; F; 1/16, 15; Cheyenne; F; S; S-Dau; 1211; Yes; Yes; None
1224; Tallwhiteman, Laura; F; 6/23, 8; Cheyenne; F; S; S-Dau; 1212; Yes; Yes; None [Tallwhiteman, Regina 1931]

1225; Tangleyellowhair, James; M; 1/69, 63; Cheyenne; F; M; Head; 1213; Yes; Yes; None [Tangledyellowhair with a "d" in 1930 - the whole family]
1226; Tangleyellowhair, Minnie; F; 12/70, 61; Cheyenne; F; M; Wife; 1214; Yes; Yes; None
1227; Tangleyellowhair, Josie; F; 3/48, 82; Cheyenne; F; Wd; Mother; 1215; Yes; Yes; None

1228; Teeth, Charles; M; 3/63, 69; Cheyenne; F; M; Head; 1216; Yes; Yes; None
1229; Teeth, Fannie (Hardrobe, Fannie); F; 10/80, 51; Cheyenne; F; M; Wife; 1217; Yes; Yes; None

Census of the **Tongue River** reservation of the **Tongue River** jurisdiction, as of **April 1**, 1932, taken by **W. R. Centerwall**, Superintendent.

**Key:** Number; NAME: Surname, Given; Sex; Birthdate, Age At Last Birthday; Tribe; Degree of Blood; Marital Status; Relationship To Head of Family; Last Census Roll Number; At Jurisdiction Where Enrolled (Yes or No); At Another Jurisdiction; ELSEWHERE: Post office, County, State; Ward (Yes or No); Allotment, Annuity, and Identification Numbers.

1230; Teeth, Franklin; M; 10/09, 22; Cheyenne; F; M; Head; 1218; Yes; Yes; None
1231; Teeth, Mabel D.; F; 7/13, 18; Cheyenne; F; M; Wife; 1219; Yes; Yes; None

1232; Teeth, John; M; 5/89, 42; Cheyenne; F; M; Head; 1220; Yes; Yes; None
1233; Teeth, Edith (Romannose, Edith); F; 10/02, 29; Cheyenne; F; M; Wife; 1221; Yes; Yes; None
1234; Teeth, Earl; M; 6/16, 15; Cheyenne; F; S; Son; 1222; Yes; Yes; None
1235; Teeth, Montana; F; 4/22, 9; Cheyenne; F; S; Dau; 1223; Yes; Yes; None
1236; Teeth, Elsie; F; 4/12/25, 7; Cheyenne; F; S; Dau; 1224; Yes; Yes; None
1237; Teeth, Logan; M; 11/15/28, 3; Cheyenne; F; S; Son; 1225; Yes; Yes; None
1238; Americanhorse, Flora; 1861, 71; Cheyenne; F; Wd; G-Mother; 1226; Yes; Yes; None

---- ~~Threefingers, John; M; 3/62, 70; Cheyenne; F; M; Head; 1227; Yes; Yes; None Died October 10, 1931~~
---- ~~Threefingers, Pansy (Wolfchief, Pansy); F; 7/76, 55; Cheyenne; F; M; Wife; 1228; Yes; Yes; None Died September 5, 1931~~

1239; Threefingers, William; M; 9/01, 30; Cheyenne; F; M; Head; 1230; Yes; Yes; None
1240; Threefingers, Lucy (Hardground, Lucy); F; 9/11, 21; Cheyenne; F; M; Wife; 1231; Yes; Yes; None
1241; Threefingers, Isaac; M; 1/22/31, 1; Cheyenne; F; S; Son; 1232; Yes; Yes; None

1242; Turkeylegs, John; M; 7/59, 72; Cheyenne; F; M; Head; 1233; Yes; Yes; None
1243; Turkeylegs, Lydia (Bearblack, Lydia); F; 8/74, 57; Cheyenne; F; M; Wife; 1234; Yes; Yes; None
1244; Redbird, Dorothy; F; 7/08, 23; Cheyenne; F; S; G-Dau; 1235; Yes; Yes; None [1/4+ 1931]
1245; Redbird, David; M; 5/22/28, 3; Cheyenne; F; S; G G-Son; 1236; Yes; Yes; None [1/4+ 1931]

1246; Turkeylegs, Lawrence; M; 7/06, 25; Cheyenne; F; M; Head; 1237; Yes; Yes; None [Name James in 1926.]
1247; Turkeylegs, Eva (Ghostbull, Eva); F; 3/08, 24; Cheyenne; F; M; Wife; 352; Yes; Yes; None

1248; Twin, James L.; M; 12/87, 44; Cheyenne; F; M; Head; 1238; Yes; Yes; None [Twin, Louis J. 1931; Louis James 1930]
1249; Twin, Bessie (Bigbeaver, Bessie); F; 3/86, 46; Cheyenne; F; M; Wife; 1239; Yes; Yes; None
1250; Twin, Margaret; F; 4/18, 13; Cheyenne; F; S; Dau; 1240; Yes; Yes; None

Census of the **Tongue River** reservation of the **Tongue River** jurisdiction, as of **April 1**, 1932, taken by **W. R. Centerwall**, Superintendent.

**Key:** Number; NAME: Surname, Given; Sex; Birthdate, Age At Last Birthday; Tribe; Degree of Blood; Marital Status; Relationship To Head of Family; Last Census Roll Number; At Jurisdiction Where Enrolled (Yes or No); At Another Jurisdiction; ELSEWHERE: Post office, County, State; Ward (Yes or No); Allotment, Annuity, and Identification Numbers.

1251; Twobirds, Peter; M; 5/78, 53; Cheyenne; F; M; Head; 1241; Yes; Yes; None
1252; Twobirds, Lenora (Arapahochief, Lenora); F; 7/72, 58; Cheyenne; F; M; Wife; 1242; Yes; Yes; None
1253; Twobirds, Jacob; M; 1/01, 30; Cheyenne; F; S; Son; 1243; Yes; Yes; None

1254; Twobulls, Martin; M; 7/91, 41; Cheyenne; F; M; Head; 1244; Yes; Yes; None
1255; Twobulls, Eleanor (Twin, Eleanor); F; 5/00, 31; Cheyenne; F; M; Wife; 1245; Yes; Yes; None
1256; Twobulls, William; M; 9/20, 11; Cheyenne; F; S; Son; 1246; Yes; Yes; None
1257; Twobulls, Alice; F; 8/27, 4; Cheyenne; F; S; Dau; 1247; Yes; Yes; None
1258; Twobulls, Ruth; F; 1/15/31, 1; Cheyenne; F; S; Dau; 1248; Yes; Yes; None

1259; Twofeathers, John; M; 4/57, 74; Cheyenne; F; M; Head; 1249; Yes; Yes; None
1260; Twofeathers, Clara; F; 5/70, 61; Cheyenne; F; M; Wife; 1250; Yes; Yes; None
---- ~~Twofeathers, Ethel; F; 9/08, 23; Cheyenne; F; S; Dau; 1251; Yes; Yes; None Died August 30, 1931~~

1261; Twomoons, Bert; M; 11/87, 44; Cheyenne; F; M; Head; 1252; Yes; Yes; None

1262; Twomoons, John; M; 4/55, 76; Cheyenne; F; Wd[sic]; Head; 1253; Yes; Yes; None
1263; Bigheadman, Betty N.; F; 1/15, 17; Cheyenne; F; S; G-Dau; 1254; Yes; Yes; None
1264; Bigheadman, Frank B.; M; 8/17, 14; Cheyenne; F; S; G-Son; 1255; Yes; Yes; None

1265; Twomoons, William; M; 5/84, 47; Cheyenne; F; M; Head; 1256; Yes; Yes; None
1266; Twomoons, Emma (Bites, Emma); F; 7/95, 36; Cheyenne; F; M; Wife; 1257; Yes; Yes; None [Rowland]

N.E. Two Two, Stephen; M; [--]; Sioux; F; M; Head; --
1267; Two Two, Thelma (Foot, Thelma); F; 6/13, 18; Cheyenne; 5/8; M; Wife; 345; Yes; Yes; None [1/4+ 1930] [1917 Census name Daisy.]

1268; Vassau, Jessie; F; 5/07, 24; Cheyenne; F; D; Head; 1258; No; Miles City, town, Custer, Mont.; Yes; None

1269; Walkingbear, Charles; M; 5/76, 74; Cheyenne; F; M; Head; 1259; Yes; Yes; None
1270; Walkingbear, Jennie; F; 9/72, 59; Cheyenne; F; M; Wife; 1260; Yes; Yes; None

Census of the **Tongue River** reservation of the **Tongue River** jurisdiction, as of **April 1**, 1932, taken by **W. R. Centerwall**, Superintendent.

**Key:** Number; NAME: Surname, Given; Sex; Birthdate, Age At Last Birthday; Tribe; Degree of Blood; Marital Status; Relationship To Head of Family; Last Census Roll Number; At Jurisdiction Where Enrolled (Yes or No); At Another Jurisdiction; ELSEWHERE: Post office, County, State; Ward (Yes or No); Allotment, Annuity, and Identification Numbers.

1271; Walkingbear, David; M; 6/97, 34; Cheyenne; F; M; Head; 1229; Yes; Yes; None
1271; Walkingbear, Olive (Plentycrows, Olive); F; 8/91, 40; Cheyenne; F; M; Wife; 892; Yes; Yes; None    [Redwoman, Olive 1931]
1272; Redwoman, Edna; F; 7/3/26, 5; Cheyenne; F; S; S-Dau; 893; Yes; Yes; None
1273; Redwoman, Donald; M; 7/10/28, 3; Cheyenne; F; S; S-Son; 894; Yes; Yes; None
1274; Redwoman, John; M; 1/18/31, 1; Cheyenne; F; S; S-Son; ---; Yes; Yes; None

1276; Walkinghorse, John; M; 8/57, 74; Cheyenne; F; M; Head; 1261; Yes; Yes; None
1277; Walkinghorse, Olive (Whitebull, Olive); F; 9/66, 65; Cheyenne; F; M; Wife; 1262; Yes; Yes; None

1278; Walksalong, Hugh; M; 4/85, 46; Cheyenne; F; M; Head; 1263; Yes; Yes; None
1279; Walksalong, Mamie (Limberhand, Mamie); F; 3/97. 34; Cheyenne; F; M; Wife; 1264; Yes; Yes; None
1280; Walksalong, Flora; F; 5/15, 16; Cheyenne; F; S; Dau; 1265; Yes; Yes; None [Previous censuses 1916-19, Fred, son.]
1281; Walksalong, Mary E.; F; 6/20, 11; Cheyenne; F; S; Dau; 1266; Yes; Yes; None
1282; Walksalong, Carol; F; 1/10/28, 3; Cheyenne; F; S; Dau; 1267; Yes; Yes; None
1283; Walksalong, Joseph; M; 4/26/31, 1; Cheyenne; F; S; Son; ----; Yes; Yes; None
1284; Killsontop, Ida; F; 10/24, 7; Cheyenne; F; S; S-Dau; 1268; Yes; Yes; None

1285; Walkslast, Frank; M; 3/08, 24; Cheyenne; F; M; Head; 1269; Yes; Yes; None
1286; Walkslast, Carrie (Killsnight, Carrie); F; 5/11, 20; Cheyenne; F; M; Wife; 1270; Yes; Yes; None
1287; Walkslast, Lloyd; M; 9/2/30, 1; Cheyenne; F; S; Son; 1271; Yes; Yes; None

1288; Walkslast, James; M; 9/05, 26; Cheyenne; F; M; Head; 1272; Yes; Yes; None [Clement in 1926.]
1289; Walkslast, May (Littlewolf, May); F; 3/11,21; Cheyenne; F; M; Wife; 1273; Yes; Yes; None    [Walkslast, May L.W. 1931]
1290; Walkslast, Gilbert; M; 3/13/31, 1; Cheyenne; F; S; Son; 1274; Yes; Yes; None

1291; Walkslast, Richard; M; 3/56, 76; Cheyenne; F; M; Head; 1275; Yes; Yes; None
---- ~~Walkslast, Anne; F; 7/62, 69; Cheyenne; F; M; Wife; 1276; Yes; Yes; None Died Spetember[sic] 27, 1931~~

1292; Walksnice, Adolph; M; 4/78, 53; Cheyenne; F; M; Head; 1277; Yes; Yes; None
1293; Walksnice, Flora; F; 10/84, 46; Cheyenne; F; M; Wife; 1278; Yes; Yes; None

Census of the **Tongue River** reservation of the **Tongue River** jurisdiction, as of **April 1**, **1932**, taken by **W. R. Centerwall**, Superintendent.

**Key:** Number; NAME: Surname, Given; Sex; Birthdate, Age At Last Birthday; Tribe; Degree of Blood; Marital Status; Relationship To Head of Family; Last Census Roll Number; At Jurisdiction Where Enrolled (Yes or No); At Another Jurisdiction; ELSEWHERE: Post office, County, State; Ward (Yes or No); Allotment, Annuity, and Identification Numbers.

1294; Walksnice, Dick; M; 5/11, 20; Cheyenne; F; S; Son; 1279; Yes; Yes; None
1295; Wolfchum, Lily; F; 5/16, 15; Cheyenne; F; S; G-Son; 1280; Yes; Yes; None [1917 Census name Betty.]

1296; Walksnice, John; M; 9/05, 26; Cheyenne; F; M; Head; 1281; Yes; Yes; None
1297; Walksnice, Mary (Crookednose, Mary); F; 1/03, 29; Cheyenne; F; M; Wife; 1282; Yes; Yes; None
1298; Walksnice, Mae; F; 11/1/29, 2; Cheyenne; F; S; Dau; 1283; Yes; Yes; None

1299; Wallowing, Rufus; M; 11/87, 44; Cheyenne; F; M; Head; 1284; Yes; Yes; None [Dustybuffalo, Rollingbull] Name changed to "Wallowing" see 57750-26. [First name Rutherford misspelled starting in 1918.]
1300; Wallowing, Stella (Parker, Stella); F; 7/85, 46; Cheyenne; F; M; Wife; 1285; Yes; Yes; None [1/4+ 1931]
1301; Redwoman, George P.; M; 4/4/28, 3; Cheyenne; F; S; A-Son; 1286; Yes; Yes; None

1302; Walters, George; M; 9/97, 34; Cheyenne; 3/8; M; Head; 1287; Yes; Yes; None [1/4+ 1931]

1303; Waters, Frank; M; 3/75, 57; Cheyenne; F; M; Head; 1289; Yes; Yes; None
1304; Waters, Joseph; M; 9; Cheyenne; F; S; A-Son; 1290; Yes; Yes; None [1346; 1377; Woodenlegs, Martin; son; 1922; in 1926. Step-son in 1928.]

1305; Weaselbear, Frank; M; 9/61, 70; Cheyenne; F; M; Head; 1291; Yes; Yes; None
1306; Weaselbear, Mary; F; 2/70, 62; Cheyenne; F; M; Wife; 1292; Yes; Yes; None

---- ~~Weaselbear, Hugh; M; 1889, 42; Cheyenne; F; D; Head; 1293; Yes; Yes; None Died March 4, 1932~~
1307; Weaselbear, Andrew; M; 4/15, 17; Cheyenne; F; S; Son; 1294; Yes; Yes; None
1308; Weaselbear, Busby; M; 7/22, 9; Cheyenne; F; S; Son; 1295; Yes; Yes; None

N.E. Weaselbear, Sam; M; [--]; Chey. & Sioux; F; M; Head
1309; Weaselbear, Martha (Wolfname, Martha); F; 6/10, 21; Cheyenne; F; M; Wife; 1296; Yes; Yes; None

1310; Wheeler, DeWitt C.; M; 12/92, 39; Cheyenne; 1/2; M; Head; 1297; Yes; Yes; None [1/4+ 1931; Listed as Sioux in 1930 & 1931; 1/4- in 1930]
1311; Wheeler, DeWitt P.; M; 11/16, 15; Cheyenne; 1/2; S; Son; 1298; Yes; Yes; None [1/4+ 1930; Listed as Sioux in 1930 & 1931]

Census of the **Tongue River** reservation of the **Tongue River** jurisdiction, as of **April 1**, 19**32**, taken by **W. R. Centerwall**, Superintendent.

**Key:** Number; NAME: Surname, Given; Sex; Birthdate, Age At Last Birthday; Tribe; Degree of Blood; Marital Status; Relationship To Head of Family; Last Census Roll Number; At Jurisdiction Where Enrolled (Yes or No); At Another Jurisdiction; ELSEWHERE: Post office, County, State; Ward (Yes or No); Allotment, Annuity, and Identification Numbers.

1312; Whirlwind, Thomas; M; 10/76, 55; Cheyenne; F; M; Head; 1299; Yes; Yes; None
1313; Whirlwind, Minnie (Ironshirt, Minnie); F; 6/82, 58; Cheyenne; F; M; Wife; 1300; Yes; Yes; None
1314; Killsnight, Susan; F; 5/17, 14; Cheyenne; F; S; S-Dau; 1301; Yes; Yes; None
1315; Killsnight, Bessie; F; 2/20, 12; Cheyenne; F; S; S-Dau; 1302; Yes; Yes; None
1316; Ironshirt, Jennie; F; 7/58, 73; Cheyenne; F; Wd; Mother-in-law; 1303; Yes; Yes; None

1317; Whistlingelk, Charles; M; 1/76, 56; Cheyenne; F; M; Head; 1333; Yes; Yes; None
1318; Whistlingelk, Rose (Whitebird, Rose); F; 12/92, 39; Cheyenne; F; M; Wife; 1334; Yes; Yes; None
1319; Whitebird, Lena; F; 10/55, 76; Cheyenne; F; Wd; Mother-in-law; 1335; Yes; Yes; None

1320; Whistlingelk, John; M; 4/04, 27; Cheyenne; F; M; Head; 1304; Yes; Yes; None
1321; Whistlingelk, Carrie (Deafy, Carrie); F; 6/10, 21; Cheyenne; F; M; Wife; 1305; Yes; Yes; None [Whistlingelk, Carrie D. 1931]
---- ~~Whistlingelk, Maynora; F; 10/25/31, 2/12; Cheyenne; F; S; Dau; ----; Yes; Yes; None Died December 31, 1931~~

1322; White, Stamper; M; 4/98, 33; Cheyenne; F; M; Head; 1306; Yes; Yes; None
1323; White, Lottie (Rowland, Lottie); F; 3/03, 29; Cheyenne; 3/4; M; Wife; 1307; Yes; Yes; None [1/4+ 1931; 1/4- 1930]
1324; White, Pearl; F; 823, 8; Cheyenne; 7/8; S; Dau; 1308; Yes; Yes; None [1/4+ 1931; 1/4- 1930]
1325; White, Willis; M; 3/31/30, 2; Cheyenne; 7/8; S; Son; 1309; Yes; Yes; None [1/4+ 1931; 1/4- 1930]

1326; Whitebear, Joseph; M; 1896, 35; Cheyenne; F; M; Head; 1310; Yes; Yes; None
1327; Whitebear, Alice (Blackree, Alice); F; 3/09, 22; Cheyenne; F; M; Wife; 1311; Yes; Yes; None
1328; Blackree, Anna; F; 8/23, 8; Cheyenne; F; S; S-Dau; 1312; Yes; Yes; None [Whitebear, Anna in 1931]

1329; Whitebird, Frank; M; 2/02, 30; Cheyenne; F; M; Head; 1313; Yes; Yes; None
1330; Whitebird, Julia (Redwoman, Julia); F; 7/09, 22; Cheyenne; F; M; Wife; 1314; Yes; Yes; None [Whitebird, Julia R. 1931] [1926 Nicetalker, Clarice; s-dau; 1909; F. Also s-dau John Chubby.]
1331; Whitebird, Edward; M; 3/4/30, 2; Cheyenne; F; S; Son; 1315; Yes; Yes; None

Census of the __Tongue River__ reservation of the __Tongue River__ jurisdiction, as of __April 1__, 1932, taken by __W. R. Centerwall__, Superintendent.

**Key:** Number; NAME: Surname, Given; Sex; Birthdate, Age At Last Birthday; Tribe; Degree of Blood; Marital Status; Relationship To Head of Family; Last Census Roll Number; At Jurisdiction Where Enrolled (Yes or No); At Another Jurisdiction; ELSEWHERE: Post office, County, State; Ward (Yes or No); Allotment, Annuity, and Identification Numbers.

1332; Whitebuffalo, John; M; 3/71, 61; Cheyenne; F; Wd[sic]; Head; 1316; Yes; Yes; None

1333; Woundedeye, Paul; M; 6/11, 20; Cheyenne; F; S; G-Son; 1317; Yes; Yes; None

1334; Medicineelk, Spencer; M; 7/17, 14; Cheyenne; F; S; G-Son; 1318; Yes; Yes; None

Whiteman family see under Littlewhiteman page [311, #665-667].
Changed to Whiteman

1335; Whitecrane, Leo; M; 6/95, 36; Cheyenne; F; M; Head; 1319; Yes; Yes; None
1336; Whitecrane, Ella (Tangleyellowhair, Ella); F; 7/01, 30; Cheyenne; F; M; Wife; 1320; Yes; Yes; None [Littlebird]
1337; Whitecrane, Victor; M; 7/19/24, 7; Cheyenne; F; S; Son; 1321; Yes; Yes; None
1338; Whitecrane, Eva; F; 12/5/28, 3; Cheyenne; F; S; Son[sic]; 1322; Yes; Yes; None
1339; Whitecrane, Anna; F; 2/6/31, 1; Cheyenne; F; S; Son[sic]; 1323; Yes; Yes; None
1340; Littlebird, Harry; M; 8/18, 13; Cheyenne; F; S; S-Son; 1324; Yes; Yes; None
1341; Littlebird, James; M; 7/19, 12; Cheyenne; F; S; S-Son; 1324; Yes; Yes; None
[Previous #1274; Littlebird, Elsie; s-dau; birth year 1920; F in 1926.]

1342; Whitecrow, Alfred; M; 12/10, 21; Cheyenne; F; S; Head; 1326; No; Cheyenne & Arap., Okla.; Yes; None    [Teddy Redcherries- Fthr.]

1343; Whitedirt, Charlie; M; 6/05, 26; Cheyenne; F; M; Head; 1327; Yes; Yes; None
1344; Whitedirt, Julia (Whistlingelk, Julia); F; 7/09, 22; Cheyenne; F; M; Wife; 1328; Yes; Yes; None
1345; Whitedirt, Leona; F; 12/7/28, 3; Cheyenne; F; S; Dau; 1329; Yes; Yes; None
1346; Whitedirt, May; F; 5/26/30, 1; Cheyenne; F; S; Dau; 1330; Yes; Yes; None
1347; Whitedirt, Maggie; F; 6/75, 54[sic]; Cheyenne; F; Wd; Mother; 1331; Yes; Yes; None
1348; Whitedirt, Jennie; F; 2/11, 21; Cheyenne; F; S; Sister; 1332; Yes; Yes; None

1349; Whitehawk, Charles J.; M; 4/99, 32; Cheyenne; F; M; Head; 1336; Yes; Yes; None
1350; Whitehawk, Alice (Crook, Alice); F 1/08, 24; Cheyenne; F; M; Wife; 1337; Yes; Yes; None   [Whitehawk, Alice C. in 1931]
1351; Whitehawk, Mary; F; 9/19, 12; Cheyenne; F; S; Dau; 1338; Yes; Yes; None
1352; Whitehawk, Marguerite; F; 11/20, 11; Cheyenne; F; S; Dau; 1339; Yes; Yes; None   [Same #1251 John, 1922-25, son, M.; Same prev., #1289 Emma; dau; 1922 in 1926.]
1353; Whitehawk, Andrew; M; 12/20/27, 3; Cheyenne; F; S; Son; 1340; Yes; Yes; None

Census of the __Tongue River__ reservation of the __Tongue River__ jurisdiction, as of __April 1__, 1932, taken by __W. R. Centerwall__, Superintendent.

**Key:** Number; NAME: Surname, Given; Sex; Birthdate, Age At Last Birthday; Tribe; Degree of Blood; Marital Status; Relationship To Head of Family; Last Census Roll Number; At Jurisdiction Where Enrolled (Yes or No); At Another Jurisdiction; ELSEWHERE: Post office, County, State; Ward (Yes or No); Allotment, Annuity, and Identification Numbers.

---- Whitehawk, James; M; 7/3/29, 3; Cheyenne; F; S; Son; 1341; Yes; Yes; None Died April 1, 1931

1354; Whitehawk, George; M; 12/6/30, 1; Cheyenne; F; S; Son; 1342; Yes; Yes; None

1355; Whitehawk, Mary; F; 7/58, 73; Cheyenne; F; Wd; Head; 1346; Yes; Yes; None

---- Whitemoon, George; M; 11/54, 76; Cheyenne; F; M; Head; 1347; Yes; Yes; None Died May 2, 1931

1356; Whitemoon, Kate; F; 8/65, 66; Cheyenne; F; M; Wife; 1348; Yes; Yes; None

1357; Whitemoon, Hugh; M; 4/81, 50; Cheyenne; F; M; Head; 1349; Yes; Yes; None
1358; Whitemoon, Eva (Littleeyes, Eva); F; 38; Cheyenne; F; M; Wife; 1350; Yes; Yes; None   [Whitemoon, Eva L.E. in 1931]
1359; Whitemoon, Clarence; M; 8/8/30, 1; Cheyenne; F; S; Son; 1351; Yes; Yes; None

1360; Whitewolf, Belle (Littleeagle, Belle); F; 5/02, 29; Cheyenne; F; Wd; Head; 1352; Yes; Yes; None
1361; Whitewolf, Joseph; M; 3/21, 11; Cheyenne; F; S; Son; 1353; Yes; Yes; None
1362; Whitewolf, George; M; 6/23, 8; Cheyenne; F; S; Son; 1354; Yes; Yes; None
1363; Whitewolf, Fred; M; 2/20/28, 3; Cheyenne; F; S; Son; 1355; Yes; Yes; None

N.E. Whitewolf, Grover; M; [--]; Cheyenne; F; Wd[sic]; Head; 1352; Yes; Yes; None
1364; Whitewolf, Everett; M; 3/14, 18; Cheyenne; F; S; Son; 1356; Yes; Yes; None
1365; Whitewolf, Carrie; F; 6/16, 16; Cheyenne; F; S; Dau; 1357; Yes; Yes; None [Philip son, M., 1920 census.]
1366; Whitewolf, Wilson; M; 5/19, 12; Cheyenne; F; S; Son; 1358; Yes; Yes; None
1367; Whitewolf, Thomas; M; 11/21, 10; Cheyenne; F; S; Son; 1359; Yes; Yes; None
1368; Whitewolf, Martin O.; M; 2/23, 9; Cheyenne; F; S; Son; 1360; Yes; Yes; None
1369; Whitewolf, Calvin M.; M; 1/25, 7; Cheyenne; F; S; Son; 1361; Yes; Yes; None

1370 Whitewolf, Frank; M; 3/47, 85; Cheyenne; F; M; Head; 1362; Yes; Yes; None
1371; Whitewolf, Julia; F; 7/54, 77; Cheyenne; F; M; Wife; 1363; Yes; Yes; None

N.E. Whitewolf, Charles; M; [--]; Cheyenne; F; M; Head
1372; Whitewolf, Susie (Grasshopper, Susie); F; 4/09, 22; Cheyenne; F; M; Wife; 1364; Yes; [Grasshopper; Dau. of Mrs. Stanley Lamewoman.]
1373; Whitewolf, Leo; M; 12/18/29, 2; Cheyenne; F; S; Son; 1365; Yes; Yes; None

N.E. Whitright, William; M; [--]; Sioux; [--]; M; Head

Census of the __Tongue River__ reservation of the __Tongue River__ jurisdiction, as of __April 1__, 1932, taken by __W. R. Centerwall__, Superintendent.

**Key:** Number; NAME: Surname, Given; Sex; Birthdate, Age At Last Birthday; Tribe; Degree of Blood; Marital Status; Relationship To Head of Family; Last Census Roll Number; At Jurisdiction Where Enrolled (Yes or No); At Another Jurisdiction; ELSEWHERE: Post office, County, State; Ward (Yes or No); Allotment, Annuity, and Identification Numbers.

1374; Whitright, Rhoda (Parker, Rhoda); F; 3/82, 50; Cheyenne; 1/4; M; Wife; 1366; Yes; Yes; None [Whitright, Rhoda S. in 1931 also 1/4+]
1375; Seminole, Lorraine; F; 6/16, 15; Cheyenne; 1/2; S; S-Dau; 1367; Yes; Yes; None [1/4+ 1931]
1376; Seminole, David; F; 12; Cheyenne; 1/2; S; S-Son; 1368; Yes; Yes; None [1/4+ 1931]

1377; Wildhog, Bird; M; 6/69, 62; Cheyenne; F; M; Head; 1369; Yes; Yes; None
1378; Wildhog, Lydia (Littlewolf, Lydia); F; 10/72, 59; Cheyenne; F; M; Wife; 1370; Yes; Yes; None
1379; Wildhog, Anne; F; 9/95, 36; Cheyenne; F; S; Dau; 1341; Yes; Yes; None
1380; Wildhog, John; M; 10/98, 33; Cheyenne; F; S; Son; 1342; Yes; Yes; None
1381; Wildhog, Mary; F; 12/03, 28; Cheyenne; F; S; Dau; 1343; Yes; Yes; None
1382; Wildhog, Vida; F; 3/05, 27; Cheyenne; F; S; Dau; 1344; Yes; Yes; None [Viola in 1906-25. Shows as 2 months old in 1906 yet majority of census years show the year of birth as 1907.]
1383; Wildhog, Julia; F; 7/13, 18; Cheyenne; F; S; Dau; 1345; Yes; Yes; None
1384; Wildhog, Opal; F; 1/25, 7; Cheyenne; F; S; G-Dau; 1376; Yes; Yes; None
1385; Blackstone, Arthur Jr.; M; 5/8/31, 11/12; Cheyenne; F; S; G-Son; xxxx; Yes; Yes; None

1386; Wilson, Martha; F; 5/94, 37; Cheyenne; 1/2; M; Head; 1377; Yes; Yes; None [Fullblood in 1931; 1/4+ 1930]
1387; Wilson, Arthur; M; 9/18, 13; Cheyenne; 1/4; S; Son; 1378; Yes; Yes; None [1/4- 1931] [1/4+ 1930] [1919 name James Jr.]
1388; Wilson, Esther M.; M; 8/20, 11; Cheyenne; 1/4; S; Dau; 1379; Yes; Yes; None [1/4- 1931] [1/4+ 1930]
1389; Wilson, Alice; F; 7/21, 10; Cheyenne; 1/4; S; Dau; 1380; Yes; Yes; None [1/4- 1931] [1/4+ 1930]
1390; Wilson, Florence; F; 9/22, 9; Cheyenne; 1/4; S; Dau; 1381; Yes; Yes; None [1/4- 1931] [1/4+ 1930]
1391; Wilson, Josephine; F; 11/26/24, 7; Cheyenne; 1/4; S; Dau; 1382; Yes; Yes; None [1/4- 1931] [1/4+ 1930]
1392; Wilson, James Jr.; M; 12/2/26, 6; Cheyenne; 1/4; S; Son; 1383; Yes; Yes; None [1/4- 1931] [1/4+ 1930] [#1383 was listed as 1384 in 1931]
1393; Wilson, George; M; 5/24/29, 2; Cheyenne; 1/4; S; Son; 1384; Yes; Yes; None [1/4- 1931] [1/4+ 1930]
1394; Wilson, William; M; 9/3/30, 1; Cheyenne; 1/4; S; Son; ----; Yes; Yes; None

1395; Windsor, Sarah (Spang, Sarah); F; 8/04, 27; Cheyenne; 1/8; M; Head; 1385; No; Easton, town, Kittitas, Wash.; Yes; None
1396; Windsor, Lee Roland; M; 5/23/30, 1; Cheyenne; 1/16; S; Son; 1386; No; Easton, town, Kittitas, Wash.; Yes; None

Census of the **Tongue River** reservation of the **Tongue River** jurisdiction, as of **April 1**, 1932, taken by **W. R. Centerwall**, Superintendent.

**Key:** Number; NAME: Surname, Given; Sex; Birthdate, Age At Last Birthday; Tribe; Degree of Blood; Marital Status; Relationship To Head of Family; Last Census Roll Number; At Jurisdiction Where Enrolled (Yes or No); At Another Jurisdiction; ELSEWHERE: Post office, County, State; Ward (Yes or No); Allotment, Annuity, and Identification Numbers.

1397; Wolfblack, Dallas; M; 4/82, 49; Cheyenne; F; M; Head; 1387; Yes; Yes; None
1398; Wolfblack, Rose (Whitemoon, Rose); F; 6/90, 41; Cheyenne; F; M; Wife; 1388; Yes; Yes; None
1399; Wolfblack, Gladys; F; 12/15, 16; Cheyenne; F; S; Dau; 1389; Yes; Yes; None[
1400; Wolfblack, Oran; M; 4/12/24, 7; Cheyenne; F; s; Son; 1390; Yes; Yes; None
1401; Wolfblack, Harry; M; 1/12/26, 6; Cheyenne; F; S; Son; 1391; Yes; Yes; None
1402; Wolfblack, Mary; F; 4/8/29, 3; Cheyenne; F; S; Dau; 1392; Yes; Yes; None

---- ~~Wolfchief, Harshey; M; 8/52, 79; Cheyenne; F; M; Head; 1393; Yes; Yes; None Died October 31, 1931~~

1403; Wolfchief, Flora (Bigbeaver, Flora); F; 9/91, 30; Cheyenne; F; Wd; Head; 1394; Yes; Yes; None
1404; Wolfchief, Ann; F; 5/27/27, 4; Cheyenne; F; S; Dau; 1395; Yes; Yes; None
1405; Wolfchief, Norman; M; 3/7/29, 3; Cheyenne; F; S; Son; 1396; Yes; Yes; None
1406; Wolfchief, Mary; F; 3/1/31, 1; Cheyenne; F; S; Dau; 1397; Yes; Yes; None

1407; Wolfchum, Paul; M; 10/93, 38; Cheyenne; F; M; Head; 1398; Yes; Yes; None
1408; Wolfchum, Bessie (Powderface, Bessie); F; 6/90, 41; Cheyenne; F; M; Wife; 1399; Yes; Yes; None   [Littlesun in 1927.]
---- ~~Wolfchum, Walker; M; 12/4/26, 5; Cheyenne; F; S; Son; 1400; Yes; Yes; None Died May 12, 1937[sic]~~
1409; Wolfchum, John F.; M; 11/10/28, 3; Cheyenne; F; S; Son; 1401; Yes; Yes; None
---- ~~Wolfchum, Espy; M; 4/1/30, 2; Cheyenne; F; S; Son; 1402; Yes; Yes; None Died August 31, 1931~~

1410; Wolfear, Willis; M; 1/84, 48; Cheyenne; F; M; Head; 1403; Yes; Yes; None
1411; Wolfear, Sophia (Elkshowshorn, Sophia); F; 5/72, 59; Cheyenne; F; M; Wife; 1404; Yes; Yes; None

1412; Wolfname, Bessie; F; 5/54, 77; Cheyenne; F; M; Head; 1405; Yes; Yes; None
1413; Wolfname, Grace; F; 6/16, 15; Cheyenne; F; S; G-Dau; 1406; Yes; Yes; None

1414; Wolfroads, Mack; M; 7/78, 53; Cheyenne; F; Wd[sic]; Head; 1407; Yes; Yes; None
1415; Wolfroads, Maude; F; 7/10, 21; Cheyenne; F; S; Dau; 1408; Yes; Yes; None
1416; Medicineelk, Leo; M; 9/6/29, 2; Cheyenne; F; S; G-Son; 1409; Yes; Yes; None   [Wolfroads in 1930]

1417; Wolftooth, Young; M; 11/81, 50; Cheyenne; F; M; Head; 1410; Yes; Yes; None
1418; Wolftooth, Mary; F; 5/18, 13; Cheyenne; F; M; Wife; 1411; Yes; Yes; None
1419; Wolftooth, Norman; M; 7/20, 11; Cheyenne; F; S; Son; 1412; Yes; Yes; None

Census of the **Tongue River** reservation of the **Tongue River** jurisdiction, as of **April 1**, 1932, taken by **W. R. Centerwall**, Superintendent.

**Key:** Number; NAME: Surname, Given; Sex; Birthdate, Age At Last Birthday; Tribe; Degree of Blood; Marital Status; Relationship To Head of Family; Last Census Roll Number; At Jurisdiction Where Enrolled (Yes or No); At Another Jurisdiction; ELSEWHERE: Post office, County, State; Ward (Yes or No); Allotment, Annuity, and Identification Numbers.

1420; Wolftooth, Doris; F; 11/14/25, 6; Cheyenne; F; S; Dau; 1413; Yes; Yes; None

1421; Wolfvoice, Grover; M; 4/90, 41; Cheyenne; F; M; Head; 1414; Yes; Yes; None
1422; Wolfvoice, Jennie (Blackcrane, Jennie); F; 5/82, 49; Cheyenne; F; M; Wife; 1415; Yes; Yes; None
1423; Wolfvoice, Anne; F; 2/18, 14; Cheyenne; F; S; Dau; 1516; Yes; Yes; None
1424; Wolfvoice, Dewey; M; 3/12/27, 5; Cheyenne; F; S; Son; 1517; Yes; Yes; None
1425; Bearquiver, Grace; F; 5/15/27, 5; Cheyenne; F; S; A-Dau; 1518; Yes; Yes; None
1426; Blackcrane, Clara; F; 12/66, 65; Cheyenne; F; Wd; Mother-in-law; 1419; Yes; Yes; None

1427; Womanleggins, Edward; M; 4/88, 43; Cheyenne; F; M; Head; 1420; Yes; Yes; None
1428; Womanleggins, Nannie (Blackbird, Nannie); F; 11/91, 40; Cheyenne; F; M; Wife; 1421; Yes; Yes; None [Mannie in 1931] [Lamewoman]
1429; Badhorse, Mabel; F; 8/15, 16; Cheyenne; F; S; Step-Dau; 1422; Yes; Yes; None [1917-20 son, Junior, M.; Name is June in 1926. Womanleggins in 1929.]
1430; Lamewoman, Mary; F; 7/17, 14; Cheyenne; F; S; S-Dau; 1423; Yes; Yes; None
1431; Bearchum, Benjamin; M; 3/19, 12; Cheyenne; 7/8; S; S-Son; 1424; Yes; Yes; None [1/4+ 1931]

1432; Woodenlegs, John; M; 11/09, 22; Cheyenne; 3/4; M; Head; 1425[sic]; Yes; Yes; None [#1429 1931; Fullblood 1931]]
1433; Woodenlegs, Clara C. (Littleeagle, Clara C); F; 8/05, 26; Cheyenne; F; M; Wife; 588; Yes; Yes; None
---- Woodenlegs, (Unnamed); M; 8/17/31; Cheyenne; 7/8; S; Son; --; Yes; Yes; None Died August 17, 1931

1434; Woodenlegs, Richard; M; 8/59, 72; Cheyenne; F; M; Head; 1425; Yes; Yes; None
1435; Woodenlegs, Sophia; F; 5/59, 71; Cheyenne; F; M; Wife; 1426; Yes; Yes; None

1436; Woodenlegs, Tom; M; 7/87, 44; Cheyenne; 1/2; M; Head; 1427; Yes; Yes; None
1437; Woodenlegs, Alice (Whistlingelk, Alice); F; 6/13, 18; Cheyenne; F; M; Wife; 1428; Yes; Yes; None
1438; Woodenlegs, Tom Jr.; M; 6/12; Cheyenne; 3/4; S; Son; 1429; Yes; Yes; None

1439; Woodenthigh, Arthur; M; 11/83, 48; Cheyenne; F; M; Head; 1430; Yes; Yes; None

Census of the **Tongue River** reservation of the **Tongue River** jurisdiction, as of **April 1**, 1932, taken by **W. R. Centerwall**, Superintendent.

**Key:** Number; NAME: Surname, Given; Sex; Birthdate, Age At Last Birthday; Tribe; Degree of Blood; Marital Status; Relationship To Head of Family; Last Census Roll Number; At Jurisdiction Where Enrolled (Yes or No); At Another Jurisdiction; ELSEWHERE: Post office, County, State; Ward (Yes or No); Allotment, Annuity, and Identification Numbers.

1440; Woodenthigh, Eva (Whitecow[sic], Eva); F; 12/87, 44; Cheyenne; F; M; Wife; 1431; Yes; Yes; None
1441; Woodenthigh, Esther C.; F; 4/10, 21; Cheyenne; F; S; Dau; 1432; Yes; Yes; None
1442; Woodenthigh, Alice M.; F; 2/14, 18; Cheyenne; F; S; Dau; 1433; Yes; Yes; None
1443; Woodenthigh, Peter; M; 5/18, 13; Cheyenne; F; S; A-Son; 1434; Yes; Yes; None

1444; Woodenthigh, Chester; M; 9/84, 47; Cheyenne; F; M; Head; 1435; Yes; Yes; None
1445; Woodenthigh, Lena (Sponge, Lena); F; 9/90, 41; Cheyenne; F; M; Wife; 1436; Yes; Yes; None
1446; Woodenthigh, Philip; M; 5/15, 16; Cheyenne; F; S; Son; 1437; Yes; Yes; None
1447; Woodenthigh, John; M; 6/16, 15; Cheyenne; F; S; Son; 1438; Yes; Yes; None
1448; Woodenthigh, Melvin; M; 11/23, 8; Cheyenne; F; S; Son; 1439; Yes; Yes; None

1449; ~~Woodepecker~~[sic] Bird, James; M; 3/03, 31; Cheyenne; F; M; Head; 1440; Yes; Yes; None Authority Letter 12-13-3
1450; ~~Woodepecker~~[sic] Bird, Gladys (Littlehead, Gladys); F; 8/00, 31; Cheyenne; F; M; Wife; 596; Yes; Yes; None
1451; Blackstone, Louis; M; 10/21/27, 4; Cheyenne; F; S; S-Son; 597; Yes; Yes; None
1452; Blackstone, Joseph; M; 6/20/29, 2; Cheyenne; F; S; S-Son; 598; Yes; Yes; None

1453; Woodepecker[sic], Mary; F; 5/04, 27; Cheyenne; 3/4; D; Head; 1441; Yes; Yes; None [Littlewhiteman]

1454; Woundedeye, Davis; M; 6/95, 36; Cheyenne; F; M; Head; 1442; Yes; Yes; None
1455; Woundedeye, Susie (Standingelk, Susie); F; 8/03, 28; Cheyenne; F; M; Wife; 1443; Yes; Yes; None
1456; Woundedeye, Milton; M; 4/20, 11; Cheyenne; F; S; Son; 1444; Yes; Yes; None
1457; Woundedeye, Veta E.; F; 1/14/27, 5; Cheyenne; F; S; Son; 1445; Yes; Yes; None
1458; Woundedeye, Waldo; M; 8/22/29, 2; Cheyenne; F; S; Son; 1446; Yes; Yes; None

1459; Woundedeye, Ford; M; 4/82, 49; Cheyenne; F; M; Head; 1447; Yes; Yes; None

Census of the __Tongue River__ reservation of the __Tongue River__ jurisdiction, as of __April 1__, 1932, taken by __W. R. Centerwall__, Superintendent.

**Key:** Number; NAME: Surname, Given; Sex; Birthdate, Age At Last Birthday; Tribe; Degree of Blood; Marital Status; Relationship To Head of Family; Last Census Roll Number; At Jurisdiction Where Enrolled (Yes or No); At Another Jurisdiction; ELSEWHERE: Post office, County, State; Ward (Yes or No); Allotment, Annuity, and Identification Numbers.

1460; Woundedeye, Florence (Stronglefthand, Florence); F; 5/90, 41; Cheyenne; F; M; Wife; 1448; Yes; Yes; None

1461; Woundedeye, Victoria; F; 1/22, 10; Cheyenne; F; S; Dau; 1449; Yes; Yes; None

1462; Woundedeye, Ruth; F; 4/25/27, 4; Cheyenne; F; S; Dau; 1450; Yes; Yes; None

1463; Goggles, Laura; F; 11/09, 22; Cheyenne; F; S; Dau; 1451; Yes; Yes; None

1464; Goggles, Hayes; M; 6/26/28, 3; Cheyenne; F; S; G-Son; 1452; Yes; Yes; None

1465; Woundedeye, Winfield; M; 4/08, 23; Cheyenne; F; M; Head; 1453; Yes; Yes; None

1466; Woundedeye, Alice (Wolfchief, Alice); F; 11/12, 19; Cheyenne; F; M; Wife; 1454; Yes; Yes; None

---- ~~Woundedeye, Iva Ruth; F; 10/18/30, 1; Cheyenne; F; S; Dau; 1455; Yes; Yes; None Died July 6, 1931~~

1467; Yelloweagle, Kate; F; 4/52, 79; Cheyenne; F; Wd; Head; 1456; Yes; Yes; None

1468; Yelloweyes, Abram; M; 7/74, 57; Cheyenne; F; F[sic]; Head; 1457; Yes; Yes; None

1469; Yelloweyes, Nora (Whitehorse, Nora); F; 2/77, 54; Cheyenne; F; M; Wife; 1458; Yes; Yes; None

1470; Yelloweyes, Oliver; M; 7/01, 30; Cheyenne; F; M; Head; 1460; Yes; Yes; None

---- ~~Yelloweyes, Gertrude (Brownbird, Gerturde[sic]); F; 5/05, 26; Cheyenne; F; M; Wife; 1461; Yes; Yes; None Died March 3, 1932~~

1471; Yelloweyes, Mary; F; 11/8/24, 7; Cheyenne; F; S; Dau; 1462; Yes; Yes; None

1472; Yelloweyes, David; M; 12/26/29, 2; Cheyenne; F; S; Son; 1463; Yes; Yes; None

1473; Yellowfox, Charles; M; 10/08, 23; Cheyenne; F; M; Head; 1467; Yes; Yes; None

1474; Yellowfox, Sarah W.; F; 6/13, 18; Cheyenne; F; M; Wife; 1468; Yes; Yes; None

1475; Yellowfox, Paul; M; 12/28/31, 3/12; Cheyenne; F; S; Son; xxxx; Yes; Yes; None

1476; Yellowfox, Robert; M; 7/75, 56; Cheyenne; F; M; Head; 1464; Yes; Yes; None

1477; Yellowfox, Carrie; F; 11/82, 49; Cheyenne; F; M; Wife; 1465; Yes; Yes; None

1478; Yellowfox, Frank; M; 7/01, 30; Cheyenne; F; S; Son; 1466; Yes; Yes; None

Census of the **Tongue River** reservation of the **Tongue River** jurisdiction, as of **April 1**, 19**32**, taken by **W. R. Centerwall**, Superintendent.

**Key:** Number; NAME: Surname, Given; Sex; Birthdate, Age At Last Birthday; Tribe; Degree of Blood; Marital Status; Relationship To Head of Family; Last Census Roll Number; At Jurisdiction Where Enrolled (Yes or No); At Another Jurisdiction; ELSEWHERE: Post office, County, State; Ward (Yes or No); Allotment, Annuity, and Identification Numbers.

1479; Yellowfox, William; M; 5/00, 31; Cheyenne; F; M; Head; 1469; Yes; Yes; None

1450; [sic] Yellowfox, Margaret (Yellownose, Margaret); F; 3/05, 27; Cheyenne; F; M; Wife; 1470; Yes; Yes; None [Number should be 1480]

1451; [sic] Yellowfox, Mary J.; F; 3/1/30, 2; Cheyenne; F; S; Dau; 1471; Yes; Yes; one [Number should be 1481]

1452; [sic] Yellownose, George; M; 11/96, 35; Cheyenne; F; M; Head; 1472; Yes; Yes; None [Number should be 1482]

1453; [sic] Yellownose, Marie (Bigbeaver, Marie); F; 6/11, 20; Cheyenne; F; M; Wife; 1473; Yes; Yes; None [Yellownose, Marie B. in 1931] [Number should be 1483]

---- Yellownose, Mary; F; 7/27, 4; Cheyenne; F; S; Dau; 1474; Yes; Yes; None

1454; [sic] Yellownose, Lena; F; 11/24/30, 1; Cheyenne; F; S; Dau; 1475; Yes; Yes; None [Number should be 1484]

1455; [sic] Yellownose, Robert; M; 9/57, 54; Cheyenne; F; M; Head; 1476; Yes; Yes; None [Number should be 1485]

1456; [sic] Yellownose, Rosa; F; 5/77, 54; Cheyenne; F; M; Wife; 1477; Yes; Yes; None [Number should be 1486]

1457; [sic] Wolf, Fannie L.; F; 3/16, 16; Cheyenne; F; S; S-Dau; 1478; Yes; Yes; None [Number should be 1487]

1488; Yellowrobe, Charles; M; 6/92, 3; Cheyenne; F; M; Head; 1479; Yes; Yes; None

1489; Yellowrobe, Alice (Seminole, Alice); F; 5/98, 33; Cheyenne; F; M; Wife; 1480; Yes; Yes; None

1490; Yellowrobe, Ruth; F; 3/17, 14; Cheyenne; F; S; Dau; 1481; Yes; Yes; None

1491; Yellowrobe, Martha; F; 1/26, 6; Cheyenne; F; s; Dau; 1482; Yes; Yes; None

1492; Yellowrobe, Theodore; M; 7/5/30, 1; Cheyenne; F; S; Son; 1483; Yes; Yes; None

1493; Yellowrobe, Jasper; M; 12/94. 37; Cheyenne; F; M; Head; 1484; Yes; Yes; None

1494; Yellowrobe, Jean (Turkeylegs, Jean); F; 7/99, 32; Cheyenne; f; M; Wife; 1485; Yes; Yes; None [Whiteshirt]

1495; Yellowrobe, Moses; M; 2/7/29, 3; Cheyenne; F; S; Son; 1486; Yes; Yes; None

---- ~~Yellowrobe, Hilda; F; 4/7/30, 1; Cheyenne; F; S; Dau; 1487; Yes; Yes; None~~ [Died November 10, 1930]

1496; Yellowrobe, Nancy C.; F; 2/23/32, 1/12; Cheyenne; F; S; Dau; xxxx; Yes; Yes; None

1497; Whiteshirt, Caroline; F; 11/21, 10; Cheyenne; F; S; S-Dau; 1487; Yes; Yes; None [Name Alice in 1926.]

Census of the **Tongue River** reservation of the **Tongue River** jurisdiction, as of **April 1**, 1932, taken by **W. R. Centerwall**, Superintendent.

**Key:** Number; NAME: Surname, Given; Sex; Birthdate, Age At Last Birthday; Tribe; Degree of Blood; Marital Status; Relationship To Head of Family; Last Census Roll Number; At Jurisdiction Where Enrolled (Yes or No); At Another Jurisdiction; ELSEWHERE: Post office, County, State; Ward (Yes or No); Allotment, Annuity, and Identification Numbers.

1498; Yellowrobe, William; M; 10/65, 66; Cheyenne; F; M; Head; 1488; Yes; Yes; None
1499; Yellowrobe, Minnie; F; 1/58; 75; Cheyenne; F; M; Wife; 1489; Yes; Yes; None

1500; Youngbear, George; M; 8/82, 49; Cheyenne; F; M; Head; 1490; Yes; Yes; None
1501; Youngbear, Cora (Seminole, Cora); F; 7/88, 43; Cheyenne; 3/4; M; Wife; 1491; Yes; Yes; None   [Fullblood 1931]
1502; Youngbear, Arthur; M; 8/13, 18; Cheyenne; 7/8; S; Son; 1492; Yes; Yes; None [Fullblood 1931]
1503; Youngbear, Ralph H.; M; 10/21, 10; Cheyenne; 7/8; S; Son; 1493; Yes; Yes; None [Fullblood 1931]
---- Youngbear; M; 6/6/30; Cheyenne; 7/8; S; Son; Son; ---; Yes; Yes; None Stillbirth

1504; Youngbird, James; M; 9/57, 74; Cheyenne; F; M; Head; 1494; Yes; Yes; None
1505; Youngbird, Clara; F; 5/63, 68; Cheyenne; F; M; Wife; 1495; Yes; Yes; None

1506; Youngbird, John Beans; M; 9/84, 47; Cheyenne; F; M; Head; 1496; Yes; Yes; None
1507; Youngbird, Anne (Woundedeye, Anne); F; 2/85, 47; Cheyenne; F; M; Wife; 1497; Yes; Yes; None   [Looksbehind]
1508; Youngbird, Carl; M; 4/22/22, 10; Cheyenne; F; S; Son; 1498; Yes; Yes; None

Census of the **Tongue River** reservation of the **Tongue River** jurisdiction, as of **April 1**, 1932, taken by **W. R. Centerwall**, Superintendent.

Key:  Number; NAME: Surname, Given; Sex; Birthdate, Age At Last Birthday; Tribe; Degree of Blood; Marital Status; Relationship To Head of Family; Last Census Roll Number; At Jurisdiction Where Enrolled (Yes or No); At Another Jurisdiction; ELSEWHERE: Post office, County, State; Ward (Yes or No); Allotment, Annuity, and Identification Numbers.

---

53617

1932 Annual Statistical Report        Office of Indian Affairs

Section II. Population.

State **Montana**      Reservation **Tongue River**

Agency or Jurisdiction **Tongue River**    Tribe **Cheyenne**

I. CENSUS RECAPITULATION SHEET

Sheet compiled by.... **Elizabeth A. Rowland**

Population as of April 1, 1932:   Sheet verified by.... **W. R. Centerwall**

ATTENTION:
The base of this schedule will have to be Table 2, Commissioner's Annual Report of June 30, 1930, as the Census Rolls were not tabulated last year. Give all changes since that date on this sheet. Must check with pages 16 and 17 and supplemental rolls.

|  | Total | Male | Female |
|---|---|---|---|
| 1. Total Census April 1, 1930 (Table 2, Commissioner's Annual Report).............. | 1479 | 725 | 754 |
| 2. Additions since April 1, 1930........................ | 152 | 102 | 50 |
|    a. Because of enrollment by Departmental authority........................ | 3 | 1 | 2 |
|    b. Because of omission from previous census rolls........................ | 2 | 2 | 0 |
|    c. Births unreported, but occurring prior to April 1, 1930............... | 4 | 0 | 4 |
|    d. Because of error in sex................ | 27 | 24 | 3 |
|    e. Births during the two years (April 1, 1930 and March 31, 1932, only.)........ | 116 | 75 | 41 |
| 3. Total Census April 1, 1930 Table 2, Commissioner's Annual Report, plus additions to roll........................ | 1631 | 827 | 804 |
| 4. Deductions........................ | 122 | 50 | 72 |
|    a. Because of illegal or wrongful enrollment by Departmental authority since April 1, 1930................ | 1 | 0 | 1 |
|    b. Deaths unreported, but occurring prior to April 1, 1930........................ | 2 | 1 | 1 |
|    c. Duplications........................ | 0 | 0 | 0 |
|    d. Because of error in sex................ | 27 | 3 | 24 |
|    e. Deaths during the two years (April 1, 1930 and March 31, 1932, only)........ | 92 | 46 | 46 |
| 5. Total this census (should agree with last number on current roll)................ | 1509 | 777 | 732 |
| (See instructions on back of sheets 16 and 17.) Unaccounted for. | 1 | 0 | 1 |
| | 1508 | 777 | 731 |

14
(over)

Census of the **Tongue River** reservation of the **Tongue River** jurisdiction, as of **April 1**, 19**32**, taken by **W. R. Centerwall**, Superintendent.

**Key:** Number; NAME: Surname, Given; Sex; Birthdate, Age At Last Birthday; Tribe; Degree of Blood; Marital Status; Relationship To Head of Family; Last Census Roll Number; At Jurisdiction Where Enrolled (Yes or No); At Another Jurisdiction; ELSEWHERE: Post office, County, State; Ward (Yes or No); Allotment, Annuity, and Identification Numbers.

Census of the **TONGUE RIVER** reservation of the **TONGUE RIVER** jurisdiction, as of **APRIL 1**, 1932, taken by **W. R. CENTERWALL**, Superintendent.

**Key:** 1932 Census Roll Number; NAME: Surname, Given; Sex; Birthdate, Age At Last Birthday; Tribe; Degree of Blood; Marital Status; At Jurisdiction Where Enrolled (Yes or No); At Another Jurisdiction; ELSEWHERE: Post office, County, State; Ward (Yes or No); Allotment, Annuity, and Identification Numbers.

## ADDITION ROLL

### Added by Indian Office Authority for year ended March 31, 1932.

461; Redbird, Ellen; F; 12/15/26, 5; Cheyenne; F; S; Yes; Yes; None
1076; Sooktis, Andrew; M; 3/12/26, 6; Cheyenne; F; S; No; Cheyenne & Arap. Agency, Okla.; Yes; None
1075; Sooktis, Josie; F; 1889, 43; Cheyenne; F; M; No; Cheyenne & Arap. Agency, Okla.; Yes; None

### Added unreported births prioer[sic] to March 31, 1931.

341; Fisher, Emeline; F; 2/10/31, 1; Cheyenne; 11/16; S; Yes; Yes; None
532; Kingfisher, Elizabeth; F; 8/1/30, 8/12; Cheyenne; F; S; Yes; Yes; None
DBE Know-His-Gun, Genevieve; F; 7/13/30, 1; Cheyenne; F; S; Yes; Yes; None
DBE Limberhand, George; M; 3/23/31, 1; Cheyenne; F; S; Yes; Yes; None
DBE Littlemouth, Fred; M; 1/27/31, 9/12; Cheyenne; F; S; Yes; Yes; None
1275; Redwoman, John; M; 1/18/31, 1; Cheyenne; F; S; Yes; Yes; None
1118; Spottedelk, Eugene; M; 1/28/31, 1; Cheyenne; F; S; Yes; Yes; None
1134; Spottedwolf, James; M; 3/15/31, 1; Cheyenne; 11/16; S; Yes; Yes; None
1394; Wilson, William; M; 9/3/30, 1; Cheyenne; 1/4; S; Yes; Yes; None

### Added unreported birth prior to April 1, 1930

235; Cooley, Charlotte; F; 2/15/27, 5; Cheyenne; 1/16; S; Yes; Yes; None

### Added erroneously ommitted[sic] from Census April, 1931.

268; Deafy, James; M; 8/70, 61; Cheyenne; F; Wd; Yes; Yes; None

## DEDUCTION ROLL

Deducted by Indian Office authority for year ended March 31, 1932
1931- 240; Crazymule, Eva; F; 5/09, 21; Cheyenne; F; S; No; Chey. & Arap. Agency, Okla.; Yes; None
    Deducted unreported deaths prior to March 31, 1931
1931- 664; Littleyellowman, Rose; F; 3/22/24, 7; Cheyenne; F; S; No; Chey. & Arap. Agency, Okla.; Yes; None
    Deducted unreported deaths prior to April 1, 1930.
1931- 310; Fightingbear, Emma; F; 5/19/26, 4; Cheyenne; F; S; Yes; Yes; None
1931-1400; Wolfchum, Walker; M; 12/4/26, 4; Cheyenne; F; S; Yes; Yes; None

BIRTH ROLL

LIVE BIRTHS

TONGUE RIVER AGENCY

TONGUE RIVER RESERVATION

MONTANA

July 1, 1924 - June 30, 1925
July 1, 1925 - June 30, 1926
July 1, 1926 - June 30, 1927
July 1, 1927 - June 30, 1928
July 1, 1928 - June 30, 1929
July 1, 1929 - June 30, 1930
April 1, 1930 - March 31, 1931
April 1, 1931 - March 31, 1932

## LIVE BIRTHS

State **Montana** Reservation **Tongue River** Agency or jurisdiction, **Tongue River** Office of Indian Affairs

Key: Census Roll Number; Surname, Given; Date of Birth (Year-Month & Day); Live Births (Yes unless otherwise given); Still Births (blank unless otherwise given); Sex; Tribe; Ward (Yes/No); Degree of Blood (Father; Mother; Child); At Jurisdiction Where Enrolled (Yes/No); (If no – Where)

Births Occurring Between the Dates of July 1, 1924 and June 30, 1925 to Parents Enrolled at Jurisdiction
[For the year dates to the left (1926, 1927) there is no explanation.]

|      | 1925 Census Roll # | |
|------|------|---|
| 1927 | 22;  | Ant, Bertha; 1925-Jan 1; F; Cheyenne; Yes; F; F; F; Yes |
|      | 182; | BeMent, Jesse; 1925-Mar. 14; M; Cheyenne; Yes; W; 1/8; 1/16; Yes |
| 1927 | 87;  | Bigheadman, Julia; 1924-Dec. --; F; Cheyenne; Yes; F; F; F; Yes |
| 1927 | 97;  | Bigheadman, Kathleen; 1925-Mar. --; F; Cheyenne; Yes; F; F; F; Yes |
|      | 71;  | Bigheadman, Lucy; 1924-Oct. 30; F; Cheyenne; Yes; F; F; F; Yes |
| 1927 | 120; | Bixby, William L.; 1925-Mar. 2; M; Cheyenne; Yes; 1/4; W; 1/8; Yes |
| 1927 | 134; | Blackhorse, Alice; 1924-Sept. 10; F; Cheyenne; Yes; F; F; F; Yes |
|      | 125; | Blackstone, James Jr.; 1924-Nov. 10; M; Cheyenne; Yes; F; F; F; Yes |
|      | 160; | Brady, Roy; 1925-Jan. --; M; Cheyenne; Yes; F; F; F; Yes |
| 1927 | 207; | Chasingbear, Robert; 1924-July --; M; Cheyenne; Yes; F; F; F; Yes |
|      | 225; | Cooley, Vera; 1925-Jan. --; F; Cheyenne; Yes; W; 1/8; 1/16; Yes |
|      | 244; | Curley, Joseph; 1925-Apr. --; M; Cheyenne; Yes; F; F; F; Yes |
| 1927 | 271; | Divesbackward, Grace; 1925-Feb. 22; F; Cheyenne; Yes; F; F; F; Yes |
|      | 265; | Duster, Bessie; 1924-July 12; F; Cheyenne; F; F; F; Yes |
|      | 520; | Killsontop, Ida; 1924-Sept. 15; F; Cheyenne; F; F; F; Yes |
|      | 480; | Kinzel, Celia L.; 1924-July 23; F; Cheyenne; W; 1/4; 1/8; Yes |
| 1926 | 550; | Littlebird, James Wm.; 1925-June 25; M; Cheyenne; Yes; F; F; F; Yes |
| 1927 | 646; | Littlewolf, Eva; 1925-April 5; F; Cheyenne; Yes; F; F; F; Yes |
|      | 629; | Longjaw, Thomas; 1925-Jan. --; M; Cheyenne; Yes; F; F; F; Yes |
| 1926 | 726; | Medicineflying, Phyllis; 1924-July --; F; Cheyenne; Yes; F; F; F; Yes |
|      | 694; | Medicinetop, Roy; 1925-Aug. 19; M; Cheyenne; Yes; F; F; F; Yes |
|      | 703; | Mexican Cheyenne, Rudolph; 1925-Feb. --; M; Cheyenne; Yes; 1/2; F; 3/4; Yes |
|      | 714; | Parker, Verda F.; 1924-Sept. 2; F; Cheyenne; Yes; 1/4; W; 1/8; Yes |
| 1926 | 776; | Pine, Sarah; 1924-Aug. 4; F; Cheyenne; Yes; F; F; F; Yes |
|      | 760; | Redbird, Allen; 1925-May 25; M; Cheyenne; Yes; F; F; F; No; Cheyenne & Arap. Okla. |
| 1926 | 817; | Redbreath, Elina Jane; 1925-June --; F; Cheyenne; Yes; F; F; F; Yes |
|      | 790; | Redneck, John; 1925-May --; M; Cheyenne; Yes; F; F; F; Yes |
| 1926 | 879; | Risingsun, James; 1925-Dec. --; M; Cheyenne; Yes; F; F; F; Yes |
| 1926 | 966; | Russell, Ford; 1925-Mar. --; M; Cheyenne; Yes; F; F; F; Yes |
|      | 899; | Russell, Herman; 1925-May --; M; Cheyenne; Yes; F; F; F; Yes |
|      | 905; | Sandcrane, Annie May; 1925-Apr. --; F; Cheyenne; Yes; F; F; F; Yes |
|      | 0;   | Seminole, Falling; 1924-Aug. 26; M; Cheyenne; Yes; 3/4; F; 7/8; Yes |
|      | 1117; | Seminole, Max; 1924-Nov. --; M; Cheyenne; Yes; 3/4; F; 7/8; Yes |
|      | 0;   | Seminole, Rising; 1924-Aug. 26; M; Cheyenne; Yes; 3/4; F; 7/8; Yes |
|      | 963; | Shoulderblade, Alice Thurla; 1925-Apr. --; F; Cheyenne; Yes; F; 3/4; 7/8; Yes |
|      | 975; | Small, Melvin; 1925-Feb. 17; M; Cheyenne; Yes; W; 1/2; 1/4; Yes |

## LIVE BIRTHS

State **Montana** Reservation **Tongue River** Agency
or jurisdiction, **Tongue River** Office of Indian Affairs

Key: Census Roll Number; Surname, Given; Date of Birth (Year-Month & Day); Live Births (Yes unless otherwise given); Still Births (blank unless otherwise given); Sex; Tribe; Ward (Yes/No); Degree of Blood (Father; Mother; Child); At Jurisdiction Where Enrolled (Yes/No); (If no – Where)

|  |  |  |
|---|---|---|
|  | 1013; | Spottedelk, Nelson Miles; 1925-Mar. --; M; Cheyenne; Yes; F; F; F; Yes |
|  | --  | Standingelk, Henry; 1924-July 20; M; Cheyenne; Yes; F; F; F; Yes |
|  | 1046; | Standingelk, Margaret; 1924-Nov. 10; F; Cheyenne; Yes; F; F; F; Yes |
|  | 1120; | Tangledyellowhair, Roberta; 1924-Sept. --; F; Cheyenne; Yes; F; F; F; Yes |
|  | 1159; | Twin, Edna; 1924-July --; F; Cheyenne; Yes; F; F; F; Yes |
|  | 1273; | Whitewolf, Calvin M.; 1925-Jan. --; M; Cheyenne; Yes; F; F; F; Yes |
|  | 1283; | Wildhog, Opal; 1925-Jan. --; F; Cheyenne; Yes; F; F; F; Yes |
|  | 1287; | Wilson, Josephine; 1924-Nov. 26; F; Cheyenne; Yes; W; 1/2; 1/4; Yes |
|  | 1366; | Woundedeye, Rose; 1925-Jan. 24; F; Cheyenne; Yes; F; F; F; Yes |
|  | 1381; | Yelloweyes, Mary; 1924-Nov. 8; F; Cheyenne; Yes; F; F; F; Yes |
| 1926 | 645; | *Lonewolf, Ella; 1924-May 10; F; Cheyenne; Yes; F; F; F; Yes |

* Last name on the list is out of alphabetical order.

<u>Births Occurring Between the Dates of July 1, 1925 and June 30, 1926 to Parents Enrolled at Jurisdiction</u>
[For the year dates to the left (1927, 1931, 1932) there is no explanation.]

|  | 1926 Census Roll # |  |
|---|---|---|
| 1931 | 11; | Americanhorse, Ruth; 1925-Aug. 11; F; Cheyenne; No; Chey. & Arap. Okla. |
|  | 43; | Beartusk, Jerome Jr.; 1925-Dec. 23; M; Cheyenne; Yes; F; 1/8; 9/16; Yes |
|  | 185; | Beirdneau, Barbara Marie; 1926-Apr. 21; F; Cheyenne; Yes; W; 1/8; 1/16; Yes |
|  | -- | Bigfoot, Mary Lota; 1926-Mar. 12; F; Cheyenne; Yes; F; F; F; Yes |
| 1927 | 98; | Bigheadman, Dorla; 1926-June 30; F; Cheyenne; Yes; F; F; F; Yes |
|  | 127; | Blackstone, Paul Chas.; 1926-Jan. 7; M; Cheyenne; Yes; F; F; F; Yes |
|  | 173; | Burns, Phyllis R.; 1926-Mar. 21; F; Cheyenne; Yes; Yes; 1/8; W; 1/16; Yes |
|  | 247; | Deafy, Elsie; 1925-July 17; F; Cheyenne; Yes; F; F; F; Yes |
|  | 273; | Eaglefeathers, Rosie; 1925-July 7; F; Cheyenne; Yes; F; F; F; Yes |
|  | 291; | Elkshoulder, George; 1925-Dec. 8; M; Cheyenne; Yes; F; F; F; Yes |
|  | 305; | Fightingbear, Emma; 1926-May 19; F; Cheyenne; Yes; F; F; F; Yes |
|  | 369; | Hardground, Elda; 1926-Apr. 5; F; Cheyenne; Yes; F; F; F; Yes |
|  | 430; | Hollowbreast, Richard; 1925- Oct. --; M; Cheyenne; Yes; F; F; F; Yes |
|  | 485; | Killsnight, James; 1926-Apr. 2; M; Cheyenne; Yes; F; F; F; Yes |
| 1927 | 509; | Kingfisher, Ellen; 1926-June 17; F; Cheyenne; Yes; F; F; F; Yes |
|  | 501; | LaFever, Kenneth; 1925-Dec. --; M; Cheyenne; Yes; W; 1/8; 1/16; No; Crow Agency Mont. |
|  | 507; | Lamebear, Will; 1926-Jan. 10; M; Cheyenne; Yes; F; F; F; Yes |
|  | 540; | Limpy, Cora; 1925-Nov. 8; F; Cheyenne; Yes; 1/2; F; 3/4; Yes |

## LIVE BIRTHS

State **Montana** Reservation **Tongue River** Agency
or jurisdiction, **Tongue River** Office of Indian Affairs

Key: Census Roll Number; Surname, Given; Date of Birth (Year-Month & Day); Live Births (Yes unless otherwise given); Still Births (blank unless otherwise given); Sex; Tribe; Ward (Yes/No); Degree of Blood (Father; Mother; Child); At Jurisdiction Where Enrolled (Yes/No); (If no – Where)

|      |      |                                                                                        |
|------|------|----------------------------------------------------------------------------------------|
|      | 600; | Littlewhiteman, Albert Chas.; 1925-Sept. 18; M; Cheyenne; Yes; F; F; F; Yes            |
| 1927 | 626; | Littlewhiteman, Bessie; 1926-May 10; F; Cheyenne; Yes; F; F; F; Yes                    |
| 1927 | 611; | Littlewhiteman, John; 1925-Oct. 6; M; Cheyenne; Yes; 3/4; F; 7/8; Yes                  |
|      | 657; | Longjaw, Bessie; 1926-Mar. 26; F; Cheyenne; Yes; F; F; F; Yes                          |
|      | 682; | Magpie, Rose; 1925-Sept. 7; F; Cheyenne; Yes; F; F; F; Yes                             |
|      | 708; | Medicinebull, Fred; 1925-Oct. 28; M; Cheyenne; Yes; F; F; F; Yes                       |
|      | 712; | Medicineelk, May; 1926-May 10; F; Cheyenne; Yes; F; F; F; Yes                          |
|      | 719; | Medicineelk, Peter; 1926-Mar. 12; M; Cheyenne; Yes; F; F; F; Yes                       |
|      | 734; | Medicinetop, Andrew; 1926-Jan. 20; M; Cheyenne; Yes; F; F; F; Yes                      |
|      | 749; | MexicanCheyenne, Mary; 1925-July --; F; Cheyenne; Yes; 1/2; F; 3/4; Yes                |
|      | 756; | Onebear, Robert; 1925-Dec. 5; M; Cheyenne; Yes; 3/4; 3/4; 3/4; Yes                     |
|      | 766; | Parker, Vincent; 1925-July 30; M; Cheyenne; Yes; 1/4; 1/4; 1/4; Yes                    |
|      | 805; | Redbird, Fred C.; 1926-Mar. 17; M; Cheyenne; Yes; F; 3/4; 7/8; Yes                     |
|      | 808; | Redbird, Ellen; 1925-Dec. 15; F; Cheyenne; Yes; F; F; F; Yes                           |
|      | 833; | Redfox, Alice; 1926-Jan. 13; F; Cheyenne; Yes; F; F; F; Yes                            |
|      | 896; | Rockroads, Mary; 1926-Feb. 28; F; Cheyenne; Yes; F; F; F; Yes                          |
|      | 904; | Romannose, Sarah; 1925-Oct. 25; F; Cheyenne; Yes; F; F; F; Yes                         |
|      | 929; | Rowland, Allen Edsel; 1926-Feb. 9; M; Cheyenne; Yes; 3/4; 1/4; 1/2; Yes                |
|      | 922; | Rowland, Blanche; 1925-AUG. 29; F; Cheyenne; Yes; 3/4; F; 7/8; Yes                     |
|      | 991; | Shavedhead, Anna; 1925-Sept. 6; F; Cheyenne; Yes; F; F; F; Yes                         |
| 1927 | 1002;| Shavedhead, Anna Marjorie; 1925-Oct. --; F; Cheyenne; Yes; F; F; F; No; Shoshone, Wyo. |
|      | 996; | Shell, Elsie; 1926-Jan. 5; F; Cheyenne; Yes; F; F; F; Yes                              |
|      | 1037;| Soldierwolf, Veta; 1925-Dec. --; F; Cheyenne; Yes; F; F; F; Yes                        |
| 1932 |      | Sooktis, Andrew; 1926-Mar. 19; F[sic]; Cheyenne; Yes; F; F; F; Yes                     |
|      | --   | Sponge, Angeline; 1926-June 26; F; Cheyenne; Yes; F; F; F; Yes                         |
|      | 1075;| Spottedwolf, Eugene; 1926-Jan. 1; M; Cheyenne; Yes; F; 3/8; 11/16; Yes                 |
|      | 1155;| Tallwhiteman, Agnes; 1925-July --; F; Cheyenne; Yes; F; F; F; Yes                      |
|      | 1181;| Teeth, Elsie; 1925-Sept. 12; F; Cheyenne; Yes; F; F; F; Yes                            |
| 1927 | --   | Threefingers, Patrick; 1926-Jan. 1; M; Cheyenne; Yes; F; F; F; Yes                     |
| 1927 | 689; | Walters, Coolidge; 1926-Feb. 6; M; Cheyenne; Yes; 1/2; F; 3/4; Yes                     |
| 1927 | 1263;| Whistlingelk, May; 1926-Mar. 9; F; Cheyenne; Yes; F; F; F; Yes                         |
|      | --   | Whitehawk, Thomas; 1925-Nov. 18; M; Cheyenne; Yes; F; F; F; Yes                        |
|      | 1303;| Whitewolf, Goldstein; 1925-Dec. 6; M; Cheyenne; Yes; F; F; F; Yes                      |
|      | 1336;| Wolfblack, Harry; 1926-Jan. 12; M; Cheyenne; Yes; F; F; F; Yes                         |
|      | 1344;| Wolfchief, Jerome John; 1925-Oct. 24; M; Cheyenne; Yes; F; F; F; Yes                   |
|      | 1365;| Wolftooth, Doris; 1925-Nov. 14; M[sic]; Cheyenne; Yes; F; F; F; Yes                    |
|      | --   | Woundedeye, Edelson; 1926-Jan. 24; M; Cheyenne; Yes; F; F; F; Yes                      |

## LIVE BIRTHS

State _____ **Montana** _____ Reservation _____ **Tongue River** _____ Agency
or jurisdiction, _____ **Tongue River** _____ Office of Indian Affairs

Key: Census Roll Number; Surname, Given; Date of Birth (Year-Month & Day); Live Births (Yes unless otherwise given); Still Births (blank unless otherwise given); Sex; Tribe; Ward (Yes/No); Degree of Blood (Father; Mother; Child); At Jurisdiction Where Enrolled (Yes/No); (If no – Where)

Births Occurring Between the Dates of July 1, 1926 and June 30, 1927 to Parents Enrolled at Jurisdiction
[For the year dates to the left (1928, 1930, 1931) there is no explanation.]

|      | 1927 Census Roll # | |
|------|------|---|

1931    12;  Americanhorse, Ella; 1927-June 21; F; Cheyenne; Yes; F; F; F; No; Chey. & Arap. Mont.
          26;  Ant, Paul; 1927-Mar. 4; M; Cheyenne; Yes; F; F; F; Yes
          45;  Bearquiver, Grace; 1927-May 15; F; Cheyenne; Yes; F; F; F; Yes
1928    63;  BeMent, Geraldine; 1927-Feb. 1; F; Cheyenne; Yes; W; 1/8; 1/16; Yes
          88;  Bigheadman, Mary; 1927-June 20; F; Cheyenne; Yes; F; F; F; Yes
         111;  Bites, Florence; 1926-July 17; F; Cheyenne; Yes; F; F; F; Yes
          --;  Blackhorse, Dan; 1926-Nove[sic]. 28; M; Cheyenne; Yes; F; F; F; Yes
         149;  Blackwolf, Ruth; 1927-Jan. 22; F; Cheyenne; Yes; F; F; F; Yes
          --;  Clubfoot, Frank Jr.; 1927-Mar. 25; M; Cheyenne; Yes; F; F; F; Yes
         230;  Colhoff, George; 1927-Jan. 19; M; Cheyenne; Yes; 1/2; 3/4; 5/8; No; Pine Ridge, S. Dak.
         258;  Curley, Logan; 1927-Feb. 25; M; Cheyenne; Yes; F; F; F; Yes
         336;  Fisher, Bernidine; 1926-Dec. 29; M[sic]; Cheyenne; Yes; 1/2; 1/8; 5/16; Yes
          99  Hisbadhorse, Baby; 1927-Jan. 29; F; Cheyenne; Yes; F; F; F; Yes
         449;  Horn, Margaret; 1926-July 18; F; Cheyenne; Yes; F; F; F; Yes
         454;  Horseroads, Cora; 1926-Nov. 26; F; Cheyenne; Yes; F; F; F; Yes
         461;  Ironhand, Jane; 1927-Feb. 21; F; Cheyenne; Yes; F; F; F; Yes
         483;  Killsnight, Dorothy; 1927-Feb. 19; F; Cheyenne; Yes; F; F; F; Yes
          --;  Killsontop, Baby; 1927-Jan. 26; F; Cheyenne; Yes; F; F; F; Yes
         499;  Killsontop, June; 1927-Apr. 1; F; Cheyenne; Yes; F; F; F; Yes
1928   512;  Knows-His-Gun, Sylvester; 1926-Sept. [--]; M; Cheyenne; Yes; F; F; F; Yes
1928    --  Limpy, Elnora; 1927, June 18; F; Cheyenne; Yes; F; 1/2; 3/4; Yes
         563;  Littlebear, Lucille; 1926-July 14; F; Cheyenne; Yes; F; F; F; Yes
          --;  Littlemouth, Sallie; 1926-Oct. 1; F; Cheyenne; Yes; F; F; F; Yes
1930   624;  Littlewhiteman, Philip; 1927-Mar. 29; M; Cheyenne; Yes; 3/4; F; 7/8; Yes
         634;  Littlewhiteman, Sadie; 1927-Jan. 23; F; Cheyenne; Yes; 3/4; F; 7/8; Yes
         667;  Longjaw, Robert; 1927-Mar. 25; M; Cheyenne; Yes; F; F; F; Yes
         868;  Longroach, May; 1926-Aug. 26; F; Cheyenne; Yes; F; F; F; Yes
         690;  Looksbehind, James Jr.; 1927-May --; M; Cheyenne; Yes; F; F; F; No; Cheyenne & Arap. Okla.
1930   737;  Medicinebull, Bert; 1927-Jan. 1; M; Cheyenne; Yes; F; F; F; Yes
         775;  Parker, Gabriel; 1926-Oct. 22; M; Cheyenne; Yes; 1/4; 1/4; 1/4; Yes
         772;  Parker, Shirley Ross; 1927-Jan. 8; M; Cheyenne; Yes; 1/4; W; 1/8; Yes
         839;  Redfox, Edna; 1927-Mar. 13; F; Cheyenne; Yes; F; F; F; Yes
         871;  Redwoman, Edna; 1927-July 7; F; Cheyenne; Yes; F; F; F; Yes

## LIVE BIRTHS

State __Montana__ Reservation __Tongue River__ Agency
or jurisdiction, __Tongue River__ Office of Indian Affairs

Key: Census Roll Number; Surname, Given; Date of Birth (Year-Month & Day); Live Births (Yes unless otherwise given); Still Births (blank unless otherwise given); Sex; Tribe; Ward (Yes/No); Degree of Blood (Father; Mother; Child); At Jurisdiction Where Enrolled (Yes/No); (If no – Where)

|  |  |
|---|---|
| 878; | Ridgebear, Anna; 1927-Jan. 22; F; Cheyenne; Yes; F; F; F; Yes |
| 885; | Risingsun, Teddy; 1926-Oct. 26; M; Cheyenne; Yes; F; F; F; Yes |
| 924; | Roundstone, Ruth; 1926-July 16; F; Cheyenne; Yes; F; F; F; Yes |
| 941; | Rowland, Carrie; 1926-Nov. --; F; Cheyenne; Yes; 3/4; F; 7/8; Yes |
| 973; | Sandcrane, Harry; 1927-June 6; M; Cheyenne; Yes; F; F; F; Yes |
| -- | Sharpnose, Baby; 1927-May --; M; Cheyenne; Yes; F; F; F; Yes |
| 1004; | Shavedhead, Marjorie; 1926-Sept. 30; F; Cheyenne; Yes; F; F; F; No; Shoshone, Wyo. |
| -- | Shoulderblade, Theodore; 1926-Oct. 7; M; Cheyenne; Yes; F; 3/4; 7/8; Yes |
| 1043; | Small, Worth; 1927-Feb. 2; M; Cheyenne; Yes; W; 1/2; 1/4; Yes |
| 1047; | Spang, Dale Cooper; 1926-July 8; M; Cheyenne; Yes; 1/8; W; 1/16; No; Fort Peck, Mont. |
| 1086; | Spottedwolf, Earl; 1926-July 25; M; Cheyenne; Yes; F; F; F; Yes |
| 1105; | Standingelk, Clara Jennie; 1927-May 5; F; Cheyenne; Yes; F; F; F; Yes |
| 1099; | Standingelk, Roy; 1926-Aug. 11; M; Cheyenne; Yes; F; F; F; Yes |
| 1930   142; | Star, Charles; 1927-Mar. 9; M; Cheyenne; Yes; F; F; F; Yes |
| 1154; | Tallbull, Cecil Russell; 1927-Jan. 1; M; Cheyenne; Yes; F; F; F; Yes |
| 1176; | Tangledyellowhair, Bert; 1926-Oct. 14; M; Cheyenne; Yes; F; F; F; Yes |
| -- | Twentystands, [Blank]; 1927-Jan. 10; M; Cheyenne; Yes; F; F; F; Yes |
| -- | Twentystands, [Blank]; 1927-Jan. 10; F; Cheyenne; Yes; F; F; F; Yes |
| 1216; | Twomoons, Austin; 1927-Feb. 2; M; Cheyenne; Yes; F; F; F; Yes |
| 1239; | Walksnice, Agnes; 1926-Aug. 18; F; Cheyenne; Yes; F; F; F; Yes |
| 1267; | White, Ben; 1926-Dec. 23; M; Cheyenne; Yes; F; 3/4; 7/8; Yes |
| 1276; | Whitecrane, Elmer; 1926-Dec. 27; M; Cheyenne; Yes; F; F; F; Yes |
| -- | Whitewolf, Grace; 1926-Sept. 28; F; Cheyenne; Yes; F; F; F; Yes |
| -- | Whitewolf, Baby; 1927-Jan. 10; F; Cheyenne; Yes; F; F; F; Yes |
| 1326; | Wilson, James Jr.; 1926-Dec. 2; F[sic]; Cheyenne; Yes; W; 1/2; 1/4; Yes |
| 1341; | Wolfchief, Ann; 1927-May 27; F; Cheyenne; Yes; F; F; F; Yes |
| 1344; | Wolfchum, Walker; 1926-Dec. 4; M; Cheyenne; Yes; F; F; F; Yes |
| -- | Wolfname, Margaret; 1926-Sept. 9; F; Cheyenne; Yes; F; F; F; Yes |
| -- | Wolfname, Peter; 1927-June 9; M; Cheyenne; Yes; F; F; F; Yes |
| 1367; | Wolfvoice, Dewey; 1927-Mar. 12; M; Cheyenne; Yes; F; F; F; Yes |
| 1376; | Woodenleg, Mabel; 1927-Mar. 9; F; Cheyenne; Yes; 3/4; F; 7/8; Yes |
| 1403; | Woundedeye, Ruth; 1927-Apr. 25; F; Cheyenne; Yes; F; F; F; Yes |
| 1395; | Woundedeye, Veta Alice; 1927-Jan. 14; F; Cheyenne; Yes; F; F; F; Yes |
| -- | Youngbear, Anna; 1926-July 14; F; Cheyenne; Yes; F; 3/4; 7/8; Yes |
| -- | Youngbear, George; 1926-July 14; M; Cheyenne; Yes; F; 3/4; 7/8; Yes |
| *   -- | Bigback, Susie; 1926-Oct. 19; F; Cheyenne; Yes; F; F; F; Yes |
| *   -- | Hart, Elnora Fern; 1926-Aug. 16; M[sic]; Cheyenne; Yes; F; F; F; Yes |

\* The last two names are out of alphabetical order.

## LIVE BIRTHS

State **Montana** Reservation **Tongue River** Agency
or jurisdiction, **Tongue River** Office of Indian Affairs

Key: Census Roll Number; Surname, Given; Date of Birth (Year-Month & Day); Live Births (Yes unless otherwise given); Still Births (blank unless otherwise given); Sex; Tribe; Ward (Yes/No); Degree of Blood (Father; Mother; Child); At Jurisdiction Where Enrolled (Yes/No); (If no – Where)

<u>Births Occurring Between the Dates of July 1, 1927 and June 30, 1928 to Parents Enrolled at Jurisdiction</u>
[For the year dates to the left (1929 & 1930) there is no explanation.]

|      | 1928 Census Roll # | |
|---|---|---|
|      | -- | Atwood, Baby; 1928-Jan. 24; M; Cheyenne; Yes; F; F; F; Yes |
|      | -- | Atwood, Walter; 1928-Jan. 24; M; Cheyenne; Yes; F; F; F; Yes |
|      | 58; | Beirdneau, Albert; 1928-Feb. 16; M; Cheyenne; Yes; W; 1/8; 1/16; Yes |
|      | 64; | Bement, Celia Camille; 1928-Jan, 19; F; Cheyenne; Yes; W; 1/8; 1/16; Yes |
|      | 86; | Bigfoot, James; 1927-Dec. 15; M; Cheyenne; Yes; F; F; F; Yes |
|      | 91; | Bigheadman, Laura; 1927-July 27; F; Cheyenne; Yes; F; F; F; Yes |
| 1929 | -- | Blackhorse, Charles; 1928-Feb. 15; M; Cheyenne; Yes; F; F; F; Yes |
|      | 148; | Blackstone, Louis; 1927-Oct. 21; M; Cheyenne; Yes; F; F; F; Yes |
|      | -- | Burns, Robert J. Jr.; 1928-Feb. 15; M; Cheyenne; Yes; 1/8; W; 1/16; Yes |
| 1932 |      | Cooley, Charlotte; 1927-Nov. 15; F; Cheyenne; Yes; W; 1/8; 1/16; Yes |
|      | 298; | Elliott, Edwin Francis; 1928-Jan. 8; M; Cheyenne; Yes; W; 3/8; 3/16; Yes |
|      | 1406; | Goggles, Hayes; 1928-June 26; M; Cheyenne; Yes; F; F; F; Yes |
|      | 399; | Harris, Inez; 1927-Dec. 9; F; Cheyenne; Yes; 1/4; F; 5/8; Yes |
| 1929 | 414; | Hart, Edna; 1927-Nov. 16; F; Cheyenne; Yes; 5/8; F; 15/16; Yes |
|      | 441; | Horn, Celia; 1928-May 7; F; Cheyenne; Yes; F; F; F; Yes |
|      | 449; | Huff, Elsie M.; 1927-Dec. 23; F; Cheyenne; Yes; 1/2; 1/8; 5/16; Yes |
|      | 490; | Killsnight, Ralph; 1928-Apr. 7; M; Cheyenne; Yes; F; F; F; Yes |
|      | 505; | Kingfisher, Angela; 1928-May 23; M[sic]; Cheyenne; Yes; F; F; F; Yes |
|      | 510; | Kinzel, Virgil Bruce; 1927-Oct. 9; M; Cheyenne; Yes; W; 1/4; 1/8; Yes |
| 1930 | 507; | Knows-His-Gun, Edith; 1928-May 11; F; Cheyenne; Yes; F; F; F; Yes |
| 1930 | 548; | Limpy, Eunice; 1927-Sept. 23; F; Cheyenne; Yes; F; F; F; Yes |
|      | -- | Littlemouth, Baby; 1928-Mar. 20; M; Cheyenne; Yes; F; F; F; Yes |
|      | -- | Littlewhirlwind, Ellen; 1927-July 7; F; Cheyenne; Yes; F; F; F; Yes |
|      | 642; | Littlewolf, Laban; 1928-June 4; M; Cheyenne; Yes; F; F; F; Yes |
| 1929 | -- | Littleyellowman, J. Ernest; 1928-Mar. 17; M; Cheyenne; Yes; F; F; F; No; Chey. & Arap. Okla. |
|      | 672; | Longjaw, Donald; 1927-Nov. 27; M; Cheyenne; Yes; F; F; F; Yes |
|      | 725; | Medicineelk, Alice Sarah; 1928-Apr. 20; F; Cheyenne; Yes; F; F; F; Yes |
|      | 735; | Medicineelk, Claude; 1927-Dec. 12; M; Cheyenne; Yes; F; F; F; Yes |
|      | 731; | Medicineelk, William; 1928-Mar. 5; M; Cheyenne; Yes; F; F; F; Yes |
|      | 749; | Medicinetop, Lena; 1927-Oct. 27; F; Cheyenne; F; F; F; Yes |
|      | 763; | MexicanCheyenne, Mabel Ann; 1928-Feb. 1; F; Cheyenne; Yes; F; F; F; Yes |
|      | 817; | Redbird, David; 1928-May 22; M; Cheyenne; Yes; F; F; F; Yes |
|      | 824; | Redbreath, George; 1927-July 8; M; Cheyenne; Yes; F; F; F; Yes |
|      | 834; | Redcherries, Late; 1927-Sept. 3; F; CHEYENNE; Yes; F; F; F; Yes |

## LIVE BIRTHS

State __Montana__ Reservation __Tongue River__ Agency or jurisdiction, __Tongue River__ Office of Indian Affairs

Key: Census Roll Number; Surname, Given; Date of Birth (Year-Month & Day); Live Births (Yes unless otherwise given); Still Births (blank unless otherwise given); Sex; Tribe; Ward (Yes/No); Degree of Blood (Father; Mother; Child); At Jurisdiction Where Enrolled (Yes/No); (If no – Where)

|      |      |
|------|------|
|      | 812; Redwoman, George Philip; 1928-Apr. 4; M; F; F; F; Yes |
|      | 946; Rowland, Ardeth Faye; 1928-Apr. 30; F; Cheyenne; Yes; 3/4; 1/4; 1/2; Yes |
|      | 939; Rowland, Don Edward; 1928-Jan. 22; M; Cheyenne; Yes; 3/4; F; 1/2; Yes |
|      | 956; Rowland, Eugene A.; 1927-Aug. 13; M; Cheyenne; Yes; 3/4; F; 7/8; Yes |
|      | --   Seminole, [Blank]; 1927-Nov. ~~30~~ 24; F; Cheyenne; Yes; F; F; F; Yes |
|      | 1009; Shavedhead, Lucille; 1927-Nov. 31; F; CHEYENNE; Yes; F; F; F; Yes |
|      | 1031; Shoulderblade, Fern Ruth; 1928-Feb. 23; F; Cheyenne; Yes; F; 3/4; 7/8; Yes |
|      | 1076; Spang, Norman; 1927-Sept. 20; F; Cheyenne; Yes; 1/8; F; 9/16; Yes |
|      | 1064; Spang, Shirley Ann; 1928-May 19; F; Cheyenne; Yes; 1/8; W; 1/16; Yes |
|      | 1081; Sponge, Paul; 1927-Dec. 11; M; Cheyenne; Yes; F; F; F; Yes |
|      | 1094; Spottedwolf, Gertrude Rena; 1927-Nov. 22; F; Cheyenne; Yes; F; F; F; Yes |
|      | 1100; Spottedwolf, Mollie; 1927-Sept. 28; F; Cheyenne; Yes; F; 1/2; 3/4; Yes |
| 1930 | 1138; Standingelk, Aiden; 1928-May 17; M; Cheyenne; Yes; F; F; F; Yes |
|      | --   Standingelk, Mary; 1927-Oct. 24; F; Cheyenne; Yes; F; F; F; Yes |
|      | 1123; Standsintimber, Ruth Elva; 1928-Apr. 21; F; Cheyenne; Yes; F; F; F; Yes |
|      | 1187; Tangledyellowhair, John Laraith; 1928-Apr. 14; M; Cheyenne; Yes; F; F; F; Yes |
|      | 1216; Twobulls, Alice; 1927-Aug. 2; F; Cheyenne; Yes; F; F; F; Yes |
|      | 1237; Walksalong, Carol; 1928-Jan. 10; M; Cheyenne; Yes; F; F; F; Yes |
| 1930 | 1324; Whitehawk, Andrew; 1927-Dec. 20; M; Cheyenne; Yes; F; F; F; Yes |
| 1930 | 1328; Whitehawk, Thersa[sic]; 1927-Aug. 3; F; Cheyenne; Yes; F; F; F; Yes |
|      | 1312; Whitewolf, Fred; 1928-Feb. 20; M; Cheyenne; Yes; F; F; F; Yes |
| 1929 | 1387; Wolftooth, Wayne; 1928-May 30; M; Cheyenne; Yes; F; F; F; Yes |
|      | 1416; Yelloweyes, Ruth Elsie; 1927-Nov. 6; F; Cheyenne; Yes; F; F; F; Yes |
|      | --   Yellowfox, John Arthur; 1927-Nov. 1; M; Cheyenne; Yes; F; F; F; Yes |
|      | 1425; Yellownose, Mary; 1927-July 7; F; Cheyenne; Yes; F; F; F; Yes |
|      | 1436; Youngbear, Mary; 1927-Dec. 20; F; Cheyenne; Yes; F; F; F; Yes |

Births Occurring Between the Dates of July 1, 1928 and June 30, 1929 to Parents Enrolled at Jurisdiction
[For the year dates to the left (1929 & 1930) there is no explanation.]

1929 Census Roll #

23; Ant, ~~Thelma~~ Ralph; 1928-Oct. 18; ~~F~~ M; Cheyenne; Yes; F; F; F; Yes
1148; Bearcomesout, Herbert; 1928-Sept. 18; M; Cheyenne; Yes; F; F; F; Yes
106; Bigheadman, Elizabeth; 1928-Nov. 16; F; Cheyenne; Yes; F; F; F; Yes
120; Bites, James Jr.; 1929-May 5; M; Cheyenne; Yes; F; F; F; Yes
129; Bixby, Hattie C.; 1928-July 24; F; Cheyenne; Yes; 1/4; W; 1/8; Yes
183; Brady, Pearl; 1928-July 14; F; Cheyenne; Yes; F; F; F; Yes

## LIVE BIRTHS

State **Montana** Reservation **Tongue River** Agency
or jurisdiction, **Tongue River** Office of Indian Affairs

Key: Census Roll Number; Surname, Given; Date of Birth (Year-Month & Day); Live Births (Yes unless otherwise given); Still Births (blank unless otherwise given); Sex; Tribe; Ward (Yes/No); Degree of Blood (Father; Mother; Child); At Jurisdiction Where Enrolled (Yes/No); (If no – Where)

|   | | |
|---|---|---|
| | 282; | Eaglefeathers, Milton; 1929-Jan. 12; M; Cheyenne; Yes; F; F; F; Yes |
| | 301; | Elkshoulder, Calvin; 1928-Aug. 5; M; Cheyenne; Yes; F; F; F; Yes |
| | 304; | Elliott, Loretta May; 1929-Apr. 16; F; Cheyenne; Yes; W; 3/8; 3/16; Yes |
| | 00 | Fightingbear, Baby; 1929-June 11; M; Cheyenne; Yes; F; F; F; Yes |
| | 351; | Foot, Sylvia; 1928-Nov. 19; F; Cheyenne; Yes; 1/2; F; 3/4; Yes |
| | -- | Hardground, Mary; 1929-Mar. 12; F; Cheyenne; Yes; F; F; F; Yes |
| | 432; | Hollowbreast, Edward; 1929-Apr. 7; M; Cheyenne; Yes; F; F; F; Yes |
| | 585; | Killsnight, Kitty Belle; 1928-Nov. 8; F; Cheyenne; Yes; F; F; F; Yes |
| | 576; | Killsnight, Jennie; 1929-Mar. 12; F; Cheyenne; Yes; F; F; F; Yes |
| | 595; | Killsontop, Levern; 1929-Jan. 1; M; Cheyenne; Yes; F; F; F; Yes |
| | 634; | Limberhand, Doris; 1928-Oct. 15; F; Cheyenne; Yes; F; F; F; Yes |
| | 655; | Limpy, Benjamin; 1929-June 10; M; Cheyenne; Yes; F; F; F; Yes |
| | 663; | Littlebear, Carol; 1929-Dec. 2; F; Cheyenne; Yes; F; F; F; Yes |
| | -- | Littleeyes, Baby; 1929-Oct. 19; M; Cheyenne; Yes; F; F; F; Yes |
| 1929 | 600; | Littlewhirlwind, Anna; 1928-Nov. 30; F; Cheyenne; Yes; F; F; F; Yes |
| | 631; | Littlewhiteman, Willis; 1928-Aug. 9; M; Cheyenne; Yes; 3/4; F; 7/8; Yes |
| | -- | Littlesun, Baby; 1929-Mar. 13; M; Cheyenne; Yes; F; F; F; Yes |
| | 745; | Medicineflying, Clifford; 1929-May 12; M; Cheyenne; Yes; F; F; F; Yes |
| | 754; | Medicinetop, Edward; 1929-Mar. 15; M; Cheyenne; Yes; F; F; F; Yes |
| | 762; | MexicanCheyenne, Anna Joyce; 1928-Aug. 15; F; Cheyenne; Yes; 1/2; F; 3/4; Yes |
| | 779 | Parker, Donald Edw.; 1928-Aug. 28; M; Cheyenne; Yes; 1/4; W; 1/8; Yes |
| | 812; | Prairiebear, Louis; 1928-Nov. 2; M; Cheyenne; Yes; F; F; F; Yes |
| | 826; | Redbird, Samuel; 1928-Nov. 22; M; Cheyenne; Yes; F; 3/4; 7/8; Yes |
| | 841; | Redcherries, Wallace; 1929, Feb. 4; M; Cheyenne; Yes; ?; F; F; Yes |
| | 887; | Redwoman, Donald; 1928-July 10; M; Cheyenne; Yes; F; F; F; Yes |
| | 894; | Ridgebear, James; 1929-Mar. 2; M; Cheyenne; Yes; F; F; F; Yes |
| | 907; | Risingsun, Pearl; 1928-Aug. 19; F; Cheyenne; Yes; F; F; F; Yes |
| | 908; | Risingsun, Ruby; 1928-Aug. 19; F; Cheyenne; Yes; F; F; F; Yes |
| | 918; | Robinson, Buell; 1928-July 30; M; Cheyenne; Yes; 1/8; 1/8; 1/8; Yes |
| | 931; | Romonnose[sic], Louise; 1928-July 26; F; Cheyenne; Yes; F; F; F; Yes |
| | 971; | Russell, John Jr.; 1929-Mar. 31; M; Cheyenne; Yes; F; F; F; No; Chey. & Arap. Okla. |
| | 365; | Sandcrane, Peter; 1928-Nov. 29; M; Cheyenne; Yes; F; F; F; Yes |
| | -- | Seminole, Helen May; 1929-Jan. 13; F; Cheyenne; Yes; 3/4; F; 7/8; Yes |
| | 1002; | Seminole, Beatrice; 1928-Aug. 27; F; Cheyenne; Yes; 3/4; F; 7/8; Yes |
| | -- | Small, Vera Sue; 1928-Dec. 20; F; Cheyenne; Yes; W; 1/2; 1/4; Yes |
| | 1072; | Spang, Edward F.; 1929-Mar. 16; M; Cheyenne; Yes; 1/8; W; 1/16; Yes |
| | 1199; | Tangledyellowhair, Marie; 1929-Mar. 31; F; Cheyenne; Yes; F; F; F; Yes |
| | 1182; | Tallbull, Nellie; 1929-Jan. 5; F; Cheyenne; Yes; F; F; F; Yes |

## LIVE BIRTHS

State __Montana__ Reservation __Tongue River__ Agency or jurisdiction, __Tongue River__ Office of Indian Affairs

Key: Census Roll Number; Surname, Given; Date of Birth (Year-Month & Day); Live Births (Yes unless otherwise given); Still Births (blank unless otherwise given); Sex; Tribe; Ward (Yes/No); Degree of Blood (Father; Mother; Child); At Jurisdiction Where Enrolled (Yes/No); (If no – Where)

| | | |
|---|---|---|
| 1930 | 1216; | Teeth, Logan; 1928-Nov. 11; M; Cheyenne; Yes; F; F; F; Yes |
| | 1304; | Whitecrane, Eva; 1928-Dec. 5; F; Cheyenne; Yes; F; F; F; Yes |
| | 1311; | Whitedirt, Leona; 1928-Dec. 7; F; Cheyenne; Yes; F; F; F; Yes |
| | 1351; | Wilson, George; 1929-May 24; M; Cheyenne; Yes; W; 1/2; 1/4; Yes |
| | 1359; | Wolfblack, Mary; 1929-Apr. 8; F; Cheyenne; Yes; F; F; F; Yes |
| | 1367; | Wolfchief, Norman; 1929-Mar. 7; M; Cheyenne; Yes; F; F; F; Yes |
| | -- | Yellowfox, Baby; 1928-Sept. 8; Cheyenne; Yes; F; F; F; Yes |
| | -- | Yellowrobe, Alfred; 1929-May 12; M; Cheyenne; Yes; F; F; F; Yes |
| | 1448; | Yellowrobe, Moses; 1929-Feb. 7; M; Cheyenne; Yes; F; F; F; Yes |
| | -- | Youngbear, Baby; 1928-Sept. 28; M; Cheyenne; Yes; F; F; F; Yes |
| | 593; | *Blackstone, Joseph; 1929-June 20; M; Cheyenne; Yes; F; F; F; Yes |
| | | Bigheadman, James 1929-Feb 24; M; Cheyenne; Yes; F; [--]; [--]; Yes |
| | | Soldierwolf, Baby; 1929-Nov. 29; F; Cheyenne; Yes; F; [--]; [--]; Yes |

\* The last name on the list is out of alphabetical order.

__Births Occurring Between the Dates of July 1, 1929 and June 30, 1930 to Parents Enrolled at Jurisdiction__
[For the year date to the left (1931) there is no explanation.]

1930
Census
Roll #

| | | |
|---|---|---|
| 1931 | -- | Americanhorse, Esther; 1930-Mar. 22; F; Cheyenne; Yes; F; F; F; No; Cheyenne & ARAP. Okla. |
| | 29; | Atwood, David; 1929-Aug. 16; M; Cheyenne; Yes; F; F; F; Yes |
| | -- | Atwood, Paul; 1929-Aug. 16; M; Cheyenne; Yes; F; F; F; Yes |
| | -- | Bigback, Eugene; 1930-May 7; M; Cheyenne; Yes; F; F; F; Yes |
| | 70; | Bigback, Marie; 1929-Sept. 8; F; Cheyenne; Yes; F; F; F; Yes |
| 1931 | 80; | Bigfoot, Hoover; 1930-June 10; M; Cheyenne; Yes; F; F; F; Yes |
| 1931 | 129; | Bixby, Juanita; 1930-May 24; F; Cheyenne; Yes; 1/4; W; 1/8; Yes |
| | 131; | Blackhorse, Lafe C.; 1929-July 8; M; Cheyenne; Yes; F; F; F; Yes |
| | -- | Blackstone, [Blank]; 1929-Nov. 18; M; Cheyenne; Yes; F; F; F; Yes |
| | 183; | Brein, Myron; 1929-Oct. 12; M; Cheyenne; Yes; 1/2; 1/9; 5/16; Yes |
| | 200; | Burns, George E.; 1929-Aug. 13; M; Cheyenne; Yes; 1/8; W; 1/16; Yes |
| | 262; | Deafy, Irene; 1929-July 15; F; Cheyenne; Yes; F; F; F; Yes |
| | 336; | Fisher, Burton; 1929-July 27; M; Cheyenne; Yes; F; F; F; Yes |
| | 373; | Hardground, Susan; 1930-Mary[sic] 28; F; Cheyenne; Yes; F; F; F; Yes |
| 1931 | 372; | Hardground, Thomas; 1930-Apr. 26; M; Cheyenne; Yes; F; F; F; Yes |
| | 387; | Harris, Elmer; 1939-Sept. 1; M; Cheyenne; Yes; 1/4; F; 5/8; Yes |
| | -- | Killsnight, Eugene; 1929-Sept. 17; M; Cheyenne; Yes; F; F; F; Yes |
| 1931 | 501; | Killsontop, Harold; 1930-June 21; M; Cheyenne; Yes; F; F; F; Yes |
| | 518; | Lamebear, Susie; 1930-Feb. 12; F; Cheyenne; Yes; F; F; F; Yes |
| | 521; | Lamewoman, Ruth; 1929-Oct. 15; M[sic]; Cheyenne; Yes; F; 3/4; 7/8; Yes |
| | -- | Limberhand, Harry; 1930-Jan. 3; M; Cheyenne; Yes; F; F; F; Yes |

## LIVE BIRTHS

State **Montana** Reservation **Tongue River** Agency
or jurisdiction, **Tongue River** Office of Indian Affairs

Key: Census Roll Number; Surname, Given; Date of Birth (Year-Month & Day); Live Births (Yes unless otherwise given); Still Births (blank unless otherwise given); Sex; Tribe; Ward (Yes/No); Degree of Blood (Father; Mother; Child); At Jurisdiction Where Enrolled (Yes/No); (If no – Where)

|      |       |                                                                                              |
|------|-------|----------------------------------------------------------------------------------------------|
|      | 564;  | Littlebear, Lester; 1929-Sept. 16; M; Cheyenne; Yes; F; F; F; Yes                            |
|      | 572;  | Littlebird, Theresa; 1929-Dec. 8; F; Cheyenne; Yes; F; F; F; Yes                             |
|      | --    | Littlewhiteman, Elmer; 1929-Oct. 28; M; Cheyenne; Yes; 3/4; F; 7/8; Yes                       |
|      | --    | Littlewhiteman, Mabel; 1930-June 9; F; Cheyenne; Yes; 3/4; F; 7/8; Yes                        |
|      | 635;  | Littlewhiteman, Mona; 193-Mar. 30; F; Cheyenne; 3/4; F; 7/8; Yes                              |
|      | 658;  | Littlewolf, Herbert; 1930-Mar. 19; M; Cheyenne; Yes; F; F; F; Yes                             |
|      | --    | Littleyellowman, Eddie Jr.; 1929-Nov. 16; M; Cheyenne; Yes; F; F; F; No; Chey. & Arap. Okla.  |
|      | 1281; | Looksbehind, Inez; 1929-Aug. 19; F; Cheyenne; Yes; F; F; F; Yes                              |
| 1931 | 739;  | Medicinebull, Mae; 1930-Apr. 30; F; Cheyenne; Yes; F; F; F; Yes                              |
|      | 1394; | Medicineelk, Leo; 1929-Sept. 6; M; Cheyenne; Yes; F; F; F; Yes                               |
|      | 741;  | Medicineelk, Margaret; 1930-Feb. 2; F; Cheyenne; Yes; F; F; F; Yes                            |
|      | 785;  | Onebear, Louise; 1929-Oct. 18; F; Cheyenne; Yes; 3/4; 3/4; 3/4; Yes                          |
|      | 799;  | Parker, Charlotte; 1929-July 23; F; Cheyenne; Yes; 1/4; 1/4; 1/4; Yes                        |
| 1931 | 853;  | Redcherries, Della; 1930-May 18; F; Cheyenne; Yes; F; F; F; Yes                              |
|      | 860;  | Redfox, Ralph; 1929-Sept. 24; M; Cheyenne; Yes; F; F; F; Yes                                 |
|      | 931;  | Rockroads, Flossie; 1929-July 10; F; Cheyenne; Yes; F; F; F; Yes                             |
|      | 1019; | Shavedhead, Mabel; 1930-Jan. 30; F; Cheyenne; Yes; F; F; F; Yes                              |
|      | 1064; | Small, Clinton; 1929-Nov. 19; M; Cheyenne; Yes; W; 1/2; 1/4; Yes                             |
| 1931 | 1074; | Soldierwolf, Doris; 1930-APR. 5; F; Cheyenne; Yes; F; F; F; Yes                              |
|      | 1097; | Speelman, Wm. Lawrence; 1929-July 26; M; Cheyenne; Yes; W; 1/4; 1/8; Yes                     |
|      | 1103; | Sponge, Lena; 1929-Aug. 28; F; Cheyenne; Yes; F; F; F; Yes                                   |
|      | 1117; | Spottedwolf, Della; 1930-Jan. 1; F; Cheyenne; Yes; F; F; F; Yes                              |
|      | 1139; | Standingelk, Benno; 1930-Feb. 21; M; Cheyenne; Yes; F; F; F; Yes                             |
| 1931 | 1136; | Swallow, Elsie; 1930-Apr. 12; F; Cheyenne; Yes; F; F; F; Yes                                 |
|      | 1269; | Walksnice, Mae; 1929-Nov. 1; F; Cheyenne; Yes; F; F; F; Yes                                  |
|      | 1269;[sic] | White, Willis; 1930-Mar. 31; M; Cheyenne; Yes; F; 3/4; 7/8; Yes                         |
|      | 1300; | Whitebird, Edward; 1930-Mar. 4; M; Cheyenne; Yes; F; F; F; Yes                               |
| 1931 | 1330; | Whitedirt, Mae; 1930-May 26; F; Cheyenne; Yes; F; F; F; Yes                                  |
|      | 1325; | Whitehawk, James; 1929-July 3; M; Cheyenne; Yes; F; F; F; Yes                                |
|      | 1348; | Whitewolf, Leo; 1930-Dec. 18; M; Cheyenne; Yes; F; F; F; Yes                                 |
| 1931 | 1386; | Winsor, Lee Roland; 1930-May 23; M; Cheyenne; Yes; W; 1/8; 1/16; No; Easton, Wash.           |
|      | 1386; | Wolfchum, Espy; 1930-Apr. 1; M; Cheyenne; Yes; F; F; F; Yes                                  |
|      | 1432; | Woundedeye, Waldo; 1929-Aug. 28; M; Cheyenne; Yes; F; F; F Yes                               |
|      | 1448; | Yelloweyes, David; 1929-Dec. 26; M; Cheyenne; Yes; F; F; F; Yes                              |
|      | 1455; | Yellowfox, Mary Josephine; 1930-Mar. 1; F; Cheyenne; Yes; F; F; F; Yes                       |
|      | --    | Yellowrobe, Hilda; 1930-Apr. 7; F; Cheyenne; Yes; F; F; F; Yes                               |

## LIVE BIRTHS

State __Montana__ Reservation __Tongue River__ Agency or jurisdiction, __Tongue River__ Office of Indian Affairs

Key: Census Roll Number; Surname, Given; Date of Birth (Year-Month & Day); Live Births (Yes unless otherwise given); Still Births (blank unless otherwise given); Sex; Tribe; Ward (Yes/No); Degree of Blood (Father; Mother; Child); At Jurisdiction Where Enrolled (Yes/No); (If no – Where)

Births Occurring Between the Dates of April 1, 1930 and March 31, 1931 to Parents Enrolled at Jurisdiction
[For the year date to the left (1932) there is no explanation.]

|      | 1931 Census Roll # | |
|---|---|---|
|      | 25;   | Ant, Francis; 1930-July 15; M; Cheyenne; Yes; F; F; F; Yes |
|      | 425;  | Badhorse, Esther; 1930-Aug. 18; F; Cheyenne; Yes; F; F; F; Yes |
|      | 80;   | Bigfoot, Hoover; 1930-June 10; M; Cheyenne; Yes; F; F; F; Yes |
|      | 72;   | Bigback, Eugene; 1930-May 7; M; Cheyenne; Yes; F; F; F; Yes |
|      | --    | Bigheadman, Anthonly[sic]; 1931-Jan. 9; M; Cheyenne; Yes; F; F; F; Yes |
|      | 87;   | Bigheadman, [Blank]; 1931-Mar. 13; F; Cheyenne; Yes; F; F; F; Yes |
|      | 96;   | Bigheadman, [Blank]; 1931-Mar. 6; F; Cheyenne; Yes; F; F; F; Yes |
|      | 129;  | Bixby, Juanita; 1930-May 24; F; Cheyenne; Yes; 1/4; W; 1/8; Yes |
|      | 149;  | Blackstone, Leo; 1930-Oct. 22; M; Cheyenne; Yes; F; F; F; Yes |
|      | 189;  | Brady, Clifford; 1930-Oct. 10; M; Cheyenne; Yes; F; F; F; Yes |
|      | 303;  | Elliott, Myron Leonard; 1930-Nov. 13; M; Cheyenne; Yes; W; 3/8; 3/16; Yes |
| 1932 |       | Fisher, Emeline; 1931-Feb. 10; F; Cheyenne; Yes; F; 3/8; 11/16; Yes |
|      | 328;  | Fisher, Virginia Mae; 1930-Dec. 14; F; Cheyenne; Yes; 1/2; 1/8; 5/16; Yes |
|      | 364;  | Gray, Buddy; 1930-Sept. 17; M; Cheyenne; Yes; F; F; F; Yes |
|      | 372;  | Hardground, Thomas; 1930-Apr. 26; M; Cheyenne; Yes; F; F; F; Yes |
|      | 384;  | Harris, Chester; 1931-Feb. 25; M; Cheyenne; Yes; 1/4; F; 5/8; Yes |
|      | 410;  | Hart, Hilda; 1930-Aug. 29; F; Cheyenne; Yes; 7/8; F; 15/16; Yes |
|      | 442;  | Horn, Denver Sherman; 1930-Dec. 13; M; Cheyenne; Yes; F; F; F; Yes |
|      | 501;  | Killsontop, Harold; 1930-June 21; F[sic]; Cheyenne; Yes; F; F; F; Yes |
| 1932 |       | Kingfisher, Elizabeth; 1930-Aug. 1; F; Cheyenne; Yes; F; F; F; Yes |
| 1931 |       | Knows-His-Gun, Genevieve; 1930-July 13; F; Cheyenne; Yes; F; F; F; Yes |
| 1932 |       | Limberhand, George; 1931-Mar. 23; M; Cheyenne; Yes; F; F; F; Yes |
|      | --    | Littlewhiteman, Mabel; 1930-June 9; F; Cheyenne; Yes; 3/4; F; 7/8; Yes |
| 1932 |       | Littlemouth, Fred; 1931-Jan. 27; M; Cheyenne; Yes; F; F; F; Yes |
|      | 678;  | Loneelk, George; 1931-Mar. 14; M; Cheyenne; Yes; F; F; F; Yes |
|      | 694;  | Longjaw, Claudia; 1930-Oct. 7; F; Cheyenne; Yes; F; F; F; Yes |
|      | 739;  | Medicinebull, Mae; 1930-Apr. 30; F; Cheyenne; Yes; F; F; F; Yes |
|      | 790;  | Parker, Lyle Neal; 1930-SEPT. 8; M; Cheyenne; Yes; 1/4; W; 1/8; Yes |
|      | 832;  | Redbird, Diva; 1930-Dec. 8; F; Cheyenne; Yes; F; F; F; Yes |
|      | 853;  | Redcherries, Della; 1930-May 18; F; Cheyenne; Yes; F; F; F; Yes |
| 1932 |       | Redwoman, John; 1931-Jan. 18; M; Cheyenne; Yes; F; F; F; Yes |
|      | 961;  | Rowland, Julia; 1930-Aug. 11; F; Cheyenne; Yes; 3/4; F; 7/8; Yes |
|      | 977;  | Russell, Clifford; 1930-Sept. 17; M; Cheyenne; Yes; F; F; F; Yes |
|      | 1014; | Seminole, Lucille; 1931-Feb. 24; F; Cheyenne; Yes; 3/4; F; 7/8; Yes |
|      | 1045; | Shoulderblade, Claudia; 1930-July 8; F; Cheyenne; Yes; F; 3/4; 7/8; Yes |

## LIVE BIRTHS

State **Montana** Reservation **Tongue River** Agency
or jurisdiction, **Tongue River** Office of Indian Affairs

Key: Census Roll Number; Surname, Given; Date of Birth (Year-Month & Day); Live Births (Yes unless otherwise given); Still Births (blank unless otherwise given); Sex; Tribe; Ward (Yes/No); Degree of Blood (Father; Mother; Child); At Jurisdiction Where Enrolled (Yes/No); (If no – Where)

|      |       |                                                                                                 |
|------|-------|-------------------------------------------------------------------------------------------------|
|      | 1074; | Soldierwolf, Doris; 1930-Apr. 5; F; Cheyenne; Yes; F; F; F; Yes                                 |
|      | 1083; | Spang, Darrell Dean; 1930-Aug. 11; M; Cheyenne; Yes; 1/8; W; 1/16; No; ~~Fort Peck Mont~~. Poplar, Mont Letter 6/18/32 Mac. |
|      | 1090; | Spang, Joyce; 1931-Jan. 5; F; Cheyenne; Yes; 1/8; W; 1/16; Yes                                  |
|      | 1077; | Spang, Peter Albert; 1931-Feb. 24; M; Cheyenne; Yes; 1/8; W; 1/16; Yes                          |
| 1932 |       | Spottedelk, Eugene; 1931-Jan. 28; M; Cheyenne; Yes; F; F; F; Yes                                |
| 1932 |       | Spottedwolf, James; 1931-Mar. 15; M; Cheyenne; Yes; F; F; F; Yes                                |
|      | 1155; | Standsintimber, Gilbert; 1930-Oct. 24; M; Cheyenne; Yes; F; F; F; Yes                           |
|      | 1136; | Swallow, Elsie; 1930-Apr. 12; F; Cheyenne; Yes; F; F; F; Yes                                    |
|      | 1182; | Tallbear, Erma Jean; 1931-Feb. 17; F; Cheyenne; Yes; F; F; F; Yes                               |
|      | 1232; | Threefingers, Isaac; 1931-Jan. 22; M; Cheyenne; Yes; F; F; F; Yes                               |
|      | 1248; | Twobulls, Ruth; 1931-Jan. 15; F; Cheyenne; Yes; F; F; F; Yes                                    |
|      | 1271; | Walkslast, Lloyd; 1930-Sept. 2; M; Cheyenne; Yes; F; F; F; Yes                                  |
|      | 1274; | Walkslast, ~~Gilbert~~ Tom; 1931-Mar. 13; M; Cheyenne; Yes; F; F; F; Yes                        |
|      | 1323; | Whitecrane, Anna; 1931-Feb. 16; F; Cheyenne; Yes; F; F; F; Yes                                  |
|      | 1330; | Whitedirt, Mae; 1930-May 26; F; Cheyenne; Yes; F; F; F; Yes                                     |
|      | 1342; | Whitehawk, George; 1930-Dec. 6; M; Cheyenne; Yes; F; F; F; Yes                                  |
|      | 1351; | Whitemoon, Clarence; 1930-Aug. 8; M; Cheyenne; Yes; F; F; F; Yes                                |
| 1932 |       | Wilson, Wm.; 1930-Sept. 3; M; Cheyenne; Yes; F; F; F; Yes                                       |
|      | 1386; | Windsor, Lee Roland; 1930-May 23; M; Cheyenne; Yes; W; 1/8; 1/16; ~~Yes~~ No; Easton Wash. Letter 6/18/32 Mac. |
|      | 1397; | Wolfchief, Mary; 1931-Mar. 1; F; Cheyenne; Yes; F; F; F; Yes                                    |
|      | 1455; | Woundedeye, Iva Ruth; 1930-Oct. 18; F; Cheyenne; Yes; F; F; F; Yes                              |
|      | 1475; | Yellownose, Lena; 1930-Nov. 24; F; Cheyenne; Yes; F; F; F; Yes                                  |
|      | --    | Yellownose, Hilda; 1930-Apr. 7; F; Cheyenne; Yes; F; F; F; Yes                                  |
|      | 1483; | Yellowrobe, Theodore; 1930-July 5; M; Cheyenne; Yes; F; F; F; Yes                               |

Births Occurring Between the Dates of April 1, 1931 and March 31, 1932 to Parents Enrolled at Jurisdiction

1932 Census Roll #

- 415; Akin, Vernon Hart; 1931-June 28; M; Cheyenne; Yes; W; 5/8; 5/16; Yes
- 37; Bearchum, Frank Jr.; 1931-~~Dec. 29~~ Sept 26; M; Cheyenne; Yes; 3/4; F; 7/8; Yes
- 401; Beckman, Eugene Veloe; 1931-Dec. 29; M; Cheyenne; Yes; W; 5/8; 5/16; Yes
- 64; Bement, Albert Raymond; 1931-Apr. 14; M; Cheyenne; Yes; W; 1/8; 1/16; Yes
- 85; Bigfoot, White; 1931-July 2; M; Cheyenne; Yes; F; F; F; No; Cheyenne & Arap. Okla.
- 121; Bites, Mamie; 1931-Nov. 10; F; Cheyenne; Yes; F; F; Yes
- 135; Bixby, Lloyd James; 1932-Mar. 18; M; Cheyenne; Yes; 1/4; W; 1/8; Yes

## LIVE BIRTHS

State **Montana** Reservation **Tongue River** Agency or jurisdiction, **Tongue River** Office of Indian Affairs

Key: Census Roll Number; Surname, Given; Date of Birth (Year-Month & Day); Live Births (Yes unless otherwise given); Still Births (blank unless otherwise given); Sex; Tribe; Ward (Yes/No); Degree of Blood (Father; Mother; Child); At Jurisdiction Where Enrolled (Yes/No); (If no – Where)

DBE Blackhorse, Ruben; 1931-Dec. 18; M; Cheyenne; Yes; F; F; F; Yes
1385; Blackstone, Arthur; 1931-May 8; M; Cheyenne; Yes; F; F; F; Yes
186; Brein, Lorraine; 1932-Jan. 12; F; Cheyenne; Yes; 1/2; 1/8; 5/16; Yes
236; Cooley, Odessa Marie; 1931-Nov. 6; F; Cheyenne; Yes; W; 1/8; 1/16; Yes
238; Crawford, Lyman Eugene; 1931-Apr. 30; M; Cheyenne; Yes; 1/2; 3/8; 7/16; Yes
306; Elkshoulder, Fred; 1931-July 9; M; Cheyenne; Yes; F; F; F; Yes
DBE Fightingbear, Francis; 1931-Nov. 13; M; Cheyenne; Yes; F; F; F; Yes
345; Fisher, Floyd; 1932-Mar. 30; M; Cheyenne; Yes; F; F; F; Yes
358; Foot, Joseph; 1931-Apr. 30; M; Cheyenne; Yes; 1/2; F; 3/4; Yes[sic]; Ft. Peck Agency, Mont.
367; Gray, Joseph; 1931-July 11; M; Cheyenne; Yes; F; F; F; Yes
442; Hollowbreast, Fern; 1931-Sept. 1; F; Cheyenne; Yes; F; F; F; Yes
467; Ironhand, Rufus Grant; 1932-Feb. 20; M; Cheyenne; Yes; F; F; F; Yes
509; Killsontop, Paul; ~~1931-Sept. 20~~ 1932-Mar 4; M; Cheyenne; Yes; F; F; Yes
516; King, Stephen; 1932-Mar. 8; M; Cheyenne; Yes; 1/2; F; 3/4; Yes
541; Knows-His-Gun, Hector Jr.; 1932-Mar. 5; M; Cheyenne; Yes; F; F; Yes
DBE Lamebear, Ethel; 1931-Sept. 20; F; Cheyenne; Yes; F; F; F; Yes
555; Lamewoman, Sam Jr.; 1931-May 14; M; Cheyenne; Yes; F; F; F; Yes
~~Limberhand, George; 1931-Mar. 21; M; Cheyenne; Yes; F; F; F; Yes~~
734; Limpy (Romannose), Lee; 1931-Nov. 14; M; Cheyenne; Yes; F; F; F; Yes
DBE Littlebear, (Unnamed); 1831-Nov. 27; F; Cheyenne; Yes; F; F; F; Yes
632; Littlewhirlwind, Levi; 1931-Sept. 6; M; Cheyenne; Yes; F; F; F; Yes
649; Littlewhiteman, Clara; 1921-Mar. 24; F; Cheyenne; Yes; 3/4; F; 7/8; Yes
667; Littlewhiteman, Richard J.; 1931-May 3; M; Cheyenne; Yes; 3/4; F; 7/8; Yes
686; Littleyellowman, Hugh Everett; 1931-June 19; M; Cheyenne; Yes; 3/4; 3/4; 3/4; Yes[sic]; Chey. & Arap. Agency, Okla.
895; Ridgebear, Jerry K.; 1931-Nov. 12; M; Cheyenne; Yes; F; F; F; Yes
915; Risingsun, Irvin Wm.; 1931-Aug. 29; M; Cheyenne; Yes; F; F; F; Yes
904; Risingsun, Jordan; 1931-May 13; M; Cheyenne; Yes; F; F; F; Yes
921; Robinson, James M.; 1932-Feb 16; M; Cheyenne; Yes; 1/8; 1/8; 1/8; Yes
749; Roundstone, Victoria; 1931-Aug. 20; F; Cheyenne; Yes; F; F; F; Yes
980; Russell, Hubert; 1931-Oct. 5; M; Cheyenne; Yes; F; F; F; Yes
1192; Salzer, Frances; 1931-Aug. 4; F; Mexican & Cheyenne; Yes; M; F; 1/2; Yes[sic]; Chey. & Arap. Agency, Okla.
1002; Seminole, Eva; 1931-Aug. 24; F; Cheyenne; Yes; 3/4; F; 7/8; Yes
1007; Seminole, Jule; 1931-Dec. 15; M; Cheyenne; Yes; 3/4; f; 7/8; Yes

## LIVE BIRTHS

State **Montana** Reservation **Tongue River** Agency
or jurisdiction, **Tongue River** Office of Indian Affairs

Key: Census Roll Number; Surname, Given; Date of Birth (Year-Month & Day); Live Births (Yes unless otherwise given); Still Births (blank unless otherwise given); Sex; Tribe; Ward (Yes/No); Degree of Blood (Father; Mother; Child); At Jurisdiction Where Enrolled (Yes/No); (If no – Where)

DBE  Seminole (Woodenleg), (Unnamed); 1931-Aug. 17; M; Cheyenne; Yes; 3/4; F; 7/8; Yes
1082;  Spang, Alfonso Jr.; 1931-Aug. 15; M; Cheyenne; Yes; 1/8; 7/8; 1/2; Yes
1100;  Spang, Lawrence R.; 1931-July 6; M; Cheyenne; Yes; 1/8; F; 9/16; Yes
1105;  Speelman, Orville; 1931-Apr. 20; M; Cheyenne; Yes; W; 1/4; 1/8; Yes
1113;  Sponge, Charles; 1931-July 1; M; Cheyenne; Yes; F; F; F; Yes
~~1134; Spottedwolf, James; 1931-July 1[?]; M; Cheyenne; Yes; F; 3/8; 11/16; Yes~~
1148;  Standingelk, Isaac; 1931-Nov. 27; M; Cheyenne; Yes; F; F; F; Yes
1142;  Standingelk, Jordan; 1931-Sept. 1; M; Cheyenne; Yes; F; F; F; Yes
1155;  Standingelk, George; 1931-Feb. 22; M; Cheyenne; Yes; F; F; F; Yes
1182;  Swallow, Herbert; 1931-Nov. 11; M; Cheyenne; Yes; F; F; F; Yes
1204;  Tallbull, Charles Jr.; 1931-Sept. 11; M; Cheyenne; Yes; F; F; F; Yes
1218;  Tangledyellowhair, Ruth; 1932-Feb. 2; F; Cheyenne; Yes; F; F; F; Yes
1283;  Walksalong, Joseph; 1931-Apr. 26; M; Cheyenne; Yes; F; F; F; Yes
DBE  Whistlingelk, Maynora; 1931-Oct. 25; F; Cheyenne; Yes; F; F; F; Yes
1438;  Woodenleg, Tom, Jr.; 1931-~~Dec. 28~~ Sept. 11; M; Cheyenne; Yes; 1/2; F; 3/4; Yes
1475;  Yellowfox, Paul; 1931-Dec. 28; M; Cheyenne; Yes; F; F; F; Yes
1496;  Yellowrobe, Nancy Coed; 1932-Feb. 23; F; Cheyenne; Yes; F; F; F; Yes
DBE  Zettle, Frank; 1931-Nov. 7; M; Cheyenne; Yes; W; 3/8; 3/16; Yes
* 784;  Onebear, Wayne; 1931-June 10; M; Cheyenne; Yes; 7/8; 3/4; 13/16; Yes

*(The last name on this list is out of alphabetical order.)

DEATH ROLL

(EXCLUSIVE OF STILLBIRTHS)

TONGUE RIVER AGENCY

TONGUE RIVER RESERVATION

MONTANA

July 1, 1924 - June 30, 1925
July 1, 1925 - June 30, 1926
July 1, 1926 - June 30, 1927
July 1, 1927 - June 30, 1928
July 1, 1928 - June 30, 1929
July 1, 1929 - June 30, 1930
April 1, 1930 - March 31, 1931
April 1, 1931 - March 31, 1932

## EXCLUSIVE OF STILLBIRTHS

State **Montana** Reservation **Tongue River** Agency or jurisdiction, **Tongue River** Office of Indian Affairs

Key: Last Census Roll: Year & Number; Surname, Given; Date of Death (Year-Month & Day); Age At Death; Sex; Tribe; Ward (Yes/No); Degree of Blood; Cause of Death; At Jurisdiction Where Enrolled (Yes/No); (If no – Where)

Deaths Occurring Between the Dates of July 1, 1924 and June 30, 1925 of Indians Enrolled at Jurisdiction

1924  22; Badger, John; 1925-Apr. 29; 79; M; Cheyenne; Yes; F; Cancer of Rectum; Yes
1924  30; Bearcomesout, Angel; 1924-Nov. 22; 2; F; Cheyenne; Yes; F; Diphtheria; Yes
1925  61; Bigfoot, Rosa; 1925-June 15; 5; F; Cheyenne; Yes; F; Valvular Disease; Yes
1925  128; Blackwhiteman, Nellie; 1924-Nov. 24; 84; F; Cheyenne; Yes; F; Senility; Yes
1924  144; Boxelder, David; 1924-Oct. 19; 60; M; Cheyenne; Yes; F; Pulm. Tuberculosis; Yes
1924  173; Bullsheep, Sadie; 1924-Dec. 8; 74; F; Cheyenne; Yes; F; Senility; Yes
----  ---- Duster, Augusta; 1925-Apr. 27; 3; F; Cheyenne; Yes; F; Pulm. Tuberculosis; Yes
1924  970; Eastman, Emma; 1924-July 15; 24; F; Cheyenne; Yes; F; Pulm. Tuberculosis; Yes
1924  309; Firecrow, Alice Eva; 1924-Dec. 5; 25; F; Cheyenne; Yes; F; Pulm. Tuberculosis; Yes
1924  319; Fisher, Floyd; 1925-Apr. 24; 50; M; Cheyenne; Yes; F; Pneumonia; Yes
1924  350; Gray, Russell; 1925-Apr. 11; 3; M; Cheyenne; Yes; F; Pulm. Tuberculosis; Yes
1924  344; Grasshopper, Ida; 1925-Apr. 18; 63; F; Cheyenne; Yes; F; Pulm. Tuberculosis; Yes
1924  353; Hail, Inez; 1924-Dec. 31; 73; F; Cheyenne; Yes; F; Senility; Yes
1924  384; Harris, Elsie; 1925-June 7; 24; F; Cheyenne; Yes; F; Pulm. Tuberculosis; Yes
1924  425; Hollowbreast, Agnes; 1925-Apr. 20; 29; F; Cheyenne; Yes; F; Pulm. Tuberculosis; Yes
1924  461; Killsnight, Edward; 1924-Dec. 20; 45; M; Cheyenne; Yes; F; Apoplexy; Yes
1924  494; Kingfisher, Payton; 1925-Spring --; 8; M; Cheyenne; Yes; F; No Data; Yes
1924  647; Lostleg, George; 1925-Mar. 1; 71; M; Cheyenne; Yes; F; Pulm. Tuberculosis; Yes
1924  653; Magpie, Annie; 1925-Mar. 27; 5; F; Cheyenne; Yes; F; Pulm. Tuberculosis; Yes
1924  685; Medicineelk, Alice; 1924-Sept. 25; 3; F; Cheyenne; Yes; F; Pulm. Tuberculosis; Yes
1924  664; Manuel, Mexican; 1925-Mar. 28; 84; M; Mexican; Yes; F; Senility; Yes
1924  731; Pine, Bessie; 1924-Nov. 22; 60; F; Cheyenne; Yes; F; Septicemia; Yes
1924  841; Risingsun, Henry L.; 1924-Nov. 22; 9/12; M; Cheyenne; Yes; F; Convulsions; Yes

## EXCLUSIVE OF STILLBIRTHS

State___**Montana**_____ Reservation___**Tongue River**_____ Agency
or jurisdiction,_____**Tongue River**_____ Office of Indian Affairs

Key: Last Census Roll: Year & Number; Surname, Given; Date of Death (Year-Month & Day); Age At Death; Sex; Tribe; Ward (Yes/No); Degree of Blood; Cause of Death; At Jurisdiction Where Enrolled (Yes/No); (If no – Where)

1924 965; Sanchez, Grace E. 1924-July 11; 7; F; Cheyenne; Yes; 3/4; T.B. of Lungs; Yes
1924 914; Sandstone, Bessie; 1925-May 17; 70; F; Cheyenne; Yes; F; No data; Yes
---- --- Seminole, Falling; 1924-Aug. 27; 1 da; M; Cheyenne; Yes; 7/8; Prematurity; Yes
---- --- Seminole, Rising; 1924-Sept. 1; 7 da; M; Cheyenne; Yes; 7/8; Prematurity; Yes
1924 941; Sharpnose, Daisy; 1925-Apr. 2; 67; F; Cheyenne; Yes; F; Pulm. T.B.; Yes
1924 1033; Squinteye, Nellie; 1924-Dec. 20; 59; F; Cheyenne; Yes; F; Unknown; Yes
---- ---- Standingelk, Henry Jr.; 1924-Oct. 21; 1; M; Cheyenne; Yes; F; Pulm. T.B.; Yes
1924 1174; Twobulls, Joseph; 1924-Oct. 16; 1; M; Cheyenne; Yes; F; Unknown; Yes
1924 1190; Walkingbird, Seth; 1925-May 31; 70; M; Cheyenne; Yes; Pulm. T.B.; Yes
1924 1199; Walkseasy, David; 1924-Apr. 14; 70; M; Cheyenne; Yes; F; Killed by horse; Yes
1924 1220; Weaselbear, John; 1924-Aug. 21; 33; M; Cheyenne; Yes; F; Pulm. T.B.; Yes
1924 1217; Weaselbear, Minnie; 1925-Apr. 1; 33; F; Cheyenne; Yes; F; Pulm. T.B.; Yes
1924 1264; Whitehorse, Emma; 1924-July 4; 81; F; Cheyenne; Yes; F; Fatally injured by run away team; Yes
---- ---- Whitehawk, Paula; 1925-Feb. 5; 1; F; Cheyenne; Yes; F; Pneumonia; Yes
1924 1360; Woodenthigh, Hugh; 1924-Dec. 25; 77; M; Cheyenne; Yes; F; Senility; Yes
1924 1378; Yellowfox, Wm. Wayne; 1925-Jan. 8; 1; M; Cheyenne; Yes; F; Pneumonia; Yes
1924 1388; Yellowfox, Harriet M.; 1925-Feb. 3; 7: F; Cheyenne; Yes; F; Pulm. T.B.; Yes
1924 111; Blackeagle, Ada; 1924-Oct. --; 32; F; Cheyenne; Yes; F; Unknown; Yes
1924 266; Eaglefeathers, Laura; 1925-Feb. 14; 45; F; Cheyenne; Yes; F; Pulm. T.B.; Yes
1924 427; Hollowbreast, Anna; 1925-May 20; 1; F; Cheyenne; Yes; F; Unknown; Yes
1925 581; Littlewhiteman, Jennie; 1924-Oct. 25; 1; F; Cheyenne; Yes; 7/8; Unknown; Yes
1925 661; Medicine, Sampson; 1925-Mar. 27; 5; M; Cheyenne; Yes; F; No data; Yes

Note: Names on this page are out of alphabetical order. This roll would have been rewritten had there been enough blanks.

## EXCLUSIVE OF STILLBIRTHS

State __Montana__ Reservation __Tongue River__ Agency
or jurisdiction, __Tongue River__ Office of Indian Affairs

Key: Last Census Roll: Year & Number; Surname, Given; Date of Death (Year-Month & Day); Age At Death; Sex; Tribe; Ward (Yes/No); Degree of Blood; Cause of Death; At Jurisdiction Where Enrolled (Yes/No); (If no – Where)

Deaths Occurring Between the Dates of July 1, 1925 and June 30, 1926 of Indians Enrolled at Jurisdiction

1926    64; Bigfoot, James Peter; 1926-Mar. 15; 3; M; Cheyenne; Yes; F; Unknown; Yes
1925    71; Bigheadman, Maxine Lucy; 1926-Feb. 1; 3; F; Cheyenne; Yes; F; Acute Pulm. T.B.; Yes
1926    364; Hankeringwolf, Helen; 1926-June 26; 82; F; Cheyenne; Yes; F; Senility; Yes
1926    383; Hardrobe, Ruth; 1926-Mar. 6; 6; F; Cheyenne; Yes; F; Unknown; Yes
----    --- Issue, Donald; 1926-Jan. 27; 3/12; M; Cheyenne; Yes; F; Erysiplas[sic]; Yes
1925    560; Littlewhirlwind, Levi; 1926-Jan. 3; 58; M; Cheyenne; Yes; F; Gun shot wound; Yes
1925    461; Lonewolf, Romeo; 1925-Oct. 3; 15; M; Cheyenne; Yes; F; Fits; Yes
1926    734; Medicinetop, Andrew; 1926-Jan. 21; 1 da; M; Cheyenne; Yes; F; No data; Yes
1926    753; Oldbull, Ross; 1926-Mar. 25; 10; M; Cheyenne; Yes; F; Pulm. T.B.; Yes
1925    757; Redbird, Willis; 1925-Oct. 30; 42; M; Cheyenne; Yes; F; Pulm. T.B.; Yes
1926    833; Redfox, Myrtle Alcie; 1926-Jan. 24; 10 da; F; Cheyenne; Yes; F; No Data; Yes
1925    ~~804~~ Redwoman, Lucy; 1925-Dec. 1; 19; F; Cheyenne; Yes; F; Epilepsy; Yes
        435
1925    858; Rondeau, Hattie; 1925-Aug. 21; 39; F; Cheyenne; Yes; F; Pulm. T.B.; Yes
----    --- Roundstone, David; 1925-Sept. 25; 2/12; M; Cheyenne; Yes; F; Intestinal T.B.; Yes
1925    866; Roundstone, Louis; 1925-Dec. 27; 77; M; Cheyenne; Yes; F; Senility; Yes
1925    905; Sandcrane, Annie May; 1926-June 30; 1; F; Cheyenne; Yes; F; Unknown; Yes
---     --- Seminole, [Blank]; 1925-July 16; 3 da; M; Cheyenne; Yes; F; Premature; Yes
1926    973; Seminole, Mary; 1926-June 18; 66; F; Cheyenne; Yes; F; Cancer of Stomach; Yes
1925    1028; Standingelk, Eugene; 1926-Mar. 11; 66; M; Cheyenne; Yes; F; Lobar Pneumonia; Yes
1925    1122; Tangledyellowhair, Olive; 1926-Apr. 16; 25; F; Cheyenne; Yes; F; Unknown; Yes
1925    1120; Tangledyellowhair, Regina; 1925-Oct. 18; 2; F; Cheyenne; Yes; F; Dysentery; Yes
1925    1139; Texas, Augusta; 1926-Apr. 21; 18; F; Cheyenne; Yes; F; Pulm. T.B.; Yes
1925    1155; Twentystands, Paul; 1926-Mar. 7; 9/12; M; Cheyenne; Yes; F; Suffocation; Yes

## EXCLUSIVE OF STILLBIRTHS

State __Montana__ Reservation __Tongue River__ Agency or jurisdiction, __Tongue River__ Office of Indian Affairs

Key: Last Census Roll: Year & Number; Surname, Given; Date of Death (Year-Month & Day); Age At Death; Sex; Tribe; Ward (Yes/No); Degree of Blood; Cause of Death; At Jurisdiction Where Enrolled (Yes/No); (If no – Where)

\--- --- Walksnice, Susie; 1925-Oct. 4; 1/12; F; Cheyenne; Yes; F; Unknown; Yes

1925 1212; Whirlwind, Dick; 1926-Jan. 30; 17; M; Cheyenne; Yes; F; Pulm. T.B.; Yes

1925 1251; Whitehawk, Charles John; 1925-Dec. 27; 3; M; Cheyenne; Yes; F; Croup; Yes

\--- --- Whitehawk, Thomas; 1926-Mar. 1; 4/12; M; Cheyenne; Yes; F; Unknown; Yes

1925 1269; Whitewolf, Pius; 1926-Mar. 17; 8; M; Cheyenne; Yes; F; Pulm. T.B.; Yes

1925 1310; Wolfear, Mary; 1926-Apr. 15; 16; F; Cheyenne; Yes; F; Pneumonia; Yes

\--- --- Woundedeye, Edelson; 1926-Jan. 28; 9 da; M; Cheyenne; Yes; F; Premature; Yes

1925 1366; Woundedeye, Rose; 1926-Mar. 24; 1; F; Cheyenne; Yes; F; Broncho-pneumonia; Yes

\--- --- Yellowrobe, Arthur; 1926-Jan. 24; 3; M; Cheyenne; Yes; F; Fractured Skull; Yes

1925 1204; Youngbear, Frank; 1926-Mar. 3; 20; M; Cheyenne; Yes; 3/4; Pulm. T.B.; Yes

Deaths Occurring Between the Dates of July 1, 1926 and June 30, 1927 of Indians Enrolled at Jurisdiction

1926 25; Bearcomesout, Hilda; 1926-Sept. 13; 40; F; Cheyenne; Yes; F; Tapeworm & T.B.; Yes

\--- -- Bigback, Susie; 1926-Oct. 29; 6 da; F; Cheyenne; Yes; F; No data; Yes

\--- -- Bigfoot, Mary Lota; 1927-Feb. 15; 11/12; F; Cheyenne; Yes; F; Pneumonia-Measles; Yes

\--- -- Blackhorse, Alice; 1927-May --; 2; F; Cheyenne; Yes; F; Unknown; Yes

1926 126; Blackstone, James; 1927-Mar. 29; 2; M; Cheyenne; Yes; F; Pulm. Tuberculosis; Yes

1926 127; Blackstone, Paul; 1927-Feb. 19; 1; M; Cheyenne; Yes; Measles-Pneumonia; Yes

1926 128; Blackwhetstone, David; 1927-Apr. 22; 83; M; Cheyenne; Yes; F; Senility-Paralized[sic]; Yes

1926 170; Bullsheep, Martin; 1927-Feb. 10; 87; M; Cheyenne; Yes; F; Senility; Yes

1926 197; Chubby, Andrew; 1927-Feb. 28; 18; M; Cheyenne; Yes; F; Pulm. Tuberculosis; Yes

1926 224; Crawling, Mary; 1926-Sept; 16, 61; F; Cheyenne; Yes; Unknown; Yes
Allot.

1926 283; Eyesyellow, Lizzie; 1927-Apr. 9; 81; F; Cheyenne; Yes; F; Senility; Yes

\--- --- Gray, Margaret; 1927-Jan. 28; 4/12; F; Cheyenne; Yes; F; Pneumonia; Yes

\--- --- Hart, Elnora F.; 1927-Mar. 31; 8/12; F; Cheyenne; Yes; F; T.B.-Pneumonia; Yes

## EXCLUSIVE OF STILLBIRTHS

State____**Montana**_____ Reservation____**Tongue River**_____ Agency or jurisdiction, _____**Tongue River**_____Office of Indian Affairs

Key: Last Census Roll: Year & Number; Surname, Given; Date of Death (Year-Month & Day); Age At Death; Sex; Tribe; Ward (Yes/No); Degree of Blood; Cause of Death; At Jurisdiction Where Enrolled (Yes/No); (If no – Where)

1926  393; Harris, Robert; 1927-Feb. 3; 3; M; Cheyenne; Yes; 5/8; Bronchitis-Relapse; Yes
---    --- Hisbadhorse, Baby; 1927-Feb. 21; 23 da; F; Cheyenne; Yes; F; No Data; Yes
1926  425; Hisbadhorse, Mary; 1927-Feb. 4; 26; F; Cheyenne; Yes; F; Childbirth; Yes
1926  456; Issues, Minnie; 1926-Nov. 4; 27; F; Cheyenne; Yes; F; Pulm. Tuberculosis; Yes
---    --- Limberhand, Baby; 1927-Feb. 9; 14 da; F; Cheyenne; Yes; F; Unknown; Yes
1926  598; Littlewhiteman, James; 1927-May 25; 6; M; Cheyenne; Yes; F; Pulm. Tuberculosis; Yes
1926  630; Littlewolf, Laban; 1927-Mar. 8; 76; M; Cheyenne; Yes; F; Intestinal Obstruction; Yes
1926  657; Longjaw, Bessie; 1927-Mar. 3; 1; F; Cheyenne; Yes; F; Bronchitis; Yes
1926  660; Longjaw, Thomas; 1927-Mar 3; 2; M; Cheyenne; Yes; F; Broncho-pneumonia; Yes
Allot.
1926  663; Magpie, Anna; 1927-May 13; 27; F; Cheyenne; Yes; F; Larg. & Pulm. T.B.; Yes
1926  712; Medicineelk, May; 1927-Feb. 6; 8/12; F; Cheyenne; Yes; F; Pneumonia; Yes
1926  725; Medicineflying, Leoris; 1927-Jan. 1; 2; F; Cheyenne; Yes; F; Measles-Exposure; Yes
1926  787; Powderface, Jennie; 1927-Jan. 7; 73; F; Cheyenne; Yes; F; Senility; Yes
1926  800; Redbird, Evelyn; 1927-May 12; 18; F; Cheyenne; Yes; F; T.B.-Childbirth; Yes
1926  805; Redbird, Fred C.; 1927-Feb. 15; 11/12; M; Cheyenne; Yes; 7/8; No data; Yes
1926  895; Rockroads, Bert; 1927-Mar. 3; 4; M; Cheyenne; Yes; F; Pneumonia; Yes
1926  889; Rockroads, James; 1927-Apr. 15; 65; M; Cheyenne; Yes; F; Pulm. Tuberculosis; Yes
1926  941; Rowland, James; 1927-Apr. 11; 16; M; Cheyenne; Yes; 7/8; Pulm. & Bone T.B.; Yes
1926  904; Romannose, Ruth; 1927-Jan. 12; 1; F; Cheyenne; Yes; F; Pneumonia; Yes
---    --- Seminole, Jules; 1927-Jan. 28; 10/12; M; Cheyenne; Yes; 7/8; Measles-Pneumonia; Yes
1926  972; Seminole, Sadie; 1927-Feb. 1; 38; F; Cheyenne; Yes; F; Pulm. Tuberculosis; Yes
1926  994; Shell, Paul; 1926-Nov. 26; 49; M; Cheyenne; Yes; F; Fractured Skull Fell from roof; Yes
1926 1014; Shoulderblade, Alice T.; 1926-Nov. 19; 1; F; Cheyenne; Yes; 7/8; Pneumonia; Yes

## EXCLUSIVE OF STILLBIRTHS

State **Montana** Reservation **Tongue River** Agency or jurisdiction, **Tongue River** Office of Indian Affairs

Key: Last Census Roll: Year & Number; Surname, Given; Date of Death (Year-Month & Day); Age At Death; Sex; Tribe; Ward (Yes/No); Degree of Blood; Cause of Death; At Jurisdiction Where Enrolled (Yes/No); (If no – Where)

1926 1006; Shoulderblade, Lucy; 1927-Jan. 18; 50; F; Cheyenne; Yes; F; Paralysis; Yes
--- --- Shoulderblade, Theodore; 1927-Feb. 27; 4/12; M; Cheyenne; Yes; 7/8; Bronchopneumonia; Yes
1926 1017; Sioux, Bessie; 1926-Nov. 23; 54; F; Cheyenne; Yes; F; T.B.-Pneumonia; Yes
1926 1037; Soldierwolf, Veta; 1927-Jan. 29; 2; F; Cheyenne; Yes; F; Measles-Pneumonia; Yes
--- --- Sponge, Angeline; 1927-Jan. 7; 1; F; Cheyenne; Yes; F; Measles-Pneumonia; Yes
1926 1024; Sponge, Henry; 1927-June 9; 3; M; Cheyenne; Yes; F; Pulm. T.B.; Yes
1926 1023; Sponge, Rose; 1927-Jan. 12; 4; F; Cheyenne; Yes; F; Measles-Pneumonia; Yes
1926 1025; Sponge, Susie; 1927-Jan. 15; 2; F; Cheyenne; Yes; F; Measles-Pneumonia; Yes
1926 1063; Spottedelk, Mary; 1927-Jan. 25; 26; F; Cheyenne; Yes; F; Pulm. T.B.; Yes
1926 1064; Spottedelk, Nelson M.; 1927-Mar. 25; M; Cheyenne; Yes; F; Toxic Gastritis; Yes
1926 1076; Standingelk, Susan; 1927-Mar. 27; 67; F; Cheyenne; Yes; F; Pulm. T.B.; Yes
1926 1147; Tallwhiteman, Frances; 1926-Oct. 26; 32; F; Cheyenne; Yes; F; Pulm. T.B.; Yes
1926 1161; Tanglehornelk, Joseph; 1926-July 28; 89; M; Cheyenne; Yes; F; Senility; Yes
Allot
1926 1149; Threefingers, Patrick; 1927-Jan. 31; 1; M; Cheyenne; Yes; F; Measles-Pneumonia; Yes
1926 1193; Turtlewoman, Mary; 1926-Nov. 22; 65; F; Cheyenne; Yes; F; No data; Yes
--- --- Twentystands, Baby; 1927-Jan. 10; 1 hr.; M; Cheyenne; Yes; F; Premature Twin; Yes
--- --- Twentystands, Baby; 1927-Jan. 26; 16 da; M; Cheyenne; Yes; F; Premature Twin; Yes
1926 1218; Twomoons, Lena; 1927-May 15; 62; F; Cheyenne; Yes; F; Pulm. T.B.; Yes
--- --- Walksnice, Susie; 1926-Oct. 4; 1/12; F; Cheyenne; Yes; F; Unknown; Yes
Allot
1926 1182; Walksnight[sic]; Lilly; 1927-Mar. 27; 12; F; Cheyenne; Yes; F; Pulm. T.B.; Yes
1926 1282; Whitehawk, Andrew; 1927-Apr. 7; 50; M; Cheyenne; Yes; F; Cardiac Failure; Yes

## EXCLUSIVE OF STILLBIRTHS

State __Montana__ Reservation __Tongue River__ Agency or jurisdiction, __Tongue River__ Office of Indian Affairs

Key: Last Census Roll: Year & Number; Surname, Given; Date of Death (Year-Month & Day); Age At Death; Sex; Tribe; Ward (Yes/No); Degree of Blood; Cause of Death; At Jurisdiction Where Enrolled (Yes/No); (If no – Where)

--- --- Whitewolf, Baby; 1927-Feb. 18; 1/12; F; Cheyenne; Yes; F; Pneumonia-Exposure; Yes
--- --- Whitewolf, Grace; 1926-Sept. 30; 2 da; F; Cheyenne; Yes; F; No data; Yes
1926 1303; Whitewolf, Goldstein; 1927-Mar. 28; 1; M; Cheyenne; Yes; F; T.B. Pneumonia; Yes
1926 1328; Wolf, Mary; 1926-July 3; 13; F; Cheyenne; Yes; F; Pulm. T.B. Yes
1926 1333; Wolfblack, John; 1926-Dec. 9; 16; M; Cheyenne; Yes; F; Instant death by Auto accident; Yes
1926 1344; Wolfchief, Jerome; 1927-Jan. 9; 1; M; Cheyenne; Yes; F; Broncho-pneumonia; Yes
1931[sic]1400; Wolfchum, Walker; 1927-May 27; 5/12; M; Cheyenne; Yes; F; Dysentery; Yes
--- --- Wolfname, Peter; 1927-June 12; 4 da; M; Cheyenne; Yes; F; Umbilical Hemorrhage; Yes
1926 1404; Yellowfox, Thaddeus; 1927-Jan. 13; 1; M; Cheyenne; Yes; F; Measles-Pneumonia; Yes
--- --- Youngbear, Annie; 1926-July 19; 6 da; F; Cheyenne; Yes; 7/8; Premature Twin; Yes
--- --- Youngbear, George; 1926-July 19; 6 da; M; Cheyenne; Yes; 7/8; Premature Twin; Yes
1926 1331; Youngbird, Edith; 1926-Nov. 15; 3/11; F; Cheyenne; Yes; F; Gastro Enteritis; Yes

Deaths Occurring Between the Dates of July 1, 1927 and June 30, 1928 of Indians Enrolled at Jurisdiction

1927 27; Arapahoechief, Maude; 1928-Apr. 15; 82; F; Cheyenne; Yes; F; Senility
-- -- Atwood, Baby; 1928-Jan. 26; 2 da.; F; Cheyenne; Yes; F; Premature Twin; Yes
-- -- Atwood, Walter; 1928-Feb. 16; 26 da.; M; Cheyenne; Yes; F; Premature Twin; Yes
1927 40; Bearquiver, Maggie; 1928-Apr. 1; 47; F; Cheyenne; Yes; F; Pulm. T.B.; Yes
1927 88; Bigheadman, Mary; 1928-Mar. 4; 9/12; F; Cheyenne; Yes; F; Pneumonia; Yes
1927 82; Bigheadman, Lucy; 1928-Apr. 17; 3; F; Cheyenne; Yes; F; Pneumonia; Yes
1927 99; Biglefthand, Peter; 1928-Feb. 18; 61; M; Cheyenne; Yes; F; Diabetis[sic]; Yes
1927 124; Blackcrane, Charles; 1928-Mar. 18; 63; M; Cheyenne; Yes; F; Broken Neck Fell from Horse; Yes
1927 137; Blackree, Emma; 1927-Nov. 24; 76; F; Cheyenne; Yes; F; Senility; Yes
1927 144; Blackstone, Blackwhetstone, Nellie; 1928-May 23; 64; R; Cheyenne; F; Heart Trouble; Yes

## EXCLUSIVE OF STILLBIRTHS

State___**Montana**_____ Reservation___**Tongue River**_____ Agency or jurisdiction, _____**Tongue River**_____Office of Indian Affairs

Key: Last Census Roll: Year & Number; Surname, Given; Date of Death (Year-Month & Day); Age At Death; Sex; Tribe; Ward (Yes/No); Degree of Blood; Cause of Death; At Jurisdiction Where Enrolled (Yes/No); (If no – Where)

1927   167; Brady, James; 1927-Dec. 4; 18; M; Cheyenne; Yes; F; Pulm. T.B.; Yes
--     -- Burns, Robert J.; 1928-Feb. 15; 2 hrs.; M; Cheyenne; Yes; 1/16; Premature; Yes
1927   231; Comestogether, Ida; 1928-June 19; 68; F; Cheyenne; Yes; F; Senility-Acute Indigestion; Yes
1927   286; Eaglefeathers, Bernice; 1927-Dec. 26; 10; F; Cheyenne; Yes; F; Pulm. T.B.; Yes
1927   355; Foot, Jennie; 1927-Sept. 27; 37; F; Cheyenne; Yes; 3/4; Laryn. & Hip T.B.; Yes
1928   384; Hardground, Elda; 1927-Jan. 31; 1; F; Cheyenne; Yes; F; Pulm. T.B.; Yes
1927   433; Hisbadhorse, Richard; 1927-Sept. 6; 79; M; Cheyenne; Yes; F; Senility; Yes
1927   442; Hollowbreast, Richard; 1928-Apr. 16; 2; M; Cheyenne; Yes; F; Pneumonia; Yes
1927   452; Horseroads, Sallie; 1928-Feb. 29; 6; F; Cheyenne; Yes; F; Pneumonia; Yes
192[?] 558; Irontooth, Susan; 1928-May --; 94; F; Cheyenne; Yes; F; Senility; Yes
1927   484; Killsnight, Rose; 1928-June 25; 47; F; Cheyenne; Yes; F; Pulm. T.B.; Yes
1927   523; Lamebear, Will; 1928-June 10; 2; M; Cheyenne; Yes; F; Pulm. T.B.; Yes
--     -- Limpy, Eleanora; 1927-Sept. 9; 3/12; F; Cheyenne; Yes; 3/4; Dysentery; Yes
--     -- Littlemouth, Baby; 1928-Mar. 29; 9 da; M; Cheyenne; Yes; F; Unknown; Yes
--     -- Littlewhirlwind, Ellen; 1927-Sept. 17; 2/12; F; Cheyenne; Yes; F; Unknown; Yes
1929[sic] 665; Longjaw, Cora S.; 1927-Sept. --; 26; F; Cheyenne; Yes; F; Pulm. T.B.; Yes
1927   678; Longjaw, James; 1927-Dec. 3; 4; M; Cheyenne; Yes; F; Unknown; Yes
1927   686; Longroach, May; 1928-Mar. 3; 1; F; Cheyenne; Yes; F; Pneumonia; Yes
1927   695; Lostleg, Gertrude; 1927-Aug. 12; 88; F; Cheyenne; Yes; F; Senility; Yes
1927   702; Magpie, Rose; 1927-Dec. 10; 2; F; Cheyenne; Yes; F; Pneumonia; Yes
1927   724; Medicinebull, Donald; 1928-Mar. 23; 5; M; Cheyenne; Yes; F; Pneumonia-T.B.; Yes
1927   780; Parker, Vincent; 1928-Mar. 11; 2; M; Cheyenne; Yes; 1/4; Accidental Drowning; Yes
1927   803; Plentycamps, Clara; 1927-Sept. 16; 82; F; Cheyenne; Yes; F; Senility; Yes
1927   865; Redwoman, Ella; 1928-Apr. 21; 28; F; Cheyenne; Yes; F; Laryngeal & Pulm. T.B.; Yes
1927   905; Rockroads, Mary; 1928-Feb. 8; 2; F; Cheyenne; Yes; F; Pneumonia; Yes
1927   955; Russell, Joseph M.; 1927-Aug. 29; 2; M; Cheyenne; Yes; F Unknown; No; Chey. & Arap. Okla.
1927   958; Russell, Sadie; 1927-Sept. 28; 41; F; Cheyenne; Yes; F; Pulm. T.B.; Yes

## EXCLUSIVE OF STILLBIRTHS

State __Montana__ Reservation __Tongue River__ Agency or jurisdiction, __Tongue River__ Office of Indian Affairs

Key: Last Census Roll: Year & Number; Surname, Given; Date of Death (Year-Month & Day); Age At Death; Sex; Tribe; Ward (Yes/No); Degree of Blood; Cause of Death; At Jurisdiction Where Enrolled (Yes/No); (If no – Where)

1927 971; Sandcrane, Anne; 1927-Sept. 12; 32; F; Cheyenne; Yes; F; Pulm. T.B.; Yes
1927 973; Sandcrane, Harry; 1928-Jan. 30; 6/12; M; Cheyenne; Yes; F; Unknown; Yes
-- -- Seminole, Baby; 1927-Dec. 1; 7 da; F; Cheyenne; Yes; F; No data; Yes
-- -- Sharpnose, Baby; 1927-Aug. 25; 3/12; M; Cheyenne; Yes; F; Dysentery; Yes
1927 998; Sharpnose, Edward C.; 1927-Aug. 23; 31; M; Cheyenne; Yes; F; Pulm. T.B.; Yes
1927 997; Sharpnose, Bessie; 1927-Sept. 28; 81; F; Cheyenne; Yes; F; Senility; Yes
1927 1010; Shell, Elsie; 1928-Feb. 21; 2; F; Cheyenne; Yes; F; Pneumonia; Yes
1927 1086; Spottedwolf, Earl; 1928-Jan. --; 1; M; Cheyenne; Yes; F; Unknown; Yes
1927 --- Standingelk, Mary; 1928-Jan. 26; 3/12; R; Cheyenne; Yes; F; Unknown; Yes
1927 1157; Tallwhiteman, John A.; 1927-Sept. 19; 13; M; Cheyenne; Yes; F; Convulsions; Yes
1927 1167; Tallwhiteman, Joseph; 1928-Feb. 16; 81; M; Cheyenne; Yes; F; Senility; Yes
1927 1184; Teeth, Sallie; 1928-Apr. 17; 55; F; Cheyenne; Yes; F; T.B. Peritonitis; Yes
1927 1276; Whitecrane, Elmer; 1928-Feb. 23; 1; M; Cheyenne; Yes; F; Pneumonia; Yes
1927 1296; Whiteshirt, Dottie; 1928-Mar. 29; 3; F; Cheyenne; Yes; F; Convulsions; Yes
1927 1313; Wildhog, Willie; 1928-May 12; 17; M; Cheyenne; Yes; F; Pulm. T.B.; Yes
1927 1349; Wolfname, Anna; 1927-Aug. 21; 35; F; Cheyenne; Yes; F; Miliary T.B.; Yes
1927 1357; Wolfroads, Jennie; 1928-Apr. 11; 51; F; Cheyenne; Yes; F; T.B. Bone; Yes
1927 1389; Woodpecker, Ralph; 1927-Sept. 28; 20; M; Cheyenne; Yes; F; Pulm. T.B.; Yes
1927 1394; Woundedeye, Charles; 1928-June 27; 6; M; Cheyenne; Yes; F; T.B. Meningitis; Yes
1927 1402; Woundedeye, Fordson; 1928-Apr. 17; 9; M; Cheyenne; Yes; F; Pulm. T.B.; Yes
-- -- Yellowfox, Arthur J.; 1927-Nov. 26; 26 da; M; Cheyenne; Yes; F; Accidental Smothering; Yes
1927 1416; Yellowfox, William; 1927-Nov. 11; 5; M; Cheyenne; Yes; F; Pulm. T.B.; Yes
1927 1421; Yellownose, Lizzie; 1927-July 10; 35; F; Cheyenne; Yes; F; Childbirth; Yes

## EXCLUSIVE OF STILLBIRTHS

State **Montana** Reservation **Tongue River** Agency or jurisdiction, **Tongue River** Office of Indian Affairs

Key: Last Census Roll: Year & Number; Surname, Given; Date of Death (Year-Month & Day); Age At Death; Sex; Tribe; Ward (Yes/No); Degree of Blood; Cause of Death; At Jurisdiction Where Enrolled (Yes/No); (If no – Where)

Deaths Occurring Between the Dates of July 1, 1928 and June 30, 1929 of Indians Enrolled at Jurisdiction

| | |
|---|---|
| 1928 | 86; Bigfoot, James 1928-Dec. 3; 86; M; Cheyenne; Yes; F; Pneumonia Bronchial; Yes |
| 1928 | 87; Bighead, Kate; 1929-Feb. 23; 81; F; Cheyenne; Yes; F; Senility; Yes |
| 1929 | 132; Blackbird, Sallie; 1929-Apr. 9; 65; F; Cheyenne; Yes; F; Apoplexy; Yes |
| 1929 | ---  Blackhorse, Charles; 1928-Aug. 4; 5/12; M; Cheyenne; Yes; F; Cleft Palate-Starved; Yes |
| 1928 | 212; Clubfoot, Verle; 1928-Oft. 27; 5; M; Cheyenne; Yes; F; T.B. Meningitis; Yes |
| 1928 | 259; Deafy, Mary; 1928-Dec. 30; 54; F; Cheyenne; Yes; F; Lobar Pneumonia; Yes |
| -- | --  Fightingbear, Baby; 1929-June 15; 5 da; M; Cheyenne; Yes; F; Unknown; Yes |
| 1931[sic] | 310; Fightingbear, Emma; 1928-Nov. --; 2; F; Cheyenne; Yes; F; Unknown; Yes |
| 1928 | 346; Flying, Margaret; 1928-Sept. 21; 62; F; Cheyenne; Yes; F; Unknown; Yes |
| 1928 | 385; Hardground, Thomas; 1928-Dec. 3; 25; M; Cheyenne; Yes; F; Pulm. T.B.; Yes |
| 1928 | 383; Hardground, Ruth; 1929-June 12; 21; F; Cheyenne; Yes; F; Pulm. T.B.; Yes |
| 1928 | 436; Hollowwood, Minnie; 1929-May 14; 72; F; Cheyenne; Yes; F; Exphalmic[sic] Goiter; Yes |
| 1928 | 456; Ironshirt, Fred; 1929-Mar. 18; 97; M; Cheyenne; Yes; F; Senility; Yes |
| 1928 | 485; Killsnight, Alice Farr; 1929-June 6; 19; F; Cheyenne; Yes; 1/8; Pulm. T.B.; Yes |
| 1928 | 470; Killsnight, Robert; 1929-Jan. 12; 16; M; Cheyenne; Yes; F; Pulm. T.B; Yes |
| 1928 | 497; Kingfisher, Herman; 1928-Dec. 2; 61; M; Cheyenne; Yes; F; T.B. Peritonitis; Yes |
| -- | --  Littleyes[sic], Baby; 1928-Oct. 19; 8 min.; M; Cheyenne; Yes; F; Unknown; Yes |
| -- | --  Littlesun, Baby; 1929-Mar. 17; 5 da.; M; Cheyenne; Yes; F; Unknown; Yes |
| -- | --  Littleyellowman, Ernest J.; 1928-July 11; 4/12; M; Cheyenne; Yes; F; Natural Causes; No; Chey. & Arap. Okla. |
| 1928 | 711; Medicinebear, Maggie; 1928-July 8; 81; F; Cheyenne; Yes; F; Senility; Yes |
| 1928 | 797; Porcupine, Albert; 1929-May 19; 80; M; Cheyenne; Yes; F; Senility; Yes |
| 1928 | 892; Risingsun, Bessie; 1928-Aug. 19; 36; F; Cheyenne; Yes; F; Childbirth - T.B.; Yes |
| 1928 | 971; Russell, Ford; 1928-Aug. 9; 3; M; Cheyenne; Yes; F; T.B. Meningitis; Yes |

**EXCLUSIVE OF STILLBIRTHS**

State_____**Montana**_____ Reservation____**Tongue River**_____ Agency or jurisdiction, _____**Tongue River**_____Office of Indian Affairs

Key: Last Census Roll: Year & Number; Surname, Given; Date of Death (Year-Month & Day); Age At Death; Sex; Tribe; Ward (Yes/No); Degree of Blood; Cause of Death; At Jurisdiction Where Enrolled (Yes/No); (If no – Where)

1928 947; Rowland, George; 1929-Jan. 29; 31; M; Cheyenne; Yes; 3/4; Accidental Traumatism; No; Southard Okla.
--- --- Seminole, Helen; 1929-Jan. 19; 6 da; F; Cheyenne; Yes; F; Unknown; Yes
--- --- Small, Vera Sue; 1929-Feb. 24; 2/12; F; Cheyenne; Yes; 1/4; Pneumonia; Yes
1928 1104; Standingelk, George; 1928-AUG. 7; 18; M; Cheyenne; Yes; F; Pulm. T.B; Yes
1928 1135; Sunbear, John; 1929-Feb. 19; 85; M; Cheyenne; Yes; F; Senility Broncho-pneumonia; Yes
1928 1175; Tallwhiteman, Pat; 1928-Sept. 23; 40; M; Cheyenne; Yes; F; Pulm. T.B; Yes
1928 1201; Threefingers, Ruth Maud; 1927-Jan. 10- 21; F; Cheyenne; Yes; F; Pulm. T.B.; Yes
1928 1208; Twin, Edna; 1929-May 1; 4; F; Cheyenne; Yes; F; T.B. Intestinal; Yes
1928 1212; Twobirds, Walter; 1929-June 15; 20; M; Cheyenne; Yes; F; Pulm. T.B; Yes
1928 1286; Whitecrane, Charles; 1928-Oct. 20; 52; M; Cheyenne; Yes; F; Epileptic Fit; Yes
1928 1307; Whitewolf, Anna L.; 1928-Dec. 29; 24; F; Cheyenne; Yes; F; Bronch-pneumonia[sic]; Yes
1928 1313; Whitewolf, Maude; 1929-Mar. 25; 37; F; Cheyenne; Yes; F; Pulm. T.B.; Yes
1928 1356; Wolfname, Paul; 1928-July 28; 42; M; Cheyenne; Yes; F; Pleurisy & Gallstones; Yes
1928 1416; Yelloweyes, Ruth; 1928-Sept. 18; 10/12; F; Cheyenne; Yes; F; Cough-so reported; Yes
1928 --- Yellowfox, Baby; 1929-Apr. 16; 7/12; M; Cheyenne; Yes; F; Unknown; Yes
1928 1423; Yellownose, Anne; 1929-Mar. 10; 62; F; Cheyenne; Yes; F; Gangrene of Foot; No; Cheyenne & Arap. Okla.
1928 1431; Yellowrobe, Adolph; 1928-Oct. 24; 28; M; Cheyenne; Yes; F; Pulm. T.B.; Yes
--- --- Yellowrobe, Alfred; 1929-May 14; 2 da; M; Cheyenne; Yes; F; Umbilical Hemorrhage; Yes
--- --- Youngbear, Baby; 1928-Sept. 26; 1 da; F; Cheyenne; Yes; 7/8; Unknown; Yes

Deaths Occurring Between the Dates of July 1, 1929 and June 30, 1930 of Indians Enrolled at Jurisdiction

1929 9; Americanhorse, Minnie; 1929-Nov. 5; 45; F; Cheyenne; Yes; F; Broncho-pneumonia; Yes
1929 27; Ant, Paul; 1930-Feb. 13; 2; M; Cheyenne; Yes; F; T.B. Meningitis; Yes

## EXCLUSIVE OF STILLBIRTHS

State **Montana** Reservation **Tongue River** Agency
or jurisdiction, **Tongue River** Office of Indian Affairs

Key: Last Census Roll: Year & Number; Surname, Given; Date of Death (Year-Month & Day); Age At Death; Sex; Tribe; Ward (Yes/No); Degree of Blood; Cause of Death; At Jurisdiction Where Enrolled (Yes/No); (If no – Where)

1929 -- Atwood, Paul; 1929-Oct. 12; 1/12; M; Cheyenne; Yes; F; Malnutrition; Yes

1929 114; Bignose, Rachel; 1929-Aug. 10; 74; F; Cheyenne; Yes; F; Cancer-Liver Ascitis[sic]; Yes

1929 135; Blackeagle, Carl; 1929-Nov. 29; 18; M; Cheyenne; Yes; F; Pulm. T.B.; Yes

--- --- Blackstone, Baby; 1929-Nov. 18; 3 min.; M; Cheyenne; Yes; F; Probably Exposure; Yes

1929 186; Braidedlocks, Gertie; 1930-Mar. 14; 87; F; Cheyenne; Yes; F; Senility; Yes

1929 196; Burns, Gertrude; 1929-Sept. 26; 83; F; Cheyenne; Yes; F; Senility; Yes

1929 214; Clubfoot, Floyd; 1930-Apr. 2; 42; M; Cheyenne; Yes; F; Pulm. T.B.; Yes

1929 257; Curley, Logan; 1930-Mar. 3; 3; M; Cheyenne; Yes; F; Diarrhea-Acute Indisgestion[sic]; Yes

1929 353; Ghostbull, Sarah; 1930-Jan. 5; 62; F; Cheyenne; Yes; F; Acute dilatation of the heart; Yes

1929 368; Hankeringwolf, Peter; 1929-Nov. 24; 95; M; Cheyenne; Yes; F; Senility; Yes

1929 1099; Hardground, Jane; 1930-May 5; 15; F; Cheyenne; Yes; F; Pulm. T.B.; Yes

1929 283; Hardground, Mary; 1930-Apr. 12; 34; F; Cheyenne; Yes; F; Pulm. T.B; Yes

-- -- Hardground, Mary; 1929-Sept. 29; 6/12; F; Cheyenne; Yes; F; Diphtheria; Yes

1929 379; Hardground, Roland; 1929-Oct. 18; 20; M; Cheyenne; Yes; F; Pulm. T.B.; Yes

-- -- Killsnight, Eugene; 1929-Nov. 4; 1/12; M; Cheyenne; Yes; F; Broncho-pneumonia; Yes

-- -- Limberhand, Harry; 1930-Feb. 4; 1/12; M; Cheyenne; Yes; F; Malnutrition; Yes

1929 615; Littlewhiteman, Charles; 1929-July 1; 3; M; Cheyenne; Yes; F; Unknown; Yes

-- -- Littlewhiteman, Elmer; 1930-Apr. 15; 5/12; M; Cheyenne; Yes; F; Broncho-pneumonia; Yes

-- -- Littleyellowman, Ed Jr.; 1929-Nov. 18; 2 da.; M; Cheyenne; Yes; F; Hemophilia; No; Cheyenne & ARAP. Okla.

1929 692; Looksbehind, Thomas; 1929-July 17; 22; M; Cheyenne; Yes; F; Pulm. T.B.; Yes

-- -- Looksbehind, Inez; 1930-Apr. 12; 8/12; F; Cheyenne; Yes; F; Broncho-pneumonia; Yes

1929 700; Lostleg, Nelson; 1930-June 3; 36; M; Cheyenne; Yes; F; Pulm. T.B.; Yes

1929 739; Medicineelk, Claude; 1929-Oct. 29; 1; M; Cheyenne; Yes; F; Malnutrition; Yes

## EXCLUSIVE OF STILLBIRTHS

State __Montana__ Reservation __Tongue River__ Agency or jurisdiction, __Tongue River__ Office of Indian Affairs

Key: Last Census Roll: Year & Number; Surname, Given; Date of Death (Year-Month & Day); Age At Death; Sex; Tribe; Ward (Yes/No); Degree of Blood; Cause of Death; At Jurisdiction Where Enrolled (Yes/No); (If no – Where)

1929 745; Medicineflying, Clifford; 1929-Oct. 11; 5/12; M; Cheyenne; Yes; F; Unknown; Yes
1929 802; Playingbear, John; 1929-Nov. 7; 14; M; Cheyenne; Yes; F; Pulm. T.B.; Yes
1929 847; Redfox, Cora; 1930-Apr. 15; 62; F; Cheyenne; Yes; F; Broncho-pneumonia; Yes
1929 944; Rowland, Sally; 1929-Dec. 16; 75; F; Cheyenne; Yes; F; Senility; Yes
1929 1022; Shavedhead, Lucille; 1930-Jan. 23; 2; F; Cheyenne; Yes; Pulm. T.B; Yes
1929 1042; Shoulderblade, Everett J.; 1930-June 17; 7; M; Cheyenne; Yes; 7/8; Hemiplegia Infantile; Yes
1929 -- Soldierwolf, Baby; 1929-Oct. 29; 11/12; F; Cheyenne; Yes; F; Broncho-pneumonia; Yes
1929 1090; Spang, Alice Y.; 1930-Feb. 1; 21; F; Cheyenne; Yes; F; Pulm. T.B.; Yes
1929 1103; Spottedhawk, Hugh; 1929-Oct. 13; 62; M; Cheyenne; Yes; F; Injuries rec'd from horse; Yes
1929 1109; Spottedwolf, Gertrude R.; 1929-Nov. 25; 2; F; Cheyenne; Yes; F; Unknown; Yes
1929 1198; Tangledyellowhair, Bert; 1930-Jan. 19; 3; M; Cheyenne; Yes; F; Broncho-pneumonia; Yes
1929 1267; Walksnice, Agnes; 1929-July 5; 1; F; Cheyenne; Yes; F; Broncho-pneumonia; Yes
1929 1271; Wanderingmedicine, William; 1930-Apr. 25; 61; M; Cheyenne; Yes; F; Lobar-pneumonia; Yes
1929 1291; White, Ben; 1929-July 22; 2; M; Cheyenne; Yes; 7/8; Summer Complaint; Yes
1929 1297; Whitebuffalo, Ella; 1930-May 11; 62; F; Cheyenne; Yes; F; Pulm. T.B.; Yes
1929 1306; Whitedirt, Arthur; 1930-Feb. 15; 54; M; Cheyenne; Yes; F; Pulm. T.B; Yes
1929 1319; Whitehorse, George; 1929-Aug. 18; 79; M; Cheyenne; Yes; F; Senility; Yes
1929 1324; Whitewolf, Isadore C; 1930-Apr. 11; 39; M; Cheyenne; Yes; F; Peritonitis T.B.; Yes
1929 1352; Wolf, William; 1939-Sept. 1; 57; M; Cheyenne; Yes; F; Pulm. T.B.; Yes
1929 1361; Wolfchief, Anna; 1930-June 22; 69; F; Cheyenne; Yes; F; Senility; Yes
1929 1362; Wolfchief, Josie; 1930-Jan. 27; 86; F; Cheyenne; Yes; F; Senility; Yes
1929 1382; Wolfroads, Rose; 1930-Mar. 20; 16; F; Cheyenne; Yes; F; T.B. Pulm.-T.B. of Skin; Yes
1930 1399; Wolftooth, Wayne; 1930-June 1; 1; M; Cheyenne; Yes; F; Unknown; Yes
1929 1399; Woodenlegs, Jessie; 1930-Feb. 4; 24; F; Cheyenne; Yes; F; Pulm. T.B.; Yes

## EXCLUSIVE OF STILLBIRTHS

State __Montana__ Reservation __Tongue River__ Agency or jurisdiction, __Tongue River__ Office of Indian Affairs

Key: Last Census Roll: Year & Number; Surname, Given; Date of Death (Year-Month & Day); Age At Death; Sex; Tribe; Ward (Yes/No); Degree of Blood; Cause of Death; At Jurisdiction Where Enrolled (Yes/No); (If no – Where)

Deaths Occurring Between the Dates of April 1, 1930 and March 31, 1931 of Indians Enrolled at Jurisdiction

1930    64; Bigback, Stephen; 1930-Aug. 3; 38; M; Cheyenne; Yes; F; Pulm. T.B.; Yes

--    -- Bigheadman, Anthony; 1931-Mar. 18; 2/12; M; Cheyenne; Yes; F; Unknown; Yes

1930    243; Crazymule, John; 1930-AUG. 12; 61; M; Cheyenne; Yes; F; Acute Endororditis[sic]; Yes

1930    211; Clubfoot, Floyd; 1930-Apr. 2; 43; M; Cheyenne; Yes; F; Pulm. T.B.; Yes

1930    1106; Hardground, Jane; 1930-May 5; 15; F; Cheyenne; Yes; F; Pulm. T.B.; Yes

1930    380; Hardground, Mary; 1930-Apr. 12; 35; F; Cheyenne; Yes; F; Pulm. T.B; Yes

1930    476; Killsnight, Dorothy; 1931-Feb. 16; 4; F; Cheyenne; Yes; F; Broncho-pneumonia; Yes

1930    357; Limpy, Fred Jr.; 1930-Oct. 15; 1; M; Cheyenne; Yes; 3/4; Enteritis; Yes

1930    601; Littlesun, Frank; 1930-Dec. 11; 46; M; Cheyenne; Yes; F; Pulm. T.B.; Yes

--    -- Littlewhiteman, Elmer; 1930-Apr. 15; 1; M; Cheyenne; Yes; 7/8; Broncho-pneumonia; Yes

--    -- Littlewhiteman, Mabel; 1930-Aug. 16; 10/12; F; Cheyenne; Yes; 7/8; Starvation; Yes

1930    650; Littlewolf, Laura; 1931-Mar. 27; 78; F; Cheyenne; Yes; F; Senility; Yes

1931    665; Littleyellowman, Rose; 1930-Aug. 7; 6; F; Cheyenne; Yes; F; Typhoid; No; Cheyenne & Arap. Okla.

1930    1281; Looksbehind, Inez; 1930-Apr. 11; 1; F; Cheyenne; Yes; F; Broncho-pneumonia; Yes

1930    709; Lostleg, Nelson; 1930-June 3; 39; M; Cheyenne; Yes; F; Pulm. T.B.; Yes

1930    743; Medicineelk, Harold; 1930-Oct. 31; 65; M; Cheyenne; Yes; F; Lobar-pneumonia; Yes

1930    855; Redfox, Cora; 1930-Apr. 15; 63; F; Cheyenne; Yes; F; Broncho-pneumonia; Yes

1930    890; Redwoman, Manuel; 1930-Dec. 9; 49; M; Cheyenne; Yes; F; Pulm. T.B.; Yes

1930    969; Rowland, Helen; 1931-Jan. 15; 62; F; Cheyenne; Yes; F; Lobar Pneumonia; Yes

1930    980; Russell, May; 1930-July 7; 6; F; Cheyenne; Yes; 7/8; T.B. Meningeal; No; Cheyenne & Arap. Okla.

1930    981; Russell, Inez I.; 1931-Mar. 5; 4; F; Cheyenne; Yes; 7/8; T.B. Meningitis with Influenza; No; Cheyenne & Arap. Okla.

1930    982; Russell, John Jr.; 1931-Mar. 2; 2; M; Cheyenne; Yes; 7/8; Pneumonia follow Influenza

1930    1039; Shoulderblade, Pius; 1931-Jan. 3; 41; M; Cheyenne; Yes; F; Pulm. T.B.; Yes

## EXCLUSIVE OF STILLBIRTHS

State___Montana___Reservation___Tongue River___Agency or jurisdiction,___Tongue River___Office of Indian Affairs

Key: Last Census Roll: Year & Number; Surname, Given; Date of Death (Year-Month & Day); Age At Death; Sex; Tribe; Ward (Yes/No); Degree of Blood; Cause of Death; At Jurisdiction Where Enrolled (Yes/No); (If no – Where)

1930 1044; Shoulderblade, Everett J.; 1930-June 17; 7; M; Cheyenne; Yes; 7/8; Hemeplegia[sic] Infantile; Yes
1930 1117; Spottedwolf, Della; 1930-Oct. 6; 1; F; Cheyenne; Yes; F; Enteritis; Yes
1930 1169; Swallow, Percy R.; 1930-Aug. 22; 11; M; Cheyenne; Yes; F; Pulm. T.B.; Yes
1930 1274; Wanderingmedicine, William; 1930-Apr. 25; 62; M; Cheyenne; Yes; F; Lobar-Pneumonia; Yes
1930 1302; Whitebuffalo, Ella; 1930-May 11, 63; F; Cheyenne; Yes; F; Pulm. T.B.; Yes
1930 1334; Whitewolf, Chas. Isadore; 1930-Apr. 11; 40; M; Cheyenne; Yes; F; Peritonitis T.B.; Yes
1930 1377; Wolfchief, Anna; 1930-June 22; 69; F; Cheyenne; F; Senility; Yes
1930 1378; Wolfchief, Richard; 1931-Feb. 8; 38; M; Cheyenne; Yes; F; Nephritis Int. Chron.; Yes
1930 1389; Wolfname, William; 1931-Jan. 15; 77; M; Cheyenne; Yes; F; Senility; Yes
1930 1399; Wolftooth, Wayne; 1930-June 1; 2; M; Cheyenne; Yes; F Unknown; Yes
1930 586; Woodepecker[sic], Donald C.; 1931-Feb. 12; 21; M; Cheyenne; Yes; F; Pulm. T.B; Yes
---- --- Yellowrobe, Hilda; 1930-Nov. 10; 7/12; F; Cheyenne; Yes; F; Lobar-Pneumonia; Yes

### Deaths Occurring Between the Dates of April 1, 1931 and March 31, 1932 of Indians Enrolled at Jurisdiction

1931 23; Ant, Bertha; 1931-Sept. 24; 6; F; Cheyenne; Yes; F; T.B. Pulm.; Yes
-- "D.B.E." Blackhorse, Ruben Jr.; 1931-Dec. 23; 5 da.; M; Cheyenne; Yes; F; Unknown; Yes
1931 148; Blackstone, Anna; 1932-Jan. 11; 20; F; Cheyenne; Yes; F; T.B. Pulm.; Yes
1931 145; Blackstone, Charles; 1931-Aug. 18; 70; M; Cheyenne; Yes; F; Pneumonia Broncho; Yes
1931 164; Bobtailhorse, Gertrude; 1931-Aug. 17; 79; F; Cheyenne; Yes; Senility; Yes
1931 190; Buffalohump, Samuel; 1932-Feb. 2; 86; M; Cheyenne; Yes; F; Senility; Yes
1931 251; Crook, Albert; 1932-Mar. 28; 30; M; Cheyenne; Yes; F; T.B. Pulm; Yes
1931 299; Elkshoulder, Calvin; 1931-Dec. 21; 3; M; Cheyenne; Yes; F; Pneumonia Broncho; Yes
1931 305; Eyesyellow, Daisy; 1931-June 22; 74; F; Cheyenne; Yes; F; Senility; Yes
1931 307; Fightingbear, Alice; 1931-Dec. 31; 38; F; Cheyenne; Yes; F; T.B. Pulm; Yes
-- DBE Fightingbear, Francis; 1932-Mar. 16; 4/12; M; Cheyenne; Yes; F; Convulsions; Yes

## EXCLUSIVE OF STILLBIRTHS

State_____ **Montana**_____ Reservation____ **Tongue River**_____ Agency
or jurisdiction, _____ **Tongue River**_____ Office of Indian Affairs

Key: Last Census Roll: Year & Number; Surname, Given; Date of Death (Year-Month & Day); Age At Death; Sex; Tribe; Ward (Yes/No); Degree of Blood; Cause of Death; At Jurisdiction Where Enrolled (Yes/No); (If no – Where)

1931   906; Fightingbear, Julia; 1932-Mar. 27; 20; F; Cheyenne; Yes; F; T.B. Pulm; Yes
1931   344; Foot, Ruth Y.; 1931-July 28; 32; F; Cheyenne; Yes; F; Broncho-Pneumonia; Yes
1931   394; Harris, Anna B.; 1921-Dec. 10; 18; F; Cheyenne; Yes; F; T.B. Pulm.; Yes
1931   385; Harris, Sallie; 1932-Feb. 23; 81; F; Cheyenne; Yes; 1/2; Senility; Yes
1931   144; Ironshirt, Nora; 1931-Sept. 27; 81; F; Cheyenne; Yes; F; Accidental Drowning; Yes
--   DBE   Knows-His-Gun, Genevieve; 1931-May 14; 10/12; F; Cheyenne; Yes; F; Pneumonia Bronchial; Yes
--   DBE   Lamebear, Ethel; 1931-Sept. 20; 12 hrs.; F; Cheyenne; Yes; F; Unknown; Yes
1931   531; Lamewoman, Ruth; 1932-Mar. 7; 2; F; Cheyenne; Yes; 7/8; Poloemyelitis[sic]; Yes
1931   DBE   Limberhand, George; 1931-Oct. 23; 7/12; M; Cheyenne; Yes; F; Starvation Marasmus; Yes
1931   561; Limpy, Amelia; 1931-Apr. 20; 45; F; Cheyenne; Yes; F; Nephritis; Yes
--   DBE   Littlebear, [Blank]; 1931-Nov. 27; 3 min; F; Cheyenne; Yes; F; Exposure; Yes
--   DBE   Littlemouth, Fred; 1931-Oct. 12; 8/12; M; Cheyenne; Yes; F; Starvation Marasmus; Yes
1931   986; Littleoldman, Thomas; 1931-Dec. 17; 18; M; Cheyenne; Yes; F; T.B. Pulm.; Yes
1931   607; Littlesun, Cora; 1931-Dec. 21; 67; F; Cheyenne; Yes; F; Pneumonia-Lobar; Yes
1931   606; Littlesun, Samuel; 1931-May 17; 73; M; Cheyenne; Yes; F; Senility; Yes
1931   614; Littlewhiteman, Aaron; 1931-Dec. 13; 69; M; Cheyenne; Yes; 1/2; Heart Trouble; Yes
1931   1002; Littlewhiteman, Charles; 1032-Feb. 14; 17; M; Cheyenne; Yes; 7/8; T.B. Pulm.; Yes
1931   617; Littlewhiteman, David; 1931-Oct. 15; 62; M; Cheyenne; Yes; 1/2; Pneumonia Lobar; Yes
1931   669; Littleyellowman, Lena; 1931-Nov. 15; 55; F; Cheyenne; Yes; F; T.B. Peritonitis; Yes
1931   681; Longjaw, Clara; 1931-Dec. 6; 69; F; Cheyenne; Yes; F; T.B. Bone; Yes
1931   703; Looksatbareground, Julia; 1932-Feb. 13; 79; F; Cheyenne; Yes; F; Senility; Yes
1931   735; Medicinebull, James; 1931-June 28; 20; M; Cheyenne; Yes; F; T.B. Pulm.; Yes
1931   747; Medicineelk, Thomas; 1931-Sept. 13; 25; M; Cheyenne; Yes; f; Broken Neck in Car Accident; Yes
1931   834; Redbird, Florence; 1932-Jan. 19; 54; F; Cheyenne; Yes; 3/4; Suicide by Firearms; Yes
1931   858; Redfox, Jennie; 1931-Aug. 9; 58 F; Cheyenne; Yes; F; Pulm. T.B.; Yes

## EXCLUSIVE OF STILLBIRTHS

State **Montana** Reservation **Tongue River** Agency or jurisdiction, **Tongue River** Office of Indian Affairs

Key: Last Census Roll: Year & Number; Surname, Given; Date of Death (Year-Month & Day); Age At Death; Sex; Tribe; Ward (Yes/No); Degree of Blood; Cause of Death; At Jurisdiction Where Enrolled (Yes/No); (If no – Where)

1931 1048; Sioux, Jane W.; 1931-Aug. 18; 65; F; Cheyenne; Yes; F; T.B. Peritonitis; Yes

-- DBE Seminole (Woodenleg), [Blank]; 1931-Aug. 17; 1 hr.; [?]; Cheyenne; Yes; 7/8; Unknown; Yes

1931 1143; Standingelk, Aiden; 1931-Aug. 25; 2; M; Cheyenne; Yes; F; T.B. Pulm.; Yes

1931 1147; Standingelk, Ella J.; 1931-Nov. 12; 13; F; Cheyenne; Yes; F; T.B. Pulm.; Yes

1931 1174; Swallow, Edward; 1931-Apr. 13; 29; M; Cheyenne; Yes; F; T.B. Pulm; Yes

1931 1185; Tallbull, Charles; 1931-May 15; 43; M; Cheyenne; Yes; F; Pneumonia-Lobar; Yes

1931 1227; Threefingers, John; 1931-Oct. 10; 69; M; Cheyenne; Yes; F; T.B. Pulm.; Yes

1931 1228; Threefingers, Pansy; 1931-Sept. 5; 55; F; Cheyenne; Yes; F; Peritonitis; Yes

1931 1251; Twofeathers, Ethel; 1931-Aug. 30; 22; F; Cheyenne; Yes; F; T.B. Pulm.; Yes

1931 1272; Walkslast, Anne; 1931-Sept. 27; 69; F; Cheyenne; Yes; F; Senility; Yes

1931 1293; Weaselbear, Hugh; 1932-Mar. 4; 43; M; Cheyenne; Yes; F; T.B. Pulm.; Yes

---- DBE Whistlingelk, Maynora; 1931-Dec. 31; 2/12; F; Cheyenne; Yes; F; Acute Cold; Yes

1931 1341; Whitehawk, James; 1931-Apr. 1; 2; M; Cheyenne; Yes; F; Pneumonia Broncho; Yes

1931 1345; Whitehawk, Theresa; 1931-Dec. 13; 4; F; Cheyenne; Yes; F; Unknown; Yes

1931 1347; Whitemoon, George; 1931-May 2; 76; M; Cheyenne; Yes; F; Senility; Yes

1931 1393; Wolfchief, Harshey; 1931-Oct. 31; 79; M; Cheyenne; Yes; M; Dilatation Cardic[sic] Acute; Yes

1931 1402; Wolfchum, Espy; 1931-Aug. 31; 1; M; Cheyenne; Yes; M; Unknown; Yes

1931 1455; Woundedeye, Iva Ruth; 1931-July 6; 9/12; F; Cheyenne; F; Summer Complaint; Yes

1931 1461; Yelloweyes, Gertrude; 1932-Mar. 3; 25; F; Cheyenne; F; T.B. Pulm.; Yes

1931 1474; Yellownose, Mary; 1931-July 15; 4; F; Cheyenne; Yes; F; Intestinal Influenza; Yes

-- DBE Zettle, Frank; 1931-Nov. 13; 6 da.; M; Cheyenne; Yes; 3/16; Infection Umbilicus; Yes

# Books and Resources

Brill, Charles J., Norman, Paperback Edition 2002, *Custer, Black Kettle, and The Fight on The Washita,* University of Oklahoma Press, published by author 1938.

Cook, John R., *The Border and The Buffalo,* New York; The Citadel Press, published by author 1967.

Fast, Howard, Garden City, New York, 1944, *The Last Frontier,* Sun Dial Press, published by author 1941.

Greene, Jerome A., *January Moon, The Northern Cheyenne Breakout from Fort Robinson, 1878-1879,* Norman, 2020, University of Oklahoma Press.

Grinnell, George Bird, New York, October 1915, *The Fighting Cheyennes,* Charles Scribner's Sons.

Grinnell, George Bird, Bison Books, 1972, Lincoln and London, *The Cheyenne Indians, Their History and Ways of Life; History and Society Volume I,* University of Nebraska Press, published by author Yale University Press 1923.

Grinnell, George Bird, Bison Books, 1972, Lincoln and London, *The Cheyenne Indians, Their History and Ways of Life; War, Ceremonies, and Religion, Volume II,* University of Nebraska Press, published by author Yale University Press 1923.

Hoig, Stan, Norman, Paperback Published 1994, *The Sand Creek Massacre,* University of Oklahoma Press, published by author 1961.

Leiker, James N., Powers Ramon, Norman, 2011, *The Northern Cheyenne Exodus in History and Memory,* University of Oklahoma Press.

Monnett, John H., *Tell Them We Are Going Home,* Norman, 2001, University of Oklahoma Press.

Monnett, John H., Albuquerque, 2008, *Where A Hundred Soldiers Were Killed,* University of New Mexico Press.

Sandoz, Mari, New York, 1975, *Cheyenne Autumn,* Hastings House Publishers, published by author 1953.

Starita, Joe, New York, 1995, *The Dull Knifes of Pine Ridge,* Berkley Books, G.P. Putnam's Sons Edition April 1995, Berkley Trade Paperback Edition March 1996.

Susan Straight Editor, National Geographic, Washington, D.C., 2010, *Indian Nations of North America,* National Geographic Society.


Paper
Dusenberry, Verne, 1956, B.S. Montana State College, 1927, The Varying Culture of The Northern Cheyenne, Master of Arts, Montana State University.

# Index

AIKIN, Mattie L .......................... 232
AKIN
   Mattie L .................................. 299
   Vernon H ................................. 299
   Vernon Hart ............................ 368
AMERICANHORSE
   (Peter) George ......................... 57
   Albert ........................ 5,57,117,182
   Albert M ........................... 233,307
   Austin ......... 5,57,117,169,219,281
   Bessie ......... 5,57,117,169,219,306
   David .......... 13,66,125,177,227,292
   Ella ..................... 219,277,281,360
   Ernest ......... 5,57,117,169,219,281
   Esther .................. 219,277,281,365
   Flora ............ 5,57,117,207,260,338
   George ......... 5,57,117,169,219,281
   George (Peter) ............................ 5
   Grace ............................... 5,57,117
   Grace J ...................... 169,219,281
   James ........... 5,57,117,169,219,281
   Josie ........................................ 330
   Laura Martha ................... 5,57,117
   Lucy ............ 5,57,117,169,219,281
   Lucy May .................. 169,219,281
   Madge ..................... 5,57,117,169
   Madge L ........................... 219,281
   Mae ......................................... 307
   Margaret .. 46,101,158,169,219,281
   Marie ........... 5,57,117,169,219,281
   Martha ............................... 219,281
   Martha L ................................. 169
   Maude ......... 5,57,117,169,219,281
   Minnie ...................... 5,57,117,383
   Reuben ................................ 5,117
   Rueben ................. 57,203,255,330
   Ruth ..................... 219,277,281,358
   Walter ......... 5,57,117,169,219,281
   Willis ........... 5,57,117,169,219,281
ANT
   Bertha ............... 5,57,117,169,219,
   281,357,387
   Francis ................. 219,273,282,367
   Hannah ........ 5,57,117,169,219,281
   Helen ........... 5,57,117,169,219,282
   James ........... 5,57,117,169,219,281
   June ............. 5,57,117,169,219,282
   Paul ..................... 5,57,117,360,383

   Ralph ...................................... 117
   Thelma ...................... 169,219,281
   ~~Thelma~~ Ralph ....................... 363
   Walter ......... 5,57,117,169,219,282
ARAPAHO, Ruth ........................ 326
ARAPAHOCHIEF, Lenora .......... 339
ARAPAHOECHIEF, Maude 5,57,379
ATWOOD
   Baby ........................... 58,362,379
   Cecelia ........ 5,57,117,169,219,282
   David ................. 169,219,282,365
   Herbert ...................... 6,58,117,169
   Herbert W ........................ 219,282
   James ........... 5,57,117,169,219,282
   Mary ................... 117,169,219,282
   Mary Lucy ............................. 5,57
   Paul .................................. 365,384
   Walter ......................... 58,362,379
BADGER, John ........................... 373
BADHORSE
   Esther ..................................... 367
   June ......................... 213,267,347
   Junior ...................... 213,267,347
   Mabel ...................... 213,267,347
   Mike ................................. 5,57,117
BADHORSES, Mabel ...... 51,107,163
BALDEAGLE
   Hugh ........... 6,58,117,169,220,282
   Minnie ........ 6,58,118,169,220,282
BALLARD, Clara ........................ 323
BEARBLACK, Lydia .................. 338
BEARCHUM
   Alex ......................................... 58
   Anna ....................................... 282
   Anna R C ................................ 220
   Benjamin .................. 213,267,347
   Benjamin, Jr .................... 6,58,118
   Flossie .................................... 288
   Frank ............. 58,118,169,220,282
   Frank, Jr .............................. 282,368
   Junior ............................... 58,118
   Nellie ...................................... 322
   Wallace ............................. 220,282
BEARCOAL
   Clara ....................................... 336
   Rose ........................................ 310
   Sallie ....................................... 313
BEARCOMESOUT

# Index

Angel..........................................373
Charles........ 6,58,118,169,220,282
Harold........ 6,58,118,170,220,282
Herbert........ 155,170,220,282,363
Hilda..........................................376
Mary..........................169,220,282
Pius............ 6,58,118,170,220,282
BEARQUIVER
   Clara.........................................267
   Claud........................................282
   Claude........ 6,58,118,170,220,282
   Dewey.......................................213
   Edna....................................6,58,118
   Edna Josie................................322
   Edward........ 6,58,118,170,220,282
   Grace........... 6,58,118,267,347,360
   James........... 6,58,118,170,220,282
   Maggie........ 6,30,58,83,192,244, 315,379
   Martin ............... 6,58,118,170,282
   Martin Frank.....................220,282
   Minnie.......................................282
BEARTUSK
   Alice............ 6,58,118,170,233,283
   Bertha.......................170,233,283
   Bertha Eliz ...............................118
   Bertha Elizabeth.....................6,58
   Edith..................6,58,118,178,228,294
   Gladys.......... 6,58,118,170,233,283
   Ida S ........................170,220,283
   Jerome.......... 6,58,118,170,220,283
   Jerome, Jr.......... 6,58,118,170,233, 283,358
   Julia..............................................15
   Kenneth....... 6,58,118,170,233,283
   Lucy........ 6,15,58,67,118,126,170, 178,228
   Mary...........................................293
   Myrtle .........................................15
   Nellie...................6,58,118,170,233
BEAVERHEART
   David........... 6,58,118,170,220,283
   Davis............ 6,58,118,170,220,283
   Nellie............ 6,58,118,170,220,283
   Thomas ....... 6,58,118,170,220,283
BEAVERQUIVER, Maggie ........141
BECKMAN
   Eugene V...................................298

Eugene Veloe ..........................368
May...........................................298
BEIRDNEAU
   Adeline..... 11,58,118,170,220,292
   Al..................................................58
   Albert........................................362
   Albert L ..................... 170,220,292
   Albert Lee.........................58,118
   Barbara M................. 170,220,292
   Barbara Marie......... 11,58,118,358
   Betty B..................... 170,220,292
   Betty Belle.................... 11,58,118
BEMENT
   Albert R ...................................283
   Albert Raymond .....................368
   Celia ..........................................170
   Celia C............................. 220,283
   Celia Camille............... 59,119,362
   Clarence..................... 175,225,289
   Clarence, Jr.................... 11,59,118
   Emma ................. 118,170,220,283
   Emma Burns....................... 11,59
   Geraldine 59,118,170,220,283,360
   Jacqueline. 11,59,118,170,220,283
   Jesse.......... 11,59,118,220,283,357
   Jessie..........................................170
   Joseph........ 11,59,118,170,220,283
   Mas............................................289
   Max.................. 11,59,118,175,225
   Maxine.........................................11
   Mickie....... 11,59,118,175,225,289
BIGBACK
   Charles......... 6,59,119,170,220,283
   Clara ............ 6,59,119,170,220,283
   Eugene.......... 221,273,284,365,367
   Gladys.......... 6,59,119,171,221,283
   Henry................ 6,119,171,221,283
   James ........... 6,59,119,171,221,283
   Jennie........... 6,59,119,171,221,283
   John ............. 6,59,119,171,221,283
   Marie .................. 171,221,283,365
   Nina..........................................283
   Nina S E .......................... 171,221
   Robert.......... 6,59,119,171,221,283
   Stephen 7,59,119,170,220,275,386
   Susie ................................. 361,376
BIGBEAVER
   Annie Marie.................... 7,59,119

August......... 7,59,119,171,221,284
Bessie .............................................338
Emma................................................62
Flora..............................................346
Marie.............................................350
Rosa .........................50,105,162
BIGCROW
   Andrew ....... 7,59,119,171,221,284
   Jennie .......... 7,59,119,171,221,284
   Sarah A ......................................312
   Sarah Angela...................7,59,119
BIGFOOT
   Alice............. 7,59,119,171,221,284
   Davis ........... 7,59,119,171,221,284
   Hoover ........ 221,273,284,365,367
   James......................59,119,362,382
   James Peter ...............................375
   John............. 7,59,119,171,221,284
   Louis .................................7,59,119
   Louis Paul .................. 171,221,284
   Louisa ......... 7,59,119,171,221,284
   Lucy ............ 7,59,119,171,221,284
   Martha......... 7,59,119,171,221,284
   Mary............ 7,59,119,171,221,284
   Mary Lota ........................358,376
   May ..............................................171
   Rosa ............................................373
   White.... 7,59,119,171,221,284,368
BIGHEAD, Kate ............ 7,59,119,382
BIGHEADMAN ..............221,273,367
   Anthonly ....................................367
   Anthony ..............222,273,275,386
   August......... 7,60,119,171,221,284
   Ben ......................................7,60,120
   Benjamin ..... 7,59,119,171,221,284
   Betty N ........................208,261,339
   Betty Nora.........................7,60,120
   Biddle............................................. 7
   Blair ............ 7,60,119,171,221,284
   Clara............ 7,60,119,171,221,284
   Cora.............................................284
   Doris ............................................... 8
   Dorla ................................60,120,358
   Elizabeth .............................120,363
   Emma..........................................313
   Esther Stella ...............................285
   Frank ............................................. 7
   Frank (Biddle)..............................60

Frank B ..................... 208,261,339
Frank Biddle ........................... 120
Gladys.......... 7,60,119,171,221,284
Grace .............................. 8,60,120
Grace M ..................... 172,222,285
Grover ................................ 7,60,119
Helen E ...................... 172,222,285
James ................. 171,221,284,365
John ............ 7,60,120,171,222,285
Julia .7,59,60,119,171,221,284,357
Kathleen ................... 8,60,120,357
Laura....... 60,119,171,221,284,362
Lucille ............... 7,60,119,171,221
Lucy .................. 7,60,120,357,379
Majorie ................................... 285
Marjorie .......................... 172,222
Mary ....................... 7,60,360,379
Maxine Lucy........................... 375
Nellie .......... 7,60,120,171,222,285
Richard ....... 8,60,120,172,222,285
Susie D ..................... 172,222,285
William........ 7,60,120,171,222,285
Wm Grover ................ 171,221,284
BIGLEFTHAND
   Daisy........... 8,60,129,181,231,297
   Patty...................................8,60,129
   Peter..................................8,60,379
   Raphael..............................8,60,129
   Rapheal......................181,231,297
BIGLEG
   Anne ............................................ 60
   Annie ............... 8,120,172,222,285
   Hinton............ 8,37,60,91,120,172,
   222,285
BIGNOSE
   George ........ 8,60,120,172,222,285
   James .......... 8,60,120,172,222,285
   Nora............................................317
   Rachael ........................................ 8
   Rachel ............................. 61,120,384
   Samuel ........ 8,60,120,172,222,285
BIRD
   Gladys....................................348
   James ................................. 285,348
BITES
   Clara ................................. 222,285
   Emma .......................................339
   Florence............ 8,61,120,172,222,

285,360
Herman .............................. 222,286
James ............ 8,61,120,172,222,285
James, Jr ....... 120,172,222,285,363
Mamie ..................... 285,368
Mary ................................... 300
Sally ............ 8,61,120,172,222,285
BIXBY ....................................... 61
Anne ............................................ 8
Annie ....... 61,120,172,222,285,286
Benjamin ..... 8,61,120,172,222,286
Clara ............ 8,61,121,172,222,286
Edward ........ 8,61,121,172,222,286
Edward G .................... 172,222,286
Edward George ............... 8,61,121
Elsie ..................................... 222
Elsie V .............................. 172,286
Elsie Virginia ................... 8,61,121
Eva Kelsey .................................. 8
Gertrude ....... 8,61,120,172,222,286
Hattie C ............... 172,223,286,363
Hattie Caroline ......................... 121
Jack ..................... 61,121,172,222
James ................ 8,121,172,222,286
Jessie ........... 8,61,121,198,250,323
Juanita ........... 223,273,286,365,367
Lloyd James ............................. 368
Louise ..................................... 323
Loyd James .............................. 286
Mary G .................................... 293
Vianna .................................... 286
Vianne ................. 8,61,121,172,222
William L .................................. 357
William Lawrence ................... 8,61
Wm L ......................... 172,223,286
Wm Lawrence .......................... 121
BLACKBEAR
Maude ..................................... 292
Nellie ....................................... 307
BLACKBIRD
Isaac ............. 9,61,121,172,223,286
Nannie .................................... 347
Sallie ........................ 9,61,121,382
BLACKCRANE
Charles ........................... 9,61,379
Clara ..................... 9,61,121,213,347
Edith ................................. 61,121
Jennie ..................................... 347

Julia .......... 31,85,143,194,246,317
BLACKEAGLE
Ada ........................................ 374
Carl ........................... 9,61,121,384
Charles ......................................... 9
Clara ............................... 9,61,121
Edith ............................................ 9
William ....... 9,61,121,172,223,286
BLACKHORSE
Ada ........................... 9,61,121,173
Alex ........... 9,61,121,172,223,286
Alice ................. 9,62,121,357,376
Anna ................. 9,61,121,173,298
Arthur ....................... 9,61,121,173
Charles ..................... 121,362,382
Dan ........................................ 360
Francis ........ 9,62,121,173,223,286
Ida ............................ 9,61,121,173
Jennie ..................................... 326
Lafe ....................................... 173
Lafe C ...................... 223,286,365
Lena .......... 9,61,121,173,223,286
Mary .......... 9,61,121,172,223,286
Merton .................... 9,121,223,286
Reuben ......................................... 9
Ruben ..................................... 369
Ruben, Jr ........................... 286,387
Rueben ........... 61,121,173,223,286
BLACKMEDICINE
Clara ......... 20,74,132,183,234,302
Rose ....................................... 302
BLACKREE
Alice ................... 9,62,121,173,342
Anna ................. 9,62,121,173,342
Emma ............................. 9,62,379
Jennie ......... 9,62,121,173,223,286
Paul ............ 9,62,121,173,223,286
BLACKSTONE
Anna ............................... 287,387
Anna K ............................ 173,223
Arthur .. 9,62,122,173,223,287,369
Arthur, Jr ................................. 345
Baby ....................................... 384
Charles. 9,62,121,173,223,287,387
Gladys ............................. 187,238
James ..................................... 376
James, Jr ................................. 357
Joseph ................ 187,238,348,365

# Index

Lafe C ................................. 365
Lena ............ 9,62,121,173,223,287
Leo ....................... 223,273,287,367
Louis ....... 62,122,187,238,348,362
Nellie ......................... 9,62,122,379
Paul ..................................... 376
Paul Chas ............................ 358
Sallie ............................. 9,62,122
BLACKWHETSTONE
   Amelia ................................. 307
   David .................................. 376
   Nellie ........................... 9,62,379
BLACKWHITEMAN, Nellie ....... 373
BLACKWOLF
   Alex ........ 9,10,62,122,173,223,287
   Alfred ..................... 9,62,122,173
   Bennie ......... 9,62,122,173,223,287
   Busby ............................ 223,287
   Ella ............... 9,62,122,173,223,287
   Gertrude ............................. 316
   Gladys .................................. 10
   Helen ................................. 282
   Henry ......... 9,62,122,173,223,287
   James .......... 9,62,122,173,223,287
   John ........... 10,62,122,173,223,287
   Mary .......... 10,62,122,173,224,325
   Nellie ......... 10,62,122,173,223,287
   Ruth ...... 9,62,122,173,223,287,360
   Thomas ....... 9,62,122,173,223,287
BLINDMAN
   Arthur ........ 10,62,122,173,224,287
   Minnie ................................ 299
BLUEHAWK .............................. 174
   Louis ................ 10,62,122,224,287
BOBTAILHORSE ....................... 224
   Gertrude .... 10,62,122,174,287,387
   Thomas ..... 10,62,122,174,224,287
BOLSON
   Frank ......... 10,63,122,185,236,305
   Gail ............. 10,63,122,185,312
   Roy ........................... 185,236,305
   Roy Buy ............................... 63
   Roy Guy .......................... 10,122
BOXELDER
   David .................................. 373
   Laura ......... 10,63,122,174,224,287
BRADY
   Alex ............ 10,63,122,174,224,288

Arthur ....... 10,63,122,174,224,288
Charles ..... 10,63,122,174,224,288
Clifford .............. 224,273,288,367
Ellen ......... 10,63,122,174,224,288
Elmore ...... 10,63,122,174,224,288
Flossie ....... 10,63,122,174,224,288
George ...... 10,63,122,174,224,288
Howard ..... 10,63,123,174,224,288
James ................................... 380
James H ..................... 174,224,288
James Henry .................. 10,63,123
James R ............................ 10,63
Josie .......... 10,63,122,174,224,288
Martha ...... 10,63,123,174,224,288
Mary .................................... 336
Mrs Geo ................................ 69
Paul ............................. 69,123,174
Pauline ................................. 224
Pearl ............. 123,174,224,288,363
Ramona .................... 174,224,288
Romona Lucy ............... 10,63,123
Roy .... 10,63,123,174,224,288,357
Wilson ...... 10,63,123,174,224,288
BRAIDEDLOCKS
   Gertie .................... 10,63,123,384
   William ..... 10,63,123,174,224,288
BRAVEWOLF, Nellie .......... 287,319
BREIN
   Frederick ............................. 288
   Lorraine ........................... 288,369
   Margaret ................... 174,224,288
   Myron ................ 174,224,288,365
BROWNBIRD
   Anna ......... 10,63,123,174,224,288
   Gertrude ............. 108,165,214,268
   Gerturde ............................. 349
   Jennie ................................. 307
   Joseph ....... 10,63,123,174,224,288
BUFFALOCHUMP
   Nora ................................ 174,225
   Samuel ............................ 174,225
BUFFALOHORN
   John ......... 11,63,123,174,224,288
   Lena ......... 11,63,123,174,225,288
BUFFALOHUMP
   Nora ............... 11,63,123,174,288
   Samuel ...... 11,63,123,174,288,387
BULLARD, Esther ..................... 292

## Index

BULLSHEEP
    Martin ..................................376
    Sadie ...................................373
BURNS
    Adeline................................292
    Anna....................................289
    Anna G...........................175,225
    Anna Grace ....................11,64,123
    Belle................................11,63
    Emma..................118,170,220,283
    George.......11,63,123,174,225,289
    George E .............175,225,289,365
    Gertrude ...................11,64,123,384
    Hattie..........................................11
    Hattie Walker..............................64
    James...........................................11
    James C ......................175,225,289
    James C, Jr.....................11,64,123
    Josephine...11,64,123,175,225,289
    Julia............11,64,123,175,225,289
    Lizzie ........11,64,123,175,225,289
    Margaret....11,64,123,175,225,289
    Mary.................................23,306
    Patrick............................... 11,64
    Phyllis R..............175,225,289,358
    Phyllis Roberta...............11,64,123
    Robert .........................175,225,289
    Robert J....................11,64,123,380
    Robert J, Jr............................64,362
    Veta.....................................329
BUSBY, Alex ...............10,62,122,173
CAIN
    Edith...........................................289
    Edith S ................................175,225
    Leslie...........................................289
CALLSFIRST
    Andres.....................................225
    Andrew ............11,64,123,175,289
    Annie.......................................11,64
    Jennie .........11,64,123,175,225,289
    Mary...........11,64,152,203,255,330
CENTERWALL, W R ....279,281,352
CHASINGBEAR
    Flora...............................11,64,123
    Laura ...............11,64,123,176,226
    Madge .......12,64,124,175,225,289
    Robert ........11,64,124,176,226,357
    Willis..........12,64,124,175,225,289

CHUBBY
    Andrew ....................................376
    Anna..........................................301
    Anne......... 12,64,124,175,225,289
    John ...... 12,34,64,88,124,160,175,
210,225,263,289,342
    Mrs Jno......................................34
    Mrs John.........................17,70,88
    Rhoda ....... 12,64,124,175,225,289
CLUBFOOT
    Flossie....... 12,64,124,175,226,290
    Floyd......... 12,64,124,175,225,275,
384,386
    Frank......... 12,64,124,175,225,290
    Frank, Jr.............. 175,225,290,360
    James ........ 12,64,124,175,225,290
    John .......... 12,65,124,175,226,290
    Joseph....... 12,65,124,175,226,290
    Lucy..........................................290
    Lucy A.............................. 175,225
    Lucy Alice ......................... 12,124
    Lucy Ann...................................64
    Minnie ...... 12,65,124,175,226,290
    Norman..... 12,64,124,175,226,290
    Stella...................... 12,64,124,175
    Stella M .................................. 290
    Stella Mary .............................226
    Verle..................... 12,64,124,382
    Willis ........ 12,65,124,175,226,290
COLHOFF
    Annie G ..................... 176,226,290
    Annie Gladys................. 12,65,124
    Edward ..... 12,65,124,176,226,290
    Emma ....... 12,65,124,176,226,290
    George ..... 12,65,124,176,226,290,
360
    Maxine...... 12,65,124,176,226,290
    William............ 12,65,176,226,290
    William R ...............................290
    William Rowland................... 12,65
    Wm Rowland.........................124
COMESTOGETHER, Ida .. 12,65,380
COOLEY
    Al......................................... 12,65
    Charlotte ................... 290,354,362
    Francis ...... 12,65,124,176,226,290
    Julia .......... 12,65,124,176,226,290
    Junior........ 12,65,124,176,226,290

# Index

Odessa ................................. 291
Odessa Marie ..................... 369
Rachel ................................ 290
Vera .... 12,65,124,176,226,290,357
Violet ........ 12,65,124,176,226,290
CRAWFORD
  Francis ............................ 291
  Lillian ............................. 291
  Lyman E .......................... 291
  Lyman Eugene ................ 369
CRAWLING
  Charles ...... 13,65,125,176,226,291
  Flora ..................... 176,226,291
  Laura ............................... 291
  Martha ....... 13,65,125,176,226,291
  Mary ................................ 376
  Robert ............................. 291
CRAZYHEAD
  Edna ................................ 325
  Lizzie .............................. 335
  Lucy ................................ 329
CRAZYMULE
  Charles ...................... 13,65,125
  Charles R ........................ 291
  Chas R ...................... 176,227
  Eva ..... 13,65,125,176,226,291,354
  James ................ 125,176,226,291
  James Paul ................ 13,65,125
  Jennie ........ 13,65,125,176,226,291
  John .... 13,65,125,176,226,275,386
  Joseph ....... 13,65,125,176,227,291
  Lizzie ......................... 53,109
  Raymond ... 13,65,125,176,227,291
  Sally .............. 61,120,172,222,285
  Sarah ......... 13,65,125,176,227,291
  Wyoming .. 13,65,125,176,226,291
  Xavier ........ 13,65,125,176,227,291
CROOK
  Albert . 13,66,125,176,227,291,387
  Alice ..................... 13,66,125,343
  George ....... 13,66,125,176,227,291
  Rosa ........... 13,66,125,176,227,291
  Theresa ....... 13,66,125,176,227,291
CROOKEDNOSE
  Mary ......... 46,102,159,209,262,341
  Nicholas .... 13,66,125,176,227,291
  Susie ........... 13,66,125,176,227,291
CROW, Rosa .................. 50,105,162

CURLEY
  Baby ................................. 13
  Ella ................. 13,66,125,177,227
  Esther ......... 13,66,125,177,227,292
  Hattie ..................... 13,66,125,177
  Joseph ............................ 292,357
  Logan .................. 66,125,360,384
  Thomas ..... 13,66,125,177,227,291
DAHLE, Adeline ...................... 292
DEAFY
  Anna ......... 13,66,125,177,227,292
  Carrie .............. 14,66,126,177,342
  David ........ 13,66,125,177,227,292
  Elsie .... 13,66,125,177,227,292,358
  Geo ................................... 5
  Irene ................. 177,227,292,365
  James ........ 13,66,125,177,292,354
  Jessie .......................... 66,126,177
  Louisa .............................. 308
  Mary ..................... 14,66,125,382
  Willie .............................. 177,227
  Willis ................. 13,66,125,292
DIVESBACKWARD
  Grace ........... 126,177,227,292,357
  Irving .............................. 126
  John ................. 126,177,227,292
  Louisa ...................... 201,253,327
  Mary ................................ 327
  May ......................... 33,87,145
  Nancy ................. 126,177,227,292
  Rufus ................. 126,177,227,292
  Sam .................... 126,177,227,292
  Strane ................ 126,177,227,292
DIVESBACKWARDS
  Grace ............................... 14,66
  Henry ......................... 40,94,151
  Irving .............................. 14,66
  John ............................. 14,66,227
  Louisa ......................... 14,66,150
  Nancy .............................. 14,66
  Rufus ............................... 14,66
  Sam ................................... 14
  San .................................... 66
  Strane .............................. 14,66
DOG
  Louis .......... 14,66,126,177,227,292
  Maude ....... 14,66,126,177,227,292
DULLKNIFE, Bessie ........ 14,67,126,

399

# Index

186,237,307
DUSTER
  Albert . 14,67,126,177,227,293,316
  Anie...........................................126
  Annie................ 14,67,177,228,293
  Augusta.....................................373
  Bessie. 14,67,126,177,228,293,357
  Mabel ............................14,67,126
  Vinnie ....... 14,67,126,177,227,293
DUSTYBUFFALO, Rufus......47,102,
159,209,262,341
EAGLEFEATHERS
  Bernice...........................14,67,380
  Jacob ......... 14,67,126,177,228,293
  Jennie.............29,141,187,238,308
  Jennie E........................................83
  Julia............ 14,67,126,177,228,293
  Laura.........................................374
  Mildred ..... 14,67,126,177,228,293
  Milton .......... 126,177,228,293,364
  Oliver........... 14,24,67,78,126,177,
  228,293
  Rosie .. 14,67,126,177,228,293,358
  Simon........ 14,67,126,177,228,293
EASTMAN
  Carl ..............................................14
  Charles ............. 15,67,126,228,293
  Chas ..........................................178
  Emma........................................373
  Ida ........................31,143,194,246
  Julia.......................67,126,178,228
  Letha ....... 14,109,166,200,252,326
  Louisa ....... 15,67,126,178,228,293
  Margaret................. 14,67,126,288
  Mary.......... 15,67,127,178,228,293
  Mary G...... 14,67,126,178,228,293
  Mike.....................................14,67
  Myrtle ............. 67,126,178,228,293
  Pearl ............... 14,132,183,234,301
  Perry........ 15,67,127,178,228,293
  Rena....................................22,305
  Robert ....... 14,67,126,178,228,293
  Rose ......... 14,67,126,178,228,293
ELKSHOULDER
  Adolph ...... 15,67,127,178,228,294
  Bessie........ 15,67,127,178,228,294
  Calvin.... 127,178,228,294,364,387
  Curtis.......... 15,67,127,178,228,294

Fred................................. 294,369
George 15,67,127,178,228,294,358
Henry......... 15,67,127,178,228,294
Lucy........... 15,67,127,178,228,294
Sylvia......... 15,67,127,178,228,294
ELKSHOULDERS, Julia .. 28,82,140,
191,242
ELKSHOWSHORN, Sophia........ 346
ELLEN, Daisy............................... 324
ELLIOT
  ---................................................ 15
  Edwin F ..................................... 178
  Edwin Francis.................... 68,127
  Elizabeth..................... 67,127,178
  Elizabeth Harris........................ 15
  Lafe............................................. 67
  Loretta M.................................. 178
  Loretta May ............................ 127
ELLIOTT
  Edwin F ............................ 228,294
  Edwin Francis........................ 362
  Elizabeth.......................... 228,294
  Loretta ..................................... 228
  Loretta M................................... 294
  Loretta May ............................. 364
  Myron L................... 229,273,294
  Myron Leonard....................... 367
EYESYELLOW
  Daisy...15,68,127,178,229,294,387
  Lizzie......................................... 376
  Wilbur........ 15,68,127,178,229,294
FARR .............................................. 15
  Alice ............................................ 15
  Evelyn............ 68,127,203,256,331
  Frank.......... 15,68,127,204,256,331
  Jessie................................ 15,68,127
FASTHORSE
  Clara .......... 15,68,132,183,233,301
  Raymond ................................... 68
  Raymond M.............................. 15
FIGHTINGBEAR
  Alice ...15,68,127,178,229,294,387
  Baby .......................... 127,364,382
  Daisy........................................... 324
  Dora .......... 15,68,127,197,249,321
  Edgar ......... 15,68,127,178,229,294
  Ellen ................ 36,90,148,199,251
  Elmer ......... 15,68,127,178,229,294

400

Emma ............ 15,68,127,178,229, 294,354,382
Fannie ........................... 15,68,127
Francis ........................ 294,369,387
Herbert ...... 15,68,127,178,229,294
Julia.... 15,68,127,197,249,321,388
Willie ....................... 180,231,297
Willis .............................. 15,68,127
FINGERS
　Joseph ....... 15,68,127,178,229,295
　Josie .......... 15,68,127,178,229,295
　Nellie ................................... 294
　Otis ............ 15,68,127,178,229,294
FIRECROW
　Alice Eva ............................... 373
　Joseph ....... 15,68,127,179,229,295
　Josephine... 15,68,127,179,229,295
　Peter .......... 15,68,127,179,229,295
FIREWOLF
　John ........... 16,68,127,179,229,295
　Josephine... 16,68,127,179,229,295
FISHER
　Alice .......... 16,69,139,190,241,312
　Alliwitchie 16,68,128,179,229,295
　Bernidine ......... 16,68,128,179,229, 295,360
　Burton ................ 179,229,296,365
　Calleaus ..... 16,68,128,179,229,295
　Earl ............ 16,68,128,179,229,295
　Emeline .................... 296,354,367
　Eugene ...... 16,68,128,179,229,295
　Eugene, Jr.. 16,68,128,179,229,295
　Floyd ........................ 296,369,373
　Harold ....... 16,69,139,190,241,312
　Helen ........................ 179,229,295
　Henry ........ 16,69,139,179,229,295
　Ira ............... 16,68,128,179,229,295
　Isabelle ...... 16,69,139,190,241,312
　J Allen ..................... 16,68,128
　James A ..................... 179,229,295
　John ........... 16,69,128,179,229,296
　Kitty ........... 16,68,128,179,229,295
　Langburn... 16,68,128,179,229,295
　Lena ................................... 16,69
　Lucy ......................... 179,229,295
　Mary ........................................ 296
　Mary P ..................... 128,179,229
　Pearl .......... 16,68,128,179,229,295

Phyllis Helen ................. 16,68,128
Richard ..... 16,69,139,190,241,312
Russell ....... 16,68,128,179,229,295
Virginia ........................... 229,295
Virginia Mae .................... 273,367
FLIESABOUT
　June ........... 16,69,128,179,230,282
　Martin .................... 16,69,128,179
　Minnie ............ 16,69,128,179,230
　William ..... 16,69,128,179,230,296
FLYING ........................................ 16
　Debs ........... 16,69,128,179,230,296
　Elizabeth ........ 35,146,197,250,322
　Elizabeth Martha ...................... 89
　Frank ......... 16,69,128,179,230,296
　Margaret ................ 16,69,128,382
　Martha ....................................... 35
　Myra ......... 16,69,128,179,230,296
　Parker ....... 16,69,128,179,230,296
　Paul ............................ 16,224,288
　Pauline ........... 69,123,174,224,288
　Ruth .............................. 16,69,128
　Thomas ..... 16,69,128,179,230,296
FONTENELLE
　Frances ........................... 128,296
　Francis ............................ 179,230
　Sherman ............................... 296
FOOT
　Albert ............................ 16,69,296
　Bertha ....... 16,69,128,180,230,296
　Daisy ............... 16,69,128,180,230
　Edward ..... 16,69,128,180,230,296
　Eva ............ 16,69,128,180,230,296
　Jennie ............................. 16,69,380
　Joseph ............................. 296,369
　Ruth ........................................ 296
　Ruth Y ..................... 180,230,388
　Ruth Yellownose .... 69,71,128,130
　Sylvia ........... 128,180,230,296,364
　Thelma ...... 16,69,128,180,230,339
FOX
　Jessie ......... 17,69,150,201,253,327
　Margaret ... 17,69,150,201,253,327
　Marie ........ 17,69,150,201,253,327
　Max ............... 69,150,201,253,327
　Max M .................................... 17
GHOSTBULL
　Arthur ....... 17,69,128,180,230,296

Eva .............................. 180,230,338
Eva (Mary) ................................. 17
Eva Mary ............................. 69,128
Sarah ...................... 17,69,128,384
GILLISPIE
   George ...................................... 296
   Mary .......................................... 296
   May P .................................. 180,230
   May Parker ......................... 69,128
   Parker May ................................. 53
GOGGLES
   Hayes ................. 214,268,349,362
   Laura ......................... 214,268,349
GRASSHOPPER
   Arthur ........ 17,70,129,180,230,297
   Frank ......... 17,70,129,180,230,297
   Ida ............................................. 373
   Isaac .......... 17,70,129,180,230,297
   Mary ................. 17,70,134,185,324
   Susie ................. 17,70,161,211,344
   Susie G ...................................... 265
GRAY
   Baby ............................................ 70
   Bessie ........ 17,70,129,180,230,297
   Buddy .................. 231,273,297,367
   Edward ...... 17,70,129,180,230,297
   Ida .............. 17,70,129,180,231,297
   John ............ 17,70,129,180,230,297
   Joseph ............................... 297,369
   Kate ............................ 180,231,297
   Kate Wolfname .............. 17,70,129
   Margaret ................................... 376
   Nellie ......... 17,70,129,180,230,297
   Peter .......................................... 129
   Rose Marie 17,70,129,180,230,297
   Russell ...................................... 373
   Teddy ........ 17,70,129,180,230,297
GREASYDOG, Fannie ...... 17,70,129, 176,227,291
HAIL, Inez ..................................... 373
HAIRLESSBEAR
   Alice ..................... 130,181,232,299
   Hilda ......... 17,70,124,175,225,289
   Rosa Alice .................................. 72
   Rose Alice ................................. 19
HAIRYHAND, Henry ....... 17,70,129, 180,231,297
HANKERINGWOLF

Helen ........................................ 375
Peter ....................... 17,70,129,384
HARDGROUND
   Albert ........ 18,70,129,180,231,297
   Elda ....................... 17,70,358,380
   Ernest ........ 17,70,129,180,231,297
   Ethel ......... 17,70,129,180,231,297
   George ...... 18,71,129,180,231,297
   Jane .......... 17,70,153,204,256,275, 384,386
   Katie ......... 17,70,129,180,231,297
   Lucy ............... 18,70,129,180,338
   Lyla ........... 18,70,129,181,231,297
   Mary ..17,70,129,180,231,275,364, 384,386
   Nancy Susan ..................... 231,297
   Patty .......................................... 297
   Patty B L ............................ 180,231
   Rena ................................... 18,180
   Robert ....... 17,70,129,180,231,297
   Roland .................... 17,70,129,384
   Rowland ............................ 17,129
   Ruth ...................... 18,70,129,382
   Susan ................................ 180,365
   Thomas .... 18,71,129,231,273,297, 365,367,382
HARDROBE
   Albert ...................... 18,71,130,298
   Albert J .............................. 181,231
   Colonel ..... 18,71,130,181,231,298
   Fannie .............. 18,71,130,181,337
   Lucy .............................. 18,71,130
   Margaret ... 18,71,130,180,230,296
   Mira ........................................... 314
   Mollie ....... 18,71,130,191,243,314
   Ruth .......................................... 375
HARRIS
   Agnes ........ 18,71,130,181,232,299
   Alice .......................................... 304
   Allie ...................... 71,130,181,231
   Anna ................................. 232,298
   Anna B ...................................... 388
   Bessie ....... 18,71,130,181,231,298
   Bryan ........ 18,71,130,181,231,298
   Carl ........... 18,71,130,181,231,298
   Chester ................. 231,273,298,367
   Dorothy ..... 18,71,130,181,231,298
   Edward ..... 18,71,130,181,231,298

# Index

Elizabeth ................................. 294
Elmer ........................................ 365
Elmer F ..................... 181,231,298
Elsie ......................................... 373
Florence .... 18,71,130,181,232,299
Francis E ................................. 231
Francis R ................................. 298
George ....... 18,71,130,181,232,298
Hubert ................ 130,181,231,298
Hubert Geo ............................... 71
Hubert George .......................... 18
Inez .......................................... 362
Inez R ....................... 181,231,298
Inez Romona ..................... 71,130
Joseph ............... 130,181,232,299
Joseph M ............................. 18,71
Julia .... 18,71,130,181,232,289,299
Lawrence Edw ....... 18,71,130,181,
231,298
Leota ......... 18,71,130,181,232,299
Lizzie ...................................... 289
Louisa ..................................... 299
Lucy ...................... 18,71,130,295
Margaret .... 18,71,130,181,232,298
Mary .......... 18,71,130,181,232,299
May ....... 18,26,71,80,130,138,181,
189,231,240,311
Nellie .......... 18,71,130,181,231,298
Raymond ... 18,71,130,181,232,299
Robert .................................... 377
Ruth .................................. 181,298
Ruth M B .............................. 231
Sallie .. 18,71,130,181,231,298,388
William ..... 18,71,130,181,232,298
HART
  Alice .................. 130,181,232,299
  Charles ....... 19,71,130,181,232,299
  Edna .............. 130,181,232,299,362
  Elnora F .................................. 376
  Elnora Fern ........................... 361
  Eva ............ 19,72,130,181,232,299
  Frank ............. 18,72,130,181,232,299
  Hilda .................. 232,273,299,367
  Jessie .................................... 299
  Jessie D .......................... 181,232
  Jessie Diana ..................... 72,130
  Jessie Dianna .......................... 19
  Katie ..................... 19,71,130

Louisa ....... 19,71,130,181,232,299
Mattie L ................................. 181
Mattie Lizzie ................. 19,71,130
Rosa Alice ............................... 72
Rose Alice ............................... 19
HAWK
  Hannah ................................. 299
  Nelson................................... 299
HEADSWIFT
  Charles ...... 19,72,131,182,232,299
  Frank ......... 19,72,131,182,232,299
HIGHBEAR
  Margaret ..................... 16,69,128
  Minnie ...... 19,72,131,182,232,299
  William ..... 19,72,131,182,232,299
HIGHWALKING
  Belle ......... 19,72,131,182,232,300
  David ........ 19,72,131,182,232,300
  Floyd ........ 19,72,131,182,232,300
  George ...... 19,72,131,182,232,300
  Hannah ....... 5,57,117,169,219,281
  Max........... 19,72,131,182,232,300
  Nellie ........ 19,72,131,182,232,300
HILLMAN, Adrain..................... 138
HISBADHORSE
  Baby ............................. 360,377
  Bird........................... 182,232,300
  Ernest ...................... 182,232,300
  Esther ..................... 233,273,300
  Eugene .................... 182,232,300
  Fannie ..................... 182,232,300
  Josephine ................ 182,232,300
  Mary ...................................... 377
  Medaris .................... 182,232,300
  Rhoda ....... 19,72,131,182,233,300
  Richard ......................... 19,72,380
  Willis ....................... 182,232,300
HISBADHORSES ....................... 19
  Bird............................... 72,131
  Ernest ............................ 19,72,131
  Eugene ........................... 19,72,131
  Fannie ............................ 19,72,131
  Hattie ........ 19,72,131,182,233,300
  Josephine .......... 19,38,93,131,201,
253,327
  Medaris ....................... 19,72,131
  Rhoda .................................. 19,72
  Richard ................................ 19,72

## Index

Willis .............................. 19,72,131
HOLLOWBREAST
   Agnes ................................... 373
   Anna .................................... 374
   Donald ....... 19,72,131,182,233,300
   Edith ................................ 20,73
   Edward ......... 131,182,233,300,364
   Fern ............................... 300,369
   Hubert ...... 19,72,131,182,233,300
   Jack ..................................... 182
   Jack R .................................. 300
   Jack Richard .......................... 233
   James ............................. 19,72,131
   Mary .......... 19,72,131,182,233,300
   Richard .................. 19,72,358,380
   William ..... 20,72,131,182,233,300
   Willie ............................ 20,72,131
HOLLOWWOOD
   Flora ................................... 291
   Hattie .............................. 233,301
   Minnie .................... 20,73,131,382
   Richard ...... 20,73,131,182,233,300
HORN
   Alice .......... 20,73,131,182,233,301
   Anna .................................... 301
   Annie W ...................... 182,233,301
   Annie Wolfname ............. 20,73,131
   Celia .............................. 73,132,362
   Celia M ....................... 182,233,301
   Denver ................................ 273
   Denver S ........................... 233,301
   Denver Sherman ..................... 367
   Margaret 20,73,132,182,233,301,360
   Miles .............................. 20,73,301
   Rose .......... 20,73,131,182,233,301
   Wilena ....... 20,73,131,182,233,301
HORSEROADS
   Anna .......... 13,66,125,177,227,292
   Cora .... 20,73,132,183,233,301,360
   Ida ................. 20,73,132,182,233,301
   Lucy .......... 20,73,132,182,233,301
   Sallie .............................. 20,73,380
   Thomas ..... 20,73,132,182,233,301
HOWE, Lucy ....................... 233,301
HOWLINGANTELOPE
   Albert ........ 20,73,132,183,233,301
   Ellen .................................. 325
   Eva ........... 20,73,132,183,233,301

HOWLINGWOLF, Julia .............. 308
HUFF
   Elsie ......................... 183,234,301
   Elsie M ................................ 362
   Elsie Margaret .................... 73,132
   Patrick ............................... 73,301
   Pearl .................. 132,183,234,301
   Pearl Eastman .......................... 73
   Percy ......................... 183,234,301
IRONHAND
   Henry ........ 20,73,132,183,234,301
   Jane ..... 20,73,132,183,234,302,360
   Mamie ............................. 234,301
   Rufus Grant ..................... 301,369
   Sally .......... 20,73,132,183,234,302
   William ..... 20,73,132,183,234,301
   Willis ........ 20,73,132,183,234,302
IRONSHIRT
   Fred ..................... 20,73,132,382
   Jennie ........ 20,73,132,210,263,342
   Minnie ................................ 342
   Nora .... 20,73,132,173,223,287,388
   Robert ............. 20,73,132,249,321
IRONTOOTH, Susan .. 20,73,132,380
ISSUE
   Clara .................................. 234
   Donald ................................ 375
   John ................................... 234
ISSUES
   Clara .......... 20,74,132,183,234,302
   Francis ....... 20,74,132,183,234,302
   George ....... 21,74,132,183,234,302
   Ira .............. 21,74,132,183,234,302
   Irene ........... 21,74,132,183,234,302
   Jennie ................... 13,125,226,291
   John .......... 20,73,132,183,234,302
   Mamie ................................ 302
   Mamie L .......................... 183,234
   Mamie Limpy ......................... 132
   Mary .................................. 303
   Minnie ................................ 377
JUNIOR .................................... 6
KILLSACROSS
   Hallie ......... 23,76,135,186,237,306
   Joseph ....... 21,74,132,183,234,302
KILLSBACK
   Amelia ...... 21,74,132,183,234,302
   Hattie ................................ 306

# Index

James ......... 21,74,132,183,234,302
KILLSNIGHT
   Alice .......... 34,88,146,197,249,321
   Alice Farr ..................... 74,133,382
   Anna ......................... 21,74,133,287
   Bessie ........ 21,74,133,210,263,342
   Brighton .... 21,74,133,183,234,302
   Carrie . 21,74,133,184,235,303,340
   Charles ....... 21,74,132,183,234,302
   Clara .......... 21,74,133,183,234,302
   Cole ........... 21,74,133,184,235,303
   Cora ........... 21,74,133,184,235,302
   Dorothy .......... 21,74,133,184,235, 275,360,386
   Edward ..................................... 373
   Eugene .............................. 365,384
   Florence ........................ 21,74,133
   Flossie ..................... 21,74,133,184
   Flossie A ................................ 302
   Harold ..................................... 303
   Hubert ....... 21,74,133,183,234,302
   Hugh ......... 21,74,133,183,234,302
   James .. 21,75,133,184,235,303,358
   Jennie ........... 133,184,235,302,364
   Jessie .................................. 74,133
   Julia ........................................ 328
   June ........................................ 303
   Kitty ....................................... 235
   Kitty B .............................. 183,332
   Kitty Belle ........................ 133,364
   Levern .................................... 303
   Mabel ..................................... 303
   Mabel L .................................. 235
   Margaret .... 21,74,133,183,235,302
   Martin ....... 21,74,133,183,234,302
   Mary ....................................... 330
   Mary Flossie ..................... 235,303
   Minnie ...................... 21,39,94,151
   Paul ........................................ 303
   Ralph ....... 75,133,184,235,303,362
   Rilla ....................................... 321
   Robert ..................... 21,74,133,382
   Rosa ............................... 21,74,133
   Rose ... 21,74,183,234,235,302,380
   Rose L W ........................ 183,234
   Ruth ........................ 179,230,296
   Rutherford . 21,74,133,184,235,303
   Sage .......... 21,74,133,184,235,303
   Susan ....... 21,74,133,210,263,342
   William ........................ 184,235,302
   William, Jr 21,74,133,184,235,302
   William, Sr .................... 21,74,133
   Willis ........ 21,74,133,184,235,303
KILLSNIGHTWOMAN ... 21,75,133, 235,303
   Ralph ..................................... 184
KILLSONTOP
   Baby ....................................... 360
   Harold .......... 235,273,303,365,367
   Ida ....... 22,75,133,208,262,340,357
   John .......... 21,75,133,184,235,303
   June ..... 21,75,133,184,235,303,360
   Levern .......... 133,184,235,303,364
   Mamie ............................ 22,75,133
   Mary ................. 133,184,235,303
   Mary Strangeowl ..................... 75
   Paul ................................ 303,369
KING
   Anabelle ................................ 193
   Anna Joyce ............... 193,245,303
   Emma ....................... 193,245,304
   Ernest ....................... 193,244,303
   Ethel .............................. 193,304
   Harriet ...................... 193,245,303
   Hilda ...................................... 193
   James ........................ 193,245,304
   M Victoria ................ 193,245,303
   Mabel Ann ....................... 193,304
   Margaret .................... 193,245,304
   Marion ....................... 193,245,303
   Mary .................. 193,245,303,304
   Rosa .......................... 193,245,304
   Rudolph ..................... 193,245,303
   Stephen ............................ 303,369
KINGFISHER
   Angela .... 75,134,184,235,304,362
   Carrie ........ 22,75,133,184,235,304
   Charles ...... 22,75,134,184,235,304
   Elizabeth ................... 304,354,367
   Ellen ... 22,75,134,184,235,304,358
   Herman ................... 22,75,133,382
   Isabelle ..... 22,75,134,184,235,304
   James W ................................ 304
   Julia .......... 31,85,143,194,246,317
   Louise ....... 22,75,134,184,235,304
   Minnie ...... 22,75,134,184,235,304

# Index

Payton .................................. 373
Willis ............................ 22,75,134
Willis J ..................... 184,235,304
KINSEL
   Alice ......................... 184,235,304
   Cecelia L ......................... 184,236
   Celia L .................................. 304
   Emma L ...................... 184,236,304
   Helen L ...................... 184,236,304
   Virgil B ...................... 184,236,304
KINZEL
   -- ............................................ 304
   Alice ....................... 22,75,134,304
   Cecelia Leah ................. 22,75,134
   Celia L .............................. 304,357
   Emma L ................................. 304
   Emma Loua ................... 22,75,134
   Helan Louise ............................ 22
   Helen L ................................... 304
   Helen Louise ..................... 75,134
   Jerry ........................................ 22
   Virgil B .................................. 304
   Virgil Bruce ................. 75,134,362
KNOW-HIS-GUN, Genevieve ...... 354
KNOWS-HIS-GUN
   Edith .................... 184,236,305,362
   Frances ...... 22,75,134,184,236,304
   Genevieve .................. 305,367,388
   Hector ........................... 22,75,304
   Hector, Jr ........................... 305,369
   Sylvester .......... 22,75,134,184,236, 305,360
LAFEVER
   Herman ................... 22,75,134,185
   I B ............................................ 75
   Kenneth .......... 22,75,134,185,236, 305,358
   Rena ............... 22,122,184,236,305
   Rena Eastman ..................... 75,134
LAMEBEAR
   Benjamin ... 22,75,134,185,236,305
   Charles ...... 22,75,134,185,236,305
   Clara .......... 22,75,134,185,236,305
   Cora ........... 22,75,134,185,236,305
   Ethel ............................ 305,369,388
   Eva ............. 22,75,134,185,236,305
   Susie ................... 185,236,305,365
   Will ........................ 22,76,358,380

LAMEWOMAN
   Alice ......................... 185,236,305
   Alice R .................................. 134
   Augusta ..... 22,76,134,185,236,306
   Jessie ......... 23,76,134,185,236,306
   Mannie ........... 51,107,163,213,267
   Mary .... 22,23,76,163,213,267,347
   Maude ............................... 236,305
   Minnie ........................ 22,76,163
   Mrs Stanley ..... 17,70,129,161,180, 211,230,265,297,344
   Nannie .................................. 347
   Nellie ........ 22,76,134,185,236,306
   Ruth ............. 185,236,305,365,388
   Sally ...................................... 302
   Sam ........... 22,76,134,185,236,305
   Sam, Jr ............................. 305,369
   Stanley . 17,22,76,134,185,236,305
   Virgil ........ 22,76,134,185,236,306
LASTBULL
   Fred .......... 23,76,134,185,236,306
   Maywoman ......................... 23,76
LEFEVER, Rena ...................... 10,63
LENNON
   Arthur G .................... 185,236,306
   Arthur George ............... 23,76,134
   Mary ................................. 23,306
   Mary B .............................. 185,236
   Mary Burns ....................... 76,134
   Thomas ................................ 23,76
LIGHTNING
   Emma ....... 25,79,137,188,239,309
   Frank ......... 23,76,135,185,236,306
LIMBERHAND .......................... 237
   Aerie .................................... 185
   Artie ................. 23,76,135,236,306
   Baby .................................... 377
   Bennie ....... 23,76,135,185,237,306
   Bessie ................................... 306
   Doris ........ 23,76,135,185,186,237, 306,364
   Elmore ...... 23,76,135,185,237,306
   George ......... 306,354,367,369,388
   Harry ............................... 365,384
   James ........ 23,76,135,185,237,306
   Jennie ............... 23,76,135,185,331
   Jessie ................. 135,186,237,306
   Mamie .................................. 340

# Index

N ............................................... 135
Nathan .. 23,76,77,135,185,236,306
Richard ............. 23,76,135,186,306
LIMPY
Amelia ... 14,23,67,77,126,135,186, 237,307,388
Anna ............ 23,76,135,186,237,307
Benjamin ......... 23,76,135,186,237, 306,364
Bessie ......................... 186,237,307
Charles ...... 23,76,135,186,237,307
Cora ............. 23,77,135,186,237,358
Cora Eva ..................................307
Eleanora ..................................380
Elnora ... 23,76,77,186,237,307,360
Eunice ................. 186,237,307,362
Frank ......... 23,77,135,186,237,307
Fred 23,24,77,78,135,149,186,200, 237,252,307,326
Fred, Jr ..... 23,77,135,186,237,275, 386
Hallie .......... 23,76,135,186,237,306
Hattie .......... 23,76,135,186,237,306
Henry .......... 23,77,135,186,237,306
Jack ............ 23,76,135,186,237,307
Jean ............ 23,76,135,186,237,307
Jessie ................. 23,76,135,237,307
Lee ...................................323,369
Lena ........................................312
Mamie ...........................23,77,302
Mary ............ 23,77,135,186,237,307
May ....... 14,23,67,77,126,135,186, 237,307
Nellie ........... 23,77,135,186,237,307
Rosa ............ 23,76,135,186,237,307
LITTLEBEAR .............................388
(Unnamed) ........................307,369
Anne ................. 23,77,135,186,238
Carol ................................135,364
Clara ........... 24,77,135,186,237,307
Flossie ........ 24,77,135,186,237,307
Lenora ................................186,238
Lenora C ................................307
Lester ................ 186,238,307,366
Lucille 24,77,135,186,237,307,360
Mary ........... 24,77,135,186,237,307
May ................. 23,77,135,186,238
Paul ............ 23,77,135,186,237,307

Peter T ...................... 186,237,307
Rosa .............................. 23,77,135
Rose .......................... 186,237,307
Sam ........... 22,76,134,185,236,305
Two Birds ....................................77
Two-Birds ................................ 135
Two-birds ..................................24
LITTLEBIRD
Ella ........ 48,103,160,210,264,343
Elsie .......... 24,77,160,210,264,343
Harry ......... 24,77,160,210,264,343
James ........ 24,77,160,210,264,343
James Wm77,136,187,238,308,357
Jennie ....... 24,77,136,186,238,307
Joseph ....... 24,77,136,186,238,308
Julia ................. 24,77,136,186,238
Peter .......... 24,77,136,186,238,307
Theresa ............... 187,238,308,366
LITTLECHIEF
Lizzie ........................................ 24
Louisa ....... 24,77,136,187,238,308
Lucille ............. 24,77,136,187,318
Maude .................................... 281
Victor ........ 24,77,136,187,238,308
LITTLECOYOTE
Daniel .......................... 24,77,136
Daniel E .................... 187,238,308
Henry ........ 24,77,136,187,238,308
Julia .................................. 187,308
Julia P .................................238,308
LITTLEEAGLE
Belle ........................................ 344
Charles ...... 24,77,136,187,238,308
Clara ................ 24,77,136,187,238
Clara C ................................. 347
Mary ......... 24,77,136,187,238,308
LITTLEEYES
Baby ............................... 136,364
Eva ....................... 24,77,136,344
LITTLEHAWK, Dora ....... 24,78,136, 187,238,308
LITTLEHEAD
Charles ...... 24,78,136,187,238,308
Frank ......... 24,78,136,187,238,308
George ............ 24,78,136,238,308
Gladys .................................... 348
Jennie .................................... 308
John .......... 24,78,136,187,238,308

# Index

Mildred ............ 24,78,126,228,293
Nellie ........ 9,24,62,78,122,136,187, 238,308
Rena .......... 24,78,126,178,228,293
Sallie ........................................ 122
LITTLEMAN, Julia ........... 24,78,149, 200,252,326
LITTLEMOUTH
    Baby ............................ 78,362,380
    Clara .......... 24,78,136,187,239,308
    Evelyn ....... 25,78,136,187,239,308
    Fred .................... 309,354,367,388
    James ......... 25,78,136,187,239,308
    Jennie ........ 25,78,136,187,238,308
    John ............ 25,78,136,187,238,308
    Mary .......... 25,78,136,187,239,308
    Sallie ........................................ 360
LITTLEOLDMAN
    Bertha ...................................... 315
    Fern ........... 24,78,149,200,252,326
    Ida ........................................... 315
    Thomas ........... 25,78,136,187,252, 325,388
LITTLESUN
    Alfred ........ 25,78,136,187,252,325
    Anna ........................ 25,78,136,187
    Baby ........................... 136,364,382
    Bessie ........... 106,163,213,266,346
    Cora .... 25,78,137,188,239,309,388
    Frank .. 25,78,136,187,239,275,386
    Gusta ......... 25,79,137,188,240,310
    Horace ....... 25,78,137,188,239,309
    Jack ........... 25,78,137,188,239,309
    Samuel ............ 25,78,137,187,239, 309,388
LITTLEWHIRLWIND
    Anna .............. 137,188,239,309,364
    Ellen ............................. 78,362,380
    George ....... 25,78,137,188,239,309
    Georgia ................................... 337
    Levi ......................... 309,369,375
    Martha ..... 25,78,137,188,239,309
LITTLEWHITEMAN ................... 343
    Aaron .... 25,26,78,79,137,138,188, 189,239,240,309,311,388
    Adrain ............ 79,138,189,240,311
    Adrian ........................................ 26
    Agnes .......... 25,26,79,137,188,239, 309,310
    Albert ......................................... 25
    Albert Chas ............................. 359
    Bessie .26,79,137,188,259,336,359
    Charles ....... 25,26,79,137,150,200, 253,326,384,388
    Charles (Albert) .................. 79,137
    Clara ................................. 310,369
    Cora .............................. 36,91,148
    David ..25,79,137,188,239,309,388
    Edith ......... 26,79,137,188,239,310
    Elmer ......... 239,275,366,384,386
    Emma .............. 25,79,137,188,309
    Emma F .................................. 239
    Florence .......... 26,79,153,204,257, 319,332
    Frank ......... 25,79,137,188,239,309
    Grace ........ 26,79,138,189,240,310
    Gusta ......... 25,79,137,188,240,310
    Henry .26,79,103,137,146,188,197, 239,249,310,321
    Hillman ............ 26,79,189,240,311
    James ..25,79,137,188,240,310,377
    Jennie ....................................... 374
    John ....25,79,137,188,239,310,359
    Josie ....................... 26,79,137,188
    Kitty .......... 25,79,137,188,240,310
    Leon .......... 25,79,137,188,239,309
    Mabel .... 240,273,275,366,367,386
    Margaret ... 25,79,137,188,239,310
    Mary .52,107,164,214,268,310,348
    Mary R ............................. 239,310
    Milton ......... 26,52,79,108,137,138, 188,189,240,310,311
    Mona ................................. 240,366
    Mona F ............................. 188,310
    Mrs Henry ................................. 47
    Peter .......... 25,79,137,188,239,309
    Philip .................. 188,239,310,360
    Richard .................................... 311
    Richard J .................................. 369
    Rosa ................. 26,79,137,188,239
    Rose ............................ 188,240,310
    Sadie ..... 25,26,79,80,137,138,188, 189,239,240,311,360
    Stanley ....... 26,79,138,189,240,310
    Warren ............................. 138,189
    Wesley ............. 25,79,137,188,239

# Index

Willis ........................................... 364
Willis Warren .................... 240,311
Winn ........................ 188,240,310
LITTLEWOLF
   Anna Mary ............................... 311
   Charles ................ 26,189,240,311
   Charles Homer .................... 80,138
   Claude ....... 27,80,138,189,241,311
   Esther G ................................... 311
   Esther Geraldine ..................... 240
   Eva ..... 26,80,138,189,240,311,357
   Frank ......... 26,80,138,189,240,311
   Geraldine ............... 26,80,138,189
   Herbert ................ 189,240,311,366
   Homer ........................................ 26
   Kate .......... 26,80,138,189,240,311
   Laban ............ 80,138,189,240,311, 362,377
   Laura .. 26,80,138,189,240,275,386
   Lena .......... 26,80,138,189,240,311
   Lydia ....................................... 345
   Mamie .............. 27,80,138,189,301
   Mary .... 26,27,80,131,138,182,189, 233,240,300
   May ..... 26,27,80,138,189,240,241, 311,340
   Robert ....... 26,80,138,189,240,311
   Susan .......... 26,80,138,189,240,311
   William ..... 27,80,138,189,241,311
   William, Jr 27,80,138,189,241,311
LITTLEYELLOWMAN
   Ed, Jr ....................................... 384
   Eddie ......... 27,80,138,189,241,311
   Eddie, Jr .................................. 366
   Ernest J .................................... 382
   Gertrude ........... 27,80,159,209,262
   Hugh .......... 27,80,139,189,241,312
   Hugh E .................................... 312
   Hugh Everett .......................... 369
   Ida S ........................................ 283
   J Ernest ............................ 138,362
   Jake ............ 27,80,139,190,241,312
   Lena ................... 190,241,312,388
   Lena Fisher ............................. 139
   May ........... 53,80,138,189,241,312
   Richard ....... 27,81,139,190,241,312
   Rose ......... 53,80,138,189,241,311, 354,386
   Susie ........ 53,80,138,189,241,311
LITTLEYES, Baby ..................... 382
LIVINGSTON
   Gail .......................................... 312
   Gail Bolson ............................. 241
LOHMILLER, C B ...... 3,5,55,57,113, 114,117,169,217,219,271,273
LONEBULL, Louis .......... 27,81,139, 177,227,292
LONEELK
   George ................ 241,273,312,367
   Sarah A ...................... 190,241,312
   Wilson ............ 27,81,190,241,312
LONEJAW, Claudia .................... 273
LONELEK, Wilson ..................... 145
LONETRAVELINGWOLF, Mabel
   ........................... 27,81,158,202,303
LONEWOLF
   Charles ...... 27,81,139,190,241,312
   Ella ..... 27,81,139,183,234,302,358
   James ........ 27,81,139,183,234,302
   Lloyd .................................. 27,81
   Mary ............................. 27,81,139
   Romeo .................................... 375
   Rosa .............................. 27,81,139
   Rose .................................. 81,139
LONGEARS .................. 202,254,328
   Maggie ......................... 39,94,151
LONGJAW
   Albert ........ 28,81,139,190,241,312
   Bernice ..................... 139,242,313
   Bernice M ............................... 190
   Bessie ............................... 359,377
   Charles ...... 27,81,139,190,241,312
   Charles, Jr. 27,81,139,190,241,312
   Clara ......... 27,28,81,139,190,241, 312,388
   Claudia ..................... 242,313,367
   Cora ........................................ 139
   Cora S ..................................... 380
   Cora Sharpnose .................... 27,81
   Donald .... 81,139,190,242,313,362
   Elmer ........ 27,81,139,190,241,312
   Frank ........ 27,81,139,190,242,313
   Henry ........ 28,81,139,190,241,312
   James ......... 27,28,81,139,190,242, 313,380
   Jennie ............................... 139,190

# Index

Lena ......... 28,81,139,190,241,312
Nellie......... 27,81,139,190,242,313
Robert 27,81,139,190,242,313,360
Thomas ............................ 357,377
LONGROACH ............................. 242
   Emma.......................................313
   Frank ......... 28,81,140,190,242,295
   George....... 28,81,139,190,242,313
   Harry......... 28,81,139,190,242,295
   James......... 28,81,140,190,242,295
   Mary.......... 28,81,140,190,242,295
   May ........................ 28,81,360,380
   Nellie................ 28,81,139,190,242
   Regina ....... 28,81,140,190,242,295
   Veria ......... 28,81,140,190,242,295
   Vita ................. 28,81,140,190,295
LOOKSATBAREGROUND
   James................... 140,190,242,313
   Jas .........................................28,82
   Julia.... 28,82,140,191,242,313,388
LOOKSBEHIND
   Anne......... 53,109,166,215,270,351
   Camilla...... 53,82,140,191,242,313
   Charles ...... 28,82,140,191,242,313
   Fannie .....................................320
   Inez ....... 209,263,275,366,384,386
   James.... 28,53,82,140,191,242,313
   James, Jr........... 28,82,140,191,242, 313,360
   Pius ........................ 28,82,242,313
   Roy............ 53,82,140,191,242,313
   Sallie ......... 28,82,140,191,242,313
   Sarah .........................................209
   Sarah W B ................................140
   Thomas ................... 28,82,140,384
LOSTLEG
   Ernest George......... 28,82,140,191, 242,313
   George.....................................373
   Gertrude ........................ 28,82,380
   James......... 28,82,140,191,242,313
   Nelson ....... 28,82,140,191,242,275, 384,386
   Sally ........................................334
   Theodore ........... 28,82,140,191,313
   Theodorea ................................. 28
   Virgina ....................................191
   Virginia ................ 28,140,243,313

   Virginia Theodorea................... 82
LOW BROW
   Anna ....................................... 288
   Sadie........................................ 309
MAGPIE
   Albert........ 28,82,140,191,243,314
   Anna ....................................... 377
   Anna Mary 28,82,140,191,243,314
   Anne ........ 28,82,140,191,243,314
   Annie ...................................... 373
   Eddie........ 29,82,140,191,243,314
   Eddy ............................. 29,82,140
   Edward ..................................... 82
   Eva................................. 28,82,140
   Gilbert....... 28,82,140,191,243,314
   Julia ......... 28,82,140,191,243,314
   Louis......... 29,82,140,191,243,314
   Minnie ............ 28,82,191,243,314
   Mira .......... 29,82,140,191,243,314
   Mrs Louis ..................... 18,71,130
   Rose ....................... 29,82,359,380
MANBEAR
   Lena.......... 29,82,140,191,243,314
   Lizzie ........ 29,82,140,191,243,314
   Walters Collidge..................... 140
   Walters Coolidge ................. 29,82
MANUEL, Mexican .................... 373
MARROWBONE, Jessie... 29,82,141, 191,243,314
MEDICINE
   Anna ......... 29,83,141,191,243,314
   Jennie........ 29,83,141,192,243,314
   Sampson ......... 29,83,141,191,243, 314,374
MEDICINEBEAR
   Ella ........................................... 29
   Homer....................................... 29
   Maggie.................... 29,83,141,382
   Nelson....................................... 29
MEDICINEBIRD
   Ella ................ 83,141,192,243,314
   Homer....................................... 83
   Homer J ..................... 192,243,314
   Homer James .......................... 141
   Nelson.......... 83,141,192,243,314
   Ruth .......... 41,96,130,181,231,298
   Ruth Maude ................ 45,100,157
MEDICINEBULL

# Index

Anne..........29,83,141,192,243,315
Bert ................192,243,315,360
Donald.....................29,83,380
Fred....29,83,141,192,243,315,359
James........29,141,192,243,315,388
Mae ..............243,273,315,366,367
Maggie ......29,83,141,192,243,314
Robert .......29,83,141,192,243,314
Ruth................29,141,192,243,333
Willis............18,29,71,83,130,141,
192,243,314
MEDICINEELK
Alice......................................373
Alice Sarah............................362
Andrew .....30,83,141,192,244,315
Basil .........29,83,141,192,244,315
Claude..................83,141,362,384
Harold 29,83,141,192,244,275,386
James.................141,192,244,315
James Edw ..........................30,83
Jennie............29,141,187,238,308
Jennie E.................................83
John...........29,83,141,192,244,315
Leo ..............267,346,366
Maggie ...................30,83,141,315
Maggie B........................192,244
Margaret.............192,244,315,366
May ......................359,377
Nellie T ...............83,141
Nellie Teeth..............................30
Peter...30,83,141,192,244,315,359
Sarah A ......................187,238,308
Sarah Alice.........................83,141
Spence...............................141
Spencer ............29,83,210,264,343
Thomas ..........30,83,141,192,244,
315,388
William ...83,141,204,257,332,362
MEDICINEFLYING
Agnes ........................30,84,142
Agnes S .....................192,244,315
Alice..........39,93,150,201,253,327
Bernice............30,84,139,190,313
Bertha........30,84,141,192,244,315
Clifford ..................142,364,385
Helen....................30,84,141
Helen J ......................192,244,315
Jennie ...................30,84,242,313

John .........30,84,141,192,244,315
Leoris....................................377
Phyllis..................30,84,142,357
Phyllis A ....................192,244,315
MEDICINETOP
Andrew.....................359,375
Clarance.....................................84
Clarence.........30,142,193,244,316
Edward ........142,193,244,316,364
Ida..............30,84,142,193,244,315
James ........30,84,142,192,244,315
John ..........30,84,142,192,244,315
Lena........84,142,193,244,316,362
Majorie .....................193,244,316
Marjorie........................30,84,142
Phyllis........30,84,142,193,244,316
Roy .....30,84,142,193,244,316,357
MERITT
Josie........................................316
Wesley.....................................316
MERRITT
Josie..........30,84,142,193,244,316
Wesley......30,84,142,193,244,316
MEXICAN CHEYENNE, Rudolph ...
357
MEXICANCHEYENNE
Anabelle ........................30,84,142
Anna Joyce ..142,193,245,303,364
Annabelle........................193,245
Dorothy........................30,86,144
Emma ........30,84,142,193,245,304
Ernest........30,84,142,193,244,303
Ethel .........30,84,142,193,245,304
Harriet.................142,193,245,303
Hilda................30,84,142,193,245
James ........30,84,142,193,245,304
M Victoria .................193,245,303
Mabel Ann...........84,142,193,245,
304,362
Margaret ...30,84,142,193,245,304
Marion ......30,84,142,193,245,303
Mary ........30,84,142,193,245,303,
304,359
Mary Victoria ................30,84,142
Rosa..........30,84,142,193,245,304
Rudolph ....30,84,142,193,245,303
Stephen.....................................303
MILES......................37,92,149,252

411

# Index

Rhoda .................................... 200
MONOTHY, Albert ............... 293,316
NICETALKER
    Clarice ....... 34,88,160,210,263,342
    Nora ..................................... 320
NIGHTWALKING
    James ............... 28,82,191,242,313
    Roy ........................................ 53
OLDBULL
    Clara .................................. 284,332
    Daniel ........ 30,84,142,193,245,316
    Gertrude ............................... 316
    Lena ..................................... 312
    Lucy ..................................... 290
    Ross ...................................... 375
    Thomas ..... 30,84,142,193,245,316
ONEBEAR
    James ......... 31,84,142,193,245,316
    Josie ..................................... 334
    Louise ....................... 245,316,366
    Maggie ....... 31,84,142,193,245,316
    May ....................................... 311
    Robert ....... 31,84,142,245,316,359
    Wayne ............................. 316,370
PARKER
    Alice .......... 31,85,143,194,246,317
    Alvin O ..... 31,84,142,193,245,316
    Charles A ................... 194,245,317
    Charles A, Jr ................. 31,85,143
    Charlotte ............. 194,246,317,366
    Clyde S ....................... 193,245,316
    Clyde Spencer ................ 31,85,142
    Donald E ................... 193,245,317
    Donald Edw ........................... 364
    Donald Edward ...................... 143
    Edwin ................. 143,194,246,317
    Edwin H .............................. 31,85
    Ethel ..................................... 328
    Gabriel ............. 31,85,143,194,245, 317,360
    Gertrude ............................. 31,85
    Guy ......... 31,85,143,194,246,317
    Lyle Neal ............. 245,273,317,367
    Marie ................................... 31,85
    May ...................................... 296
    Mildred ............................... 31,84
    Rhoda .................................. 345
    Shirley R ................... 193,245,316
Shirley Rose .................. 31,85,142
Shirley Ross ........................... 360
Stella ... 31,85,143,194,246,317,341
Theresa ..... 31,85,143,194,245,317
Verda .................................... 316
Verda F ...................... 193,245,357
Verda Faye .................... 31,85,142
Vincent ............................ 359,380
Vincent Albert ..................... 31,85
Winfred ..... 31,85,143,194,246,317
PEASE
    George ................................ 31,85
    Ida .................. 31,143,194,246,317
    Ida (Eastman) ........................... 85
PINE
    Alexander . 31,85,143,194,246,317
    Bessie ................................... 373
    Cecelia ...... 31,85,143,194,246,317
    Daniel ....... 31,85,143,194,246,317
    Frank ......... 31,85,143,194,246,317
    John ......... 31,85,143,194,246,317
    Josie ......... 10,63,122,174,224,288
    Julia .......... 31,85,143,194,246,317
    Nora .......... 31,85,143,194,246,317
    Nora W ........................... 194,246
    Rutherford 31,85,143,194,246,317
    Sarah ......... 31,85,143,194,246,357
    Sarah Mary ........................... 318
    Wilson ......... 31,32,85,86,137,143, 194,246,317
PLAYINGBEAR ........................ 143
    Henry ........ 31,85,143,194,246,318
    John ............................... 32,85,385
    Mary ............... 32,85,179,229,296
    Mary P ................................. 128
    Mildred ..... 31,85,143,194,246,318
PLENTYCAMPS
    Clara ...................... 32,85,143,380
    Flora ..................................... 323
PLENTYCROWS
    Lena ..................................... 288
    Olive .................................... 340
PORCUPINE
    Albert ..................... 32,86,143,382
    Julia ............................. 32,86,143
POWDERFACE
    Bessie ................................... 346
    Fern ........... 32,86,143,194,246,318

# Index

Jennie ... 377
John ... 32,86,143,194,246,318
Julia ... 32,86,137,188,239,309
Madge ... 12,64,124,175,225
POWELL
  Clay ... 32,86,144,194,246,318
  Deyo ... 32,86,144,194,246,318
  Edward ... 32,86
  Howard ... 32,86,144,194,246,318
  Mary ... 32,86,143,194,246,318
  Ollie ... 32
PRAIRIEBEAR
  Arthur ... 32,86,144,195,246,318
  A Louis ... 246,318
  Louis ... 144,195,364
  Sallie ... 195,246,318
  Sally ... 32,86,144
REDBEAD
  Clara ... 195,247,318
  Georgia ... 195,247,318
  Gloria ... 195,247,318
  John ... 195,247,318
  Nancy ... 195,247,318
  Susie ... 195,247,318
REDBEADS
  Clara ... 32,86,144,318
  Georgia ... 32,86,144,318
  Gloria ... 32,86,144,318
  John ... 32,86,144,318
  Nancy ... 32,86,144,318
  Susie ... 32,86,144,318
REDBIRD
  Allen .. 32,86,144,195,247,319,357
  David ... 86,144,207,261,338,362
  Diva ... 247,273,319,367
  Dorothy ... 144,207,261,338
  Dorothy M C ... 86
  Ellen ... 301,354,359
  Eva ... 301
  Evelyn ... 377
  Florence ... 32,86,144,195,247,388
  Flornce ... 319
  Fred C ... 359,377
  Helena ... 32,86,144,195,247,319
  Joseph ... 32,86,144,195,247,318
  Joseph Francis ... 32,86,144,195, 247,318
  Lena ... 32,86,144,195,247,319
  Lucille ... 247,318
  Mary ... 17,32,38,93,150,201, 253,326
  Maxine ... 38,93,150,201,253,326
  Samuel ... 144,195,247,319,364
  Susie ... 32,86,144,195,247
  William ... 32,86,144,195,247, 318,319
  Willis ... 375
REDBREATH
  Betty ... 32,86,144,195,247,319
  Charles ... 32,86,144,195,247,319
  Elina J ... 195,247,319
  Elina Jane ... 32,86,144,357
  Elina June . 32,86,144,195,247,319
  George .... 86,144,195,247,319,362
  Gertrude ... 43,98,155,206,259
  Percy ... 98
  Percy (Walter) ... 43
REDCHERRIES
  Alice ... 33,87,144,195,247,319
  Anna ... 33,87,145,177,282
  Anne ... 289
  Bessie ... 33,87,144,195,247,319
  Della ... 248,273,319,366,367
  Frank ... 33,87,144,195,247,319
  Katie ... 87,144,195,248,319
  Late ... 362
  Margaret ... 33,87,144,195,248,319
  Mille ... 319
  Miller ... 53,86,144,195,247
  Rose ... 33,87,144,195,247,319
  Teddy ... 33,53,86,144,160,195, 210,247,264,319,343
  Wallace ... 145,177,364
  William ... 33,87,144,195,247,319
REDEAGLE
  Jennie ... 33,87,145,192,243,314
  Nellie 27,33,81,87,145,196,248,319
  Willis ... 33,87,145,196,248,319
REDFOX
  Alice ... 359
  Cecelia. 33,37,87,145,196,248,320
  Cecleia ... 92
  Cora ... 33,87,145,196,248,275, 385,386
  Edna ... 33,87,145,360
  Edna S ... 196,248,320

# Index

James........ 33,87,145,196,248,320
Jennie. 33,87,145,196,248,320,388
Myrtle Alcie.............................. 375
Nora ........................................ 320
Ralph................. 196,248,320,366
Robert ...... 33,87,145,196,248,320
Vinnie ..................................... 293
REDNECK
    Clyde........ 33,87,120,197,248,320
    Curtis........ 33,87,145,196,248,320
    David........ 33,87,145,196,248,320
    Dora .......... 33,87,145,196,248,320
    Fannie ...... 33,87,145,196,248,320
    Florence .... 33,87,145,196,248,320
    Grace ....................... 33,87,145,334
    Henry ....... 33,87,145,196,248,320
    Homer ...... 33,87,145,196,248,320
    John.... 33,87,145,196,248,320,357
    Josei ........................................ 87
    Josie .............. 33,145,196,248,320
    Minnie....... 33,87,145,196,248,320
    Nora ....................................... 333
    Pius ........... 28,82,140,191,242,313
REDNOSE
    Lucy .......... 33,88,145,196,248,320
    Mae ........................................... 34
    Paul ........... 33,88,145,196,248,320
    Sarah ......................................... 34
    Sarah Mae ...... 88,145,214,268,335
REDOWL, Mabel ............. 34,88,145,
170,220,283
REDROBE
    Alice .......... 34,88,146,197,249,321
    Carrie ...................................... 303
    Flora ..................... 47,103,160,327
    Fred ........... 34,88,145,196,248,320
    Jasper ....... 34,88,146,196,248,320
    Jennie ..................................... 284
    Louis ......... 34,88,146,196,248,320
    Madge .................................... 289
    Nora ........... 34,88,145,196,248,320
    William ..... 34,88,146,196,249,321
REDSLEEVES, Kate .................... 311
REDWATER
    Cecelia ...... 34,88,146,197,249,321
    Martha ................................ 34,88
    Thaddeus... 34,88,146,197,249,321
REDWOMAN

Donald ......... 146,197,249,340,364
Edna....34,88,146,197,249,340,360
Ella ................................. 34,88,380
Eugene ...... 34,88,146,197,249,321
Flossie................................. 34,302
Flossie A ......................... 197,249
Flossie Alice ...................... 88,146
Frank....... 34,88,146,197,249,321
George ............................. 88,146
George P ................. 209,262,341
George Philip........................ 363
Joe ............ 34,88,146,197,249,321
John ...... 197,249,321,340,354,367
Julia ............................. 34,88,342
Lucy........................................ 375
Manuel............ 34,88,146,197,249,
275,386
Olive ......... 34,88,146,197,249,340
Paul .................................... 88,146
RIDGEBEAR
    Anna ...34,88,146,197,249,321,361
    Bessie A .................... 197,249,321
    Bessie Agnes ................ 34,88,146
    Carrie ........ 34,88,146,197,249,321
    Chares................................... 197
    Charles............. 34,88,146,249,321
    James ........... 146,197,249,321,364
    Jerry K ............................. 321,369
    Katie ....................... 34,88,146,197
    Rilla .......... 34,88,146,197,249,321
    Willis ........ 34,88,146,197,249,321
RIDGEWALKER
    Ethel ......... 34,89,146,197,249,321
    Frank......... 34,89,146,197,249,321
    Robert ....... 34,88,146,197,249,321
RISINGFIRE, Bessie ......... 34,89,146,
197,249,321
RISINGSUN
    Alice ....... 34,35,39,88,89,146,147,
197,249,321,325
    Bessie ..................... 35,89,147,382
    Edna Josie................. 198,250,322
    Elizabeth......... 35,146,197,250,322
    Elizabeth Martha ...................... 89
    Harry.......... 35,89,147,198,250,322
    Henry L ................................. 373
    Irvin Wm ........................ 322,369
    James ..35,89,147,198,250,322,357

# Index

Jennie ................................ 283
Jessie ............................. 35,89
John ............ 35,89,147,198,250,322
Jordan ......................... 322,369
Lyman ........ 35,89,147,198,250,322
Margaret ............................ 281
Martha ............................... 35
Maude ............ 35,89,147,197,305
Nora ............ 35,89,147,198,250,322
Oliver ......... 35,89,146,197,249,322
Pearl ............... 147,198,250,322,364
Peter ......... 35,89,147,197,250,322
Philip ......... 35,89,147,198,250,322
Ruby ............. 147,202,255,329,364
Shell .................................. 34
Teddy . 35,89,146,197,250,322,361
William ..... 35,89,147,198,250,322
ROBINSON
   Buell ............................. 147,364
   Buell D ...................... 198,250,322
   Cornelius .......................... 198,250
   Cornelius Clay ............. 35,89,147
   Cornelius D ............................ 322
   David ............................ 35,89,147
   David C ..................... 198,250,322
   Eloise E ...................... 198,250,322
   Eloise Elaine ................ 35,89,147
   James M ........................ 322,369
   Major ............................... 35,89
   Nellie ......... 35,89,147,198,250,322
ROCKROADS
   Bert ................................... 377
   Buell D ............................... 198
   Flossie .............. 198,250,322,366
   James ................................ 377
   Jessie ............................... 306
   Lettie ......... 35,89,147,198,250,322
   Mack ............... 35,89,147,250,322
   Mary ........ 35,89,147,198,250,323, 359,380
   Nellie .. 35,89,147,198,250,313,322
   Nora ........... 35,89,147,198,250,323
   Rhoda ............... 37,92,135,186,237
   Thomas ..... 35,89,147,198,250,322
ROLLINGBULL
   Emma ............................... 304
   Rufus ....... 47,102,159,209,262,341
ROMANNOSE

Blanche ..... 35,90,147,198,250,323
Edith .................................. 338
Eva L ........................ 198,240,310
Eva Louise ............................ 147
George ...... 35,90,147,198,250,323
Helen ........ 35,90,147,198,250,323
Julia ......... 35,90,147,198,250,323
Lee .................................... 369
Louis ......... 35,89,147,198,250,323
Mary ..................... 35,90,147,198
May ................. 35,90,147,198,323
Montana .... 35,90,147,198,250,323
Ruth .................................. 377
Sarah ................................ 359
Willeatte ... 35,90,147,198,250,323
Willette ............................... 323
ROMONNOSE, Louise ............... 364
RONDEAU
   Antoine ..... 35,90,147,198,250,323
   Charles ...... 36,90,148,198,250,323
   Clara ............... 35,90,148,198,250
   Hattie ................................ 375
   Henry ........ 36,90,148,198,251,323
   John ......................... 198,251,323
   John R ......................... 36,90,148
   Louisa ......................... 35,90,148
   Louise ...................... 198,250,323
   Marie .................................. 90
   William ..... 36,90,148,198,251,323
ROUNDSTONE
   David ................................ 375
   Flora ......... 36,90,148,199,251,323
   Fred ............................. 36,90,323
   Louis ................................ 375
   Martin ....... 36,90,148,199,251,323
   Mary ................................. 324
   Mary G ........................... 251,324
   Nellie ................................ 294
   Paul .......... 36,90,148,199,251,323
   Ruth ....36,90,148,199,251,323,361
   Sallie ................................ 318
   Sarah ........ 36,90,148,199,251,323
   Victoria ......................... 324,369
ROWLAND
   Alice ............... 37,91,185,236,305
   Alice R .............................. 134
   Allen E ..................... 199,251,324
   Allen Edsel ............ 36,91,148,359

# Index

Annie .................................. 37,91
Annie-Anna .................... 36,90,148
Ardeth F ..................... 199,251,324
Ardeth Faye ............................. 363
Ardith Faye ........................ 91,148
Benjamin ... 37,91,120,172,222,285
Benton ........ 37,91,149,199,251,324
Blanche36,90,148,199,251,324,359
Carrie . 36,91,149,182,233,300,361
Chester C .................... 199,251,324
Chester Clay .................. 36,91,148
Claude ....... 37,91,120,172,222,285
Clay .................................. 36,90,148
Clay T ........................ 199,251,324
Daisy .......... 36,90,148,199,251,324
Don ................ 90,148,199,251,324
Don Edward ............................. 363
Edna ........ 37,91,149,199,251,325
Elizabeth .......... 36,91,195,247,324
Elizabeth A ............................. 352
Emma .............................. 290,339
Emma Bites ............ 37,91,158,261
Eugene ..................... 199,251,324
Eugene A ..................... 91,149,363
Frances .................................... 91
Frank .... 36,90,91,148,199,251,325
George ..................... 36,91,148,383
Grace .......... 36,91,148,199,251,325
Helen .. 36,91,148,199,251,275,386
James ................................... 377
Jennie ................................ 36,90
Jesse ..................... 36,90,148,325
Jessie ................................. 199,251
Joe ............. 36,90,148,199,251,324
Jose ........... 36,90,148,199,251,324
Julia .................... 251,273,324,367
Lillian ......... 36,90,148,195,247,324
Lizzie ............................ 36,90,148
Lottie ....... 48,103,160,210,263,342
Marie ......... 37,91,149,199,251,324
Mary .................................... 318
Richard ........... 8,60,120,172,222,285
Sally ......................... 36,90,148,385
Sarah .................... 36,91,148,199
Thomas ..... 36,90,148,199,251,324
William ..... 36,91,148,199,251,324
Willis ......... 36,91,148,199,251,324
Wilma ............................... 36,91

Zac24,37,77,91,136,149,199,251,325
RUSSELL
Alice ................................... 325
Alice R ......................... 199,252
Clara ..................... 37,92,149,172
Clifford ............ 252,273,325,367
Earl .......... 37,92,149,200,252,325
Ellen ............... 149,199,252,325
Ford ............... 37,92,149,357,382
Frank ....... 37,92,135,149,186,199,
237,252,325
Fred .......... 37,92,149,200,252,325
Herman ........... 37,92,149,172,357
Hubert ........................... 325,369
Inez I ................ 200,252,275,386
Inez Irma ..................... 37,91,149
Jessie ............... 37,92,135,186,237
John ......... 37,91,149,199,252,325
John, Jr . 149,200,252,275,364,386
Joseph M ............................... 380
Joseph Melvin ..................... 37,91
Mary ........ 37,92,149,200,252,325
May .....37,91,149,200,252,275,386
Mildred ........... 37,92,149,200,325
Sadie ............................ 37,92,380
Sallie ...................................... 92
Stella ..................... 199,252,325
Stella Mildred .............. 37,91,149
William ..... 37,92,149,200,252,325
SALZER
Alta ................................... 336
Frances ......................... 336,369
SANCHEZ
Cecelia ...... 37,92,145,196,248,320
Grace E ................................ 374
Pauline ....... 37,92,145,196,248,320
SANDCRANE
Anna ............................. 252,325
Anne ........................... 37,92,381
Annie May ..................... 357,375
Bessie ....... 17,70,129,180,230,297
Emily May .................... 37,92,149
Harry ..................... 37,92,361,381
Henry ........ 37,92,149,200,252,325
Isabelle ..... 38,92,149,200,252,326
John .......... 38,92,149,200,252,325
Margaret .................. 200,252,325
Peter ................. 180,230,297,364

# Index

Ruth.......... 38,92,149,200,252,326
SANDSTONE, Bessie ................374
SANDWOMAN, John .......29,83,141, 192,244,315
SANSAVER, Lillian..........37,92,149, 200,252,291
SANSOVER
   Lillian......................37,92,149,252
   Rhoda.....................................200
SCABBY, Lucy ..........................284
SCALPCANE
   August................. 149,200,252,326
   August Paul.........................38,92
   Henry........ 38,92,149,200,252,326
   Otto ........... 38,92,149,200,252,326
   Rudolph..... 38,92,149,200,252,326
SCHAFFER
   Carl ..................... 109,166,200,326
   George..............................109,326
   Letha .................. 109,200,252,326
   Letha E ...................................166
SCOTT, Josie...........................41,96
SEMINOLE ........................363,375
   (Unnamed) ..............................370
   Alfred........ 38,92,150,200,253,326
   Alice.......................................350
   Anna.......... 38,92,150,200,253,326
   Baby ..................................93,381
   Beatrice ........ 150,200,253,326,364
   Cora........................................351
   Dan........ 26,38,92,150,200,253,326
   David.......... 38,93,150,212,265,345
   Delbert ...... 38,93,150,173,223,286
   Eva ..................................326,369
   Falling ...............................357,374
   Flora.......................................327
   Fred ........... 38,92,150,200,253,326
   Gertrude .................................286
   Hannah...... 38,93,150,173,223,299
   Helen......................................383
   Helen May.........................150,364
   Jennie . 38,92,150,200,253,289,326
   John........... 38,92,149,200,253,326
   Joseph ....................................150
   Josephine.......... 38,93,201,253,327
   Jule .................................326,369
   Jules ......................................377
   Julia........................................293

Lawrence ....... 38,150,201,253,327
Lawrence (Smoky) .....................93
Lorraine .... 38,93,150,212,265,345
Louis.......... 38,93,150,201,253,327
Louise.....................................193
Lucille................. 253,273,327,367
Maggie...... 31,84,142,193,245,316
Margaret ... 38,92,150,200,253,326
Mary ............................... 326,375
Mary R.......................... 200,253
Mary Redbird .................... 92,149
Max.....38,93,150,201,253,326,357
Miles.......... 38,93,150,201,253,327
Mollie .................................... 328
Rhoda .......... 37,38,92,93,149,150, 200,252
Rising ............................. 357,374
Robert .................................... 193
Sadie....................................... 377
Smoky....................................... 38
Theodore..................... 38,93,150
Tom .......................... 51,107,267
SEMINOLE (WOODENLEG), [Blank] ................................................. 389
SHARPNOSE
   Baby ........................ 93,361,381
   Bessie .......................... 38,93,381
   Chas .......... 24,78,149,200,252,326
   Cora ....................................... 139
   Daisy....................................... 374
   Edward C ............................... 381
   Edward Chas...................... 38,93
   Josephine .. 38,93,150,201,253,327
SHAVEDHEAD
   Alice ......... 39,93,150,201,253,327
   Anna ...39,93,151,201,253,327,359
   Anna M...................... 201,254,327
   Anna Marjorie ........ 38,93,150,359
   Charles...... 38,93,150,201,254,327
   Hyacinth ... 39,93,151,201,253,327
   James ........ 39,93,150,201,253,327
   Jean...................... 38,93,150,327
   Jean S............................. 201,253
   Jeffrey................................ 38,93
   Jeffrey, Jr .. 38,93,150,201,254,327
   Lucille.................. 93,151,363,385
   Mabel................. 201,253,327,366
   Marjorie ................................ 361

## Index

Marjorie A. ................................. 327
Mary ............. 14,39,66,93,150,201,
253,327
SHEBEAR, Blanche ..................... 330
SHELL
   Alice ................. 39,88,146,249,321
   Alice [Risingsun] ........ 94,151,201,
254,328
   Elsie ......................... 39,94,359,381
   Joseph ....... 39,93,151,201,254,328
   Julia ........... 39,94,151,201,254,328
   Minnie ............................ 39,94,151
   Paul ............................................ 377
SHEPHERD
   Clarence ......................... 39,94,328
   Mollie ........ 39,94,151,201,254,328
SHERMAN
   Carl ............ 39,94,151,201,254,328
   Clarence ......... 94,151,202,254,328
   Clarence Oliver ......................... 39
   Ethel ..................... 151,201,254,328
   Ethel Parker .......................... 39,94
   Frances ........................... 39,94,128
   Francis .............................. 179,230
   George ............. 39,94,201,254,328
   George, Jr ........................ 39,94,151
   Otto ........... 39,94,151,201,254,328
   Wretha ....... 39,94,151,201,254,328
SHIELDS, Maude ........................ 161
SHORTSIOUX ..... 25,79,137,239,309
   Anna ............................................ 98
   Annie ................ 42,98,155,205,335
   Emma ........................................ 188
   Lucy .......................................... 301
   Mary .......... 39,94,151,202,254,328
SHOULDERBLADE
   Alice T ..................................... 377
   Alice Thurla ............................. 357
   Benedict .... 39,94,151,202,254,328
   Claudia ................ 254,273,329,367
   Ethel .......... 39,94,151,202,254,328
   Everett J ....... 202,254,276,385,387
   Everett John .................. 39,94,151
   Fannie ........................ 202,254,328
   Fern ................. 94,151,202,254,329
   Fern Ruth ................................. 363
   Francis ....... 39,94,151,202,254,328
   Fred ........... 39,94,151,202,254,328

Josie ................. 41,96,153,204,256
Lucy .......................................... 378
Mary Josie ............................... 332
Pius .....39,94,151,202,254,276,386
Richard ..... 39,94,151,202,254,328
Theodore ........................... 361,378
Thomas ..... 39,94,151,202,254,328
Wendel ..... 39,94,151,202,254,328
William ..... 39,94,151,202,254,328
SILLOWAY
   Lloyd ..................................... 39,94
   Veta ................... 151,202,254,329
   Veta (Burns) ............................. 39
   Veta Burns ................................ 94
SIOUX
   Bessie ...................................... 378
   Henry ........ 40,94,151,202,255,329
   Jacob ............................. 40,94,151
   Jane W ................ 202,255,329,389
   Nellie ....................................... 308
   Thomas ..... 39,94,151,202,255,329
SITTINGMAN
   Charles ...... 40,94,151,202,255,329
   Edw Chas ................................ 329
   Edward ............ 40,95,152,202,255
   Edwin ................. 40,152,202,255
   Ida Whitehawk .................. 95,152
   Lucy .......... 40,95,151,202,255,329
SMALL
   Clinton ................. 202,255,329,366
   Edward ..... 40,95,152,202,255,329
   Horace ...... 40,95,152,202,255,329
   Ivan ........... 40,95,152,202,255,329
   Josephine ..... 11,40,64,95,123,152,
202,255,289,329
   Kitty .......... 11,64,123,175,225,289
   Max J ......................... 202,255,329
   Max Joe ......................... 40,95,152
   Melvin ............ 40,95,152,202,255,
329,357
   Thomas ..... 40,95,152,202,255,329
   Vera Sue .................... 152,364,383
   Victor ........ 40,95,152,202,255,329
   Worth..40,95,152,202,255,329,361
SMITH
   Blanche ..... 40,95,152,203,255,330
   John .......... 40,95,152,203,255,329
SNOWBIRD, Anna ..................... 325

# Index

SOLDIERWOLF
  Annie K .................. 203,255,330
  Aurora ...................... 40,95,152
  Baby ............................ 365,385
  Bessie L .................. 203,255,330
  Doris ............ 255,273,330,366,368
  James K ................... 203,255,330
  James Kenneth ..................... 152
  John .......... 40,95,152,203,255,330
  Josie A .................... 203,255,330
  Katherine .................. 40,95,152
  Kenneth ................................ 40
  Kenneth Jas ........................... 95
  Lucy .......................... 40,95,152
  Mary .......................... 40,95,152
  Mary K .................... 203,255,330
  Thomas ................... 203,255,330
  Thos Chas ................ 40,95,152
  Veta ............................... 359,378
SOOKTIS
  Andrew .................. 330,354,359
  Josie ............................ 330,354
SPANG
  Alban ..................... 40,95,203,255
  Alban D ............................... 330
  Alfonso ..... 40,95,152,203,255,330
  Alfonso, Jr ........................ 330,370
  Alice Y ................................. 385
  Alice Y H ............................. 153
  Alice Yellowhorse ............... 41,96
  Annie .................. 152,203,255,330
  Bruce S .................... 203,255,330
  Bruce Spencer ................ 40,95,152
  Cash .......... 41,96,152,203,256,331
  A D ................................... 40,96
  Dale C ..................... 203,256,330
  Dale Coo[Er ........................... 95
  Dale Cooper ................ 40,152,361
  Darrel D ........................... 273,331
  Darrel Dean .......................... 256
  Darrell Dean .......................... 368
  Deyo .......... 40,95,152,203,255,330
  Edith ..................... 41,96,152,289
  Edward ................................ 203
  Edward F ................. 255,330,364
  Harriet ...... 41,96,152,203,256,331
  James .......... 40,95,152,203,256,331
  James R ..................... 203,256,331

James Russell .................. 95,152
Jennie ................................. 331
Jennie L ............................. 256
Jessie ......................... 41,96,153
Joyce ................. 256,273,331,368
Julia .................................. 290
Kitty .................................. 295
Lawrence R .................... 331,370
Lucille ............................. 40,95
Lucy ......... 40,96,152,203,256,331
Lyman ...... 41,96,153,203,256,331
Margie ............................. 40,95
Mary .................................. 330
Mary C ......................... 152,203
May C ................................ 255
Nellie ................................. 322
Nina Dawson ......................... 95
Norman ... 96,153,203,256,310,363
Peter A .................... 255,273,330
Peter Albert ......................... 368
Regina ................................ 203
Regina Rosetta
    ............ 41,96,153,203,256,331
Regina S ........................ 256,331
Regina Susanna ............ 41,96,153
Roy .......... 41,96,152,203,256,331
Ruth ................................... 95
Sarah ................... 40,96,152,345
Shirley A .................. 203,256,331
Shirley Ann ................ 95,152,363
Viola ........................ 203,256,331
Viola Alice ........................ 153
Wilfred ..... 41,96,153,203,256,331
SPEELMAN
  Jessie ....................... 203,256,331
  Orville ........................... 332,370
  William L ................. 204,256,331
  Wm Lawrence ..................... 366
SPONGE
  Alfred ....... 41,96,153,204,256,332
  Angeline ......................... 359,378
  Charles ........................... 332,370
  Clara ........ 41,96,153,204,256,332
  Henry ................................. 378
  Josie ............... 41,96,153,204,256
  Lena ......... 204,256,332,348,366
  Mary Josie ........................... 332
  Oliver ....... 41,96,153,204,256,332

## Index

Paul ......... 96,153,204,256,332,363
Rose ............................................. 378
Scott ........................... 204,256,332
Susie ............................................. 378
SPOTTEDBLACKBIRD
   Clara......... 41,96,153,204,256,332
   Lee ....... 17,41,96,153,204,256,332
   Leo ............ 41,96,153,204,256,332
SPOTTEDELK
   Alex........... 41,96,153,204,257,332
   August....... 41,96,153,204,257,332
   Charles ...... 41,96,153,204,257,332
   Eugene ....................... 332,354,368
   Jessie ............................ 51,107,164
   Mary........................................378
   Nellie.......................................332
   Nellie T ..................... 204,257,332
   Nelson ....................................378
   Nelson Miles...........................358
SPOTTEDHAWK
   Hugh ...................... 41,96,153,385
   Ruth................ 41,96,130,181,298
   Ruth M B ................................231
SPOTTEDWOLF
   Baby...........................................96
   Charles ...... 41,96,153,204,257,332
   Chas ....................................26,79
   Clarence Eugene ............... 257,333
   Della............. 204,257,276,366,387
   Earl........................ 41,96,361,381
   Eldora P...................................333
   Eldora Phyllis....................257,333
   Ella............................................314
   Eugene ............. 41,97,153,204,359
   Eugene C................................333
   Gertrude R..............................385
   Gertrude Rena .......................363
   James................... 333,354,368,370
   Jean ........... 41,97,153,204,257,333
   John............ 41,96,153,204,257,332
   Julia..................................41,204
   Julia E ................................257,332
   Julia Eva............................96,153
   Lena .......... 41,96,153,204,257,332
   Martha P..................... 204,257,332
   Mollie...... 97,154,204,257,333,363
   Patrick ....... 41,97,153,204,257,333
   Phyllis .................... 41,97,153,204

Piney............................... 41,96,153
Ruby ......... 41,97,153,204,257,333
SQUINTEYE
   John ........................................ 333
   Josie................. 154,204,257,333
   Nellie ..................................... 374
STANDINGELK
   (Clara) Jennie ....................... 42,97
   Aiden ........... 205,258,334,363,389
   Alex ........... 42,97,154,204,257,333
   Annie ........ 42,97,154,192,257,333
   Benno ................. 205,258,334,366
   Bessie .................................... 298
   Clara ...................................... 305
   Clara Jennie ........................... 361
   Ella .................... 42,97,154
   Ella J.................. 205,258,334,389
   Eugene .................................. 375
   Fannie ....... 42,97,154,205,257,334
   Flora ......... 42,97,154,205,257,334
   Francis ...... 42,97,154,205,257,333
   Frank......... 42,97,154,205,257,333
   Geneva............ 42,97,154,204,333
   Geneva S ............................... 257
   George ...... 42,97,154,334,370,383
   Henry ..42,97,154,205,257,334,358
   Henry, Jr ................................ 374
   Isaac................................. 333,370
   Jennie........................ 205,258,334
   Jennie Clara ........................... 154
   Jordan ............................... 333,370
   Lockwood. 42,97,154,205,258,334
   Margaret ......... 42,97,154,204,257,
   333,358
   Mary ..................... 97,334,363,381
   Mary S ........................... 205,257
   Nina ...................... 41,97,154,283
   Nora ......... 42,97,154,204,257,333
   Robert B ... 42,97,154,205,258,334
   Roy .....42,97,154,192,257,333,361
   Ruth ...................... 18,70,129,333
   Sally.......... 42,97,154,205,258,334
   Susan ..................................... 378
   Susie ...................................... 348
   Wayne...................... 205,257,333
STANDINGWOLF, Lena............. 332
STANDSINTIMBER
   Elva................ 97,154,205,258,334

## Index

Gilbert ............... 258,273,334,368
John ........... 42,97,154,205,258,334
John, Jr ...... 42,97,154,205,258,334
Josephine... 42,97,154,205,258,334
Josie ......... 42,97,154,205,258,334
Ruth Elva ............................... 363
STANDSOUT, Sallie ......... 42,97,154, 177,227,292
STAR
   Charles ............... 173,223,287,361
   May ........................ 173,223,286
   May Blackree ............... 42,97,154
   Minnie .................................... 154
STARVINGBEAR
   Jack .................. 42,98,155,205,258
   Jack J ................................... 335
   James ........ 42,97,155,205,258,335
   Lottie ......................... 42,98,155
   Mary ........................... 42,98,155
   Rosco .............. 42,98,155,258,335
STRANGEOWL
   Gertie ........ 42,98,155,205,258,335
   Grace .................................... 334
   Grace R ..................... 205,258,334
   James ........ 42,98,155,205,258,334
   John ........... 42,98,155,205,258,335
   Mary .......... 21,42,133,184,235,303
STRONGLEFTHAND
   Florence .................................. 349
   Josie ....................................... 333
STUMPHORN
   Anna ............... 43,155,196,248,319
   Annie ........ 42,98,155,205,258,335
   Frank .... 42,58,98,155,205,258,335
SUNBEAR
   Deyo .......... 43,98,155,205,258,335
   Florence ................................. 337
   Herman ..... 43,98,155,205,258,335
   John ....................... 43,98,155,383
   Louisa .................................... 284
   Michael ......................... 43,98,155
   Micheal .................... 205,258,335
SUNROADS
   David ......... 43,98,155,206,258,335
   John ........... 43,98,155,206,258,335
   Lena .......... 43,98,155,206,258,335
   Lizzie ........ 43,98,155,206,258,335
SWALLOW

Anne ........... 29,43,83,98,141,155, 192,243,315
Edward .......... 43,98,155,206,259, 335,389
Elsie ............ 257,273,333,366,368
Gertrude.... 43,98,155,206,259,335
Herbert ............................ 335,370
Jean ............................ 38,201,327
Johnnie ................................. 335
Julia ....................................... 284
Mae ........................................ 335
Mary ..................... 43,98,155,334
Oliver ........ 43,98,155,206,259,335
Percy .................................... 155
Percy R .............. 206,259,276,387
Rednose ................................ 335
William ..... 43,98,155,206,258,335
SWEETMEDICINE
   Alta ........... 43,99,156,206,259,336
   Clara ......... 43,98,155,206,259,336
   David ............. 98,155,206,259,335
   Davie ....................................... 43
   Ellen ..................... 43,99,199,325
   Jacob ......... 43,98,155,206,259,336
   Joseph ....... 43,98,155,206,259,336
   Thomas ..... 43,99,156,206,259,336
   William ..... 43,99,155,206,259,336
   Wm .......................................... 43
TALKS
   David ..................................... 260
   Florence ................................ 260
   Georgia .............. 156,207,260,337
   Georgia Marion ........................ 44
   Marie ..................................... 260
   Roberta .................................. 260
TALLBEAR
   DeForest ............................... 336
   Erma Jean ....................... 273,368
   Ermajean ......................... 259,336
   Josie ............................... 259,336
TALLBULL
   Albert ........ 43,99,156,206,259,336
   Cecil R ...................... 206,259,336
   Cecil Russell ........... 44,99,156,361
   Charles ............. 43,99,156,206,259, 336,389
   Charles, Jr ...................... 336,370
   Henry ........ 44,99,156,206,259,336

Joseph ....... 43,99,156,206,259,336
Mary.......... 43,99,156,206,259,336
Nellie............ 156,206,259,336,364
Nelson ....... 44,99,156,206,259,336
Nora ................ 44,99,156,206,259
William ..... 44,99,156,206,259,336
TALLWHITEMAN
 Agnes .............. 44,99,156,179,206, 229,295,359
 Agnes V ...................................337
 Agnes Virginia..................260,337
 Alice.......... 44,99,156,157,206,207, 259,260,337
 Clarence .... 44,99,156,206,259,336
 Dan.................................44,99,156
 Eleanor...... 44,99,156,206,259,336
 Elsie ..................................259,337
 Florence .......... 44,99,156,206,259, 260,337
 Frances....................................378
 Gertrude ............. 8,61,120,172,222
 Jasper . 44,99,156,206,259,336,337
 John........... 44,99,156,206,259,336
 John A .....................................381
 John E ......................................44
 Joseph ...........................44,99,381
 Laura ......................44,99,157,337
 Pat............................................383
 Patrick ...........................44,99,156
 Regina .......................207,260,337
 Rilla................................44,99,156
 Tug............ 44,99,156,206,259,337
TANGLEDHORNELK
 Bert .........................................100
 Chas ..........................................99
 Clara ........................................100
 David .......................................100
 Georgia Marion........................100
 James.......................................100
 Joseph ....... 38,93,150,201,253,326
 Josie .........................................100
 Lariath..............................100,157
 Minnie......................................100
 Nellie.......... 44,99,156,195,247,319
 Robert ......................................100
 Winona.....................................100
TANGLEDYELLOWHAIR
 Bert ....................44,156,361,385

Chas..................... 44,156,207,260
Clara ............. 44,157,207,260,332
David .......................... 44,156,207
Florence............................. 156,207
Georgia ...................... 156,207,260
Georgia Marion ........................ 44
James ................... 44,157,207,260
John Laraith............................. 363
Josie..................... 45,157,207,260
Marie ........................ 156,207,364
Minnie .................. 45,157,207,260
Nellie ........................................ 156
Olive ........................................ 375
Regina...................................... 375
Roberta ................. 44,156,207,358
Ruth ......................................... 370
Winona ................. 44,157,207,260
TANGLEHORNELK, Joseph ...... 378
TANGLEYELLOWHAIR
 Chas ........................................ 337
 Clara ......... 41,96,153,204,256,337
 David P .................................... 337
 Ella .......................................... 343
 Florence................................... 337
 Georgia .................................... 337
 James ...................................... 337
 Josie ........................................ 337
 Marie ...................................... 337
 Minnie ..................................... 337
 Roberta ................................... 337
 Ruth ........................................ 337
 Winona .................................... 337
TAYLOR, Mary .......................... 310
TEETH
 Belle ........................................ 300
 Charles.... 45,100,157,207,260,337
 Earl ......... 45,100,157,207,260,338
 Edith ....... 45,100,157,207,260,338
 Elsie..45,100,157,207,260,338,359
 Fannie .............................. 260,337
 Franklin .. 45,100,157,207,260,338
 John ........ 45,100,157,207,260,338
 Logan ................... 207,260,338,365
 Mabel D ..................... 207,260,338
 Montana.. 45,100,157,207,260,338
 Nellie ....................................... 332
 Sallie........................... 45,100,381
TEXAS, Augusta ......................... 375

THREEFINGERS
  Isaac .................. 260,274,338,368
  John .. 45,100,157,207,260,338,389
  Lucy .................................260,338
  Pansy 45,100,157,207,260,338,389
  Patrick ..............................359,378
  Ruth Maud ...............................383
  Ruth Maude ..................45,100,157
  William ... 45,100,157,207,260,338
TIMBER
  Elva ........................................334
  Gilbert ....................................334
  John ........................................334
  John, Jr ...................................334
  Josephine ................................334
  Josie .......................................334
TURKEYLEGS
  Eva .........................................338
  James .............. 45,157,207,261,338
  Jean ........................................350
  John ......... 45,100,157,207,261,338
  Lawrence. 45,100,157,207,261,338
  Lydia ........ 45,100,157,207,261,338
TURTLEWOMAN, Mary ..............378
TWENTYSTANDS
  [Blank] ..................................361
  Baby .......................................378
  James ............... 57,117,169,219,282
  Margaret .................................298
  Paul ........................................375
TWIN
  Bessie ...... 45,100,157,208,261,338
  Edna ............... 45,101,157,358,383
  Eleanor ...................................339
  James L ..................................338
  Louis J ..............................261,338
  Louis James .......... 45,100,157,207,
    261,338
  Margaret .. 45,100,157,208,261,338
TWO TWO
  Daisy ......................................339
  Stephen ..................................339
  Thelma ...................................339
TWOBIRDS
  Edna .......................................101
  Frances ...................................304
  Jacob ....... 45,101,158,208,261,339
  Lenora ........ 101,158,208,261,339

Leonora ..................................... 45
Minnie ..................................... 304
Peter ......... 45,101,157,208,261,339
Walter .................. 45,101,158,383
TWOBULLS
  Alice ..... 101,158,208,261,339,363
  Eleanor ... 45,101,158,208,261,339
  Flora ......... 36,90,148,199,251,323
  Joseph .................................... 374
  Kate .......................... 45,101,158
  Martin ..... 45,101,158,208,261,339
  Ruth .................. 261,274,339,368
  William ... 45,101,158,208,261,339
TWOFEATHERS
  Clara ....... 46,101,158,208,261,339
  Ethel .46,101,158,208,261,339,389
  John ........ 45,101,158,208,261,339
TWOMMONS, William ................ 46
TWOMOON
  Agnes ..................................... 309
  J ............................................. 120
TWOMOONS
  Austin .......... 46,101,158,169,219,
    281,361
  Bert ......... 46,101,158,208,261,339
  Emma ............................... 37,339
  Emma Bites .......... 91,158,208,261
  George .... 46,101,158,193,244,316
  John .7,46,60,101,158,208,261,339
  Lena ....................................... 378
  Margaret ..................... 46,101,158
  William ... 46,101,158,208,261,339
VASSAU, Jessie ............. 208,261,339
WALKINGBEAR
  Charles .... 46,101,158,208,261,339
  David ...... 46,101,158,207,260,340
  Grace ........ 26,79,138,189,240,310
  Jennie ...... 46,101,158,208,261,339
  Mamie ............................ 101,158
  Mannie .......... 46,101,158,193,244
  Nannie ................................... 316
  Olive ...................................... 340
WALKINGBIRD
  Jane ................... 27,46,81,101,158
  Seth ........................................ 374
WALKINGHORSE
  John ........ 46,101,158,208,261,340
  Olive ....... 46,101,158,208,262,340

WALKINGWOMAN.................66
  Maria...........................14,66,125
  Mary.............................14,66,125
WALKSALONG
  (Mary) Eugenia........................101
  Carol ..... 102,158,208,262,340,363
  Eugenia ......................................46
  Fannie ..............25,78,137,188,239
  Flora........ 46,101,158,208,262,340
  Fred......... 46,101,158,208,262,340
  Hugh ....... 46,101,158,208,262,340
  Joseph ...............................340,370
  Mamie ........................208,262,340
  Mary E .......................208,262,340
  Mary Eugenia...........................158
WALKSEASY
  David........................................374
  Nora ...............................46,102,158
WALKSLAST
  Anne. 46,102,159,209,262,340,389
  Carrie ........................208,262,340
  Clement... 46,102,159,209,262,340
  Ella............................................287
  Frank....... 46,102,159,208,262,340
  Gilbert .........................262,273,340
  ~~Gilbert~~ Tom.............................368
  James....... 46,102,159,209,262,340
  Lloyd................... 262,273,340,368
  May ..........................................340
  May L ......................................209
  May L W ..........................262,340
  Richard.... 46,102,159,209,262,340
WALKSNICE
  Adolph ..... 46,50,102,106,159,209,
  262,340
  Agnes .............. 46,102,159,361,385
  Dick.......... 46,102,159,209,262,341
  Flora......... 46,102,159,209,262,340
  John.......... 46,102,159,209,262,341
  Mae ......................209,262,341,366
  Mary......... 46,102,159,209,262,341
  Susie.............................376,378
WALKSNIGHT, Lilly ...................378
WALLOWING
  Rufus........ 47,102,159,209,262,341
  Rutherford47,102,159,209,262,341
  Stella ........ 47,102,159,209,262,341
WALTERS

  Coolidge ............ 191,243,314,359
  George .... 47,102,159,209,262,341
  Jean...........................................333
  Lillian Cook........................47,102
WANDERINGMED, Bessie ........294
WANDERINGMEDICINE
  Gertrude............. 159,209,262,316
  William............... 159,276,385,387
  Wm ...................... 47,102,209,262
WATER
  Frank............. 47,102,159,209,263
  Joseph ........... 47,102,159,209,263
  Sarah................................. 47,102
WATERS
  Frank....... 47,102,159,209,263,341
  Joseph ..... 47,102,159,209,263,341
  Sarah................................. 47,102
WEASELBEAR
  Andrew ... 47,102,159,209,263,341
  Busby...... 47,102,159,209,263,341
  Clarice .... 47,103,146,197,249,321
  Cordelia ..................... 47,103,146
  Frank....... 47,102,159,209,263,341
  Hugh.47,102,159,209,263,341,389
  John .........................................374
  Josie............................ 26,137,188
  Martha .....................................341
  Martha W................................263
  Mary ....... 47,102,159,209,263,341
  Minnie ....................................374
  Sam..........................................341
  Sarah........................... 47,102,140
  Stella......... 12,64,124,175,290,321
  Stella C ............... 197,249
  Stella Mary .....................226
WHEELER
  DeWitt C ................................341
  Dewitt C ........................210,363
  Dewitt Carlton ............. 53,103,159
  DeWitt P ................................341
  Dewitt P.........................210,363
  Dewitt Philip................ 53,103,159
WHIRLWIND
  Dick..........................................376
  Martha .....................................309
  Minnie .....................................342
  Minnie S .........................210,263
  Rose............................ 47,103,160

# Index

Thomas ... 47,103,159,210,263,342
WHISTLINGELK
  Alfred ...... 47,103,154,204,257,333
  Alice ........................... 103,154,347
  Blanche Alice ............................ 47
  Carrie ..................................... 342
  Carrie D ............................ 263,342
  Charles .... 47,103,160,211,264,342
  Flora ..................... 47,103,160,196
  Harriet Julia .............................. 47
  Henry ....................................... 47
  John ......... 47,103,160,210,263,342
  Josie ........ 47,103,154,204,257,333
  Julia ........................... 161,210,343
  Julia W .................................. 264
  Lois .............................. 47,103,154
  Mary ...................................... 286
  May .. 47,103,160,196,253,327,359
  Maynora ..................... 342,370,389
  Rise ........................................ 211
  Rose ................................. 264,342
WHITE
  Ben ................ 48,103,160,361,385
  Lottie ....... 48,103,160,210,263,342
  Pearl ........ 48,103,160,210,263,342
  Stamper ... 47,103,160,210,263,342
  Willis ................... 210,263,342,366
WHITEBEAR
  Alice ................................ 263,342
  Anna ................................ 263,342
  Joseph ..... 48,103,160,210,263,342
WHITEBIRD
  Edward ................ 210,263,342,366
  Frank ....... 48,103,160,210,263,342
  George .............................. 48,103,160
  Julia ...................................... 342
  Julia R ....................... 210,263,342
  Julia Redwoman ..................... 160
  Lena ........ 48,103,160,211,264,342
  Rose ...................................... 342
WHITEBUFFALO
  Ella ......... 48,103,160,210,264,276,
  385,387
  John ......... 48,103,160,210,264,343
WHITEBULL, Olive ................... 340
WHITECOW, Eva ....................... 348
WHITECRANE
  Anna ................... 264,274,343,368

Charles ................. 48,103,160,383
Eleanor ................................... 336
Ella ........ 48,103,160,210,264,343
Elmer .................... 48,103,361,381
Eva ............. 160,210,264,343,365
Leo ........... 24,48,77,103,160,210,
264,343
Victor ...... 48,103,160,210,264,343
WHITECROW, Alfred .... 53,104,160,
210,264,343
WHITEDIRT
  Alfred .................................... 104
  Arthur ................. 48,104,160,385
  Charlie .... 48,104,161,210,264,343
  Henry .................................... 104
  Jennie ...... 48,104,160,210,264,343
  Julia ................................ 210,343
  Julia W .................................. 264
  Julia W E ............................... 161
  Julia Whistlingelk .................. 104
  Leona .......... 161,210,264,343,365
  Mae ................................ 366,368
  Maggie .... 48,104,160,210,264,343
  May ......................... 264,274,343
WHITEELK, Anna .......... 50,106,162,
212,266
WHITEFROG, Nellie ...... 48,104,161,
187,238,308
WHITEHAWK
  Alice ..................................... 343
  Alice C ...................... 211,264,343
  Andrew ........ 211,264,343,363,378
  Charles J .................... 211,264,343
  Charles Jno ........................ 48,104
  Charles John .................... 161,376
  Chase .......................... 48,104,161
  Emma .......... 48,104,161,211,264,
313,343
  George ................ 264,274,344,368
  Ida ........................................... 48
  James ........... 211,264,344,366,389
  John ........ 48,104,161,211,264,343
  Marguerite .......... 48,104,161,211,
264,343
  Mary ....... 48,104,161,211,264,343
  Mary F .................................. 344
  Paula ..................................... 374
  Theresa .............. 211,264,313,389

Thersa ....................................... 363
Thomas ............................. 359,376
Verlie ...... 48,104,161,211,264,313
WHITEHORSE
    Emma ........................................ 374
    George .................... 48,104,161,385
    Nora .......................................... 349
    William ...................... 120,171,222
WHITEMAN .............................. 343
    Sadie ......................................... 309
    Wesley ...................................... 309
WHITEMOON
    Carrie ........ 21,74,133,184,235,303
    Cecelia ..................................... 320
    Clarence .............. 265,274,344,368
    Eva ...................................... 211,344
    Eva L E ............................. 265,344
    George ........... 48,104,161,211,265, 344,389
    Hugh ....... 49,104,161,211,265,344
    Kate ........................................... 344
    Kate T ............................... 211,265
    Rosa .......................................... 162
    Rose ............... 50,106,212,266,346
WHITEPOWDER, Gertrude ....... 8,61, 120,172,222
WHITESHIRT
    Alice ............... 49,104,215,269,350
    Caroline .......... 49,104,215,269,350
    Dottie .......................... 49,104,381
    Jean ......... 49,104,165,215,269,350
WHITEWOLF
    Anna L ..................................... 383
    Anne Lucy .................... 49,104,161
    Baby .................................. 361,379
    Belle ........ 49,104,161,211,265,344
    Calvin M .............. 211,265,344,358
    Calvin Mexican ............ 49,105,162
    Carrie ...... 49,105,161,211,265,344
    Charles ..................................... 344
    Charles I ..................... 211,265,276
    Charles Isadore ............. 49,104,161
    Chas Isadore ............................ 387
    Clara ............... 49,105,162,211,265
    Everett ..... 49,105,161,211,265,344
    Frank ....... 49,104,161,211,265,344
    Fred ....... 105,161,211,265,344,363
    George ..... 49,105,161,211,265,344

Goldstein ......................... 359,379
Grace ................................ 361,379
Grover .............................. 49,105,344
Isadore C ................................ 385
Joseph ..... 49,104,161,211,265,344
Julia ........ 49,104,161,211,265,344
Leo .................... 211,265,344,366
Martin O .................... 211,265,344
Martin Owen ................. 49,105,161
Maude ............................... 161,383
Maude Shields ... 33,49,87,105,120
Philip ...... 49,105,161,211,265,344
Pius ......................................... 376
Susie ........................................ 344
Susie G ............................. 211,265
Susie G H ................................ 161
Thomas ... 49,105,161,211,265,344
Wilson .... 49,105,161,211,265,344
WHITRIGHT
    Rhoda ....................................... 345
    Rhoda S ..................... 212,265,345
    William .................................... 344
WILDHOG
    Alice Viola ......................... 49,105
    Anne ....... 49,105,162,212,265,345
    Bessie ...................................... 319
    Bird ......... 49,105,162,212,265,345
    John ........ 49,105,162,212,265,345
    Julia ........ 49,105,162,212,265,345
    Lydia ....... 49,105,162,212,265,345
    Mary ......................... 212,265,345
    Mary Anne ................... 49,105,162
    Opal ..49,105,162,212,265,345,358
    Susie ............. 49,105,162,212,265
    Vida ........ 49,105,162,212,265,345
    Viola ...... 49,105,162,203,212,256, 265,331,345
    Viola Alice ............................. 153
    Willie ........................... 49,105,381
WILSON
    Alice ........ 50,105,162,212,266,345
    Arthur ..... 49,105,162,212,266,345
    Esther ...................................... 212
    Esther M .......................... 266,345
    Esther Martha ............... 50,105,162
    Florence .. 50,105,162,212,266,345
    George ......... 162,212,266,345,365
    James ................................. 49,105

James, Jr.......... 49,50,105,162,212, 266,345,361
Josephine....... 50,105,162,212,266, 345,358
Martha..... 49,105,162,212,266,345
William .............................345,354
Wm ...........................................368
WINDSOR
 Lee Roland.......... 266,274,345,368
 Sarah ........................212,266,345
WINSOR, Lee Roland ..................366
WOLF
 Fannie L .....................212,269,350
 Fannie Lucy ..................50,105,162
 Mary...........................................379
 Rosa .....................50,105,162,212
 William .................50,105,162,385
WOLFBLACK
 Anna..........................................162
 Dallas ....... 50,106,162,212,266,346
 Gladys ..... 50,106,162,212,266,346
 Harry ........ 50,106,266,277,346,359
 Harshey ....................................162
 John...........................................379
 Mary............. 162,212,266,346,365
 Oran ........ 50,106,162,212,266,346
 Rosa ..........................................162
 Rose ........ 50,106,162,212,266,346
WOLFCHIEF
 Alice...................... 50,106,162,349
 Ann ......... 50,106,163,266,346,361
 Anna. 50,106,212,266,276,385,387
 Artie ..........................................306
 Flora........ 50,106,162,212,266,346
 Harshey ... 50,106,212,266,346,389
 Jerome.......................................379
 Jerome John ..............................359
 Josie ...................... 50,106,162,385
 Mary.................... 266,274,346,368
 Norman ........ 163,212,266,346,365
 Pansy.........................................338
 Richard........... 50,106,162,212,266, 276,387
WOLFCHUM
 Bessie........................................346
 Bessie L..........................213,266
 Bessie L Sun ............................163
 Bessie Littlesun ..........25,50,78,137

Bessie Sun ............................... 106
Betty ....... 50,106,159,209,262,341
Espy............. 213,266,346,366,389
John ......................... 163,213,266
John F ...................................... 346
Lily ......... 50,106,159,209,262,341
Paul......... 50,106,163,213,266,346
Walker ... 50,106,163,213,266,346, 354,361,379
WOLFEAR
 Josie.......................................... 320
 Mary ......................................... 376
 Sophia..... 50,106,163,213,266,346
 Willis ...... 50,106,163,213,266,346
WOLFNAME ............................. 106
 Anna .................................. 106,381
 Annie .......................................... 50
 Bessie ..... 50,106,163,213,267,346
 Grace ...... 51,106,163,213,267,346
 Henry ...... 50,106,163,173,224,287
 Ida............................................. 297
 Kate .................................. 180,231
 Margaret ................................... 361
 Martha ................ 106,163,173,341
 Martha Grace ............................. 50
 Paul...................... 50,106,163,383
 Peter.................................. 361,379
 Wilbur P .................... 173,224,287
 Wilbur Paul................. 50,106,163
 William .......... 50,163,213,267,387
WOLFROADS
 Jennie........................... 51,106,381
 Leo............................. 213,267,346
 Mack........ 51,106,163,213,267,346
 Maude..... 51,106,163,213,267,346
 Norman ........................ 51,106,163
 Rosa .................................. 106,163
 Rosa Charlotte ............................ 51
 Rose.......................................... 385
 Rose Charlotte .................. 106,163
WOLFTOOTH
 Doris.51,107,163,213,267,347,359
 Mary ....... 51,107,163,213,267,346
 Norman... 51,107,163,213,267,346
 Wayne......... 163,213,267,276,363, 385,387
 Young..... 51,107,163,213,267,346
WOLFVOICE

Anne........ 51,107,163,213,267,347
Dewey............ 51,107,163,213,267, 347,361
Grover...... 51,107,163,213,267,347
Jennie..........................213,267,347
Jennie Brady........... 10,51,107,163
WOMANLEGGINS
  Amelia...............23,77,135,237,307
  Ed..........................6,22,58,76,118
  Edward............ 23,51,107,163,213, 267,347
  June...............................51,107,163
  Junior............................51,107,163
  Mabel...... 51,107,163,213,267,347
  Mannie.... 51,107,163,213,267,347
  May...........................................311
  Nannie......................................347
WOODENLEG
  (Unnamed)..............................370
  Ethel.........................................328
  Mabel.................. 175,225,289,361
  Tom, Jr......................................370
WOODENLEGS
  (Unnamed)..............................347
  Alice......................... 213,267,347
  Clara C....................................347
  Jessie..................... 51,107,164,385
  John.......... 51,107,164,213,267,347
  Josie............................ 26,137,188
  Mabel..........................51,107,164
  Martin...... 47,102,159,209,263,341
  Richard.... 51,107,163,213,267,347
  Sophia...... 51,107,164,213,267,347
  Tom.......... 51,107,164,213,267,347
  Tom, Jr......................................347
WOODENTHIGH
  Alice............................51,107,164
  Alice M....................... 214,267,348
  Arthur....... 51,107,164,214,267,347
  Chester.... 51,107,164,214,268,348
  Esther..........................51,107,164
  Esther C.......................214,267,348
  Eva........... 51,107,164,214,267,348
  Hugh..........................................374
  John........... 51,107,164,214,268,348
  Lena.......... 51,107,164,214,268,348
  Melvin...... 51,107,164,214,268,348
  Pater.........................................268

Peter............. 51,107,164,214,348
Philip....... 51,107,164,214,268,348
WOODENTHIGH-KILLSONTOP,
  Anna.................................. 33,87,145
WOODEPECKER
  Donald C................................. 387
  Gladys..................................... 348
  James...................................... 348
  Mary........................................ 348
WOODPECKER
  Donald............................... 52,107
  Donald C......................... 238,276
  Donald Charles...................... 164
  Donald Chas.......................... 187
  James...... 52,107,164,214,268,285
  Mary............. 52,107,164,214,268
  Ralph........................ 52,107,381
WOUNDEDEYE
  Alice.............................. 214,268,349
  Anne......................................... 351
  Charles........................ 52,108,381
  Davis........ 52,108,164,214,268,348
  Edelson............................. 359,376
  Florence.. 52,108,164,214,268,349
  Ford......... 52,108,164,214,268,348
  Fordson........................ 52,108,381
  Hayes................................ 108,164
  Iva Ruth........ 268,274,349,368,389
  Laura............................. 52,108,164
  Milton..... 52,108,164,214,268,348
  Paul.......... 52,108,160,210,264,343
  Rose................................. 358,376
  Ross...................................... 52,108
  Ruth ..52,108,164,214,268,349,361
  Susie............................. 214,268,348
  Susie May..................... 52,108,164
  Veta................................ 52,108,164
  Veta Alice................................ 361
  Veta E........................ 214,268,348
  Victoria... 52,108,164,214,268,349
  Waldo................. 214,268,348,366
  Winfield.. 52,108,164,214,268,349
YELLOWEAGLE, Kate.. 52,108,165, 214,268,349
YELLOWEYES
  Abram..... 52,108,165,214,268,349
  David.................. 214,268,349,366
  Gertrude......... 52,108,165,214,268,

# Index

349,389
Mary. 52,108,165,214,268,349,358
Nora ........ 52,108,165,214,268,349
Oliver ...... 52,108,165,214,268,349
Ruth ............................ 108,165,383
Ruth Elsie ................................ 363
YELLOWFOX
   Arthur ...................................... 108
   Arthur J .................................. 381
   Baby ............................... 164,365,383
   Carrie ...... 52,108,165,214,268,349
   Cecelia .................................... 282
   Charles .... 52,108,165,215,269,349
   Frank ....... 52,108,165,214,268,349
   Harriet M. ............................... 374
   John Arthur ............................ 363
   Margaret ............... 52,108,164,350
   Margaret Y ....................... 215,269
   Mary J ....................... 215,269,350
   Mary Josephine ...................... 366
   Paul .................................. 349,370
   Robert ..... 52,108,165,214,268,349
   Sarah W. ............................ 269,349
   Thaddeus ................................ 379
   William ........ 52,108,164,215,269, 350,381
   Wm Wayne ............................. 374
YELLOWHORSE
   Alice ....................................... 153
   Julia ......... 52,108,137,188,240,310
YELLOWNOSE
   Anne ............................. 52,108,165
   Betty .......... 32,86,144,195,247,319
   George ..... 52,109,165,215,269,350
   Gertrude ................................. 335
   Hilda ...................................... 368
   Lena ..................... 269,274,350,368
   Lizzie ............. 52,65,109,125,381
   Lizzie Crazymule ...................... 13
   Margaret ................. 52,164,215,350
   Margaret Y ............................. 269
   Marie ................................ 215,350
   Marie B .............................. 269,350
   Mary ............ 109,165,215,269,350, 363,389
   Nellie ...................................... 285
   Robert ..... 52,108,165,215,269,350
   Rosa .................................. 269,350

Ruth ................ 18,29,53,83,296
YELLOWROBE
   Adolph ................ 53,109,165,383
   Alfred ............................. 165,365
   Alice ........ 53,109,165,215,269,350
   Arthur ..................................... 376
   Caroline .................................. 165
   Charles.... 53,109,165,215,269,350
   Hilda ..... 269,274,276,350,366,387
   Jasper ...... 53,109,165,215,269,350
   Jean ........................................ 350
   Jean W S ................... 165,215,269
   Martha .... 53,109,165,215,269,350
   Minnie .... 53,109,165,215,269,351
   Moses .......... 165,215,269,350,365
   Nancy C .................................. 350
   Nancy Coed ............................ 370
   Ruana ............ 53,109,165,215,269
   Ruth ........ 53,109,165,215,269,350
   Theadore ................................. 274
   Theodore ........................... 350,368
   Theordore ............................... 269
   William ... 53,109,165,215,269,351
YOUNGBEAR
   [--] .......................................... 351
   Anna ....................................... 361
   Annie ...................................... 379
   Arthur ..... 53,109,165,215,269,351
   Baby ......................... 166,365,383
   Cora ........ 53,109,165,215,269,351
   Frank ...................................... 376
   George .......... 53,109,165,215,269, 351,361,379
   Mary .......................... 109,166,363
   Ralph ............................. 53,109,166
   Ralph H ..................... 215,269,351
YOUNGBIRD
   Anne ....... 53,109,166,215,270,351
   Carl ................................ 53,109,351
   Carl J .............................. 215,270
   Carl James ............................. 166
   Clara ........ 53,109,166,215,269,351
   Edith ....................................... 379
   James ...... 53,109,166,215,269,351
   John ............... 53,109,166,215,270
   John Beans ............................. 351
YOUNGMAGPIE, Albert . 28,82,140, 191,243,314

# Index

ZETTLE, Frank ............... 323, 370, 389

www.ingramcontent.com/pod-product-compliance
Lightning Source LLC
Chambersburg PA
CBHW020238030426
42336CB00010B/519